THE BIRTH OF
CARIBBEAN CIVILISATION

THE BIRTH OF CARIBBEAN CIVILISATION

A Century of Ideas about
Culture and Identity, Nation and Society

O. Nigel Bolland

Ian Randle Publishers
Kingston • Miami

James Currey Publishers
Oxford

First published in Jamaica 2004 by
Ian Randle Publishers, 11 Cunningham Avenue, Box 686, Kingston 6

National Library of Jamaica Cataloguing in Publication Data

Bolland, O. Nigel
      The birth of Caribbean civilisation : a century of ideas about culture and identity, nation and society / O. Nigel Bolland

          p. ;   cm

          Bibliography : p.   . – Includes index

          ISBN 976-637-109-1 (paperback)
          ISBN 976-637-149-0 (hardback)

1. Caribbean Area – Civilisation   2. Caribbean Area – Culture   3. Caribbean
      Area –   History
I.   Title

      305.8009729   dc 21

and in the United States by
Ian Randle Publishers, Inc

          ISBN 0-9742155-8-9 (paperback)
          ISBN 0-9742155-9-7 (hardback)

First published in the United Kingdom, 2004 by
James Currey Publishers
73 Botley Road
Oxford, OX2 0BS
www.jamescurrey.co.uk

British Library Cataloguing in Publication Data

Bolland, O. Nigel
      The birth of Caribbean civilisation: a century of ideas about culture and identity, nation and society
      1. Caribbean Area - Civilization
      I. Title

      306'.9729

      ISBN 0-85255-872-4 (paperback)

Cover design by Robert Harris
Book design by Shelly-Gail Cooper
Printed in the United States of America

Cover painting "Mayan Galaxy" by Denis Williams
Courtesy of the Orange Park Trust

Table of Contents

PREFACE & ACKNOWLEDGEMENTS vii

PUBLISHER'S ACKNOWLEDGEMENTS ix

INTRODUCTION xvi

PART ONE - THE HISPANOPHONE INTELLECTUALS

1. José Martí 3
2. Lola Rodríguez de Tío 18
3. Ramiro Guerra y Sánchez 21
4. Fernando Ortiz 36
5. Luis Muñoz Rivera 60
6. Pedro Albizu Campos 71
7. Luis Muñoz Marín 80
8. Juan Antonio Corretjer 99
9. Fidel Castro 106
10. Roberto Fernández Retamar 123
11. José Luis González 135
12. Esmeralda Santiago 157
13. Antonio Benítez-Rojo 160

PART TWO - THE FRANCOPHONE INTELLECTUALS

14. Anténor Firmin 173
15. Jean Price-Mars 190
16. Aimé Césaire 210
17. Frantz Fanon 228
18. René Despestre 236
19. Jean Bernabé, Patrick Chamoiseau and Raphaël Confiant . 250
20. Edourd Glissant 267
21. Maryse Condé 279
22. Edwidge Danticat 287

PART THREE - THE ANGLOPHONE INTELLECTUALS

23. J.J. Thomas 294
24. Marcus Mosiah Garvey 313
25. Elma Francois 331
26. Eric Williams 336
27. M.G. Smith 362
28. V.S. Naipaul 373
29. C.L.R. James 394
30. Elsa Goveia 421
31. Cheddi Jagan 446
32. Rex M. Nettleford 461
33. Walter Rodney 474
34. Michael Manley 492
35. Kamau Brathwaite 504
36. W. Arthur Lewis 516
37. Merle Hodge 524
38. Maurice Bishop 531
39. Michelle Cliff 548
40. Clive Y. Thomas 562
41. Stuart Hall 577
42. Derek Walcott 591
43. Shridath Ramphal 607
44. George Lamming 617
45. Orlando Patterson 632

BIBLIOGRAPHY 652
INDEX 655

✎ *Preface & Acknowledgements* ✎

This book exists because I wanted to see such a book and it did not yet exist. I have long admired the quality and range of the work of Caribbean intellectuals and I have always tried to read widely, beyond whatever project I was currently working on. In my reading I have noticed several similarities and recurrent themes, both within and across the linguistic divisions of the region, even when these intellectuals made no reference to (and in some cases were unaware of) the work of their neighbours, so this had to be a pan-Caribbean selection. Moreover, in the interdisciplinary course on Caribbean culture and societies that I have been teaching for 30 years, I have wanted to use a broad anthology like this, in which Caribbean intellectuals would speak for themselves, to stimulate discussions and a variety of research projects. Of course, I had to impose limits both on the number and size of the selections and also on the range of topics covered by them. I believe that the focus on ideas about culture and identity, nation and society, reflects the emphasis of Caribbean intellectual traditions since the late nineteenth century.

With the benefit of a sabbatical I was able to take the time to re-read, and read more widely in, the work of the large number of Caribbean intellectuals that I have admired since, as an undergraduate, I first read C.L.R. James, Eric Williams and M.G. Smith. So, with brief introductions and a few notes, here are the works I selected. I know that there is much work that I do not know, so I would appreciate suggestions, especially from people who choose to teach with this book, that I could consider if there is another edition.

I am indebted to Colgate University for the semester's sabbatical in 2000 that gave me a good start on this project and to the skilled members of our library, especially Ann Ackerson, Ellie Bolland and David Hughes, who helped me a great deal with my reference questions and inter-library loans. They were generous with their time and patient with their 'problem patron'. I want to mention all the people who have helped with ideas and encouragement but, as I am unable to do that, I will single out Howard Johnson, Linden Lewis, Teresita Martinez-Vergne and Cami Townsend for special mention. I owe a good deal to the people who invited me to participate in two conferences at the University of the West Indies. The first, on Caribbean Intellectual Traditions at Mona, Jamaica, in 1998 and the second on (Re)Thinking Caribbean Culture at Cave Hill, Barbados, in 2001. I am indebted to Trudy King and Amy Rawson who patiently helped prepare the manuscript and to

Ian Randle and his capable crew who turned it into a book. To all these people who gave support and assistance, I offer my sincere thanks, and I hope they like the result to which they generously contributed. In addition, of course, I owe my thanks to all the authors and publishers, listed separately, who gave permission for these works to be reprinted here.

Finally, and with due respect, I wish to dedicate this anthology to all the Caribbean intellectuals, (some of whom it has been my pleasure and honour to know) whose works have been included. I hope they, or their spirits, will approve.

✒ Publisher's Acknowledgements ✒

The editor and publisher would like to thank the following for permission to reproduce the material in this volume:

José Martí:

'Our America', from *Jose Marti: Selected Writings* by Jose Marti, introduction by Roberto Gonzalez Echevarria, edited by Esther Allen, translated by Esther Allen, copyright © 2002 by Esther Allen. Reprinted by permission of Viking Penguin, a division of Penguin Group (USA) Inc.

Ramiro Guerra y Sánchez:

'Sugar and Society in the Caribbean' (translated by Marjory M. Urquidi) excerpts from *Sugar and Society in the Caribbean: An Economic History of Cuban Agriculture*. Copyright © 1964. Reprinted by permission of Yale University Press.

Luis Muñoz Rivera:

'Give Us Our Independence' [1916], speech given to the US House of Representatives, May 5, 1916 from *Hearings of the United States-Puerto Rico Commission,* 89th Cong 2nd Sess., Document 108, 1965.

Roberto Fernández Retamar:

'Caliban. Notes Toward a Discussion of Culture in Our America' (translated by Lynn Garofola, David Arthur McMurray and Roberto Márquez) from *Caliban and Other Essays*. Copyright © 1989. Reprinted by permission of University of Minnesota Press.

José Luis González:

'Puerto Rico: The Four-Storeyed Country' (translated by Gerald Guinness) from *Puerto Rico: The Four-Storeyed Country and Other Essay*. Copyright © 1993. Reprinted by kind permission of Markus Wiener Publishers.

Kamau Brathwaite:

'Timehri'. Copyright © 1970. Reprinted by kind permission of the author.

W. Arthur Lewis:

'On Being Different' from *The Aftermath of Sovereignty: West Indian Perspectives*, edited by David Lowenthal and Lambros Comitas. Copyright © 1973. Reprinted by kind permission of David Lowenthal.

Clive Y. Thomas:

'An Alternative Conception of Development' from *The Poor and the Powerless*. Copyright © 1988 by Monthly Review Press. Reprinted by permission of Monthly Review Foundation.

Derek Walcott:

The Antilles: Fragments of Epic Memory by Derek Walcott. Copyright © 1992 by the Nobel Foundation. Published by Farrar, Straus and Giroux, LLC. Reprinted by permission of Farrar, Straus and Giroux, LLC.

George Lamming:

'Caribbean Labor, Culture and Identity' from *Caribbean Cultural Identities*, edited by Glyne Griffith. Copyright © 2001. Reprinted by permission of Bucknell University Press.

While every effort has been made to contact the copyright holders of the following material, we have been unsuccessful in our attempts. As such, the editor and publishers would be pleased to hear from any interested parties:

Lola Rodríguez de Tío:

'The Song of Borinquen' and 'Cuba and Puerto Rico' (translated by José Nieto) from *Borinquen: An Anthology of Puerto Rican Literature,* edited by Maria Teresa Babin and Stan Steiner (New York: Vintage, 1974).

Fernando Ortiz:

'Cuban Counterpoint' (translated by Harriet de Onís) excerpts from *Cuban Counterpoint: Tobacco and Sugar* (New York: Vintage, 1970).

Pedro Albizu Campos:

'The Day of the Race' (translated by Joseph Michael Ferri) from 'Pedro Albizu Campos, "El Maestro": Translation and rhetorical analysis of selected speeches' (PhD dissertation, Temple University, 1988).

'Puerto Rican Nationalism' (translated by Roberto Santiago) from *Boricuas: Influential Puerto Rican Writings – An Anthology*, edited by Roberto Santiago (New York: Ballantine, 1995).

Luis Muñoz Marín:

Speech from *The Puerto Ricans: A Documentary History,* edited by Kal Wagenheim with Olga Jiménez de Wagenheim (New York: Anchor/Doubleday, 1973).

'A Good Civilization', speech to the Legislative Assembly, San Juan, from *Borinquen: An Anthology of Puerto Rican Literature,* edited by María Teresa Babín and Stan Steiner (New York: Vintage, 1974).

Juan Antonio Corretjer:

'The Day Puerto Rico Became a Nation' from *San Juan Star Sunday Magazine* Sept 22, 1968

Fidel Castro:

'History Will Absolve Me' (New York: Fair Play for Cuba Committee, 1961)

'Words to the Intellectuals' in *The Revolution and Cultural Problems of Cuba* (Havana, 1962), reprinted from *Radical Perspectives in the Arts* edited by Lee Baxandall (Harmondsworth: Penguin, 1972).

Anténor Firmin:

'The Equality of the Human Races' (translated by Asselin Charles), excerpts from *The Equality of the Human Races: Positivist Anthropology* (New York: Garland Publishing, 2000).

Jean Bernabé, Patrick Chamoiseau and Raphaël Confiant:

'In Praise of Creoleness' (translated by Mohamed B. Taleb Khyar), *Callaloo* 13 (1990).

Maryse Condé:

'Conversations with Maryse Condé', excerpts from Françoise Pfaff *Conversations with Maryse Condé* (Lincoln: University of Nebraska, 1996).

J.J. Thomas:

'Froudacity', excerpts from *Froudacity: West Indian Fables by James Anthony Froude* (London: New Beacon, 1969).

Elma Francois:

'Speech in her Self-Defence at her Sedition Trial' from Rhoda Reddock *Elma Francois: The NWCSA and the Workers' Struggle for Change in the Caribbean in the 1930's* (London: New Beacon, 1988)

Eric Williams:

'Race Relations in Caribbean Society' in *Caribbean Studies: A Symposium*, edited by Vera Rubin (Seattle: University of Washington, 1957).
'The Future of the Caribbean' from *Columbus to Castro: The History of the Caribbean, 1492-1969* (London: André Deutsch, 1970).

V.S. Naipaul:

'The Middle Passage', excerpts from *The Middle Passage: Impressions of Five Societies – British, French and Dutch – in the West Indies and South America* (Harmondsworth: Penguin, 1969)

C.L.R. James:

'From Toussaint L'Ouverture to Fidel Castro' from *The Black Jacobins: Toussaint L'Ouverture and the San Domingo Revolution,* second edition (New York: Vintage, 1963).

Elsa Goveia:

'Slave Society in the British Leeward Islands', excerpts from *Slave Society in the British Leeward Islands at the End of the Eighteenth Century* (New Haven: Yale University, 1965).

Cheddi Jagan:

'The West on Trial', excerpts from *The West on Trial* revised edition (Berlin: Seven Seas, 1971)

Merle Hodge:

'The Shadow of the Whip: A Comment on Male-Female Relations in the Caribbean' from *Is Massa Day Dead? Black Moods in the Caribbean,* edited by Orde Coombs (New York: Anchor/Doubleday, 1974)

Maurice Bishop:

'Address Celebrating the First National Day of Culture' from *One Caribbean: Two Speeches by Maurice Bishop* (Epsom: Britian/Grenada Friendship Society, n.d.).

Michelle Cliff:

'If I Could Write This in Fire, I Would Write This in Fire' from *If I Could Write This in Fire: An Anthology of Literature from the Caribbean* edited by Pamela Maria Smorkaloff (New York: New Press, 1994).

Stuart Hall:

'Myths of Caribbean Identity', Walter Rodney Memorial Lecture, (Oct 1991), University of Warwick.

Shridath Ramphal:

'A Commonwealth of the Caribbean for the Twenty-first Century' from *No Island is an Island: Selected Speeches of Sir Shridath Ramphal,* edited by David Dabydeen and John Gilmore (London: Macmillan Education, 2000).

Orlando Patterson:

'Ecumenical America: Global Culture and the American Cosmos' in *World Policy Journal* 11:2 (1994).

Introduction

When C.L.R. James, one of the Caribbean's foremost intellectuals, said that it is 'clear that the birth of a nation is in process', he was referring, with his characteristic vision, to the unity of the Caribbean experience, not to a political unity which remains far beyond reach.[1] Few people would claim that a pan-Caribbean nation, in the sense of a 'nation-state', is in the process of being born, though many do claim that the common experiences of Caribbean people have already given rise to the consciousness and expression of an emerging civilisation. In George Lamming's words, 'I hold no stronger conviction than that the Caribbean is our own experiment in a unique equation of human civilisation'.[2] The word 'civilisation' is generally used in contrast with 'barbarism', to refer to an achieved state of order and refinement, but it also conveys the consciousness of an historical process through which a distinctive culture and society are achieved. 'The birth of Caribbean civilisation', therefore, conveys a claim that the unique historical experience of the region is giving rise to a culture and society unlike any other, a civilisation that reflects this unique experience in its own way through its social and political ideas, literature, music and art, as is true of other civilisations.

During the last 500 years people from various parts of the world have met, exchanged ideas and activities, and created varied and vibrant cultures in the Caribbean. The cross-fertilisation of the indigenous cultures of Taino and Carib peoples with those from Europe, Africa and Asia resulted not only in a culturally heterogeneous region but also many culturally heterogeneous countries within the region. Cultural pluralism and hybridity have been more the norm than the exception in the Caribbean. In the last two centuries, a growing sense of attachment to the various homelands in the region has given rise to nationalism, both cultural and political, that unites people of different ethnicity. However, this nationalism reflects the pluralism and often the insularity that characterises the region as a whole, resulting in what the Jamaican historian Franklin Knight calls a 'fragmented nationalism'.[3] Consequently, people identify strongly as Haitians or Cubans or Jamaicans, but rarely as 'Caribbeans'.

The political history of certain nations has also given rise to varied and changing relationships to other places, both within and outside the Caribbean. For example, at one time some nationalists in Cuba and Puerto Rico identified with each other in their struggle against Spain,[4] but soon after the United States invaded these islands in 1898 their paths diverged. Cuba became independent in 1902 while Puerto Rico remained a colony of the United States. Some Puerto Ricans are fiercely nationalistic, others have come to accept that since 1917 they have been US citizens, and many remain ambivalent about their relationship with the United States.[5] Haiti has been an independent nation since 1804, but there is still a sense of cultural connection between Haitians and the people of Guadeloupe and Martinique who are French citizens and think of themselves as both French and West Indian. In the English-speaking Caribbean, following the unsuccessful attempt at federation between 1958 and 1962, the nations have gone their independent political ways, but there remain cultural and organisational connections through the West Indies cricket team, the University of the West Indies and CARICOM, the Caribbean Community and Common Market.

In the history of the Caribbean, many people have moved from one place to another within the region and started families in their new homes, so there are Cubans of Haitian and Jamaican origin, Trinidadians of Barbadian and Grenadian origin, and there are Cubans, Haitians and Dominicans in Puerto Rico. As George Lamming points out, a household may consist of 'a family of islands', with a Grenadian mother, a Vincentian father, a Barbadian grandfather, an Antiguan aunt and Trinidadian children.[6] Maryse Condé says, 'If you ask four West Indians, at least one of them had a grandfather who went to Panama',[7] and today there are millions of people of Caribbean origin in Europe and North America as well as Central America. Migration experiences have made many Caribbean people bilingual and even multilingual; family members are scattered in several nations and people move comfortably between, say, Jamaica, Panama, London and New York. If by 'Caribbean' we mean more than a geographical expression, then the Caribbean in a cultural sense is wherever Caribbean people live and cultivate their religions, music, food, and families. Although few people think of themselves as 'a Caribbean', they recognise that people from the region share something and when they have moved outside the region they sometimes associate with each other across national boundaries. The question of what constitutes Caribbean culture, identity, and nationalism is complex, dynamic and flexible.

If we mean by 'culture' a common language, religion and lifestyle, then there is clearly no pan-Caribbean culture, nor is there a strong pan-Caribbean identity. There are obvious major divisions by language, as is reflected in the organisation of this book. These linguistically-defined regions are generally characterised and categorised by the languages of the four European powers that dominated the region in the colonial period, hence the Spanish-speaking, French-speaking, English-speaking and Dutch-speaking Caribbean. This linguistic division is an important component of cultural or ethnic identity. For example, by the 'Hispanic Caribbean' we refer to people who share a common language and other aspects of their culture, even though Cubans, Dominicans and Puerto Ricans are separated by nationality. Many people from the English-speaking Caribbean talk of 'the Caribbean' when they are referring only to the former British colonies which, although numerous, amount to less than 16 per cent of the 38 million people in the region. When they refer to themselves as Caribbean in this way, they are indicating their identity, to be sure, but they are also implicitly separating themselves from the majority of Caribbean people.

Religious affiliations and national identities, like languages, unite people into groups while separating the groups from each other. These divisions may coincide with or cross-cut linguistic distinctions, thereby creating a more complex mosaic of identities. Most Caribbean people identify themselves, at least nominally, as Catholic, for example. This includes not only most people in the Hispanic and Francophone Caribbean, but also many people in the former British colonies of Belize, Grenada, St Lucia and Trinidad. They are more united in their Catholicism than are the members of a variety of Protestant churches that predominate in most of the former British colonies and that are also making inroads in Haiti and Puerto Rico. Large minorities in Trinidad, Guyana and Suriname are Hindu or Muslim, and there are small but old and significant Jewish communities in several places, such as Jamaica and Suriname. These religious identities are often cross-cut by 'racial' or ethnic categories, which are important, but by no means straightforward, everywhere in the Caribbean. In Belize, for example, there are Catholics who speak different languages and are of African, Mestizo or Garifuna descent, while in Trinidad there are people of Indian origin who are Presbyterian, Muslim or Hindu.

In terms of political status and national identity, most of the Caribbean, following the early lead of Haiti (1804) and the Dominican Republic (1844), became independent in the twentieth century, beginning with Cuba in 1902, most of the British colonies during and after 1962, and Suriname in 1975. Only the smallest British islands remain colonies in the twenty-first century. Puerto Rico, however, despite its considerable size, remains a colony, as are the US Virgin Islands, which were Danish colonies until 1917, and the Netherlands Antilles retain a relationship with Holland. French Guiana, Guadeloupe and Martinique moved in a different direction, away from independence, when they became politically integrated departments of France in 1946. Along with this variety of political status, the strength of nationalist feeling and identity varies a great deal. Most Caribbean nations achieved constitutional independence before acquiring a strong national identity. Countries as different as Haiti and Belize, which became independent in 1804 and 1981, respectively, were forming their national identities long after independence. Cuba and Puerto Rico are notable exceptions to this pattern, though for different reasons: Cuba achieved a strong national identity through its long struggle for independence, while Puerto Rico has a strong national identity but is not independent.

Given all this cultural division and political fragmentation, is there any underlying unity in the region? There are four ways, at least, that we may perceive some underlying – and possibly growing –unity within the obvious diversity of the Caribbean: in regional organisations, in common historical experiences, in shared Afro-creole culture, and in some distinctive ideas about culture and identity, nation and society. Before focusing on the intellectual traditions, I will comment briefly on the other features.

First, there is an increase in the number and variety of regional organisations that link the otherwise – fragmented parts of the Caribbean. These organisations include ones that engage in economic, labour, educational, media, religious, health and sporting activities. Many are limited to a single linguistic area of the Caribbean, but some reach beyond these divisions. For example, since 1926, when the British Guiana Labour Union hosted a West Indies Labour Conference, efforts have been made to develop regional trade union confederations. The Caribbean Labour Congress (CLC) was founded in 1945 and, although it was essentially a confederation of trade unions from the British colonies, it did include representatives from Suriname and Aruba and efforts were made to include representation from trade unions in Cuba, Puerto Rico, Guadeloupe and Martinique. Its successor, the Caribbean Area Division of the Inter-American Regional Organisation of Workers (CADORIT), was launched in 1952 as a subsidiary of the International Confederation of Free Trade Unions. The University of the West Indies, founded as a college of the University of London in 1948, is a multinational institution with major campuses in Jamaica, Trinidad and Tobago and Barbados, and with university centres in other countries of the Commonwealth Caribbean. Academic organisations, such as the Association of Caribbean Historians which began meeting in 1969, and the Caribbean Studies Association, which was founded in 1974, bring hundreds of teachers and scholars together in annual conferences that are held in locations all over the region, from the Bahamas to the Guianas. There is a growing number of other non-government organisations, such as the Caribbean Conference of Churches, associations of women and of media workers, and organisations for the visually impaired and of indigenous peoples of the region. These bring together people of the Caribbean who, despite their different languages, religions and nationalities, share common concerns and who feel that, *as Caribbean people*, they can work better together than they can separately.

These non-government organisations are important, although they generally focus on a specific issue. The most important pan-Caribbean organisation is CARICOM, which was established in 1973, replacing CARIFTA, the Caribbean Free Trade Area, which was formed in 1968. This group of 15 countries, consisting of the former British colonies plus Haiti and Suriname, links over 13 million people in an effort to achieve economic cooperation and greater coordination of services, such as education and health, and foreign policy. An even larger organisation, the Association of Caribbean States (ACS), consisting of 25 members, including Cuba, the Dominican Republic, the Central American states, Colombia, Mexico and Venezuela as well as the members of CARICOM, was formed in 1994. This organisation has yet to achieve much, but it does represent an aspiration towards regional cooperation, if not regional unity.

The second unifying aspect of the Caribbean lies in certain common historical experiences that are shared, more or less, by all the societies in the region. The American anthropologist, Sidney Mintz, who has worked in Puerto Rico, Haiti and Jamaica, identified several regional commonalities, some of which are closely related and overlap.[8] These historical commonalities, which Mintz says 'consist largely of parallels of economic and social structure and organization, the consequence of lengthy and rather rigid colonial rule', include these features:

1. The common lowland, subtropical, insular ecology.
2. The rapid extirpation of most of the indigenous people.
3. The unusual pervasiveness and persistence of colonialism.
4. The dominance of the plantation system of production, using mostly coerced labour to produce sugar, coffee and a few other items for export to distant markets, upon which the societies are highly dependent.
5. The concomitant development of bipolar social structures of extreme inequality and limited social mobility, as epitomised by slavery, that are sustained by overseas domination.
6. The successive introduction of immigrants on a massive scale into the lower, labouring levels of these societies, from Africa, India, China and elsewhere, resulting in a high degree of cultural pluralism.
7. The continuous interplay between the dominant plantation sector and a struggling sector of small-scale or peasant agriculture.
8. A high degree of economic individualisation and the relative weakness of national identity and ideology.

These features vary considerably from place to place and also from time to time in the same place. For example, some indigenous people have survived in several territories and some colonies, such as Puerto Rico, had a much smaller proportion of enslaved people than most other colonies. We can also see that Haiti became a peasant society while Cuba was vigorously developing plantations based on slavery, passing each other on different trajectories in the nineteenth century. As Mintz suggests, the various societies of the Caribbean may be viewed in terms of a 'multidimensional continuum' along these lines, rather than characterised in terms of a single general model. Nevertheless, these features generally relate to each other to form a quite coherent picture: it was the *de*population of the region that required its massive *re*population; sugar, slavery and the plantation went together, forming not just a kind of agricultural enterprise but also a kind of society that included a bipolar social structure, the cultural dominance of a minority over the majority, the weakness of national identity and the persistent struggle with the peasant alternative. Essentially, Mintz's point is that, even if we cannot say there is a common culture throughout the Caribbean, there are sufficient common historical experiences and features for it to be defined as a 'socio-cultural area.'

The third way of thinking of Caribbean unity follows from the second, namely that the most massive immigration into the Caribbean, between the beginning of the sixteenth century and the late nineteenth century, was of African people (about 6 million people in 350 years), most of them enslaved. Despite the fact that they suffered from physical and psychological abuse, degraded social status and appallingly high mortality rates, these people created a culture that pervades the entire region and has even spread beyond it. This is the 'Afro-creole' culture in which African components of religion, language and music, for example, were adapted along with elements of Amerindian, European and Asian cultures into a new culture that was created in the Caribbean. Jean Price-Mars showed that Vodou, the most common religion in Haiti, like Santería in Cuba and Orisha in Trinidad, has African roots (see chapter 15). Other Caribbean religions, like Comfa in Guyana, show European and Asian influences, but grew within a framework shaped by the heritage of African beliefs and practices.

When we examine the languages actually spoken by people in the Caribbean, we see that it is far too simple to classify them by the labels of the dominant European powers. As the Trinidadian linguist, Mervyn Alleyne, says: if these labels are taken literally they are 'misleading, inadequate, or inaccurate in some cases, and they certainly mask a great deal of linguisitic complexity'.[9] Only the term 'Spanish-speaking' has any accurate application; the other terms 'provide only approximate references'. The so-called French, English and Dutch-speaking territories are quite complex linguistically and generally include creole languages that have developed historically through the influence of the African languages that were initially spoken by the majority of people. Linguistic research shows that these creole languages have great lexical diversity but a high degree of structural similarity. Far from being mere corruptions of European languages, as biased commentators have long claimed, these creole languages, which are often the mass vernacular or national language, are just as genuine as any other languages that have developed through centuries of cultural interaction and creativity. Moreover, it is not only in the forms of speech that there are strong African influences but also in the content, as the pan-Caribbean similarities in proverbs and folktales, which are often adapted from African sources, clearly demonstrate.

As in religion and language, so also in music and food. There is a huge variety of music and food throughout the Caribbean, and influences from Asia and Europe as well as the original Taino and Carib peoples are obvious. It must have been chiefly Africans who learned the cultivation and use of local foods, such as manioc (yucca, cassava), as well as aspects of music and religion from the indigenous Amerindians, while they were also learning from and adapting each others' cultures. In the historical process of creolisation, it was largely the Africans and their descendants who adapted and combined cultural elements from various origins to create what is most widely shared and *distinctively Caribbean* in religion, music and cuisine. Certainly, African cultural influences are pervasive in the Caribbean and they are widely shared by people who are not of African descent.

Finally, I turn to the development of some distinctive intellectual traditions in the Caribbean. Several excellent books have addressed aspects of this topic. Gordon Lewis wrote an outstanding book, *Main Currents of Caribbean Thought* (1983), which examines the historical development of ideologies in the region from 1492 to 1900, but there is no comparable study of Caribbean thought in the twentieth century. Paget Henry's *Caliban's Reason: Introducing Afro-Caribbean Philosophy* (2000) makes an important contribution and other collections of essays explore aspects of this huge subject. Among these are the two volumes edited by Alistair Hennessy, *Intellectuals in the Twentieth Century Caribbean* (1992), a reader edited by Brian Meeks and Folke Lindahl, *New Caribbean Thought* (2001), and *Caribbean Cultural Identities* (2001) edited by Glyne Griffith. Most of the content of these collections, however, is limited to the anglophone Caribbean. I hope that this collection will show that, despite the divisions of language and nationality, there are several pan-Caribbean themes and even a growing sense of what may be called 'Caribbeanness'. The collection of works, largely essays and excerpts from books, included in this volume are by distinguished Caribbean men and women who are, or were, for the most part writers, scholars and politicians. Although there are disagreements, contradictions and debates among them, they have contributed to the emerging pan-Caribbean civilisation.

I have tried to select as wide a variety as possible for this collection, by people from the Hispanic, Francophone and Anglophone Caribbean from the 1880s to the end of the twentieth century. The earliest works are Anténor Firmin's *The Equality of the Human Races* (1885), J.J. Thomas's *Froudacity* (1889) and José Martí's 'Our America' (1891), and the latest are by George Lamming (1994), Orlando Patterson (1994), Edwidge Danticat (1996) and Antonio Benítez-Rojo (1998). Inevitably, there are omissions and imbalances in this selection, some of which may result from my own biases and ignorance (I am more familiar with works from the Anglophone Caribbean than the Hispanic and Francophone, and am quite ignorant of the Dutch Caribbean). Other omissions and imbalances, however, reflect some of the social and cultural biases within the intellectual traditions of the Caribbean. One of these, of course, has to do with gender. For most of the period covered by this collection, middle-class women were expected to lead domestic lives, dependent on their husbands, and working-class women lacked education. None of them were expected, much less encouraged, to make public statements about their identities, cultures and societies. Nationalism and politics were public business and therefore the business of men and it was men alone who were expected to pronounce on these matters. The rare exceptions to this pattern were extraordinary individuals who refused to accept such social constraints. Lola Rodríguez de Tió and Elma Francois were revolutionaries, the former expressing her nationalistic feelings about Puerto Rico and Cuba in poetry and the latter defending her militant activities in a speech during her trial. In later generations, more women accepted the task of analysing and expressing their region's history and culture, among them such distinguished scholars and writers as Elsa Goveia, Maryse Condé, Merle Hodge, Esmeralda Santiago, Michelle Cliff and Edwidge Danticat, and some of them contribute a gendered perspective.

Some writers in this collection are more famous than others, particularly Marcus Garvey, Luis Muñoz Marín, Cheddi Jagan, Eric Williams, Fidel Castro, Michael Manley and Maurice Bishop, who had important political careers; or C.L.R. James, Frantz Fanon and Shridath Ramphal, who are known internationally for their political acumen and activities. Several were or are outstanding writers of poetry and fiction, coming from a region that is renowned for these fields, including Aimé Césaire, V.S. Naipaul, George Lamming, Derek Walcott, Edouard Glissant, Patrick Chamoiseau, Maryse Condé, Michelle Cliff and Edwidge Danticat. Others are known more for their scholarship, including such internationally famous scholars as W. Arthur Lewis, M.G. Smith, Elsa Goveia, Rex Nettleford, Clive Thomas, Stuart Hall, Walter Rodney, Antonio Benítez-Rojo and Orlando Patterson. Then there are writers, like Jean Price-Mars, Fernando Ortiz and Kamau Brathwaite, who are hard to pigeon-hole because they excel in more than one sphere.

Given the colonial history of the region and its limited career opportunities, it is not surprising that many of these writers made their careers largely outside the region, in exile from their homelands. Among these are José Martí, José Luis González, C.L.R. James, W. Arthur Lewis, Frantz Fanon, M.G. Smith, Stuart Hall, V.S. Naipaul, Maryse Condé, Antonio Benítez-Rojo, Orlando Patterson, Michelle Cliff, Esmeralda Santiago and Edwidge Danticat. Some moved from their homeland to another Caribbean country which became their new home; Elma Francois moved from St Vincent to Trinidad and René Depestre from Haiti to Cuba. Undoubtedly the writers' individual experiences, as well as the cultures in which they were brought up, influenced their self-identities and their views about their societies and the region as a whole.

There are some writers who think of themselves not simply in terms of nationality, such as Cuban or Jamaican, but rather in a 'hyphenated' identity, such as East Indian-Trinidadian or Afro-Cuban, linking their nationality with an ethnic origin. José Martí considered himself Cuban and therefore also Latin American (chapter 1), while Anténor Firmin, a Haitian, and Marcus Garvey, who was Jamaican and West Indian, were pioneers of Pan-Africanism (chapters 14 and 24). As identities cross-cut or overlap one another, depending on the social context, an individual may identify or be identified in different ways, for example, as Jamaican or as African, as East Indian or as Guyanese. These racial, ethnic and national identities may also cross-cut with identities by religious community, language group, and gender or sexual orientation. Michelle Cliff, for example, points out that in different social contexts she thinks of herself as white, or Jamaican, or a lesbian, and consequently may identify with or separate herself from the same person: in one situation, sharing her Jamaicanness with someone from whom she later feels alienated because he is homophobic (chapter 39). As this example shows, identity is not simply what a person chooses, nor is it fixed. Rather, identities are flexible and shifting, and are negotiated between the individual and others from one context to another. Different identities, therefore, may not be mutually exclusive but may follow each other in series, or they may be simultaneous and multiple. Like Russian dolls that nest inside each other, a man may identify himself as Jamaican and West Indian, and as a member of the African diaspora, while he holds a British passport and lives in New York; or a US citizen may identify herself as a creolised Chinese-Trinidadian.[10] Both these people may think of themselves also as Caribbean. In fact, Caribbean people are frequently experts in these complexities of identity, because they are as complex as the cultures in which they are embedded, and are a function of the history of migration and transculturation that began in 1492. It is this rich complexity that makes the Caribbean such a unique and dynamic civilisation in which people are, in Stuart Hall's words, 'constantly producing and reproducing themselves anew, through transformation and difference'.[11]

These writers speak well for themselves. In this introduction, I will simply suggest some ways to compare and contrast them by mentioning three broad themes that run through much of their work. First, a common theme among these Caribbean intellectuals concerns their reactions to the political, cultural and psychological impact of colonialism, slavery and racism. This dialectic with oppression has taken two chief roads which show a different emphasis even while they overlap. On the one hand, there are responses that emphasise the ideological and psychological impact of racism, which is identified as one of the primary legacies of colonialism and slavery. This may be seen clearly in the works of Anténor Firmin, Marcus Garvey, Aimé Césaire and Frantz Fanon. It is a less prominent response in the Hispanic Caribbean, perhaps because people of African descent are a smaller proportion of the population there than in the Francophone and Anglophone Caribbean. One the other hand, there are responses that are more explicitly political, that draw attention to the problems associated with the plantation system, and that are often influenced by Marxist analysis. Examples of this emphasis are the work of Ramiro Guerra y Sánchez, Elma Francois, Fidel Castro, C.L.R. James, Elsa Goveia, Cheddi Jagan, Juan Antonio Corretjer, René Depestre, José Luis González and Walter Rodney. The first group emphasised the African roots of their identity and the psychological damage of colonialism and racism which devalued the African cultural heritage. The second group, while certainly not denying that there was such damage, was less focused on, and even rejected, the idea that a set of essential traits constituted their identity, as advocates of *negritude* suggested. Their analysis, on the contrary, focuses on the social, economic and political conditions that had created, among many other problems, those of identity and culture. However, the differences between these approaches should not be exaggerated at the expense of acknowledging their similarities. What all these intellectuals share is a basic conviction that the far-reaching problems of culture, identity and nation in Caribbean societies are rooted in the history of oppression and that the solution to these problems must lie in a profound cultural and political struggle.

A second broad theme in the work of Caribbean intellectuals concerns the development of a creole culture and society out of the synthesis of elements from various sources, primarily, but not exclusively, African and European. This may be seen in the work of Jean Price-Mars and Fernando Ortiz, and more recently in work by Rex Nettleford, Kamau Brathwaite, Stuart Hall, Antonio Benítez-Rojo, Jean Bernabé, Patrick Chamoiseau and Raphael Confiant, Edouard Glissant, and Derek Walcott. Across all their differences, these writers share an emphasis on the process of creolisation, or of 'transculturation', a word coined by Ortiz (chapter 4), in the shaping of a unique and authentic Caribbean culture and identity. Their reaction is generally less explicitly political and confrontational than the groups of intellectuals listed above, and their emphasis is more on cultural creativity as the source of Caribbean identity. Consequently, their attention focuses more on the emergence of distinctive languages, musics, religions and cuisine, rather than on political struggle.

The third group contains something of the first two, but with a slightly different emphasis. These intellectuals emphasise the differences and the relations between the Caribbean, seen as the inside or 'us,' and the non-Caribbean, the outside, or 'them.' Among the earliest expressions of this view are the response of J.J. Thomas to Professor Froude's attack on the abilities of West Indians (chapter 23) and José Martí's essay 'Our America' (chapter 1). Other intellectuals who have contributed to this theme include Roberto Fernandez Retamar, Edouard Glissant, Shridath Ramphal and George Lamming. Many of these writers express the concern that the cultural and political struggles of the Caribbean for autonomy, unity and independence are not merely historical. On the contrary, the huge influence of the United States, the hegemonic 'other America', is seen as a persistent threat to the cultural and political sovereignty of the small nations of the Caribbean. Hence, many of these writers, from Martí to Lamming and Ramphal, perceive the need for the peoples and nations of the Caribbean to cooperate in order to survive. Although they are not all political federalists, they do tend to think in terms of a unitary Caribbean identity, that is of a Caribbean 'we' that is distinct from and threatened by 'them', meaning chiefly the United States. The final piece in this collection, however, contradicts some of these basic assumptions. Orlando Patterson argues that Caribbean people are actively participating in shaping what he calls the 'ecumenical culture' of the West Atlantic region, that includes Miami, New York and Toronto as well as the Caribbean.

This last comment shows that the intellectual tradition of the Caribbean is one of continuing debate, and debate at a very high level. It would be foolish to try to place these intellectuals into little boxes with simple labels on them, and that has not been my intention. Simple categories cannot contain the rich and subtle thought of such people as Fernando Ortiz, C.L.R. James and Edouard Glissant. All I have tried to do here is to identify some of the principal themes and concerns regarding Caribbean culture and identity, nation and society, to which these people have contributed. There is, of course, no substitute for reading their works and I hope that this book makes a sample of them more widely available and will encourage more people to study the intellectual traditions that are shaping a Caribbean civilisation.

NOTES

1. C.L.R. James, 'The Birth of a Nation', in *Contemporary Caribbean: A Sociological Reader*, edited by Susan Craig (Maracas, 1981), vol. 1, p. 31.
2. George Lamming, 'Caribbean Labor, Culture, and Identity,' in *Caribbean Cultural Identities,* edited by Glyne Griffith (Lewisburg, PA: Bucknell University, 2001), 20; see chapter 44 of this volume.
3. Franklin W. Knight, *The Caribbean: The Genesis of a Fragmented Nationalism* (New York: Oxford University Press, 1978).
4. See Lola Rodríguez de Tió's poem 'Cuba and Puerto Rico,' in chapter 2 of this volume.
5. See the selections in Part One of this volume by Luis Muñoz Rivera, Pedro Albizu Campos, Luis Muñoz Marín, Juan Antonio Corretjer, José Luis González and Esmeralda Santiago.
6. Lamming, *Caribbean Cultural Identities*, 20.

7. Françoise Pfaff, *Conversations with Maryse Condé* (Lincoln: University of Nebraska, 1996) p. 67, see chapter 21 of this volume.

8. Sidney Mintz, 'The Caribbean as a Socio-cultural Area,' *Journal of World History*, 9:4 (1966): 912-37.

9. Mervyn Alleyne, 'A Linguistic Perspective on the Caribbean' in *Caribbean Contours,* edited by Sidney W. Mintz and Sally Price (Baltimore: Johns Hopkins University Press, 1985), 155.

10. Christine Ho, 'Hold the Chow Mein, Gimme Soca: Creolization of the Chinese in Guyana, Trinidad and Jamaica,' *Amerasia* 15:2 (1989): 3-25.

11. Stuart Hall, 'Cultural Identity and Diaspora' in *Colonial Discourse and Post-Colonial Theory*, edited by Patrick Williams and Laura Chrisman (New York: Columbia University Press, 1994), 402.

Part One
The Hispanophone Intellectuals

One

José Martí

José Martí (1853–1895), the Cuban poet, journalist, and political philosopher, was tremendously influential in shaping a distinct cultural identity for Latin America and predicting the imperialistic tendencies of the United States. More than any other patriot, he is revered in Cuba as the founding father who organised the last stage of the revolution against Spanish colonialism, for which he gave his life.

Born in Havana on January 28 1853, Martí contributed patriotic articles and brought out a newspaper, La Patria Libre, *while still at school. The first stage of the war for independence began in 1868 and lasted for ten years. At the age of 16, Martí was sentenced to six years of hard labour for disloyalty. He worked in stone quarries, cutting and hauling stone, and was so maltreated that he became ill. He was released after six months and, in January 1871, deported to Spain. While studying law in Madrid, he continued to agitate for Cuban independence. After the first Spanish Republic was declared in 1873, Martí wrote to the prime minister that the freely elected body of deputies who had just proclaimed a democratic republic should grant the same rights to Cuba. However, Spain would not relinquish its colonies and the army overthrew the new government in 1874.*

Martí sailed to Mexico where he lived for two years. Mexico had a democratic government at that time and Martí approved of its progressive anti-feudal and anti-clerical policies. However, in November 1876 a military coup ended the democracy and Porfirio Diaz established a dictatorship. Martí, travelling under a pseudonym, briefly visited Cuba in 1877 before he took up a position teaching literature and the history of philosophy at a school in Guatemala City. He was initially impressed by the educational and legal reforms and some signs of economic development in Guatemala but he was dismayed by the political squabbles. After he was himself attacked by both the Liberals and Conservatives, he resigned and left Guatemala in 1878. He was disillusioned by Guatemala's failure to overcome the social divisions and traditions of despotism that he understood were the legacy of its brutal colonial history.

Back in Havana, Martí was arrested for conspiracy and again deported to Spain in 1879. After brief stays in Spain and France he sailed for New York, where he arrived in January 1880. Apart from about six months in Venezuela in 1881, and trips to Haiti, Santo Domingo, Jamaica, and Costa Rica in 1892–93 to promote the cause of the Cuban revolution, Martí lived the rest of his life in the United States. During his exile in the United States Martí's views of that country became more critical and he developed an understanding of the relations between the 'Two Americas', these being essentially the United States and Latin America. His most important essay, 'Nuestra America', published in 1891, summed up his views of these relations and the future possibilities of Latin America. A year later he founded the Cuban Revolutionary Party and devoted himself to organising and raising funds for the independence movement. In April 1895 he reached Cuba via Haiti and Santo Domingo and joined Máximo Gómez and Antonio Maceo in the insurrection that began the final struggle with Spain. On May 19, 1895, Martí, ignoring orders to stay in the rear, rode into the front line of battle and was killed.

The war Martí had launched was close to achieving its goal when the United States intervened in 1898 and the 'Cuban war of liberation was transformed into a U.S. war of conquest' (Pérez 1995, 178). What the United States calls the 'Spanish-American War' soon ended, but no Cubans participated in the peace negotiations. As Martí had feared, the United States, emerging as a world power for the first time, controlled Cuba, along with Puerto Rico, Guam, and the Philippines. Three decades of revolutionary activity (1868–98), of which Martí was the outstanding spokesman, had created a powerful nationalist movement and the deeply-rooted national pride with which the United States has had to contend for over a century.

Martí defined what he meant by the patria, *or fatherland, in a letter to the Spanish prime minister in 1873: 'Fatherland means a community of interests, unity of traditions, unity of goals, the sweetest and most consoling fusion of loves and hopes . . . Cubans do not live as Spaniards live . . . They are nourished by a different system of trade, have links with different countries, and express their happiness through quite contrary customs. There are no common aspirations or*

*identical goals linking the two peoples, or beloved memories to unite them'
(quoted in Turton 1986, 8). Martí understood a people and their homeland to be
defined in terms of their distinct culture. Every* patria *has a unique history that is
shaped by the economic, political and cultural relations it has with other
countries as well as by its own emerging aspirations and traditions. This is what
gives a people, like the Cuban people, the 'community of interests' and 'beloved
memories' that unite them by ties of fraternity and love.*

*Martí's idealism was shaped by the romantic and humanistic movements
of the nineteenth century and especially by the philosophy of the German, Karl
Friedrich Krause (1781–1832), which he encountered in Madrid between 1871
and 1874. Krause emphasised 'the ultimate harmony of the universe and the
brotherhood of man, who by an even fuller exercise of his reason was progressing
towards a realization of these two truths' (Turton 1986, 147). This 'harmonic
rationalism' was the philosophical basis of Martí's conviction that each society
should pursue its own goals with its people living in harmony with each other. It
followed that Cuba, as a distinct society, should be free to define and follow its
own goals. Martí's argument for Cuban independence was not based on narrow
legal points, therefore, but on a philosophical conception of his own culture and
society, and the conviction that it was unjust for any other society to dictate to
Cubans what they should and should not do. Cuba would not only have to
achieve its constitutional independence from Spain, but would also have to
overcome the legacies of its colonial history. Not only that, Martí realised, it
would also have to avoid any future domination by another society, and
particularly one like the United States that had such different memories and
traditions, aspirations and interests.*

A real patria, *in Martí's view, would be a homeland where every person
could achieve fulfilment because major social differences, such as those of an
economic or a racial kind, would be overcome by everyone's love for their common
country, and so, presumably, for each other. Part of Martí's disillusionment with
Mexico, Guatemala and Venezuela resulted from his observation that the
despotism of Porfirio Diaz, Justo Rufino Barrios and Antonio Guzmán Blanco,
respectively, the selfishness and racism of certain social groups, and the huge
inequalities between towns and the countryside, made social harmony impossible.
Despite having become independent, these countries continued to suffer from the
legacies of colonialism, including the ruling class' monopoly of power, the
pervasive racist ideology and the problem of unequal economic development. In
his notebooks of 1881, Martí developed two ideas that became increasingly
important to him: 'the need for home-grown institutions as opposed to those
imported into Latin American countries, and the equally desirable search for*

unity of those peoples' (Turton 1986, 76). He came to see the peoples and countries of Latin America as a kind of family who, though quarreling incessantly, are nevertheless bound by unbreakable ties' (Turton 1986, 77). What he defined as 'Our America', therefore, was shaped, like the particular homelands of which it was composed, by common memories, traditions and aspirations that set them apart from the other America.

Martí's experience of the United States between 1880 and 1895 led him to become increasingly critical until, on the eve of his death, he wrote to a friend, 'I have lived in the monster and I know its entrails; my sling is David's' (to Manuel Mercado, May 18, 1895, in Foner 1977, 440). Martí, as the leader of the Cuban war for independence from Spain, foresaw the imminent danger of the Goliath of the north seizing this opportunity for imperialistic expansion, 'annexing our American nations to the brutal and turbulent North which despises them' (ibid., 440). Even before Cuba had achieved its independence from Spain, therefore, he warned of the dangers of recolonisation by the United States. In this, his last and unfinished letter, Martí accepted the risk of being in personal danger because of 'the duty of preventing the United States from spreading through the Antilles as Cuba gains its independence, and from overpowering with that additional strength our lands of America' (ibid., 439).

The chief problems that the United States posed, from Martí's Cuban point of view, were its growing economic predominance, its jingoism and contempt for its neighbours, the pervasive nature of its racism, and the oppression of working people that resulted from the polarisation of capital and labour. Martí became aware of the dangers of US economic power when a projected trade agreement between Mexico and the United States favoured the latter. Having developed its own industries under a protectionist system, the United States was moving towards a monopoly capitalism in the last decades of the nineteenth century. A country like Mexico would become increasingly dependent on US-manufactured goods. Optimistically, Martí thought that Latin America could become unified into a 'great spiritual nation' that could avoid and counterbalance the hard calculating mentality of the United States. He considered the United States to be a 'country which is in danger . . . putting at risk the decency of the nation, the independence of its neighbours and, perhaps, the independence of the human spirit itself' (letter to El Partido Liberal [Mexico], Aug. 2, 1886, quoted in Turton 1986, 80). Martí was not against economic development but he saw it not so much as an ultimate goal, but as a means of achieving a more just, generous and spiritual society.

In 1886, Martí became more critical of the United States because of its expansionist foreign policy, open racism and violent labour relations. An organisation of US businessmen and politicians, the American Annexation League, was advocating the take-over of territories in Latin America and Canada in order to expand their markets and opportunities for investment. After the Mexican government arrested Colonel Francis Cutting, a US agitator, Martí was shaken by the jingoistic US press and angry mobs of Texans who advocated invading Mexico. He understood that Americans were contemptuous and ignorant of Latin Americans and viewed societies like Mexico and Cuba merely as desirable possessions.

Martí was shocked by the racism that characterised US culture. Articles on Mexico that appeared in Harper's Monthly *in 1887, for example, were openly racist, asserting the superiority of Teutonic and Anglo-Saxon 'races' and arguing that the mixed race of Mexico was inherently degenerate. Martí, on the contrary, was proud of 'our* mestizo *America' and considered the acceptance of miscegenation in Latin America was better than the US efforts to keep 'races' separate. Early in 1888, Martí wrote of 'the serious news that is already coming to light concerning the dangerous and haughty way in which this country [the USA] is proposing to treat our countries . . . plans that I see which tend, in private and public, to an unjust advancement of its power amongst the Spanish peoples of America' (letter to Manuel Mercado, Feb. 19, 1888, quoted in Turton 1986, 84).*

The prejudice against Latin American peoples and the desire for economic expansion reinforced each other in US culture and Martí understood how the demand for new markets was provoked by monopoly capitalism and overproduction. He also understood how this was related to racial and class conflicts within the United States. When Martí lived in the United States, the social advances of Reconstruction that followed Emancipation were being rolled back by Jim Crow laws that segregated the 'races' in order to keep African-Americans unequal. The former slaves, despite having legally become citizens in 1868, became entrapped in rural poverty in the segregated southern states while millions of immigrants came from European countries, like Germany and Italy, to work in the expanding industrial cities of the northern states. In 1886, class tensions exploded in Chicago when 60,000 workers went on strike. Martí at first criticised the trade unionists. However, after police fired on a demonstration in Haymarket Square, killing several people, he became increasingly sympathetic to the workers. When four men were hanged for throwing a bomb that killed several policemen, Martí was outraged because he did not believe any of these men had been responsible. 'This republic,' he wrote, 'through the excessive cult of wealth, has fallen, unchecked by any traditional shackles, into the inequality, injustice and violence of the monarchies' (letter to La Nation *[Argentina], Nov. 13, 1887, quoted in Turton 1986, 139).*

    While Cuba was struggling for independence from Spain, Martí believed that the United States, shaped by its expansionist economy and racist culture, had become corrupt, oppressive and imperialistic. He did not want an independent Cuba to imitate or be dominated by the United States. He hoped that Cuba, as part of 'our America', could be politically independent from Spain and economically and culturally independent of the United States. His important article, 'Our America', published in January 1891, echoes Simón Bolívar's 'Letter to a Jamaican Gentleman' (1815) which argued that Latin American systems of government, rather than being imported from outside, should be appropriate to the country. 'Our America' expressed his mature fears and hopes, and inspired countless Cubans and Latin Americans throughout the twentieth century.

Our America

    The prideful villager thinks his hometown contains the whole world, and as long as he can stay on as mayor or humiliate the rival who stole his sweetheart or watch his nest egg accumulating in its strongbox he believes the universe to be in good order, unaware of the giants in seven-league boots who can crush him underfoot or the battling comets in the heavens that go through the air devouring the sleeping worlds. Whatever is left of that sleepy hometown in America must awaken. These are not times for going to bed in a sleeping cap, but rather, like Juan de Castellanos's[1] men, with our weapons for a pillow, weapons of the mind, which vanquish all others. Trenches of ideas are worth more than trenches of stone.

    A cloud of ideas is a thing no armored prow can smash through. A vital idea set ablaze before the world at the right moment can, like the mystic banner of the last judgment, stop a fleet of battleships. Hometowns that are still strangers to one another must hurry to become acquainted, like men who are about to do battle together. Those who shake their fists at each other like jealous brothers quarreling over a piece of land or the owner of a small house who envies the man with a better one must join hands and interlace them until their two hands are as one. Those who, shielded by a criminal tradition, mutilate, with swords smeared in the same blood that flows through their own veins, the land of a conquered brother whose punishment far exceeds his crimes, must return that land to their brother if they do not wish to be known as a nation of plunderers. The honorable man does not collect his debts of honor in money, at so much per slap. We can no longer be a nation of fluttering leaves, spending our lives in the air, our treetop crowned in flowers, humming or creaking, caressed by the caprices of sunlight or thrashed and felled by tempests. The trees must form ranks to block the seven-league giant! It is the hour of reckoning and of marching in unison, and we must move in lines as compact as the veins of silver that lie at the roots of the Andes.

Only runts whose growth was stunted will lack the necessary valor, for those who have no faith in their land are like men born prematurely. Having no valor themselves, they deny that other men do. Their puny arms, with bracelets and painted nails, the arms of Madrid or of Paris, cannot manage the lofty tree and so they say the tree cannot be climbed. We must load up the ships with these termites who gnaw away at the core of the patria that has nurtured them; if they are Parisians or Madrileños then let them stroll to the Prado by lamplight or go to Tortoni's for an ice. These sons of carpenters who are ashamed that their father was a carpenter! These men born in America who are ashamed of the mother that raised them because she wears an Indian apron, these delinquents who disown their sick mother and leave her alone in her sickbed! Which one is truly a man, he who stays with his mother to nurse her through her illness, or he who forces her to work somewhere out of sight, and lives off her sustenance in corrupted lands, with a worm for his insignia, cursing the bosom that bore him, sporting a sign that says 'traitor' on the back of his paper dress-coat? These sons of our America, which must save herself through her Indians, and which is going from less to more, who desert her and take up arms in the armies of North America, which drowns its own Indians in blood[2] and is going from more to less! These delicate creatures who are men but do not want to do men's work! Did Washington, who made the land for them, go and live with the English during the years when he saw the English marching against his own land? These *incroyables* who drag their honor across foreign soil, like the *incroyables* of the French Revolution, dancing, smacking their lips, and deliberately slurring their words!

And in what patria can a man take greater pride than in our long-suffering republics of America, erected among mute masses of Indians upon the bloodied arms of no more than a hundred apostles, to the sound of the book doing battle against the monk's tall candle? Never before have such advanced and consolidated nations been created from such disparate factors in less historical time. The haughty man thinks that because he wields a quick pen or a vivid phrase the earth was made to be his pedestal, and accuses his native republic of irredeemable incompetence because its virgin jungles do not continually provide him with the means of going about the world a famous plutocrat, driving Persian ponies and spilling champagne. The incapacity lies not in the emerging country, which demands forms that are appropriate to it and a grandeur that is useful, but in the leaders who try to rule unique nations, of a singular and violent composition, with laws inherited from four centuries of free practice in the United States and nineteen centuries of monarchy in France. A gaucho's pony cannot be stopped in midbolt by one of Alexander Hamilton's[3] laws. The sluggish blood of the Indian race cannot be quickened by a phrase from Sieyès.[4] To govern well, one must attend closely to the reality of the place that is governed. In America, the good ruler does not need to know how the German or Frenchman is governed, but what elements his own country is composed of and how he can marshal them so as to reach, by means and institutions born from the country itself, the desirable state in which every man knows himself and is active, and all men enjoy the abundance that Nature, for the good of all, has bestowed on the country they make fruitful by their labor and defend with their lives. The government must be born from the country. The spirit of the government must be the spirit of the country. The form of the government must be in harmony with the country's natural constitution. The government is no more than an equilibrium among the country's natural elements.

In America the natural man has triumphed over the imported book. Natural men have triumphed over an artificial intelligentsia. The native mestizo has triumphed over the alien, pure-blooded criollo.[5] The battle is not between civilization and barbarity, but between false erudition and nature. The natural man is good, and esteems and rewards a superior intelligence as long as that intelligence does not use his submission against him or offend him by ignoring him – for that the natural man deems unforgivable, and he is prepared to use force to regain the respect of anyone who wounds his sensibilities or harms his interests. The tyrants of America have come to power by acquiescing to these scorned natural elements and have fallen as soon as they betrayed them. The republics have purged the former tyrannies of their inability to know the true elements of the country, derive the form of government from them, and govern along with them. *Governor*, in a new country, means *Creator*.

In countries composed of educated and uneducated sectors, the uneducated will govern by their habit of attacking and resolving their doubts with their fists, unless the educated learn the art of governing. The uneducated masses are lazy and timid about matters of the intellect and want to be well-governed, but if the government injures them they shake it off and govern themselves. How can our governors emerge from the universities when there is not a university in America that teaches the most basic element of the art of governing, which is the analysis of all that is unique to the peoples of America? Our youth go out into the world wearing Yankee- or French-colored glasses and aspire to rule by guesswork a country they do not know. Those unacquainted with the rudiments of politics should not be allowed to embark on a career in politics. The literary prizes must not go to the best ode, but to the best study of the political factors in the student's country. In the newspapers, lecture halls, and academies, the study of the country's real factors must be carried forward. Simply knowing those factors without blindfolds or circumlocutions is enough – for anyone who deliberately or unknowingly sets aside a part of the truth will ultimately fail because of the truth he was lacking, which expands when neglected and brings down whatever is built without it. Solving the problem after knowing its elements is easier than solving it without knowing them. The natural man, strong and indignant, comes and overthrows the authority that is accumulated from books because it is not administered in keeping with the manifest needs of the country. To know is to solve. To know the country and govern it in accordance with that knowledge is the only way of freeing it from tyranny. The European university must yield to the American university. The history of America from the Incas to the present must be taught in its smallest detail, even if the Greek Archons go untaught. Our own Greece is preferable to the Greece that is not ours; we need it more. Statesmen who arise from the nation must replace statesmen who are alien to it. Let the world be grafted onto our republics, but we must be the trunk. And let the vanquished pedant hold his tongue, for there is no patria in which a man can take greater pride than in our long-suffering American republics.

Our feet upon a rosary, our heads white, and our bodies a motley of Indian and criollo we boldly entered the community of nations. Bearing the standard of the Virgin, we went out to conquer our liberty. A priest, a few lieutenants, and a woman built a republic in Mexico upon the shoulders of the Indians.[6] A Spanish cleric, under cover of his priestly cape, taught French liberty to a handful of magnificent students who chose a Spanish general to lead Central America against Spain.[7] Still accustomed to monarchy, and with the sun on their chests, the Venezuelans in the north and the Argentines in the south set out to construct nations. When the two heroes clashed and the continent was about to be rocked, one of them, and not the lesser one, turned back.[8] But heroism is less glorious in peacetime than in war, and thus rarer, and it is easier for a man to die with honor than to think in an orderly way. Exalted and unanimous sentiments are more readily governed than the diverging, arrogant, alien, and ambitious ideas that emerge when the battle is over. The powers that were swept up in the epic struggle, along with the feline wariness of the species and the sheer weight of reality, undermined the edifice that had raised the flags of nations sustained by wise governance in the continual practice of reason and freedom over the crude and singular regions of our mestizo America with its towns of bare legs and Parisian dress-coats. The colonial hierarchy resisted the republic's democracy, and the capital city, wearing its elegant cravat, left the countryside, in its horsehide boots, waiting at the door; the redeemers born from books did not understand that a revolution that had triumphed when the soul of the earth was unleashed by a savior's voice had to govern with the soul of the earth and not against or without it. And for all these reasons, America began enduring and still endures the weary task of reconciling the discordant and hostile elements it inherited from its perverse, despotic colonizer with the imported forms and ideas that have, in their lack of local reality, delayed the advent of a logical form of government. The continent, deformed by three centuries of a rule that denied man the right to exercise his reason, embarked – overlooking or refusing to listen to the ignorant masses that had helped it redeem itself – upon a government based on reason, the reason of all directed toward the things that are of concern to all, and not the university-taught reason of the few imposed upon the rustic reason of others. The problem of independence was not the change in form, but the change in spirit.

Common cause had to be made with the oppressed in order to consolidate a system that was opposed to the interests and governmental habits of the oppressors. The tiger, frightened away by the flash of gunfire, creeps back in the night to find his prey. He will die with flames shooting from his eyes, his claws unsheathed, but now his step is inaudible for he comes on velvet paws. When the prey awakens, the tiger is upon him. The colony lives on in the republic, but our America is saving itself from its grave blunders – the arrogance of the capital cities, the blind triumph of the scorned campesinos, the excessive importation of foreign ideas and formulas, the wicked and impolitic disdain for the native race – through the superior virtue, confirmed by necessary bloodshed, of the republic that struggles against the colony. The tiger waits behind every tree, crouches in every corner. He will die, his claws unsheathed, flames shooting from his eyes.[9]

But 'these countries will be saved', in the words of the Argentine Rivadavia,[10] who erred on the side of urbanity during crude times; the machete is ill-suited to a silken scabbard, nor can the spear be abandoned in a country won by the spear, for it becomes enraged and stands in the doorway of Iturbide's Congress[11] demanding that 'the fair-skinned man be made emperor'. These countries will be saved because, with the genius of moderation that now seems, by nature's serene harmony, to prevail in the continent of light, and the influence of the critical reading that has, in Europe, replaced the fumbling ideas about phalansteries[12] in which the previous generation was steeped, the real man is being born to America, in these real times.

What a vision we were: the chest of an athlete, the hands of a dandy, and the forehead of a child. We were a whole fancy dress ball, in English trousers, a Parisian waistcoat, a North American overcoat, and a Spanish bullfighter's hat. The Indian circled about us, mute, and went to the mountaintop to christen his children. The black, pursued from afar, alone and unknown, sang his heart's music in the night, between waves and wild beasts. The campesinos, the men of the land, the creators, rose up in blind indignation against the disdainful city, their own creation. We wore epaulets and judge's robes, in countries that came into the world wearing rope sandals and Indian headbands. The wise thing would have been to pair, with charitable hearts and the audacity of our founders, the Indian headband and the judicial robe, to undam the Indian, make a place for the able black, and tailor liberty to the bodies of those who rose up and triumphed in its name. What we had was the judge, the general, the man of letters, and the cleric. Our angelic youth, as if struggling from the arms of an octopus, cast their heads into the heavens and fell back with sterile glory, crowned with clouds. The natural people, driven by instinct, blind with triumph, overwhelmed their gilded rulers. No Yankee or European book could furnish the key to the Hispanoamerican enigma. So the people tried hatred instead, and our countries amounted to less and less each year. Weary of useless hatred, of the struggle of book against sword, reason against the monk's taper, city against countryside, the impossible empire of the quarreling urban castes against the tempestuous or inert natural nation, we are beginning, almost unknowingly, to try love. The nations arise and salute one another. 'What are we like?' they ask, and begin telling each other what they are like. When a problem arises in Cojimar they no longer seek the solution in Danzig.[13] The frock-coats are still French, but the thinking begins to be American. The young men of America are rolling up their sleeves and plunging their hands into the dough, and making it rise with the leavening of their sweat. They understand that there is too much imitation, and that salvation lies in creating. *Create* is this generation's password. Make wine from plantains; it may be sour, but it is our wine! It is now understood that a country's form of government must adapt to its natural elements, that absolute ideas, in order not to collapse over an error of form, must be expressed in relative forms; that liberty, in order to be viable, must be sincere and full, that if the republic does not open its arms to all and include all in its progress, it dies. The tiger inside came in through the gap, and so will the tiger outside. The general holds the cavalry's speed to the pace of the infantry, for if he leaves the infantry far behind, the enemy will surround the cavalry. Politics is strategy. Nations must continually criticize themselves, for criticism is health, but with a single heart and a single mind. Lower yourselves to the unfortunate and raise them up in your arms! Let the heart's fires unfreeze all that is motionless in America, and let the country's natural blood surge and throb through its veins! Standing tall, the workmen's eyes full of joy, the new men of America are saluting each other from one country to another. Natural statesmen are emerging from the direct study of nature; they read in order to apply what they read, not copy it. Economists are studying problems at their origins. Orators are becoming more temperate. Dramatists are putting native characters onstage. Academies are discussing practical subjects. Poetry is snipping off its wild, Zorilla-esque[14] mane and hanging up its gaudy waistcoat on the glorious tree. Prose, polished and gleaming, is replete with ideas. The rulers of Indian republics are learning Indian languages.[15]

America is saving herself from all her dangers. Over some republics the octopus sleeps still, but by the law of equilibrium, other republics are running into the sea to recover the lost centuries with mad and sublime swiftness. Others, forgetting that

Juárez[16] traveled in a coach drawn by mules, hitch their coach to the wind and take a soap bubble for coachman – and poisonous luxury, enemy of liberty, corrupts the frivolous and opens the door to foreigners. The virile character of others is being perfected by the epic spirit of a threatened independence. And others, in rapacious wars against their neighbors, are nurturing an unruly soldier caste that may devour them. But our America may also face another danger, which comes not from within but from the differing origins, methods, and interests of the continent's two factions. The hour is near when she will be approached by an enterprising and forceful nation that will demand intimate relations with her, though it does not know her and disdains her. And virile nations self-made by the rifle and the law love other virile nations, and love only them. The hour of unbridled passion and ambition from which North America may escape by the ascendancy of the purest element in its blood – or into which its vengeful and sordid masses, its tradition of conquest, and the self-interest of a cunning leader could plunge it – is not yet so close, even to the most apprehensive eye, that there is no time for it to be confronted and averted by the manifestation of a discreet and unswerving pride, for its dignity as a republic, in the eyes of the watchful nations of the Universe, places upon North America a brake that our America must not remove by puerile provocation, ostentatious arrogance, or patricidal discord. Therefore the urgent duty of our America is to show herself as she is, one in soul and intent, rapidly overcoming the crushing weight of her past and stained only by the fertile blood shed by hands that do battle against ruins and by veins that were punctured by our former masters. The disdain of the formidable neighbor who does not know her is our America's greatest danger, and it is urgent – for the day of the visit is near – that her neighbor come to know her, and quickly, so that he will not disdain her. Out of ignorance, he may perhaps begin to covet her.[17] But when he knows her, he will remove his hands from her in respect. One must have faith in the best in man and distrust the worst. One must give the best every opportunity, so that the worst will be laid bare and overcome. If not, the worst will prevail. Nations should have one special pillory for those who incite them to futile hatreds, and another for those who do not tell them the truth until it is too late.

There is no racial hatred, because there are no races.[18] Sickly, lamp-lit minds string together and rewarm the library-shelf races that the honest traveler and the cordial observer seek in vain in the justice of nature, where the universal identity of man leaps forth in victorious love and turbulent appetite. The soul, equal and eternal, emanates from bodies that are diverse in form and color. Anyone who promotes and disseminates opposition or hatred among races is committing a sin against humanity. But within that jumble of peoples which lives in close proximity to our peoples, certain peculiar and dynamic characteristics are condensed – ideas and habits of expansion, acquisition, vanity, and greed – that could, in a period of internal disorder or precipitation of a people's cumulative character, cease to be latent national preoccupations and become a serious threat to the neighboring, isolated and weak lands that the strong country declares to be perishable and inferior. To think is to serve. We must not, out of a villager's antipathy, impute some lethal congenital wickedness to the continent's light-skinned nation simply because it does not speak our language or share our view of what home life should be or resemble us in its political failings, which are different from ours, or because it does not think highly of quick-tempered, swarthy men or look with charity, from its still uncertain eminence, upon those less favored by history who, in heroic stages, are climbing the road that republics travel. But neither should we seek to conceal the obvious facts of the problem, which can, for the peace of the centuries, be resolved by timely study and the urgent, wordless union of the continental soul. For the unanimous hymn is already ringing forth, and the present generation is bearing industrious America along the road sanctioned by our sublime forefathers. From the Rio Bravo to the Straits of Magellan, the Great Cemi,[19] seated on a condor's back, has scattered the seeds of the new America across the romantic nations of the continent and the suffering islands of the sea!

NOTES

1. Juan de Castellanos (1522–1607) a Spanish poet, soldier and trader in the Caribbean, and later a parish priest in Colombia, wrote an epic chronicle in verse about the creative and heroic men he had known, *Elegies of Famous Men of the Indies* (Madrid, 1589).
2. On December 29, 1890, just before Martí wrote 'Our America', most of a group of 350 unarmed Sioux Indians, men, women and children, were massacred by the US cavalry at Wounded Knee, South Dakota.
3. Alexander Hamilton (1755 or 1757–1804), who was born in Nevis, was the first US secretary of the treasury (1789–95) and an advocate of a strong national government.
4. Emmanuel Joseph Sieyès (1748–1836), a French priest who was prominent in the French Revolution, participated in drafting the Declaration of the Rights of Man in 1789. His views on government influenced Simón Bolívar, who led the wars of independence that liberated Bolivia, Colombia, Ecuador, Peru and Venezuela from Spanish rule.
5. Martí contrasts the 'natural man' (*el hombre natural*), who in the Americas is of mixed 'races', with the American-born 'white' man (*criollo*) who has European habits which, however well learned, are inappropriate ('false') in America. Martí rejects the idea of a struggle between civilisation and barbarism, as declared by the Argentine statesman Domingo Faustino Sarmiento in *Facundo* (1845), because this poses a false dichotomy between progress based on foreign ideas, on the one hand, and ignorance and backwardness, on the other. The 'natural man' is good and is capable of governing for the common good because he is educated in the culture of his own society and

understands the local realities more than those who are 'wearing Yankee- or French-colored glasses'.

6. The priest was Padre Miguel Hidalgo y Costilla (1753–1811) who led the struggle for Mexican independence in 1810, and José María Morelos was one of his lieutenants who drew up a constitution in 1814. The woman was Doña Josefa Ortíz de Domínguez, the wife of a chief magistrate, who defied her husband to join the revolutionary movement.

7. Martí was probably referring to José Antonio Liendo y Goicoechea (1735–1814) who was a Franciscan. He was born in what is now Costa Rica but he studied in Spain in the 1780s and Martí may have considered him to be Spanish. Returning to Guatemala in 1788, he taught an experimental approach to science and a progressive social attitude to his students at the University of San Carlos. The generation of Guatemalans who led the colony to independence was influenced by him. The 'Spanish general' was probably Gabino Gaínza (1753–1824). Born in Spain, he had a military career in South America and became the acting captain-general of Guatemala in 1821. He tolerated the rebellion against Spain and remained the chief executive after independence was declared.

8. Simón Bolívar (1783–1830) and the Argentine José de San Martín (1778–1850), the leader of the southern revolution, clashed in 1822 over the control of Guayaquil, Ecuador, a major port and naval base that Bolívar claimed for Colombia and San Martín for Peru. San Martín withdrew, leaving the way open for Bolívar to complete the liberation of Peru.

9. The colonial spirit of despotism, 'the tiger', was a persistent threat within the newly independent republics of 'Our America' and Martí, without analysing the problem in terms of the struggle between antagonistic social groups, thought that it could be overcome by 'a change of spirit'. The new *patria* could be unified and the tiger kept at bay, Martí believed, if people would commit themselves to the 'higher virtue' of the common good.

10. Bernadino Rivadavia (1780–1845), an Argentine revolutionary who advocated policies of enlightened reform and economic development, became president in 1826. He alienated powerful interests and was forced to resign in 1827, spending most of the rest of his life in exile.

11. Augustín de Iturbide (1783–1824), a Mexican landowner, fought against the revolution of Hidalgo and Morelos but led Mexico to independence in 1821. When he made himself emperor, the Mexican Congress ratified the proclamation but a republican revolution forced him into abdication and exile in 1823. When he returned he was executed.

12. A phalanstery was a planned self-sufficient community, rather like a monastery but organised according to the philosophy of the French Cooperative Socialist Charles Fournier (1772–1837). It was only a utopian idea because Fournier could not raise the money to start one.

13. Cojímar is a small Cuban port just east of Havana and Danzig is a major Polish port, now called Gdansk, that was controlled by Germany in Martí's time.

14. José Zorilla (1817–93) was a popular romantic Spanish poet, whose work Martí did not like.

15. Martí's romantic vision powerfully expresses the nationalistic aspirations of 'our America' but his reliance on love and reason underestimated the persistent social antagonisms of these post-colonial nations. For example, in Guatemala, where the

majority of the people are Indian, the government did not accept the official status and use of the indigenous peoples' languages until 1995.

16. Benito Pablo Juárez (1806–72), a Mexican of Indian descent, reduced the power of the army and the church when he was minister of justice. After a long struggle against conservatives he was elected president of Mexico in 1861. His integrity and commitment to the poor were legendary. France invaded Mexico, ostensibly to collect debts, and installed an emperor in 1864. Republican armies drove out the French and restored democracy. In 1867, Juárez was restored as president, which he remained until his death.

17. This was very perceptive and prophetic. The United States not only invaded Cuba and Puerto Rico in 1898, but it also developed military intervention as a standard element of its policy. In 1904, when Santo Domingo could not pay its debts, President Theodore Roosevelt announced his 'Big Stick' policy, threatening the use of force whenever the United States decided there was 'wrongdoing or impotence' anywhere in the western hemisphere. During the next 30 years, the United States repeatedly invaded and occupied Cuba (1906–9, 1912, 1917–22), Haiti (1914, 1915–34) and the Dominican Republic (1904, 1914, 1916–24).

18. Martí was correct to say that 'there are no races'. Modern biologists and anthropologists agree that there is no objective, biological or scientific reason for grouping certain people together as a 'race', distinct from others. Humanity is, in fact, one species. The idea of 'race' is a social construction, developed out of colonial relationships in order to try to justify the oppression of one people by another. Unfortunately, however, Martí is engaged in wishful thinking when he says 'there can be no racial animosity'. It is true that reason would conclude there can be no racial animosity if there are no races, but racial prejudice and racist ideology, which are not based on reason or science, are both real and widespread social phenomena.

19. The Great Cemí ('*el Gran Zemi*') refers to a deity or guardian spirit, one of the ancient *zemis* of the Taino Arawak which were a personification of natural forces. They usually took anthropomorphic form, were associated with dreams and ceremonies, and were represented in objects made of bone, clay, wood, shell, cotton or stone, or in carved designs on rocks. Many had specialized powers, such as influencing the weather, crops, hunting and health. The most powerful deities were Yúcahu, lord of cassava and the sea, and Atabey, his mother, the goddess of fresh water and human fertility.

Two

Lola Rodríguez de Tío

Lola Rodríguez de Tío (1843–1924) was a lyrical poet and political revolutionary from Puerto Rico. Like her friend Eugenio María de Hostos (1839–1903), who also advocated Puerto Rican self-determination and Caribbean unity, she spent much of her life in exile, and she died in Cuba. She helped José Martí plan the Cuban War for Independence when she lived in New York. When Martí created the Cuban Revolutionary Party in 1892, he said one of its aims was to help Puerto Rico in its struggle against Spain and 18 patriots formed a Puerto Rican section of the party in New York in 1895. Rodríguez de Tío encountered sexism from her compatriots and became an early feminist.

Puerto Rico, like Cuba, had its nationalist independentistas in the nineteenth century. On September 23, 1868, just before the beginning of the Ten Years' War in Cuba, El Grito de Lares [The Cry of Lares], initiated an insurrection in Puerto Rico when the insurgents declared independence in the town of Lares. In 1896, in the middle of Cuba's war, there was an uprising in Yauco, Puerto Rico. These uprisings in Puerto Rico were quickly suppressed but some concessions were made. In 1873, slavery was abolished and in 1897, Spain agreed that Puerto Rico would have universal suffrage, representation in the Cortes in Madrid, and a degree of self-government. Within months, however, on July 25, 1898, US troops invaded Puerto Rico and this autonomist constitution was overthrown. Ironically, it was not so much a unified revolutionary struggle that Puerto Rico shared with Cuba, as the patriots had hoped, as the common experience of invasion and occupation by the United States.

Rodríguez de Tío's poems exemplify the romantic idealism of the nineteenth century patriots and gave voice to a national sentiment. Her poems were collected in several volumes, including My Songs *(1876),* Clarities and Mists *(1885) and* My Book of Cuba *(1893). 'The Song of Borinquen' became the* independentista *anthem of Puerto Rico, 'La Borinqueña'. (After the US invasion more sentimental and less militant lyrics were written by Manuel Fernández Juncos).*

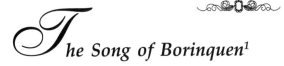

The Song of Borinquen[1]

Awake, Borinqueños,
for they've given the signal!

Awake from your sleep
for it's time to fight!

Come! The sound of cannon
will be dear to us.

At that patriotic clamor
doesn't your heart burn?

Look! The Cuban will soon be free,
the machete will give him freedom.

The drum of war announces in its beating
that the thicket is the place, the meeting place!

Most beautiful Borinquen, we have to follow Cuba;
you have brave sons who want to fight!

Let us no more seem fearful!
Let us no more, timid, permit our enslavement!

We want to be free already
and our machete is well sharpened!

Why should we, then, remain so asleep
and deaf, asleep and deaf to that signal?

There's no need to fear, Ricans, the sound of cannon,
for saving the homeland is the duty of the heart!

We want no more despots! Let the tyrant fall!
Women, likewise wild, will know how to fight!

We want freedom and our machete will give it to us![2]

Let's go, Puerto Ricans, let's go already,
for LIBERTY is waiting, ever so anxious!

Cuba and Puerto Rico

Cuba and Puerto Rico are
the two wings of a bird,
they receive flowers and bullets
on the very same heart.
What a lot if in the illusion
that glows red in a thousand tones,
Lola's muse dreams
with fervent fantasy
of making one single homeland
of this land and of mine.

NOTES

1. *Borinquen* or *Boriquen* was the Taino's name for the island the Spanish called Puerto Rico.
2. A militant group of Puerto Rican revolutionaries called *Los Macheteros* announced themselves in 1978 as a 'People's Army' against the United States. Operating in small cell-like units, they carried out several actions, including the destruction of nine National Guard planes at the airport in San Juan, the robbery of a Wells Fargo armoured car in Santurce, and an explosion at the US courthouse in Old San Juan.

Three

Ramiro Guerra y Sánchez

Ramiro Guerra y Sánchez (1880–1970), a leading Cuban historian and intellectual, was educated at Harvard University and the University of Havana. He backed General Gerardo Machado, the Liberal party candidate for president in 1924, and later became his secretary, supporting him until his resignation and flight from Cuba in 1933. In 1927, Guerra published his most influential book, which had first appeared as a series of newspaper articles, called Sugar and Society in the Caribbean. *This is an analysis of the history and consequences of the system of land exploitation that has predominated in much of the Caribbean since the middle of the seventeenth century.*

The plantation, or latifundium *as Guerra called it, is a large-scale enterprise that produces a single crop for export. It tends to monopolise land ownership and needs to control a large labour force. Consequently, the social and political structure of a 'plantation society' is generally bipolar, with a small group of rich and powerful landowners (often absentees and, later, foreign corporations) exploiting a large mass of impoverished and powerless workers. Guerra showed how this pattern developed in Barbados and other parts of the British West Indies long before it came to predominate in Cuba. He described how the evolution of this kind of economy and society is related to its dependency on overseas markets and how this leads to 'economic servitude and social and political decay' even in a society, like Cuba, that was nominally an independent republic. He showed also how this evolution is related to the importation of cheap labour, first slaves and contract labourers (African, Chinese, and Mayan Mexicans) and then free but poor*

*immigrants (Haitian and Jamaican) who depress wages and drive down the
living standards of most of the Cuban people.*

*In relating the particular history of Cuba to a general economic and
sociological analysis, Guerra developed a powerful thesis and many of his
predictions came true. His wide-ranging study was one of the first to provide
insight into the complex relationships that have shaped twentieth-century Cuba.*

✧◈❀◈✧

Sugar and Society in the Caribbean: An Economic History of Cuban Agriculture (excerpts)

From 1840 to 1860 sugar production increased rapidly in Cuba, and sugar
exports rose from 12,867,698 arrobas for the five years from 1841 through 1845 to
23,139,245 arrobas for the period 1856 through 1859,[1] according to Pezuela. This
rapid development was assisted by a fall in the price of coffee which almost
completely ruined the coffee plantations. Consequently, almost all of the farms,
capital, and labor that had been engaged in coffee cultivation were turned to the
production of sugar. In other words, the sugar industry was strengthened by the
destruction of one of the economy's four pillars – livestock, sugar cane, tobacco,
and coffee. Coffee, although the last to appear, had come to be one of the strongest
and most prosperous.

Meanwhile, advances in processing methods and mechanical improvements
forced constant renewal of machinery and other factory installations in the sugar
mills. They expanded continually and were already enterprises requiring large
amounts of capital. It became necessary to abandon the old practice whereby each
farmer, no matter how few caballerías[2] he had planted, would set up his own grinding
mill for his cane; by 1850 or 1860 the number of mills had leveled off. Future
development would occur no longer through an increase in the number of mills but
through an increase in the capacity of each. It was no longer possible to be a sugar
planter without being a large landowner or capitalist. Small sugar mills, less effective
in cane juice extraction and often producing sugar of lower quality, could not meet
the competition and, at first barely surviving, began to fail and disappear. Many
were destroyed during the Ten Years' War. For example, in 1862 in the Bayamo area
there were twenty-four sugar mills, including one steam-driven; in the Manzanillo
area there were six steam-driven mills out of a total of eighteen. In 1877 not a single
mill was recorded for these areas, and around Holguín they had been reduced from
sixteen to only four. The number of sugar mills fell from 2,000 in 1860 to 1,190 in 1877.

One of the first effects of this twofold process – reduction in the number of sugar mills and increase in the manufacturing capacity of those that continued to operate – was the appearance of a new type of producer, the colono,[3] who planted cane but did not own a mill to grind and convert it into sugar. Instead, he had his cane ground at the nearest sugar mill and, paying the owner with part of his product, disposed of the rest as he wished. The colono symbolized the division of the production of sugar into separate growing and processing phases and the decline of the traditional planter who also processed and sold his sugar. Nevertheless, farmers continued to be independent producers. They had their cane ground at the mills under specified conditions and received a share of the sugar to dispose of on whatever terms they could get. Mills that received cane from independent farmers in these circumstances came to be called *centrales* at the end of the Ten Years' War. The existence of the central and the system of colonos date approximately from that time.

This new arrangement came about spontaneously to meet the needs of both the mill owners and the farmer turned colono. In the 1850s and 1860s mill owners were hampered by the lack of the capital they required to modernize and expand their factory machinery and by the size of their mills, which presented enormous problems of organization and administration. The Count of Pozos Dulces and other economists of that period advanced the principle of division of labor as a means for solving the industry's problems: sugar manufacture and agriculture should be kept distinct and separate. By devoting himself exclusively to processing, the manufacturer would reduce the extent of his enterprise and could employ all his capital in improving, and enlarging, and operating the mill. He would free himself from the immense expense and burden of seeing to the purchase of lands and the cultivation of cane and its transportation to the factory. The mill owner never completely gave up growing sugar cane but, adapting his financial and administrative problems to the problems of the farmer who could not afford to maintain a mill, he began to grind his neighbors' cane and charge for this service in sugar. This opened a new era in the history of the sugar industry by creating and extending a new social class, the colono, which has slowly but surely become economically dependent on the central.

The establishment of the central and colono system at first did not lead to the appearance of the latifundium,[4] but delayed it instead. If the expanding central had not been supplied by the colono, its stock of cane would have had to be ensured by land purchases and farm administration, in spite of capital shortages and the scarcity of labor after the abolition of slavery. Mills could be and were enlarged, therefore, without additional farm land. Although mills were becoming huge, there was no over-all movement in the direction of the latifundium. Subdivision of properties continued at a slower rate, creating 'cane colonies', and at the end of the century there was a total of 60,711 farms in cane, representing 30 per cent of Cuba's total area. The general obstacles to rapid development have been enumerated and, still existing, they stood in the way of the latifundium.

After 1868 another powerful obstacle was added: the insecure conditions for capital and business, especially outside the cities, during the long and bloody wars of independence. Production developed very slowly and even suffered serious setbacks, for example in the years 1885–90, when it was much lower than in 1870–75.

But before the close of the nineteenth century and the end of Spanish rule in Cuba, a new factor came into play that is mainly responsible for the latifundium: the competition among the mills for their raw material, sugar cane.

Mills had not competed with each other formerly because each was limited to a circumscribed area by the lack of adequate and economical transportation. No mill invaded the lands of its neighbor mill, and more than a hundred small mills might be contained in one municipal district.

As mills grew into centrales they required a much greater supply of cane. Although the supply area was constantly being expanded, its boundaries were set by the high cost of carting; but in 1836 the introduction of the railroad[5] finally resulted in bitter competition among the centrales and eventually brought about the latifundium. Until 1878 the railroads developed slowly all over the world because, in spite of their enormous advantages, they were an expensive and still imperfect means of transportation. But after 1870, when iron rails began to be replaced by steel and the price of steel rails in the United States decreased from $106 per ton in 1870 to $44 in 1878, railroads developed amazingly and came into wide use.

The centrales of Cuba, consuming more and more cane as they grew in size, began to lay down their own narrow gauge tracks, which enabled them to bring cane to the mill at moderate cost from regions previously outside the central area. At the same time, the network of public railways made it feasible to move cane over long distances. In theory, the central could now expand endlessly but, in practice, for long hauls the zone of each factory was circumscribed by the expense of laying lines or by freight charges.

From the moment a central was able to invade another's traditional supply area, rivalry between the two was inevitable. At first there was an increase in the amount of sugar offered the colono in exchange for grinding his sell cane and, until a few years ago, it was still possible to identify these competing zones by the higher number of arrobas of sugar that the farmer received from the central for his cane. In Havana, Matanzas, and Santa Clara, where there were many centrales and a public railroad promoting their rivalry, the colono was free to sell his cane to the highest bidder and was given more than seven arrobas of sugar for every hundred of cane. In Camagüey, Oriente, and parts of Pinar del Río, where there were no railroads, only four – or at the most, five and a half – were offered.

Competition created a new problem for the centrales: how to guarantee that each would have enough cane for each zafra[6] at the lowest possible cost. This could be accomplished through one of two means: by economic domination of the colono – reducing his independence and making him a vassal of the mill, bound by contract and prevented from freely selling his product – or by purchasing lands and administering them as cane farms or having them sharecropped or rented by colonos dependent on the mill.

The first means twisted the original colono system by changing a class of free farmers into feudal vassals of the central; the second led directly to the latifundium by destroying small and medium-sized rural properties and replacing the old-style colono with either a kind of unpaid employee whose earnings would derive from his farming of lands owned and financed by the mill and under its strict supervision and accounting or, in the case of 'administration' farming, with a day laborer.

This marked the beginning of the contest between colono and central. The last decades of the century passed without any appreciable change in the situation because the capital resources of each continued to be fairly evenly matched. But independence created new conditions for industry and, through the Cuban government's lack of foresight, permitted foreign capital to weigh overwhelmingly on the side of the factory . . . .

With the end of Spanish rule in Cuba, very favorable conditions were created for the development of the sugar industry. Some were general and affected business as a whole, others were related only to the sugar sector; but all in one way or another contributed to the transformation of the central into the immense modern latifundium.

Once the country was at peace, it became safe for business. Absolute guarantees were offered capital investment not only by the Cuban government but also by the formidable strength of the United States. The terms of the Treaty of Paris, which in 1898 ended the Spanish-American War, and the Permanent Treaty between Cuba and the United States, drawn up in accordance with the Platt Amendment, ended the fear of revolutionary damage and eliminated one of the obstacles that had inhibited foreign investment in Cuba since the middle of the nineteenth century.

Another very important consideration was the conquest of yellow fever and the extraordinary improvement in sanitary conditions. From a disease-ridden island which took a high toll in foreign lives, Cuba was transformed into a healthy country with a low mortality rate. Precautions against epidemics were strictly enforced, and measures were taken to combat them at the first outbreak.

Also, because of its interest in railway development, the government gave generous subsidies to the railroad companies, as well as to other public utilities enterprises, thus helping to open up new and extensive regions to development through the initiative of organizers and entrepreneurs. At the same time, the lowering of most of the customs barriers, formerly designed to protect the interests of Spain against the trade of the rest of the world, offered opportunities hitherto unknown to foreign commerce.

Finally, investment of foreign capital was welcomed as a demonstration of faith in the Republic and special laws were enacted for banks and their branches, which were subject to minimal state control and paid insignificant taxes. These were but the most salient factors that contributed effectively to opening Cuba to the unhindered activity of capitalist enterprise. In Cuba such enterprise was free from any of the restrictions placed on it in the United States itself, the land of big business, by the Sherman antitrust laws and all the other regulations for maintaining a sound balance among the various forces behind industrial, financial, and commercial development.

Aside from the influence of these general causes, the sugar industry received a powerful stimulus from the Reciprocal Treaty clause which reduced by 20 per cent the United States tariff on Cuban sugar. Cuba is better located than any other sugar-producing country to sell its commodity to the United States. During the colonial period, customs barriers separated Cuba from its neighbor. But when that wall was not only demolished but replaced by a treaty that gave Cuba special privileges in the United States tariff system, foreign capital interested in the sugar industry decided that Cuba was an ideal country for investment.

Also of special and direct interest to the mills was the railroad legislation enacted by the military government of General Wood,[7] which has provided and still provides exceptional facilities for the construction of private railways. When a private railway dominates a region, it inevitably outstrips the public railroad by depriving it of its most important freight and therefore eliminates competition. It also aids the mills in the endless expansion by which they become absolute masters of the landowner or farmer, who lacks economical transportation for his products. The government's concession of the so-called *subpuertos* (private coastal piers) was to give the private railway a final advantage. By guaranteeing to each central exclusive transportation for domestic and foreign trade, the subpuertos not only permitted great economies but protected the central against all competition in its particular zone.

Opposing these very favorable conditions for the development of a powerful sugar industry was only one measure that, by relating its growth to the country's increase in population, could restrict its drive or contain its force. This was the wise and provident legislation, enacted under General Wood, which limited so-called undesirable immigration. Promoted energetically and with patriotic zeal by the Cuban public from the time of Saco and Pozos Dulces, its inclusion in the Reciprocal Treaty of 1902 was insisted upon by North American beet sugar interests.[8] But this obstacle was easily overcome by the most powerful companies, when it was a question of their making more money at the expense of the Cuban worker and of national welfare. Who would have imagined that Cuba's presidents and ministers of state, almost all of them men of the revolution, with their special permits to contract for and import Haitians and Jamaicans, would vindicate the captains-general O'Donnell, Roncali, Cañedo, and Concha, who, little more than fifty years before, had facilitated the traffic of slave dealers on the grounds that the cultivation of cane made the slaves indispensable! The complicity of these governors, said to be purchased at the rate of an ounce of gold for each slave, was always held up to Spain by Cuban revolutionaries as one of the most shameful aspects of the colonial period and as one of the most heinous crimes committed against Cuba by Spain in its effort to continue dominating our country.

Wood's measure has now been amended by the highest Cuban authorities, who no doubt mistakenly believe that they are serving the best interests of the national economy. But it is sad to reflect that all the past thinking, writing, and efforts of Cuba's most eminent statesmen and patriots have been in vain, and that public and high government circles are so slow to realize certain truths which are basic to the country's security and welfare but are outweighed by powerful material influences when they are placed on the scale of national destinies.[9]

With the country opened up to world progress and swept clean of the last obstructions of the colonial period, with extraordinary incentives and the elimination of the only possible hindrance to its growth, the sugar industry could and did extend itself by using the two invincible courses of action employed in Barbados: very cheap labor and foreign capital in search of profit. It consolidated itself in about 180 sugar mills and more than 170,000 caballerías of property, a fifth of the national territory and perhaps more than half the arable land of Cuba. In addition, it controlled many more caballerías, either by renting them or by isolating them within the mills' zones of influence.

But precisely here lies Cuba's tragedy. For four centuries its people had been settling the country little by little, clearing it and making it a healthy place to live in. They imported its principal commercial crops; they adapted cattle and domestic livestock to its climate; they found suitable locations for towns and cities on its coasts and in its interior; they courageously defended the island against invasion; they allotted and divided its land among farmers; they laid out and built its modern railways as well as its old but useful country roads; they fought for liberty and independence in the hope of establishing a vigorous republic that would be shared by and would serve all; and, thanks to the genius of a Cuban – Finlay[10] – not only Cuba but the whole world was freed of one of its worst plagues.

When all this toil of centuries seemed to be almost completed and the fruits could at last be enjoyed by their children, the sugar latifundium, which had ruined the West Indies with its two formidable instruments, foreign capital and imported cheap labor, invaded the island. Its appearance marked the beginning of the wholesale destruction of our small and medium-sized properties and the reduction of our rural landowners and independent farmers, backbone of our nation, to the lowly condition of a proletariat being stifled by that economic asphyxiation which afflicts the country today from one end to the other . . . .

It is said that the latifundium is indispensable to the existence of the sugar industry. This is an error. The latifundium is indispensable to the domination and exploitation of the colono by the central, which can then set its own conditions; that is, it enables forty, or at the most fifty, companies to control hundreds of thousands of farmers; but it is not essential to the planting or processing of cane. There are more just and humane bases upon which to organize sugar production. If there were not, Cuba would have no interest at all in an industry that subjects the farmer to such cruel and destructive economic servitude . . . .

Cuban land originally was allotted, divided, and cultivated by the first Spanish settlers and their descendants. A thriving community was gradually established, one whose members were deeply attached to the soil they tilled and were better adapted than any other Europeans to the natural and social environment. Mainly rural folk and landowners, they believed in their national identity and fought first for Spain and later for political independence until they became a sovereign state. Cuba existed as a nation from the time the native-born colonists, who far outnumbered the peninsular Spanish residents, divided up and took possession of the island territory and fashioned for themselves an economic life, based on their agricultural activities, distinct from that of Spain. Economic independence was the essential precondition of spiritual and political independence.

The latifundium system is reversing this process. It consolidates thousands of small farms into immense agrarian units; it uproots the farmer from his land; it destroys the rural landowning and independent farming class, backbone of the nation; and finally, it puts an end to national economic independence by converting the society into a mere dependency, a satellite, a workshop, at the service of some foreign power. It reverses the lengthy process which shaped Cuban society and polity and undermines, subverts, and obliterates its national identity. Just as a field is prepared for new farming and different crops by tearing down its fences, abolishing its boundaries, and clearing away its plants and vegetation, so the latifundium is wiping out four centuries of growth in Cuba and is reducing Cuba to an enormous plantation producing sugar for the benefit of foreign consumers.

The sugar latifundium, in addition to attacking the foundation of Cuba's economic, social, and political structure, must inevitably impoverish the Cuban masses. Economists of all periods and of all schools have recognized that agriculture is the activity most productive and most conducive to real wealth for the general population, much more so than forestry, fishing, and mining, with industry and commerce trailing far behind. For this reason, national welfare depends on how widely land is divided and distributed among the people. When the latifundium deprives the Cuban farmer of his land, it takes away his most effective and often his only means of self-support.

The collective ability of the Cuban to create wealth, to produce, and to increase his properties, is rapidly disappearing. The Cuban capitalist has to live from income or accumulated capital, spending it gradually, and the Cuban daily wage-earner can never hope to own anything more than a little house in some poor section of the city outskirts. The rate of growth of Cuban-held wealth is bound to slow down until it comes to a standstill, and this process, already noticeable, will eventually result in a progressive reduction of national wealth. Like a spring that has dried at its source or wandered from its course, Cuban productive capacity, attacked and destroyed where it originates, is failing little by little. When the money they received for their land is spent, native Cubans will be left paupers in the country where their grandparents owned tobacco fields, pastures, sugar mills, coffee plantations, and estancias, and they will vanish by the thousands into the insatiable maw of the latifundium.

The colono system on company latifundium land is certain to annihilate the Cuban farming class. The colono, dependent on the sugar mill, can only accept the conditions set for him by the mill or abandon his farm; he has no alternative. And what conditions are laid down by the latifundium company? Knowing the exact production cost, the company makes sure that the colono, working carefully and efficiently, can barely earn a living. Business is business, and it would be ridiculous or stupid – and corporation directors would have to account for it to shareholders – for the company knowingly to grant five arrobas to the colono who can make ends meet on four and a half. Every company calculates down to the last cent the terms under which the farmer will continue to plant cane. Since the colono takes all the risks – drought, fire, carry-over crops, restricted zafra, a fall in price below that expected by the company when it made up the contract – the colono system is ideal for the company, which can never lose.

The colono, in economic bondage, has only one hope: an unforeseen price rise. Such a rise, by introducing a new factor into the year's business, may yield him some profit. Nevertheless, colonos work under such harsh, adverse conditions that almost all of them owe money to the company. Unexpected earnings from a sudden price rise only serve to reduce their debts and encourage them to believe that eventually they will be independent and solvent; so they continue to engage in a ruinous occupation. Against the present diabolical system, colonos have only two possible weapons: association in a union in order to obtain more favorable conditions until that day when the company will be able to do without them entirely and will grow all of its own cane; or government intervention, with a law ensuring a fairer distribution of the industry's profits.[11] Both weapons are dangerous to use and of doubtful efficacy. There is no hope within the latifundium.

In areas where it prevails, the latifundium is creating a society as simple as that of Barbados: high and low employees of the company, and field hands earning a small daily wage, paid by the week. Moreover, employees and field hands have work during only three or four months of the year. Once the grinding period is finished, they have nothing to do, because they have no subsistence plots and there are no occupations except those related to sugar cane. Idle field hands must set out for other parts of the country, which every day becomes poorer and more destitute, to look for some uncertain employment until the next year's zafra . . . .

The latifundium is gradually strangling every type of independent farmer, ruining him economically, lowering his standard of living, and making his existence intolerable. It is therefore a powerful agent for impoverishing and urbanizing a people, even in regions it has not occupied, by disrupting the rural economy. The farmer's poverty decreases his purchasing power, and Cuban industry and commerce languish as from a disease that robs the nation of its vitality . . . .

The sugar latifundium company carries on its battle to strengthen its position and increase its profits on three different fronts: against sugar production in the United States and its island possessions (Hawaii, Puerto Rico, and the Philippines[12]), against sugar production in other countries, and against the Cuban farmer and laborer. On this last, domestic, front it has achieved absolute superiority. We will try here to describe its futile and destructive struggle against an invulnerable rival, the North American sugar industry. The Cuban latifundium company's adversary is not, strictly speaking, a special branch of North American production; rather, it is the total economic and social organization of the United States, a formidable instrument for expansion and for national defense, conceived and created through the combined efforts of its industrial magnates, statesmen, and workers. We are moved to study such a fruitless and unequal battle not out of idle intellectual curiosity but out of concern with the effects of a silent economic war on the Cuban people, whose ruin will follow on the destruction of the national sugar industry.

On the United States front, the sugar latifundium is in direct conflict with the beet sugar producers of the Western states and the cane sugar producers of Louisiana, Puerto Rico, Hawaii, and the Philippines; and it competes indirectly with all the sugars from other sources that reach the North American market. Since sugar is a commodity that hardly varies in quality, the struggle is based on a single factor – price. And the Cuban industry has recourse to only one weapon – the reduction of production costs. This is the basis for the continued existence of the latifundium and the sacred banner in the name of which all Cuba is supposed to make any sacrifice demanded of it. In order to lower production costs, Cuba is expected to allow the unlimited concentration of rural property in the hands of a few companies, less numerous but more powerful every year; to facilitate the company railway and the subpuerto; to permit the importation of cheap labor which depresses local wages; and to accept without argument the fact that the colono will lose his economic independence and will receive less and less sugar for his cane. At the same time, so as not to blunt the only weapon available to the industry at present, the Cuban people are expected to put the welfare of the latifundium company before their own destiny and autonomy.

Lowering production costs, the only weapon the industry possesses and the one to which it entrusts the defense of Cuba's interests, is completely ineffectual, because the North American economic organization has another weapon that automatically nullifies Cuba's: the raising of its tariff.[13] Every cent saved in production costs, at the expense of the Cuban laborer's redoubled efforts and standard of living, is canceled by the cent that is thereupon added to the North American tariff. The enemy is invulnerable and the latifundium owners know it. But since the Cuban people are the ones to suffer the consequences, the owners beguile themselves, or they beguile the people, by encouraging the vain hope that the United States will, for Cuba's sake, renounce the system and industrial methods that have made it so incredibly prosperous. This attitude is either very naïve or very disingenuous.

The United States, with a population of 120 million scattered over an immense territory abounding in natural resources and free from customs barriers, has developed industrial production on a scale never before known to humanity. Although North American industrial genius, initiative, enterprise, and energy have been very important factors, historians, economists, and statesmen agree that the unlimited consumption capacity of its vast domestic market has been essential to the magnificent development of its production . . . .

North American economic and social organization, the basis of its extraordinary prosperity, can be thrown out of balance in only two ways: by the immigration of foreign labor that would compete with the American for factory jobs and force down wages or by imports of foreign goods manufactured by cheaper labor that could profitably compete with domestic products in the local market. Against these two dangers, statesmen, capitalists, and the working class together have erected two formidable and absolutely effective barriers, immigration laws and customs tariffs, which have eliminated any threat from abroad . . . .

When, during this century, Cuba managed to reduce production costs by obtaining higher yields, opening up new farm lands, giving less sugar in payment to the colono, and importing cheap labor from the other islands, all our savings disappeared in United States customs houses. In order to sell sugar in New York, additional duties had to be paid in exactly the same amount as production costs had been lowered. The North American producer and his workers suffered no loss; neither did the North American consumer. As Mr. Coolidge, advised by Mr. Hoover,[14] had foreseen, the price of sugar did not go up; and the United States Government profited by becoming the principal beneficiary of Cuba's industry, collecting at its ports of entry all that was saved in Cuba. The only losers were the Cuban people, who worked more and earned less . . . .

To complete this exposition of the evils of the latifundium, it remains only to explain how the Cuban sugar manufacturers' obsession with lowered production costs will inevitably complete the latifundium cycle and, as in the other Antilles, convert Cuba into a poverty-ridden country, devoted entirely to the production of sugar, and completely dependent – economically, socially, and politically – on an export market.

Lowering of production costs is the procedure normally employed by the industrialist to earn a profit, when he cannot force up the price. In the case of a product for domestic consumption, the economy as a whole is always benefited, especially if it is a basic commodity, because the cheaper article is placed within reach of the local consumer. However, if it is an export product, lowering production costs is useless unless it serves to overcome foreign competition; otherwise, the consumer in other countries simply pays less money for the labor that produced the article. Only when competition forces us should we resort to the desperate expedient of lowering production costs, in effect thereby earning less money for our labor.

If the sales price did not change, lowered production costs could result in a gain for the whole society, if distributed equitably among the central, the colono, and the laborer; but the history of the price of all consumer goods sold in a competitive market shows that any reduction in cost is always reflected in a lower sales price, since whoever reduces costs is prepared to utilize part of his profit margin to increase his sales volume by selling his product more cheaply than that of his competitor. Over the last century, sugar prices have declined every year in value, in absolute or relative terms, compared with the steady rise in the cost of living for almost all civilized peoples. Prices have gone up when wars or other such events have disturbed the normal balance of production; but they have soon resumed their downward trend. This trend, together with the advantage derived from a reduction in overhead expenses, is the most powerful and constant incentive to large-scale production which, by stimulating consumption, increases the volume of business. To produce more at less cost is the desideratum of modern industry.

All of this is commonplace and easy; we are dealing with simple and familiar economic facts. But when we come to an agricultural industry such as Cuban sugar production, which is based on extensive cultivation of an 'export crop', the facts take on an ominous cast. More sugar at less cost means that a greater proportion of our national territory will be devoted to raising a single crop; it means lower wages for the Cuban laborer, without any benefit to the Cuban consumer, who lives on imported articles, not on sugar.

With declining prices, the central is compelled to produce and sell more sugar every year, because only in that way can it show a profit. Otherwise, invested capital would earn lower dividends or none at all. The latifundium is relentlessly forced to continue growing, to expand, to improve its machinery in order to extract more sugar, and to acquire more terrain until it has devoured all the country's arable land. This has happened throughout the Antilles; under the present system it is happening in Cuba in full view of anyone who cares to see. The constant expansion of the latifundium, driven by inescapable economic forces, cannot help but extend monoculture and will consequently leave less land, capital, and labor for other productive activities. The more Cuba comes to depend on sugar cane, the less possibility there is that it will ever be able to diversify its agriculture and supply its population with consumer goods. Cuba's economic dependence will increase and we shall be completely and hopelessly at the mercy of the sugar buyers and of foreign governments. The day that Cuba finally becomes one huge cane plantation, the republic and its sovereignty will vanish; and we are embarked on this course.

Just as the company tries to maintain its dividends by manufacturing more sugar in order to compensate for the lower price per bag, so the farmer and the laborer try to plant a larger crop and to have more cane ground in order to maintain their annual earnings by working additional days at lower wages. Hence, not only the company, but also the workers, advocate an expanding industry, because their lower wages make it imperative that they work longer hours. 'More sugar, more sugar!' urges the latifundium company. 'More sugar, more sugar!' the laborer also shouts, though both are being crushed ruthlessly between the rollers of a giant grinding mill. But more sugar results in overproduction, which depresses the market and lowers the company's dividends and the worker's wages, and both must cry out again: 'More sugar, more sugar!' Cuba is caught in this vicious circle. Meanwhile, the latifundium spreads, defended by the selfishness of those who are concerned only with how to maintain profits and by the intellectual shortsightedness of those who look only at one small part of the picture, instead of at the whole panorama.

Cuba is going through the same experiences and the same stages as the British West Indies, whose culture and social progress have been enthralled until now by a dreadful system of land exploitation. When this system is introduced into a national economy, it can only be neutralized by wise, forward-looking, and firm measures. Cuba has taken some action, thanks to Necessity, that harsh, implacable teacher whose lessons are always learned *a posteriori*. In the last two years, the government has imposed a limit on the zafra and has prohibited the clearing of new lands for cane cultivation. These are the first steps toward curbing the evil, the recognition of the existence of a danger that only the state can combat. If the zafra had not been restricted by the government, the companies – driven by those forces that compel them to produce more and more – would have sent to market more than five million tons of sugar, thereby intensifying further the fall in prices caused by overproduction. The zafra has been reduced and, consequently, the farmer and the laborer have had less work, less income, more poverty.

But we should not look for the remedy within the vicious circle of the latifundium system itself. More sugar at less cost will sooner or later turn Cuba into a new Barbados. We have nothing to say to those who accept that fate for their country and are satisfied with the present situation. We do have a message for those who love Cuba in another way: all their intelligence, resolution, and faith should be used to solve this tremendous problem and to ensure the economic independence of their country. The latifundium, which has stained history with suffering and misery, which brought about the downfall of Rome, which has led to innumerable wars and revolutions, which has produced the decline of the Antilles, is now slowly and relentlessly strangling the Cuban people.

NOTES

1. An *arroba* is 25.35 pounds or 11.5 kilograms, so Cuban sugar exports rose from about 29,100 tons per year in the early 1840s to 65,500 tons per year in the late 1850s.
2. A *caballería* is a land measure of 13.42 hectares or 33.16 acres.
3. A *colono* is a small-scale farmer. The term was generally used in Cuba to refer to an independent cane farmer who owned his own land and had a contractual grinding agreement with a mill to which he delivered his cane, or to a tenant farmer who produced cane on land owned by the mill, essentially as a sharecropper. The *colono* generally received a certain amount of sugar, more or less determined by the market price, for each hundred *arrobas* of cane he delivered to the mill.
4. The *latifundium* is a large, often corporately-owned, enterprise combining large amounts of land and a factory.
5. The first Cuban railroad was actually inaugurated on November 19, 1837 along just 16 miles of track. A year later this was extended, linking Havana and Güines, to about 50 miles. Cuba was the seventh country in the world with a railroad (Zanetti and Garcia 1998, 33-4). Within 25 years, another 400 miles of track, chiefly connecting sugar zones with the principal ports, were completed.
6. *Zafra* is the period of cane harvesting and grinding, the crop season.
7. General Leonard Wood was the US military governor of Cuba from 1899 to 1902, when the first Cuban president, Tomás Estrada Palma, took office.
8. General Wood issued the law restricting the immigration of labour into Cuba in order to satisfy the demands of US beet sugar growers who feared the competition of the growing Cuban sugar industry.
9. There was a substantial increase in immigration after 1902 and a change in the people's origins. In the three years ending in 1902, some 93,000 immigrants entered Cuba, about 77 per cent of them Spanish. Between 1902 and 1919, some 700,000 immigrated to Cuba, many of them Spanish, but only about 40 per cent of these Spaniards remained on the island. It was the influx of cheap contract labour from Haiti and Jamaica, at least

309,000 of them between 1912 and 1930, and the growing strength of organised labour, that led to opposition to this immigration. In 1931, there were some 80,000 Haitians and 40,000 Jamaicans legally residing in Cuba. In 1933, soon after President Machado was overthrown, with unemployment soaring, the Nationalization of Labour Decree was signed, requiring that 50 per cent of the employees in all industrial, commercial and agricultural enterprises should be native Cubans, and foreigners without work or resources were forcibly repatriated.

10. Carlos Juan Finlay (1833–1915), a Cuban doctor, discovered that yellow fever was transmitted by the bite of a mosquito. He was the chief medical officer of Cuba between 1902 and 1908.

11. In the third edition of his book (1944) Guerra noted that these two measures were put into practice in 1937, when the *colonos* started the Association of Cuban Colonos and the government passed the Sugar Coordination Law to provide them with protection.

12. The United States annexed Hawaii in 1898, the same year that Spain ceded its colonies of Puerto Rico and the Philippines. Hawaii became the 50th state of the union in 1959, the Philippines became an independent republic in 1946, and Puerto Rico, as an *Estado Libre Asociado* since 1952, remains in a colonial status.

13. From 1934, the United States also established sugar quotas which limited the amount of sugar that could be imported each year.

14. Calvin Coolidge was the 30th president of the United States, from 1923 to 1929. Herbert C. Hoover, who was the secretary of commerce between 1921 and 1928, succeeded Coolidge and was president from 1929 to 1933.

Four

Fernando Ortiz

Fernando Ortiz (1881–1969), a Cuban lawyer, judge, diplomat and professor, is best known for his pioneering and prolific studies of Cuban history, culture and politics, and especially those concerning Afro-Cuban culture and social life. After being educated in Havana, Barcelona, Madrid and Italy, Ortiz had a long and distinguished career in public service. He was a member of Cuba's diplomatic-consular corps, a professor of law at the University of Havana, a member of the Cuban Congress for ten years, the director of the Legislative Office of Cuba, and a judge in the Cuban courts. In addition to the many articles and books he wrote, he edited collections of Cuban literature and was the director of several magazines. His important collection of Afro-Cuban religious artifacts is displayed in Africa House, a museum in Havana.

In 1923, Ortiz led the Junta Cubana de Renovación Nacional *which denounced the previous two decades of misgovernment and demanded social reforms. The Junta sought to defend local economic interests by calling for the protection of Cuban industry, commerce and agriculture, and for the renegotiation of trade relations with the United States in order to promote national economic development. It demanded labour reform, prison reform, electoral reform, the expansion of the health services, and an end to graft, electoral fraud, and political corruption. Following the lead of José Martí, the Junta also protested the growing domination of Cuba by the United States. 'The Cuban people,' proclaimed the Junta, 'want to be free as much from the foreigners who abuse the flag as from the citizens who violate it and will end up burying it' (Pérez 1995, 236). This expression of Cuban nationalism and summons to national renewal was supported by many professionals and business people, as well as Afro-Cuban, Catholic, and women's organisations. Ortiz wrote a book called* La decadencia cubana *just 22 years after Cuba's independence (Havana 1924).*

Cubans united around the demand to revise the Permanent Treaty with the United States and the abrogation of the Platt Amendment. This amendment, named after the senator who drafted it, was passed in the US Congress in 1901 when Cuba was still under US military occupation. It stated that the Cuban government should 'never enter into any treaty or other compact with any foreign power or powers which will impair or tend to impair the independence of Cuba', but this is precisely what the statute required. Article 3 stated 'That the government of Cuba consents that the United States may exercise the right to intervene for the preservation of Cuban independence, the maintenance of a government adequate for the protection of life, property, and individual liberty...' (Treaty Between the United States and Cuba, signed in Havana May 22, 1903, U.S. Statutes at Large, *xxi, 897–898). Cubans demonstrated against this proposed amendment but the US Secretary for War warned that if Cuba did not accept it there would be no end to the military occupation that had begun in 1898. The Cuban constituent convention accepted the Platt Amendment by a margin of a single vote, so it became an appendix to the constitution of 1901 and was incorporated into the Permanent Treaty of 1903. Nominal independence, therefore, was achieved only after it was agreed that the United States had a right to intervene, which infringed on Cuban sovereignty. The patriotic movement for the regeneration of Cuba and the Liberal party called for eliminating the amendment from the constitution and revising the treaty in order to achieve a genuine independence.*

In the presidential election of 1924, Ortiz and other Cuban patriots and reformers endorsed Gerardo Machado, the Liberal candidate. Although Machado, as a candidate, 'intuitively adopted the rhetoric of reform' (Pérez 1995, 249), he became increasingly corrupt when elected president. With the economy deteriorating, the major political parties cooperated in supporting Machado, who won uncontested re-election in 1928. When the Great Depression hit the Cuban economy in 1929, unemployment soared, wages fell, and business came to a standstill. Much of the government's reduced revenues were transferred overseas to service its debt while thousands of public employees were cut and the salaries of those who remained were drastically reduced. The result was growing political confrontation, including a general strike in 1930 and waves of repression in which many demonstrators were killed and injured and thousands jailed. Opponents of the government were kidnapped, tortured and murdered and Machado became the personification of oppression. By 1931, more or less open warfare broke out and the imprisonment of about 400 of the moderate opposition further polarised the political situation. Ortiz was one of many Cubans who thought that the United States, under the terms of the Platt Amendment, was obliged to intervene 'to protect the Cubans' right to vote for a government of their own choosing' (quoted in Pérez 1995, 259), but that was not why the United States had insisted on the amendment.

The social crisis of the early 1930s led the new United States government of Franklin D. Roosevelt to decide that Machado, who had initially provided order and security, had outlived his usefulness. Sumner Welles was appointed US ambassador to Cuba with instructions to mediate the crisis by finding common ground between the Cuban government and the 'responsible leaders' of the opposition. He sought to ease out Machado and, in an orderly fashion, ease new political leaders in, thereby avoiding a revolution and ensuring that Cuba's new leaders would feel indebted to the United States. When the crisis deepened in August 1933, after many people were killed during a general strike and demonstrations, Welles threatened that the United States would withdraw recognition of Machado's government. Many Cubans who opposed Machado were reluctant to see his government removed solely by US pressure and on August 12, the army forced him into exile. Carlos Manuel de Céspedes was the US choice for the new president but strikes by tobacco workers in Pinar del Río, stevedores in Havana, railroad workers in Camaguey and coffee workers in Oriente persisted unabated. Workers seized sugar mills, created 'soviets' and, together with a radical student organisation, threatened revolution. On September 4, the Céspedes government was overthrown by mutinous troops led by sergeant Fulgencio Batista and supported by many civilian groups. A revolutionary government was quickly created under Ramón Grau San Martín. On the day of his inauguration, President Grau unilaterally abrogated the Platt Amendment and initiated a comprehensive programme of political, economic and social reforms. The United States withheld recognition of his government.

On October 19, Grau invited Ortiz to join his cabinet and to propose a plan to unite all the revolutionary groups. Ortiz, whose support for Grau's government did not waver, accepted only the second part of the invitation. He suggested that the government, with Grau as provisional president, should include representatives of all major political groups and work towards a genuine national government. Grau and the radical students accepted this compromise plan but Batista and the army, who were the emerging power, sought to force Grau's resignation. The US government regarded Batista 'as the only factor capable of changing the situation and toppling the revolutionary government . . . . Batista's moment had come' (Aguilar 1972,199). On January 15,1934, Grau was forced by military pressure to resign. The United States, which had never recognised his government, recognised his successor, Colonel Carlos Mendieta, within five days. Batista, however, was the real power in Cuba, so long as he had the support of the United States. Batista's power increased as he 'ruled Cuba through puppet presidents and shadow governments' (Pérez 1995, 277) and in 1940 he was elected president for a four-year term.

During this revolutionary and counter-revolutionary period, Ortiz wrote an outstanding analysis of the relations between the economy, society and culture in Cuban history. What he called the 'counterpoint' between tobacco and sugar was the contrast between peasant and plantation systems of agriculture, a contrast between forms of agricultural enterprise that had profound social and cultural implications. Some of these implications were subsequently explored by anthropologists in other parts of the Caribbean, including Julian Steward's team in Puerto Rico (Robert A. Manners, Sidney W. Mintz, Elena Padilla and Eric R. Wolf) and Edith Clarke in Jamaica. These studies focused on different examples and aspects of the relationship between the systems of production of different crops – sugar, tobacco, coffee and mixed farming – and the cultures and social relations of their associated types of community. The variations in types of family and household, for example, tend to be associated with the 'subcultures' of the different crops. Ortiz, in a more ambitious analysis than most ethnographers undertake, linked the production of sugar and tobacco, through their prevailing patterns of land distribution, labour systems and markets, to the history of colonialism and the struggle for independence in the Caribbean. He argued that the connection of sugar production with the concentration of land ownership, the need for abundant cheap labour for a limited season, and the dependence on a single foreign market, has profound consequences for Cuba's politics, social structure and sovereignty. Ortiz also drew attention to the interactions between people of many cultures in Cuba's history and he coined a new word, 'transculturation', to refer to the process in which Cuba's complex culture is formed through these interactions.

$\mathscr{C}$uban Counterpoint: Tobacco and Sugar (excerpts)

Sugar cane and tobacco are all contrast. It would seem that they were moved by a rivalry that separates them from their very origins. One is a gramineous plant, the other a solanaceous; one grows from cuttings of stalk rooted down, the other from tiny seeds that germinate. The value of one is in its stalk, not in its leaves, which are thrown away; that of the other in its foliage, not its stalk, which is discarded. Sugar cane lives for years, the tobacco plant only a few months. The former seeks the light, the latter shade; day and night, sun and moon. The former loves the rain that falls from the heavens; the latter the heat that comes from the earth. The sugar cane is ground for its juice; the tobacco leaves are dried to get rid of the sap. Sugar achieves its destiny through liquid, which melts it, turns it into syrup; tobacco through fire, which volatilizes it, converted into smoke. The one is white, the other dark. Sugar is sweet and odorless; tobacco bitter and aromatic. Always in contrast! . . .

In the economy of Cuba there are also striking contrasts in the cultivation, the processing, and the human connotations of the two products. Tobacco requires delicate care, sugar can look after itself; the one requires continual attention, the other involves seasonal work; intensive versus extensive cultivation; steady work on the part of a few, intermittent jobs for many; the immigration of whites on the one hand, the slave trade on the other; liberty and slavery; skilled and unskilled labor; hands versus arms; men versus machines; delicacy versus brute force. The cultivation of tobacco gave rise to the small holding; that of sugar brought about the great land grants. In their industrial aspects tobacco belongs to the city, sugar to the country. Commerically the whole world is the market for our tobacco, while our sugar has only a single market. Centripetence and centrifugence. The native versus the foreigner. National sovereignty as against colonial status. The proud cigar band as against the lowly sack.

Tobacco and sugar cane are two gigantic plants, two members of the vegetable kingdom which both flourish in Cuba and are both perfectly adapted, climatically and ecologically, to the country. The territory of Cuba has in its different zones the best land for the cultivation of both plants. And the same happens in the combinations of the climate with the chemistry of the soil . . . .

The special requirements of tobacco cultivation have made it necessary (a most imperative economic need) for tobacco to be grown in small plots, like vegetable gardens, and not on great acreage like the canefields of the sugar plantations. Each of these tobacco fields was called, and should still be called a *tabacal*; but the preferred name is *vega*, which was applied to the river bottom lands, which were the best for the growing of tobacco because of their fertility, the ease with which they could be watered, and their sheltered location. *Veguerío* now is used to designate all of the vegas of a region.

Each vega is a unit in itself, where the complete agricultural cycle of tobacco begins and ends. It is in no way connected with the subsequent operations of the tobacco industry. The vega is independent, unlike the canefields and the colony that springs up about them, which is dependent upon the industrial processing and the marketing of sugar through its final stage. The vega is not the slave of a mechanical installation whose voracity it must feed as is the sugar plantation of the tentacled structure of the mill. In the tobacco industry there are no centrals.

With the cutting of the cane the work of the sugar-raiser is finished. It is loaded, weighed, and all his work is turned into a figure that tells him the number of arrobas he has delivered and a voucher for the money due him. But the work of the tobacco-raiser is not over with the cutting of the leaves from the plant. On the contrary, it is now redoubled, and requires great skill. The drying of the leaves involves delicate and patient handling. And once more weather conditions become a factor. The *enmatulado*, for instance, must be done at daybreak and under the right conditions, for the wrong temperature could spoil the whole crop. The tobacco leaves then go through three stages, in the *cujes*, in the *pilones*, and in the *tercios*, and in all of them the tobacco is cured or fermented more or less, depending on the quality of the leaf and the amount of sap in it, and the help given it. On the care and success of the curing much of the value of the product depends, its aroma, taste, appearance, flexibility, combustibility.

The grower visits his treasure every day, first to touch the leaves and gauge their degree of dryness, then to smell them and judge the progress of curing by their scent. If the tobacco gets too dry it may crumble to powder in handling. It is here that the painstaking skill of the grower comes into play to keep the leaves at the right degree of flexibility. Thus they wait for the *pilón*, which consists in piling up the tobacco leaves, one by one and one on top of another, in prescribed formation and with many precautions to beautify and make uniform the color of the leaf, get rid of the excess of resin, attenuate its bitterness, and soften it so it will be more flexible and silky.

Then comes the stripping, which is removing from each leaf the stem left on it. After this comes the tedious process of selection, in which, after pulling out all the threads on which they have been strung together, those leaves to be used for filler must be separated from the wrappers, which are like fillets of tobacco. These are delicate operations, generally performed by women, *abridoras*, *rezagadoras* or *apartadoras*, and *repasadoras*. And finally the leaves must be reclassified, according to whether they are fillers or wrappers, in hands, hanks, bunches, and bales, prepared and ready for the market. There is no exaggeration in saying that in the cultivation and harvesting of tobacco in Cuba the human contribution is the most important element because of the great variety of special skills, physical and mental, involved in achieving the best results, as though it were a question of a work of art, the miracle of an ever changing and harmonious symphony of smells, tastes, and stimuli.

After the selection of each tobacco crop, or, to be more exact, after the selection of each leaf of each plant of each field, tobacco emerges from its agricultural cycle into that of industry, business, pleasure; it goes forth, as Martí[1] wrote, 'to employ workmen, to enrich merchants, to amuse the idle, while away sorrow, accompany lonely thoughts'.

In the olden days the selection of leaf tobacco was made by the planter himself.

But even before the war of independence (1895)[2] a division of labor was introduced and the selection was made in the towns nearest the fields, where it was easier and cheaper to find adequate space and workers. In this, too, the production of tobacco differs from that of sugar. The only centers of population with which the latter is concerned is the *batey*, the mill yard around the central, and the port of embarkation alongside the warehouses. The tobacco industry, on the contrary, gives life to selected rural centers . . . .

In the canefields and in the mills there is no selection. All canes go to the conveyor belt and the grinder together, and all the juice is mixed together in the same syrup, the same evaporating-dishes, the same filters, the same centrifugals, and the same sacks.

Whereas the steps in the harvesting and selection of tobacco are slow and studied, those connected with sugar cane always demand haste. The cane must be ground as soon as it is cut or else the yield of juice shrinks, ferments, and spoils. This characteristic of the sugar cane is responsible for social and historical consequences of incalculable importance. The workmen who do the cutting cannot be the same as those who, later on, carry out the grinding and boiling of the syrup. With tobacco, as with wheat, the agro-industrial operations are consecutive over a whole cycle. The same farmers can carry out the different phases of the work one after another. This is not the case with sugar cane. The offhand manner in which it can be treated in the field is transformed into the most breathless haste once it has been mutilated to steal its juice, and not a moment can be lost. Cut cane begins to ferment and rot in a few days. The operations of cutting, hauling, grinding, clarification, filtration, evaporation, and crystallization must theoretically be carried out one after the other, but without interruption; nearly all of them are going on at the same time in the mill. While one field of cane is being cut, others are being converted into sacks of sugar. And all at top speed. From the time the machete fells the cane until the receptacle of the sugar is closed, there is only a short lapse, a few hours. The grinding season of a plantation lasts months because of the volume of cane, but the conversion of each stalk into sugar is always quick. For this reason the milling season requires the simultaneous co-operation of many workers for a short time. The rapidity with which the cane must be ground after cutting and milled in an unavoidably brief space of time gave rise to the need for having on hand plenty of cheap, stable, and available labor for work that is irregular and seasonal. The intermittent concentration of cheap and abundant labor is a fundamental factor in the economy of Cuban sugar production. And as there was not sufficient labor available in Cuba, for centuries it was necessary to go outside the country to find it in the amount, cheapness, ignorance, and permanence necessary. The result has been that this urgent agricultural-chemical nature of the sugar industry has been the fundamental factor in all the demogenic and social evolution of Cuba. It was due principally to these conditions governing the production of sugar that slave-trading and slavery endured there to such a late date.

It was not the existence of latifundia that was responsible for the large Negro population of Cuba, as has been erroneously supposed, but the lack of native labor, of Indians and white men, and the difficulty of bringing in from other parts of the world except Africa workers who would be equally cheap, permanent, and submissive. The latifundium in Cuba was only a consequence of stock-raising first, and then of cane cultivation, and of other concomitant factors, just as was the influx of Negro population. Both have been the almost parallel effects of the same basic causes, sugar being mainly responsible, and the Africanoid population is not a direct result of latifundism. There was an abundance of Negroes in Cuba even when there was no shortage of land, and the great sugar plantations did not constitute a primordial economic factor . . . .

For this reason, also, the division of labor in a sugar factory is different from that in a tobacco workshop. In the sugar central many workmen are needed to carry on the different industrial operations necessary from the time the cane is put on the conveyor belt to the grinder until the sugar comes out of the centrifugals into the sacks in which it is packed. In the making of sugar certain workmen tend to the fires, others to the grinding, others to the syrup, others to the chemical clarification, others to the filtering, others to the evaporating, and so on, through the successive steps involved in the sugar cycle. Each workman attends to one single job. No workman of the mill can by himself make sugar out of the cane; but each cigar worker can make a cigar out of a leaf of tobacco unassisted. The same tobacco worker can take charge of making each cigar from beginning to end, from cutting with his own knife the leaf for the filler to twisting the wrapper to its final turn. And any smoker can do it, too, as the tobacco-planter does with the leaf of his own harvest for his own smoking. He can cut the leaf, dry it, shred it, stuff it into a pipe or roll it in a cigarette paper, and light it and smoke it, as he pleases. At the mill many work together in joint and successive operations, which in their totality produce sugar in great quantities. In the tobacco industry many workers are occupied in individual but identical tasks, all of which when added together produce many cigars. The manufacture of sugar is a collective job; that of tobacco is by individual efforts . . . .

Tobacco was taken to the rest of the world from America; sugar was brought to America. Tobacco is a native plant,[3] which the Europeans who came with Columbus discovered, in Cuba, to be exact, at the beginning of November of the year 1492. Sugar cane is a foreign plant of remote origin that was brought to Europe from the Orient, thence to the Canary Islands, and it was from there that Columbus brought it to the Antilles in 1493. The discovery of tobacco in Cuba was a surprise, but the introduction of sugar was planned.

It has been said, though I do not know on what authority the statement is based, that when Columbus returned from his second voyage he took tobacco seed with him to Andalusia, as did the Catalonian friar Ramün Pané later, and planted it, but without success. It would seem that it was Dr. Francisco Hernández de Toledo who gave a scientific account of tobacco half a century later in a report to King Philip II, who had sent him to Mexico to study the flora of that country. The cultivation of tobacco was spread less through a desire for gain than through the spontaneous and subversive propaganda of temptation. Tobacco was the delight of the people before it became that of the upper classes. Its appeal was natural and traditional rather than studied and commercial. It was the sailors who spread its use through the ports of Europe in the forms in which they used it aboard ship, either for chewing or for pipe smoking. The courtiers of Europe made its acquaintance later through travelers returning from America.

Centuries and even millenniums went by before sugar left Asiatic India, passing into Arabia and Egypt, then traveling along the islands and shoreline of the Mediterranean to the Atlantic Ocean and the Indies of America. A few decades after a handful of adventurers discovered it in Cuba, tobacco had already been carried not only through America, where the Indians used it before the arrival of the Spaniards, but through Europe, Africa, and Asia, to the distant confines of Muscovy, the heart of darkest Africa, and Japan. In 1605 the Sultan Murad had to place severe penalties on the cultivation of tobacco in Turkey, and the Japanese Emperor ordered the acreage that had been given over to its cultivation reduced. Even today many nations still lack sugar, but hardly any lack tobacco or some substitute for it, however unworthy. Tobacco is today the most universal plant, more so than either corn or wheat. Today the world lives and dreams in a haze of blue smoke spirals that evoke the old Cuban gods. In the spread of this habit of smoking the island of Cuba has played a large part, not only because tobacco and its rites were native to it, but because of the incomparable excellence of its product, which is universally recognized by all discerning smokers, and because Havana happened to be the port of the West Indies most frequented by sailors in bygone days. Even today to speak of a Havana cigar is to refer to the best cigar in the world. And that is why, as a general thing, in lands remote from the Antilles the geographical name of Havana is better known than that of Cuba.

The economy of sugar was from the start capitalistic in contrast to that of tobacco. From the earliest days of the economic exploitation of these West Indies this was perfectly evident to Columbus and his successors who settled the islands. Aside from the fertility of the land and the favorable climate, the efficient production of sugar always required large acreage for plantations, pastures, timberland, and reserves of land – in a word, extensions that verged upon the latifundium. As the historian Oviedo[4] said, 'an ample supply of water' and accessible 'forests for the hot and continuous fires' and, in addition, 'a large and well-constructed building for making the sugar and another in which to store it'. And, besides, a great number of 'wagons for hauling the cane to the mill and to fetch wood, and an uninterrupted supply of workers to wash the sugarloaves and tend and water the cane'. Even all this was not enough, for there was the investment in the required number of those automotive machines known as slaves, on which Oviedo commented: 'At least from eighty to one hundred Negroes must be on hand all the time, or even a hundred and twenty and more to keep things running smoothly,' and, besides, other people, 'overseers and skilled workmen to make the sugar'. And to feed all this crew still another and larger investment. According to Oviedo, 'a good herd of cattle, from one thousand to three thousand head, close by the mill to feed the workers' was necessary. For this reason he concludes logically enough that 'the man who owns a plantation free from mortgage and well equipped has a property of great value'. Sugar is not made from patches of cane but from plantations of it; cane is not cultivated by the plant but in mass. The industry was not developed for private or domestic consumption, nor even for that of the locality, but for large-scale production and foreign exportation.

Tobacco is born complete. It is nature's gift to man, and his work with tobacco is merely that of selection. Sugar does not spring full-fledged; it is a gift man makes to himself through the creative effort of his labor. Sugar is the fruit of man's ingenuity and the mill's engines. Ingenuity where sugar is concerned consists in the human and mechanical power of creation. In the case of tobacco it is rather in the personal selection of that which has been naturally created.

Of the tobacco leaves, the invention and gift of nature, the knowing countryman selects the best, and, with the simple effort of his hands to roll them into shape, he can smoke the best cigar that can be made. Just with the hands, without tools, machinery, or capital, one can enjoy the finest tobacco in the world; but one cannot get sugar that way, not even the poorest grade.

There can be no manufacture of sugar without machinery, without milling apparatus to grind the cane and get out its sweet juice, from which saccharose is obtained. The mill may be an Indian *cunyaya* – a pump-handle device resting against the branch of a tree, which as it moves up and down presses the cane against the trunk – or a simple two-cylinder roller moved by animal or human power, or a titanic system of mills, wheels, cogs, pumps, evaporating-pans, boilers, and ovens, powered by water, steam, or electricity; but it is always a machine, fundamentally a lever that squeezes. Sugar is made by man and power. Tobacco is the voluntary offering of nature.

It is possible for the *guajiro*[5] living on his small farm to make a little sugar squeezing the juice out of the cane by the pressure of the *cunyaya*, that simple device with its single lever which the Indians used, simpler even than the *cibucán* with which they pressed the yucca. Probably it was with the Indian *cunyaya* that the first juice was squeezed out in America, from the cane planted in Hispaniola[6] by Christopher Columbus. But it was impossible to develop production on a commercial scale with so rudimentary an instrument. The first settlers in Hispaniola devised and set up grinding mills operated by water or horse power.

To be sure, these mills which were known in Europe before the discovery of America were all of wood, including the rollers. The maximum of juice that could be extracted from the cane was thirty-five per cent, and the sugar yield was only six per cent. But in the manufacture of sugar the grinder was always as essential as the evaporating-dishes and the other vessels for the filtration of the settlings and the clarification of the syrup.

For centuries sugar was manufactured in these *cachimbos*. In the year 1827 Cuba had over one thousand centrals. The limited capacity of the mills was the cause of the small scale of their operations. At this time the average size of the numerous plantations in Matanzas, for example, was only about 167 acres of cane, and some 750 in wood and pasture land. For a good central 1,000 acres was enough.

In 1820 the steam engine was introduced into Cuba and marked the beginning of an industrial revolution. The steam engine changed everything on the central. The process of the penetration of the steam engine into the sugar industry was slow; half a century went by from the time it was first employed in the grinding mill in 1820 until 1878, when it was applied to the last step of the process – that is, in the separation centrifugals. By the end of the nineteenth century everything about the central was mechanical, nothing was done by hand. Everything about the organism was new. The framework continued the same, but the organs, the joints, the viscera had been adapted to new functions and new dimensions. For as a result of the introduction of steam not only was completely new machinery installed, but everything grew in size. The increased potential of energy called for enlarged grinding capacity of the mills, and this, in turn, made it necessary for all the other apparatus in the sugar-milling process to expand. But only in the last third of the nineteenth century did the Cuban sugar central begin that intense growth which has brought it to its present-day dimensions.

The Cuban sugar mill, despite the complete transformation of its machinery brought about by the steam engine, grew slowly in productive capacity, both in machinery and in acreage. As late as 1880 the size of the centrals was not extremely large. At that time the centrals of Matanzas Province, for example, averaged some 1,650 acres all together, of which only about 770 were planted to cane. This delay in the growth in size of the centrals, despite the possibilities afforded by the introduction of steam-powered machinery, was not due so much to the revolutions and wars that harassed the colony and laid much of its land waste for years as to the economic difficulties that impeded the development of transportation by steam – that is, the railroads. Railways were first introduced into Cuba in the year 1837, before Spain had them, by a company of wealthy Creoles. But it was after the ten-year revolution that steel rails were invented and that they became cheap enough so they could be used on a large scale on the centrals, not only on lines from the mill yard to the canefields, but to link up the mills and the cane-growing zones with each other and with the ports where sugar was stored and shipped. From this time on, the railway lines reached out steadily toward the sugar cane and wrapped themselves about it like the tentacles of a great iron spider. The centrals began to grow in size, giving way to the great latifundium. By 1890 there was a central in Cuba, the Constancia, that produced a yield as high as 135,000 sacks of sugar, at that time the largest in the world.

The machine won a complete victory in the sugar-manufacturing process. Hand labor has almost completely disappeared. The mechanization has been so thorough that it has brought about a transformation in the industrial, territorial, judicial, political, and social structure of the sugar economy of Cuba through an interlinked chain of phenomena which have not been fully appreciated by Cuban sociologists.

In the twentieth century the sugar production of Cuba reached the peak of its historical process of industrialization, even though it has not yet passed through all the phases necessary for its perfect evolutionary integration. Mechanization, which reached Cuba in the nineteenth century with the steam engine, began to triumph in that century and created the central; but it is in this twentieth century that the machine has given rise to the typical present-day organization, the *supercentral*. This type of mill has been the logical outgrowth of mechanization, and from it have streamed a whole series of derivations that because of their complicated interlocking structure and the relation of cause and effect have not been clearly understood or properly analyzed. It is sufficient to point out here that the principal characteristics typical of the Cuban sugar industry today, and the same holds true in a greater or lesser degree of the other islands of the Antilles, and happens to a certain extent in other similar industries, are the following: mechanization, latifundism, sharecropping, wage-fixing, supercapitalism, absentee landlordism, foreign ownership, corporate control, and imperialism.

Mechanization is the factor that has made possible and necessary the increased size of the centrals. Prior to this the central's radius of activity was the distance suitable for animal-drawn haulage. Now, with railroads, the limits of extension of a central are measured by the cost of transportation. It is a known fact that cane cut in Santo Domingo is milled in Puerto Rico and transported to the mill in ships. The mill and the railroad have developed simultaneously and their growth has made necessary planting on a larger scale, which explains the need for vast areas for cane plantations. This phenomenon also gave rise to the occupation of virgin lands in the provinces of Camagüey and Oriente and the consequent shifting of the agricultural center of Cuba. These Cyclopean machines and those great tentacles of railways that have turned the centrals into monstrous iron octopuses have created the demand for more and more land to feed the insatiable voracity of the mills with canefields, pasture land, and woodland.

On the heels of the mechanization came the great latifundism – that is, the use of a great extension of land by a single private owner. Latifundism was the economic basis of feudalism, and it has often reproduced this state. The struggle of the modern age has always been, particularly since the eighteenth century, to give man freedom and sever him from his bondage to the land, and for the freedom of the land, liberating it from the monopolistic tyranny of man. Today this process is on the way to being repeated in the Antilles, and one day we shall see agrarian laws enacted to disentail the lands held in the grasp of mortmain. The agrarian latifundism today is a fatal consequence of the present universal system of the concentration of capital. Every day industry needs more and more means of production, and the land is the most important of them all.

The central is now more than a mere plantation; there are no longer any real planters in Cuba. The modern central is not a simple agricultural enterprise, nor even a factory whose production is based on the raw materials at hand. Today it is a complicated 'system of land, machinery, transportation, technicians, workers, capital, and people to produce sugar'. It is a complete social organism, as live and complex as a city or municipality, or a baronial keep with its surrounding fief of vassals, tenants, and serfs. The latifundium is only the territorial base, the visible expression of this. The central is vertebrated by an economic and legal structure that combines masses of land, masses of machinery, masses of men, and masses of money, all in proportion to the integral scope of the huge organism for sugar production.

Today the sugar latifundium is so constituted that it is not necessary for the tracts of land or farms that constitute it to be contiguous. It is generally made up of a nuclear center around the mill yard, a sort of town, and of outlying lands, adjacent or distant, linked by railroads and under the same general control, all forming a complete empire with subject colonies covered with canefields and forests, with houses and villages. And all this huge feudal territory is practically outside the jurisdiction of public law; the norms of private property hold sway there. The owner's power is as complete over this immense estate as though it were just a small plantation or farm. Everything there is private – ownership, industry, mill, houses, stores, police, railroad, port. Until the year 1886 the workers, too, were chattels like other property.[7]

The sugar latifundium was the cause of important agro-social developments, such as the monopolizing of land that is not cultivated but lies fallow; the scarcity of garden produce or fruits that would complement the basic crop, which is sugar – the reason for the latifundium's existence – because the effort required for this can be turned to more profitable use from the economic standpoint; the depreciation in value of land that it does not need within the zone monopolized by the central, and so on.

Within the territorial scope of the central, economic liberty suffers serious restrictions. There is not a small holding of land nor a dwelling that does not belong to the owner of the central, nor a fruit orchard or vegetable patch or store or shop that does not form part of the owner's domain. The small Cuban landowner, independent and prosperous, the backbone of a strong rural middle class, is gradually disappearing. The farmer is becoming a member of the proletariat, just another laborer, without roots in the soil, shifted from one district to another. The whole life of the central is permeated by this provisional quality of dependence, which is a characteristic of colonial populations whose members have lost their stake in their country.

The economic organization of the latifundium in Cuba has been blamed for consequences that are not properly attributable to it, such as the importation of cheap labor, especially colored. First Negro slaves were brought into the country, then laborers from Haiti and Jamaica.[8] But this immigration, which lowers the wage level of the whole Cuban proletariat and the living standard of Cuban society and upsets its racial balance, thus retarding the fusion of its component elements into a national whole, is not the result of the latifundium system. The use of colored slaves or laborers has never been nor is it a social phenomenon due to latifundism or to the monopolizing of the land. Both these economic developments are essentially identical: with the concentration of the ownership of land comes the concentration of laborers, and both depend directly upon the concentration of capital resulting from industry, especially when the process of mechanization demands more land for the plantations upon whose crop it depends, more labor to harvest it, and, in an endless progression, more machines and more and more money. The land and the laborer, like the machine itself, are only means of production, which, as a rule, are simultaneously augmented, but often the increment of one is followed by that of the others. When there was an abundance of land and before the machines had reached their full development, sugar-planting used large numbers of Negro slaves brought in from Africa; at this time the latifundium had not yet come into being. Later, as the machines grew in power, they demanded more and more cane plantations, and these, in turn, more and more labor, which was supplied by white immigration[9] and the natural growth of population. But as the speed of the development of the sugar industry outpaced that of the population, and great centrals were established on vast tracts of virgin land, everything had to be brought in: machines, plantations, and – population. It was the swift occupation of large and new sections of Camagüey and Oriente that, aside from other secondary economic considerations such as the scale of wages, brought about a revival of 'traffic in Negroes', who were now hired on terms of miserable peonage instead of being bought outright, as under the earlier system of slavery. In Puerto Rico the latifundium developed after its great demographic expansion, and as it has a dense and poverty-stricken white population, it has not been necessary to bring in cheap labor from the other islands.

In the tobacco industry the process is exactly the reverse. It was an industry without machinery. In the beginning it used very few manual devices, and these of the simplest, to twist the tobacco or grind it to powder or shred it. The largest of these apparatuses was a simple wheel. At the Quinta de los Molinos in Havana one can still see the insignificant stream of water that turned the little mills, from which it derived its name, that were formerly used to make the snuff that was exported. In addition to the preparation of snuff and cut tobacco, it was in the manufacture of cigarettes that the machine began to be used; but for hundreds of years these were made by hand at home. Machinery did not come into the life of tobacco with the invention of the steam engine, but years after the Jamaica engines had been invented for the sugar mills and were introduced into Cuba.

There is always a stationary quality to sugar. Where the canefields are planted, there they stay and last for years, around the mill installation, which is permanent and immovable, The canefields are vast plantings and the central is a great plant. Tobacco is a volatile thing. The seeds are planted in a seed-bed, then transplanted to another spot; sometimes even from one vega to another, and tobacco's cycle ends with the year's harvest. Nothing is left in the field, and it has to be planted all over again.

The rental arrangements for tobacco lands are usually for a brief period; the crop-sharing may be on an annual basis. In the case of sugar they are of lengthy duration, depending on how long the root stock continues to produce cane before it turns into worthless stubble.

Without a large investment of money in lasting plantations and powerful machinery it is impossible to set up a central or produce any form of sugar, unless one excepts the honey produced by the communistic bees in their hives. Tobacco's economical arrangements could be limited to a small patch of fertile land and a pair of skillful hands to twist the leaf into cigars or shred it for pipe smoking. For the widespread distribution of sugar great advances had to be made first in the secrets of chemistry, in machinery, in maritime shipping capacity, in tropical colonization, in the securing of slave labor, and, above all, in the accumulation of capital and in banking organization. In the case of tobacco all that was required was for a few sailors and traders to scatter about the world a few handfuls of seed, which are so small they will fit anywhere, even in a cabin-boy's duffel-bag.

The social consequences deriving from tobacco and sugar in Cuba and originating in the different conditions under which the two crops are produced can be easily grasped. The contrast between the vegas where tobacco is grown and the sugar plantation, particularly if it is a modern central, is striking. Tobacco gave origin to a special type of agricultural life. There is not the great human agglomeration in the tobacco region that is to be found around the sugar plants. This is due to the fact that tobacco requires no machinery; it needs no mills, nor elaborate physical and chemical equipment, nor railway transport systems. The vega is a geographical term; the central is a term of mechanics.

In the production of tobacco intelligence is the prime factor; we have already observed that tobacco is liberal, not to say revolutionary. In the production of sugar it is a question of power; sugar is conservative, if not reactionary.

I repeat, the production of sugar was always a capitalistic venture because of its great territorial and industrial scope and the size of its long-term investments. Tobacco, child of the savage Indian and the virgin earth, is a free being, bowing its neck to no mechanical yoke, unlike sugar, which is ground to bits by the mill. This has occasioned profound economic and social consequences.

In the first place, tobacco was raised on the land best suited for the purpose, without being bound to a great indispensable industrial plant that was stationary and remained 'planted' even after it had impoverished all the land about it. This gave rise to the central, which even in olden times was at least a village, and today is a city. The vega was never anything but a rural holding, like a garden. The vega was small; it was never the site of latifundia, but belonged to small property-owners. The central required a plantation; in the vega a small farm was enough. The owners of a central are known as *hacendados* and live in the city; those of the vegas remained *monteros*, *sitieros*, or *guajiros* and never left their rural homes.

The cultivation of tobacco demands a yearly cycle of steady work by persons who are skilled and specialized in this activity. Tobacco is often smoked to kill time, but in the tobacco industry there is no such thing as 'dead time', as is the case with sugar. This, together with the circumstance that the vega was a small holding, has developed in the *veguero* a strong attachment to his land, as in the rancher of old, and made it possible for him to carry on his tasks with the help of members of his family. Only when this is not feasible does he hire workers, but in small groups, never in gangs or by the hundred, as happens with sugar cane. The vega, I repeat, is merely a topographical denomination; the *colonia* is a term having complex political and social connotations.

For these same reasons, while during slavery Negroes were employed as sugar-plantation hands, the cultivation of the vegas was based on free, white labor. Thus tobacco and sugar each have racial connections. Tobacco is an inheritance received from the Indian, which was immediately used and esteemed by the Negro, but cultivated and commercialized by the white man. The Indians at the time of the discovery raised tobacco in their gardens, considering it 'a very holy thing', in the words of Oviedo, distinguishing between the mild cultivated variety and the stronger wild species, according to Cobo. The whites were familiar with it, but did not develop a taste for it at once. 'It is a thing for savages'. The historians of the Indies did not smoke, and some abominated the habit. Benzoni tells that the smell of tobacco was so offensive to him that he would run to get away from it. When Las Casas wrote his *Apologética Historia de las Indias*,[10] in the second quarter of the sixteenth century, he called attention to the unusual fact that he had known 'an upright, married Spaniard on this island who was in the habit of using tobacco and the smoke from it, just as the Indians did, and who said that because of the great benefit he derived from it he would not give it up for anything'.

It was the Negroes of Hispaniola who quickly came to esteem the qualities of tobacco and not only copied from the Indians the habit of smoking it, but were the first to cultivate it on their owners' plantations. They said it 'took away their weariness,' to use Oviedo's words. But the Spaniards still looked askance at it. 'Negro stuff'.

In Cuba the same thing probably happened; tobacco was a thing 'for Indians and Negroes', and only later, as it worked its way up from the lower strata of society, did the whites develop a taste for it. But by the middle of the sixteenth century in Havana, where each year the Spanish fleets assembled and set out across the ocean in convoy, tobacco had already become an article of trade, and it was the Negroes who carried on the business. The whites realized that they were missing a good venture, and the authorities issued ordinances forbidding the Negroes to go on selling tobacco to the fleets. The Negro could no longer sell or cultivate tobacco except for his own use; the Negro could not be a merchant. From then on, the cultivation and trade in tobacco was the economic privilege of the white man.

Sugar was mulatto from the start, for the energies of black men and white always went into its production. Even though it was Columbus who brought the first sugar cane into the Antilles from the Canary Islands, sugar was not a Spanish plant, nor even European. It was native to Asia, and from there it was carried along the Mediterranean by the Arabs and Moors. For the cultivation of the cane and the extraction of its juice the help of stout slaves and serfs was required, and in Portugal, as in Spain and Sicily in Europe, in Mauritania and Egypt in Africa, in Arabia, Mesopotamia, Persia, and India in Asia, these workers were as a rule of Negroid stock, those dark people who from prehistoric times had penetrated into that long strip of supertropical areas and gave them their permanent dark coloring, the same stock that in the Middle Ages invaded it anew with the waves of Moslems, who never felt any hostile racial prejudice toward the Negro. Sugar cane and Negro slaves arrived together in the island of Cuba, and possibly in Hispaniola, from across the sea. And since then Negro labor and sugar cane have been two factors in the same economic binomial of the social equation of our country.

For centuries the workers in the centrals were exclusively Negroes; often even the overseers were colored. This was true of the mill workers as well as of the field workers, with the exception of the technicians and the management. It was not until the abolishment of slavery, the influx of Spanish immigrants after the Ten Years' War, and the introduction of the sharecropping system that white farmers were to be found on the Cuban sugar plantations.

The nineteenth century in Cuba was marked by the change in the labor system brought about by the prohibition of the slave trade and, much later, by the abolition of slavery and the substitution for it of hired workers. The abolition was proclaimed by the Cubans fighting a war of secession against the mother country, and later by Spain in 1880–6. The cessation of the slave trade coincided with the introduction of the steam engine, which increased the productive capacity of the mills, and the abolition of slavery (1886) was simultaneous with the use of steel rails and the development of the railroads, which increased the radius of activity of the centrals. Cheap labor was an imperative need, so Spain, no longer able to smuggle in slaves or bring in more Chinese coolies or peons from Yucatán,[11] began to export her own white laborers. As a result the proportion of Negroes in the Cuban population began to diminish. In the distribution of colored population in Cuba today the greatest density is to be found in the old sugar-growing sections, not in the tobacco-raising areas, which were settled in the main by white immigrants from the Canary Islands and peasants of old Cuban stock. Tobacco drew upon the free white population, whereas for sugar cane black slaves were imported. This also explains why there are no invasions of migrant seasonal workers in the tobacco industry, and still less of Haitians and Jamaicans, who were brought in to make the harvesting of cane cheaper.

It should be noted that this process which took place in Cuba was not paralleled in other countries, such as Virginia, for example, whose early economy was based on tobacco. In Virginia, at that time an English colony, when the settlers began to raise tobacco they depended wholly on slave labor to cultivate it – white or black slaves, but preferably black.

This was due to the fact that the growing of tobacco there did not follow the same pattern as in Cuba, where, just as the Indians had done, it was treated as a small-scale, garden product, but in Virginia it employed the system of large plantations. The reason for this was that from the start the growing of tobacco in Virginia was a business, and the product was for foreign export, with the largest possible profit. That is to say, from its beginnings it was a capitalistic enterprise. For this reason, in the Anglo-American colonies there were never small growers nor any concern with the distinctive qualities of the leaf. There capitalism was in control of tobacco production from the first moment, and its objective was quantity rather than quality . . . .

On the Social Phenomenon of 'Transculturation' and Its Importance in Cuba

I am going to take the liberty of employing for the first time the term *transculturation*, fully aware of the fact that it is a neologism. . .as a substitute for the term *acculturation*, whose use is now spreading.

Acculturation is used to describe the process of transition from one culture to another, and its manifold social repercussions. But *transculturation* is a more fitting term.

I have chosen the word *transculturation* to express the highly varied phenomena that have come about in Cuba as a result of the extremely complex transmutations of culture that have taken place here, and without a knowledge of which it is impossible to understand the evolution of the Cuban folk, either in the economic or in the institutional, legal, ethical, religious, artistic, linguistic, psychological, sexual, or other aspects of its life.

The real history of Cuba is the history of its intermeshed transculturations. First came the transculturation of the paleolithic Indian to the neolithic, and the disappearance of the latter because of his inability to adjust himself to the culture brought in by the Spaniards. Then the transculturation of an unbroken stream of white immigrants. They were Spaniards, but representatives of different cultures and themselves torn loose, to use the phrase of the time, from the Iberian Peninsula groups and transplanted to a New World, where everything was new to them, nature and people, and where they had to readjust themselves to a new syncretism of cultures. At the same time there was going on the transculturation of a steady human stream of African Negroes coming from all the coastal regions of Africa along the Atlantic, from Senegal, Guinea, the Congo, and Angola and as far away as Mozambique on the opposite shore of that continent. All of them snatched from their original social groups, their own cultures destroyed and crushed under the weight of the cultures in existence here, like sugar cane ground in the rollers of the mill. And still other immigrant cultures of the most varying origins arrived, either in sporadic waves or a continuous flow, always exerting an influence and being influenced in turn: Indians from the mainland, Jews, Portuguese, Anglo-Saxons, French, North Americans, even yellow Mongoloids from Macao, Canton, and other regions of the sometime Celestial Kingdom.[12] And each of them torn from his native moorings, faced with the problem of disadjustment and readjustment, of deculturation and acculturation –in a word, of transculturation.

Among all peoples historical evolution has always meant a vital change from one culture to another at tempos varying from gradual to sudden. But in Cuba the cultures that have influenced the formation of its folk have been so many and so diverse in their spatial position and their structural composition that this vast blend of races and cultures overshadows in importance every other historical phenomenon.

Even economic phenomena, the most basic factors of social existence, in Cuba are almost always conditioned by the different cultures. In Cuba the terms Ciboney, Taino, Spaniard, Jew, English, French, Anglo-American, Negro, Yucatec, Chinese, and Creole do not mean merely the different elements that go into the make-up of the Cuban nation, as expressed by their different indications of origin. Each of these has come to mean in addition the synthetic and historic appellation of one of the various economies and cultures that have existed in Cuba successively and even simultaneously, at times giving rise to the most terrible clashes. We have only to recall that described by Bartolomé de las Casas as the 'destruction of the Indies.'. . .

First there was the culture of the Ciboneys and the Guanajabibes, the paleolithic culture, our stone age. Or, to be more exact, our age of stone and wood, of unpolished stone and rough wood, and of sea shells and fish bones, which were like stones and thorns of the sea.

After this came the culture of the Taino Indians, which was neolithic. This was the age of polished stone and carved wood. With the Tainos came agriculture, a sedentary as opposed to a nomadic existence, abundance, tribal chieftains, or caciques, and priests. They entered as conquerors and imposed the first transculturation. The Ciboneys became serfs, . . . or fled to the hills and jungles, . . . Then came a hurricane of culture: Europe. There arrived together, and in mass, iron, gunpowder, the horse, the wheel, the sail, the compass, money, wages, writing, the printing-press, books, the master, the King, the Church, the banker . . . A revolutionary upheaval shook the Indian peoples of Cuba, tearing up their institutions by the roots and destroying their lives. At one bound the bridge between the drowsing stone ages and the wide-awake Renaissance was spanned. In a single day various of the intervening ages were crossed in Cuba . . . . If the Indies of America were a New World for the Europeans, Europe was a far newer world for the people of America. They were two worlds that discovered each other and collided head-on. The impact of the two on each other was terrible. One of them perished, as though struck by lightning. It was a transculturation that failed as far as the natives were concerned, and was profound and cruel for the new arrivals. The aboriginal human basis of society was destroyed in Cuba, and it was necessary to bring in a complete new population, both masters and servants. This is one of the strange social features of Cuba, that since the sixteenth century all its classes, races, and cultures, coming in by will or by force, have all been exogenous and have all been torn from their places of origin, suffering the shock of this first uprooting and a harsh transplanting.

With the white men came the culture of Spain, and together with the Castilians, Andalusians, Portuguese, Galicians, Basques, and Catalonians. It could be called a crosscut of the Iberian culture of the white Pyrenean subrace. And in the first waves of immigration came Genoese, Florentines, Jews, Levantines, and Berbers – that is to say, representatives of the Mediterranean culture, an age-old mixture of peoples, cultures, and pigmentation, from the ruddy Normans to the sub-Sahara Negroes. Some of the white men brought with them a feudal economy, conquerors in search of loot and peoples to subjugate and make serfs of; while others, white too, were urged on by mercantile and even industrial capitalism, which was already in its early stages of development. And so various types of economy came in, confused with each other and in a state of transition, to set themselves up over other types, different and intermingled too, but primitive and impossible of adaptation to the needs of the white men at that close of the Middle Ages. The mere fact of having crossed the sea had changed their outlook; they left their native lands ragged and penniless and arrived as lords and masters; from the lowly in their own country they became converted into the mighty in that of others. And all of them, warriors, friars, merchants, peasants, came in search of adventure, cutting their links with an old society to graft themselves on another, new in climate, in people, in food, customs, and hazards. All came with their ambitions fixed on the goal of riches and power to be achieved here, and with the idea of returning to their native land to enjoy the fruits of their labors in their declining years. That is to say, the undertaking was to be bold, swift, and temporary, a parabolic curve whose beginning and end lay in a foreign land, and whose intersection through this country was only for the purpose of betterment.

There was no more important human factor in the evolution of Cuba than these continuous, radical, contrasting geographic transmigrations, economic and social, of the first settlers, this perennial transitory nature of their objectives, and their unstable life in the land where they were living, in perpetual disharmony with the society from which they drew their living. Men, economies, cultures, ambitions were all foreigners here, provisional, changing, 'birds of passage' over the country, at its cost, against its wishes, and without its approval.

With the whites came the Negroes, first from Spain, at that time full of slaves from Guinea and the Congo, and then directly from all the Dark Continent. They brought with them their diverse cultures, some as primitive as that of the Ciboneys, others in a state of advanced barbarism like that of the Tainos, and others more economically and socially developed, like the Mandingas, Yolofes (Wolofs), Hausas, Dahomeyans, and Yorubas, with agriculture, slaves, money, markets, trade, and centralized governments ruling territories and populations as large as Cuba; intermediate cultures between the Taino and the Aztec, with metals, but as yet without writing.

The Negroes brought with their bodies their souls, but not their institutions nor their implements. They were of different regions, races, languages, cultures, classes, ages, sexes, thrown promiscuously into the slave ships, and socially equalized by the same system of slavery. They arrived deracinated, wounded, shattered, like the cane of the fields, and like it they were ground and crushed to extract the juice of their labor. No other human element has had to suffer such a profound and repeated change of surroundings, cultures, class, and conscience. They were transferred from their own to another more advanced culture, like that of the Indians; but the Indians suffered their fate in their native land, believing that when they died they passed over to the invisible regions of their own Cuban world. The fate of the Negroes was far more cruel; they crossed the ocean in agony, believing that even after death they would have to recross it to be resurrected in Africa with their lost ancestors. The Negroes were torn from another continent, as were the whites; but not of their own will or choice, and forced to leave their free and easy tribal ways to eat the bitter bread of slavery, whereas the white man, who may have set out from his native land in despair, arrived in the Indies in a frenzy of hope, converted into master and authority. The Indians and the Spaniards had the support and comfort of their families, their kinfolk, their leaders, and their places of worship in their sufferings; the Negroes found none of this. They, the most uprooted of all, were herded together like animals in a pen, always in a state of impotent rage, always filled with a longing for flight, freedom, change, and always having to adopt a defensive attitude of submission, pretense, and acculturation to a new world. Under these conditions of mutilation and social amputation, thousands and thousands of human beings were brought to Cuba year after year and century after century from continents beyond the sea. To a greater or lesser degree whites and Negroes were in the same state of dissociation in Cuba. All, those above and those below, living together in the same atmosphere of terror and oppression, the oppressed in terror of punishment, the oppressor in terror of reprisals, all beside justice, beside adjustment, beside themselves. And all in the painful process of transculturation.

After the Negroes began the influx of Jews, French, Anglo-Saxons, Chinese, and peoples from the four quarters of the globe. They were all coming to a new world, all on the way to a more or less rapid process of transculturation.

I am of the opinion that the word *transculturation* better expresses the different phases of the process of transition from one culture to another because this does not consist merely in acquiring another culture, which is what the English word *acculturation* really implies, but the process also necessarily involves the loss or uprooting of a previous culture, which could be defined as a deculturation. In addition it carries the idea of the consequent creation of new cultural phenomena, which could be called neoculturation. In the end, as the school of Malinowski's[13] followers maintains, the result of every union of cultures is similar to that of the reproductive process between individuals; the offspring always has something of both parents but is always different from each of them.

These questions of sociological nomenclature are not to be disregarded in the interests of a better understanding of social phenomena, especially in Cuba, whose history, more than that of any other country of America, is an intense, complex, unbroken process of transculturation of human groups, all in a state of transition. The concept of transculturation is fundamental and indispensable for an understanding of the history of Cuba, and, for analogous reasons, of that of America in general.

NOTES

1. José Martí, leader of the Cuban Revolutionary Party and author of 'Our America', was killed in action fighting for independence in 1895. See Chapter 1 in this volume).
2. The Cuban war for independence, 1895–98, continued the armed struggle that began with the Ten Years' War, 1868–78.
3. Tobacco is a plant native to the Caribbean. In Taino language, *tabaco* was the name of a bifurcated tube by which the powder (*cohoba*), made from the pulverised leaves of the plant, was inhaled through the nose. The Spaniards' confusion of these words led to the spread of the name for the tube as the name for the plant in several European languages.
4. Gonzalo Fernández de Oviedo y Valdés wrote one of the first histories of the Caribbean in 1535, *Historia general y natural de las Indias*, reprinted in 5 volumes (Madrid publishers 1959).
5. The *guajiro*, a peasant of Spanish origin, was generally viewed as the 'typical Cuban', which pushed Afro-Cubans to the margin of their society.
6. Hispaniola was the name given by the Spanish to the island where they first settled. It was later divided and the western part, ceded to France, became Haiti and the eastern part the Dominican Republic.
7. Emancipation was planned to take place gradually over an eight-year period of 'apprenticeship', called *patronato*, beginning in 1880. This was abolished two years ahead of schedule, so slavery finally ended in Cuba in 1886.
8. The rapid expansion of sugar production that resulted from heavy US investments depended on the immigration of thousands of workers, many of them contract workers from Haiti and Jamaica. Between 1912 and 1930, almost 200,000 Haitians and 113,000 Jamaicans entered Cuba legally and many more entered through extralegal channels. During the Great Depression, there was antagonism between Cubans, including Afro-Cuban workers, and immigrants from Haiti and Jamaica, many of whom were repatriated.
9. In the nineteenth century Spain was a poor country with a rapidly growing population. In the last decades of the century, as the slave trade and then slavery ended in Cuba, about 250,000 Spaniards emigrated to Cuba. Between 1902 and 1919 some 700,000 immigrants arrived, most of them from Spain.
10. Bartolomé de Las Casas (1474–1566) settled in Hispaniola in 1502. He became a priest and denounced the system of forced labour which was destroying the native population. His critical *Historia de las Indias* is an indictment of Spanish colonial policies and practices.
11. Some 125,000 Chinese workers were brought to Cuba under 8-year indentures between 1848 and 1874, most of them men between the ages of 20 and 39. Like the earlier trade in enslaved Africans, this trade was profitable in itself and also contributed a pool of coerced labour to the sugar industry. A smaller number of Maya Indians were brought to Cuba from the Yucatán peninsula of Mexico.

12. Celestial Kingdom refers to the ancient Chinese Empire. The Chinese words *T'ien Ch'ao*, meaning Heavenly Dynasty, referred to the kingdom ruled by a dynasty which claimed to have been appointed by heaven.

13. Bronislaw Malinowski (1884–1942) was a British anthropologist of Polish origin who taught at the University of London and then at Yale University from 1939 until his death. Best known for his book *Argonauts of the Western Pacific,* he contributed an introduction to the first edition of Ortiz's *Contrapunteo Cubano* in 1940.

Five

Luis Muñoz Rivera

Luis Muñoz Rivera (1859–1916), a journalist, poet, and leader of the Partido Liberal Fusionista *(Liberal Fusionist party), helped Puerto Rico achieve autonomy from Spain in 1898. When the United States invaded Puerto Rico that year, Muñoz Rivera was the leading advocate of self-government. He died shortly before US citizenship was imposed on Puerto Ricans.*

The Autonomic Charter gave Puerto Rico 16 representatives and three senators in the Spanish Cortes *(parliament), a governor who represented the crown and was responsible for security and the appointment of members of the judiciary, and a bicameral parliament consisting of a house of representatives and an administrative council. The latter would consist of 15 members, eight of them elected and the others appointed by the governor. To be eligible for election, a candidate had to be a native Puerto Rican or resident of the island for four consecutive years. The house of representatives consisted of 32 members who were elected for five-year terms and had the power to legislate on a variety of matters, including the monetary system, electoral procedures, the local judicial system, and tariff duties, and it had exclusive authority over the island's educational and transportation systems and welfare institutions. It had the power even to negotiate commercial treaties with foreign nations, while treaties negotiated by the Spanish* Cortes *that affected the island were to be submitted to the insular government for its approval. This charter, which not only provided for considerable self-government but also for Puerto Rican representation in Spain, could not be amended except at the request of the insular legislature. In the first elections under this charter Muñoz Rivera won by a wide margin and, with his party having control of the cabinet and legislature, he became the undisputed leader. The new government, which was to have taken office in May 1898, was delayed because the United States declared war on Spain on April 19. The Puerto Rican legislature convened on July 17, the day after the Spanish army in Cuba surrendered, and eight days later the United States invaded Puerto Rico and terminated this experiment in autonomy.*

Muñoz Rivera, distrusting US intentions, immediately emphasised that Puerto Rico was an autonomous state with its own identity which should be respected. However, when the Treaty of Paris was signed on December 10, 1898, Spain conceded Puerto Rico to the United States, with the political status and civil rights of the islanders to be determined solely by the US Congress. US military rule ended on May 1, 1900 with the appointment of a civilian governor by the president, but it was clear that the US political philosophy of government by consent, based on the inalienable rights of the people, as stated in the Declaration of Independence, would not be applied in Puerto Rico. Half a century elapsed between the US invasion and the first opportunity for Puerto Ricans to elect their own governor. Puerto Rico, which is defined by the United States as its 'unincorporated territory', was firmly in the hands of presidential appointees and the US Congress. The Foraker Act, passed in 1900, created an elected House of Delegates but the real government was still run by Washington.

The US Republican party rejected Puerto Rican demands for self-government for 14 years. Muñoz Rivera wrote to Woodrow Wilson, the Democratic president who was inaugurated in 1913, to affirm his hope that Puerto Ricans would be given 'the home rule to which they aspire with the same right as other countries in the world' (Muñoz Rivera to Wilson, Jan. 14, 1913, in Wilson Papers, Library of Congress, *Mss. Division, ser. 2, reel 39). Wilson vaguely promised to Puerto Ricans the 'ample and familiar rights and privileges accorded our own citizens in our territories' (quoted in Cabranes 1979, 72) without any commitment on home rule or self-determination. Muñoz Rivera wanted to be assured that US citizenship would not rule out the option of independence in the future and he continued to demand home rule as a step towards independence.*

As the United States came closer to involvement in the great war that was being fought in Europe the question of Puerto Rico's status became part of its defense strategy which included its control of the Caribbean. The United States occupied Haiti in 1915 and the Dominican Republic in 1916 and, in 1917, purchased the Danish Virgin Islands for $25 million. On January 20, 1916, Congressman William H. Jones introduced a bill dealing with Puerto Rico and on May 5 Muñoz Rivera, as the island's Resident Commissioner in Washington, spoke to the House, eloquently and passionately arguing for the United States to *live up to its democratic principles and give Puerto Rico self-government. Puerto Ricans were Latin Americans, he asserted, and second-class US citizenship should not be imposed on them. The bill passed in the House on May 23 but ran into trouble in the Senate. Muñoz Rivera died on November 15, 1916.*

At a time when the international situation was worsening, the United States was anxious about the strength of agitation for independence in Puerto Rico. Concerns over the defense of the United States and the independence movement in Puerto Rico coincided and convinced the Senate to pass the bill on February 20, 1917, a few weeks before war was declared on Germany. The Jones Act imposed US citizenship on all Puerto Ricans, and those who declined to accept it were disenfranchised. As citizens they could and did join the US army. About 18,000 Puerto Ricans served in the US armed forces in World War I. Self-government, the issue that was central to Muñoz Rivera, was not addressed and Puerto Ricans had far less autonomy as US citizens than they had temporarily achieved under Spain in 1898.

⋯⋯⋯

'Give Us Our Independence', Speech to the U.S. House of Representatives, May 5, 1916

On the 18th day of October 1898, when the flag of this great Republic was unfurled over the fortresses of San Juan, if anyone had said to my countrymen that the United States, the land of liberty, was going to deny their right to form a government of the people, by the people, and for the people of Porto Rico,[1] my countrymen would have refused to believe such a prophecy, considering it sheer madness. The Porto Ricans were living at that time under a regime of ample self-government, discussed and voted by the Spanish Cortes, on the basis of the parliamentary system in use among all the nations of Europe. Spain sent to the islands a Governor, whose power, strictly limited by law, made him the equivalent of those constitutional sovereigns who reign but do not govern. The members of the Cabinet, without whose signature no executive order was valid, were natives of the island; the representatives in the Senate and in the House were natives of the island; and the administration in its entirety was in the hands of natives of the island. The Spanish Cortes, it is true, retained the power to make statutory laws for Porto Rico, but in the Cortes were 16 Porto Rican representatives and 3 Porto Rican senators having voice and vote. And all the insular laws were made by the insular parliament.

Two years later, in 1900, after a long period of military rule, the Congress of the United States approved the Foraker Act. Under this act, all of the 11 members of the executive council were appointed by the President of the United States; 6 of them were the heads of departments; 5 exercised legislative functions only. And this executive council, or, in practice, the bureaucratic majority of the council, was, and is in reality, with the Governor, the supreme arbiter of the island and of its interests. It represents the most absolute contradiction of republican principles.

For 16 years we have endured this system of government, protesting and struggling against it, with energy and without result. We did not lose hope, because if one national party, the Republican, was forcibly enforcing this system upon us, the other national party, the Democratic, was encouraging us by its declarations in the platforms of Kansas City, St. Louis, and Denver. Porto Rico waited, election after election, for the Democratic Party to triumph at the polls and fulfill its promises. At last the Democratic Party did triumph. It is here. It has a controlling majority at this end of the Capitol and at the other end: it is in possession of the White House. On the Democratic Party rests the sole and undivided responsibility for the progress of events at this juncture. It can, by a legislative act, keep alive the hopes for the people of Porto Rico or it can deal these hopes their death blow.

The Republican Party decreed independence for Cuba and thereby covered itself with glory; the Democratic Party is bound by the principles written into its platforms and by the recorded speeches of its leaders to decree liberty for Porto Rico. The legislation you are about to enact will prove whether the platforms of the Democratic Party are more than useless paper, whether the words of its leaders are more than soap bubbles, dissolved by the breath of triumph. Here is the dilemma with its two unescapable horns: You must proceed in accordance with the fundamental principles of your party or you must be untrue to them. The monarchies of the Old World, envious of American success and the republics of the New World, anxious to see clearly the direction in which the American initiative is tending, are watching and studying the Democratic administration. Something more is at stake than the fate of Porto Rico – poor, isolated, and defenseless as she is – the prestige and the good name of the United States are at stake. England learned the hard lessons of Saratoga and Yorktown in the 18th century. And in the 19th century she established self-government, complete, sincere, and honorable in Canada, Australia, and New Zealand. Then in the 20th century, immediately after the Anglo-Boer War, she established self-government, complete, sincere, and honorable, for the Orange Free State and the Transvaal, her enemies of the day before. She turned over the reins of power to insurgents who were still wearing uniforms stained with British blood.

In Porto Rico no blood will be shed. Such a thing is impossible in an island of 3,600 square miles. Its narrow confines never permitted and never will permit armed resistance. For this very reason Porto Rico is a field of experiment unique on the globe. And if Spain, the reactionary monarchy, gave Porto Rico the home rule which she was enjoying in 1898, what should the United States, the progressive Republic, grant her? This is the mute question which Europe and America are writing today in the solitudes of the Atlantic and on the waters of the Panama Canal. The reply is the bill which is now under discussion. This bill cannot meet the earnest aspirations of my country. It is not a measure of self-government ample enough to solve definitely our political problem or to match your national reputation, established by a successful championship for liberty and justice throughout the world since the very beginning of your national life. But, meager and conservative as the bill appears when we look at its provisions from our own point of view, we sincerely recognize its noble purposes and willingly accept it as a step in the right direction and as a reform paving the way for others more acceptable and satisfactory which shall come a little later, provided that my countrymen will be able to demonstrate their capacity, the capacity they possess, to govern themselves. In regard to such capacity, it is my duty, no doubt a pleasant duty, to assure Congress that the Porto Ricans will endeavor to prove their intelligence, their patriotism, and their full preparation to enjoy and to exercise a democratic regime.

Our behavior during the past is a sufficient guarantee for our behavior in the future. Never a revolution there, in spite of our Latin blood; never an attempt to commercialize our political influence; never an attack against the majesty of law. The ever-reigning peace was not at any time disturbed by the illiterate masses, which bear their suffering with such stoic fortitude and only seek comfort in their bitter servitude, confiding in the supreme protection of God.

There is no reason which justifies American statesmen in denying self-government to my country and erasing from their programs the principles of popular sovereignty. Is illiteracy the reason? Because if in Porto Rico 60 percent of the electorate cannot read, in the United States in the early days of the Republic, 80 percent of the population were unable to read; and even today there are 20 Republics and 20 monarchies which acknowledge a higher percentage of illiteracy than Porto Rico. It is not the coexistence of two races on the island, because here in North America more than 10 States show a higher proportion of Negro population than Porto Rico and the District of Columbia has precisely the same proportion, 67 white to 33 percent colored.[2] It is not our small territorial extent, because two States have a smaller area than Porto Rico. It is not a question of population, for by the last census there were 18 States with a smaller population than Porto Rico. Nor is it a matter of real and personal property, for the taxable property in New Mexico is only one-third that of Porto Rico. There is a reason and only one reason – the same sad reason of war and conquest which let loose over the South after the fall of Richmond thousands and thousands of office seekers, hungry for power and authority, and determined to report to their superiors that the rebels of the South were unprepared for self-government. We are the southerners of the 20th century.

The House of Representatives has never been influenced by this class of motive. The House of Representatives has very high motives, and, if they are studied thoroughly, very grave reasons, for redeeming my country from bureaucratic greed and confiding to it at once the responsibility for its own destinies and the power to fix and determine them. They are reasons of an international character which affect the policy of the United States in the rest of America; Porto Rico, the only one of the former colonies of Spain in this hemisphere, which does not fly its own flag or figure in the family of nations, is being closely observed with assiduous vigilance by the Republics of the Caribbean Sea and the Gulf of Mexico. Cuba, Santo Domingo, Venezuela, Colombia, Costa Rica, Honduras, Nicaragua, Salvador, Guatemala maintain with us a constant interchange of ideas and never lose sight of the experiment in the colonial government which is being carried on in Porto Rico. If they see that the Porto Ricans are living happily, that they are not treated with disdain, that their aspirations are being fulfilled, that their character is respected, that they are not being subjected to an imperialistic tutelage, and that the right to govern their own country is not being usurped, these nations will recognize the superiority of American methods and will feel the influence of the American government. This will smooth the way to the moral hegemony which you are called by your greatness, by your wealth, by your traditions, and your institutions to exercise in the New World. On the other hand, if these communities, Latin – like Porto Rico – speaking the same language as Porto Rico, branches of the same ancestral trunk that produced Porto Rico, bound to Porto Rico by so many roots striking deep in a common past, if these communities observe that your insular experiment is a failure and that you have not been able to keep the affections of a people who awaited from you their redemption and their happiness, they will be convinced that they must look, not to Washington but to London, Paris, or Berlin when they seek markets for their products, sympathy in their misfortunes, and guarantees for their liberty.

What do you gain along with the discontent of my countrymen? You as Members of Congress? Nothing. And the Nation loses a part of its prestige, difficulties are created in the path of its policies, its democratic ideals are violated, and it must abdicate its position as leader in every progressive movement on the planet. Therefore if you undertake a reform, do it sincerely. A policy of subterfuge and shadows might be expected in the Italy of the Medicis, in the France of the Valois, in the England of the Stuarts, or the Spain of the Bourbons, but it is hard to explain in the United States of Cleveland, McKinley, Roosevelt, and Wilson.

This bill I am commenting on provides for a full elective legislature. Well, that is a splendid concession you will make to your own principles and to our own rights. But now, after such a magnificent advance, do not permit, gentlemen, do not permit the local powers of the legislature to be diminished in matters so important for us as the education of the children. We are citizens jealous of this dignity . . . .

I come now to treat of a problem which is really not a problem for Porto Rico, as my constituents look at it, because it has been solved already in the Foraker Act. The Foraker Act recognizes the Porto Rican citizenship of the inhabitants of Porto Rico.[3] We are satisfied with this citizenship and desire to prolong and maintain it – our natural citizenship, founded not on the conventionalism of law but on the fact that we were born on an island and love that island above all else, and would not exchange our country for any other country, though it were one as great and as free as the United States. If Porto Rico were to disappear in a geological catastrophe and there survived a thousand or 10,000 or a hundred thousand Porto Ricans, and they were given their choice of all citizenships of the world, they would choose without a moment's hesitation that of the United States. But so long as Porto Rico exists on the surface of the ocean, poor and small as she is, and even if she were poorer and smaller, Porto Ricans will always choose Porto Rican citizenship. And the Congress of the United States will have performed an indefensible act if it tries to destroy so legitimate a sentiment and to annul through a law of its own making a law of the oldest and wisest legislators of all time – a law of nature.

It is true that my countrymen have asked many times, unanimously, for American citizenship. They asked for it when through the promise of General Miles on his disembarkation in Ponce,[4] and through the promises of the Democratic Party when it adopted the Kansas City platform – they believed it not only possible but probable, not only probable but certain, that American citizenship was the door by which to enter, not after a period of 100 years nor of 10, but immediately into the fellowship of the American people as a State of the Union. Today they no longer believe it. From this floor the most eminent statesmen have made it clear to them that they must not believe it. And my countrymen, who, precisely the same as yours, have their dignity and self-respect to maintain, refuse to accept a citizenship of an inferior order, a citizenship of the second class, which does not permit them to dispose of their own resources nor to live their own lives nor to send to this Capitol their proportional representation. To obtain benefits of such magnitude they were disposed to sacrifice their sentiments of filial love for the mother- land. These advantages have vanished, and the people of Porto Rico have decided to continue to be Porto Ricans; to be so each day with increasing enthusiasm, to retain their own name, claiming for it the same consideration, the same respect, which they accord to the names of other countries, above all to the name of the United States. Give us statehood and your glorious citizenship will be welcome to us and to our children. If you deny us statehood, we decline your citizenship, frankly, proudly, as befits a people who can be deprived of their civil liberties but who, although deprived of their civil liberties, will preserve their conception of honor, which none can take from them because they bear it in their souls, a moral heritage from their forefathers.

This bill which I am speaking of grants American citizenship to all my compatriots. It authorizes those who do not accept American citizenship to so declare before a court of justice, and thus retain their Porto Rican citizenship. It provides that –

'No person shall be allowed to register as a voter in Porto Rico who is not a citizen of the United States'.

My compatriots are generously permitted to be citizens of the only country they possess, but they are eliminated from the body politic; the exercise of political rights is forbidden them and by a single stroke of the pen they are converted into pariahs and there is established in America, on American soil, protected by the Monroe Doctrine, a division into castes like the Brahmans and Sudras of India. The Democratic platform of Kansas City declared 14 years ago, ' A nation can not long endure half empire and half republic', and 'Imperialism abroad will lead rapidly and irreparably to despotism at home'. These are not Porto Rican phrases reflecting our Latin impressionability; they are American phrases, reflecting the Anglo-Saxon spirit, calm in its attitude and jealous – very jealous – of its privileges.

We have a profound consideration for your national ideas; you must treat our local ideas with a similar consideration. As the representative of Porto Rico I propose that you convoke the people of the island to express themselves in full plebiscite on the question of citizenship and that you permit the people of Porto Rico to decide by their votes whether they wish the citizenship of the United States or whether they prefer their own natural citizenship. It would be strange, if, having refused it so long as the majority of people asked for it, you should decide to impose it by force now that the majority of the people decline it.

Someone recently stated that we desire the benefits but shirk the responsibilities and burdens of citizenship. I affirm in reply that we were never consulted as to our status, and that in the Treaty of Paris the people of Porto Rico were disposed of as were the serfs of ancient times, fixtures of the land, who were transferred by force to the service of new masters and subject to new servitudes. The fault is not ours, though ours are the grief and humiliation; the fault lies with our bitter destiny which made us weak and left us an easy prey between the warring interests of mighty powers. If we had our choice, we would be a free and isolated people in the liberty and solitude of the seas, without other advantages than those won by our exertions in industry and in peace, without other responsibilities and burdens than those of our own conduct and our duty toward one another and toward the civilisation which surrounds us.

The bill under consideration, liberal and generous in some of its sections – as those creating an elective insular Senate; a Cabinet, the majority of whose members shall be confirmed by the Senate; and a public-service commission, two members of which shall be elected by the people – is exceedingly conservative in other sections, most of all in that which restricts the popular vote, enjoining that the right of registering as electors be limited to those who are able to read and write or who pay taxes to the Porto Rican treasury. By means of this restriction 165,000 citizens who vote at present and who have been voting since the Spanish days would be barred from the polls.

Here are the facts: There exist at present 250,000 registered electors. Seventy percent of the electoral population is illiterate. There will remain, then, 75,000 registered electors. Adding 10,000 illiterate taxpayers, there will be a total of 85,000 citizens within the electoral register and 165,000 outside of it. I cannot figure out, hard as I have tried, how those 165,000 Porto Ricans are considered incapable of participating in the elections of their representatives in the legislature and municipalities, while on the other hand they are judged perfectly capable of possessing with dignity American citizenship. This is an inconsistency which I cannot explain, unless the principle is upheld that he who incurs the greatest misfortune – not by his own fault – of living in the shadow of ignorance is not worthy of the honor of being an American citizen. In the case of this being the principle on which the clause is based, it would seem necessary to uphold such principle by depriving 3 million Americans of their citizenship, for this is the number of illiterates in the United States according to the census of 1910. There is no reason that justifies this measure, anyway. Since civil government was established in Porto Rico, superseding military government – that is, 16 years ago – eight general elections have been staged. Eight times the people with a most ample suffrage law, have elected their legislative bodies, their municipal councils, their municipal courts, and school boards. These various bodies have cooperated to the betterment and progress of the country, which gives evidence that they were prudently chosen . . . .

The aforesaid motives are fundamental ones that require careful attention from the House. But there are deeper motives yet, those that refer to the history of the United States and of the American Congress. Never was there a single law passed under the dome of the Capitol restrictive of individual rights, of the rights of humanity. Quite the contrary, Congress, even going to the extreme of amending the Constitution, restrained the initiative of the States for the purpose of making them respect the exercise of those rights without marring it with the least drawback. There is the 14th amendment.[5] Congress could not hinder States from making their electoral laws, but it could decree and did decree that in the event of any State decreasing its number of electors it would, ipso facto, decrease its number of Representatives in this House. The United States always gave to the world examples of a profound respect for the ideal of a sincere democracy.

I feel at ease when I think of the future of my country. I read a solemn declaration of the five American commissioners that signed, in 1898, the Treaty of Paris. When the five Spanish delegates, no less distinguished than the Americans, asked for a guarantee as to the future of Porto Rico, your compatriots answered thus:

> 'The Congress of a country which never enacted laws to oppress or abridge the rights of residents within its domains, and whose laws permit the largest liberty consistent with the preservation of order and the protection of property, may safely be trusted not to depart from its well-settled practice in dealing with the inhabitants of these islands.'

Congress needs not be reminded of its sacred obligations, the obligations which those words impose upon it. Porto Rico had nothing to do with the declaration of war. The Cubans were assured of their national independence. The Porto Ricans were acquired for $20 million, and my country, innocent and blameless, paid with its territory the expenses of the campaign.

The Treaty of Paris says:

> 'As compensation for the losses and expenses occasioned the United States by the war and for the claims of its citizens by reason of the injuries and damages they may have suffered in their persons and property during the last insurrection of Cuba, Her Catholic Majesty, in the name and representation of Spain, and thereunto constitutionally authorized by the Cortes of the Kingdom, cedes to the United States of America, and the latter accept for themselves, the island of Porto Rico and the other islands now under Spanish sovereignty in the West Indies, as also the island of Guam, in the Mariannas or Ladrones Archipelago,[6] which island was selected by the United States of America in virtue of the provisions of article 11 of the protocol signed in Washington on August 12 last.'

You, citizens of a free fatherland, with its own laws, its own institutions, and its own flag, can appreciate the unhappiness of the small and solitary people that must await its laws from your authority, that lacks institutions created by their will, and who does not feel the pride of having the colors of a national emblem to cover the homes of its families and the tombs of its ancestors.

Give us now the field of experiment which we ask of you, that we may show that it is easy for us to constitute a stable republican government with all possible guarantees for all possible interests. And afterward, when you acquire the certainty that you can find in Porto Rico a republic like that founded in Cuba and Panama, like the one that you will find at some future day in the Philippines,[7] give us our independence and you will stand before humanity as the greatest of the great; that which neither Greece nor Rome nor England ever were, a great creator of new nationalities and a great liberator of oppressed peoples.

NOTES

1. In the Foraker Act (1900), the US Congress, following an error made in the English text of the Treaty of Paris, established a system of civil government for 'Porto Rico'. The US Geographic Board subsequently changed the spelling of Puerto Rico to conform to this official error. The official misspelling occurred only in English language publications, such as this record of Muñoz Rivera's speech. The Puerto Rican legislature in 1930, in a symbolic act of self-assertion, unanimously passed a resolution that Congress should 'restore our island its true name of Puerto Rico in place of Porto Rico as it is now called because it is considered that full justice will thus be done to our history, our language, and our traditions'. The US Congress passed the bill to correct the spelling in 1932 (US Congress, *Correct the Spelling of the Name of the Island of Porto Rico*, 72nd Cong., 1st Sess., H. Doc. 585, 1932).
2. The ways that 'white' and 'coloured' are culturally defined in Puerto Rico and the United States were, and still are, different. Thus, a Puerto Rican who appeared white would be defined as 'white' in the island but on coming to the mainland would be defined as 'negro' or 'coloured' if it was known that this person had any African ancestry.
3. The Foraker Act did not extend US citizenship to Puerto Ricans but referred to a body of people, 'The People of Porto Rico', who had limited rights and were entitled to the protection of the United States. Muñoz Rivera chose to interpret this as recognizing Puerto Rican citizenship.
4. General Nelson A. Miles was the commander of the US forces when they occupied Ponce, the chief southern town of Puerto Rico, in 1898.
5. The 14th amendment of the constitution of the United States, which was passed soon after the abolition of slavery and ratified in 1868, states that all persons born or naturalized in the United States are citizens and that no state could deny equal rights to any citizen. The principal purpose of the amendment was to extend all the rights of citizenship to the former slaves but this was widely denied in practice until the civil rights movement of the 1960s.
6. Guam was captured by Japan in 1941 and retaken by the United States in 1944. In 1950, the United States declared Guam a 'territory' under the supervision of the department of the interior and the people became US citizens. They can elect a one-house legislature and, since 1970, their governor.
7. US forces in the Philippines surrendered to Japan in 1942 but recaptured it in 1945. The independent Republic of the Philippines was established the next year.

Six

Pedro Albizu Campos

Pedro Albizu Campos (1891–1965) was one of Puerto Rico's most distinguished nationalist leaders. He studied engineering, chemistry and law in the United States, receiving a law degree from Harvard University in 1923. He was influenced by the Irish Republican movement's struggle for independence from British rule, as it had many supporters in Boston. Albizu thought that Puerto Rico would not be allowed to become a state of the United States unless it gave up its Hispanic culture and conformed to the dominant traditions of the mainland. At first he thought that Puerto Rico could achieve something like the dominion status that Canada and Australia had with Britain, in which Puerto Ricans could continue to be US citizens but with full local sovereignty. He soon became disillusioned, however, and joined the Nationalist party that was formed in 1922.

Between 1927 and 1930, Albizu travelled in the Caribbean and Latin America, visiting anti-imperialist groups in the Dominican Republic, Haiti, Cuba, Mexico, Panama, Peru and Venezuela. Returning to Puerto Rico in 1930, he became the president of the Nationalist party. When he and his party won few votes in the 1932 elections he became more militant. The Nationalists considered the US occupation of the island since 1898 to be illegitimate and they promoted the use of national symbols, such as the Puerto Rican flag and anthem, in defiance of the United States. The economic collapse in the 1930s, caused by the world-wide depression, provoked more radical and even revolutionary responses in Puerto Rico. Albizu was an intense and inspirational leader and the Nationalists became convinced that the United States would give up Puerto Rico only after a fight. The United States tried to shore up the Puerto Rican economy with some relief measures after President Franklin Roosevelt initiated the New Deal, but there was a surge of nationalism in the island in the 1930s.

Albizu's Nationalists, a hard core of them wearing black shirts in imitation of Mussolini's Fascist party in Italy, considered the yankis *an occupying force. In October 1935, a demonstration at the university became violent and three Nationalists were killed by the police. The following February, the US chief of police, Colonel E. Francis Riggs, was assassinated by two Nationalists, Hiram Rosado and Elías Beauchamp. They were taken to the police headquarters and promptly shot. Both the killing of Riggs and the way the police took the law into their own hands caused widespread shock in Puerto Rico. The governor, Blanton Winship, resolved to put Albizu behind bars, and Senator Millard Tydings, with the administration's approval, worked on a bill to offer Puerto Rico independence. This would have been on such ruinous economic terms that it was calculated most Puerto Ricans would vote against it, thus undermining the Nationalists. The* New York Times *reported, however, 'that should a plebiscite be held today independence would win overwhelmingly' (May 3, 1936, sec. 4, p. 6).*

Albizu and seven of his supporters were put on trial, accused of conspiring to overthrow the federal government in Puerto Rico. An FBI report stated that no significant evidence had been found when several Nationalists' homes were searched and the US attorney in San Juan, who had been pressured by the governor to prosecute, concluded that they would be acquitted because all that they had said and done had been in the open. The trial ended when the jury, composed of seven Puerto Ricans and five Americans, was unable to reach agreement. A second jury, selected with only two Puerto Ricans, quickly brought in a guilty verdict and the defendants were sentenced to jail for between two and ten years (Morales Carrión 1983, 235).

While Albizu was imprisoned, a parade of unarmed Nationalists in Ponce was fired on by the police on March 21, 1937. Twenty-one people, two of them policemen, were killed and this became known as the Ponce Massacre. The violence continued. Governor Winship decided on a show of force on July 25, 1938, the anniversary of the US invasion in 1898, with a massive military parade in Ponce. A Nationalist shot at the governor but killed a National Guard colonel, and was then killed by the police. Winship, who had provoked the Nationalists, resigned in 1939. In 1940, a new era began when the United States decided to make Puerto Rico a key base in the war of the Atlantic and the Popular Democratic party, or Populares, *began its long period of political dominance.*

Albizu served his prison term and remained convinced that Puerto Rico could achieve its independence only through an armed struggle. In an uprising on October 30, 1950, the Nationalists took over two towns and attacked the governor's residence in San Juan. The uprising was quelled after 33 Nationalists were killed and many people, including Albizu, were imprisoned. Two other Nationalists attacked President Truman's residence in Washington. One of them, Oscar Collazo, and a police guard were killed. Albizu, who was in poor health in jail, was seen by many people as a martyr to US imperialism. The governor of Puerto Rico, Luis Muñoz Marín, pardoned Albizu in September 1953 but sent him back to jail in 1954 after four Nationalists, led by Lolita Lebrón, opened fire in the US House of Representatives, wounding five congressmen, to draw the world's attention to Puerto Rico's colonial status. Albizu suffered a stroke in jail in 1956. In all he spent almost 20 years in federal prisons, much of the time in solitary confinement. Muñoz Marín again pardoned him in 1964 and on April 21, 1965 the Nationalist leader died. For Albizu, who was strongly influenced by Catholicism, nationalism was a supreme value. He became, for some people, a romantic symbol of patriotism and militant resistance to the United States.

The Day of the Race

September 23 is the date of the armed proclamation of the Republic of Puerto Rico, the Proclamation of the Republic, the establishment of our nationhood in a free society – sovereign and independent. It is of vital interest and a matter of life itself for each one of you . . .

The other significant occasion which defines our character is October 12, the Discovery of the New World[1]. . . .

President Irigoyen[2] was governing the great nation of Argentina, and he came up with the idea that October 12 should be celebrated in all of Latin America as the Day of the Race. Many laughed and asked: 'Day of which race? Of the Negroes? Of the Indians? Of the Italians in America? Of the Portuguese in America? Of the French in America? Of the Spanish in America? Of the Yankees in America? Of the Germans in America? Of the British in America? Of the Chinese in America? Of the Japanese in America? To which race is he referring?'

And that brings us to the problem of resolving what is understood by the term. . . .

Ladies and gentlemen, the national structure is not the structure of the epidermis. It is not the structure of the skin because by means of the skin we can judge the cat, the goat, and even the wild animals, to see which one has a better quality skin for shoes, coats, or hats. Only ignorant minds separate men because of their epidermis. This would only cross the mind of the stupid North Americans. Only a savage nation would consider this. But civilized countries, mother countries, those countries always live with the unity that emanates from within every person, with the indestructible unity of people. They see that skin is an accident and the blondest man with the bluest eyes and the handsomest face, and the most attractive Negro with the most vibrant eyes and the most powerful physique could be either a saint or a sinner. This depends on what they carry in their spirit and on what they carry in their soul. This quality is what distinguishes man from beast.

Race, ladies and gentlemen, comes after the transformation of a people under the influence of the spirit – the transformation of the skin, of feelings, or thoughts – through the fundamental ideal which reveals life in all its details and in all transcendental acts. That is why the Latin American race exists.

Is there African blood? Yes . . . .

It flows through my veins, and I carry it with the supreme pride of human dignity.

Here we have Indian blood. Here we have pure archetypes of Indian blood. I also have Indian blood which is why I feel perfectly American, an autochthonal American in the true sense of the word.

Do we have white blood? I also carry it in my veins. My father was Biscayan, and he came from the purest race in all of Europe.

And the type of person who is creating unity of feeling and day-to-day homogeneity of action in our country is also forming racial unity in the biological sense and is restoring man to his pristine origin since man did not begin yellow, or white, or black, but only man, like the Divine Creator.

And so we come on this sacred night to live all that goes through our veins, all that is within us, to live the venerable ashes of all of our ancestors, to live all the millennium-ancient stones of the Spanish countries – and to live the millennium-ancient stones of the African countries. It is in contemporary times that we have unearthed in the Congo the grandeur of the African civilisation; it is today that we are unearthing in America the grandeur of the Indian civilisation.

We are a country predestined in history because Puerto Rico is the first nation in the world where a union of the spirit and of the body has been formed.[3]

That is why, ladies and gentlemen, we celebrate the Day of the Race. By race we refer to what has just been defined . . .

Ladies and gentlemen, we remember the man who was the instrument of this enormous deed. We remember the mother country – Spain, and Spain, ladies and gentlemen, is one of the few nations that has always been civilized . . . .

The Roman occupation also did not destroy Spain. Rome had a civilization, and the Spanish interpolated that which suited their body and soul. From the civilization of Rome, they formed their own empire. Since the Romans were civilized, they did not destroy nations . . . . Rome was a civilized nation, and the Romans never allowed more than one-third of conquered lands to go to Roman hands . . . .

What a contrast, ladies and gentlemen! Two thousand years of Roman civilization and we are still confronting barbarity. We are facing the United States, and the first thing it did was to dispossess us from our lands. The advance of barbarity, ladies and gentlemen, is as follows: from proprietor to proletariat, from proletariat to beggar, and from beggar to a disgraced tomb. Those who do not defend, with blood, the independence of their country are not worthy of a glorious tomb. This is our present situation as contrasted with the time of the Roman civilization . . . .

And Spain, despite Rome's grandeur, stayed Spanish . . . .

Much later, Spain had the invasion of the Moors and Spain kept its character. The Moors, contrary to what has been said in the history books, contrary to false history which is designed to discredit Spain's historical grandeur, did not bring any civilization to Spain . . .

After enduring other invasions and destroying the Moorish civilization, Spain accomplished its monumental work under the sponsorship of a woman . . . . Queen Isabella. And so we have it that a nation's sense of unity should be given by a woman.

When women are divided, the nation will be torn to pieces. Where the blonde woman is not the sister of the black woman, there is no nationhood, there is no civilization. There is barbarity, opposition, ruin, murder. Woman forges the unity of a race, the unity of a civilization, the unity of a nation . . . . [I]t is with Queen Isabella that the principles of Spain's unity crystallized. The moral catalyst of that unity was a woman, just as the catalyst of Puerto Rico's unity has to be the Puerto Rican woman.

Puerto Rico will be free, Puerto Rico will be sovereign, Puerto Rico will be independent when the Puerto Rican woman feels free, feels sovereign, feels independent . . . .

Queen Isabella captured a sense of unity for the New World. Spain brought to America, not the ideals of the pagan Romans, but the Roman judicial system, the Greek philosophical sense, and the mysticism of the Orient and brought to America the sublime spirit of Christianity.

Where the Spaniard went, he formed a family. He found the Indian, married her, and their children were Spaniards . . . .

Spain did not deny its highest honors to any man nor any woman, whether they were black, Indian, or white . . . .

Today, Negroes cannot even visit La Fortaleza.[4] Negroes are thrown a bone from the kitchen of La Fortaleza to pick up . . . .

Great is the work to be accomplished in our homeland! Great and immense! But you have to look at the obligations of your own origins. Whoever is not proud of his origin will never value anything because he begins by despising himself.

We honor Spain's name because, for us, it means the science of law, the positive sciences, the science of the Christian and moral tradition in our nation. We are not confused by the fact that the Moors have entered the Temple of Christianity in Puerto Rico. We shall restore the Temple, the Christian Church which has also been violated in Puerto Rico . . . .

It has been said that I once asked why we honor Spain when the Spanish colony in Puerto Rico is an enemy of the independence of Puerto Rico . . . .

We honor the nation that set the millennial foundation of civilization in Puerto Rico . . . .

Ladies and gentlemen, those are the millennial foundations of our race . . . .

Right here and now, our time starts. Let's not abandon our nation to those who are oblivious to the great civilization which shapes our blood. Let's rescue, as the Spaniards rescued the Iberian peninsula, our lands from profane hands. Puerto Rico has to start by pulling the economic, political, and cultural invasion out by the roots. Nationalism is concerned with all aspects of nationality.

Each one of you must be a landowner. Each one of you must own at least a patch of land, so you realize the value of the land. It is difficult to defend liberty when you do not realize the value of the land . . . .

And where is Ponce's dignity? I was here for the elections. It was immoral! Everyone here was selling votes for a dollar on election day . . . .

What elections? They were elections for sheep and pigs. Those voters looked like a herd of pigs, each going to dump his filth in the ballot boxes . . . .

If you want liberty, if you want to be owners of your land, rise up and hold your head up high, for you have been given the right to speak Spanish. You have no right whatsoever to speak any human language if you are defending the enslavement of a nation . . . .

We have something good to instill in America. Let us begin by guaranteeing our civilization to our descendents in Puerto Rico and by bringing, in conjunction with all Antillean nations, our civilization to North America so that it covers the world from pole to pole and endures on this planet forever.

That is why Nationalism sets forth four beautiful principles: the independence of Puerto Rico, the Antillean Confederation, the Pan American Union, and the supremacy of Latin American countries for the honor of all of us before posterity . . . .

Spanish arts, all the knowledge of our race, and above all the spiritual values, the spiritual values of the very soul of our race, are the objects of yearnings, the most vehement yearnings in an orgy of material ambition – the orgy of the golden calf – which are leading humanity to world chaos and destruction . . . .

Puerto Rico has to play its part in history and has to be free in order to look posterity straight in the eye.

$\mathcal{P}$uerto Rican Nationalism

Sixty-eight years ago, our republic was formed. On September 23, 1868, we declared our independence from Spain. Puerto Rico was rich in name and in our soil. Our Christian foundation had created a family model that was to be a vanguard of modern civilization.

Influential, independent men have made a difference in our society. Men such as musician Morel Campos; intellectuals such as Eugenio María de Hostos; and poets like Gautier Benítez[5] were among the great men who built and founded this nation.

The founders of our republic in 1868 held that our nation and its people would be sovereign –never belonging to another nation or people. This idea is not original, but is the basis of universal civilization, of international law. It is the basis of the family of free nations.

Our mother nation, Spain, founder of North and South American civilization, recognized this basic principle of sovereignty and, in 1868, paved the way for Puerto Rico to enter the family of free nations.

The United States (after the Spanish American War), on the other hand, saw Puerto Rico not as a nation, but as island property, and therefore took Puerto Rico through military intervention, and kept it.

Military intervention is the most brutal and abusive act that can be committed against a nation and a people. We demanded then, as we do today, the retreat of United States armed forces from Puerto Rico in order to embrace the liberty we held all too briefly in 1868.

We are not as fortunate as our forebears in 1868, who struggled to attain sovereignty. They never had a complaint against Spain, for Spain had every intention of granting Puerto Rico its liberty.

We stand today, docile and defenseless, because, since 1868, our political and economic power has been systematically stripped away by the United States for its own political and economic gain.

We stand as a nation forced not only to demand our liberty, but to demand reparations for having our political and economic liberty taken away.

We stand as a nation surrounded by industry, but with little of it belonging to our people. The business development in Puerto Rico since the United States intervention should have made the island one of the most prosperous islands in the world, but that is not the case.

The United States controls our economy, our commerce. Puerto Rico must determine a price for its products that is acceptable to the United States, while the United States issues their products to Puerto Rico at a rate that is comfortable to its own manufacturers and not the Puerto Rican consumer. The result is exploitation and abuses perpetrated at will, resulting in poverty for our people and wealth for the United States.

Seventy-six per cent of the wealth is in the hands of United States corporations, and their stability is ensured by the United States military. This economic exploitation will have long-lasting impact. Our family structure will be weakened, and the intellectual, spiritual, and moral advancement of our race will be jeopardized as we are made to be more 'North American'.

Already United States government agencies, under the guise of Christian virtue and goodwill, are simply controlling our people, destroying its culture. By imposing its own culture and language, the United States destroys our own culture and language.[6]

What will we have when we have nothing but dependency on those who destroyed us?

This is why I am dismayed by the effort among our own people to defeat the spirit of those who struggle for our liberation. Our own people see Puerto Rican nationalism as nothing but a path of terrorism and murder; but they defeat our spirit in denouncing themselves. They defeat our spirit by ignoring the historical terrorism and murder of the United States. In the end, they help only the United States, its industry, its imperialistic objectives.

It stands to reason – it stands to common sense – that we must be a free nation in order to survive as a people. The future of those not yet born depends on respecting the independence of Puerto Rico. That respect alone – the respecting of Puerto Rico's independence – is what Puerto Rican nationalism is all about.

NOTES

1. October 12, 1492 was the day that Columbus arrived in the Bahamas and claimed the lands for Spain. On his second voyage, he reached Puerto Rico on November 19, 1493. The beginning of Puerto Rico's existence as a colony is commemorated on the latter date and October 12 is the '*Dia de la Raza*', not 'Columbus Day' as in the United States.
2. Hipólito Irigoyen (1852–1933) was the founder of the Radical Party and the president of Argentina from 1916 to 1922. He was re-elected in 1928 but he was ill and in 1930 he was deposed by a military coup.
3. Albizu refers to the fact that when the first Africans arrived in Puerto Rico in the early sixteenth century the three elements of '*la raza*'– Indian, Spanish and African – were present.
4. The governor's mansion in San Juan.
5. Juan Morel Campos (1857– 96) was a Puerto Rican composer, known for his *danzas*. Eugenio María de Hostos (1839–1903) was a leading Puerto Rican patriot, philosopher, novelist, essayist and educator who lived much of his life in exile. Jose Gautier Benítez (1851 – 80) was a lyrical romantic poet whose principal themes were love and *patria*.

6. The Americanization of Puerto Rico that began in 1898 included the promotion of English as the official language of education until 1948. Although many Puerto Ricans learned English, the US policy failed and Puerto Rico remains a Spanish-speaking nation. The issue of language is central in the relations between the United States and Puerto Rico as it is connected to the problem of the island's political status and cultural identity.

Seven

Luis Muñoz Marín

L Luis Muñoz Marín (1898–1980), the son of Muñoz
Rivera, was the dominant politician in Puerto Rico for almost
40 years, its first elected governor, and the architect of its
current status as an Estado Libre Asociado *(Associated Free
State). He was, like his father, a poet and journalist as well
as a political leader. When he was a young man, he was a
member of the Socialist and Liberal parties. In 1938, he
founded the* Partido Popular Democratico *(Popular Democratic
Party) based on the liberal, social and economic reformers in
the pro-independence wing of the Liberals. By emphasising
a programme of economic and social reforms, including land
reform, rather than the issue of political status, Muñoz Marín
gained support from small farmers (jíbaros) whose profile in
a distinctive straw hat was adopted as the party's emblem.
In the 1940 election, the PPD won about 38 per cent of the
vote and control of the Senate. Together with Rexford
Tugwell, who was appointed governor in 1941, Muñoz Marín
created two dynamic agencies of economic growth, the
Puerto Rico Development Company and the Development
Bank of Puerto Rico. When the PPD won 65 per cent of the
vote in 1944, sweeping all the senatorial districts and 34 of
the 35 representative districts, it achieved a political
hegemony that lasted for 25 years.*

*In the face of the catastrophic decline of agriculture
and consequent rising unemployment and poverty, Muñoz
Marín embarked Puerto Rico on an ambitious programme
of industrialisation known as Operation Bootstrap.
Although the government's development company began
constructing and operating some industries itself, this was
not the accepted American way of private enterprise, so the
strategy soon changed to luring investors from the United*

States by offering incentives, including total tax exemption, low wages and free access to the mainland market. This developmental strategy did succeed in industrialising the Puerto Rican economy, but at the expense of increasing the island's dependence on the United States and of the massive emigration of Puerto Ricans. Almost a million workers and their families moved to the mainland between 1950 and 1965, many of them encountering discrimination and poor employment opportunities. Meanwhile, the US government agreed that Puerto Rico could have a little more self-government and in the first gubernatorial elections in 1948, Muñoz Marín swept in. Acting on the basis that he had a mandate from Puerto Ricans, not from Washington, he appointed Mariano Villaronga as commissioner of education who advocated education in Spanish, with English as a second language. After 50 years of enforced Americanisation in the schools, Puerto Rico was at last determining its own language policy.

While Puerto Rico was becoming more integrated into the United States economy, and thousands of Puerto Ricans migrated to the mainland, Muñoz Marín achieved some important gains in terms of self-government and cultural autonomy. Puerto Rico was becoming both more industrialised and urbanised, but the image of what Muñoz Marín called la patria-pueblo *was rooted in the traditional Hispanic values of the agrarian nineteenth century. His conception of nationalism, far from Albizu's commitment to an armed struggle of liberation, was peaceful and largely cultural. Puerto Rican identity, defined in terms of a romanticised, folkloric past, was seen in opposition to the modern commercial and materialistic culture associated with the United States. After 1948, it seemed that this identity could be maintained without a suicidal confrontation with the United States, but the social and economic changes wrought by Operation Bootstrap were actually destroying the basis of that idealised past.*

In the late 1940s, Muñoz Marín explored the possibility that Puerto Rico could achieve a political status that avoided what he called 'the divisive and futile debate' between a poverty-stricken independence, as had been offered by the Tydings bill in 1936, and the idea of statehood, that had little support in Washington or Puerto Rico. He said in a speech given on July 17, 1951 in Barranquitas, the birthplace and resting place of his father, that there was a third possibility that would enable Puerto Rico to achieve more freedom and economic development while remaining associated with the United States. A Puerto Rican convention wrote a new constitution, which was approved by the Puerto Rican people and the US Congress and on July 25, 1952 Puerto Rico became an Estado Libre Asociado, *known in English as the Commonwealth of Puerto Rico. This makes Puerto Rico self-governing in many respects, but the US*

Congress still defines it as a US territory and, although Puerto Ricans are US citizens, they cannot participate in presidential elections and are represented in Congress only by a commissioner who has no vote.

In 1960, Muñoz Marín spoke to Puerto Rico's legislature of his dream of a 'good civilisation', which included a growing economy, the development of Puerto Rican culture and education, unemployment compensation and a minimum wage, an expanded police force and improved civil rights, and the 'preservation of our natural heritage' for Puerto Ricans and tourists. 'Commonwealth status', he claimed, provides the means to create economic justice, personal freedom, and a 'good civilisation' in Puerto Rico. Four years later, Muñoz Marín handed over the governorship to his hand-picked successor, Roberto Sánchez Villela, but he remained the real leader of the PPD. When he died on April 30, 1980, after several years of failing health, he still advocated the Commonwealth status, believing that Puerto Rico could preserve its historic culture and identity within a strong political and economic bond to the United States.

<hr>

Speech at Barranquitas, July 17, 1951

Language was given to man to enable him to make himself understood by his fellow man. But one of the frailties of language is that there are some words which for a time prevent understanding. In Puerto Rico *patria* – the homeland – has been such a word. At first blush this may seem strange, as there is no people of the earth who love their native land more profoundly than do the people of Puerto Rico.

To the Puerto Rican, *patria* is the colors of the landscape, the change of season, the smell of the earth wet with fresh rain, the voice of the streams, the crash of the ocean against the shore, the fruits, the songs, the habits of work and of leisure, the typical dishes for special occasions and the meager ones for everyday, the flowers, the valleys, and the pathways. But even more than these things, *patria* is the people: their way of life, spirit, folkways, customs, their way of getting along with each other. Without these latter things *patria* is only a name, an abstraction, a bit of scenery. But with them it is an integral whole: 'the homeland *and* the people'. Those who profess to love their country while taking an irresponsible attitude towards the destiny of its people suffer from spiritual confusion. The implication of their attitude is that we must save the country even though we destroy the people!

Love of country must mean love of all of the country – both the *patria* and the people. But some of us confused love of the homeland with the narrow and bitter concept of the national state. We felt that love of Puerto Rico has as a necessary corollary the desire for separate independence. We had not yet comprehended that no law, divine or human, commands that countries must be suspicious, vain, and hostile, that they must live separate from other countries whose peoples are a part of the broad equality which the Lord created on the earth. Because of the rigidity of our thinking, we could not disentangle the concept of love for our country from the fixed idea of separate independence. Anything other than independence seemed to clash with our love for Puerto Rico.

The Dawning Light

The difficult process of clarifying these ideas began when the Tydings bill was introduced in Congress in 1936.[1] On the one hand this bill offered the separate independence for which many of us had asked because of our feeling for the abstract idea of the *patria*. On the other hand, it condemned the people of our homeland to extreme poverty from which they could never hope to escape. Suddenly what had seemed to be an integral idea – the homeland and separate independence – turned out to be two conflicting ideas: one, acceptable as an abstract idea; the other, a mortal enemy of the people. The Tydings bill would have made Puerto Rico independent; but it would have shackled the people with economic misery.

It was not easy to change our views on this subject. Our minds could grasp the point that if we could have separate independence only under the economic conditions of the Tydings bill it would be not independence but a living death of hopeless poverty for Puerto Rico. Yet our emotions led us to search for other economic conditions under which independence would be possible.

At the time, our emotions were stronger than our powers of reasoning. Rationalization works where understanding is the servant, instead of the master, of emotion. Instead of using reasoning objectively to seek the truth, we used it to justify our emotions. Just as one might confuse the glittering uniform of a doorkeeper with that of a king, our powers of reasoning were led astray by rationalization induced by our emotions. We were the victims of wishful thinking in believing that separate independence would be feasible if the economic conditions in the Tydings bill came into effect over a period of ten years instead of immediately. This was also inadequate; but it served for a time to protect, in the minds of many of us, the preconceived idea of separation.

The Untaught Wisdom

We were gripped with this emotional confusion wanting independence but not wanting economic upheaval – when the campaign to found the Popular Democratic Party was running its course between 1938 and 1940. At this point, well aware of the great economic needs of our people, and knowing our simple people well, I set out to talk with them. I learned many things from these talks.

I learned that there is a wisdom among the people in the towns and in the countryside which education may lead, but cannot improve, in its magnificent human essence. I taught many of them something, but they taught me more. I learned that the people are wise – wiser than we think. I learned that to them freedom is something deep in the heart, in the conscience, in everyday life, in personal dignity, in the furrow, the plow, and the tools. I learned that among the simple people the nationalistic concept does not exist, because in its place there is a deep understanding of freedom. I learned that in their wisdom they prefer – if they have to choose – one who governs respectfully from a distance to one who governs despotically from nearby. And that understanding is the unequaled basis and root of every great federalist concept, of great unions between countries and between men which cut across climates, races, and languages. The nationalistic concept prefers the despotic government of the nearby to the democratic government of the remote. Naturally, democratic federalism requires respect and liberty in the local as well as in the federal levels of government.

I learned many things, probably many more than I think I learned; for we learn by planting things in the mind which later bear fruit in understanding. And I learned better something I already knew: that it is unworthy of the conscience, that it is the denial of all ideals, to risk, for abstract concepts, the hope for a better life, the deep belief in the integral freedom of the good and simple people who populate the long paths, which sometimes cross the streets and squares, which are Puerto Rico. I learned all this, and I also learned that the great majority of the people of Puerto Rico prefer close association with their fellow citizens of the American Union and with all men on earth, to the bitter narrowness of separation.

I realized that with a program calling for separate independence we would never obtain the support of the people for economic development – equitable distribution and production – which the people needed so much. The profound intuition of the people was quick to point out the contradiction in a program which on the one hand talked about the struggle to reduce their extreme poverty and on the other hand talked about separate independence which would destroy any hope of ever conquering that extreme poverty – which in fact would rapidly aggravate the seriousness of that poverty.

From the instinct of the people which I observed in my journeys among them, from the doubts in my own mind and the minds of others, and from the compulsion to deal with the great economic and social problems of so many good people in Puerto Rico, there emerged the formula which made possible everything that was to come, the formula that 'the political status is not in issue'. The votes in favor of the Popular Democratic Party would not be counted either for separate independence or for federated statehood; they would be votes in favor of an economic and social program. Our political status would be decided by the people on another occasion, wholly apart from the regular elections – presumably in a plebiscite.

This new concept of separating the economic from the political problem of Puerto Rico liberated the Popular Democratic Party from a platform which was its own worst enemy – a platform in which the political plank could destroy the economic planks with the devastating fury of a tropical hurricane. This liberated those of us who had suffered from an intolerable perplexity of spirit. It enabled us to tackle the economic problems of Puerto Rico in a way that introduced a new, large movement of reform, creation, and hope. We are still engaged in that great task; in spite of the great deal which we have accomplished, there is much more to be done.

The Either/Or Concept Persists

However, we were free of this perplexity of the spirit for only a short period. We continued to be preoccupied as a collective group with the notion of a plebiscite in which we would be required to choose between separate independence and federated statehood – despite the fact that under either alternative the economic life of our people would be gravely threatened. It must be understood that it was not the people who were insisting on this course. This came from the political assemblies, who in this respect were not so representative of the people as they were in economic questions.

Those of us who participated in these assemblies were not insincere. With more learning and less wisdom, we continued to believe, although assailed by anguished doubts, that the choice must be between separate independence and federated statehood under economic conditions different from those in the Tydings bill and from those which existed for the states of the Union. We persisted in this view without examining closely the question of whether it would be possible to obtain these necessary economic conditions without any deviation from the two rigid alternatives. We were impaled on the horns of the dilemma which seemed to force an inexorable choice between separate independence and federated statehood. Actually, the instinct of the people used the idea of a plebiscite between these two classical forms of government to provide time for a better and autochthonous solution of the problem to appear. We can see this now. It was not easy to see it at that time.

In the 1944 campaign the promise to the people that the political status was not in issue was repeated. However, it was still imperative that we find a solution for that problem. The wisdom of the people, which I have mentioned, does not consist in a belief that the question of political status is of no importance whatsoever. Rather, recognizing that man does not live by bread alone and is in part a political being, the people have wisely refused to be bound by the intellectual straitjacket of rigid and preconceived formulas which stifle the creative will and energy of men. It was this instinct of the people, which at times their leaders must channel into action, which engendered the happy thought that the solution might well lie in some form other than the two inflexible formulas upon which the political assemblies had long focused their attention.

A Third Possibility Recognized

We were thus one step farther along the road to reality: in a request to Congress for a plebiscite we used language which permitted consideration of solutions other than the two rigid classical alternatives. True, we committed the error, at the insistence of some of the members of the political assembly, of inserting a deadline; we asked for a solution of the problem when World War II ended. But we had freed ourselves from the tyranny of the labels, separate independence and federated statehood. We were making progress.

In 1945 I went to Washington for discussions on the question of the political status of Puerto Rico. As a result of this visit, a bill was introduced in the Senate by Senator Tydings and in the House of Representatives by Resident Commissioner Piñero.[2] That bill presented *three* alternatives: separate independence, federated statehood, and dominion status; the economic conditions were completely different from those of the original Tydings bill and from other Tydings bills. Under either of these alternatives, free trade between the United States and Puerto Rico would continue, the internal revenue taxes which now revert to the Treasury of Puerto Rico would continue to be covered into our Treasury, and federal aid for roads, hospitals, school lunchrooms, and many other public works and services would be extended for a long period of time.

During these consultations in Washington I became aware that such a bill could not pass. However, it did serve to present graphically to Congress and to the people of Puerto Rico the minimum economic conditions we needed in order to survive, irrespective of our political status.

The Object Lesson of the Philippines

In April 1946 I went again to Washington as a member of the Status Commission which was created by the Legislature of Puerto Rico and on which all the political parties with members in the Legislature were represented. Once more we tried to find a solution to the problem of status as we saw it. During that time hearings were being held before congressional committees on a bill to establish the economic relations which would exist between the United States and the Philippines when the latter became a republic.[3] I read carefully the record of those hearings because of their obvious bearing on the question we were raising. It convinced me that Puerto Rico would never obtain the right to choose separate independence in a plebiscite except under economic conditions which would destroy any hope of continuing to improve their standard of living. The most important factor which led me to this conviction was the most-favored-nation clause found in trade treaties between the United States and many other countries.

The plan at the time was to give the Philippines economic treatment which would preserve for them the advantages of union with the United States for only eight years; this preference would be gradually reduced until the Philippines had no preference whatsoever in their economic relations with the United States. The principal reason for this treatment of the Philippines was the most-favored-nation clause in trade treaties to which the United States is a party. Under this clause the United States is required to give each nation with which it has a trade treaty containing the clause the most favorable economic treatment provided in a treaty with any other nation.

Obviously, the United States could not maintain its present good economic treatment of Puerto Rico, which is vital to our continued development, if we acquired a status which had all the legal paraphernalia of separate independence. It became clear that only under some form of status in association with the United States in which we retained our American citizenship could we preserve the good economic conditions which are necessary for our survival as a people. It could not be gainsaid that any status for Puerto Rico which connoted loss of American citizenship and disassociation from the American Union meant the discontinuance of our present favorable economic conditions, except perhaps for a few years on a diminishing graduated scale. The hard fact was that the present free trade between Puerto Rico and the United States could not be continued if Puerto Rico were a separate, independent nation. To provide for such free trade would require the same treatment for all the most-favored-treaty nations. And this, of course, was out of the question. Moreover, added to our economic situation was the affection and mutual respect which had developed between the peoples of Puerto Rico and the United States within our common citizenship.

We concluded that we must stop wasting time groping for a solution to the problem of political status which we knew beforehand was impossible for Puerto Rico to attain – impossible not for the American Union but for us. The Philippines with their greater territory and natural resources in relation to population, could manage under such stringent economic conditions. Our destiny lay in a different direction. It was incumbent upon us to devise creatively a realistically free form of political status which would not be at war with the solution of the economic problems of Puerto Rico and yet would protect the dignity of our people within our association with the American Union.

The Path of Progress

Once we forthrightly faced this task in the middle of 1946, things began to happen. The political status lost its role of enemy of the solution of our economic problems; instead we considered it in the light of and in harmony with the effort to solve the great economic difficulties of our people. We moved at an unprecedentedly accelerated pace which proved beyond peradventure that the log jam on status had finally been broken.

There had been no progress in self-government for Puerto Rico since 1917. Less than two months after this new approach to the problem of status had been adopted, the President of the United States appointed Jesús Piñero, who had been elected by the people of Puerto Rico as their Resident Commissioner in Washington, to the post of Governor of Puerto Rico. And it took only four years for Congress by Public Law 600[4] to offer to create a relationship between Puerto Rico and the United States based on a compact approved by the people of Puerto Rico and on a constitution written by the people of Puerto Rico themselves.

The wisdom of halting the divisive and futile debate on status, which paralyzed our progress towards self-government from 1917 until 1946, has been dramatically demonstrated by the swiftness of the events which occurred between 1946 and 1952. With this hindrance removed, the long-repressed political energy of our people soon created a new form of status, a new form of political relationship in the American Union and in all America, a new form of political harmony with the economic freedom of our people, in place of the rigid and sterile formulas which threatened the full development of Puerto Rico, which had immobilized for generations the great creative political powers of its people.

It should be made clear that what we have done has been to initiate a process of political creation in Puerto Rico, and not merely to invent just another formula. Precisely because it needs to grow in so many phases in its life as a people, Puerto Rico cannot become engaged in formulas. It must use its energy in development and continuous growth. Nothing could enslave us more than handicapping our great drive towards a happy future with a rigid, obsolescent, unprogressive, or inapplicable formula.

Interpretation of the Constitution

Every constitution is subject to different interpretations which are made in good faith. But our thesis is that by their votes in the referenda in which Public Law 600 and the constitution were approved, the people adopted the interpretations of these documents advanced by those who campaigned for their approval. We submit then that when the time comes for judicial review of the compact and the constitution, they should be interpreted in accordance with the understanding of the people as to their meaning and scope when they approved them. We are confident that such interpretations will prevail, and that they will yield the results which will be most favorable and liberal to Puerto Rico and which will promote fraternal understanding between Puerto Rico and the American Union.

Speech to the Legislative Assembly, January 19, 1960

We are now starting a new decade. We must surely maintain and hasten the integral development of Puerto Rico in all its phases. But something more deserves our fundamental attention, our finest dedication, in this new period.

We devoted the decade that started in 1940 to beginning the struggle to abolish poverty. To do that we set aside political status as an issue. During the decade that started in 1950 we directed our energy especially toward the creation of a new political status vitally adapted to the economic needs of Puerto Rico. During the decade that is now starting I propose that we devote special attention to what kind of civilization, what kind of culture, what deep and good manner of living the people of Puerto Rico want to make for themselves on the basis of their increasing economic prosperity.

This is the true ideal of a people, their real aim. And this is the true ideal and the real aim of the people of Puerto Rico: what kind of community and what goals of individual moral and spiritual realization, within this community, are worthy of respect in the heart of Puerto Ricans.

Decade for Education

Economic development is not an end in itself but a basis for a good civilization. Political status is not an end in itself but a means of attaining economic development and the creation of a good civilization. If a good civilization is the final goal, and if we are to devote to it the larger part of this new decade, we must set above all other duties the duty of education – education in the school and out of the school: the improvement of all means of communication, such as schools, universities, radio, television, and the press. We must do this by government action where it is legitimate, and by citizens' action where the responsibility belongs to them.

Let us start by raising the teacher to the position of prestige that is fitting to his task. Let us resolve that before the end of this decade education in Puerto Rico, in all its aspects, shall have reached a level comparable with that of the states and countries best served by education. Teachers' compensation is an integral part of the great reform. Let us therefore determine – beginning right now! – to have this recognition we owe our teachers reach the levels prevailing in the United States before this decade ends.

Growth of the Economy

Before I go on considering the challenges presented by the agenda of the future, I must now fulfill my constitutional duty to inform you of the state of the country and submit to your consideration several recommendations for legislative action.

The economy of Puerto Rico is in the full throes of expansion.

Puerto Rico weathered very well the economic recession in the United States, which ended by the middle of 1958. It continued growing in spite of that recession, although at a somewhat slower pace.

When the recession ended, the economy of Puerto Rico started again to climb rapidly. During the fiscal year 1958–59 net income increased by 7½ per cent. This is the greatest increase of past years. The income of the United States is increasing at a rate of only 3 per cent. The total net income of Puerto Rico in 1958–59 reached one billion 148 million dollars. These figures represent an increase of 78 million dollars over last year's income.

One hundred eleven (111) new factories started to operate, a record under the Industrial Development Program.

In agriculture, there were increases in the sugar and dairy industries that more than offset a decrease in coffee production. (1958–59 was the low point in the biennial cycle of coffee production.) The net result was an increase of 4 per cent in agricultural income.

Income derived from the activities of the Commonwealth and municipal governments increased by 13 per cent, while income derived from Federal Government activities remained at the level of the previous year.

Income from the remaining sector of the economy, such as commerce, transportation, and services, registered an aggregate increase of nine per cent – a little higher than the general average of the economy.

Exports increased by 9 per cent. The products of the new factories were the principal factor in this increase. These products, which were not made in Puerto Rico before 1950, now represent more than 50 per cent of the total export value.

Imports registered an even greater proportional increase. However, capital goods, including raw materials for production, were the principal items in this increase. Consumer goods increased by only 5 per cent. Tourism had a very active year.

Higher paying jobs in industry, building, and services continue to replace the decrease in the marginal sectors of the economy.[5]

Fixed capital investment, mainly in factories and machinery, reached 292 million dollars. For the third consecutive year investment represented 21 per cent of the country's total production.

Preliminary estimates indicate that the economy continues go grow at an accelerated pace, driven mainly by the large investments made in Puerto Rico for the past three years, and stimulated by economic recovery in the United States[6]. . . .

Education

Whether the kind of education given to children and young people is adequate for a free world is open to question not only in Puerto Rico but also in the United States and many other parts of the world. Public schools in Puerto Rico have performed a highly commendable function in aiding the creation of a democratic way of life and of respect for the dignity of man. For sixty years they have performed their task amid great difficulties under a highly centralized system administered until a few years ago under a colonial administration, with appointments originating outside Puerto Rico.[7]

Changes in method and attitude were frequent, often capricious, during the stage of colonial administration of public education. Teachers' salaries were low, and at one time they were reduced twice in a few years.

In the past teachers have enjoyed well-deserved prestige in the community. They continue to deserve that prestige; but a certain superficial trend in the scale of values of Puerto Rico has raised the prestige of the mere possession of a multiplicity of objects. The result is that the function and merit of the teacher is unfairly regarded as having relatively less importance in the community. Our society, in its endeavor to improve spiritually, to enlighten its understanding, to understand itself better, must restore to the teacher his legitimate position. It can do this not only by paying him a proper salary as rapidly as possible, but also by creating, with the help of the teachers themselves, a more balanced vision, a vision less superficial in the Puerto Rican scales of values. . . .

Cultural Development

A mere enumeration of the cultural activities developed in Puerto Rico with the stimulus and help of this Legislative Assembly would fill several pages. Under the direction of the Institute of Puerto Rican Culture alone, numerous programs are being carried out that help Puerto Ricans to know themselves better by understanding the positive values of their heritage.

What has been done in Puerto Rico in the field of music, from the modest but excellent Free Schools of Music to the Casals Festival, the Symphony Orchestra, and the Conservatory (which has just opened its doors) should make Puerto Rico feel very proud. The Casals Festival alone brings to our country each year outstanding interpreters and lovers of music, including distinguished Puerto Rican musicians. This has been made possible in our time by the presence among us of a man we can regard as a spiritual fellow countryman, a man eminent in music, eminent in human virtues, eminent in liberty. Of all his qualities the least is music – and he is one of the great musicians of the world: Maestro Pablo Casals![8]. . .

Sugar Industry

In my Budget Message I recommended the appropriation of $1,050,000 to continue, during the coming year, to help and encourage the sugar industry to make new plantings so that Puerto Rico might sooner reach and surpass its quota . . . .

I believe it is important to provide the means of financing the acquisition of agricultural machinery and equipment, in addition to the already existing facilities, to help sugar cane planters to attain the optimum efficiency in production. These methods, however, should go hand in hand with measures to provide social remedies for unemployment caused, as we have already seen, by technological progress. For such unemployment we are in duty bound to compensate . . . .

In the past the sugar industry dominated the country's economy.[9] Many of us Puerto Ricans had the conviction that it thus improperly exercised a large measure of the political power that in a democracy belongs properly to the people. This situation, as we all know, has changed altogether. The sugar industry exercises its economic function of helping the country's production, like many other industries that are helped by the government as part of its public policy of stimulating economic progress for the benefit of all Puerto Ricans. However, the industry still faces certain hostile attitudes created by its already extinct political power. These are mere historical vestiges that should disappear. In considering legislation presented on the subject, we should regard it very objectively, in the light of the economic realities of today, and not of the political and economic realities of yesterday . . . .

Preservation of Our Natural Heritage

Places of great beauty in Puerto Rico are a heritage of the people of Puerto Rico. They are to be used for the public benefit. There are two ways of using them for this purpose. One way is to establish hotels and great tourist attractions, which, as part of the economic development of the country, attract capital, provide employment, put money in circulation. The other is to provide easy access to these places for the people in general, whether their economic means are plentiful or scarce. I think that the public policy should be to accept both ways of using our natural heritage: that of stimulating economic progress and that of providing beauty, pleasure, serenity, and equality in the enjoyment of beauty regardless of differences in economic position.

The Planning Board is making a census of places of exceptional beauty, in order to determine which should be available for one or the other use. The Board is also surveying sites for inexpensive facilities for local tourists and tourists from the United States and other countries. Of course, in accordance with law, the great tourist installations are open to all citizens, to all inhabitants of Puerto Rico; but the prices they have to charge, due to the large investments they involve, put them out of reach of a large number of Puerto Ricans and potential visitors . . . .

Political Status

The history of Puerto Rico in the past decades has been that of two drives seeking to merge into one: the drive to abolish poverty and the drive of the people toward the ideal image of themselves. This image was once confused with the concept of political status, a grave error. The people's image of themselves is not based on their political status. From 1940 to 1948 a political movement of deep spiritual meaning – including justice, hope, respect for human dignity, the will to overcome obstacles – existed. All are qualities of the spirit. Yet this movement did not include the concept of political status.

In many former colonial countries these two drives coincided. In Puerto Rico they did not, and could not, coincide so long as political status was conceived as the ideal image, the goal, and so long as the only two alternatives to colonialism were independence and federated statehood, both of them economically inconsistent with the abolition of poverty. The objective is, I repeat, a good civilization based on the abolition of poverty.

A political status that puts obstacles in the path of that ideal cannot be, so long as it creates obstacles, the status that gives real freedom to the people of Puerto Rico. It is inconceivable that an enlightened people should seek to nullify the possibility of attaining their own high ends with the very means that should serve to fulfill them.

Commonwealth status provides us with a means adapted to the high end of creating an excellent civilization here in Puerto Rico.

There is talk as to whether the Commonwealth status is or is not permanent. Strictly speaking, nothing in the world is permanent; but, accepting this as a relative term, I will say that the Commonwealth status shall be as permanent as the people of Puerto Rico may desire. It is fruit of our people's freedom of thought, and its permanence or impermanence should be the fruit of our people's continuing freedom to make decisions.[10]

When the economic development of Puerto Rico reaches a point where any other political status may be consistent with a prosperous life and a good civilization, the people of Puerto Rico may then take up the question of political status. For they will then be free, truly free, of the coercion of destructive and inexorable economic realities, to decide whether they wish to continue using Commonwealth as a means toward the ideal of the good life, or whether they prefer to use any other status as a means to this end. What I am saying is that a political status should not be a straitjacket, a fetish, an unreasoned prejudice, but a great means toward much deeper and more significant ends.

A government is not an end in itself. It is a means for the appropriate organization of a political community. Neither is a political status – for the same reason – an end in itself. Does one, in any sense, live for a political status? Is it not perhaps truer to say that the purpose of a political status is to enable us to live in terms of a good culture, spiritual well-being, and a good economy? I repeat, the best political status for a country has the consent of its people and helps, or at least does not greatly hinder, the growth of its economy. It participates in the development of what is good in its culture – the culture that the people desire for themselves – on the basis of this economy.

I believe that if Puerto Rico had been a federated state of the Union in, say, 1945, at the end of World War II, it would never have been able to attain the economic development, with its consequent social progress, which has been observed and admired by the whole world all these years.

If Puerto Rico had had to pay direct income taxes to the Federal Treasury during these years, it would have been impossible to provide the incentives to industrialization that have produced so rich a harvest of economic development, employment opportunities, ever-increasing wages, and ever-expanding circulation of wealth for the whole Puerto Rican community. Our Legislature would have been empowered to exempt new industries from state taxes but powerless to exempt them from the high federal taxes. Puerto Rico, as a federated state, would inevitably have had to pay these taxes by mandate of the Constitution of the United States, uniformly applicable to federated states, but currently applied in a different way to Puerto Rico. Regarding indirect federal taxes on such articles and services as public shows, gasoline, etc., the poor among Puerto Rican consumers would have had their standard of living lowered in proportion to these indirect federal taxes that they do not have to pay now. Furthermore, since the Puerto Rican taxpayer could not have afforded paying both kinds of taxes – federal and state – our people would have been deprived of a large proportion of the schools, roads and other public works and services that have contributed so much to the noteworthy progress of these years.

With these impediments, could Puerto Rico have experienced the tremendous upsurge of its standards of living that it has experienced during these years? Would we have today an income of one billion 150 million dollars for the life of our entire people – almost three times the 450 million dollars (in terms of dollars adjusted to actual purchasing power), which the people of Puerto Rico had in 1940? Obviously not. Without these impediments, progress has not been easy. With these impediments, it would have been impossible . . . .

Notwithstanding the progress indicated by this, the distance to be covered is even longer than the distance we have already covered. It is evident that we must continue to progress as rapidly as possible, not to flatter our vanity by comparing ourselves with other countries, but because it is necessary and fair, for the sake of all Puerto Ricans, that this progress continue . . . .

The Agenda for the Future

A just government, deeply concerned with the welfare of our entire people, should continue the equitable distribution that has so far prevailed in the process of great economic development taking place in Puerto Rico from the end of World War II in 1945 to the present. I propose that economic justice be maintained or improved as part of the agenda of the future . . . .

We have seen that Puerto Rico could not have reached its present levels if it had been a federated state since 1945, with the great and inescapable economic burdens that this status would have imposed. I now ask: Could Puerto Rico attain the levels indicated by its agenda of the future if now, or in the near future, these burdens were to fall upon its shoulders? The honest answer must be: Obviously not.

The federal tax burden, in addition to state tax, would have been 188 million dollars by 1959, according to the Federal Bureau of the Budget. This federal organization cannot be presumed to have any interest in a political debate in Puerto Rico.

When I mention these figures, I am speaking of much more than dollars and cents. I am speaking of liberty and justice. I am speaking of the need of the people of Puerto Rico of every social class to have these projections for the years ahead come true. We must not put obstacles in the path of their realization. We must stimulate and facilitate this realization. It is not merely 188 million dollar bills and coins counted out as a miser would, or written down in account books, as in a bank. It is 188 million dollars worth of liberty for the Puerto Rican people, of individual freedom for every Puerto Rican. It is 188 million dollars in the hands of those who receive them for their work, for their contribution to the economy, to be used by them as each one of them freely decides for the education of their children, for health, security in old age, a life easier than at present, for housing, travel, recreation, study – study for the pleasure of knowledge, for the freedom that knowledge gives. It is 188 million dollars' worth of personal liberty that I speak of. It is the personal liberty of each and every Puerto Rican, because federal taxes include not only income taxes, which some pay and others do not, but also consumption taxes, which everyone has to pay.

It should be clear that when I use the word 'liberty' here, I do not refer to any political status. Political liberty – under any political status – is in itself only one of the many expressions of human liberty. And it is of every *other* expression of political liberty that I speak now. The man who knows something today that he did not know yesterday is today, in that degree, a freer man than he was yesterday, because ignorance is servitude and knowledge is freedom. Parents who know today that they can provide their children with an adequate education are much freer than they were yesterday, if yesterday they lived in uncertainty as to whether or not they could educate their children. If a family knows it can move from a slum to a public housing development and later, as its economic condition improves, to a home of its own, it has greater freedom of spirit than one that despairs of ever being able to improve its lot. (I say this fully aware of the disadvantages of some public housing regulations.) In a rapidly growing economic system such as Puerto Rico has and should continue to have, with increasing opportunities for greater economic well-being, all who now have hope, rather than despair, are freer because of this hope. It is all this that I am speaking of when I talk about 188 million dollars. My friends of the Legislative Assembly, it is *this* I speak of, and not of dollars and cents.

The political status that facilitates this personal freedom of Puerto Ricans, that facilitates the carrying out of the agenda of the future, that provides the style of life that the Puerto Rican desires to have, *that* is the political status Puerto Rico needs, call it what you will. If in the future another political status, because of our economic development, should make possible these same liberties, this same style of life, there is no reason why our people should not, at that time, give such status their most careful consideration and freely reach the decision to which their spirit guides their will.

Our Final Goal: A Good Civilization

Once more I will speak of a good civilization, our true final goal. When our income is three and a half billion dollars, we should not desire merely to possess or consume three times as much as at present. That would not be a good civilization. It would be relative economic abundance ill-spent by a bad civilization. A good civilization, it seems to me, is one which continues to work energetically to create more wealth, but directs this wealth toward the fulfillment of deeper values. Once certain basic needs are satisfied and certain basic comforts are available to all, it turns its attention to the attainment of more meaningful and lasting satisfactions than the mere possession and consumption of merchandise. It is not within anyone's competence, nor is it in anyone's power, to give an exact prescription for a good civilization. But I believe that some broad propositions worthy of general acceptance may be made and that these propositions help to shape what the political philosophy of the Puerto Rican people might be, giving unity and a firm sense of self to this good human community. Many elements of this public philosophy already exist in Puerto Rico: the democratic spirit, the religious spirit that exists even in those who do not practice any specific religion, the love of peace, the respect for human dignity, the feeling of friendliness toward other peoples, the pride of serving – in all modesty – other peoples in their techniques of development and their explorations of democracy, the willingness to see the world through the mirror of two great languages, the adherence to federalist rather than to isolationist principles.

To all this I would add the need to understand clearly that, once the basic needs and comforts are provided for, this growing economic energy should be used to create more personal freedom in all its multiple aspects. We have already pointed out what these are: more universities, more museums, more laboratories and libraries, more opportunities for adults to continue their education beyond the mere attainments of techniques for earning a living, more individuality in decisions, better neighborly feeling, better neighborhoods, greater appreciation of, rather than imitation of, the neighbor – in short, more serenity.

Preeminent among these is the freedom that education gives. Our public philosophy is a sort of consensus of what Puerto Ricans think of themselves, of what they are and what they wish to be. This is to be understood not in a merely juridical sense, but in a human sense, in the sense of human personality, under any economic changes and any political status. The public philosophy of our people should be much more than their political status; much more than their technology and their economy. It is – or should be–the deepest expression of their unity and their soul. Economy and politics are there to serve the public philosophy of the people of Puerto Rico. As to the part that education must play in all this, let us dedicate this new decade to the grand enterprise of a great education for Puerto Rico. Let's get busy!

NOTES

1. Senator Millard Tydings of Maryland introduced a bill in 1936 by which, if Puerto Ricans chose independence, the island would lose any economic preferences with the United States within four years.
2. In 1944, Jésus Toribio Piñero was elected the resident commissioner of Puerto Rico in Washington, a position in the US Congress which has no vote. In 1946, after the PPD legislature had recommended him, Piñero was appointed governor of Puerto Rico by President Harry S. Truman. He was the first Puerto Rican governor and the last to be appointed by the US government.
3. The Tydings-McDuffie Act, 1934, provided for the independence of the Philippines, which became a republic on July 4, 1946.

4. Public Law 600, passed in the US Congress in July 1950, enabled a Puerto Rican convention to write a new constitution. The convention met between September 17, 1951 and February 6, 1952 and the 'compact' with the United States was passed by Congress as Public Law 447 on July 7, 1952.

5. In 1960, there were 105,000 fewer jobs in agriculture than in 1940, but only 54,000 more jobs were available in manufacturing and construction. The largest increases in employment were in the sectors of trade and public administration, which rose between 1940 and 1960 by 43,000 jobs and 49,000 jobs respectively. Despite these dramatic changes, however, almost 23 per cent of the workforce was still in agriculture in 1960, compared to about 15 per cent in manufacturing, 18 per cent in trade, 14 per cent in services, 11 per cent in public administration and 8 per cent in construction. By 1980 only 5 per cent of the workforce was employed in agriculture, compared to 24 per cent in public administration, 19 per cent in manufacturing, 18 per cent in trade, and 18 per cent in services. This was a rapid evolution from a largely agricultural economy to a modern service and industrial economy (Dietz 1986, 258-9).

6. Puerto Rico became so integrated into the US economy that every change in the latter was reflected, and often magnified, in the former. For example, the number and percentage of unemployed persons declined from 90,000 (15 per cent) in 1940 to 88,000 (13 per cent) in 1950, 83,000 (13 per cent) in 1960 and 79,000 (10 per cent) in 1970, but the recession in the United States in the 1970s and 1980s had a severe impact in Puerto Rico where unemployment rose to 215,000 (23 per cent) in 1983. The dependence of Puerto Rico and its workers on the US economy is also evident in the fact that 750,560 people migrated from the island to the mainland between 1940 and 1970. This massive migration helped to reduce unemployment in Puerto Rico. It has been estimated that without this emigration the unemployment rate in Puerto Rico between 1960 and 1980 would have been between 24 and 27 per cent (Dietz 1986, 288).

7. The first US commissioner of education was appointed in 1900 and, in 1905, English was made the official language of instruction in all public schools. In 1934, when the first commissioner of Puerto Rican background was appointed, Spanish was restored as the language of instruction in elementary schools, with English a special subject. It was only after 1948, when Muñoz Marín appointed Mariano Villarongo as commissioner, that the policy was for instruction to be in Spanish at all levels of education in the public system, with English to be studied as a second language.

8. The *Instituto de Cultura Puertorriqueña* (Institute of Puerto Rican Culture) was created by Muñoz Marín's government in 1956 and directed for the first 18 years by an anthropologist, Ricardo Alegría. The ICP, by promoting a cultural definition of Puerto Rican nationalism, helped Muñoz Marín legitimise the island's new political status. Puerto Rican identity, as defined by the government through the ICP, emphasised European elements in the island's culture, hence the support for classical music and the annual festival led by the Spanish cellist, Pablo Casals.

9. The sugar industry, which was dominated by US corporations after 1898, dominated the island's economy. Between 50 and 60 per cent of all export value was accounted for by sugar earlier in the twentieth century. This was a typical example of 'monodependence' (Dietz 1986, 104). Sugar production declined along with the rest of agriculture after the Great Depression and the subsequent official promotion of industrialisation. By 1982, only 112,000 tons of sugar were produced, which was less than it had been since 1902.

10. The basis of Puerto Rico's Commonwealth status is an agreement between the Puerto Rican people and the US Congress that accepts their permanent association, and it is understood that modifications of this 'compact' could be proposed by Puerto Rico, subject to mutual consent (Morales Carrión 1983, 278).

Eight

Juan Antonio Corretjer

Juan Antonio Corretjer (1908–85) was a poet, journalist and life-long advocate of Puerto Rican independence. A member of the Nationalist party, he was jailed in 1936 and on other occasions. Later he became general secretary of the Puerto Rican Socialist League. This article was written to commemorate the centennial of the Grito de Lares *on September 23, 1868, when an insurrection against Spain broke out in that small town in the mountains of western Puerto Rico where thousands of* independentistas *still celebrate this historic event. Few Puerto Ricans support an armed struggle for independence but many, especially among the intellectuals, think of the* Grito de Lares *as a symbol of Puerto Rican national identity. Now, of course, this identity is defined in large part by its cultural distinctiveness from the United States, a distinctiveness conceived largely in terms of the cultural heritage of the colonial power from which Puerto Ricans sought to free themselves in the nineteenth century. The definition and defense of Puerto Rican culture and identity has become the primary activity of* independentistas, *particularly since becoming an* Estado Libre Asociado, *to some extent, stabilised the question of Puerto Rico's political status.*

The Day Puerto Rico Became a Nation

The centennial of the Grito de Lares tomorrow is a commemoration not so much of a short-lived insurrection against Spain as of the culmination of Puerto Rico's 19th Century revolutionary process. It is also the observance of an event which finally succeeded in forging a true Puerto Rican identity.

This does not mean that attempts to free Puerto Rico from Spanish colonial oppression had not occurred before or after. The red flag that waved under fire during the three attempts to take San Sebastián by assault the day after Lares was stormed, had appeared 30 years before in Carolina. The same bold spirit of Lares, with equal political intention, warmed the hearts of Fidel Vélez and his followers in Yauco, March 24, 1897.[1]

Just two years after Lares, in 1870, Captain General Laureano Sanz was forced to move to Ciales, where a serious insurrectionist organization had reached full development. Repression was severe – as was to be expected from the iron hand of General Sanz.

The Lares insurrection has been pointed out as the historical moment in which Puerto Rico's nationhood was defined. Our nationalist leaders and theoreticians have maintained that that is the deep meaning of the Lares insurrection. National thought had developed enough to see independence as a necessary condition to solve Puerto Rico's social and economic problems, and national will sufficiently developed to carry this understanding to what some consider its logical conclusion of separation by force of arms.

History, Puerto Rican life itself, shows nothing was again the same in Puerto Rico after Lares. The Spaniard became Spaniard and the Puerto Rican, Puerto Rican. In the 1890's, commenting on a servile reference to the Lares Revolt made by Luis Muñoz Rivera, Ramón Betances[2] who led the revolt, wrote to a friend: 'Without Lares, *La Democracia* (Muñoz' newspaper) would not be published now in Ponce'. Betances's clear words were a reflection of a well-guarded colonial opinion that all reform obtained from the Spanish crown after the Lares revolt originated from the Spanish fear of an independence insurrection in Puerto Rico at the time when the Spanish Army was fighting the Cuban war. That is to say, they feared a repetition of Lares.

In the 1930's, Tomás Blanco in 'Prontuario Historico' wrote that the Lares insurrection was responsible for the abolition of slavery in Puerto Rico. He said just that. No more. But one must bear in mind the fact that the abolitionist movement had reached a point where its connection with the independence movement could only result in igniting a revolution.

The provisional government formed in Lares by the successful revolutionists immediately proclaimed that every slave that took arms in defense of a free and independent Puerto Rico would become a free man. Shortly after the military defeat of the revolution, the Spanish Government decreed the gradual abolition of slavery, making the decree effective on a date previous to the Lares uprising. Five years after, in 1873, slavery came to an end.

It was not only slavery that was solved at Lares. The so-called 'free' laborer of the time was in reality a feudal serf. By decree of a General Pezuela, the 'free' laborer, who lived as an 'agregado' (something like a sharecropper) on a plantation could not leave the plantation limits without the owner's permission. Even his Sundays were spent as his master decided. He had to write his time of departure and return in a notebook that was always to be on his person and in this book he had to make note of every act of his life: work, expenses, morality. He was, in reality, a feudal serf.

And so the Liberation Army was joined not only by the Negro slaves but the laborers as well. And it was the laborers who piled up those notebooks and set them on fire in the center of Lares Plaza on Sept. 23, 1868. Shortly after, the Spanish government abolished the notebook system.[3]

It is obvious that nations are not made with slaves and serfs. Nations themselves are part of the historical development of society. Slavery and serfdom come to a point, historically, when they chain the development of society. The slave owner's acquiescence to abolition had no altruistic motive. It was an economic, historical compulsion, idealistically phrased by their intellectuals in the resounding words of 19th Century liberalism. That is why we say that the Grito de Lares brought Puerto Rico to its definition as a nation.

The social contradictions steaming within the colonial society worked themselves to the point of what Marxism calls the highest form of struggle: insurrection. The property owner's protest against Spanish taxation and restrictions on trade; the general hunger for education; the call for freedom and a cultural consciousness on the part of the intellectuals – all this came to coincide with what many consider a logical revolt against imperialistic oppression. In Puerto Rico's history, its name is Lares.

The abolition of slavery and of the labor-notebook system put the colonial landed aristocracy on the road in a long march toward greater wealth. These beneficiaries of the crown's abolition of communal property now entered into a time of new prosperity. (In 1775 Charles III had abolished communal property on the recommendation of Alejandro O'Reilly, a Spanish general he had sent to the island to make a report of its progress. Up to then, all land was owned by the crown which could deed it to individuals but it reverted to the crown again after the second generation.) If the O'Reilly reform had permitted them to monopolize the land, the abolition of slaves and the labor-notebook system now gave them the benefit of a new working class, more willing to work and learn now that it was 'free'.

Results were seen immediately. Coffee production entered a time of unprecedented growth. Sugar and tobacco production multiplied. The Junta Agricultura, Industria y Comercio were formed and shortly after unified into a government bureau. The Junta de Provincial de Estadísticas y Evaluación de la Riqueza came into being. Two agricultural experimental stations were founded, one of them in Río Piedras where the present station is located. The Asociación de Agricultores was organized and the Banco Territorial y Agrícola was founded. Agricultural 'colonies' were established by law and a system of tax exemption was created to help their development. The Sociedad Anónima Para El Fomento de la Cría Caballar, the Liga Económica and the Negociado de Montes y Terrenos Baldíos; the Banco Crédito y Ahorro Ponceño, the Banco de San Germán and the Banco Popular, are all institutions born of this great surge of the economy as a consequence of the social forces freed by the abolition of slavery and the notebook system.

But there was also a shadowy side. After the revolutionary recession, colonialism as a way of life dug deep into the Puerto Rican upper and middle classes. Defeatism was politically systemized. It became, indeed, the very center of institutional life.

In 1870 the political parties were organized. With their coming into being duplicity came to reign in a colonial kingdom that has known no democratic overthrow. The reactionary elements barricaded themselves in religion, tradition, paper nobility and other forms of social simulation, and the Partido Conservador, Incondicionalmente Español. A large section of the independence forces hid within these parties, where consequently they were castrated. In time, their leaders became the masters of this game. Wrapped in the Spanish flag, kowtowing to María Cristina, they used independence and revolution as a source of prestige before the people and of blackmail against Spain. This forced them into partisan leadership and government positions. Thus the bombing of San Juan by American guns found them ready to kneel before a new god.

The leader of the nationalist movement was Ramón Emeterio Betances . . .

Twice ordered to exile in Spain by the colonial authorities, he first fled to St. Thomas, then to New York, then to Santo Domingo. From exile, he organized the insurrection of 1868. He put into it all he had: his prestige, his fortune, his dreams of freedom and happiness for Puerto Rico. He was not, however, to be at Lares. His plans were discovered. The Dominican government seized the arms that were to be shipped to Puerto Rico. 'El Telégrafo', the steamer he had bought to take him and his closest comrades to Puerto Rico, was confiscated.

What happened to Betances in Santo Domingo happened also to the conspiracy in Puerto Rico. The secret societies did their work well, but an indiscretion caused the arrest of Manuel María González, a distinguished member of the 'Lanzador del Norte', the secret society in Arecibo. The Arecibo military found incriminating documents in González's Camuy residence which led to further arrests.

González's arrest precipitated the insurrection. The news was received by Manuel Rojas at his coffee hacienda in Lares. Rojas put the conspiratorial apparatus into immediate action. His call to the Mayagüez patriots brought 100 men to Rojas' hacienda under the command of Juan Terreforte. At the suggestion of Mathias Brugman, Rojas was named commander of the Liberation army, over 400 men strong. The night of Sept. 23, at 9 o'clock, Rojas riding at the head of the cavalry, they set off for Lares. Without meeting any resistance, a little before midnight, he took the town.

A meeting was held at the Ayuntamiento (city hall) which was located where the plaza del mercado (market place) stands now. Spanish functionaries were arrested and the Spanish symbols replaced by those of the revolution. A provisional government was formed. Francisco Ramírez Medina was elected president; Federico Valencia, minister of the treasury; Aurelio Méndez Martínez, minister of government; Clemente Millán, minister of justice; Manuel Ramírez, minister of state; and Bernabé Pol, secretary to the cabinet. Rojas was confirmed as military head.

Four decrees were immediately issued. One declared that all Puerto Ricans were duty bound to fight for the revolution; another that every foreigner who voluntarily took arms on the side of independence was to be considered a patriot; that every slave who joined the revolution would automatically cease to be a slave; and another abolished the labor-notebook system. Comments historian Lidio Cruz Monclova: 'It is obvious that the revolution was affirming with facts, from its very beginning, its decision to make a reality of the beautiful trilogy of its supreme ideals of political, economic and social freedom'.

Three flags flew at Lares. Two of them – a red flag, used 30 years before by Vizcarrondo in Carolina and a white flag ending in two points on which Capt. Manuel Cebollero Aguilar, president of the revolutionary committee, Junta Porvenir of San Sebastián, wrote with his cigar: Death or Liberty! Long Live Puerto Rico Libre! Year of 1868 – came under fire during the three attacks on San Sebastián next day.

The other, a flag created by Betances and made by Mariana Bracetti, was placed at the altar for a Te Deum celebrated by the Catholic Church and sung in a small wooden hermitage near a corner of the plaza. It was the flag we know as the flag of Lares. This was to be the official flag of the republic.

As the revolutionaries entered Lares, they say, cries were heard of 'Down with the taxes! Down with the Spaniards! Down with Spain. *Viva Puerto Rico Libre*'.

Tomorrow, Sept. 23, what we celebrate is, of course, not a defeat. It is the military success of an action that took place 100 years ago. That military success enabled the leaders of the Lares insurrection to gather at the town hall, proclaim Puerto Rico free of the Spanish crown, and organize a provisional government based on the principles of democracy. This government, sovereign in its moment, decreed the abolition of slavery and of the labor-notebook system. In doing so, Lares forced the Spanish government to free the slaves and put an end to the labor notebooks . . . .

Yet it is true that the Liberation Army was routed and disbanded at San Sebastián the day after; that this defeat put Puerto Rico under a reformist counter-revolutionary political preponderance that paved the way to both the autonomous constitution of 1897 and the American invasion of 1898.

So Puerto Rico did not become a national state independent of Spain and did become a colony of the United States. Lares failed, from this point of view. Why?

Let us go back to Sept. 23, 1868.

Was the revolution not popular? Was Puerto Rico not ready for revolution?

Betances was not a daydreamer. The whole of his life, and the whole of his activities, the testimony of his contemporaries, show him as a well-balanced, extremely intelligent, widely read person whose scientific mind and apostolic zeal in no way carried him away from reality. He loved his people and knew them well. Yet Betances to the last day of his life repeated that in 1868 the country was ripe for revolution. His testimony is worthy of respect and consideration. It is well to remember, too, that he did not say the same of subsequent uprisings . . . .

Cruz Monclova believed all the factors so far mentioned were present and adds others: bad training of the military; no help from the outside world (due to the seizure in Santo Domingo of Betances's arms and ship): disorientation because of González's sudden, unexpected arrest; 30 years of consistent anti-independence propaganda.

It is well known that the insurrection was planned on a national scale and as Pérez Moris (the best informed and most anti-Lares historian of them all) suggests, it involved a section of the most influential people in the country. And, to a degree, it was politically convenient for the government to ignore that fact. It is equally known, that, because of the moving up of the date of the uprising caused by González's arrest, practically all the revolutionary committees never received Rojas's call to arms.

I give credit to Betances, on one side and to his most bitter enemy, Pérez Moris, on the other. Betances said that the country was ready and that it was the haste that caused the revolutionary abortion. Pérez Moris, a Spaniard, so near to the Spanish General Staff, said it was lack of armament, and implicitly, not a lack of popular support.

Now, why did Rojas concentrate on attacking San Sebastián? Why his apparently stubborn attacks on that city?

There were arms in the Spanish headquarters there. That fact is known. No student of history – military, revolutionary history – ignores what an effect a resounding victory has in fortifying a people's will to fight. Or, on the contrary, the depressive effect of a confrontation with defeat. Rojas was right to try to seize San Sebastián because the weapons were there that he needed to go on to Arecibo.

He could not wait to be attacked at Lares. He was right in fighting with all he had to seize San Sebastián. If he had succeeded, the call to revolt he had issued to all the committees could have reached them on the wings of victory. Possibly, Puerto Rico's history could have been more similar to Venezuela's than to Saint Thomas's.

NOTES

1. Yauco is in southwest Puerto Rico, between Ponce and San German.
2. Ramón Emeterio Betances (1827–98), an early abolitionist and separatist, was a physician who had studied in France. The inspirational leader of the *Grito de Lares*, he organised Puerto Ricans in New York to support Martí's Cuban Revolutionary Party. He never returned to Puerto Rico and died in exile.
3. Although slavery was important to the development of sugar plantations in Puerto Rico, slaves were a smaller proportion of the population than in most other Caribbean colonies. At the peak of slavery, in the 1830s and 1840s there were between 34,000 and 52,000 slaves, less than 12 per cent of the population. Landless labourers, called *agregados*, who squatted on someone else's land in return for their labour services, exceeded the number of slaves. In the 1830s, they were nearly one third of the population and small semi-independent producers were another 45 per cent. A series of laws in the 1840s coerced many of these legally free people into becoming contract workers (*jornaleros*). Governor Juan de la Pezuela decreed in 1849 that *jornaleros* had to register in their municipality and had to have a workbook (*libreta*) to record where and for whom they were working. The *libreta* system was officially abolished in June 1873, just three months after the end of slavery.

Nine

Fidel Castro

Fidel Castro (born 1926), the son of an immigrant from Spain and his maid, grew up on the family farm in Oriente province and went to school in Santiago de Cuba. He entered the University of Havana in 1945 to study law but became involved in politics, joining the Ortodóxo party in 1947, an opposition group that spoke up against the widespread corruption in government. He took part in an attempt to overthrow the dictator of the Dominican Republic, Rafael Leonidas Trujillo in 1947, and participated in an international student congress in Bogata, Colombia in 1948. He graduated as a Doctor of Laws in 1950 and was preparing to take part in the scheduled elections when Fulgencio Batista overthrew the government and established his dictatorship in 1952.

Castro did not succeed when he filed a legal brief against Batista's takeover so he turned to revolutionary means. Without any clear goals, but hoping that they could spark a national uprising against Batista's regime, he led nearly 200 poorly armed and untrained rebels in an attack on the Moncada army barracks in Santiago de Cuba on July 26, 1953. The attack failed and many of the rebel prisoners were tortured and murdered. Castro and some others who were captured were put on trial. Castro conducted his own defense when he was tried separately on October 16, concluding with the statement, 'Condem me, it does not matter. History will absolve me'. Much of the lengthy document that is known as his defense speech was actually written in prison on the Isle of Pines in 1954. This document is not a defense so much as an attack on the oppressive regime that perpetrated injustice and corruption. Although *not attacking capitalism or imperialism as such, Castro denounced in strong terms the existing state of affairs and urged sweeping reforms, changes that could be initiated only after a revolutionary government was established.*

History Will Absolve Me (excerpts)

When we speak of the people we do not mean the comfortable ones, the conservative elements of the nation, who welcome any regime of oppression, any dictatorship, any despotism, prostrating themselves before the master of the moment until they grind their foreheads into the ground. When we speak of the struggle, the *people*[1] means the vast unredeemed masses, to whom all make promises and whom all deceive; we mean the people who yearn for a better, more dignified and more just nation; who are moved by ancestral aspirations of justice, for they have suffered injustice and mockery, generation after generation; who long for great and wise changes in all aspects of their life; people, who, to attain these changes, are ready to give even the very last breath of their lives – when they believe in something or in someone, especially when they believe in themselves. In stating a purpose, the first condition of sincerity and good faith, is to do precisely what nobody else ever does, that is, to speak with absolute clarity, without fear. The demagogues and professional politicians who manage to perform the miracle of being right in everything and in pleasing everyone, are, of necessity, deceiving everyone about everything. The revolutionaries must proclaim their ideas courageously, define their principles and express their intentions so that no one is deceived, neither friend nor foe.

The people we counted on in our struggle were these:

Seven hundred thousand Cubans without work, who desire to earn their daily bread honestly without having to emigrate in search of livelihood.

Five hundred thousand farm laborers inhabiting miserable shacks, who work four months of the year and starve for the rest of the year, sharing their misery with their children, who have not an inch of land to cultivate, and whose existence inspires compassion in any heart not made of stone.

Four hundred thousand industrial laborers and stevedores whose retirement funds have been embezzled, whose benefits are being taken away, whose homes are wretched quarters, whose salaries pass from the hands of the boss to those of the usurer, whose future is a pay reduction and dismissal, whose life is eternal work and whose only rest is in the tomb.

One hundred thousand small farmers who live and die working on land that is not theirs, looking at it with sadness as Moses did the promised land, to die without possessing it; who, like feudal serfs, have to pay for the use of their parcel of land by giving up a portion of their products; who cannot love it, improve it, beautify it or plant a lemon or an orange tree on it, because they never know when a sheriff will come with the rural guard to evict them from it.

Thirty thousand teachers and professors who are so devoted, dedicated and necessary to the better destiny of future generations and who are so badly treated and paid.

Twenty thousand small business men weighted down by debts, ruined by the crisis and harangued by a plague of filibusters and venal officials.

Ten thousand young professionals: doctors, engineers, lawyers, veterinarians, school teachers, dentists, pharmacists, newspapermen, painters, sculptors, etc., who come forth from school with their degrees, anxious to work and full of hope, only to find themselves at a dead end with all doors closed, and where no ear hears their clamor or supplication.

These are the people, the ones who know misfortune and, therefore, are capable of fighting with limitless courage!

To the people whose desperate roads through life have been paved with the brick of betrayals and false promises, we were not going to say: 'we will eventually give you what you need, but rather – Here you have it, fight for it with all your might so that liberty and happiness may be yours!'. . . .

A government acclaimed by the mass of rebel people would be vested with every power, everything necessary in order to proceed with the effective implementation of the popular will and true justice. From that moment, the Judicial Power, which since March 10th [2] has placed itself *against* the Constitution and *outside* the Constitution, would cease to exist and we would proceed to its immediate and total reform before it would again assume the power granted to it by the Supreme Law of the Republic . . . .

The problems concerning land, the problem of industrialization, the problem of housing, the problem of unemployment, the problem of education and the problem of the health of the people; these are the six problems we would take immediate steps to resolve, along with the restoration of public liberties and political democracy.

Perhaps this exposition appears cold and theoretical if one does not know the shocking and tragic conditions of the country with regard to these six problems, to say nothing of the most humiliating political oppression.

85% of the small farmers in Cuba pay rent and live under the constant threat of being dispossessed from the land that they cultivate. More than half the best cultivated land belongs to foreigners. In *Oriente*, the largest province, the lands of the United Fruit Company and West Indian Company join the north coast to the southern one. There are two hundred thousand peasant families who do not have a single acre of land to cultivate to provide food for their starving children. On the other hand, nearly three hundred thousand 'caballerias' of productive land owned by powerful interests remains uncultivated.

Cuba is above all an agricultural state. Its population is largely rural. The city depends on these rural areas. The rural people won the Independence. The greatness and prosperity of our country depends on a healthy and vigorous rural population that loves the land and knows how to cultivate it, within the framework of a state that protects and guides them. Considering all this, how can the present state of affairs be tolerated any longer?

With the exception of a few food, lumber and textile industries, Cuba continues to be a producer of raw materials. We export sugar to import candy, we export hides to import shoes, we export iron to import plows. Everybody agrees that the need to industrialize the country is urgent, that we need steel industries, paper and chemical industries; that we must improve cattle and grain products, the technique and the processing in our food industry, in order to balance the ruinous competition of the Europeans in cheese products, condensed milk, liquors and oil, and that of the Americans in canned goods; that we need merchant ships; that tourism should be an enormous source of revenue. But the capitalists insist that the workers remain under a Claudian[3] yoke; the State folds its arms and the industrialization can wait for the Greek calends.

Just as serious or even worse is the housing problem. There are two hundred thousand huts and hovels in Cuba; four hundred thousand families in the country and in the cities live cramped into barracks and tenements without even the minimum sanitary requirements; two million two hundred thousand of our urban population pay rents which absorb between one fifth and one third of their income; and two million eight hundred thousand of our rural and suburban population lack electricity. If the State proposes lowering rents, landlords threaten to freeze all construction; if the State does not interfere, construction goes on so long as the landlords get high rents, otherwise, they would not lay a single brick even though the rest of the population should have to live exposed to the elements. The utilities monopoly is no better: they extend lines as far as it is profitable and beyond that point, they don't care if the people have to live in darkness for the rest of their lives. The State folds its arms and the people have neither homes nor electricity.

Our educational system is perfectly compatible with the rest of our national situation. Where the *guajiro*[4] is not the owner of his land, what need is there for agricultural schools? Where there are no industries what need is there for technical or industrial schools? Everything falls within the same absurd logic: there is neither one thing nor the other . . . . The little rural schools are attended by only half the school-age children – barefoot, half-naked and undernourished – and frequently the teacher must buy necessary materials from his own salary. Is this the way to make a nation great?

Only death can liberate one from so much misery. In this, however, – early death – the state is most helpful. 90% of rural children are consumed by parasites which filter through their bare feet from the earth. Society is moved to compassion upon hearing of the kidnapping or murder of one child, but they are criminally indifferent to the mass murder of so many thousands of children who die every year from lack of facilities, agonizing with pain. Their innocent eyes – death already shining in them – seem to look into infinity as if entreating forgiveness for human selfishness, as if asking God to stay his wrath. When the head of a family works only four months a year, with what can he purchase clothing and medicine for his children? They will grow up with rickets, with not a single good tooth in their mouths by the time they reach thirty; they will have heard ten million speeches and will finally die of misery and deception. Public hospitals, which are always full, accept only patients recommended by some powerful politician who, in turn, demands the electoral votes of the unfortunate one and his family so that Cuba may continue forever the same or worse.

With this background, is it not understandable that from May to December over a million persons lost their jobs,[5] and that Cuba, with a population of five and a half million, has a greater per centage of unemployed than France or Italy with a population of forty million each?

When you judge a defendant for robbery, Your Honors, do you ask him how long he has been unemployed? Do you ask him how many children he has, which days of the week he ate and which he didn't, do you concern yourselves with his environment at all? You send him to jail without further thought. But those who burn warehouses and stores to collect insurance do not go to jail, even though a few human beings should have happened to [be cremated with the property insured]. The insured have money to hire lawyers and bribe judges. You jail the poor wretch who steals because he is hungry; but none of the hundreds who steal from the Government has ever spent a night in jail; you dine with them at the end of the year in some elegant place and they enjoy your respect.

In Cuba when a bureaucrat becomes a millionaire overnight and enters the fraternity of the rich, he could very well be greeted with the words of that opulent Balzac character, Taillefer,[6] who, in his toast to the young heir to an enormous fortune, said: 'Gentlemen, let us drink to the power of gold! Mr. Valentin, a millionaire six times over has just ascended the throne. He is king, can do everything, is above everything – like all the rich. Henceforward, equality before the law, before the Constitution, will be a myth for him; for he will not be subject to laws, the laws will be subject to him. There are no courts or sentences for millionaires'.

The future of the country and the solution of its problems cannot continue to depend on the selfish interests of a dozen financiers, nor on the cold calculations of profits that ten or twelve magnates draw up in their air-conditioned offices. The

country cannot continue begging on its knees for miracles from a few golden calves
. . . . The problems of the Republic can be solved only if we dedicate ourselves to
fight for that Republic with the same energy, honesty and patriotism our liberators
had when they created it . . . .

A revolutionary government with the backing of the people and the respect of
the nation, after cleaning the various institutions of all venal and corrupt officials,
would proceed immediately to industrialize the country, mobilizing all inactive capital,
currently estimated at about 500 million dollars, through the National Bank and the
Agricultural, Industrial and Development Bank, and submitting this mammoth task
to experts and men of absolute competence, completely removed from all political
machinations, for study, direction, planning and realization.

After settling the one hundred thousand small farmers as owners on land
which they previously rented, a revolutionary government would proceed
immediately to settle the land problem . . . .

A revolutionary government would solve the housing problem by cutting all
rents in half, by providing tax exemptions on homes inhabited by the owners; by
tripling taxes on rented homes; by tearing down hovels and replacing them with
modern multiple-dwelling buildings; and by financing housing all over the island
on a scale heretofore unheard of ; . . .

With these three projects and reforms, the problem of unemployment would
automatically disappear and the work to improve public health and to fight against
disease would be made much less difficult.

Finally, a revolutionary government would undertake the integral reform of the
educational system, bringing it in line with the foregoing projects with the idea of
educating those generations who will have the privilege of living in a happy land. . . .

Cuba could easily provide for a population three times as great as it now has,[7]
so there is no excuse for the abject poverty of a single one of its present inhabitants.
The markets should be overflowing with produce, pantries should be full, all hands
should be working. This is not an inconceivable thought. What is inconceivable is
that anyone should go to bed hungry, that children should die for lack of medical
attention; what is inconceivable is that 30% of our farm people cannot write their
names and that 99% of them know nothing of Cuba's history. What is inconceivable
is that the majority of our rural people are now living in worse circumstances than
were the Indians Columbus discovered living in the fairest land that human eyes
had ever seen.

To those who would call me a dreamer, I quote the words of Martí:

> 'A true man does not seek the path where advantage lies, but rather, the path
> where duty lies, and this is the only practical man, whose dream of today will be
> the law of tomorrow, because he who has looked back on the upheavals of history

and has seen civilizations going up in flames, crying out in bloody struggle, throughout the centuries, knows that the future well-being of man, without exception, lies on the side of duty.'

Castro was released from prison in 1955 after the legislature approved a bill to free all political prisoners, and within two months he flew to Mexico. On December 2, 1956, leading a group of 82 rebels in an old wooden boat, the Granma, Castro returned to liberate Cuba. Basing the armed struggle in the Sierra Maestra, the mountains of Oriente, Castro's small band of guerrillas gained support, expanded and by the end of 1958 controlled much of the country. Batista fled into exile on the first day of 1959 and the revolutionaries came to power.

Castro became prime minister in February 1959 and in May the government enacted an agrarian reform bill. Opponents of the revolution emigrated and relations with the United States quickly deteriorated when some former Batista air force men attacked Cuba from their Florida bases. In March 1960, a month after a trade delegation arrived in Havana from the Soviet Union, President Dwight D. Eisenhower told the Central Intelligence Agency to arm and train Cuban exiles for an invasion to overthrow Castro. In June, US oil companies refused to refine Soviet crude oil which was much cheaper than other imported oil, and the Cuban government nationalised the refineries. The United States retaliated by cutting the Cuban sugar quota in July, Cuba expropriated additional US properties in August, and on October 13, the United States began an economic embargo on Cuba. There was going to be no turning back on either side.

In January 1961, the United States cut diplomatic relations with Cuba and, in April, an invasion force of 1,200 exiles, organised, supplied and trained by the United States, landed at Playa Girón, the Bay of Pigs. Instead of sparking an uprising against the revolutionary government, this invasion had the opposite effect. Most Cubans rallied round their government and the invasion was crushed within 72 hours. In these circumstances, the revolution became radicalised and many opponents were imprisoned. Castro declared his government 'a socialist regime' on May 1, 1961. Invoking the great patriot José Martí, Castro condemned 'Yankee imperialism' and defined what he meant by the concept of 'motherland'.

It was the custom to talk about the motherland; there were some who had a wrong idea of the motherland. There was the motherland of the privileged ones, of a man who has a large house, while the others live in hovels. What motherland did you have in mind, sir? A motherland where a small group lives from the work of others? A motherland of the barefoot child who is asking for alms on the street? What kind of motherland is this? A motherland which belonged to a small minority? Or the motherland of today? The motherland of today where we have won the right to direct our own destiny, where we have learned to decide our own destiny, a motherland which will be, now and forever – as Martí wanted it – for the well-being of everyone and not a motherland for a few! (*Fidel Castro Speaks* edited by Martin Kenner and James Petras 1969, 72).

Castro had referred, in 'History Will Absolve Me', to the inequalities within Cuba, but in May 1961, after the US embargo and invasion, he spoke of the relations of these inequalities to foreign monopolies and of the importance of patriotism in relation to imperialist threats.

This is the context for the speech, 'Words to the Intellectuals', that Castro gave at a meeting of artists and intellectuals at the national library in Havana in June 1961. In addition to the cultural intelligentsia, there were various members of the government present, including the president, Dr Osvaldo Dorticós Torrado, the minister of education, Dr Amando Hart, and members of the National Council of Culture. Castro's statement about the relations between culture and the revolution, including his comments on 'the problem of freedom of artistic creation' and on the role of the National Council of Culture and other government agencies, is an important policy statement as well as a philosophical position.

*W*ords to the Intellectuals, June 30, 1961

Comrades:

After three sessions in which various problems related to culture and creative work were discussed, in which many interesting questions were raised and different points of view expressed, it is now our turn . . . .

We have been an active force in this Revolution, in the socio-economic Revolution taking place in Cuba. That socio-economic Revolution will inevitably produce a cultural Revolution.

On our part, we have tried to do something in this field (although the beginning of the Revolution presented more pressing problems). We might criticize ourselves by saying that we had somewhat neglected the discussion of a question as important as this . . . . Months ago we intended to call a meeting to analyse the cultural problem, but important events kept taking place in rapid succession, preventing an earlier meeting. However, the Revolutionary Government has been asking measures that express our concern with this problem. Something has been done . . . .

Comparing with the past, it is unquestionable that Cuban artists and writers now work under better conditions than in the past, which was truly discouraging for artistic endeavour. If the Revolution started off by bringing about a profound change in the atmosphere and conditions of work, why fear that this same Revolution would destroy them? . . .

If we are not mistaken, the fundamental problem that hung in the atmosphere here was the problem of freedom of artistic creation. When writers from abroad have visited our country, political writers above all, these questions have been brought up more than once. It has undoubtedly been a subject of discussion in all countries where profound revolutions like ours have taken place . . . .

I must confess that in a certain way these questions found us a little unprepared. We did not have our Yenan Conference[8] with Cuban artists and writers during the Revolution. In reality, this is a revolution whose period of gestation and arrival to power took place in what we might call record time. Unlike other revolutions, it did not have all the principal problems resolved.

One of the characteristics therefore has been the necessity of facing problems under the pressure of time. And we are like the Revolution, that is, we have improvised quite a lot. Therefore it cannot be said that this Revolution has had either the period of gestation that other revolutions have had, nor leaders with the intellectual maturity that the leaders of other revolutions have had. We believe that we have contributed as much as we could to the present happenings in our country. We believe that with the effort of all we are carrying out a true Revolution, and that this Revolution is developing and seems destined to become one of the important events of the century. However, despite that fact, we who have had an important part in these events do not consider ourselves revolutionary theoreticians or intellectuals. If men are judged by their deeds, perhaps we would have the right to consider our merit to be the Revolution itself. And yet we do not think so, and believe that we should all have similar attitudes, regardless of what our work has been. As meritorious as our work may seem, we should begin by placing ourselves in the honest position of not presuming that we know more than others, of not presuming that our points of view are infallible, and that all who do not think exactly as we do are mistaken. That is, we should place ourselves in an honest position, not of false modesty, but of true evaluation of what we know. If we place ourselves in that position, I believe that it will be easier to advance with confidence . . . .

The great concern of all should be the Revolution itself, or do we believe that the Revolution has already won all its battles? Do we believe that the Revolution is not in danger? What should be the first concern of every citizen today? Should it be the concern that the Revolution is going to go beyond what is necessary, that the Revolution is going to stifle art, that the Revolution is going to stifle the creative genius of our citizens? Should it be the dangers, real or imaginary, that might threaten the creative spirit, or the dangers that might threaten the Revolution itself? . . . It is not a question of our invoking this danger as a simple point of argument; we wish to say that the concern of all revolutionary writers and artists, of all writers and artists who understand the Revolution and find it just, should be: what dangers threaten the Revolution and what can we do to help the Revolution? We believe that the Revolution still has many battles to fight, and we believe that our first thought and first concern should be: what can we do to assure the victory of the revolution? That comes first, the Revolution itself, and then, afterwards, we can concern ourselves with other questions. This is not to say that we should not think of other problems, but that the fundamental concern in our mind should be the Revolution.

The problem that has been under discussion here and which we are going to tackle is the problem of freedom of writers and artists to express themselves.

You have been worrying about whether the Revolution will choke this freedom, whether the Revolution will stifle the creative spirit of writers and artists.

Freedom of form has been spoken of here. Everyone agrees that freedom of form must be respected. I believe there is no doubt as regards this point.

The question is more delicate, and actually becomes the essential point of discussion, when one deals with freedom of content. This is a subtle matter, as it is open to the most diverse interpretations. The most controversial point of this question is: should we or should we not have absolute freedom of content in artistic expression? It seems to us that some comrades defend the affirmative. Perhaps because of fear that what they consider prohibitions, regulations, limitations, rules, authorities, will decide on the question.

Permit me to tell you in the first place that the Revolution defends freedom; that the Revolution has brought the country a very high degree of freedom; that the Revolution cannot by its very nature be an enemy of freedom; that if some are worried about whether the Revolution is going to stifle their creative spirit, that worry is unnecessary, that worry has no reason to exist.

What can be the reason for such worry? Only those who are not sure of their revolutionary convictions can be truly worried about that problem. He who does not have confidence in his own art, who does not have confidence in his ability to create, can be worried about this matter. And it should be asked whether a true revolutionary, whether an artist or intellectual who feels the revolution and who is sure that he is capable of serving the Revolution, has to face this problem, that is, if doubts may arise for the truly revolutionary writers and artists. I feel that the answer is negative, that doubt is left only to the writers and artists who, without being counter-revolutionaries, are not revolutionaries either. And it is correct that a writer or artist who is not truly revolutionary should pose that question: that an honest writer or artist, who is capable of comprehending the cause and the justice of the Revolution without being part of it, should face that problem squarely. Because a revolutionary puts something above all other questions; a revolutionary puts something above even his own creative spirit; he puts the Revolution above everything else. And the most revolutionary artist is the one who is ready to sacrifice even his own artistic calling for the Revolution.

No one ever thought that every man, every writer, or every artist has to be a revolutionary, as no one believes that every man or every revolutionary has to be an artist, or that every honest man, for the very reason that he is honest, has to be a revolutionary. To be a revolutionary is also to have an attitude towards life, to be a revolutionary is also to have an attitude towards existing reality; there are men who are resigned and adapt themselves to reality, and there are men who are not able to resign or to adapt themselves to that reality but try to change it; that is why they are revolutionaries. But there can be men who adapt themselves to reality and are honest men, except that their spirit is not a revolutionary spirit, except that their attitude towards reality is not a revolutionary attitude. And there can be, of course, artists, and good artists, who do not have a revolutionary attitude towards life, and it is for precisely that group of artists and intellectuals that the Revolution constitutes a problem.

For a mercenary artist or intellectual, for a dishonest artist or intellectual, it would never be a problem; he knows what he has to do, he knows what is in his interest, he knows where he is going.

The real problem exists for the artist or intellectual who does not have a revolutionary attitude towards life but who is, however, an honest person . . . . For the revolutionary, those goals and objectives are directed towards the change of reality; those goals and objectives are directed towards the redemption of man. It is man himself, his fellow man, the redemption of his fellow man that constitutes the objective of the revolutionary. If they ask us revolutionaries what matters most to us, we will say *the people*, and we will always say *the people. The people* in their true sense, that is, the majority of the people, those who have had to live in exploitation and in the cruelest neglect. Our basic concern will always be the great majority of the people – that is, the oppressed and exploited classes. The point of view through which we view everything is this: whatever is good for them will be good for us; whatever is noble, useful, and beautiful for them, will be noble, useful and beautiful for us. If one does not think of the people and for the people, that is, if one does not think and does not act for the great exploited masses of the people, for the great masses which we want to redeem, then one simply does not have a revolutionary attitude.

It is from this point of view that we analyse the good, the useful, and the beautiful of every action . . . .

Whoever is more of an artist than a revolutionary cannot think exactly the same as we do. We struggle for the people without inner conflict, we know that we can achieve what we have set out to do. The principal goal is *the people*. We have to think about the people before we think about ourselves, and that is the only attitude that can be defined as a truly revolutionary attitude. And it is for those who cannot or do not have that attitude, but who are honest people, that this problem exists; and just as the Revolution constitutes a problem for them, they constitute a problem with which the Revolution should be concerned.

The case was well made that there were many writers and artists who were not revolutionaries, but were, however, honest writers and artists; that they wanted to help the Revolution, and that the Revolution is interested in their help; that they wanted to work for the Revolution and that, at the same time, the Revolution was interested in their contributing their knowledge and efforts on its behalf . . . .

It is possible that the men and women who have a truly revolutionary attitude towards reality do not constitute the greatest sector of the population: the revolutionaries are the vanguard of the people, but the revolutionaries should bend their efforts towards having all the people move along with them, the Revolution cannot renounce the goal of having all honest men and women, whether writers and artists or not, moving along with it; the Revolution should bend its efforts towards converting everyone who has doubts into a revolutionary. The Revolution should try to win over the greatest part of the people to its ideas . . . .

The Revolution should give up only those who are incorrigible reactionaries, who are incorrigible counter-revolutionaries. Towards all others the Revolution must have a policy: the Revolution has to have an attitude towards those intellectuals and writers. The Revolution has to understand the real situation and should therefore act in such a manner that the whole group of artists and intellectuals who are not genuinely revolutionaries can find within the revolution a place to work and create, a place where their creative spirit, even though they are not revolutionary writers and artists, has the opportunity and freedom to be expressed. This means: within the Revolution, everything; against the Revolution, nothing. Against the Revolution, nothing, because the Revolution has the right to exist, and no one shall oppose the right of the Revolution to exist. Inasmuch as the Revolution understands the interests of the people, inasmuch as the Revolution signifies the interests of the whole nation, no one can justly claim a right in opposition to the Revolution.

I believe that this is quite clear. What are the rights of the writers and artists, revolutionary or non-revolutionary? Within the Revolution, everything; against the Revolution, nothing.

And there is no exception for artists and writers. This is a general principle for all citizens. It is a fundamental principle of the Revolution. The counter-revolutionaries, that is, the enemies of the Revolution, have no claims against the revolution, because the Revolution has the right to exist, the right to develop, and the right to succeed . . . .

The Revolution cannot be trying to stifle art or culture when one of the goals and one of the fundamental purposes of the Revolution is to develop art and culture, so that our artistic and cultural treasures can truly belong to the people. And just as we want a better life for the people in the material sense, so do we want a better life for the people in a spiritual and cultural sense. And just as the Revolution is concerned with the development of the conditions and forces that will permit the people to satisfy all their material needs, so do we also want to create the conditions that will permit the people to satisfy all their cultural needs.

Is the cultural level of our people low? Until this year a high percentage of the people did not know how to read and write.[9] A high percentage of the people have known hunger, or at least live or used to live under wretched conditions, under conditions of misery. Part of the people lack a great many of the material goods they need, and we are trying to bring about conditions that will permit all these material goods to reach the people.

In the same way we should bring about the necessary conditions for all cultural manifestations to reach the people. This is not to say that the artist has to sacrifice the artistic worth of his creations. It is to say that we have to struggle in all ways so that the artist creates for the people and so that the people in turn raise their cultural level and draw nearer to the artist. We cannot set up a general rule: all artistic manifestations are not of exactly the same nature, and at times we have spoken here as if that were the case. There are expressions of the creative sprit that by their very nature are much more accessible to the people than other manifestations of the creative spirit. Therefore it is not possible to set up a general rule, because we have to ask the questions: What principles of expression should the artist follow in his effort to reach the people? What should the people demand from the artist? Can we make a general statement about this? No. It would be oversimplified. It is necessary to strive to reach the people in all creative manifestations, but in turn it is necessary to do all we can to enable the people to understand more, to understand better. I believe that this principle is not in contradiction to the aspiration of any artist and much less so if it is kept in mind that men should create for their contemporaries . . . .

And that is not to say that the artist who works for his contemporaries has to renounce the possibility of his work becoming known to posterity, because it is precisely by being created for the artist's contemporaries, regardless of whether his contemporaries have understood him or not, that many works have acquired historical and universal value. We are not making a Revolution for the generations to come, we are making a Revolution with this generation and for this generation, independently of its benefits for future generations and its becoming a historic event. We are not making a Revolution for posterity: this revolution will be important to posterity because it is a revolution for today and for the men and women of today . . . .

We are working and creating for our contemporaries, without depriving any artistic creation of aspirations to eternal fame . . . .

We do not see that any honest artist or writer has reason for concern. We are not enemies of freedom. No one here is an enemy of freedom. Whom do we fear? What authority is going to stifle our creative spirit? Do we fear our comrades in the National Council of Culture? . . .

Our conclusion is that our comrades in the National Council of Culture are as concerned as all of you about the bringing about of the best conditions for the creative endeavours of artists and intellectuals. It is the duty of the Revolution and the Revolutionary Government to see that there is a highly qualified organization which can be relied upon to stimulate, encourage, develop, and guide, yes, guide, that creative spirit: we consider it a duty . . . .

There has to be a Council that guides, that stimulates, that develops, that works to create the best conditions for the work of the artists and the intellectuals. And what organization could be the best defender of the interests of the artists and the intellectuals if not that very Council? What organization has proposed laws and given rise to various kinds of measures to raise those conditions, but the National Council of Culture? What organization proposed a law for the creation of the National Publishing House to remedy those defects that have been pointed out here? What organization proposed the creation of the Institute of Ethnology and Folklore, but the National Council? What organization has advocated the making available of the allocations and foreign currency necessary for importing books that had not entered the country in many months; the buying of material so that painters and plastic artists can work? What organization has been concerned with the economic problems, that is, with the material conditions of the artists? What organization has been concerned with a whole series of present-day needs of writers and artists? What organization has defended, within the government, the budgets, the buildings, and the projects directed at improving your working conditions? That organization is none other than the National Council of Culture.

The Revolution cannot arm some against others, and we believe that the writers and artists should have every opportunity to express themselves. We believe that the writers and artists, through their association, should have a broad cultural magazine open to all. Doesn't it seem to you this would be a fair solution? But the Revolution cannot put those resources in the hands of one group. The Revolution can and should mobilize those resources in such a manner that they can be widely utilized by all writers and artists. You are going to constitute an association of writers and artists soon, you are going to attend a Congress.[10] That Congress should be held in a truly constructive spirit, and we are confident that you are capable of holding it in that spirit. From it will rise a strong writers' and artists' association where all who have a truly constructive spirit can take part, because if anyone thinks we wish to eliminate him, if anyone thinks we want to stifle him, we can assure him that he is absolutely mistaken . . . .

The Revolution wants the artists to put forth their maximum effort on behalf of the people. It wants them to put the maximum interest and effort into revolutionary work. We believe that the Revolution has the right to want this.

Is that to say that we are going to tell the people here what they have to write?

No. Let each one write what he wants, and if what he writes is not good, that is his problem. We do not prohibit anyone from writing on the theme he prefers. On the contrary, let each person express himself in the form he considers best, and let him express freely the idea he wants to express. We will always evaluate his creation from the revolutionary point of view. That too is a right of the Revolutionary Government, as worthy of respect as the right of each to express what he wants to express . . . .

The National Library too is working hard on behalf of culture. It is engaged in awakening the interest of the people in music and painting. It has set up an art department with the object of making fine paintings known to the people. It has a music department, a young people's department, and a children's section . . . .

The National Publishing House is now a reality, and with the new forms of organization it is being given, it is also a victory for the Revolution that will contribute mightily to the education of the people.

The National Institute of the Motion Pictures Industry is also a reality.[11] The first stage has consisted chiefly in supplying it with needed equipment and material. The Revolution has established at least the basis of a movie industry. . . .

There are still a number of questions to resolve that are of interest to writers and artists. There are problems of a material order, that is, of an economic order. Yesterday's conditions do not exist now. Today there is no longer that small privileged class that used to buy the works of artists – although at miserable prices, we know that, since more than one artist ended in indigence and oblivion. These problems remain to be faced and solved, and the revolutionary Government should solve them, and the National Council of Culture should be concerned with them, as well as with the problem of artists who can no longer produce and are completely forsaken. They should guarantee the artists not only proper material conditions for the present, but security for the future . . . .

Long before these questions were raised, the Revolutionary Government was already concerned about the extension of culture to the people. We have always been very optimistic . . . .

The Revolution has had stages. There was a stage when different agencies took the initiative in the field of culture. Even INRA [the National Institute of the Agrarian Reform] was conducting activities of a cultural nature . . . .

In connection with our plans for the countryside, there arose the idea of spreading culture to the people of the farms and cooperatives. How? Well, by training music, dance, and drama instructors. Only optimists can propose things like this . . . . Where would we get instructors to send out to 3,000 People's Farms and 600 Cooperatives, for example? All this presents difficulties, but I am certain that all of you agree that if it is achieved it will be a positive accomplishment, especially the discovery of talents in the people and the conversion of the people from spectators into creators, for ultimately it is the people who are the great creators. We should not forget this, and neither should we forget the thousands and thousands of minds lost in our countryside and cities due to lack of opportunity to develop. Many talents have been lost in our countryside, of that we are sure . . . .

Who knows how many tens of thousands of young people, superior to all of us, have been left in ignorance by social selection. This is the truth. And he who believes himself an artist should remember that there are many, much better than he, who have not had the opportunity to become artists. If we do not admit this, we are evading reality . . . .

We are going to bring opportunity to everyone; we are going to create the conditions that permit all talent, artistic, literary, scientific, or otherwise, to develop. And think about the significance of a Revolution that permits such a thing, and that has already begun teaching all the people to read and write . . . .

Imagine when there will be a thousand dance, music, and drama groups throughout the island, in the country – we are not speaking of the city, it is somewhat easier in the city – what that will mean in cultural advance, because some have spoken here about the need to raise the level of the people – but how? The Revolutionary Government is creating conditions so that within a few years our culture, the level of the cultural background of our people, will have been raised extraordinarily . . . .

We ask the artist to develop his creative force to the fullest, we want to make conditions ideal for the creative genius of the artist and intellectual, because if we are creating for the future, how can we not want the best for the present artists and intellectuals? We are asking for maximum development on behalf of culture, and to be very precise, on behalf of the Revolution, because the Revolution means just that, more culture and more art.

We ask the intellectuals and artists to do their share in the work that, after all, is the work of this generation. The coming generation will be better than ours, but we will be the ones who have made that better generation possible. We will have shaped that future generation.

NOTES

1. The sense of *el pueblo* in Spanish is more cohesive than the English 'people', conveying more the feeling of a community with a consciousness of itself.
2. March 10, 1952 was the day Batista illegally seized power.
3. Refers to the Roman emperor, Claudius, whose power enabled his functionaries to control all public business while the assembly of people in Rome declined in importance. In other words, as in Cuba in the 1950s, when the line between the property of the ruler and the state becomes faint, the working people will suffer.
4. A *guajiro* is a peasant farmer.

5. After the crop season, from December to May, came the dead season when thousands were unemployed. About 475,000 sugar workers (25 per cent of the total labour force) averaged only 100 days of employment annually in the 1950s (Pérez 1995, 299).
6. Castro read a lot of literature when he was imprisoned. This refers to the French novelist, Honoré de Balzac (1799–1850), whose immense work, *The Human Comedy* consists of nearly 100 novels and short stories, exposing the social, political and economic movements in France between the revolutions of 1789 and 1830. Taillefer was a banker, the head partner of Frédéric Taillefer and Company, who was rumoured to have killed several people, including his best friend and his best friend's mother. The scene to which Castro refers is in *The Fatal Skin,* chapter 2 (Toronto: 1963, 180-81), in a different translation.
7. The population of Cuba in 1953 was about 5.8 million.
8. In China, unlike Cuba, the armed struggle lasted many years, from 1927 to 1949, before the revolutionaries came to power. In Yenan, where the communists established a base area in 1936, there were debates about the role of intellectuals and the place of the arts in the revolution.
9. The government declared 1961 the Year of Education and, despite the embargo and invasion, inaugurated a literacy campaign in which about 271,000 people were organised into instructional brigades. In 1958, about three-quarters of Cuba's people were illiterate or had not been able to complete primary education. By 1962, the adult literacy rate was 96 per cent, the highest in Latin America and one of the highest in the world. This was one of the most notable achievements of the revolution and provided a model for campaigns in other countries.
10. The National Union of Writers and Artists was founded in August 1961 at the first congress of Cuban writers and artists.
11. The Cuban Institute for the Art and Industry of Cinema, founded in March 1959, made a series of brilliant documentaries and started a film industry that is remarkable for the quantity and quality of its films.

Ten

Roberto Fernández Retamar

Roberto Fernández Retamar (born 1930), a Cuban poet and essayist, has been a professor of philology at the University of Havana and president of Casa de las Americas, Cuba's publishing house and cultural institute. He has also been the cultural counsellor of the Cuban embassy in Paris, the secretary of the Union of Cuban Writers and Artists and, from 1977 through 1986, director of the Martí Studies Centre. He has published several books and contributions to journals.

In his essay 'Caliban' (1971), Fernández Retamar challenges Eurocentric views of Latin American culture and draws on José Martí's vision of a mestizo *America to support an alternative revolutionary view, the symbol of which is Caliban, a metaphor of oppressed peoples. In this essay, he refers to some of the English-Speaking Caribbean writers (George Lamming and Edward Kamau Brathwaite) and French-speaking writers (Frantz Fanon and Aimé Césaire) who appear to have shared a similar view of Caribbean culture and identity in the 1950s and 1960s.*

Caliban: Notes Toward a Discussion of Culture in Our America

A Question

A European journalist, and moreover a leftist, asked me a few days ago, 'Does a Latin-American culture exist?' We were discussing, naturally enough, the recent polemic regarding Cuba that ended by confronting, on the one hand, certain bourgeois European intellectuals (or aspirants to that state) with a visible colonialist nostalgia; and on the other, that body of Latin-American writers and artists who reject open or veiled forms of cultural and political colonialism. The question seemed to me to reveal one of the roots of the polemic and, hence, could also be expressed another way: 'Do you exist?' For to question our culture is to question our very existence, our human reality itself, and thus to be willing to take a stand in favor of our irremediable colonial condition, since it suggests that we would be but a distorted echo of what occurs elsewhere. This elsewhere is of course the metropolis, the colonizing centers . . . .

While this fate is to some extent suffered by all countries emerging from colonialism – those countries of ours that enterprising metropolitan intellectuals have ineptly and successively termed *barbarians, peoples of color, underdeveloped countries, Third World*[1] – I think the phenomenon achieves a singular crudeness with respect to what Martí called 'our *mestizo* America'. Although the thesis that every man and even every culture is *mestizo*[2] could easily be defended and although this seems especially valid in the case of colonies, it is nevertheless apparent that in both their ethnic and their cultural aspects capitalist countries long ago achieved a relative homogeneity. Almost before our eyes certain readjustments have been made. The white population of the United States (diverse, but of common European origin) exterminated the aboriginal population and thrust the black population aside, thereby affording itself homogeneity in spite of diversity and offering a coherent model that its Nazi disciples attempted to apply even to other European conglomerates – an unforgivable sin that led some members of the bourgeoisie to stigmatize in Hitler what they applauded as a healthy Sunday diversion in westerns and Tarzan films. Those movies proposed to the world – and even to those of us who are kin to the communities under attack and who rejoiced in the evocation of our own extermination – the monstrous racial criteria that have accompanied the United States from its beginnings to the genocide in Indochina[3]. . . . Nor can any necessary relationship be established between *mestizaje* and the colonial world. The latter is highly complex despite basic structural affinities of its parts. It has included countries with well-defined millennial cultures, some of which have suffered (or are presently suffering) direct occupation (India, Vietnam), and others of which have suffered indirect occupation (China). It also comprehends countries with rich cultures but less political homogeneity, which have been subjected to extremely diverse forms of colonialism (the Arab world). There are other peoples, finally, whose fundamental structures were savagely dislocated by the dire activity of the European despite which they continue to preserve a certain ethnic and cultural homogeneity (black Africa). (Indeed, the latter has occurred despite the colonialists' criminal and unsuccessful attempts to prohibit it.) In these countries *mestizaje* naturally exists to a greater or lesser degree, but it is always accidental and always on the fringe of the central line of development.

But within the colonial world there exists a case unique to *the entire planet*: a vast zone for which *mestizaje* is not an accident but rather the essence, the central line: ourselves, 'our mestizo America'. Martí, with his excellent knowledge of the language, employed this specific adjective as the distinctive sign of our culture – a culture of descendants, both ethnically and culturally speaking, of aborigines, Africans, and Europeans. In his 'Letter from Jamaica' (1815), the Liberator, Simón Bolívar, had proclaimed, 'We are a small human species: we possess a world encircled by vast seas, new in almost all its arts and sciences'. In his message to the Congress of Angostura (1819), he added:

> Let us bear in mind that our people is neither European nor North American, but a composite of Africa and America rather than an emanation of Europe; for even Spain fails as a European people because of her African blood, her institutions, and her character. It is impossible to assign us with any exactitude to a specific human family. The greater part of the native peoples has been annihilated; the European has mingled with the American and with the African, and the African has mingled with the Indian and with the European. Born from the womb of a common mother, our fathers, different in origin and blood, are foreigners; all differ visibly in the epidermis, and this dissimilarity leaves marks of the greatest transcendence. . . .

This singular fact lies at the root of countless misunderstandings . . . Latin Americans are taken at times for apprentices, for rough drafts or dull copies of Europeans, including among these latter whites who constitute what Martí called 'European America'. In the same way, our entire culture is taken as an apprenticeship, a rough draft or copy of European bourgeois culture ('an emanation of Europe', as Bolívar said) . . . . The confusion lies in the root itself, because as descendants of numerous Indian, African, and European communities, we have only a few languages with which to understand one another: those of the colonizers. While other colonials or ex-colonials in metropolitan centers speak among themselves in their own language, we Latin Americans continue to use the languages of our colonizers.

These are the linguas francas capable of going beyond the frontiers that neither the aboriginal nor Creole languages succeed in crossing. Right now as we are discussing, as I am discussing with those colonizers, how else can I do it except in one of their languages, which is now also *our* language, and with so many of their conceptual tools, which are now also *our* conceptual tools? This is precisely the extraordinary outcry that we read in a work by perhaps the most extraordinary writer of fiction who ever existed. In *The Tempest*,[4] William Shakespeare's last play, the deformed Caliban – enslaved, robbed of his island, and trained to speak by Prospero – rebukes Prospero thus: 'You taught me language, and my profit on't/Is, I know how to curse. The red plague rid you/For learning me your language!'

Toward the History of Caliban

Caliban is Shakespeare's anagram for 'cannibal', an expression that he already used to mean 'anthropophagus', in the third part of *Henry IV* and in *Othello* and that comes in turn from the word *carib*. Before the arrival of the Europeans, whom they resisted heroically, the Carib Indians were the most valiant and warlike inhabitants of the very lands that we occupy today. Their name lives on in the name Caribbean Sea (referred to genially by some as the American Mediterranean, just as if we were to call the Mediterranean the Caribbean of Europe). But the name *carib* in itself – as well as in its deformation, *cannibal* – has been perpetuated in the eyes of Europeans above all as a defamation. It is the term in this sense that Shakespeare takes up and elaborates into a complex symbol . . . .

This *carib/cannibal* image contrasts with another one of the American man presented in the writings of Columbus: that of the *Arauaco* of the Greater Antilles – our *Taino* Indian primarily – whom he describes as peaceful, meek, and even timorous and cowardly.[5] Both visions of the American aborigine will circulate vertiginously throughout Europe, each coming to know its own particular development: The Taino will be transformed into the paradisiacal inhabitant of a utopic world; by 1516 Thomas More will publish his *Utopia*, the similarities of which to the island of Cuba have been indicated. . . . The Carib, on the other hand, will become a *cannibal* – an anthropophagus, a bestial man situated on the margins of civilisation, who must be opposed to the very death. . . .

The colonizer's version explains to us that owing to the Caribs' irremediable bestiality, there was no alternative to their extermination. What it does not explain is why even before the Caribs, the peaceful and kindly Arauacos were also exterminated. Simply speaking, the two groups suffered jointly one of the greatest ethnocides recorded in history . . . .

The initial destiny of the Caliban myth on our own American soil is a surprising one . . . .

José Enrique Rodó[6] . . . . published in 1900, at the age of twenty-nine, one of the most famous works of Latin-American literature: *Ariel*. North American civilisation is implicitly presented there as Caliban (scarcely mentioned in the work), while *Ariel* would come to incarnate – or should incarnate – the best of what Rodó did not hesitate to call more than once 'our civilisation' . . . .

Much sharper are the observations of the Argentine Aníbal Ponce, in his 1935 work *Humanismo burgués y humanismo proletario* . . . . In commenting on *The Tempest*, Ponce says that 'those four beings embody an entire era: Prospero is the enlightened despot who loves the Renaissance; Miranda, his progeny; Caliban, the suffering masses; and Ariel, the genius of the air without any ties to life.'[7] Ponce points up the equivocal nature of Caliban's presentation, one that reveals 'an enormous injustice on the part of a master'. In Ariel he sees the intellectual, tied to Prospero in 'less burdensome and crude a way than Caliban, but also in his service'. His analysis of the conception of the intellectual ('mixture of slave and mercenary') coined by Renaissance humanism, a concept that 'taught as nothing else could an indifference to action and an acceptance of the established order' and that even today is for the intellectual in the bourgeois world 'the educational ideal of the governing classes', constitutes one of the most penetrating essays written on the theme in our America.

But this examination, although made by a Latin American, still took only the European world into account. For a new reading of *The Tempest* – for a new consideration of the problem – it was necessary to await the emergence of the colonial countries, which begins around the time of the Second World War. That abrupt presence led the busy technicians of the United Nations to invent, between 1944 and 1945, the term *economically underdeveloped area* in order to dress in attractive (and profoundly confusing) verbal garb what had until then been called *colonial area*, or *backward areas*.

Concurrently with this emergence there appeared in Paris in 1950 O. Mannoni's book *Psychologie de la colonization*. Significantly, the English edition of this book (New York, 1956) was to be called *Prospero and Caliban: The Psychology of Colonization*. To approach this subject, Mannoni has created, no less, what he calls the 'Prospero complex', defined as 'the sum of those unconscious neurotic tendencies that delineate at the same time the "picture" of the paternalist colonial and the portrait of "the racist whose daughter has been the object of an [imaginary] attempted rape at the hands of an inferior being" '. In this book, probably for the first time, Caliban is identified with the colonial. But the odd theory that the latter suffers from a 'Prospero complex' that leads him neurotically to require, even to anticipate, and naturally to accept the presence of Prospero/colonizer is roundly rejected by Frantz Fanon in the fourth chapter ('The So-Called Dependence Complex of Colonized Peoples') of his 1952 book *Black Skin, White Masks*.

Although he is (apparently) the first writer in our world to assume our identification with Caliban, the Barbadian writer George Lamming is unable to break the circle traced by Mannoni:

> Prospero [says Lamming] has given Caliban language; and with it an unstated history of consequences, an unknown history of future intentions. This gift of language meant not English, in particular, but speech and concept as a way, a method, a necessary avenue towards areas of the self which could not be reached in any other way. It is this way, entirely Prospero's enterprise, which makes Caliban aware of possibilities. Therefore, all of Caliban's future – for future is the very name of possibilities – must derive from Prospero's experiment, which is also his risk. Provided there is no extraordinary departure which explodes all of Prospero's premises, then Caliban and his future now belong to Prospero ... Prospero lives in the absolute certainty that Language, which is his gift to Caliban, is the very prison in which Caliban's achievements will be realized and restricted[7]. . . .

At the end of that same decade, in 1969, and in a highly significant manner, Caliban would be taken up with pride as our symbol by three Antillan writers – each of whom expresses himself in one of the three great colonial languages of the Caribbean. In that year, independently of one another, the Martinican writer Aime[sic] Césaire published his dramatic work in French *Une tempête: Adapation de 'La Tempête' de Shakespeare pour un théâtre nègre,*[8] the Barbadian Edward Brathwaite, his book of poems *Islands*, in English, among which there is one dedicated to 'Caliban'[9] and the author of these lines, an essay in Spanish, 'Cuba hasta Fidel', which discusses our identification with Caliban.[10] In Césaire's work the characters are the same as those of Shakespeare. Ariel, however, is a mulatto slave, and Caliban is a black slave; in addition, Eshzú, 'a black god-devil' appears. Prospero's remark when Ariel returns, full of scruples, after having unleashed – following Prospero's orders but against his own conscience – the tempest with which the work begins is curious indeed: 'Come now!' Prospero says to him, 'Your crisis! It's always the same with intellectuals!' Brathwaite's poem called 'Caliban' is dedicated, significantly, to Cuba: 'In Havana that morning . . .' writes Brathwaite, 'It was December second, nineteen fifty-six./It was the first of August eighteen thirty-eight./It was the twelfth October fourteen ninety-two./How many bangs how many revolutions?'[11]

Our Symbol

Our symbol then is not Ariel, as Rodó thought, but rather Caliban. This is something that we, the *mestizo* inhabitants of these same isles where Caliban lived, see with particular clarity: Prospero invaded the islands, killed our ancestors, enslaved Caliban and taught him his language to make himself understood. What else can Caliban do but use that same language – today he has no other? . . .

In proposing Caliban as our symbol, I am aware that it is not entirely ours, that it is also an alien elaboration, although in this case based on our concrete realities. But how can this alien quality be entirely avoided? The most venerated word in Cuba – *mambí*[12] – was disparagingly imposed on us by our enemies at the time of the war for independence, and we still have not totally deciphered its meaning. It seems to have an African root, and in the mouth of the Spanish colonists implied the idea that all *independentistas* were so many black slaves – emancipated by that very war for independence – who of course constituted the bulk of the liberation army. The *independentistas*, white and black, adopted with honor something that colonialism meant as an insult. This is the dialectic of Caliban. To offend us they call us *mambí*, they call us *black*; but we reclaim as a mark of glory the honor of considering ourselves descendants of the *mambí*, descendants of the rebel, runaway, *independentista* black – *never* descendants of the slave holder. Nevertheless, Propero, as we well know, taught his language to Caliban and, consequently, gave him a name. But is this his true name? Let us listen to this speech made in 1971:

> To be completely precise, we still do not even have a name; we still have no name; we are practically unbaptized – whether as Latin Americans, Ibero-Americans, Indo-Americans. For the imperialists, we are nothing more than despised and despicable peoples. At least that was what we were. Since Girón they have begun to change their thinking. Racial contempt – to be a Creole, to be a mestizo, to be black, to be simply, a Latin American, is for them contemptible.

This, naturally, is Fidel Castro on the tenth anniversary of the victory at Playa Girón.[13]

To assume our condition as Caliban implies rethinking our history from the *other* side, from the viewpoint of the *other* protagonist. The *other* protagonist of *The Tempest* (or, as we might have said ourselves, *The Hurricane*)[14] is not of course Ariel but, rather, Prospero. There is no real Ariel-Caliban polarity: both are slaves in the hands of Prospero, the foreign magician. But Caliban is the rude and unconquerable master of the island, while Ariel, a creature of the air, although also a child of the isle, is the intellectual – as both Ponce and Césaire have seen.

Again Martí

This conception of our culture had already been articulately expressed and defended in the last century by the first among us to understand clearly the concrete situation of what he called—using a term I have referred to several times – 'our mestizo America': José Martí . . . .

Martí, however, dreams not of a restoration now impossible but of the future integration of our America – an America rising organically from a firm grasp of its true roots to the heights of authentic modernity . . . .

Martí's identification with our aboriginal culture was thus accompanied by a complete sense of the concrete tasks imposed upon him by his circumstances. Far from hampering him, that identification nurtured in him the most radical and modern criteria of his time in the colonial countries.

Naturally, Martí's approach to the Indian was also applied to the black. Unfortunately, while in his day serious inquiries into American aboriginal cultures (which Martí studied passionately) had already been undertaken, only in the twentieth century would then appear similar studies of African cultures and their considerable contribution to the makeup of our mestizo America . . . .

This is the way in which Martí forms his Calibanesque vision of the culture of what he called 'our America'. Martí is, as Fidel was later to be, aware of how difficult it is even to find a name that in designating us defines us conceptually. For this reason, after several attempts, he favored that modest descriptive formula that above and beyond race, language, and secondary circumstances embraces the communities that live, with their common problems, 'from the [Rio] Bravo to Patagonia', and that are distinct from 'European America' . . . .

But our America has also heard, . . . the thesis that was the exact opposite: the thesis of Prospero. The interlocutors were not called then Prospero and Caliban, but rather *Civilisation and Barbarism*, the title that the Argentinean Domingo Faustino Sarmiento gave to the first edition (1845) of his great book on Facundo Quiroga[15] . . . . 'Our America' – along with a large part of Martí's entire work – is an implicit, and at times explicit, dialogue with the Sarmiento theses. If not, what then does this lapidary sentence of Martí's mean: *'There is no battle between civilisation and barbarism*, only between false erudition and nature'. Eight years before 'Our America' appeared (1891) – within Sarmiento's lifetime –Martí had already spoken (in the sentence I have quoted more than once) of the 'pretext that civilisation, which is the vulgar name under which contemporary European man operates, has the natural right to seize the land of foreigners, which is the name given by those who desire foreign lands to every contemporary human being who does not come from Europe or European America'. In both cases, Martí *rejects* the *false* dichotomy that Sarmiento, falling into the trap adroitly set by the colonizer, takes for granted . . .

'European America', whose capitalism succeeded in expanding fabulously – unhampered as it was by the feudalistic order – added new circles of hell to England's achievements: the enslavement of the Negro and the extermination of the indomitable Indian. These were the models to which Sarmiento looked and which he proposed to follow faithfully. He is perhaps the most consequential and the most active of the bourgeois ideologues on our continent during the nineteenth century.

Martí, on the other hand, is a conscious spokesman of the exploited classes. 'Common cause must be made with the oppressed', he told us, 'so as to secure the system against the interests and customs of the oppressors'. And, since beginning with the conquest Indians and blacks have been relegated to the base of the social pyramid, making common cause with the oppressed came largely to be the same as making common cause with the Indians and blacks – which is what Martí does. These Indians and those blacks had been intermingling among themselves and with some whites, giving rise to the *mestizaje* that is at the root of our America, where – according to Martí – 'the authentic mestizo has conquered the exotic Creole'. Sarmiento is a ferocious racist because he is an ideologue of the exploiting classes, in whose ranks the 'exotic Creole' is found, Martí is radically antiracist because he is a spokesman for the exploited classes, within which the three races are fusing. Sarmiento opposes what is essentially American in order to inculcate – with blood and fire, just as the conquistadors had tried to do – alien formulas here. Martí defends the autochthonous, the genuinely American. This does not mean, of course, that he foolishly rejected whatever positive elements might be offered by other realities: 'Graft the world onto our republics,' he said, 'but the trunk must be that of our republics'. . . .

Incorporated into what is called with a bit of unintentional humor the 'free world', our countries – in spite of our shields, anthems, flags, and presidents – would inaugurate a new form of not being independent: neocolonialism. The bourgeoisie, for whom Sarmiento had outlined such delightful possibilities, became no more than a vice-bourgeoisie, a modest local shareholder in imperial exploitation – first English, then the North American.

The Future Begun

The endeavor to include ourselves in the 'free world'– the hilarious name that capitalist countries today apply to themselves and bestow in passing on their oppressed colonies and neo-colonies – is a modern version of the nineteenth-century attempt by Creole exploiting classes to subject us to a supposed 'civilization'; and this latter, in its turn, is a repetition of the designs of European conquistadors. In all these cases, with only slight variations, it is plain that Latin America does not exist except, at the very most, as a *resistance* that must be overcome in order to implant *true* culture, that of 'the modern peoples who gratify themselves with the epithet of civilized'. Pareto's[16] words here recall so well those of Martí, who wrote in 1883 of civilization as 'the vulgar name under which contemporary European man operates'.

In the face of what the conquistadores, the Creole oligarchs, and the imperialists and their flunkies have attempted, our culture – taking this term in its broad historical and anthropological sense – has been in a constant process of formation: our authentic culture, the culture created by the mestizo populace, those descendants of Indians and blacks and Europeans whom Bolívar and Artigas led so well; the culture of the exploited classes . . . .

That culture – like every living culture, especially at its dawn – *is* on the move. It has, of course, its own distinguishing characteristics, even though it was born – like every culture, although in this case in a particularly planetary way – of a synthesis. And it does not limit itself in the least to a mere repetition of the elements that formed it . . . .

Our culture is – and can only be – the child of revolution, of our multisecular rejection of all colonialisms. Our culture, like every culture, requires as a primary condition our own existence. I cannot help but cite here . . . one of the occasions on which Martí spoke to this fact in the most simple and illuminating way. 'Letters, which are expression, cannot exist,' he wrote in 1881, 'so long as there is no essence to express in them. Nor will there exist a Spanish-American literature until Spanish America exists' . . . . Latin-American culture, then, has become a possibility *in the first place* because of the many who have struggled, the many who still struggle, for the existence of that 'great people' that in 1881, Martí still referred to as Spanish America but that some years later he would prefer to name, more accurately, 'Our America'.

But this is not, of course, the only culture forged here. There is also the culture of anti-America, that of the oppressors, of those who tried (or are trying) to impose on these lands metropolitan schemes, or simply, tamely to reproduce in a provincial fashion what might have authenticity in other countries. . . . We can and must contribute to a true assessment of the history of the oppressors and that of the oppressed. But of course, the triumph of the latter will be the work, above all, of those for whom history is a function not of erudition but of deeds. It is they who will achieve the definitive triumph of the true America, reestablishing – this time in a different light – the unity of our immense continent . . . . Such a future, which has already begun, will end by rendering incomprehensible the idle question about our existence.

And Ariel Now?

The Ariel of Shakespeare's great myth, which we have been following in these notes, is, as has been said, the intellectual from the same island as Caliban. He can choose between serving Prospero . . . . or allying himself with Caliban in his struggle for true freedom.

NOTES

1. The term 'Third World' was first used in the 1950s to contrast with the 'First World' of the industrialised capitalist countries and the 'Second World' of the communist ones. Though many countries that were grouped together as the Third World were or had been colonies, and were struggling to improve their quality of life and struggling for liberation, they had little else in common. Now that some of them have become quite industrialised and the Second World has disintegrated, the term Third World has little value.

2. The term *mestizo* is used frequently to mean a person of mixed Indian (Amerindian) and European origin, with genetic and/or cultural meaning, and *mestizaje* refers to a miscegenation process or racial intermixing. Here it is being used less specifically to refer to every culture and people of mixed origins, examples of which may be found throughout the colonised world.

3. He refers to the United States' war against Vietnam, which was still in progress when this was written. It ended when the United States was forced to withdraw in 1975.

4. *The Tempest* was probably first performed in 1611 and was first published in 1623, at the time when Englishmen, such as Walter Raleigh and Thomas Warner were first seeking to establish colonies in the eastern Caribbean and Guiana.

5. This view that the Caribbean was divided between the Taino and Carib was oversimplified. In 1492 there were many different ethnic groups in the Caribbean, speaking a variety of Arawakan languages which were probably mutually unintelligible.

6. A Uruguayan essayist, Rodó (1872–1917), feared that Latin America was becoming materialistic, like the United States, and was losing its more spiritual civilisation.

7. George Lamming, *The Pleasures of Exile* (London: 1960), 109.

8. 'A Tempest: An Adaptation of Shakespeare's "The Tempest" for a Black Theatre' was published in Paris in 1969. Césaire, born in Martinique, has been mayor of Fort de France, a deputy in the French National Assembly and, until 1956, a member of the French Communist party (see chapter 16 in this volume). In his version of 'The Tempest', Césaire directly opposes Prospero and Caliban, the former as a tyrant and the latter as a rebel. In an interview Césaire said:

> I was trying to 'de-mythify' the tale. To me Prospero is the complete totalitarian. I am always surprised when others consider him the wise man who 'forgives'. What is most obvious, even in Shakespeare's version, is the man's absolute will to power. Prospero is the man of cold reason, the man of methodical conquest – in other words, a portrait of the 'enlightened' European. And I see the whole play in such terms: the 'civilized' European world coming face to face for the first time with the world of primitivism and magic. Let's not hide the fact that in Europe the world of reason has inevitably led to various kinds of totalitarianism . . . . Caliban is the man who is still close to his beginnings, whose link with the natural world has not yet been broken. Caliban can still *participate* in a world of marvels, whereas his master can merely 'create' them through his acquired knowledge. At the same time, Caliban is also a rebel – the positive hero, in a Hegelian sense. The slave is always more important than his master – for it is the slave who makes history. (Baxandall, 1972, 176).

In Shakespeare's play Prospero returns to Europe but in Césaire's, at the last moment, he decides to remain with Caliban on the island. Césaire says, 'Prospero can no more live apart from Caliban than whites and blacks can exist independently in today's world' (Ibid. 177).

9. Edward, now Kamau, Brathwaite's *Islands* (London: 1969) is the last volume of a trilogy called *The Arrivants* in which he interweaves the past and present of the African diaspora (see chapter 35).

10. 'Cuba until Fidel' was published in the Cuban magazine *Bohemia,* Sept 19, 1969.

11. Brathwaite's *Islands*, 35. These dates refer, respectively, to the day Fidel Castro and his rebels landed in Cuba to liberate their country from Batista's dictatorship, the day that full freedom came with the end of the so-called apprenticeship system after slavery was abolished in the British colonies, and the day that Columbus was discovered on a beach in the Bahamas, thereby initiating the encounter and exchange between the peoples of the Americas and those of Europe, Africa and Asia.

12. *Mambi*, or *mambises*, is what the Spanish called the Cuban soldiers, most of whom were of African descent, in the War of Independence (1895–98).

13. In April 1961, a force of Cuban exiles, organised and financed by the United States, attacked Cuba at Playa Girón (the Bay of Pigs). They were easily defeated and some 1,200 were taken prisoner.

14. The point is not only that tempests in the Caribbean are called hurricanes but that the origin of the word hurricane is from the Arawakan language of the Taino, from whom it was learned by the Spanish and then other Europeans.

15. Sarmiento (1811–88), an Argentine writer and statesman, was president of Argentina from 1868 to 1874. He wrote a biography of a provincial leader, Facundo Quiroga, in which he interpreted the great forces he felt were in conflict in his country, civilisation and barbarism. He hoped that massive European immigration and the civilising effect of the cities would overcome the barbarism of rural life and popular traditions.

16. Vilfredo Pareto (1848–1923) was an Italian economist and sociologist who interpreted history as a succession of elites.

Eleven

José Luis González

José Luis González (1926 – 96), a writer of fiction and essays, a scholar and social critic, was born in the Dominican Republic, but spent most of his childhood in Puerto Rico. González went on to receive degrees from the University of Puerto Rico and the New School of Social Research in New York, but he was unable to teach in Puerto Rico because of his politics, so he moved to Mexico in 1955 and took Mexican citizenship. As a result the United States did not allow him to visit Puerto Rico for 20 years. His book El pais de cuatro pisos y otros ensayos *(Río Piedras, 1987), published in English as* Puerto Rico: The Four-Storeyed Country and Other Essays *(Princeton, 1993), provoked considerable debate about Puerto Rican culture.*

González was raised in a time when Puerto Rican national culture was chiefly defined in opposition to that of the United States. So, ironically, the sense of nationalism that arose in resistance to Spain in the nineteenth century became transmuted into a Hispanophile culture that emphasised the Spanish legacy in Puerto Rico as a way of challenging the cultural hegemony of the United States. This Hispanophile emphasis predominated in the literature of the 1930s generation and in the Union party and the Liberal party which dominated politics from 1903 to the 1930s. The language question was of central importance, particularly in relation to education, and in general the island's intellectuals regarded hispanidad *as the embodiment of civilised values, in contrast with the crass commercialism and materialism of the United States. This went back to José Martí's distinction between the two Americas and his warning about the threat from the United States, but it was also encouraged by the intense nationalism and fascism, that was closely related to Catholicism, in the politics of Spain, Ireland and Italy in the 1920s and 1930s. Hispanic culture in Puerto Rico was associated with particular class and racial groups, especially the white land-owning class which was the group that had the most to lose in the economic, political and cultural transformation of Puerto Rico after 1898.*

González, the son of a white Puerto Rican father and a mestizo *Dominican mother, was concerned with defining a Puerto Rican culture that could be the basis of a common identity for the nation as a whole, including the black and* mestizo *working people. His architectural metaphor of the four storeys also points to the succession of historical periods, each one building on those that came before. His intention, therefore, was to criticise some of the comfortable myths of Puerto Rican nationalism and to achieve a more realistic, inclusive and complex understanding of Puerto Rican culture and identity than is possible in a simple Hispanic versus North American dichotomy. His conclusion that the African contribution to Puerto Rico is the most important one is an idea that caused some 'embarrassment and irritation', in his words, among Puerto Ricans who accept the 'established truths' of 'Puerto Ricanness'. González was not alone in this: the poet Luis Palés Matos (1898–1959) had argued since the 1930s that Puerto Rican culture should return to the vitality of its African roots. González revitalised discussions about culture, ethnicity, and nationality among Puerto Ricans on the island and the mainland.*

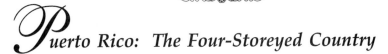

*P*uerto Rico: *The Four-Storeyed Country*

Notes Toward a Definition of Puerto Rican Culture

In September 1979 I was conducting a seminar in Latin-American Studies at the University of Puerto Rico. A group of Puerto Rican students in this seminar, enrolled in the social science faculty of the university but mostly graduates of various schools at the National Autonomous University of Mexico, put the following question to me in the course of our discussions: *How, as you see it, has American colonial intervention affected Puerto Rican culture and what do you think about the present state of that culture?* The essay that follows is my attempt to provide an answer to this question. I have sub-titled it 'Notes Toward a Definition of Puerto Rican Culture' because all I aim to do in this essay is suggest the nucleus for an interpretive study of the historical and cultural realities of Puerto Rico, something that I am sure requires a more sustained analysis and more carefully reasoned conclusions than anything I can provide here . . . .

As we all know, the question you students asked me raises an enormously important issue that has preoccupied and continues to preoccupy those many Puerto Ricans who are involved, from a variety of ideological standpoints, in the Puerto Rican situation and who are naturally concerned with how that situation will develop. But before attempting an answer I asked myself (as I am sure you asked yourselves before passing the question on to me) what you really meant by the phrase 'Puerto Rican culture'. It struck me that you might not mean exactly what I mean by it and so I thought it wise to tackle that difficulty first since I suspect that everything I shall go on to say is the rough sketch of a thesis in direct contradiction to what most Puerto Rican intellectuals have for many decades taken to represent established truths, and even, sometimes, articles of patriotic faith. I shall therefore try to be as explicit as possible within the brief space that a reply of this nature allows – which, let me again stress, makes no claim to being definitive but aims only at providing a starting-point for a dialogue that I feel sure will remain cordial in spite of any valid and productive differences of opinion between us.

Let me begin, then, by agreeing wholeheartedly with the idea, held by many sociologists, that there co-exist two separate cultures at the heart of any society divided into classes, a culture of the oppressors and another culture of the oppressed. Now it is clear that these two cultures, precisely because they *co*-exist, aren't to be seen as watertight compartments; in fact they are more like intercommunicating vessels between which there is a constant reciprocal flow. The dialectical[1] nature of that flow usually gives the impression of homogeneity, but in fact no such homogeneity really exists – indeed it could only exist in a society *without* classes, and only then after a long process of consolidation. By contrast, in any society *with* classes the true relation between the two cultures in that society is one of dominance, with the culture of the oppressors dominating and the culture of the oppressed being dominated. It follows that what is often passed off as 'the general culture', even as 'the national culture', is, naturally enough, merely a description of but one of these cultures – the dominant culture of the oppressors. So I really cannot begin to answer the question you put to me without first trying to determine precisely what that 'national culture' was really like at the time of the American arrival in Puerto Rico, although here too, if we are to treat this issue with the seriousness it merits, we first have to make sure we know the answer to another question: Just what sort of a 'nation' *was* Puerto Rico in 1898?

Needless to say, many Puerto Ricans have asked that question before and their answers to it have been various and sometimes contradictory. (I am speaking, of course, of those Puerto Ricans who have conceived of Puerto Rico as a nation; those who have denied the existence of such a nation, last century and this, pose a problem that should also be analyzed, although for the moment I intend to leave it to one side.) To make a start, then, let us consider two important figures who both *did* conceive of Puerto Rico as a nation: Eugenio María de Hostos and Pedro Albizu Campos.[2]

For Hostos in 1898, what the Spanish colonial regime had left in Puerto Rico was a society 'where life was lived under the sway of barbarity'; barely three decades later Albizu Campos defined the social reality of that same regime as 'the old collective happiness'. How is one to explain the extreme contradiction between such statements by two honorable and intelligent men, both of whom struggled to achieve the same political goal, the independence of Puerto Rico? If we recognize, as I believe we must, that it was Hostos who stuck close to the historical truth and Albizu who distorted it, and if we don't wish to fall into subjective interpretations which apart from possibly turning out to be wrong would be unjust, then we should look for explanations of this contradiction in the historical processes that caused it rather than in the personalities who gave it expression. In other words, it is not so much a matter of Hostos versus Albizu as of one historical vision versus another historical vision.

Let us begin by asking ourselves about the state of affairs that prompted Hostos to stick to the historical truth in his opinion about the condition of Puerto Rico at the time of the American invasion. In other words, what permitted Hostos to recognize, without thereby betraying his belief in Puerto Rican independence, that in 1898 'the social and individual weakness one sees on every hand seems to render our people incapable of helping themselves'? What permitted such critical frankness was without a doubt his vision of the stage Puerto Rico had then reached in the course of its political evolution. It was the vision of a society only just beginning its journey toward nationhood and then wracked by enormous collective ills (the ills Manuel Zeno Gandía[3] denounced in his novels dealing with 'a sick world' and that Salvador Brau[4] analyzed in his 'sociological disquisitions'). If the nineteenth-century Puerto Rican separatists with Ramón Emeterio Betances[5] at their head believed in and fought for national independence, it was because they understood that independence was necessary to carry forward to completion the forging of a national identity, not because any of them believed that such a national identity already existed. Not confusing politics with sociology, the separatists knew that with Puerto Rico, as with Latin-America as a whole, the creation of a national State was intended not so much to express an already fully-formed national identity as to provide the most potent and effective means of stimulating and completing the creation of that identity. In fact, *no* Latin-American country that century had arrived at independence as the culmination of a process of creating a national identity, but only by previously having forged political and judicial institutions to foster and encourage that same process.

Be that as it may, the fact remains that the Puerto Rican separatists never achieved any such independence and still today many supporters of Puerto Rican independence wonder why. Some continue to think it was because somebody or other betrayed the rebellion at Lares, or that the five hundred rifles that Betances had loaded on a boat in Saint Thomas didn't reach Puerto Rico in time. Others think it was because twenty years afterwards Puerto Rican separatists were fighting in Cuba rather than in their own country, or . . . who knows how many other 'reasons', all equally foreign to any truly scientific conception of history? But in fact the only *real* reason the separatists never achieved independence in the nineteenth century is the reason that was offered on more than one occasion by that revolutionary hero who, after his first defeat, acquired the wise habit of never pulling the wool over his own eyes: Ramón Emeterio Betances himself. The reason (and this is a direct quotation from this father of the separatist cause) is that 'Puerto Ricans don't want [their] independence'. But what do such words mean when spoken or written by a man like Betances, a man who insisted that independence was the only just and reasonable destiny for his country and who viewed that independence as Puerto Rico's necessary first step toward her incorporation into the great Antillean federation? Who exactly were those 'Puerto Ricans' Betances was talking about – and what did he mean by saying they 'don't want [their] independence'? [6]

Betances himself explained what he meant soon after the uprising at Lares in a letter from Port-au-Prince in which he attributed the failure of this uprising to the fact that 'the rich Puerto Ricans have abandoned us'. Betances didn't have to be a Marxist to know that in his day and age a revolution against the colonial powers was doomed to failure without the support of the creole ruling class. In Puerto Rico it was precisely the members of *this* class who 'didn't want [their] independence'. They didn't want it because they *couldn't* want it, because their weakness as a class, determined fundamentally though not exclusively by Puerto Rico's weak economic substructure, didn't allow the ruling class to go beyond the reformist yearnings which had always characterized it. The relative development of the economy between 1868 and 1887 and consequently of the ideology of the landowning and professional class – what then most closely resembled an incipient national bourgeoisie – is what determined the shift from assimilationism to autonomism in the political attitudes of that class. But these landowners and professionals never went as far as to believe, not even by 1898, that Puerto Rico had become a nation capable, as an independent State, of guiding its own destinies. In the case of Hostos, then, the desire for independence was never at odds with a realistic appraisal of the historical situation he lived through. And it was this appraisal that led Hostos to declare in 1898, when after an exile of several decades he came face-to-face with Puerto Rican reality, that the Puerto Rican people were incapable of governing themselves and so to propose, to overcome this incapacity, a program of moral and physical regeneration which he believed could be completed in twenty years, if the time were well employed.

By contrast, the time Albizu had to live through some thirty years later was characterized not only by the political immaturity of the creole ruling class (whose members Albizu had hoped to mobilize in the struggle for independence) but by an even more disheartening feature – the co-option, disenfranchisement, and subsequent crippling of that class by the irruption of imperialist American capitalism into Puerto Rico. Angel Quintero Rivera[7] has admirably explained the political and economic aspects of this process by showing clearly how the ever-growing economic weakness of the creole ruling class rendered it incapable of countering American imperialism with a plan of its own for the historical development of Puerto Rico and in fact finally led it to abandon the liberalism that characterized it in the last century, for the conservatism that has so far characterized it in this. The idealization – or rather, the misrepresentation – of the historical past has always been one of the typical traits of the ideology of this ruling class. Pedro Albizu Campos was without a doubt the most coherent and consistent spokesman for that conservative ideology – conservative in content, that is, but in Albizu's case radical in expression, since he spoke on especial behalf of the most desperate members of that class (and I owe that very precise adjective 'desperate' to the distinguished nationalist poet Juan Antonio Corretjer).[8] That historical desperation, so understandable that there is no reason why it should come as a surprise to anyone, was what forced Albizu to distort the truth by calling the Spanish colonial regime in Puerto Rico 'the old collective happiness'.

Now we can turn to the relevance all this has to the problem of the Puerto Rican 'national culture' today. If Puerto Rican society has always been a society divided into classes, and if, as we maintained earlier, there are in every class-divided society two cultures, the culture of the oppressors and the culture of the oppressed, moreover if what is known as 'national culture' is generally the oppressing culture – then it is necessary to recognize that what in Puerto Rico we have always called ' the national culture' is in fact nothing more than the culture of that class of landowners and professional men to which I have already referred. One should, however, make one thing clear about our use of the term 'oppressors' and 'oppressed' in the Puerto Rican context, which is that there is no denying the fact that the creole oppressors at home have at the same time been subject to oppression from abroad. It is precisely this that explains the cultural achievements of this class last century. These achievements, insofar as they expressed a resistance to Spanish domination, were essentially progressive, given the totally reactionary nature in all respects of that domination. But the same class that was oppressed by the imperial power was in turn oppressing one other social class in Puerto Rico, the class made up of slaves, until their emancipation in 1873, of landless laborers, and of small craftsmen. (As for industrial workers, strictly speaking, there were very few of them in nineteenth-century Puerto Rico, given the country's almost total lack of what could be called modern industries.) The 'culture of the oppressed' in Puerto Rico has been and is the culture produced by this 'other social class' I have just mentioned. (As a matter of fact, it is a culture that has been studied by the ruling class intellectuals only as *folklore*, that invention of the European bourgeoisie which has served so well to spirit away the true significance of popular culture.) And from now on, so as to avoid misunderstandings, let us refer to these two cultures, of oppressors and oppressed, as respectively 'élite culture' and 'popular culture'.

To answer your question we must first examine, even if it has to be in a somewhat schematic form due to lack of space, how each of these two cultures came into being and how it subsequently developed. The obvious thing would be to start with the popular culture, for the simple reason that of the two it was born first. It is by now a commonplace to assert that this culture has three historical roots: the Taino Indian, the African, and the Spanish.[9] What isn't however a commonplace – in fact just the opposite – is to say that of these three roots the one that is most important, for economic and social – and hence cultural – reasons, is the African. As is well known, the indigenous population of Puerto Rico was wiped out in a matter of mere decades by the genocidal brutality of the Spanish Conquest. (Well known *as a piece of information*, though without a doubt poorly assimilated both morally and intellectually, to judge by the fact that the principal avenue of our capital city still bears the name of that greedy adventurer and enslaver of Indians, Juan Ponce de León.)

The extermination of the Indian population couldn't of course keep aboriginal elements from figuring in our definition as a people, but it seems clear to me that their contribution to our Puerto Rican identity was achieved primarily by cultural exchange between the Indians and the other two ethnic groups, in particular the blacks, because Indians and blacks had been trapped in the most oppressed stratum of the social pyramid during the early period of colonization and therefore had more contact with one another than either had with the dominant Spanish group. It is also well known, because it has been documented, that the composition of the Spanish group was exceptionally unstable throughout the first two centuries of colonial life. For example, it is worth remembering that in 1534 the governor of the colony gave an account of his efforts to stop the Spanish population's mass exodus to the mainland in search of riches.[10] The island, he wrote, was 'so depopulated that one sees hardly any people of Spanish descent, but only Negroes'. The Spanish ingredient, then, in the formation of a popular Puerto Rican culture must have taken the form of agricultural laborers, mostly from the Canary Islands, imported to the island when the descendants of the first African slaves *had already become black Puerto Ricans*. It is because of this that I believe, as I have said on various occasions to the embarrassment and irritation of some, that the first Puerto Ricans were in fact *black* Puerto Ricans. I am not claiming, needless to say, that these first Puerto Ricans had any idea of a 'national homeland', for in fact *no one* at that time in Puerto Rico entertained, or could have entertained, such an idea. What I *am* claiming is that it was the blacks, the people bound most closely to the territory which they inhabited (they were after all slaves), who had the greatest difficulty in imagining any other place to live. Of course, it might be argued against this line of reasoning that the goal of several of the slave conspiracies that took place in Puerto Rico in the nineteenth century – at least according to the statements of official documents – was to escape to Santo Domingo, where slavery had been abolished. But it shouldn't be forgotten that many of these conspiracies were led either by slaves born in Africa, the so-called *bozales*, or by slaves imported from other Caribbean islands, *not* by *negros criollos* or creole blacks, the name given to blacks born on the island before it became customary to recognize them as *Puerto Ricans*.

As for the white *campesinos* or countrymen of those early times, in other words the first '*jíbaros*',[11] the truth is that this was a poor peasantry that found itself obliged to adopt many of the life-habits of those other poor people already living in the country, namely the slaves. In this connection, it is not irrelevant to point out that when people today speak for example of '*jíbaro* food', what they really mean is 'black food': plantains, rice, codfish, *funche*, etc. If the 'national cuisine' of all the Caribbean islands and the bordering mainland territories is virtually the same in using certain basic ingredients albeit with slight though often imaginative variants, even though the territories were colonized by European nations of such widely differing culinary traditions as the Spanish, French, English and Dutch, then I think this can be explained by the fact that all we Caribbean's eat and drink today more like blacks than like Europeans. The same thing, or something quite similar, can be said of the Puerto Rican 'national dress', the characteristics of which, to my knowledge, the folklorists haven't yet accurately defined. The truth is that the white *campesinos* for strictly economic reasons had to wear the same simple, comfortable, cheap clothing that the blacks wore. The upper-class creole tended to dress as a European as soon as that was feasible, and, as any Puerto Rican of my generation with a good memory can confirm, the popular *guayabera* or embroidered shirt of our own day arrived on the island only three decades ago from Cuba, where it had been created as a garment for casual use among country landowners.

Throughout the first three centuries of our post-Columbian history Puerto Rican popular culture, which was essentially Afro-Antillean in character, defined us as just another Caribbean population. And the social majority which produced that culture also produced the first great historical figure in Puerto Rico, Miguel Henríquez, a mulatto shoemaker who became the richest man on the island during the second half of the eighteenth century thanks to his extraordinary energies as smuggler and pirate. (Richest, that is, until the Spanish authorities became alarmed at his power and decided to remove him, first from the island and then from this world.) Our first important artist also came from this same class: José Campeche,[12] the mulatto son of an *esclavo 'coartado'* or 'limited slave', i.e. a slave purchasing his liberty in installments.[13] And if after that Puerto Rican society had gone on evolving in the same way other Caribbean islands did, then our current 'national culture' would be like theirs, a popular mestizo culture of a predominantly Afro-Antillean type.

But Puerto Rican society didn't in fact evolve this way in the course of the eighteenth and nineteenth centuries. At the beginning of the nineteenth century, when no one in Puerto Rico was thinking about a 'national culture', what one might call a *second storey* – in social, economic, cultural, and as a result of all these factors, ultimately political, terms– was being added on to our national culture. A wave of immigrants fleeing from Spanish colonies then fighting for independence in South America began building and furnishing this second storey, joined almost immediately afterward, under the aegis of the *Real Cédula de Gracias* of 1815,[14] by numerous foreigners (English, French, Dutch, Irish, etc.) and with a second wave, composed mainly of Corsicans, Majorcans, and Catalans, following them about the middle of the century.

This second wave of immigrants created virtually a second colonization, this time in the mountainous central area of the island. The institution of the *libreta*[15] or pass-book contributed to this colonization by creating a workforce at once stable, and, needless to say, servile. The world of the coffee plantations, in this century mythicized as the epitome of 'Puerto Ricanness', was in reality a world dominated by foreigners, whose wealth was founded on the expropriation of the old creole landlords and on the ruthless exploitation of a native campesino-class then existing on a subsistence level. (A splendid portrayal of this world is to be found in Fernando Picó's recent book *Libertad y servidumbre en el Puerto Rico del siglo XIX*, Ediciones Huracán, Río Piedras, 1979.)

These new Spanish, Corsican, and Majorcan coffee-plantation owners were inevitably among the main props of the Spanish colonial regime and the culture they produced was, for equally natural reasons, a seigniorial culture that looked abroad for its cultural norms. Even at the end of the century the Majorcan coffee growers spoke Majorcan among themselves and only used Spanish when they wanted to be understood by their Puerto Rican workers. And until well into the twentieth century, as many literary and historical sources attest, the Corsicans were perceived as foreigners, often as 'Frenchmen', by the native Puerto Ricans. As for the Majorcans, it's enough to point to a historical fact which merits a good deal of socio-historical examination: many of these emigrants were what in Majorca are known as *chuetas*, i.e. the descendants of converted Jews. What I am getting at is this: What social attitudes would result when a minority discriminated against in its country of origin became, as the result of emigration, a *privileged* minority in its new home? We could, of course, ask the same question about the Corsican immigrants, who were either semi- or wholly-illiterate peasants in their native country and who became gentleman landowners after a few years in Puerto Rico. The poverty of the culture which this landlord class on the coffee plantations produced throughout the second half of the nineteenth century, when compared to the culture produced by the social élite in the coastal areas, reveals a class, in social and human terms, that was basically uncultured, arrogant, and conservative, and that despised and oppressed the native poor, and were, in turn, hated by them. It is this hatred, among other things, that explains the 'seditious bands' that in 1898 attacked coffee plantations in the mountainous 'uplands' of the islands.

I have just mentioned 1898 – and this brings us, after our necessary historical excursion, to the gist of 'national culture' at the time of the American invasion, it would first be necessary to ask what kind of a nation Puerto Rico was at that time. Well then, in the light of everything I have just said it seems no exaggeration to state that Puerto Rico was a country so divided racially, socially, economically, and culturally, that it should rather be described as *two* countries than as one. Or more precisely, perhaps, as two distinct societies that hadn't yet had time to fuse into a true national synthesis. But then this shouldn't surprise anyone, since such a phenomenon is not at all exclusive to Puerto Rico but is typical of Latin America as a whole. Mexico and Peru, for example, are still debating the problem of the 'different countries': that of the Indians, that of the creoles, and that of the mestizos. In Argentina there is a long-standing conflict between the 'old creoles' and the more recent immigrants and their descendants. In Haiti there is a notorious rivalry between blacks and mulattos. And so on.

What sets the Puerto Rican case apart is that for more than half a century we have been peddled the myth of social, racial, and cultural homogeneity which it is now high time that we began to dismantle, not so as to 'divide' the country – a prospect that some people contemplate with terror – but rather so as to gain a true perspective on the country's real and objective diversity. Were we to imagine two contrasting Puerto Rican types as for example a (white) poet from Lares and a (black or mulatto) stevedore from Puerta de Tierra, we would immediately have to admit that there is a great difference between them, and I submit that it is a difference of a historically-determined *cultural tradition*, which must in no way be underestimated. (None of this implies, let me state bluntly to avoid any misunderstanding, that the one is necessarily 'more Puerto Rican' than the other.) The difference I have referred to ultimately derives from two visions of the world, two *Weltanschauungen*,[16] that are diametrically opposed in many important respects. All thinking Puerto Ricans, and more especially independentists, are distressed, and rightly so, by our people's persistent inability to agree on the final political organization of the country – in other words, the so-called 'issue of status'. In this sense at least we are responding to the reality of a 'divided people'. But what we haven't yet been able to recognize are the profound causes, the profound *historical* causes, of that division.

The traditional independence movement has maintained that this division only came into being because of the American invasion, and that what characterized Puerto Rican society during the Spanish colonial period was, in the words of Albizu Campos, 'a homogeneity among all the components and a highly developed social sense dedicated to mutual aid for the perpetuation and preservation of our nation, in other words, a deeply-rooted and unanimous sense of fatherland'. Only the obfuscating power of a profoundly conservative ideology could have produced a view of things so essentially at variance with historical reality. All mythologizing apart, the Puerto Rico of 1898 can only, in fact, be described as a country *on the way to nationhood*. So Hostos saw it and Hostos was right. And if during the nineteenth century this process of nation-building suffered profound setbacks because of the two great waves of immigrants who, to repeat my metaphor, built a second storey on Puerto Rican society, then what happened in 1898 was that the American invasion began to add a *third* storey to a second which was still not entirely habitable.

To repeat: in this nation-in-the-making, divided as we know, or should know, not only into classes but also into distinct ethnic groups which were true castes, the two cultures of which I speak always coexisted. But precisely because we are dealing with a nation-in-the-making, these two cultures were not in themselves homogeneous. To start with, the social élite was divided into two clearly distinguishable groups: plantation-owners and professional men. Quintero Rivera has explained with great clarity how these two groups of the élite were ideologically distinct, with the landowners inclining more to conservatism and the professionals to liberalism. And when we come to culture, what must be stressed is that the culture of the landowners was above all a *way of life*, seigniorial and conservative. The landowners themselves weren't capable of creating a literature that would describe or extol that way of life, and so this task fell, well into the present century, upon their descendants, members of a class in decline (but in decline *as a class* let it be understood, because individually the grandchildren of the 'ruined' landowners, now become for the most part professionals, managers, or bureaucrats, enjoyed a standard of living much higher than any known to their grandparents). Only by seeing things in such a light can one understand, for example, the ideological content of a literary work such as René Marqués's *Los soles truncos*.[17]

By contrast, the culture produced by the nineteenth-century professional men consisted of *creative works* and of *institutions*: virtually all our literature of this period, the Athenaeum, and so on. And in these creative works and institutions it was the liberal ideology of their creators that predominated, with the result that 'the culture of the dominant class' in nineteenth-century Puerto Rican colonial society isn't necessarily synonymous with 'a reactionary culture'. (It is very important to get this last point clear so as to avoid the simplifications and confusions peculiar to a certain type of underdeveloped 'Marxism'.) There certainly *were* reactionaries among cultivated Puerto Ricans at this time, but they neither formed a majority nor were they typical. Those who *did* form a majority and those who *were* typical were both liberal and progressive: Alonso, Tapia,[18] Hostos, Brau, Zeno . . . .

Then, too, there were of course some revolutionaries, but these were in the minority and, characteristically and revealingly, often mestizos: one has only to think of Betances, of Pachín Marín, and of an artisan like Sotero Figueroa who mixed culturally with the élite. The most radical of the autonomists – and who will dare say it was by chance – were also mestizos; just recall Baldorioty and Barbosa,[19] whom conservative independentists have so misunderstood and slighted this century, the former as a 'reformer' and the latter as a 'Yankophile'. (As though at least half of the separatists in the nineteenth century hadn't wanted to break with Spain so as to become part of the United States, in those days a shining symbol of republican democracy for most of the enlightened world!) There is the revealing history, for those who don't insist on ignoring the truth, of the Puerto Rican section of the Cuban Revolutionary Party in New York, where until 1898 separatist-independentists like Sotero Figueroa made common cause with separatist-annexionists (perhaps a grammatical but not a political contradiction) like Todd and Henna.[20] (And don't these very names clearly speak to us of that 'second storey' added by immigrants to Puerto Rican society in the early and middle years of the century?)

All this might seem, but in fact isn't, a digression, for Puerto Rican 'national culture' at about the time of the 1898 invasion consisted of all these elements. That is to say, in its strengths, weaknesses and contradictions it was an exact reflection of that social class which gave it life. And if that class, as we have argued, can be characterized by its historical weakness and immaturity, could the culture that resulted possibly have been strong and mature? What gave the culture a *relative* strength and maturity was, first, the fact that it had its roots in an old, rich European culture, namely the Spanish; and second, that it had already begun to put its own creole stamp, in an Hispano-Antillean sense, on whatever it produced. This last fact is undeniable and for that reason those who maintain, or at any rate maintained two or three decades ago, that there is no such thing as a 'national culture' in Puerto Rico are obviously wrong. But wrong, too, are those who ignored and continue to ignore the class basis of such a culture and describe it as the *only* culture of the Puerto Rican people, identifying its decline under the American colonial regime with a presumed decline in national identity. Seeing things in this way not only confuses the part with the whole, because that culture has in fact only been *part* of what in an all-inclusive sense might be called the 'Puerto Rican national culture'– it certainly can't claim to represent *all* the island's culture – but it also fails to recognize the existence of the *other* Puerto Rican culture which under the American colonial regime has undergone not so much a deterioration as a development, an uneven development no doubt and one that has been full of vicissitudes but a development none the less. And to say this is not, as certain conservative patriots insist, to make a leftist apology for American colonialism, but merely to recognize a historical fact: the progressive dismantling of the culture of the Puerto Rican élite under the impact of the transformations in Puerto Rican society resulting from the American colonial presence has resulted less in the 'Americanization' of Puerto Rican society than in a transformation of cultural values *from within*. The vacuum created by the dismantling of the culture of the Puerto Rican élite hasn't been filled (far from it) by intrusions of American culture; on the contrary, what *has* filled that vacuum has been the ever more perceptible rise to prominence of the culture of the Puerto Rican lower classes.

We must now ask how and why such a thing came about. I see no way of giving a valid answer to this question except by putting it in the context of the class struggle which lies at the heart of Puerto Rican society. It is high time we began to understand, in the light of a scientific theory of history, just what the change of colonial regime in 1898 really meant for Puerto Rico. And by 'what it really meant' I want to emphasize – what the change meant for the different social classes that composed Puerto Rican society. We can easily see, because it is abundantly documented, that the Puerto Rican propertied class welcomed the American invasion when it occurred with open arms. Every political spokesman of that class saw that invasion as bringing to Puerto Rico liberty, democracy, and progress, and as the prelude to the annexation of Puerto Rico by the richest and most powerful, and, we should remember, most 'democratic', nation on earth. The subsequent disenchantment only occurred when the new imperial master made it clear that the invasion did not necessarily imply annexation, or the participation of the propertied class in the sumptuous banquet of the expanding American capitalist economy, but instead their colonial subordination to that economy.

It was then and only then that the 'nationalism' of this class came into being. (Or rather to put it more exactly, the 'nationalism' of the members of that class whose economic weakness made it impossible for them to profit from the new situation.) The well-known opposition of José de Diego,[21] which is to say the opposition of the social class that he represented as President of the Chamber of Delegates, to the extending of American citizenship to Puerto Ricans, was founded on the categorical declaration by President Taft that citizenship did not necessarily pave the way for annexation or even the promise of annexation, as De Diego himself explained in a speech that all Puerto Rican independentists should read or reread. And when in addition it became clear that the new economic order, which is to say an economy based on cultivating sugar cane instead of one based on coffee, meant the ruin of the island's propertied class and the beginning of the independent participation of the working-class in the political life of the country, the "patriotic" rhetoric of the property owners reached such heights of demagoguery that not even the liberal professionals hesitated to ridicule and condemn it . . . .

The Puerto Rican working class for its part also warmly welcomed the American invasion, but for very different reasons than those that had at the same time encouraged the property-owners. For what the workers saw in the arrival of the Americans was an opportunity for an all-out *settling of scores* with the property-owning class on all fronts, and on the cultural front, which is the one that now immediately concerns us, this settling of scores has been the motive force for all the cultural changes in Puerto Rican society from 1898 until our own day. The often-denounced American cultural penetration of Puerto Rico has of course been a fact and I should be the last to deny it. But I refuse to agree that this penetration amounts to a 'transculturation', which is to say to an 'Americanization' understood as a 'de-Puerto Ricanization', in the whole of our society. Furthermore, I am convinced that the causes and consequences of this penetration can only be fully understood in the context of the struggle, which in fact is only one aspect of the class struggle at the heart of our national society, between the 'two cultures' of Puerto Rico.

The so-called 'Americanization' of Puerto Rico has had two dialectically linked aspects. On the one hand it has obeyed *from without* an imperialist policy aimed at integrating Puerto Rican society into the American capitalist system as a dependent; but on the other hand it has corresponded *from within* to the struggle of the Puerto Rican masses against the hegemony of the property-owning class. The cultural achievements of this latter class under the Spanish colonial regime had, for reasons we have already explained, a liberal-bourgeois cast; but the new relation between social classes under the American regime obliged the property-owning class, marginated and expropriated by American capitalism, to abandon the liberalism of the professionals in that same class and to struggle for the conservation of its own cultural values. The cult of the land characteristic of the literature that the Puerto Rican élite has produced in this century no longer expresses, as is generally taught in literature courses in our university, a disinterested and lyrical sensibility moved by the beauties of our tropical landscape; what in fact it expresses is a very specific and historically-determined nostalgic longing for a lost land – and not land in either a symbolic or a metaphorical but in a literal sense, as the medium for material production now in the hands of foreigners. In other words, those who could no longer continue 'doing the rounds of the farm' astride the traditional horse now devoted to themselves to 'doing the rounds' astride a *décima*, short story, or novel. And, stretching the metaphor only a little, with the same patriarchal spirit as in 'the good old days', they substituted for the work force of peons and sharecroppers a work force consisting of – their own readers!

What nonetheless complicates matters is the fact that at the time of the American invasion a very important part of the landowning class in Puerto Rico consisted not so much of Puerto Ricans as of Spaniards, Corsicans, Majorcans, Catalans, and so on. All these landowners were seen by the Puerto Rican masses for what they were: foreigners and exploiters. It was precisely this social world that the three protagonists of *Los soles truncos* longed for, idealizing that world to the point of mythification. And to pass off this world as the world of 'Puerto Ricanness', at grips with 'American adulteration', not only constitutes a flagrant misrepresentation of the historical truth but also (and this is truly serious) an aggression against the Puerto Ricanness of the popular masses, whose ancestors, in many cases within living memory, lived in that world as slaves, squatters, or peons. Hence, just as the cultural values of the property-owning class helped them to resist 'Americanization', so that same 'Americanization' has helped the masses to oppose and supplant the cultural values of the property-owning class. But it helped not only the popular masses (and I think this should be emphasized) but also certain very important elements of that same property-owning class oppressed from within their own class, particularly women. For who can deny that the women's liberation movement in Puerto Rico, essentially progressive and just, in spite of any limitations that can be alleged against it, has been in very great measure the result of the 'Americanization' of Puerto Rican society?[22]

The prevailing ignorance or underestimation of these realities has had a baleful consequence: the idea put forward and spread by the traditional independence movement, that independence is necessary to protect and shore up a national cultural identity that the Puerto Rican masses have never felt as *their* true identity. Why have these advocates of independence been accused again and again of wanting to 'return to the Spanish era'? Why have poor Puerto Ricans and black Puerto Ricans been conspicuous by their absence from the ranks of the traditional independence movement, whereas they have flocked into the populist annexationist movement? The traditional independence movement has usually answered the last question by saying that black Puerto Ricans who support annexation have become 'alienated' as a result of colonialism. And their reasoning runs as follows: if black Puerto Ricans wish to become part of a racist society like that of the United States, then such an 'aberration' can only be explained as a symptom of alienation.

However, those who reason thus either don't know or have forgotten an elementary historical truth: the experience of racism of Puerto Rican blacks came not from American, but from Puerto Rican society.[23] In other words, those who have discriminated against blacks *in Puerto Rico* haven't been Americans, but white Puerto Ricans, many of whom moreover have always taken conspicuous pride in their foreign ancestry (Spanish, Catalan, Majorcan, etc.). What a Puerto Rican black, or for that matter what any poor Puerto Rican, even a white (and everyone knows that there has always been a much higher proportion of poor people among the blacks than whites) understands by 'returning to the Spanish era' is this: returning to a society in which the white and property-owning part of the population has always oppressed and despised the non-white and non-property-owning part. For in fact how many black or poor Puerto Ricans could ever participate, even as simple voters, in Puerto Rican political life throughout the Spanish era? To be a voter in those days one had to be a property-owner or a taxpayer as well as knowing how to read and write, and how many black Puerto Ricans, or poor Puerto Ricans of any sort, could meet those requirements?

And we won't even mention what it cost a black man to become a political *leader*. There is Barbosa, of course – but who else? And then it wasn't just plain Barbosa, it was *Doctor* Barbosa. And where did Barbosa study medicine? Not in Puerto Rico, where Spain never permitted the founding of a university, nor in Spain itself, where Puerto Rican students were invariably the sons of landowners or white professionals, but in the United States, more specifically in Michigan, a northern state with an old abolitionist tradition – all of which easily explains many of the things that the traditional supporters of independence may never have been able to understand about Barbosa and his annexationism. So that, in short, if the traditional Puerto Rican independence movement this century has been – in political, social, and cultural terms – a conservative ideology, engaged in the defense of the values of the old propertied class, then why on earth blame 'alienation' for the failure of the masses to support that independence movement? Who have been and really still are the 'alienated' in a true historical sense?

But when we turn to popular culture we have to admit that this culture, too, has in the course of its historical development seldom been homogeneous. For the first and much of the second hundred years of colonial life the mass of laborers, both in the countryside and in the towns, was concentrated near the coasts, most of them being black or mulatto and with a preponderance of slaves over free men. Later this proportion became inverted and freed blacks and mulattos outnumbered slaves until the abolition of slavery in 1873 formally put an end to the latter's inferior status. The earliest popular culture in Puerto Rico was therefore basically Afro-Antillean. The white *campesinado*, which came into being at a later date and then mainly in the mountainous central region of the island, produced a variant of the popular culture which developed in a relatively autonomous way, until the decline in coffee production in the mountains coinciding with the boom in sugar production in the coastal plains caused a major population shift from the 'uplands' to the 'lowlands'. From that point on the two currents of the popular culture flowed into one channel, but with a clear predominance of the Afro-Antillean current, for demographic, social, and economic reasons.

The conservative marginated landowners, however, misrepresented these new social realities in their own literary production, proclaiming that the popular culture of the white peasantry was *the* popular culture par excellence. The literary *'jíbarismo'* of the élite has been nothing else at bottom than that class's statement of its own racial and social prejudice. And so in the Puerto Rico of our own day, where the *jíbaro* has virtually ceased to have any demographic, economic, or cultural significance, the myth of the Puerto Rican as essentially a *jíbaro* stubbornly survives – whenever the old conservative élite, whether openly or covertly racist, sets pen to paper. And this at a time when it is really the proletarian Puerto Rican of mixed race who increasingly typifies popular society!

In short, each time the ideological spokesmen for the old conservative elite accuse the Puerto Rican popular masses of 'alienation', 'unawareness', or 'loss of identity', all they are doing is to betray their own lack of confidence and their own alienation from those who, little though some people like having to admit it, constitute the immense majority of Puerto Ricans. What is more, those ideological spokesmen have done something equally negative and counter-productive: they have convinced many foreigners of good will, who are sympathetic to our independence, that the Puerto Rican people are the object of 'cultural genocide'. A particularly sad victim of this 'anti-imperialist' propaganda, which is really nothing but the swan-song of a dying social class, has been the outstanding Cuban revolutionary poet Nicolás Guillén,[24] whose 'Canción puertorriqueña', as ill-informed as it is well-intentioned, has spread around the world the image of a culturally hybrid people capable of expressing themselves only in a ridiculous stutter of English and Spanish. All Puerto Ricans, whether supporters of independence or not, know that this vision of the cultural situation in Puerto Rico bears no relation whatsoever to the truth. And there are so many good reasons to justify Puerto Rico's independence that one cannot forgive an attempt to justify it by a reason that is patently false.

In my view, the good cultural reason for supporting independence is that independence is absolutely necessary to protect, orient, and secure the full development of Puerto Rico's true national identity, the identity that has its roots in that popular culture which the independence movement – If it *really* aspires to represent the authentic national will in this country – must understand and espouse without conditions or scruples born of distrust or prejudice. What is really happening in Puerto Rico today is the spectacular and irrevocable disintegration of that *fourth storey* which an advanced American capitalism and an opportunistic Puerto Rican populism began to build onto the island's social structure from the 1940s on. The patent collapse of the idea of *Estado Libre Asociado* or Commonwealth, clearly demonstrates, if we view it from what seems to me the right historical perspective, that American colonialism, after sponsoring widespread economic transformations fundamentally in order to satisfy the needs of an expansionist imperialist economy at home, thereby creating a very real modernization-within-dependency in Puerto

Rican society, can now only lead this society into a dead-end street and into a generalized malaise, whose rightly alarming symptoms are everywhere to be seen: massive unemployment and margination, a demoralizing dependency on a false generosity from abroad and uncontrollable upsurge in delinquency and criminality, to a great extent of foreign provenance, a disenchantment with politics and civic irresponsibility resulting from institutionalized demagoguery, and a whole Pandora's box of social ills that you know better than I, since you must live with them every day.

But to speak of the *present* bankruptcy of the colonial regime in no way implies that such a regime was a 'good' regime until recently and only now becomes 'bad'. What I am trying to say – and it matters a great deal to me not to be misunderstood – is that the eighty years of American domination in Puerto Rico represent the history of a political and economic undertaking whose immediate stages were viable *as they occurred*, but which were inevitably doomed, as indeed is any historical undertaking based on colonial dependency, to founder *in the long run* into the state of *un*viability in which we are now living. This unviability of the colonial regime is precisely what for the first time in our history makes national independence viable. And not merely viable, but also, as I have just argued, absolutely necessary.

Those of us both from within and without our country committed to a socialist future for Puerto Rico have before us the daunting task of neither more nor less than the total reconstruction of Puerto Rican society. (And when I speak of 'a socialist future for Puerto Rico' I speak, as you should already know, of a *democratic* socialism, pluralist and independent, which is the only socialism worthy of the name, and not of that other 'socialism' which is bureaucratic, monolithic, and authoritarian, and instituted *in the name* only of the working class by a new ruling class one can only call a state bourgeoisie, since it is the real proprietor of the means of production, held by virtue of the at once immovable and all-powerful 'apparatus' of the State.) My well-known disagreement with the traditional independence movement in this respect is a disagreement between two conceptions of the historical aims of such a reconstruction of Puerto Rican society. I do not believe in reconstructing backward, to a past bequeathed us by Spanish colonialism and an old elite irrevocably condemned by history. I believe instead in reconstructing forward, toward a future as defined by the best proletarian socialists in Puerto Rico early in this century when they advocated a national independence capable of organizing the country into 'an industrial democracy governed by the workers'; toward a future which, basing itself on the cultural tradition of the popular masses, will rediscover and redeem the essentially *Caribbean* nature of our collective identity and thereby acknowledge, once and for all, that the natural destiny of Puerto Rico is identical to that of all the other Caribbean peoples, whether they hail from the islands or from the mainland.

In this sense I conceive the national independence of all these peoples as merely a prerequisite–albeit the indispensable prerequisite – for achieving a great confederation that will definitively unite us in a just, effective joint organization at the economic, political and cultural levels. Only by means of such an organization may we take our rightful place within the greater communities of Latin America and the world. In economic matters, far from being merely an utopian wish, such unity is an objective necessity. In political matters, it answers to a manifest historical imperative, which is the liquidation of our common colonial past by establishing popular and non-capitalist regimes. And in cultural matters, which is what now specifically concerns us, it is essential for us so that we may recognize and *assume* a reality that even the most concerned among us have consistently ignored.

Hitherto, the fact that the Caribbean peoples speak several different European languages instead of just one has been seen as a factor in our disunity – and as a factor in our disunity it has been used against us by those various imperialisms which have claimed to speak in our name. But should we then, the subjugated, regard linguistic diversity from the same viewpoint as they, the subjugators? On the contrary, we should see this diversity as a unifying and uniting factor, since it is a consequence of our shared history. The great community of the Caribbean is multilingual. This is both true and irreversible and as such it should serve less to fragment and defeat than to stimulate and enrich us. Seen in this light American imperialism, thanks to one of those 'sly tricks of history' that philosophers refer to, has imposed on us Puerto Ricans a mastery of English – but without making us forget Spanish, my dear Nicolás Guillén! – only (and unintentionally) to make it easier for us to draw into closer alliance with our English-speaking brothers of the Caribbean.

We Puerto Ricans have to learn English, not as the route to cultural suicide whereby we become dissolved into the turbulent mainstream of American life, assimilated to that 'brutal and unruly North that so despises us', to quote José Martí, but so that we may with greater ease and profit integrate ourselves into that rich Caribbean world to which we belong by historical necessity. When finally Puerto Rico becomes independent within a great confederacy of independent nations – mestizo, popular and democratic – not only will we then be able and willing to appreciate and protect our national language, the good Spanish of Puerto Rico, as we should; we will also be able and willing to institute the teaching of English and French in our schools (with particular emphasis on local dialects), not as the languages of empire, but as languages at the service of our complete and final decolonization.

NOTES

1. The dialectical analysis that González uses emphasises the unity, or co-existence, of opposites that exists in any society where there are inequalities and that gives rise to social conflict and change. Wherever there are relations of oppressors and oppressed, of domination and subordination, there is conflict and therefore the potential for change. The dominant group tries to present its own culture as if it is superior and even universal, and the culture or cultures of the subordinates as inferior, or even barbaric and uncivilised. Dialectical theory, therefore, draws attention to the inherent conflicts in any attempt by a dominant group to define its culture as the national culture.

2. Hostos (1839–1903) was one of Puerto Rico's greatest educators, intellectuals and patriots in the nineteenth century. Albizu (1891–1965) was the leader of the Nationalist party and a symbol of patriotism for many Puerto Ricans (see chapter 6 in this volume).

3. Zeno (1855–1930) was a renowned Puerto Rican physician as well as a writer of realistic fiction. His tetralogy, 'Chronicles of a Sick World', began in 1894 with the novel *La Charca* (*The Stagnant Pool*), depicting pain and misery in rural Puerto Rico, which was supposed to be the last of Spain's 'colonial jewels'.

4. Brau (1842–1912), one of the few Puerto Rican intellectuals who spoke on behalf of the underprivileged, wrote of Puerto Ricans as '*un pueblo en formación*', a people in the process of formation.

5. Betances (1827–98) was a militant opponent of slavery and colonialism. He led the revolt against Spain in 1868 and spent the rest of his life in exile.

6. However, in July 1898, shortly before the United States invaded Puerto Rico, Betances wrote to Dr Julio J. Henna, president of the Puerto Rican section of Martí's Cuban Revolutionary Party in New York:

> What are the Puerto Ricans doing? Why don't they take advantage of the [US] blockade to rise en masse? It's extremely important that when the first troops of the United States reach shore, they should be received by Puerto Rican troops, waving the flag of independence, and greeting them. Let the North Americans cooperate in the achievement of our freedom, but not push the country to annexation. If Puerto Rico does not move quickly it will be an American colony forever (Wagenheim 1973, 116).

7. Quintero is a distinguished Puerto Rican sociologist at the University of Puerto Rico and the author of many studies of Puerto Rican history, society and culture, with a particular emphasis on the working class.

8. Corretjer (1908–85) was an influential poet, journalist and militant nationalist, who became the general secretary of the Puerto Rican Socialist League (see chapter 8 in this volume).

9. The Institute of Puerto Rican Culture, created by the PPD government in 1956, popularised and gave an official status to the romantic idea of Puerto Rican culture as being a harmonious blend of Taino, African and Spanish cultures, represented in the institute's official seal and the many folkloric exhibits and performances it sponsored. Although the strands constituting this racial-cultural triad were officially declared to be equal foundational elements, in practice Puerto Rican national culture was defined

as essentially Spanish, in particular in terms of language and religiosity (Dávila 1997). The Taino existed only in the remote past and African contributions were marginalised.

10. The migration of Spanish colonists from the colonies of Cuba, Hispaniola and Puerto Rico to the mainland followed the conquest of Mexico and the exploration of Florida and Central America in the 1520s. The conquest of the Incas and the discovery of vast sources of silver in Peru and Mexico led to the further depletion of the Antilles.

11. The *jíbaro*, a small farmer, was associated with creole culture since Manuel Alonso's (1822–89) *El Gíbaro* (1849) and adopted as the symbol of the PPD. Usually portrayed as a white male whose culture was derived largely from his Spanish ancestors, 'the *jíbaro* comprises the most important building block of nationality' (Dávila 1997, 72).

12. José Campeche (1752–1809) was the principal Puerto Rican painter of the eighteenth century. His religious paintings were produced for the churches and convents and his portraits for the wealthiest homes in San Juan.

13. *Coartación* was a system of gradual self-purchase, recognised by Spanish law, whereby the slave made a substantial down payment on his or her purchase price, thus acquiring some privileges as a *coartado*. The number of *coartados* was generally small, however, as rising slave prices put the status beyond the reach of most.

14. The *Cédula de Gracias*, a 'decree of pardon', was intended to promote immigration by providing about six acres of land to every free white immigrant, with an additional three acres for each slave he owned. It also exempted these new colonists from taxes for ten years, but the local administration reduced this to five years. It contributed to the expansion of the economy and growth of the population in the nineteenth century.

15. In 1849, Governor Juan de la Pezuela decreed that all men over the age of 16 who lacked enough land or resources to be independent had to register in their municipality and carry a *libreta*, or workbook, in which they had to record where and for whom they worked. This measure to coerce and control so-called free labourers was abolished in June 1873, three months before the abolition of slavery.

16. A German word meaning literally 'world view', a philosophical vision that conceives of the spirit and course of events of the world as a whole.

17. Marqués (1919–79) was a distinguished novelist, essayist, poet and playwright who taught at the University of Puerto Rico. His most famous work, *La carreta* (The Oxcart, 1952), is about a family moving from rural Puerto Rico to San Juan and then to New York. His pessimistic response to the Americanization of Puerto Rico concludes, 'The problem was not to seek a meaning in life but to live it without hope of finding a meaning' (quoted in Carr 1984, 275).

18. Alejandro Tapia y Rivera (1827–82) was a poet-dramatist who depicted Puerto Rico as a sick society suffering under Spanish barbarism.

19. Román Baldorioty de Castro was a leading abolitionist in the mid-nineteenth century and an early advocate of autonomy within the Spanish empire. Dr. José Celso Barbosa (1857–1921), a black physician educated at the University of Michigan, and Muñoz Rivera's rival in the Autonomist Party, created a Republican Party in 1899. A believer in the United States' democracy, he sought independence within the US system, with an elected Puerto Rican governor.

20. Roberto H. Todd was a Puerto Rican Republican who became an advisor to Governor Emmet Montgomery Reily in 1921. Dr José Julio Henna, a distinguished physician, spoke with Theodore Roosevelt to obtain US help in overthrowing Spanish power and subsequently supported the idea that 'the Americans should be the mentors of the Puerto Ricans for some time' (quoted in Morales Carrion 1983, 158).

21. José de Diego, as Minister of Justice in Muñoz Rivera's short-lived government, asked the Spanish captain-general in Puerto Rico for 9,000 rifles to organise popular resistance against the US invasion, a request that was not considered. He was appointed to the executive council under the first civilian US governor, Charles H. Allen. With Muñoz Rivera, he became a leader of the *Unión de Puerto Rico* in 1904, and sought self-government. De Diego later sought full independence and, in 1915, helped to establish the *Unión Antillana*, whose purpose was to promote cultural exchanges between Puerto Rico, Cuba and Santo Domingo in preparation for a political federation. In 1917, encouraged by President Wilson's doctrine of self-determination, he campaigned for a plebiscite on Puerto Rico's political status, but he died in 1918. An eloquent lawyer, he is said to 'have realized that support for independence came from the elite and middle-class intellectuals like himself' (Carr 1984, 177).

22. As early as 1904, many women participated in Puerto Rican trade unions, often organising their own associations within them. The first feminist organisation, *Liga Femenina Puertorriqueña*, was established in 1917 and, in 1919, the Socialist Party demanded universal suffrage for women and men in its political platform. Literate Puerto Rican women were able to vote in 1932 and the literacy requirement was abolished in 1936. However, the suffrage movement did not alter the patriarchal society and for most Puerto Rican women the promise of a better quality of life was not fulfilled. The women's liberation movement was revitalised in the late 1960s, but it is an exaggeration to suggest that feminism was imported from the United States.

23. This is not to say that Puerto Ricans are not discriminated against in US society. Thousands of Puerto Ricans participated in the armed services of the United States which were racially segregated until 1948, and thousands of migrants to the mainland certainly suffer discrimination in a variety of contexts.

24. Guillén (1902–89), Cuba's greatest poet in the twentieth century, was a leading member of the *afrocubanismo* movement that influenced all the arts in the 1920s and 1930s. He was a member of the *Sociedad de Estudios Afrocubanos*, founded by Fernando Ortiz in 1936, and the Cuban Communist Party. An opponent of Batista, he lived in exile for six years, returning to Cuba after the revolution in 1959. He became president of the National Union of Writers and Artists of Cuba and a member of the Central Committee of the Communist party.

Twelve

Esmeralda Santiago

Esmeralda Santiago's 'Island of Lost Causes' was published as an op-ed article in the New York Times *(Nov. 14, 1993) when Puerto Ricans were voting in a plebiscite on the island's political status. Born in 1948 in Puerto Rico, she moved to the United States where she graduated from Harvard University and earned an MFA from Sarah Lawrence College. Her first book,* When I Was Puerto Rican *(New York, 1993), is a coming-of-age memoir, lyrically capturing her cultural transition from rural Puerto Rico in the 1950s to New York City. She has also published a novel,* América's Dream *(1996) and another memoir* Almost a Woman *(1998).*

In this brief essay, Santiago reflects on Puerto Ricans' 'elusive cultural identity' and its relation to their ambivalent feelings about their island's future. The result of the plebiscite was 48.6 per cent in favour of the existing Commonwealth status, 46.4 per cent in favour of becoming the 51st state, and 4.4 per cent in favour of independence. This confirms the decline in support for independence and the dominance of Puerto Rico's chief political parties, the Partido Popular Democratico *which is pro-Commonwealth, and the* Partido Nuevo Progressista *which is pro-statehood. The results also support Santiago's view of Puerto Ricans' ambivalence and her prediction that more people would opt for the status quo than they would for either of the other options. As there was not a majority in favour of any option, one can say, on the one hand, that most people reject the choice of statehood, and one can say, on the other, that most people prefer a status other than the present one. Although the plebiscite did not accurately reflect all opinions because many* independentistas *boycotted it, it appears that most Puerto Ricans want to maintain a distinct identity apart from the United States, but most of them cannot imagine a future entirely apart from the United States.*

Island of Lost Causes

On Oct. 30, 1950,[1] 15 policemen and 25 National Guardsmen surrounded the Salón Boricua in Villa Palmeras, Puerto Rico, a barbershop owned by the nationalist leader Vidal Santiago Diaz. The windows of the shop were shuttered, but every once in a while gunfire erupted through the slats and was returned by the police and guards armed with pistols, machine guns, rifles and tear gas.

The siege lasted more than four hours. When the police were finally able to ax their way into the shop, they found a man slumped in a corner, his torso ripped by a grenade, his head bleeding. Two policemen dragged him out to the street and threw him on a stretcher.

Vidal Santiago Diaz was my uncle. As a child, I sat on his lap and stuck my index finger into the soft hole in the middle of his forehead, the scar left from a bullet.

In the 32 years since I left Puerto Rico for the United States, I haven't told many people about Tío Vidal. No one has ever asked me much about the island other than the location of the most charming hotels and whether we cook with hot chili peppers.

Lately, however, I've been grilled politely about the plebiscite taking place there today: Should Puerto Rico become the 51st state? Should it be an independent nation? Should it remain a commonwealth?

The vote is nonbonding – not much more than a recommendation to the U.S. Congress.[2] But as the first referendum since 1967, it has excited intense interest, on the island as well as among Puerto Ricans now living in the U.S.

As a Puerto Rican born in San Juan but now living in New York, I'm not eligible to vote on these questions.[3] If I could, however, I would be filled with ambivalence approaching the ballot box.

Puerto Rico has been a colony for 500 years, first of Spain, then, since 1898, the U.S. Today's plebiscite gives Puerto Ricans only the illusion of self-determination – an illusion that deflects attention from the basic problems on the island.

The reality of Puerto Rico is an unemployment rate of 17.3 percent; 862 murders in 1992 – a number that is expected to rise in 1993; a language so quickly becoming Spanglish that we have an inferiority complex about the purity of our spoken tongue; rampant urbanization that has destroyed thousands of acres of farmland; American businesses that set up shop for as long as they can get tax breaks, then move on to another part of the world where there is no minimum wage and the workers don't expect as much.

Puerto Rico's unsettled political status is symptomatic of the internal conflicts its people struggle with every day, whether we live on the island or in the U.S. We are born American citizens but harbor an intense Latin American identity.

Yet we are looked down upon by some Latin American neighbors because our culture is a hodge-podge of American influences grafted onto 400 years of Spanish traditions. We are told that our island doesn't have the rich heritage of bloody struggles for independence that other countries do.

The truth is, we do have a history of struggle for independence, but the opposition has always won. The failure of our best hopes for independence through centuries of failed insurrections has caused many Puerto Ricans to simply give up.

To some, statehood seems a clear solution to the island's ambiguous commonwealth status and a way of making the U.S. accountable for our future. After all, many Americans already refer to Puerto Rico as 'part of the United States', as if the island were attached to the North American continent, like Kansas or Nebraska. We are viewed either as an appendage of The Mainland or as a ship lost at sea.

We are taken for granted by the U.S., and that sharpens in us a stubborn nationalist streak – yet we don't demonstrate it at the ballot box. In our hearts, we want to believe independence is the right choice, but our history forces us to see it as a lost cause. Still, we are not willing to give up so completely as to vote for statehood. It would be the ultimate statement of surrender.

This is why so many Puerto Ricans will vote for the status quo. It fosters the illusion of choosing a destiny, neither capitulating nor fighting. But it continues to evade the question of who we are as a people.

An elusive cultural identity lies at the heart of our unwillingness to declare ourselves either a nation or a state. A vote for the commonwealth insures that we don't have to commit one way or the other.

Ironically, neither violent insurrection nor the democratic process seem able to solve that question. Tío Vidal had a belief in nationhood that drove him to risk his life. How many of us Puerto Ricans would go that far? We need to look at ourselves hard and to stop hiding behind the status quo. It is not a choice. It is a refusal to choose.

NOTES

1. This was the time of the Nationalist uprising.
2. The US Congress, in agreeing to this and other plebiscites on Puerto Rico's political status, has always made it clear that this is only an expression of opinion that cannot be binding on Congress because it is Congress that has authority over Puerto Rico, which it defines as an 'unincorporated territory' of the United States.
3. Eligibility for voting in this plebiscite was based on US citizenship and residence in Puerto Rico, so a Cuban, or Californian or any other US citizen who was resident in Puerto Rico could vote on the nation's political status, whereas Puerto Ricans who, like Santiago, were born in but no longer resided on the island could not vote.

Thirteen

Antonio Benítez-Rojo

Antonio Benítez-Rojo was born in Cuba in 1931 and lived in Havana until 1980 when he moved to the United States. He was the director of the Editorial Department of Casa de las Americas, *the Cuban publishing house, and later of the* Centro de Estudios del Caribe *in Cuba. He teaches Hispanic-American literature at Amherst College. He has published several collections of short stories and his novel,* Sea of Lentils, *was published in Spanish in 1985 and in English in 1990. His book of literary criticism and cultural theory,* La isla que se repite: El Caribe y la perspectiva postmoderna *(1989) was translated into English as* The Repeating Island: The Caribbean and the Postmodern Perspective *(1992).*

Three Words Toward Creolization

In this brief essay, I examine the notion of creolization through three words: plantation, rhythm, and performance. I ought to add that I don't mean these remarks to be taken as objective; they come simply out of my desire to see myself as a person with a Caribbean identity, as I understand it.

Of course, the use of these three words in Caribbean discourse is hardly new; they have been the subject of much writing, from both inside and outside the area, since the sixteenth century. In his critique of the plantation, seen as a macrosystem that functions in the world, Fray Bartolomé de Las Casas[1] wrote, around 1520:

> As the sugar mills [of Hispaniola] grew every day, so grew the need to put Negroes to work in them. Seeing that we [Portuguese] have such a need and that we pay well for them, go out every day to capture them, through any vile and iniquitous means . . . . As they themselves see that they are looked for and desired, they make unjust wars upon each other, and in other illicit ways they steal one another to be sold to the Portuguese, so that we ourselves are the cause of the sins that one and another commits, as well as those that we ourselves commit in buying them . . . . Formerly, when there were no sugar mills . . . we had never seen a Negroe dead from disease . . . but after they were put into the sugar mills . . . they found their death and their sickness . . . and for that reason bands of them run away whenever they can, and they rise up and inflict death and cruelty upon the Spaniards, in order to get out of their captivity.

Regarding the other two words – rhythm and performance – we note that, in 1573, the town government of Havana ordered that the free Blacks should be included, with their songs and dances, in the festivals with which Corpus Christi was celebrated. These Creole manifestations, emerging from an interplay of European and African elements, reached Spain in the third quarter of the sixteenth century– particularly the so-called zarabanda – and were commented on by Cervantes, Lope de Vega, Quevedo,[2] and other writers. In fact, they were so popular in Spain that the Inquisition censured them more than once as indecent. I mention these cases to reinforce the fact that, from the earliest moments of colonization, the plantation system, as well as the Creole rhythms and performances, have been subjects of extensive commentary. And the use of the word criollo (Creole), as both noun and adjective, also dates from these early periods, as we know.[3]

Of course, what the plantation represented to Las Casas was quite different from what it represents to me. For Las Casas, the plantation was an immediate problem; it was a machine with no past that generated violence and sin in Hispaniola, Spain, and Portugal, as well as on the western coast of Africa. As he wrote the paragraph that I have quoted, Las Casas never imagined the complex dynamics unleashed by the growing demand for sugar and other plantation products would begin to figure in a new discourse – to which his words now belong – that would refer not just to the sixteenth century but also to future centuries and to large parts of America, Europe, Africa, and Asia. But if Las Casas never saw the plantation as other than a problem of his time, to me, four centuries later, it is the womb of my otherness –and of my globality, if you will allow me this word. It is the bifurcated center that exists inside and outside at the same time, near to and distant from all things that I can understand as my own: race, nationality, language, and religion.

Yes, I repeat, the plantation is my old and paradoxical homeland. It is the machine that Las Casas described, but it is also much more: the hollow center of the minuscule galaxy that gives shape to my identity. There are no organized history or family trees in that center; its tremendous and prolonged explosion has projected everything outward. There, as a child of the plantation, I am a mere fragment, or an idea that spins around my own absence, just as a drop of rain spins around the empty eye of the hurricane that set it going.

Well then, what relation do I find between the plantation and the process of creolization? Naturally, first of all, a relation of cause and effect; without the one we would not have the other. But I also see other relations. From my perspective, our cultural manifestations are not creolized, but are rather in a state of creolization. Creolization does not transform literature or music or language into a synthesis or anything that could be taken in essentialist terms, nor does it lead these expressions into a predictable state of creolization. Rather, creolization is a term with which we attempt to explain the unstable states that a Caribbean cultural object presents over time. In other words, creolization is not merely a process (a word that implies forward movement) but a discontinuous series of recurrences, of happenings, whose sole law is change. Where does this instability come from? It is the product of the plantation (the big bang of the Caribbean universe), whose slow explosion throughout modern history threw out billions and billions of cultural fragments in all directions – fragments of diverse kinds that, in their endless voyage, come together in an instant to form a dance step, a linguistic trope, the line of a poem, and afterward repel each other to re-form and pull apart once more, and so on.

In the coming together and pulling apart of those fragments, many kinds of forces are at work. In my country, Cuba, for instance, the arrival of the radio, the Victrola, the recording industry, and the cinema contributed to the popularity of the *son*, the *rumba*, and the *conga* in the decade of the 1920s. Previously, this kind of music existed only among the black population and was not accepted as a national music. However, once the majority of Cubans had internalized these rhythms, they in turn contributed to the formation of what was known then as Afro-Cuban culture, a culture that produced the symphonic music of Amadeo Roldán and Alejandro García Caturla, the *negrista* poetry of Nicolás Guillén, the magic realism of Alejo Carpentier, the essays of Fernando Ortiz and Lydia Cabrera, and the painting of Wifredo Lam.[4]

Something else was happening simultaneously. In 1916, a group of distinguished black veterans of the War with Spain (1895–98) had asked the pope to designate as Cuba's patron saint the Virgin of la Caridad, a dark-skinned virgin. The pope granted this request immediately, perhaps not knowing that to many black Cubans, the Virgin of La Caridad was also the Oshun of Santería.[5] While the so-called black music made its influence known in other cultural forms, Santería legitimized itself along with Catholicism as a national religion, influencing music, painting, dance, theater, literature, and even language – for example, words of African origin such as chévere, ashé, mayombe, bembé, ebbó, ekobio, babalawo, asere, íreme, orisha, and bilongo started being used extensively during those years.

In Cuba now, nobody speaks of Afro-Cuban manifestations: what was once something concerning Blacks before 1920 became Afro-Cuban and is now simply Cuban. One might think that all this happened because Cuban culture has been subject to an accelerated process of Africanization. But that is not the case: the public practice of Afro-Cuban religions was prohibited by the Cuban government until quite recently, negrista literature and negrista symphonic music stopped being produced many years ago, and the painting of Wifredo Lam is made now for tourists alone. In fact, Cuban culture, like any other culture born on the plantation, has for many years had African, European, Asian, and American components; and these components, in a state of creolization, approach or withdraw from one another according to situations created by unpredictable forces. If it is true that Cuba serves as an example here, it is also true that this paradigm repeats itself throughout the Caribbean. For example, both the First and Second World Wars played a part in foregrounding the African components of Caribbean culture. This seemed then to be a new thing, but in fact these components always were there and always will be there.

In short, the certainty about creolization is that it inevitably refers to the plantation. To borrow the jargon of Chaos[6] here, I would say that the plantation is the strange attractor of all the possible states of creolization, given that all of them, in their disorder, hide forms of order that look for their guiding model in the black hole of the plantation. And so it could be said that the plantation repeats itself endlessly in the different states of creolization that come out here and there in language and music, dance and literature, food and theater. These elements are summed up in the Carnival.

Now, with regard to Caribbean performance and rhythm, I shall take examples from contemporary Caribbean fiction to illustrate my points. Of course, I could use the works of Wilson Harris, Alejo Carpentier, Gabriel García Márquez, or Maryse Condé, but I prefer to cite more recent writers, such as Caryl Phillips, of St. Kitts, who writes in his novel, *Crossing the River*:[7]

> A long way from home . . . . For two hundred and fifty years I have listened. To the haunting voices. Singing: Mercy, Mercy . . . . Listened to voices hoping for Freedom. Democracy. Singing: Baby baby. Where did our love go? Samba. Calypso. Jazz. Sketches of Spain in Harlem . . . . I have listened to the voice that cried: I have a dream that one day on the red hills of Georgia, the sons of former slaves and the sons of former slaveowners will be able to sit down together at the table of brotherhood. I have listened to the sounds of an African Carnival in Trinidad. In Rio. In New Orleans, On the far bank of the river, a drum continues to be beaten . . . . A guilty father. Always listening. There are no paths in water. No signposts. There is no return. A desperate foolishness. The crops failed. I sold my beloved children. *Bought two strong man-boys, and a proud girl.* But they arrived on the far bank of the river, loved. (236–37)

How would I define this novel's performance? In the first place, I would say that the praise that English critics gave to *Crossing the River* was deserved – the critic in the *Times Literary Supplement* said that the novel was 'a triumphant piece of writing'. But I also look in these reviews for judgments about its performance. For example, praise that the novel's 'beauty lies in its very ellipses and suppressions', that 'Phillips has a fine ironic sense of time', or that the novel 'is dense with event and ingeniously structured' curiously leave out any reference to rhythm, which is one of Phillips's preoccupations. Says Phillips, 'Where did our love go? Samba. Calypso. Jazz. Sketches of Spain in Harlem . . . . I have listened to an African Carnival in Trinidad. In Rio. In New Orleans. One the far bank of the river, a drum continues to be beaten'.

It is obvious that Phillips, as a son of the plantation, performs his own literature to the rhythms of the samba, the calypso, and jazz. And that's not all: his choice of punctuation – along with the number of syllables in his words and the syntax that connects them – gives a rhythmic meaning to his narrative discourse. Where does this rhythm come from? From within Phillips. So we might say that the performance of his literary language – what the critics see as ellipses and suppressions, and so forth – is dictated by the writer's interior rhythms. And though these rhythms might seem African, they are, in fact, not entirely so. Africa, as Phillips says, is irrecoverable: 'There are no paths in water. No signposts. There is no return'. It is true that the rhythms of the samba and of calypso have their origin in Africa, but only if we understand rhythm to be a sequence of internal pulsations. For these pulsations to become rhythms, they must be wrapped in sounds. The pulsations that the rhythm of the samba follows are of African origin (we know that they belong to Bantu culture) but the sound of the samba is not a totally African one, just as it is not completely a European one. One could think, then, that it is Brazilian, but I would say that that is so only superficially. If we were to try to determine the origin of these rhythmic sounds, sounds that include many instruments along with the human voice and the rubbing of shoes against the floor (the way it is danced), we would find that this complex polyrhythmic system began to take shape on the plantation.

Natalio Galán, a Cuban musicologist, once said that within every rhythmic motif there lies a centuries-old mystery. I think that he was right; hidden within the samba there are the ancient pulsations brought by the African diaspora, the memory of sacred drums and the words of the griot.[8] But there are also the rhythms of the sugar mill's machines, the machete stroke that cuts the cane, the overseer's lash, and the planter's language, music, and dance. Later there came other rhythms, from India, from China, and from Java. And finally, all these rhythms mixed with one another to form a network of rhythmic flows whose most notable expressions today are salsa, Latin jazz, and West Coast African music. This complex polyrhythmic orchestration was born on the plantation and now lies within the memory of the people of the Caribbean. It is what inspires Phillips's performance; that is, the way the novel is written and the way it sounds. 'On the far bank of the river, a drum continues to be beaten' marks *Crossing the River* as a novel in a state of creolization.

Let's take another example from a recent novel, also praised by the critics. In *The Longest Memory* by Fred D'Aguiar[9] of Guyana, we read: 'You do not want to know my past nor do you want to know my name for the simple reason that I have none and would have to make it up to please you . . . . I just was boy, mule, nigger, slave or whatever else anyone chose to call me' (1). Here, first of all, we have the reproduction of the plantation's void. Of course the slave in the novel has a name: Whitechapel, his master's name. But is this his real name? In my own case, do I see myself as Spanish simply because my name is Spanish? Then what is my real name, the one that corresponds to my real identity? Needless to say, had I been born in Spain with the same name, my name would reflect my identity without conflict. However, no Caribbean person – that is, no person with a truly Caribbean identity – carries his or her own true name, just as his or her skin pertains to no fixed race. The same observations pertain to language. The novels of Phillips and D'Aguiar, like others I will mention, are written in English, but none of them is totally English: they are Caribbean because of their poetics – structure, theme, character, conflict, technique, language – which I call performance.

More specifically, the stylistic performance of *The Longest Memory* is manifest in the difference between its chapters: the first is formed by a monologue spoken by a slave who has betrayed his son; the second by a planter's monologue; the third is an overseer's diary; the fourth is the words of a slave woman; the fifth, a poem; and the sixth, a dialogue among planters. Another chapter is formed by the words of a white woman who teaches a slave to read, and still another by an editorial in a Virginia newspaper, and so on. What adjectives did the critics use to describe this brilliant performance? They used terms such as dense, intense, compact, and controversial. No European critic said of *The Longest Memory* that it was a novel of great rhythmic complexity. Nevertheless, in his attempt to describe the plantation, D'Aguiar wrote a text for a symphony for percussion, in which each character interprets a different rhythm; that is, a work of polyrhythmic density that gathers rhythms from the whole world.

It is precisely because of these performances that I believe Caribbean literature to be the most universal of all. I will go a step further and argue that the more Caribbean a text is – the more complex and artistic its state of creolization – the more readers it will find in the world. Some publishing houses have already understood this reality, and they are going to do a good business.

Obviously, one cannot say that all Caribbean fiction has the historic character of the examples I present here. Nevertheless, even when the action of a Caribbean novel takes place in the twentieth century, it always refers back to the plantation through its rhythm and its performance. Take for instance, 'Children of the Sea', a story by Haitian-American writer Edwidge Danticat.[10] She writes:

> Do you want to know how people go to the bathroom on the boat? Probably the same way they did on those slave ships years ago. They set aside a little corner for that. When I have to pee, I just pull it, lean over the rail, and do it very quickly. When I have to do the other thing, I rip a piece of something, squat down and do it, and throw the waste into the sea. I am always embarrassed by the smell. It is so demeaning having to squat in front of so many people. People turn away, but not always. At times I wonder if there is really land on the other side of the sea. Maybe the sea is endless. Like my love for you. (1995, 15)

These are the words of a revolutionary student who, to avoid dying at the hands of the Tonton-Macoutes,[11] has decided to flee to the United States in a little boat. As we see, in his voyage he relives the middle passage that connects Africa with America in the plantation's macrosystem. Later, when the boat takes in water, the humiliated passengers are forced to throw all of their belongings into the sea, including the clothes that they are wearing. Finally, they all drown, and their naked bodies keep company with the innumerable children of the sea who have disappeared beneath the waters of the black Atlantic. This story's narrative discourse, like those of *Crossing the River* and *The Longest Memory*, is fragmented: in a series of fragments we read the words of the man in the boat; in another series the words of his sweetheart in Haiti, who tells a story that is no less painful. Each of the individual narratives has its own typography and its own rhythm. The title of Danticat's book is *Krik? Krak!*, written in Creole, and it alludes to the peasant custom in which the story teller says 'Krik?' to which the one who wants to hear a story answers 'Krak!' We must then associate the dialogic structure of the story with the book's title, just as the boat's passengers tell stories according to the rules of *Krik? Krak!* But it is also obvious that, through this double game, Danticat puts herself in contact with the reader. Though her text is written in American English, it is deliberately connected to Haitian Creole oral traditions. According to the silly labels that we use in the United States, Danticat is a Haitian-American; in fact her identity is in the hyphen, that is, in neither place: Danticat is a Caribbean writer.

Finally, taking another recent novel *Divina Trace*, by Robert Antoni of Trinidad,[12] let us consider the following sentence:

> . . . *oy oy oy yo-yuga, yo-yuga da-bamba da-bamba oy* benedictus que venit in nomine Domini *oy* lumen de lumine de Deum verum de Deo vero *oy* Marie conçue sans péché priez por nous qui avons recours à vous Sainte Catherine del Carmen purísima hermosa azucena maravilla ayúdame cuídame fortaléceme socorredme favoréceme fuente de bondad de gracia y de misericordia *silverfish flying starpetals* exploding bursting out sudden silent from below the bow. (231)

What kind of language is this? The language of the plantation, including Latin, the language in which the Catholic Mass was said. The *Washington Post* reviewer of *Divina Trace* referred to the novel's magical realism with an avant-garde twist, but we can express this same opinion in other words: the magic realism of the Caribbean and the experiment of the modernist European novel come together here in a chaotic performance. The result is a bifurcated novel, fractal, gaseous; a novel whose performance can be placed quite near the big bang of the plantation.

Actually, *Divina Trace* offers a touch of real genius. Pages 203 and 204 are blank. Instead, a metal page performs as a mirror through which readers look at themselves and see a grotesquely disfigured face. This, naturally, is part of the novel's double performance: in the mirror, the western reader will read a joke or an irony or a mystery, but the Caribbean reader will see any one of his/her multiple masks. However, the mirror in *Divina Trace* functions at another level. The novel's plot develops around a monstrous character, half child and half frog, conceived by a mysterious woman named Magdalena, half saint and half whore. As the novel progresses, we see that nobody knows much about this child. A character says,

> Some called him the jabjab heself, son of Manfrog, the folktale devil-sprite who waits on a tree to rape young virgins at dusk. Others saw nothing peculiar in

the child a-tall. Some even said the child was beautiful, perfect: that the child was the reflection of the viewer. Some argued the hex of an obeah spell. Others the curse of Magdalena's obsession with swamp Maraval . . . . Still others said he was the result of a congenital abnormality which caused him to appear like a Frog. . . . Son, we can resign weselves to only this: there is no logical explanation. We will never know. (58–59)

With these words Antoni pushes the reader to a site of polemics: each reader projects in the mirror not just his/her face but also his/her ideology – every mirror is a text in which the observer reads him/herself. For some the reflected image will be that of the Creole; for others it will be a native of some country in the Caribbean; for others it will be the reflection of his/her own race. These reflections, invested with the political and social ideas of the observer, will never be coherent images, but rather distorted ones; they will be images in flux or, rather, images in search of their own images. Therefore, the mirror of *Divina Trace* reflects an identity in a state of creolization, a reflection that oscillates between history and myth; that is, a paradoxical mask launched into the distance by the explosion of the plantation.

In the end, the performances of Phillips, D'Aguiar, Danticat, and Antoni can be seen as attempts to represent the trip to the origins of Caribbeanness. Or, if you prefer, they trace the journey of the fragmented Caribbean self in search of its hidden unity. Can this unity be found within the black hole of the plantation? My answer is both yes and no. A performer, through his or her performance, can resolve the paradox of his or her identity. But only poetically. As the character in *Divina Trace* says, for a paradox there is no logical explanation.

NOTES

1. Bartolomé de Las Casas (1474–1566) settled in Hispaniola in 1502. He became a priest and denounced the system of forced labour which was destroying the native population. His critical *Historia de las Indias* is an indictment of Spanish colonial policies and practices.
2. Miguel de Cervantes Saavedra (1547–1616), author of the novel *Don Quixote* (1605–15), Lope de Vega (1562–1635), who wrote hundreds of plays, and Francisco Gómez de Quevedo y Villegas (1580–1645), who wrote the novel *The Life and Adventures of Buscan* (1626), are among the greatest and most influential writers of the Golden Age of Spanish literature.
3. Author's note: 'The word *criollo* (antecedent to *Créole* and *Creole*) appears for the first time in Mexico in *Geografía y descripción general de las Indias* (1571–74) by Juan Lopez de Velasco. In Cuba it appears in a document of March 1607, upon the confiscation of the departing governor Pedro de Valdés's ship *La Criolla*, built in Havana around 1605.'

4. The composers Amadeo Roldán and Alejandro García Caturba, and the poet Nicolás Guillén (1902–89), were among the first members of the *Sociedad Estudios Afrocubanos* which Fernando Ortiz founded in 1936. Alejo Carpentier (1904–80) was one of the first Cuban writers to focus on Afro-Caribbean subjects, as in his novels *Ecué-Yamba-O (*1933) and *El reino de este mundo* (1949). Lydia Cabrera (1900–91) studied Yoruba mythology and Afro-Cuban culture. She wrote *Cuentos negros de Cuba* in 1934 and *El monte* (1954), which is about the *Santería* religion. Wifredo Lam (1902–82), whose mother was of mixed African and European descent and whose father was Chinese, was the first Caribbean painter to achieve a major international reputation. His most famous painting, 'The Jungle' (1943), showing mysterious masked figures dancing in a canefield, may be seen as an allegory of plantation slavery.

5. *Santería* is an Afro-Caribbean religion based on the Yoruba culture of West Africa and influenced by Roman Catholicism. The name means 'way of the saints', based on the Spanish word *santos* and the Yoruba belief in *orishas*, or spirits. *Oshun*, or *Ochún*, is one of the *orishas*.

6. Benítez-Rojo refers to the Chaos Theory, a scientific perspective that describes the complex and ultimately unpredictable aspects of change in a system.

7. Caryl Phillips, *Crossing the River* (1994). Phillips was born in St Kitts in 1958. His family moved to England in the same year and he grew up in Leeds and studied in Oxford. He has written many film, theatre, radio and television scripts and his novels include *The Final Passage* (1985) and *Cambridge* (1991).

8. The *griot* is an African singer whose repertoire includes praise-songs for kings, historical narratives and commentaries on current events.

9. Fred D'Aguiar was born in London in 1960 and was raised in Guyana. He has published three books of poetry, a play and two novels, *The Longest Memory* (1994) and *Dear Future* (1996).

10. Edwidge Danticat (see chapter 22 in this volume), who was born in Haiti in 1969 and went to the United States when she was 12, has published two novels, *Breath, Eyes, Memory* (1994) and *The Farming of Bones* (1998), and the collection of short stories, *Krik? Krak!* (1995).

11. The *Tontons Macoutes* were the private army of François Duvalier and his son, Jean-Claude Duvalier, who were the presidents of Haiti from 1957 to 1971, and 1971 to 1986, respectively.

12. Robert Antoni's *Divina Trace* (1992) won the 1992 Commonwealth Prize for Best First Novel.

Part Two
The Francophone Intellectuals

Fourteen

Anténor Firmin

Joseph Anténor Firmin (1850–1911) was born into a working-class family in Cap-Haitien, in northern Haiti. His formal education was conducted entirely in Haiti, at the Lycée National du Cap-Haitien and the Lycée Pétion in Port-au-Prince. He was a scholar of the classical languages and civilisations of Europe and of law. He practiced law in Cap-Haitien, where he was also appointed inspector of schools and founded a newspaper in 1878. He was Commissaire of the Republic of Haiti in Caracas, Venezuela, and he lived in Paris between 1883 and 1888 as a diplomat. Returning to Haiti, Firmin became Minister of Finance, Commerce and Foreign Relations in Florvil Hyppolite's government. When Hyppolite was replaced in 1896, Firmin returned to Paris. In 1902, there was a power struggle between Firmin and Nord Alexis, an octogenarian general. Firmin was out-manoevred by Alexis and he went into exile in St Thomas. He later tried to return to Haiti as the head of an insurrection but when this failed he returned to St Thomas where he died.

Firmin, an outstanding writer, was a pioneer of anthropology but his work was neglected outside Haiti throughout the twentieth century. As a member of the Société d'anthropologie de Paris from 1884 to 1888, he argued forcefully against the racist doctrines of such people as Count Arthur de Gobineau, whose Essai sur L'Inégalité des Races Humaines *(1853–55) was very influential, and Paul Broca, who was the leading French anthropologist until he died in 1880. In his book* De L'Egalité des Races Humaines *(Paris, 1885), Firmin wrote a more scientifically accurate account of race and racial differences than his contemporaries, an account that was decades ahead of its time. Firmin insisted that all humans belong to a single species and that there is no scientific basis for a hierarchical ranking of human races. Firmin, who was proud of his nation and its revolutionary origins, described the intellectual achievements of many Haitians in literature, law, sociology, medicine, agronomy, mathematics and political economy. He was also proud of Haiti's role in the history of the Americas, not only for the brave example it set in the struggle against slavery, but also for its assistance to Simón Bolívar in his campaign to liberate South America from Spanish colonialism. An early Pan-Africanist, Firmin restored ancient Egyptian civilisation to Africa, from which Europeans had tried to appropriate it, and he participated in the first Pan-African Congress in London in 1900. A friend of José Martí and Ramón Betances, the Cuban and Puerto Rican nationalists, Firmin was an advocate of Pan-Caribbeanism, which he thought should include regional economic development and a federal system of government* (Lettres de Saint Thomas, *Paris, 1910).*

$\mathcal{T}$*he Equality of the Human Races (excerpts)*
Preface

I am always shocked whenever I come across dogmatic assertions of the inequality of the races and the inferiority of Blacks in various books. Now that I have become a member of the *Société d'anthropologie de Paris,*[1] such assertions seem to me even more incomprehensible and illogical . . . . At the opening of our meeting at the end of last year, I could have requested a debate about the issue with the Society in order to elucidate the scientific reasons why most of my fellow scientists divide the human species into superior and inferior races. But I risked being perceived as an intruder and, being ill-disposed against me, my colleagues might have rejected my request without further thought. Common sense told me I was right to hesitate so. It was then that I conceived the idea of writing this book . . . .

I am Black. Moreover, I have always considered the religion of science as the only true one, the only one worthy of the attention and infinite devotion of any man who is guided by reason. How could I reconcile the conclusions some seem to draw, on the basis of this same science, with respect to the abilities of Blacks with this deep and passionate veneration which is, for me, an imperative need of the mind? Could I withdraw from the ranks of my congeners and consider myself an exception among other exceptions? I have too logical a mind to accept such a distinction which I consider vain, specious, and mad. There is no fundamental difference between the Blacks of Africa and those of Haiti. I could never understand how, whenever mention is made of the inferiority of the Black race, the allusion would apply more to the former than to the latter. Should I be tempted to entertain such a false and inept idea, reality itself, which never lies, would make me realize every minute that the systematic contempt hurled at the African reaches me in my entire being. If Caribbean Blacks show evidence of superior intelligence, if they exhibit abilities unknown to their ancestors, it is nonetheless to these ancestors they owe their original intelligence, which selection would later strengthen and increase . . . .

The question must be asked, however. Is not the dogma of the inequality of races, which fosters the most stupid prejudices and nurtures the most malevolent antagonism among the different elements of the Haitian people, the most obvious cause of the dissentions and internal conflicts that have repressed and indeed annihilated the best natural aptitudes of the young and proud nation? Is not the inconsiderate belief in her inferiority responsible for the lack of any real support for her social development? Are not all the calamities that have afflicted her due to the ever ridiculous pretensions of some and the often indelicate claims of others? The Haitian race will achieve all that it is capable of achieving only when all these prejudices, which constitute stumbling blocks on the path to progress, are eliminated through education, to which the masses will have been given unlimited access . . .

While recognizing that the Black race in Haiti has progressed with an astonishing rapidity, I cannot deny that today it still needs to do its best to break with certain habits that can only hold it back. When one is late, on cannot afford to dawdle *en route.*

I take myself neither for a hero nor for a scientist. I bring only my sense of dedication and my good will to the cause of the truth I wish to defend. But I will take enormous pride in knowing that all Black people, those living today and those to come, read this work and become convinced that their imperative duty is to work hard and to improve themselves in order to wash away the unjust imputations that have weighed on their race for so long. I will be very happy to see the people of my country, for whom I harbor infinite love and veneration precisely because of their misfortunes and laborious destiny, understand at last that their country has a very special and delicate duty, which is to show the whole world that all human beings, Blacks and Whites, are equal in terms of both their qualities and their rights. I am deeply convinced, indeed I entertain the radiant and active hope, that my wish will come true.

The very laws of evolution inspire and justify such an aspiration. The ineluctable destiny of all human societies is to go forward, to persevere on the road of progress once the first step has been taken. Once all paralyzing constraints have been removed and the society's moral energies, the very soul of progress, have been liberated, the gradual and harmonious movement of progress will occur as a result of the natural elasticity proper to all social organisms. All young and vigorous peoples must look to freedom as the very principle of their salvation. All natural and organic laws combine to proclaim this truth.

In Haiti as elsewhere, the Black race can progress and prosper only if it enjoys freedom, real and effective civic and political freedom. If slavery horrifies Blacks, so must despotism. For despotism is nothing but moral slavery; it allows one's hands and feet to move freely, but it chains and muzzles the human soul by repressing thought. But it is worth remembering that the transformation, redemption, and rehabilitation of a race result from the inner action of the soul, operating under the impulse of a will that is free, enlightened, and unconstrained by tyranny . . . .

The wish I formulate for the people of my race, wherever they may live and govern themselves in the world, is that they turn away from anything that smacks of arbitrary practices, of systematic contempt for the law and for freedom, and of disdain of legal procedures and distributive justice. Law, justice, and freedom are eminently respectable values, for they form the crowning structure of the moral edifice which modern civilisation has been laboriously and gloriously building on the accumulated ruins of the ideas of the Middle Ages.

The example must come from Haiti. Have not Haitian Blacks already given evidence of the highest intelligence and the most forceful drive? Statesmen and writers, young and old, all will soon realize that the regeneration of the African race will be complete only when each individual is as respectful of the freedom and the rights of others as he is of his own freedom and rights . . . .

Monogenism and Polygenism

Despite all the writings on the subject and all the attendant debates, scientists who still talk about species, in one way or another, are no closer to having a clear understanding of the meaning of the term. Yet such a lack of certainty about what properly constitutes a species has prevented no one from going to battle about whether or not human beings constitute a single species or several species. As no side can win such a battle, we will overlook this noisy clash of thundering words in which the cleverest of the antagonists win but an ephemeral victory. Still, the arguments for or against the unitarian doctrine constitute for the most part the very source from which, like Minerva from Jupiter's head, sprang fully armed the theory of the inequality of the human races. We must therefore pay close attention to them . . . .

It would be a mistake to believe that the argument between supporters of polygenism and advocates of monogenism ends with the review of the anatomical or physiological traits which, according to scientists, distinguish the races from one another. To the contrary, the anthropological school that subscribes to the idea of the plurality of the species, affirms that it considers those traits only of secondary importance . . . .

We have already mentioned that old law of the species according to which it is believed that continuous fecundity from one generation to the next exists only among individuals of the same species. That law has been accepted by every naturalist of the classical school as a transcendent scientific truth. Observing that human beings have always interbred wherever they have come in contact with one another, so that the very notion of pure races becomes questionable, monogenists have grafted onto that law the doctrine of the unity of the human species. Indeed, if not for this fact of the essential unity of humanity, it would be very difficult to explain the eugenic crossbreedings that have made the surface of the planet sparkle with more human colors than there are nuances in the rainbow.

The polygenists had to demonstrate the opposite. They had to show that different species could produce indefinitely fertile offspring over successive generations, or else they had to prove that when the different human categories interbreed they do not always produce offsprings that are consistently fertile over the generations . . . .

They could and they did raise doubts about the fecundity *inter se* of *métis*[2] born of the union of a White man and a Negress, or of a Black man and a White woman. The underlying thrust of the discussion is quite transparent. A stallion and a she-ass, two animals of different species, interbreed to produce a mule, a hybrid offspring which is usually infertile. Now, if it could be proven that the mulatto, so named by analogy with the mule, was infertile, it could be irrefutably stated that his parents belong to different species.

I will overlook the case in which the hybrid fruitfully breeds with one or the other of its two parent species . . . . But in order to overcome totally his adversaries, the great polygenist only had to prove that the union between two mulattoes is not consistently fecund.

But the fecundity of mulattoes is a fact so well known by everyone who has ever lived in countries with a *métis* population that one can only be surprised that a scientist of Broca's[3] caliber can question it . . . Wherever mulattoes are found, their very existence proves that Blacks and Whites had been in close contact . . .

The Dominican population of Hispaniola offers an initial proof. Many Whites still remain in that country, and they have continued to interbreed with people of various skin complexions. As a result, next to the first-generation mulattoes, we find many mixed-bloods, *griffes*,[4] Blacks, etc. But the existence of these different *métis* in no way impedes the research on the results of unions among first-generation mulattoes. These individuals are numerous, and there is an abundance of cases which show that their unions are as fecund as those between pure-race individuals. . . .

Of Haiti, the old French section of Hispaniola, I can speak with even greater confidence, since it is my motherland, my native country. There I have made the same observation, and the evidence is irrefutable. After independence there remained very few Whites in the country, and only a restricted number came in subsequently. These Whites usually came only to make their fortune and return to their country of origin. Only exceptionally did they marry the native. It is well known that over the last eighty years or so, unions between White women and Black men or between White men and Black women are so rare that they may be considered virtually non-existent. Despite this fact, however, the number of mulattoes in Haiti has more than doubled.

It is an irrefutable fact that their number has increased at a faster rate than that of the Black population. I know that we should not attribute this phenomenon to the higher fertility of mulattoes, as compared to that of either of the two parent races. The cause resides, rather, in certain sociological conditions, which we do not have to take into consideration at this point. But while we cannot attribute only to ethnological causes the rapid growth of the mulatto population in Haiti despite the absence of unions among Whites and Blacks, the numbers provide sufficient evidence to support the idea that the unions of mulattoes are definitely fecund. It does not take an extraordinary effort to establish this truth . . . . Let us now consider the issue of the intelligence of *métis*. I will remain consistent and, faithful to the scientific method, I will choose again as the basis of my argument the case of the Haitian mulattoes . . . .

Before Haiti's independence, particularly during the time of slavery, Haitian mulattoes were subjected to the same conditions and held in the same opinion. Mistreated and scorned by their White fathers, who saw in them the sad fruits of an unfortunate union of pure Caucasian blood and degenerate African blood, they simply vegetated in the country like some parasitic species, living the lives of idle vagabonds or engaged in the harshest and most repugnant occupations. Knowing that they had in their veins a notable percentage of the same blood of which the *petits blancs,*[5] the White trash of the colony, were so proud, they let their hatred ferment in silence and their anger grow against those who had procreated them only to condemn them to a life of shame and misery. It was truly a horrible fate.

Most often, it is undoubtedly during some drunken moment or, rather, during one of those irresistible libidinous moments when the warm and balsamic tropical air would fire the blood of the European, that the master would draw to him in a criminal embrace the vivacious female slave's generous and graceful body. How long did those frenzied unions last? As soon as the White man sobered up, he would go away, leaving in the black womb of the Black African woman the seed of a being who would perhaps never know the name of his father. And the child would grow up alone, abandoned to the care of his poor Black mother for whom he would be only one more heavy burden, albeit a burden borne with love.

Forever chained in the darkness of ignorance, he will be tormented by his skin, too light for him to recognize himself in the sadly smiling black face of his loving mother, and too brown for him to ever reflect back to his father the latter's pink complexion, already so affected by the rough tropical sun and therefore particularly prized.

This painful position of the mulatto is not a product of the imagination. Time, which heals all wounds, is slowly erasing all memories of this situation, but it was a widespread reality . . . .

It is understandable that under the circumstances the mulatto, made envious, hateful, and degenerate by Caucasian injustice, but without any sense of solidarity with the African he avoids, could never rise to the most elementary ideas of progress and morality. A few exceptions could be found here and there, though. Without going so far as to recognize their paternity legally, a few White fathers took care of their offspring, raised them, and freed them from the yoke of slavery. The mulatto children of such fathers could have the benefit of an education and thus were able to develop their intelligence up to a point. But how many were there? Such men as Ogé, Chavannes, Julien Raymond,[6] and so many others, though they were not exactly high-flying eagles, were far from being ignorant. They provided sufficient proof of this by taking such active part in the vote on the Constitutional Assembly's decree granting equal civil and political rights to the men of color of Saint-Domingue. Yet, until the French Revolution came to inspire them to great thoughts and actions, their very existence was unknown . . . .

Since the old colony of Saint-Domingue became the independent nation of Haiti, a change has taken place in the mores and the intelligence of mulattoes. In the past, they had been vagabonds out of necessity. Without political rights, often living in slavery, how could they even think of cultivating those intellectual gifts which are the most precious of man's possessions. It was materially impossible. Even if they had had the possibility, they would have found it useless.

Human intelligence must find adequate stimulation if it is to be exercised and to reach its highest point of development. Obviously, constantly living in shame was not a very stimulating situation, and the burden was made even heavier as the mulattoes were conscious of the extent of their shame. Today, since 1804, in fact, the mulatto is master of his destiny. Proud and eager to show the whole world his considerable talents, which equal those of the Caucasian, the mulatto works hard and strives to develop his intellectual faculties. His successes in this regard are unchallengeable . . . .

So, are there several human species or is there only one? Does monogenism tell the whole truth? Or is the truth to be found, rather, in polygenism? What must the answer be?

Everything suggests that there is only one human species, if we understand the term as it is defined by most scientists. However, while admitting the unity of the species, we absolutely reject the separate idea of the unity of origin, Adamic or not, according to which all human beings descend from a single couple. This idea seems so contrary to reason and to the very history of our planet that it does not deserve discussion.

It is important then to distinguish between the unitarian theory and monogenism. The unitarian theory is a wholly scientific deduction based on the physical and moral qualities of the different human races, whose characteristics present no specific difference. Its conclusions are based on the evidence that the anatomical distinctions between the different human groups are easily explained by the influence of environmental factors and of other factors which we will discuss later. As for monogenism, it is an article of faith drawn from theological traditions, and its authority rests solely on a religious belief. We would have no reason to criticize the polygenists had they confined themselves to the purely etymological sense of the word by which they designate their theory and argued only that human beings do not all descend from a single ancestor or originate from a single geographical location, as averred in the Biblical tradition.

In any discussion, confusion arises always either because the points that need elucidation are not effectively presented, or because an ill-defined word is used wrongly or in a way that stretches its meaning. Thus, the unity of the human species is a clear and intelligible fact for anyone who studies it from the point of view of the natural sciences. But as soon as one brings in the word *monogenism*, one introduces unawares an arbitrary and non-demonstrable notion which considerably weakens whatever truth there is in the original fact. Unfortunately, most of the defenders of the unitarian theory are naturalists who are very much attached to religious ideas. They cannot separate the interests of faith from those of science, and to save the former, they compromise the latter . . . .

In fact, assuming that the human species appeared in several different regions on earth, there is nothing to suggest that it has not sprung everywhere with the same organic constitution, thus confirming the existence of a single blueprint which gives to each creation its typical character . . . .

Let us suppose that the species is the natural division *par excellence*, as all living beings complete their evolutionary cycle within it, with no possibility of stepping outside its boundaries. However, given that the species determines the limits of reproduction, by which organisms perpetuate themselves, we must also suppose that its serial constitution corresponds to a certain evolution of life on our planet and that the species entertains with the environment a relationship of direct dependence, which can logically be considered a relationship of cause and effect. As evolution occurred simultaneously or successively in several areas on earth, each species arose with a particular constitution that was much the same everywhere. Once that species came into being in its recognizable form, the various groups of its member individuals around the world continued to live in the particular places where they originated.

In time and under specific circumstances, conditions changed in those various milieus. From being originally absolutely similar, they then became different from one another. As environmental changes necessarily have an impact on living beings in a particular habitat, the individual members of a species were variously affected. But since the component groups of a species have, as it were, a uniform organic blueprint, they underwent only simple variations in forms, colors, and physiognomy.

Under the persistent influence of these same circumstances, a curious struggle took place. While heredity tended to maintain the general and primitive physiognomy of the species, the no less powerful principle of adaptation, joined with the self-preservation instinct, fostered the development of increasingly distinct physiological and psychological characteristics in the variety, including its capacity for resistance.

As can easily be imagined, at the end of a struggle of hundreds of thousands of years, as the primitive heredity continuously weakened, each group was able to acquire habits, physical characteristics, and forms which were sufficiently distinct and such an integral part of their very being that these became in turn a new heredity to be transmitted to their descendants. These facts are naturally consistent with the elegant laws of natural selection formulated by Darwin, even though the transformation occurs only within the limits of the species after its constitution . . .

Dispersed over areas at opposite ends of the earth, from which its constituent groups could sally forth only after reaching a certain level of development, our species is predictably as varied as its diverse habitats. In time, as these varieties perpetuated themselves, they became the principal races of humanity. But the inner constitution of these diverse races carries the proof of the unity of the species . . .

Let us now sum up the various logical conclusions that arise from the preceding discussions. The human species, with its unique original constitution and organic uniformity, which results from the fact that it is based on a single blueprint, appeared in various parts of the world, under strictly identical conditions, at a certain point in the evolution of life on this planet. However, the species later diversified into distinct peoples and races as soon as the climate began to affect markedly the various environments in the different ways it usually does. Primitive man, the first prototype of the species, was but the rough product of animal evolution, upward from the protozoan but still a far distance from his subsequent achievements. There must have been very little resemblance between him and the most advanced human populations of today. In terms of his physiognomy and his intelligence he was undoubtedly worse than the purest savage. He was simply a bestial creature.

Man had to go through a series of evolutionary steps before he could develop these attractive features that make of him not only the most elevated being in creation, but also the most beautiful product of nature. Whatever transformations the different human groups have undergone under various influences, they all retain the primordial, constitutional, imprint of the species, bearing the same intellectual and moral traits inscribed in the original common human blueprint . . . .

To embrace the concept of the unity of the species involves, through the exercise of a great keenness of mind, rejecting all the false ideas that the existence of diverse races might inspire and seeing, instead, only the essential characteristics that make of all human beings a community of beings capable of understanding one another and of joining their individual destinies into a common destiny. That destiny is civilization, that is, the highest level of physical, moral, and intellectual achievement of the species. There can be no greater and more salutary source of fraternal sentiments among the different races and peoples than such an understanding of the idea of the unity of the species.

It is the innate, essential, belief in this unity that makes man sacred to man, without one's having to invoke vague, irregular, and inconsistent notions of speculative morality, the foundations of which change according to the time and place. At this point, we consider the idea one of those primordial truths which serve as postulates to all social principles. The idea of the unity of the species elevates those principles, and its influence thus tends to attenuate competition and conflict within nations . . . .

The notion of a hierarchy of the human races, one of the doctrinal inventions of modern times or, rather, of the present century, will be seen some day as one of the greatest proofs of the imperfection of the human mind and of the imperfection, in particular, of the arrogant race that made it into a scientific doctrine . . . .

Artificial Ranking of the Human Races

Even though Monsieur de Gobineau,[7] a man of great learning but of little understanding and proven lack of logic, believes that 'the idea of an innate, original, profound, and permanent inequality among the races is one of the oldest and most widespread opinions in the world', no student of history would support such a notion. Throughout history, civilized peoples, self-centered and proud, have always thought themselves superior to their neighbors. But there has never been the least connection between this sense of superiority, which results from a narrow but highly respectable patriotism, and the notion of some systematic hierarchy among the human races . . . .

The division of humanity into distinct races, classified on the basis of the principles of the natural sciences, took roots as an intellectual notion only with the birth of ethnographic science. While ethnographic notions appear in flashes in serious works of history, the concept of race assumed its definitive meaning only with the works of eighteenth century naturalists, as mentioned earlier. In this case, is it not absolutely inaccurate to suggest that the idea of the original inequality of the human races is one of the oldest and most widespread opinions, especially when race is understood in the sense attributed to it by modern science?

The anti-philosophical and anti-scientific doctrine of the inequality of the races rests on nothing more than the notion of man's exploitation by man . . . .

It is impossible to find a people of any race that has ever developed higher aptitudes for civilization under conditions which are harmful or unfavorable to human culture. On the other hand, social history shows that every time a people has access to certain natural advantages in a favorable environment, that people always spontaneously evolves toward a better situation, their material achievements contributing further to their intellectual and moral development. They appropriate and develop new forces, which further transform not only their external world but also their inner being, as the physical and the moral interact and influence each other . . . .

Intellectual Evolution of the Black Race in Haiti

I will continue to focus my attention on Haiti and to seek in that country the examples I need in order to corroborate and justify the different propositions submitted earlier. I believe indeed that the small Haitian Republic, a shining buoy in the Antilles archipelago, will provide sufficient evidence in support of the idea of the equality of the races in all its ramifications. There mulattoes, *griffes*, all the different hybrids of Black and White, and Blacks themselves exhibit all the intellectual and moral aptitudes which arrogant and recklessly exclusionary Europeans have always recognized only in Caucasians . . . .

These men have worked heroically to check the pretension of the White man and challenge his claim to some putatively innate superiority over the Black man. The claim of course is groundless, but it has been internalized as dogma by most Europeans and it regulates all their relations with the children of Africa. Pure reason alone has never succeeded in compelling those sclerotic minds to reconsider their prejudices . . . .

White or Black, the human races are equal to one another. None received from nature a superior organism; none was granted special gifts denied to others. All physiological, intellectual, and moral differences among them are accidental and not organic, transitory and not permanent . . . .

Imagine the slave brought like some vile merchandise to foreign shores far away from his homeland; imagine him brutalized and broken before he could even lay his eyes on the new and unfamiliar land; imagine him beaten and bent under heavy burdens, ill-fed, and over-worked. The wonder is that such a humiliated creature, such a debased being, could have kept the least spark of intelligence, entertained the least will to freedom, felt the least modicum of that natural pride we feel, everyone of us, to know that we are the masters of creation.

For my part, I confess that I take great pride in my ancestors whenever I think about those miserable days of their infernal existence, when despite the floggings, the chains, and the back-breaking labor, they managed to conserve in their heaving chest the sacred fire that was to spark the epic explosion which would lead to our freedom and independence. But there is more. Barely two generations after the proclamation of the freedom of Blacks in Haiti, a tremendous transformation occurred in their very nature. Yet everything had seemed to condemn them forever to the constantly worsening state of inferiority to which their oppressors had reduced them . . . .

Despite the vigilance of slave owners, always ready to extinguish the divine spark of liberty in the Negro's soul, the secret of his triumphant strength before oppression, the miracle occurred when it was least expected. Taking advantage of the favorable climate created by the French Revolution, the enslaved Africans were soon transformed into heroes and rose up toward the sun of freedom.

Others have already recounted the glorious deeds by which our forefathers signaled to the world their heroic resolution to erase forever from the Haitian soil the least vestiges of slavery. In their memorable struggle for freedom they found inspiration in the most sublime thoughts which inspire men to great actions. We need not recall here the magnificent spectacle of a mass of slaves bent under the most odious oppression who are suddenly transformed into a formidable army of tireless, invincible soldiers who, like Pompey's legions,[8] would march from victory to victory. Never before had the world seen such beautiful élan among the downtrodden. The history of Haitian independence, the most moving, the most dramatic of histories, is replete with all sorts of facts which show most dramatically that nature has endowed the Black race with the best of dispositions. Indeed, the children of Africa in Haiti must have been blessed with unbounded perspicacity and adroitness . . . .

Outside of Haiti we find many more accomplished Blacks whose remarkable personality constitutes an eloquent protest against the obsolete and antiscientific doctrine of the inequality of the races. In the United States, in Liberia, in many small republics of South America and central America, countless Blacks of the most brilliant intelligence stand as proof of the natural equality of all the human races. Even in the African interior, there exist individuals whose powerful personality and intellectual acumen compare favorably with those of any Caucasian, taking into account the differences in environment and education. There is more than sufficient proof that wherever Blacks are organized in society, however elementary their political and religious organization might be, they show that they carry the seeds of all the great qualities, which need only the right conditions to grow and bloom. But the figure of Toussaint Louverture[9] obscures them all. The 'first among the Blacks' shall keep his chosen title, for none is more expressive or more appropriate. His glory is that of humanity as a whole, but it ennobles and fills with particular pride all the members of the African race whose marvelous aptitudes Toussaint so perfectly embodies . . . .

Beside the ancient Ethiopian-Egyptian race, is it possible to identify another Black nation, great or small, that has directly influenced by its achievements the social evolution of the civilized peoples of Europe and America? Without succumbing to the temptation of chauvinism, I must once again return to the Black race of Haiti. It is interesting to note the extent to which this small nation made up of descendants of Africans has influenced world history since its independence. Barely a decade after 1804, Haiti played one of the most remarkable roles in modern history . . . .

The great Simón Bolívar,[10] the liberator and founder of five South American republics, had failed in the great project, in which he succeeded Miranda in 1811, aimed at shaking Spanish domination and making independent the huge territories that were the pride of the Catholic king of Spain. His resources and supplies having been depleted, Bolívar went to Jamaica to beg the help of England, whose representative was the governor of the island. His request for help was rejected. Desperate and without means, he decided to journey to Haiti and to appeal to the generosity of the Black Republic to solicit the help he needed to continue the liberation struggle which he had started with such remarkable vigor but which had lately stalled. That was a moment of the greatest import for a man who embodied the destiny of the whole continent of South America . . . . He came to Haiti perhaps with a skeptical mind. But Alexandre Pétion, the president of the western part of Haiti, welcomed him with great warmth.

With all the caution and legitimate prudence required at this delicate juncture in our national existence, the Haitian government made available to the hero of Boyaca and Carabobo all the resources he needed. Bolívar needed just about everything, and he was generously given men, weapons, and money . . . . Bolívar left Haiti with the resources he needed, full of confidence in his genius and his great courage. The basic aspirations of his countrymen favored his undertaking; they were expecting, to manifest their support, only some bold move, some resolute action. So Bolívar orchestrated a heroic landing on the coast of Venezuela. After a victory over General Morillo who tried to stop his progress, Bolívar advanced from triumph to triumph until all the Spanish troops were expelled and the independence of Venezuela was proclaimed and solemnly celebrated in Caracas.

But the great Venezuelan did not stop there. He continued his campaign with an indefatigable vigor and drive. With the celebrated victory of Boyaca, he conquered the independence of New Grenada and merged its territory with Venezuela to form the Republic of Colombia, honoring by this name the memory of the immortal Christopher Columbus. Unable to rest on his laurels, he knew no respite until he could bring the whole enterprise to its conclusion. He assisted the inhabitants of Upper Peru as they went on, with the help of the Colombians led by General Sucre, to defeat the Spanish in a decisive battle near Ayacucho. He then proclaimed the independence of the Republic of Bolivia. His victory at Junin over the Spanish troops consolidated the independence of Peru and ruined Spain's colonial power forever . . . .

Thus, when we consider the influence exercised by Bolívar directly on a considerable part of the New World and indirectly on European politics, we must admit that the original decision of the government of the Haitian republic to assist the great Venezuelan leader in his enterprise did morally and materially determine a whole sequence of remarkable events.

Beside this example, which is one of the most beautiful actions for which the Black Republic deserves the whole world's esteem and admiration, we can say that the declaration of independence of Haiti has positively influenced the fate of the entire Ethiopian race living outside Africa. At the same time, Haiti's independence has affected the economic system and moral order of all the European powers that owned colonies. In addition, it had considerable bearing on the internal economy of all the American nations where slavery existed . . . .

The actions of the Blacks of Haiti indeed offered the most complete refutation of the theory according to which the Negro was a being incapable of grand and noble actions, incapable especially of standing up to White men. The greatest military feats of the Haitian war of independence had proved the courage and energy of our ancestors . . . .

Experience and observation led then to an irrefutable conclusion. The most intelligent statesmen, following the European philanthropists, came to understand that Black slavery was forever doomed. The very existence of the Black Republic was an overwhelming negation of the specious notion that served for so long to excuse slavery, namely, that Ethiopian man was congenitally incapable of behaving like a free man . . . .

In 1831, Richard Hill, a socially prominent free man of color in Jamaica, was sent to Haiti on an observation mission and asked to report on his impressions about the country. He took note, with satisfaction but also with impartiality, of the rapid progress made by the descendants of Africans in Haiti . . . . Improved knowledge of the reality of Haiti eventually bore fruit. In 1833, England abolished slavery in all its colonies.[11] In 1848, persuaded by the generous and courageous Victor Schoelcher,[12] the provisional government of France decreed a similar measure and had it inserted in the country's Constitution . . . .

It is no exaggeration to maintain, regardless of arguments to the contrary, that the Black race has a history that is as positive and as important as the history of all the other races. Neglected and for a long time falsified by the lie that made of the ancient Egyptians a White race, that history is re-emerging at the beginning of this century . . . .

Conclusion

Will the Black race some day play a prominent role in world history, picking up again the torch it had carried on the shores of the Nile to light up the way for the whole of humanity at the dawn of civilisation? I think I have sufficiently proven that it lacks nothing to assume such a role. Everything suggests indeed that it will undergo a new transformation from which it will emerge to cause human genius to shine as never before. With its first steps on the road to civilisation and freedom it showed such precocious aptitudes that we have every reason to believe and hope that it is destined to fulfill the highest of destinies . . . .

The Negro race, which has been martyred, scorned, discriminated against, brutalized, and systematically exterminated, would be justified to feel righteous anger and to dream of crushing its persecutors and its former oppressors. But its generosity will prevail, for the more one has suffered, the more one is prepared to understand and exercise justice. From the depths of intellectual and moral poverty in which they had been thrown by the combined effects of various prejudices, the race has emerged endowed with a virile courage and an ineffable kindness, twin virtues which tend to foster a tempered sense of justice.

No one today doubts the courage of Blacks, for history offers enough bloody examples to convince even the greatest skeptics . . . . To achieve equality, which is a natural and imprescriptible right, given that science has proven that no human race is superior to any other in terms of abilities, the Black race must ceaselessly aspire to conquer the moral and intellectual forces which alone guarantee equality among human beings. The race must grow in intelligence and morality. Only education and justice will ensure its triumph, for these are irresistible weapons in both social and international struggles . . . .

My wish is that this book will enlighten minds, inspire a sense of justice in all, and compel one and all to face reality. Perhaps European scientists, who are still convinced of the superiority of their race, will stop, think, and realize that they have been the victims of an illusion. The current state of the world, the myths and legends which had shaped their thought as children, the traditions that had continuously fed their intelligence, everything necessarily led them to a doctrine, to a set of beliefs, which appearances seem to justify. But can they persevere in a proven error without renouncing the exercise of reason, the greatest endowment of humanity? Will prejudice, the belief that a more or less white complexion is a sign of superiority, remain forever in the best minds despite the facts which prove its falseness? This cannot be, for reason shall always prevail . . . .

Returning to the truth, they will realize that human beings everywhere are endowed with the same qualities and defects, without distinctions based on color or anatomical shape. The races are equal; they are all capable of rising to the most noble virtues, of reaching the highest intellectual development; they are equally capable of falling into a state of total degeneration. Throughout all the struggles that have afflicted, and still afflict, the existence of the entire species, one mysterious fact signals itself to our attention. It is the fact that an invisible chain links all the members of humanity in a common circle. It seems that in order to prosper and grow human beings must take an interest in one another's progress and happiness and cultivate those altruistic sentiments which are the greatest achievement of the human heart and mind.

The doctrine of the equality of the human races, which consecrates these rational ideas, thus becomes a regenerative doctrine, an eminently salutary doctrine for the harmonious development of the species . . . .

NOTES

1. The Anthropology Society of Paris was founded by Paul Broca in 1859 and, under his leadership, its activities focused largely on racist interpretations of physical data, such as the relative size of human heads. Firmin was nominated to the society by two French physicians, Dr Ernest Aubertin and Dr Gabriel de Mortillet, and his fellow Haitian scholar Louis-Joseph Janvier (1855–1911). Contrary to the predominant views and practices of the society, Firmin based his method, which he called 'Anthropologie Positive', on the positivist tradition established by the French sociologist August Comte (1798–1857).
2. *Métis* are people of mixed racial origin, the result of the process called *métissage*.
3. Paul Broca (1824–80), a French surgeon and physical anthropologist, founded the Anthropology Society of Paris in 1859 and the School of Anthropology in Paris in 1876. He was the leading polygenist of his day.
4. *Griffes*, who were defined in Moreau de Saint Mery's classification as 24-39 parts white, would generally have darker skin and more curly hair than mulattos. Firmin generally used the term mulatto (*mulâtre*) to refer to any mix of 'white' and 'black'.
5. Although the *blancs* (whites) as a whole constituted a caste-like group in the colonial society of Saint Domingue they were divided by social class. The *petits blancs* (small whites), as distinct from the *grands blancs*, included small landowners, craftsmen, shopkeepers and employees.
6. Vincent Ogé, Jean Baptiste Chavannes and Julien Raimond were leading *affranchis*, or free coloured, members of the colony of Saint Domingue. Ogé and Chavannes were executed for rebellion in 1791 and Raimond was a spokesman for the free coloured planter elite.
7. Comte Arthur de Gobineau (1816–82), a French diplomat and philosopher, expounded a theory that claimed the white race was superior to all others. His most famous work, *Essay on the Inequality of Human Races* (1853–55), influenced Adolf Hitler, among others.
8. Pompey the Great (106–48 BC) was a Roman general whose legions conquered huge territories in the Middle East, including Armenia and Syria, and captured Jerusalem. He finally was defeated by his former ally, Julius Caesar, in 48BC.

9. Toussaint L'Ouverture (1743–1803), born of enslaved parents, became the leader of the revolution in Saint Domingue. Captured by the French, he died in prison in France. Today he is honoured as one of the principal founders of Haiti.

10. Simón Bolívar (1783–1830) is known as the Liberator because he was the principal leader of the struggle for South American independence from Spain. Born in Caracas, Venezuela, he fought against Spain under Francisco de Miranda in 1810. After his period of exile in Haiti, he led the invasion of Venezuela in 1817 and was elected its first president before moving on to defeat the Spanish and establish the republics of Colombia, Bolivia and Peru. His vision of a united independent South American nation was not fulfilled but he remains revered throughout Latin America.

11. The British parliament passed the act to abolish slavery throughout its colonies in 1833, but it did not take effect until 1834. Even then a system of coercion, called 'apprenticeship', continued until August 1, 1838.

12. Victor Schoelcher (1804–93), the son of a French porcelain manufacturer, encountered slavery first-hand when his father sent him to the Caribbean in 1829–30 in search of colonial outlets. He wrote accounts to a Paris magazine, describing slave markets and punishments, and advocating the gradual abolition of slavery. He became the leading French abolitionist and when he became a member of the revolutionary government of 1848, he organised emancipation. He fought against the coup of Louis Napoleon and was exiled from France in 1852.

Fifteen

Jean Price-Mars

Jean Price-Mars (1876–1969), a Haitian physician, statesman, diplomat, educator, and ethno-historian, was an influential critic of the elite's preference for French over Haitian culture. He is best known for his book Ainsi Parla l'Oncle (So Spoke the Uncle), published in 1928.

Haiti was the first nation in the Americas to become free and independent, in 1804, as the result of a revolution that overthrew slavery and colonialism. Consequently, the great and growing powers in the nineteenth century which continued to maintain and depend upon slavery, treated Haiti as a pariah rather than a sovereign state. The rulers of France, Britain and the United States felt threatened by the example of a nation of former slaves who had won their freedom by the sword. However, their merchants continued to do business even while the sovereignty of Haiti was unrecognised. France extended full recognition to its former colony in 1838 only after the Haitian rulers had agreed to pay a huge and crippling indemnity. The Vatican refused to establish formal ties with Haiti, although it was nominally a Catholic nation, until 1860 and this inhibited Haiti's acceptance by Latin American nations. And in the United States, which had recognised the newly independent states of Spanish America by 1822, Congress forbade trade with Haiti and recognition of Haiti was delayed until 1862 when the Union needed to import cotton to substitute for what could not be obtained from the southern states during the civil war. Haiti's enforced isolation hurt its economy and its ability to develop a formal education system, but it also meant that this largely peasant society could maintain its culture with little external influence. Haiti was a deeply divided nation, however, and the small Francophile elite *despised the black masses and tried to disassociate itself from their African-influenced culture.* When the United States occupied Haiti between 1915 and 1934 the social divisions, marked by persistent colour prejudice, huge economic inequalities and the cultural distinctions that largely coincided with them, inhibited any national unity against the occupation.

However, the US occupation did stimulate resistance. Rebellion in Port-au-Prince was quickly crushed but thousands of peasants, led by Charlemagne Péralte and Benoit Batraville, engaged in guerrilla warfare against US marines until 1920. Intellectual resistance was slower to develop but lasted longer. Some members of the elite had to reassess what it meant to be Haitian. Their pride in being lighter-skinned and well-educated in French culture was challenged by the occupying forces which considered them all to be simply inferior Negroes. Jean Price-Mars, more than anyone, rediscovered and reevaluated Haiti's cultural heritage and, 'for the first time, Africa, and not simply France, became an important part of the nationalist dialogue' (Mintz 1974, 288).

Price-Mars, when he was the head of Haiti's mission to the World's Fair in St Louis in 1904, travelled through the segregated south of the United States and experienced its virulent form of racism first hand. Between 1912 and 1915, as Inspector-General of Public Instruction, he called for textbooks that would be written for local children to replace the French texts they were using. The schools were teaching Haitians to think of their country as a cultural colony of France, but the culture of most people, particularly those in the countryside, was obviously not French. In July 1915, just before the US occupation, Price-Mars was appointed Haitian minister to Paris. After he returned in 1916, he commenced a series of lectures and conferences in which he urged the Haitian elite to act 'as Haitians', beginning with a reappraisal of their country's culture and historical heritage. These lectures were published in 1919 as La vocation de l'élite.

In December 1920, in a historic conference on Haitian folklore, Price-Mars discussed Vodou at length. 'By elevating the pride of Haitians in their folkloric past and racial competence, Price-Mars hoped to encourage a national spirit that would weld intellectual elites and illiterate peasants together and to inspire Haitians as a whole to resist oppression of any kind' (Shannon 1983, xi). Ainsi Parla l'Oncle was the culmination of these efforts to accept the contribution of the African past to contemporary Haitian culture. It launched a cultural nationalist movement by the indigénistes whose critique 'suggested that the elites' political failure stemmed in part from their contempt of Haitian popular culture' (Trouillot 1990, 131).

Price-Mars was Professor of History and Geography in the Lycée Alexandre Petion from 1918 to 1930 and founded the Haitian Historical and Geographic Society in 1922, serving as its president between 1932 and 1947. He was also a senator in the National Legislature from 1930 to 1935. In 1941, he founded the Institute of Ethnology and was its president and occupied the chair of Africology and Sociology until 1947. He was the head of many diplomatic missions to Europe, the United States and Latin America, and was ambassador to the Dominican Republic from 1947 to 1949. In 1956, he became Rector of the University of Haiti and was president of the First Congress of Black Writers and Artists in Paris. He was Minister of Foreign Affairs from 1956 to 1957 and ambassador to Paris from 1957 to 1959, when he became the first president of the African Society of Culture, an organisation created at the Second Congress of Black Writers and Artists in Rome. He continued to speak out and to publish, including a two-volume study of Haitian-Dominican relations. His last book, about Joseph Anténor Firmin (see chapter 14 in this volume), was published posthumously in 1978.

So Spoke the Uncle (excerpts)

What is folk-lore? . . . . the term folk-lore is composed of two Saxon words, 'folk-lore', literally folk meaning people, and lore meaning knowledge, that is: the lore of the people, the knowledge of the people[1] . . . .

In other words, has the Haitian society a stock of oral traditions, legends, tales, songs, riddles, customs, observances, ceremonies, and beliefs which are its own, or which it has assimilated in a way that gives them a personal imprint? . . .

[T]hey are the fundamental beliefs upon which have been grafted or superimposed other more recently acquired beliefs . . . .

[T]ales and legends have found in the Creole language an entirely unexpected manner of expression subtle and penetratingly acute.

And it is here that our capacity for assimilation and our adaptive ability are transformed into the power of creation.

Is Creole a language which can produce an original literature which will establish the genius of our race? Ought Creole to become some day the Haitian language just as there is a French language, an Italian language, or a Russian language? . . . .

In any event we will agree without difficulty that, such as it is, our Creole is a collective creation arising from the need of former masters and slaves to communicate their thoughts to each other. In consequence it bears the imprint of the vices and qualities of the human milieu and the circumstances which developed it; . . . . It is thanks to Creole that our oral traditions exist, are perpetuated and transformed, and it is through this medium that we can hope some day to bridge the gulf which makes of us and the people two apparently distinct and frequently antagonistic entities. . . .

Creole, for those who comprehend it, is a language of great subtlety. Virtue or fault, this characteristic derives less from the clearness of the sounds it expresses than from the unsuspected depth of the ambiguities that it insinuates by its innuendoes, by the inflection of the voice itself, and especially by the mimetic face of the speaker. Perhaps this is why the written Creole loses half the flavor of the spoken language; perhaps this is why the Haitian folk-lore has not blossomed as a written literature . . . .

No study seems more worthy of testing the ambition of an observer than that which embraces the whole of the psychological phenomena designated under the generic name of popular beliefs. Undoubtedly this includes many heterogenous elements, such as relics and amalgams of old customs whose secret meaning escapes us now . . . . After all, all of our popular beliefs rest upon authentic acts of faith which in the end are concretized in a religion which has its cult and its traditions . . . .

We have just said that the practices in question are actual beliefs and are embodied in acts of faith which imply adherence to a religion. What is this religion? Would it be *Voodoo*?[2] . . . .

Voodoo is a religion because all its adherents believe in the existence of spiritual beings who live anywhere in the universe in close intimacy with humans whose activity they dominate.

These invisible beings constitute an Olympian pantheon of gods in which the greatest among them bear the title of Papa or Grand Master and have the right to special hommage.

Voodoo is a religion because the cult appertaining to its gods requires a hierarchical priestly body, a society of the faithful, temples, altars, ceremonies, and finally a whole oral tradition which has certainly not come down to us unaltered, but thanks to which the essential elements of this worship have been transmitted . . . .

We are aware that this statement will bring quick objection. You are, no doubt, wondering what is the moral value of such a religion and, as your religious education is dominated by the efficiency of the Christian moral philosophy, you use that as your standard of judgment. In the light of such rules you can only dutifully condemn Voodoo as a religion, not only because you reproach it for being immoral but, more logically, because you frankly declare it amoral. And since it is not known how an amoral religion can exist, you cannot accept Voodoo as a religion. Ah! Such an attitude would be worse than an intellectual injustice, it would be a negation of intelligence . . . .

Just how did Voodoo come to us?

Unquestionably from Africa. *Africa* however implies a geographic location that is much too large for this word alone to suffice as a precise response to the concerns that absorb us. For the question is nothing less than knowing whether Voodoo spread as a concrete religion through the entire thirty million square kilometers of the old continent or whether it was confined within limited areas. This is what we are going to examine.

Let us hasten to say that nothing is more difficult to ascertain in the present state of African ethnography. However, insofar as our investigations have enabled us to further the study of mores and customs of the people of the black continent, it seems that we have found here and there, over all of African land and among the people who live there, some rites of worship which are similar though not completely identical to the rites of Voodoo . . . .

There exists in such a center as Dahomey some spiritual representations called *Vodoun* while, under varying designations, other African countries offer us quite similar beliefs derived from the same psychological base. So, if in Saint Domingue[3] these diverse beliefs, represented by followers belonging to tribes differing in their degree of civilisation and indeed in their physical structure, have received the common designation of *Voodoo*, just as we included them all ethnographically under the classification of Negro, it is due to two causes, one of a psychological nature and one of a linguistic order . . . .

Negroes – whatever their tastes, beliefs, or aptitudes – were forced to receive instruction in order to be baptized in the Catholic religion within the week after their debarkation at Saint Domingue. We are even able to affirm that one of the first surprises which greeted the African on the threshold of entering the New World was the demonstration of violence by which he was forced to acknowledge other gods than he had known and who seemed to be outraged and were threatening him with immediate or eventual suffering . . . .

As for the Negroes, the forced Christianization to which they were subjected, gave them a pretext for distracting their adversaries and stealing a bit of Freedom from their daily harsh labor . . . .

But the baptismal ceremony was, for most of the neophytes, an occasion of feasting and reveling with their chosen godfathers and godmothers. This is why the Negroes quickly devised the dodge of having themselves baptized more than once so that they could have several opportunities for fun. It is obvious merely through this fact that the new religious state of the slave was only a facade; that his fundamental beliefs were only slightly shaken by his official conversion and remained unchanged in the mysteries of his infrangible consciousness. His beliefs had to remain all the more mysterious in order to withstand the pressures of the law and of the human surroundings. But we are well aware of the resilient power of which any belief is capable that is supported by the whole mass of time-honored sentiment. It plunges its roots into the unfathomable depths of the subconscious all the more tenaciously as it is constrained to dissimulate itself.

Such was the psychological situation in which the Sudanese of the bush, the forest-dwelling Congolese and all the rest found themselves when, tormented by oppression, they were forced to make an ostentatious show of Christianity and to repress their secret adoration of obscure forces to which they felt bound by long ancestral traditions. It is natural that these people under such circumstances should feel united each time that a sudden emotion, a secret gesture, an act of piety revealed the persistence of beliefs within them which, if not identical, had many more similarities among them than they had with those of the masters who were so detested by all, whatever the origins, the customs, and the habitat of each before deportation to and servitude in the foreign land. Thus we have an explanation for and can understand the organization of secret societies which held nocturnal meetings in the depths of the forest for the free exercise of cults whose existence has been recorded since the first days of colonial administration.

Without doubt these assemblies eventually assumed a genuinely political character, but one can affirm that they pertained to worship in the beginning. They created in the course of time an imperative obligation sustained by severe sanctions and thus maintained the existence of a truly religious community, new in many respects, daughter of the milieu and of the needs of the moment. This is very likely, it seems to us, the probable origin of *our* Voodoo. It is pre-eminently a syncretism of beliefs, a compromise of the animism of the Dahomeans, the Congolese, the Sudanese, and others. By being able to assimilate the modalities of all these varieties of beliefs to the point of giving them an apparent unity of rites and customs under a common denomination, it essentially did recapitulate within itself the essence, the substratum of all the other cults and was furthermore the form most comparable to the religious traditions of the tribes disseminated from northern Guinea to Cape Lopez, including the Grain Coast, the Ivory Coast, and the Gold Coast, the kingdom of the Ashanti, of Dahomey, and so forth . . . , and extending from the coastal regions into the hinterland, to the Sudanese plateau, as far as 20° north latitude. . . .

Moreover, Voodoo was readily diffused among the members of all the tribes wherever the beliefs were related as well as where the dialect was more or less similar. Now, the greatest number of Negroes imported to Saint Domingue belonged to the linguistic family of the Bantus or that of the Mandingos.

Which language of these two groups, Mandingo and Bantu, prevailed among the plantation Negroes?

We would surmise that it was the Bantu, not only because it constitutes the linguistic group which occupies the greatest part of inhabited Africa extending from one ocean to the other and from the upper basin of the Nile and of Lake Chad down to the Orange, but also because the slave traffic was most fruitful among these people that spoke only one tongue, the Bantu. We have corroboration of this in a large number of historical documents. Moreau de St. Méry[4] tells us that most Negroes in the colony were from the coast of the Congo and Angola, that is, that they were taken from an area between Cape Lopez and Cape Négre, which was close to three hundred leagues in a straight line. They belonged beyond all question to the linguistic group of the Bantu. And among the qualities that St. Méry recognized about them and which marked them particularly for domestic service was their great ability to speak Creole with ease. Therein lies one of the most characteristic causes of the power of the Africans to adapt to their new milieu.

For this precious faculty of assimilation enables us to understand the reason why Creole rapidly absorbed the diverse African dialects, including the Mandingo, since the most important group numerically had made it, like the masters themselves, the surest means of communication. And this explains equally why so few words of African origin, deformed or pure, have survived in our present Creole. Would the word *Voodoo* be an African survival or is it a Creole term? . . . .

There exists on the coast of Guinea a little country called Dahomey, of little importance if we compare its diminutive territorial extent to the area occupied by the Bantu, but exceedingly enterprising through the power of its military organization until conquered by the French. In Dahomey there is a religion with a structure made of the same elements as our *Voodoo*. In Dahomey certain deities, the *Spirits*, are generally called *Vôdoun*, and . . . it is curious how one finds in certain formal rituals, almost word for word, the most common expressions in the 'language' of our Voodoo adherents . . . .

But by what process were a handful of men, tied to the same ignominy, bent under the same yoke of infamy, able to exercise a sort of domination over the rest of the group to the point of leading it to embrace some of the rites and forms of the Dahomean religion? This is what we will attempt to demonstrate.

Let us remember henceforth that it is highly probable that the forms of incantation, of chants, of prophesy in which the same words often were repeated, engraved themselves on the minds of the sect followers as much as on those of the occasional spectators; that these forms have lost their peculiar meaning little by little in past ages to the point that those who repeat them at the present time are totally ignorant of their original sense; that in the end it was at this moment of colonial life that the term was adopted which defined the syncretism of beliefs and at the same time gave concordance to the religious rites and dances of the slaves of Saint Domingue; that if for more than a century we found no reference authenticating the term 'Voodoo' . . . . we should recall that the colonial world, in Saint Domingue as well as in the other French islands, did not begin to take umbrage at the religious demonstrations of the slaves until they seemed to become the symbol of revolt around 1740–1750. We know that this was the time when a great many slaves escaped into the hills and the mysterious drum summoned numerous nocturnal meetings . . . .

It was the power of faith which led Negroes to martyrdom. It was at the same time the supreme guide which compelled them to accept the discipline ordered by the ringleaders. You see, these commanders did not exercise just religious authority.

Because of the audacity and energy of their action, they wielded political and religious power simultaneously. Thus they were in the position of provoking and of accomplishing the ruin of the regime through the double mystical influence that they exercised over their followers. From this proposition follows a logical outcome. Only those among the conspirators who had been known in their tribes as leaders of people and doctors of the faith offered the greatest guarantee in the eyes of their co-religionists. The Dahomeans answered both criteria. It is therefore highly probable that they served as leaders in these political and religious movements and that it was through their influence that the term *Voodoo* (the Spirit) has been attributed to the whole religious manifestation of the slaves because the word conveyed the essence of their beliefs and embodied all the nuances of African animism. Therein it seems to us lies the double genesis and the evolution of African beliefs that we designate as Voodoo . . . .

What seems certain to us is the fundamental unity of Negro animism, despite its apparent morphological diversity. Whether one studies it on the Sudanese plateau where it is sometimes influenced by the probable contribution of foreign elements, whether one considers it as a religion of the State in certain social organisms, such as the Mossi, or better yet in its harsh form on the western coast in Dahomey, African animism may be summed up in a few very simple propositions: 1st, each man is composed of a double personality, one physical, tangible, material – the body; the other, intangible, immaterial, embodied in the first as its animator – the soul; 2nd, death is the operation by which these two elements are broken apart – the soul is separated from the body . . . .

The Dahomeans possess a system of theogony in which we notice, first of all, their belief in a Supreme Being, *Mahou* or *Sê, Intelligence*. Mahou is the creator of the heavens and of earth.

If they invoke him at times as if to give witness of his supremacy over every visible thing, the Dahomeans, as most of the other black peoples, do not translate their veneration of the supreme god into a tangible worship. Mahou is too highly placed to attend to human beings; in return, humans are not troubled if they do not reach him. Besides there is no way to do so. They believe that Mahou cannot be approached through their prayers, their sacrifices, and their offerings and they feel that he is indifferent to things immediate to this world. But, below him, on another level, there is another category of divine beings, derived from him and upon which he has bestowed omniscience and complete power. These are the Spirits, the *Vodoun*. Nothing on the earth or in the heavens happens without their participation. Their wrath arouses fear and their benevolence spreads over all who merit it. It appears that Mahou expresses his will through the Vodoun: *Vodoun e gui Mahounou, the Spirit is a thing (a creature)* of God. The Vodoun are embodied in human beings whom they use to make known their wishes as well as in natural phenomena which represent manifestations of their anger, vengeance, and power.

There are Vodoun of the sea, rivers, mountains, sky, earth, thunder, wind, smallpox, and so on . . . It is the divinization of natural forces and phenomena as a whole dynamic process. Outside these diverse incarnations, Vodoun are sometimes devoted to the protection of a city, a tribe, or a family. As such they may dwell in a famous or sacred place, may assume the material or symbolic form of a rock or an eponymic animal; they may personify the ancestral totem of a family. Thus the *Tô-Vodoun* are the protective spirits of certain collectivities and reside particularly in trees, bushes, or rocks and are venerated in the places where they have revealed their presence and their power. The *Ako-Vodoun* or *Hennou-Vodoun* personify the ancestral founders of such tribes and receive pious homage . . . .

In the nomenclature which we have just given, we have only included (except for Mahou) divinities of a dynamic character, the protective deities of collectivities as families, cities, and tribes. To these categories we must add *Legba* and *Fa* who play a particular role in the Dahomean theogony. They are personal gods . . . .

To all these divinities, to their symbols, to their multiple and varied incarnations, the Dahomeans dedicate a public worship which is completely organized. In order to conserve tradition and to resolve theological difficulties, there exists a hierarchical priestly body composed of four categories: the *Vodoûn-non*, the *Houn-so*, the *Vodoun-si*, and the *Vodoun-legbanon*.

The *Vodoûn-non* (*non* meaning embodied in him, he possesses *Vodoûn*, the spirit) is the high priest and the principal sacrificer. He is the supreme depositary of the wishes of the divinity. He lives in the sacred enclosure where the temple is built. He is the one who instructs disciples in the sacred and esoteric language (formed from the early Dahomean). Through tradition, he knows the virtue of plants, prayers, and incantations. He alone sacrifices at the altars. For any ceremony outside the temple, he invests his minister the *Houn-so* with special authority by which he confers upon him the privileges attached to the exercise of his high office, *Houn-so e so Houn, il porte l'esprit* (meaning, he is the transitory agent of the spirit). For in the ceremonies of worship, his role as Houn-so consists of dancing some ritual steps while carrying the sacrificial victim on his shoulders. Then the spirit descends upon him to sanctify his gestures and his action.

The Vodoun-si are the apprentices, the scholars destined for service to the divinity. They are instructed under special conditions by the high priest and live in the sacred enclosure until the end of their studies.

Finally, the Legba-non (*non*, signifying embodied in him, he possesses) is the individual who is possessed with the spirit of Legba. In the religious dances he performs the role of an obscene buffoon.

That is, in a few words, what makes up the priestly organization. One will easily understand the exceptional importance which these personnages enjoy if he remembers that their theological science is not to be found in any sacred book, but is transmitted from age to age by oral tradition, that it assumes ipso facto an esoteric character, and that initiation is obtained only through procedures which submit their nervous systems to ordeals of extreme severity . . . .

The Religious Sentiment of the Haitian Masses

All Haitians are Christian, Catholic, Apostolic, and Roman. In the large cities and more rarely in the country, there are also some followers of reformed religions – Baptists, Adventists, Methodists, Wesleyans – who form an active and zealous minority.

One is correct, however, in assuming that the authenticity of the above proposition is of little relevance. And if we needed to be convinced of this fact, it would be sufficient to recall to mind the mode of social and ethnic formation of the Haitian nation which has had a logical repercussion on the development of religion.

We know, do we not, what elements have produced the Haitian society. We know how gangs of slaves imported from the immense expanse of the western coast of Africa to Saint Domingue presented as a whole a microcosm of all the black races of the continent. We know how the promiscuity of the white and of his black concubine, how the unauthorized conditions of a society governed by the caste system, gave birth to an intermediate group between masters and the captive mass. We know, furthermore, how the conflict of interests and passions, how the confrontation of egoisms and principles created by the revolutionary mystique, precipitated the revolt which led the former slaves to found a nation . . . .

In the glow of the conflagration that enflamed the former colony, the basic system was broken up, dismembered. But, by nature, social phenomena are rather irrepressible. The will of man condensed in legal texts, translated into administrative measures is for the most part powerless to alter their free development. Violence itself which disrupts the arrangement, only masks its irreducibility all the more. Thus, despite the severity of bloody battles which revolutionary factions undertook on our soil and which generated a transformation of the colonial social status, despite the successive upheaval which led to the ruin of the old regime and the advent of the new nation, one is astonished to find that the change has been more apparent than real, that it was realized much more on the surface than in depth, that the mutations were brought about in a displacement of political power which slipped from the hands of the white aristocracy to those of the sangs-mêlées[5] and the black populace. But again, there was only a substitution of masters. As radical as this change of regime appeared to be, it was only accomplished through a monopoly of public authority by an audacious and energetic minority. In fact, the social system remained unchanged. The possession of large seigneurial estates which was the principal mark of power and fortune, preserved its age old traditional meaning. The great planters of the past were simply dispossessed by the new political leaders who gave themselves these privileges and prerogatives with a certain prudence consistent with unpredictable conditions in the public life.

As for the common people in whose name the creation of the principle of equality had been proclaimed, it was considered expedient to testify to their participation in the new order of things by assigning to each the right to vote and the possession of a few acres of land. But, confined by economic necessity to the task of producing without a supply of tools and technical knowledge, reduced to the cultivation of small and isolated farms, their situation, in a century of liberty and political independence, is that of servitude minus the presence of the Code Noir[6] and the whip of the commander. Yet the moral philosophy remained quite unscathed since the magic formula – liberty, equality, and fraternity – was inscribed on the facade of the reconstructed edifice. But, for the one who is not reluctant to raise the veil of appearances, the Haitian society of the present time closely resembles the one from which it issued. We know that the arrogant vanity of our elite forces them into an obstinate and fierce denial of this. The elite closes his eyes to the evidence. He has only to note, however, the demographic development of our people in order to realize how vain is his stupid claim that he alone typifies the whole Haitian society. For the bourgeoisie, as they exist now, are no more than a symbol. Having fallen from their historic role as leaders of the nation because of inertia, cowardice, or failure to adapt, although they still illustrate through their thinkers, artists, and industrial chiefs the height of intellectual development to which a part of the society has risen, yet by shirking their duty to mix with the rest of the nation they exercise only a sort of mandarinate which weakens and atrophies more each day. But even if they have lost their grand vocation of leadership, they should jealously guard their role as representatives of our intellectual potentialities . . . .

As for the Haitian peasants, or the modern descendants of the Negroes of Saint Domingue, we believe we have shown at what state of colonial servitude that compulsory Christianization was conferred on them en mass as supreme justification of the regime. We dwelt upon the ineffectiveness of the initiation rites performed under such conditions, given that they were not acts of spontaneous acceptance by the neophytes. Besides, they were no more than an occasion for feasting and revelry since they would justify certain hours of respite from the constraint of labor. We indicated, at length, how these unpolished souls remained attached to their primitive faith despite everything and we followed them to the moment where, because of the revolutionary crisis, their ancestral beliefs became the leaven of the revolt against odious oppression. It is truly during the beginning of these troubled times, at the nocturnal meetings in the woods that the Haitian cult called *vaudou* was organized. But of what did this cult consist? . . .

Heavy prejudice prevented seeing anything other than superstition in all religious sentiment among Negroes which was not an act of Christian devotion . . .

At . . . around 1760, the religion of the slaves had not yet received any particular name . . .

The unconscious force of syncretism, however, operates silently and less than thirty years later we will find under the name of 'Vodou' a religious manifestation which Moreau de St-Méry was the first to analyze in detail. This analysis grew famous and became the theme, amplified and plagiarized, for most of the accounts which have been made of the cultic ceremonies of 'Vodou' by writers who have not even had the opportunity to observe them.

The author of the *Description de la parti française de Saint Domingue* first points out the external conditions of the worship – the decor. The ceremony requires the complicity of darkness and unfolds only in an exclusive spot safe from any indiscretion. 'There, each initiate puts on a pair of sandals and places around his body various numbers of red or predominantly red handkerchiefs. The Roi Vaudoux has more and finer handkerchiefs with a completely red one encircling his forehead as a diadem. A twisted cord, generally blue, completes the mark of his eminent office'. For there is a King and a Queen of Vaudoux who exercise the most effective influence over the faithful of the cult. They preside over the ceremonies and order the ritual. They are themselves the interpreters of the divinity and this divinity is no other than the grass snake . . . .

But through what medium is this communication obtained? Might it be that the grass snake has recovered the privilege of using the human language as of old in the Garden of Eden? . . .

No, the times have changed. It concerns an infinitely more subtle operation, it is a question of nothing less than a spiritual incarnation, as we shall see.

'The King and the Queen take their place at one end of the room near a sort of altar on which is a box where the serpent is kept and where each follower may see it through some wooden bars.

'When it has been confirmed that no prying persons have penetrated the place, the ceremony begins with the worship of the grass snake, with assurances of being faithful to him and of submitting to all that he will prescribe. Each renews the oath of secrecy, the fundamental principle of the association, before the King and Queen, and this act is accompanied by the most frightful frenzy imaginable in order to make it more impressive'. All this is only the outward aspect of the ceremony – we mean that part which demonstrates the profound influence of the faith – the trust which unites the faithful with his god.

A counterpart remains, the rite which shows the god becoming incarnate in his representative and being identified with him. Here accordingly the followers of the cult have rendered homage to the divinity, each has placed at the foot of the altar his offerings and his prayers, each has murmured the wish of realizing that for which he longs by invoking the almighty power of the god. It is the propitious moment for supernatural intervention.

'During all of these invocations, the Roi Vaudoux mediates, the Spirit moves in him. Suddenly, he takes the box which contains the snake, places it on the ground, and has the Reine Vaudaux stand on it. As soon as the sacred sanctuary is under her feet, instantly pythoness, she is imbued with her god, she becomes disturbed, her whole body shakes uncontrollably, and the oracle speaks through her lips.

'At times she is soothing and promises happiness, at times she thunders and bursts into reproaches, and at the whim of her desires, self-interest, or caprices, she dictates as final laws anything it pleases her to prescribe, in the name of the grass snake, to the simple flock which will never have the least thought of objecting to the preposterous nonsense and will only obey what is despotically prescribed for them.

'After all the questions have led to some sort of response from the Oracle, who is also somewhat ambiguous, a circle is formed, and the snake is replaced on the altar'.

This is the first act of the drama.

The second, which intensifies it and augments its value, follows immediately. This is the dance.

'If there is a new member, the dance is opened with his admittance. The Roi Vaudoux traces a large circle with a dark substance and places within it the person who wishes to be initiated and puts in his hand a small packet of herbs, coarse hair, kernels of corn, and other such revolting objects.

'While tapping him on the head with a small flat piece of wood, he intones an African song . . . . which those who surround the circle repeat in chorus, and then the new member begins to shake and dance what is called *monter vaudoux*. If he becomes carried away by his frenzy and steps by chance outside the circle, the chant ceases immediately, and the King and Queen *Vaudoux* turn their backs to dispel the omen. The dancer regains control of himself, reenters the circle, becomes agitated again, drinks, and finally reaches a convulsive state which the Roi Vaudoux regulates by tapping him on the head with his wooden paddle or spoon, or even by a blow of a bull lash if he deems it appropriate. He is led to the altar to take an oath and from this moment on he belongs to the sect.

'The ceremony is finished. The King puts his hand or foot on the box containing the snake and soon he is moved. He communicates this sensation to the Queen and, through her, the agitation spreads circularly and everyone experiences movements in which the upper part of the body, the head and shoulders seem to become disjointed. The Queen especially is a prey to the most violent agitations; from time to time she goes near the grass snake to renew the spell; she shakes his box and the little bells that adorn it, creating the effect of the cap and bells of the fool; the delirium grows. It is augmented further by the use of spirituous liquors which the initiates do not use sparingly in the ecstasy of their imagination and which helps, in turn, to sustain it. Exhaustion and fainting fits overcome some and a sort of fury overcomes others but within all there is a nervous agitation that they cannot seem to control. They whirl themselves about unceasingly. And while there are some who, in this kind of bacchanalia, tear their clothing to pieces and even bite themselves, others who have only lost their senses and fallen on the spot are carried, while the dancing goes on, into a neighboring room . . . . '

This page of Moreau de St. Méry, in our eyes, is of primary importance not only because it is the only authentic document which contains substantial data on the religious manifestations of the Negroes of Saint Domingue but also because in the abundance of details, the precision of references, and the general expression one immediately recognizes the stamp of authenticity. Although the author tells us that the sect was a secret one – and it still is in our time [1928] – his report to us leaves the impression that he was an eye witness . . . . They appear to us to constitute the fundamental elements of Voodoo.

The most characteristic of these traits is the state of *trance* into which the individual possessed by the god is plunged . . . .

The second trait which imparts tonality to the ceremony is the dance, a dance made rhythmic by the sound of a trio of tall drums to the cadence of the *assons* [sacred rattles], performed according to the syncopated tunes improvised by a leader whose voice is echoed by an enraptured audience...

May we be permitted to point out that these three elements: the *dance*, the *ecstasy*, and the *sacrifice* did form or do form the most persevering parts of religious rites and that we experience them, either joined together or separately, in the most exalted religions . . .

But Music and Dance equally condition another manifestation of religious sentiment, the study of which offers a scientific interest of the first order.

This concerns the ecstasy, the trance, or possession . . .

In every case, the state of trance, ecstasy, or possession appears as a delirium in which the delirious idea is characterized by a form of hallucination.

In the cult of Voodoo, this delirium has received various names.

In the West and in the South of the Republic, an individual tormented by this crisis is said to be possessed by his *loi*[7] of his *mystère*, in the North, that he is *monté par les Anges ou les Saints*. It is well understood that the terminology is not absolute or exclusive, that it is interchangeable in any part of the country. For in the end, to have *his loi* or *his mystère, to be mounted by the Angels or Saints* signifies merely the possession by a spirit which dominates you and dictates his will to you. We will note, by the way, that these expressions have borrowed from the French as well as some Catholic terminology. Does not obeying the *laws* of the Church, humbling oneself before the *Mystères* of Religion, performing one's devotion *to the angel and saints* of Paradise, form part of the teaching of the Church? The fact that the Voodoo cult uses its own terms to convey one of the essential modalities of the faith is not as banal as one might believe. It denotes one of the forms of influence exercised by Catholicism on the evolution of Voodoo . . . .

The Haitian people are preoccupied with the 'loi' or the 'mystère' of Voodoo to an indescribable degree.

The believers see it as a proof of the supernatural character of the cult and they are unperturbed by this.

The others – and these form the greatest number – grant freely that while these phenomena do not reveal rational explanations, they are not to be included whatsoever in the ensemble of demoniac acts condemned and prohibited by the Church . . . .

Nevertheless the greatest, the most vibrant aspect of the voodooistic arrangement is not the ecstasy. One would be still less likely to search for it in majestic hommages rendered to deified natural Forces. It resides almost entirely in the imperative fulfillment of sacrifice. Worship can dispense with choreographic meetings, with orgiastic festivities, with the display of nocturnal and processional pageantry, but whatever the social or legal contention may be for holding it, it positively confirms itself through the ritual obligation of the sacrifice. But why is the sacrifice the mainstay of worship? To what does it correspond? What is its proper significance?

It is difficult to condense the complex ritual included in the term sacrifice into a formula. It would be necessary to comprehend therein the idea of oblation, of mystical communion, of reverential hommage, of participation of the faithful in the life of the god or intercommunication between the profane and the sacred worlds. Each of these aforesaid considerations envisage an aspect of the rite, and together they bring about a sacrifice so rich in content that it expresses the general sense and the perfect symbol of the ceremony . . . .

In the cult of Voodoo, sacrifice assumes several forms. It is fulfilled in acts of thanksgiving to the gods for their attention, their benevolence toward the sacrificer, individual or group. It is an act of expiation to appease the wrath of the divinity irritated by some voluntary or unconscious offense the effects of which have been translated into calamities of all sorts: maladies, sorrows, unsuccessful enterprises, and so forth. It is manifested by annual hommage in compliance with family tradition which if overlooked could engender misdeeds against the individual or family. It is the communal feast in initiation ceremonies where consecrations to the Priesthood take place and where the sacrificer is accorded participation in mysterious forces through which he acquires supernatural powers of invisibility, invulnerability, success in his affairs, and so forth. It is a pledge or a pact with the Invisibles in the fulfillment of which both sides find benefits and satisfactions. It is a duty toward the dead whose existence in the supraterrestrial world would be disturbed if people neglected to accord it to them and who, to avenge themselves, would return to the living the pains and torments that could have been spared them.

We do not claim to enumerate all the aspects of the voodooistic sacrifice . . . .

It would appear to us that in this fundamental area a syncretism took place whose principal factors are easily disclosed.

Just as Dahomey has supplied us till now with the most notorious structural elements of Voodoo, so we have also observed that the cult has made impressions elsewhere.

We find ourselves confronting an analogous situation as to the functional arrangement of the voodooistic sacrifice. Let us say immediately that this concerns a form of rite that has come directly to us from the Guinean region and which quite specifically bears the Dahomean imprint. This is the agrarian sacrifice *du manger yam* [of eating yam] with a tradition that is slowly being corrupted and obliterated. It exists now as no more than a symbol with its meaning expressed by the annual obligation of Voodoo adherents to conduct some sort of ritual oblation under pain of severe penalty, immediately or in the future, directly or indirectly against responsible transgressors of the pact . . .

The symbolism of this rite is so apparent that there is no need for explanation. It accepts the ancient, universal belief that the earth and its fruits, the seasons and their rhythm belong to the mystical cycle of things to which man owes reverence and homage as a token of piety toward the Divinity who is the giver and creator of these movements.

Homage, for the primitive man, becomes concrete in an offering of the first fruits – the first fruits of the harvest and of the hunt, of the first-born of man and of beast, the improper consummation of which could be detrimental to the well-being of the individual or community . . .

But the ecstatic delirium, the ritual sacrifice, the liturgical dance express only a part of the Voodoo complex or at any rate the cultic expression of which they are the coordinated elements has given us so far only a modest figurative representation of the problem in its entirety according to the explanation we have given in the course of this study.

Its content is richer in psychological synthesis. It has assimilated other ideas, it has assumed disparate principles, it has undergone transformations, it has submitted to productive compromises in its historical evolution. This is what we will bring out while considering more closely the role played by the ideas, the ceremonial of the Catholic Church in the ascendancy of souls already shaped or simply moved by voodooistic dynamism.

For one of the most startling and certainly the most curious aspects of Voodoo, is its association with Catholicism in the present-day faith of the Haitian masses.

The confrontation of the two beliefs goes back quite far in the course of time dating from the remote period when the Portuguese planted the cross on the western coasts of Africa and catechised a good number of pagans on the shores of the Congo as far as the active period of the slave trade undertaken in the name of religious proselytism by His Very Christian Majesty. Is this not what Saint-Méry means to denounce when he speaks of the Catholicism of the Congolese mixed with idolatry and Islamism? In any case, at Saint Domingue, the justification of colonial enterprise implied total and obligatory conversion in the terms we have already precisely stated. Most certainly many elite spirits were transfigured by the Christian miracle and remained active proselytes in the recruitment of the new cult . . .

On the other hand, if the savage battles which inaugurated the demand for the rights of man at Saint Domingue were expressed in the explosion of 1791 by a wholly voodooistic ceremony – the oath of blood – if, during the thirteen years of violence, of privations, of torture, the Negroes drew from their faith in African gods the heroism which permitted them to confront death and achieve the miracle of 1804 – the creation of a Negro nation in the Antilles – it is strange indeed to note how vigorously the leaders, in the dawn of victory, declared war upon the old ancestral beliefs.

As early as 1801 Dessalines,[8] inspector general of culture for the Department of the West, learning that there had been a voodooistic ceremony somewhere on the plain of the Cul de Sac, led a battalion from the eighth regiment to the place and put fifty of the followers to the sword. A rather harsh display of police action. This was the first official repression of creed as a misdemeanor. Later the Charter,[9] having declared Catholicism as the official religion, assured it the official protection of the State. The Penal Code specified superstition as an offense. Since then, the secular authority has arrogated to itself the right to punish any action attacking the orthodoxy of the official form of worship. And so the old primitive religion of the Negro, outlawed, persecuted as the undesirable legacy of a shameful past and as inadequate for the new political status of the Haitian citizen, searched in the obscurity of consciences and in the darkness of the *hounforts* [Voodoo temples] to adapt itself to the new state of affairs. The traditions of the African cult became difficult to preserve in this conscious or unconscious effort to assimilate.

People began to search not only for ritual analogies between the two religions, but also to identify the deities of Voodoo with the principle saints of the Church.

They went so far as to prescribe an identical practice of sacraments in the two cults in order to be entitled to the favor of the gods of Voodoo. As for the minor devotions such as the wearing of scapulars, votive offerings, novenas, the use of candles, requiem masses, and so on, these were found to be functionally useful in the ritual ordinances prescribed by the *Hougan* to his followers because they harmonized readily with the most intimate tendencies of Voodoo. And a slow, subtle transformation began in the very foundations of the ancient belief. And now, it no longer rests alone on the latent or formal spiritual power that is in every being and phenomenon of our universe, it no longer implores the Natural Forces endowed with consciousness and will, rather *it teaches that the world is governed by a Supreme Being who delegates his power to intermediary spirits to whom it is necessary to pay homages [sic] and reverences. It says that men are not merely made of flesh and bone, they are also composed of a soul, which, beyond death and in spite of its imponderability, has need of the assistance of the living to fulfill the other condition, unknown, unsuspected, of its supraterrestrial existence. If the living were to fail in this task, the souls would not only be tormented on high, but would descend down here to torment the living.*

Such are the two poles of the new belief. So, since they are in accordance with the Catholic orthodoxy on a great many points, it is not surprising that the festivals of the Roman calendar have been adopted and practiced as their own festivals by adherents of Voodoo who embellish the ritual of the church on those days with ceremonies according to the traditions and in the temple of the Voodoo gods. Also people, paradoxically, by their own inclination have simply confused the denomination of saints and their functions in the two cults – a natural translation from one liturgical language to another . . .

Having reached the end of our inquiry, we can take a glance at our research as a whole and from it draw some information useful to the way of life and character of our social group.

To begin with, the demonstration has not contradicted the premises posed at the beginning of these studies when we suggested that our folklore was rich in diversified materials.

Tales, legends, riddles, songs, proverbs, beliefs thrive with an extraordinary exuberance, magnanimity, and ingenuity. These are the superb human materials from which are molded the warm heart, the multi-consciousness, the collective mind of the Haitian people! . . . [T]he tales, the songs, the legends, the proverbs, the beliefs are the works or products spontaneously springing at a given moment from an indigenous conception, adopted by all because of being faithful expositors of a common sentiment grown dear to everyone and, in the end, cast into original creations through the obscure process of the subconscious . . . .

[F]inally, if this miracular thinking which is at the base of Haitian life and confers upon it its own identity – the mystical tonality – if all of that is drawn from the common reservoir of ideas, sentiments, acts, gestures which constitute the moral patrimony of the Haitian society, then it will be in vain for the arrogant among elite and plebian to jibe at the joint responsibility for faults and transgressions, for dilettantist bovaryism to dictate to both acts of cowardice and falsehood, for imbecilic class egotisms to trigger attitudes of antipathy and measures of ostracism – nothing will know how to prevent tales, legends, songs received from the past or created and transformed by us from being a part of ourselves, revealed as an exteriorization of our collective ego, no one can hinder latent or formal beliefs from the past that have been transformed, recreated by us from having been the driving elements of our conduct and having conditioned the irresistible heroism of the throng which was slaughtered in the days of glory and sacrifices for the sake of implanting Negro freedom and independence on our soil; nothing in fact can prevent, in the period of transition and uncertainty that we endure at this moment, these same imponderable elements from being the mirror which reflects most accurately the restless countenance of the nation. They constitute in an unexpected and breathtaking fashion the materials of our spiritual unity. Therefore where could one find a more genuine image of our society?

What else has ever expressed the Haitian mind more completely? . . .

But, in fact, what is the origin of most of the customs about which we have just spoken? Are they daughters of our soil or rather do they come to us from across the seas?

We are skeptical of either explanation. None of them are entirely local creations, yet none have reached us without alteration. They exist as our personality itself, the whole charged with reminiscences and stamped by successive mutations which mark the complexity of our ethnic origins, and since the evolution of our people operates in such a divergent manner that a small number among us acquires a social and intellectual culture that puts them in a separate world, very proud and very haughty from living in an ivory tower with only a distant and formal contact with the remainder lost in misery and ignorance, it is among the multitude that we will have the chance to discover the thread of traditions that came from across the seas. If we submit these traditions to a comparative examination they will reveal immediately that Africa is the country of origin for most of them . . . .

Ah! I understand full well the repugnance with which I am confronted in daring to speak of Africa and African things! The subject seems vulgar to you and entirely devoid of interest, am I not right?

Beware, my friends, are not such sentiments resting on the groundwork of scandalous ignorance? We subsist on ideas rancid from the stupendous stupidity of an ill-balanced culture and our puerile vanity is not satisfied until we mumble phrases written to please others in which we glorify *'the Gauls our ancestors'.*

Well, our only chance to be ourselves is by not repudiating any part of our ancestral heritage.

NOTES

1. Price-Mars refers to Paul Sébillot's *Le folk-lore* (Paris, 1913) which credits an English antiquarian, William J. Thoms (1803–85), with the origin of the term folk-lore. In 1846 Thoms wrote in favour of using 'a good Saxon compound, Folk-lore – the Lore of the People', and in 1878, he led a Folk-Lore Society.
2. There are several variant spellings of this word. Price-Mars used *Vaudou*, the common French spelling, and the translator chose Voodoo, despite the negative associations frequently attached to this spelling in English. The preferred contemporary English spelling is Vodou.
3. Saint Domingue was the name of the French colony in the western part of the island the Spanish called Hispaniola, conceded by Spain to France in 1697. The republic of Haiti, whose name is derived from an Arawak word meaning highlands, extends further east than did the French colony.
4. Médéric Louis Elie Moreau de Saint-Méry, a Frenchman born in Martinique in 1750, a colonial official and historian, was the chief apologist of the planters during the revolutionary period. He wrote *Description topographique, physique, civile, politique et historique de la partie française de l'îsle Saint-Domingue* (Philadelphia, 1797–98).
5. People of mixed African and European ancestry, believed to be 125-127 parts white, were the lightest social category short of being 'pure white'.
6. The *Code Noir*, promulgated in 1685, was the first attempt by a European power to regulate the juridical, moral and material conditions of slavery and the rights of free people of colour in its colonies, but there were wide discrepancies between the law and actual practice.
7. The *loa* or *lwa*, or *mystère*, is a spirit or deity, always active in peoples' lives, which is said to mount a person during spirit possession.
8. Jean-Jacques Dessalines, a former slave, reorganised the revolutionary forces after their leader, Toussaint Louverture, was kidnapped and exiled to France in 1802. He led them to victory, proclaimed the independence of Haiti on January 1, 1804 and ruled despotically until he was assassinated on October 17, 1806.
9. Roman Catholicism was declared the official religion of Haiti in 1806 and Vodou, although by far the most popular religion, was often suppressed. After the Vatican formally recognised Haiti in the Concordat of 1860, a system of church schools further privileged the Francophile and Catholic culture of the small elite.

Sixteen

Aimé Césaire

Aimé Césaire, born in Martinique in 1913, is the most distinguished poet of the Francophone Caribbean. In Paris he was a founder of a review, Etudiant Noir *(The Black Student). Although there was only a single issue in 1935, this journal contributed to debates about black racial and cultural identity and thus to the origins of the négritude movement. Césaire was one of the leading ideologists of négritude, the others being Léopold Sédar Senghor of Senegal and Léon Damas of Cayenne (French Guiana). The first version of Césaire's epic poem,* Cahier d'un retour au pays natal *(Return to My Native Land), was published in 1939, the year he left Paris to return to Martinique. A Spanish edition, with illustrations by the great Cuban artist Wifredo Lam, appeared in Havana in 1942 and André Breton, the leader of the French surrealist movement who met Césaire after fleeing to Martinique from the Nazis, promoted the book in New York and Paris.* Cahier *is a political poem that powerfully discredits the 'Western' system of representations of Africans from the vantage point of someone who is thoroughly versed in French culture while also a member of that besieged people.*

Elected mayor of Fort-de-France and a deputy in the Constituent Assembly in France in 1945, Césaire cosponsored the bill that made Martinique, Guadeloupe and French Guiana Départements d'Outre-Mer, overseas departments of France, in 1946. Martinique, a French colony since 1635, thus became legally and politically integrated, if not culturally assimilated, into the French state. Césaire resigned from the French Communist party in 1956 and, in 1958, he founded le Parti Progressiste Martiniquai . *He has written several plays, including one about Henri*

Christophe, the first king of Haiti, and another about Patrice Lumumba, a leader of independent Congo until his assassination in 1961. Césaire's Une Tempête, *a reinterpretation of Shakespeare's* The Tempest, *was published in 1968 and his complete works were published in three volumes in 1976. He became president of the* conseil régional, *created in 1982 for Martinique and Guadeloupe as part of France's policy of decentralisation. He retired from electoral politics in 1993.*

The first version of Césaire's Discours sur le colonialisme *appeared in 1950 and a revised version in 1955. These were years marked by armed struggle in French colonies in southeast Asia and Africa. The French were decisively beaten at Dien-Bien-Phu in Vietnam in 1954 and, in 1955, Césaire joined a committee of French intellectuals, including François Mauriac and Jean-Paul Sartre, who opposed France's attempt to destroy the Algerian liberation struggle. Césaire and Frantz Fanon, another Martiniquan intellectual, wrote indictments of European colonialism and warnings about its successor, US imperialism. Césaire, with scathing sarcasm, exposed the hypocrisy of those who defend and propagate oppression, using even torture and genocide, in the name of civilisation. Colonialism, he argued, destroys not only the cultures of the people it oppresses, but also the humanity of the colonisers themselves. Césaire is the leading advocate of the view that cultural as well as political independence is a necessary condition for the re-emergence of Africa and all peoples of African origin. The ideology and movement called* négritude *is thus related to, but distinct from, Haiti's* mouvement indigéniste. *Whereas the latter was a cultural movement focused on the particularities of Haiti, the scope of* négritude *is much wider. Léopold Senghor declared Jean-Price Mars to be the father of* négritude *but he was a precursor rather than a founder of that movement. Significantly,* négritude *began in Paris in the 1930s, led by black students from the French colonies. In an interview with the Haitian poet René Depestre in 1967, Césaire referred to Haiti's* mouvement indigéniste, *the Garvey movement, and the* afrocubanismo *movement as 'parallel movements' to* négritude.

iscourse on Colonialism (excerpts)

A civilization that proves incapable of solving the problems it creates is a decadent civilization.

A civilization that chooses to close its eyes to its most crucial problems is a stricken civilization.

A civilization that uses its principles for trickery and deceit is a dying civilization.

The fact is that the so-called European civilization – 'Western' civilization – as it has been shaped by two centuries of bourgeois rule, is incapable of solving the two major problems to which its existence has given rise: the problem of the proletariat and the colonial problem; that Europe is unable to justify itself either before the bar of 'reason' or before the bar of 'conscience'; and that, increasingly, it takes refuge in a hypocrisy which is all the more odious because it is less and less likely to deceive . . . .

'Europe' is morally, spiritually indefensible.

And today the indictment is brought against it not by the European masses alone, but on a world scale, by tens and tens of millions of men who, from the depths of slavery, set themselves up as judges.

The colonialists may kill in Indochina,[1] torture in Madagascar,[2] imprison in Black Africa, crack down in the West Indies. Henceforth the colonized know that they have an advantage over them. They know that their temporary 'masters' are lying.

Therefore that their masters are weak.

And since I have been asked to speak about colonization and civilization, let us go straight to the principal lie which is the source of all the others.

Colonization and civilization?

In dealing with this subject, the commonest curse is to be the dupe in good faith of a collective hypocrisy that cleverly misrepresents problems, the better to legitimize the hateful solutions provided for them.

In other words, the essential thing here is to see clearly, to think clearly – that is, dangerously – and to answer clearly the innocent first question: what, fundamentally, is colonization? To agree on what it is not: neither evangelization, nor a philanthropic enterprise, nor a desire to push back the frontiers of ignorance, disease, and tyranny, nor a project undertaken for the greater glory of God, nor an attempt to extend the rule of law. To admit once for all, without flinching at the consequences, that the decisive actors here are the adventurer and the pirate, the wholesale grocer and the ship owner, the gold digger and the merchant, appetite and force, and behind them, the baleful projected shadow of a form of civilization which, at a certain point in its history, finds itself obliged, for internal reasons, to extend to a world scale the competition of its antagonistic economies.

Pursuing my analysis, I find that hypocrisy is of recent date; that neither Cortez discovering Mexico from the top of the great teocalli, nor Pizzaro before Cuzco . . . . claims that he is the harbinger of a superior order; that they kill; that they plunder; that they have helmets, lances, cupidities; that the slavering apologists came later; that the chief culprit in this domain is Christian pedantry, which laid down the dishonest equations *Christianity=civilization, paganism=savagery*, from which there could not but ensue abominable colonialist and racist consequences, whose victims were to be the Indians, the yellow peoples, and the Negroes.

That being settled, I admit that it is a good thing to place different civilizations in contact with each other; that it is an excellent thing to blend different worlds; that whatever its own particular genius may be, a civilisation that withdraws into itself atrophies; that for civilizations, exchange is oxygen; that the great good fortune of Europe is to have been a crossroads, and that because it was the locus of all ideas, the receptacle of all philosophies, the meeting place of all sentiments, it was the best center for the redistribution of energy.

But then I ask the following question: has colonization really *placed civilizations in contact?* Or, if you prefer, of all the ways of *establishing contact,* was it the best?

I answer *no.*

And I say that between *colonization* and *civilization* there is an infinite distance; that out of all the colonial expeditions that have been undertaken, out of all the colonial statutes that have been drawn up, out of all the memoranda that have been despatched by all the ministries, there could not come a single human value.

First we must study how colonization works to *decivilize* the colonizer, to *brutalize* him in the true sense of the word, to degrade him, to awaken him to buried instincts, to covetousness, violence, race hatred, and moral relativism; and we must show that each time a head is cut off or an eye put out in Vietnam and in France they accept the fact, each time a little girl is raped and in France they accept the fact, each time a Madagascan is tortured and in France they accept the fact, civilization acquires another dead weight, a universal regression takes place, a gangrene sets in, a center of infection begins to spread; and that at the end of all these treaties that have been violated, all these lies that have been propagated, all these punitive expeditions that have been tolerated, all these prisoners who have been tied up and 'interrogated', all these patriots who have been tortured, at the end of all the racial pride that has been encouraged, all the boastfulness that has been displayed, a poison has been instilled into the veins of Europe and, slowly but surely, the continent proceeds toward *savagery.*

And then one fine day the bourgeoisie is awakened by a terrific reverse shock: the gestapos are busy, the prisons fill up, the torturers around the racks invent, refine, discuss.

People are surprised, they become indignant. They say: 'How strange! But never mind – it's Nazism, it will pass!' And they wait, and they hope; and they hide the truth from themselves, that it is barbarism, but the supreme barbarism, the crowning barbarism that sums up all the daily barbarisms; that it is Nazism, yes, but that before they were its victims, they were its accomplices; that they tolerated that Nazism before it was inflicted on them, that they absolved it, shut their eyes to it, legitimized it, because, until then, it had been applied only to non-European peoples; that they have cultivated that Nazism, that they are responsible for it, and that before engulfing the whole of Western, Christian civilization in its reddened waters, it oozes, seeps, and trickles from every crack.

Yes, it would be worthwhile to . . . reveal to the very distinguished, very humanistic, very Christian bourgeois of the twentieth century that without his being aware of it, he has a Hitler inside him, that Hitler *inhabits* him, that Hitler is his *demon*, that if he rails against him, he is being inconsistent and that, at bottom, what he cannot forgive Hitler for is not *crime* in itself, *the crime against man*, it is not *the humiliation of man as such*, it is the crime against the white man, the humiliation of the white man, and the fact that he applied to Europe colonialist procedures which until then had been reserved exclusively for the Arabs of Algeria,[3] the coolies of India, and the blacks of Africa.

And that is the great thing I hold against pseudo-humanism: that for too long it has diminished the rights of man, that its concept of those rights has been – and still is – narrow and fragmentary, incomplete and biased and, all things considered, sordidly racist . . . .

'We aspire not to equality but to domination. The country of a foreign race must become once [a]gain a country of serfs, of agricultural laborers, or industrial workers. It is not a question of eliminating the inequalities among men but of widening them and making them into a law.' . . .

Who is speaking? I am ashamed to say it: it is the Western *humanist*, the 'idealist' philosopher... Renan[4]... the passage is taken from a book entitled *La Réforme intellectuelle et morale*...

> The regeneration of the inferior or degenerate races by the superior races is part of the providential order of things for humanity. With us, the common man is nearly always a déclassé nobleman, his heavy hand is better suited to handling the sword than the menial tool. Rather than work, he chooses to fight, that is, he returns to his first estate . . . . Pour forth this all-consuming activity onto countries which, like China, are crying aloud for foreign conquest . . . . Nature has made a race of workers, the Chinese race, who have wonderful manual dexterity and almost no sense of honor; govern them with justice, levying from them, in return for the blessing of such a government, an ample allowance for the conquering race, and they will be satisfied; a race of tillers of the soil, the Negro; treat him with kindness and humanity, and all will be as it should; a race of masters and soldiers, the European race . . . . In Europe, every rebel is, more or less, a soldier who has missed his calling, a creature made for the heroic life, before whom you are setting *a task that is contrary to his race* – a poor worker, too good a soldier. But the life at which our workers rebel would make a Chinese or a fellah happy, as they are not

military creatures in the least. *Let each one do what he is made for, and all will be well.*

Hitler? Rosenberg ?[5] No, Renan . . . .
Who protests? No one, so far as I know. . . .
No one.

I mean not one established writer, not one academician, not one preacher, not one crusader for the right and for religion, not one 'defender of the human person'.

And yet, through the mouths . . . of all those who considered – and consider – it lawful to apply to non-European peoples 'a kind of expropriation for public purposes' for the benefit of nations that were stronger and better equipped, it was already Hitler speaking!

What am I driving at? At this idea: that no one colonizes innocently, that no one colonizes with impunity either; that a nation which colonizes, that a civilization which justifies colonization – and therefore force – is already a sick civilization, a civilization that is morally diseased, that irresistibly, progressing from one consequence to another, one repudiation to another, calls for its Hitler, I mean its punishment.

Colonization: bridgehead in a campaign to civilize barbarism, from which there may emerge at any moment the negation of civilization, pure and simple.

Elsewhere I have cited at length a few incidents culled from the history of colonial expeditions . . . . [T]hese hideous butcheries . . . these heads of men, these collections of ears, these burned houses, these Gothic invasions, this steaming blood, these cities that evaporate at the edge of the sword, are not to be so easily disposed of. They prove that colonization, I repeat, dehumanizes even the most civilized man; that colonial activity, colonial enterprise, colonial conquest, which is based on contempt for the native and justified by that contempt, inevitably tends to change him who undertakes it; that the colonizer, who in order to ease his conscience gets into the habit of seeing the other man as *an animal*, accustoms himself to treating him like an animal, and tends objectively to transform *himself* into an animal. It is this result, this boomerang effect of colonization, that I wanted to point out . .

But let us speak about the colonized.

I see clearly what colonization has destroyed: the wonderful Indian civilizations . . . .

I see clearly the civilizations, condemned to perish at a future date, into which it has introduced a principle of ruin: the South Sea islands, Nigeria, Nyasaland. I see less clearly the contributions it has made.

Security? Culture? The rule of law? In the meantime, I look around and wherever there are colonizers and colonized face to face, I see force, brutality, cruelty, sadism, conflict, and, in a parody of education, the hasty manufacture of a few thousand subordinate functionaries, 'boys', artisans, office clerks, and interpreters necessary for the smooth operation of business.

I spoke of contact.

Between colonizer and colonized there is room only for forced labor, intimidation, pressure, the police, taxation, theft, rape, compulsory crops, contempt, mistrust, arrogance, self-complacency, swinishness, brainless élites, degraded masses.

No human contact, but relations of domination and submission which turn the colonizing man into a classroom monitor, an army sergeant, a prison guard, a slave driver, and the indigenous man into an instrument of production . . . . societies drained of their essence, cultures trampled underfoot, institutions undermined, lands confiscated, religions smashed, magnificent artistic creations destroyed, extraordinary *possibilities* wiped out.

They throw facts at my head, statistics, mileages of roads, canals, and railroad tracks.

I am talking about ... millions of men torn from their gods, their land, their habits, their life –from life, from the dance, from wisdom.

I am talking about millions of men in whom fear has been cunningly instilled, who have been taught to have an inferiority complex, to tremble, kneel, despair, and behave like flunkeys.

They dazzle me with the tonnage of cotton or cocoa that has been exported, the acreage that has been planted with olive trees or grapevines.

I am talking about the natural *economies* that have been disrupted – harmonious and viable *economies* adapted to the indigenous population – about food crops destroyed, malnutrition permanently introduced, agricultural development oriented solely toward the benefit of the metropolitan countries, about the looting of products, the looting of raw materials.

They pride themselves on abuses eliminated.

I too talk about abuses, but what I say is that on the old ones – very real – they have superimposed others – very detestable. They talk to me about local tyrants brought to reason; but I note that in general the old tyrants get on very well with the new ones, and that there has been established between them, to the detriment of the people, a circuit of mutual services and complicity.

They talk to me about civilization, I talk about proletarianization and mystification.

For my part, I make a systematic defense of the non-European civilizations.

Every day that passes, every denial of justice, every beating by the police, every demand of the workers that is drowned in blood, every scandal that is hushed up, every punitive expedition, every police van, every gendarme and every militiaman, brings home to us the value of our old societies.

They were communal societies, never societies of the many for the few.

They were societies that were not only ante-capitalist, as has been said, but also *anti-capitalist.*

They were democratic societies, always.

They were cooperative societies, fraternal societies.

I make a systematic defense of the societies destroyed by imperialism . . . .

My only consolation is that periods of colonization pass, that nations sleep only for a time, and that peoples remain.

This being said, it seems that in certain circles they pretend to have discovered in me an 'enemy of Europe' and a prophet of the return to the ante-European past.

For my part, I search in vain for the place where I could have expressed such views; where I ever underestimated the importance of Europe in the history of human thought; where I ever preached a *return* of any kind; where I ever claimed that there could be a *return.*

The truth is that I have said something very different: to wit, that the great historical tragedy of Africa has been not so much that it was too late in making contact with the rest of the world, as the manner in which that contact was brought about; that Europe began to 'propagate' at a time when it had fallen into the hands of the most unscrupulous financiers and captains of industry; that it was our misfortune to encounter that particular Europe on our path, and that Europe is responsible before the human community for the highest heap of corpses in history.

In another connection, in judging colonization, I have added that Europe has gotten on very well indeed with all the local feudal lords who agreed to serve, woven a villainous complicity with them, rendered their tyranny more effective and more efficient, and that it has actually tended to prolong artificially the survival of local pasts in their most pernicious aspects.

I have said – and this is something very different – that colonialist Europe has grafted modern abuse onto ancient injustice, hateful racism onto old inequality.

That if I am attacked on the grounds of intent, I maintain that colonialist Europe is dishonest in trying to justify its colonizing activity *a posteriori* by the obvious material progress that has been achieved in certain fields under the colonial regime … since no one knows at what stage of material development these same countries would have been if Europe had not intervened; since the technical outfitting of Africa and Asia … their 'Europeanization', was (as is proved by the example of Japan) in no way tied to the European *occupation*; since the Europeanization of the non-European continents could have been accomplished otherwise than under the heel of Europe; since this movement of Europeanization *was in progress*; since it was even slowed down; since in any case it was distorted by the European takeover.

The proof is that at present it is the indigenous peoples of Africa and Asia who are demanding schools, and colonialist Europe which refuses them; that it is the African who is asking for ports and roads, and colonialist Europe which is niggardly on this score; that it is the colonized man who wants to move forward, and the colonizer who holds things back.

To go further, I make no secret of my opinion that at the present time the barbarism of Western Europe has reached an incredibly high level, being only surpassed – far surpassed, it is true – by the barbarism of the United States . . . .

Once again, I systematically defend our old Negro civilizations: they were courteous civilizations.

So the real problem, you say, is to return to them. No, I repeat. We are not men for whom it is a question of 'either-or'. For us, the problem is not to make a utopian and sterile attempt to repeat the past, but to go beyond. It is not a dead society that we want to revive. We leave that to those who go in for exoticism. Nor is it the present colonial society that we wish to prolong, the most putrid carrion that ever rotted under the sun. It is a new society that we must create, with the help of all our brother slaves, a society rich with all the productive power of modern times, warm with all the fraternity of olden days . . . .

Therefore comrade, you will hold as enemies – loftily, lucidly, consistently – not only sadistic governors and greedy bankers, not only prefects who torture and colonists who flog, not only corrupt, check-licking politicians and subservient judges, but likewise and for the same reason, venomous journalists, goitrous academicians, wreathed in dollars and stupidity, ethnographers who go in for metaphysics, presumptuous Belgian theologians, chattering intellectuals born stinking out of the thigh of Nietzsche,[6] the paternalists, the embracers, the corrupters, the back-slappers, the lovers of exoticism, the dividers, the agrarian sociologists, the hoodwinkers, the hoaxers, the hot-air artists, the humbugs, and in general, all those who, performing their functions in the sordid division of labor for the defense of Western bourgeois society, try in divers ways and by infamous diversions to split up the forces of Progress – even if it means denying the very possibility of Progress – all of them tools of capitalism, all of them, openly or secretly, supporters of plundering colonialism, all of them responsible, all hateful, all slave-traders, all henceforth answerable for the violence of revolutionary action.

And sweep out all the obscurers, all the inventors of subterfuges, the charlatans and tricksters, the dealers in gobbledygook. And do not seek to know whether personally these gentlemen are in good or bad faith, whether personally they have good or bad intentions. Whether personally – that is, in the private conscience of Peter or Paul – they are or are not colonialists, because the essential thing is that their highly problematical subjective good faith is entirely irrelevant to the objective social implications of the evil work they perform as watchdogs of colonialism . . . .

One of the values invented by the bourgeoisie in former times and launched throughout the world was *man* … The other was the nation.

It is a fact: the *nation* is a bourgeois phenomenon.

Exactly; but if I turn my attention from *man* to *nations*, I note that here too there is a great danger; that colonial enterprise is to the modern world what Roman imperialism was to the ancient world: the prelude to Disaster and the forerunner of Catastrophe. Come, now! The Indians massacred, the Moslem world drained of itself, the Chinese world defiled and perverted for a good century; the Negro world disqualified; mighty voices stilled forever; homes scattered to the wind; all this wreckage, all this waste, humanity reduced to a monologue, and you think that all that does not have its price? The truth is that this policy *cannot but bring about the ruin of Europe itself*, and that Europe, if it is not careful, will perish from the void it has created around itself.

They thought they were only slaughtering Indians, or Hindus, or South Sea islanders, or Africans. They have in fact overthrown, one after another, the ramparts behind which European civilization could have developed freely....

And now I ask: what else has bourgeois Europe done? It has undermined civilizations, destroyed countries, ruined nationalities, extirpated 'the root of diversity'. . . . The hour of the barbarian is at hand. The modern barbarian. The American hour. Violence, excess, waste, mercantilism, bluff, gregariousness, stupidity, vulgarity, disorder.

In 1913, the Ambassador Page[7] wrote to Wilson:[8]

'The future of the world belongs to us ... Now what are we going to do with the leadership of the world presently when it clearly falls into our hands?'

And in 1914: 'What are we going to do with this England and this Empire, presently, when economic forces unmistakably put the leadership of the race in our hands'?

This Empire ... And the others ...

And indeed, do you not see how ostentatiously these gentlemen have just unfurled the banner of anti-colonialism?

'*Aid to the disinherited countries*', says Truman[9]. 'The time of the old colonialism has passed'. That's also Truman.

Which means that American high finance considers that the time has come to raid every colony in the world. So, dear friends, here you have to be careful!

I know that some of you, disgusted with Europe, with all that hideous mess which you did not witness by choice, are turning – oh! in no great numbers – toward America and getting used to looking upon that country as a possible liberator.

'What a godsend!' you think.

'The bulldozers! The massive investments of capital! The roads! The ports!'

'But American racism!'

'So what? European racism in the colonies has inured us to it!'

And there we are, ready to run the great Yankee risk.

So, once again, be careful!

American domination – the only domination from which one never recovers. I mean from which one never recovers unscarred.

And since you are talking about factories and industries, do you not see the tremendous factory hysterically spitting out its cinders in the heart of our forests or deep in the bush, the factory for the production of lackeys; do you not see the prodigious mechanization, the mechanization of man; the gigantic rape of everything intimate, undamaged, undefiled that, despoiled as we are, our human spirit has still managed to preserve; the machine, yes, have you never seen it, the machine for crushing, for grinding, for degrading peoples?

So that the danger is immense . . . .

Aimé Césaire was interviewed by Haitian poet and militant René Depestre at the Cultural Congress of Havana in 1967. Published in Poesias, *an anthology of Césaire's writings (Casa de las Americas, 1968), this interview was translated from the Spanish by Maro Riofrancos.*

Interview with Aime Cesaire

RENÉ DEPESTRE: Your *Return to My Native Land* bears the stamp of personal experience, your experience as a Martinican youth, and it also deals with the itineraries of the Negro race in the Antilles, where French influences are not decisive.

AIMÉ CÉSAIRE: I don't deny French influences myself. Whether I want to or not, as a poet I express myself in French and clearly French literature has influenced me. But I want to emphasize very strongly that – while using as a point of departure the elements that French literature gave me – at the same time I have always strived to create a new language, one capable of communicating the African heritage. In other words, for me French was a tool that I wanted to use in developing a new means of expression. I wanted to create an Antillean French, a black French that, while still being French, had a black character.

RD: Has surrealism[10] been instrumental in your effort to discover this new French language?

AC: I was ready to accept surrealism because I already had advanced on my own, using as my starting points the same authors that had influenced the surrealist poets. Their thinking and mine had common reference points. Surrealism provided me with what I had been confusedly searching for. I have accepted it joyfully because in it I have found more of a confirmation than a revelation. It was a weapon that exploded the French language. It shook up absolutely everything. This was very important because the traditional forms – burdensome, overused forms – were crushing me.

RD: This was what interested you in the surrealist movement ...

AC: Surrealism interested me to the extent that it was a liberating factor.

RD: So you were very sensitive to the concept of liberation that surrealism contained. Surrealism called forth deep and unconscious forces.

AC: Exactly. And my thinking followed these lines: Well then, if I apply the surrealist approach to my particular situation, I can summon up these unconscious forces. This, for me was a call to Africa. I said to myself: it's true that superficially we are French, we bear the marks of French customs; we have been branded by Cartesian philosophy, by French rhetoric; but if we break with all that, if we plumb the depths, then what we will find is fundamentally black.

RD: In other words, it was a process of disalienation.

AC: Yes, a process of disalienation, that's how I interpreted surrealism.

RD: That's how surrealism has manifested itself in your work: as an effort to reclaim your authentic character, and in a way as an effort to reclaim the African heritage.

AC: Absolutely.

RD: And as a process of detoxification.

AC: A plunge into the depths. It was a plunge into Africa for me.

RD: It was a way of emancipating your consciousness.

AC: Yes, I felt that beneath the social being would be found a profound being, over whom all sorts of ancestral layers and alluviums had been deposited.

RD: Now, I would like you to go back to the period in your life in Paris when you collaborated with Léopold Sédar Senghor and Léon Damas on the small periodical *L'Etudiant noir*. Was this first stage of the Negritude expressed in *Return to My Native Land*?

AC: Yes, it was already Negritude, as we conceived of it then … I maintained that the political question could not do away with our condition as Negroes. We are Negroes, with a great number of historical peculiarities. I suppose that I must have been influenced by Senghor in this. At the time I knew absolutely nothing about Africa. Soon afterward I met Senghor, and he told me a great deal about Africa. He made an enormous impression on me: I am indebted to him for the revelation of Africa and African singularity. And I tried to develop a theory to encompass all of my reality.

RD: You have tried to particularize Communism …

AC: Yes, it is a very old tendency of mine. Even then Communists would reproach me for speaking of the Negro problem – they called it my racism. But I would answer: Marx is all right, but we need to complete Marx. I felt that the emancipation of the Negro consisted of more than just a political emancipation.

RD: Do you see a relationship among the movements between the two world wars connected to *L'Etudiant noir*, the Negro Renaissance Movement in the United States, *La Revue indigène* in Haiti, and *Negrismo* in Cuba?

AC: I was not influenced by those other movements because I did not know of them. But I'm sure they are parallel movements.

RD: How do you explain the emergence, in the years between the two world wars, of these parallel movements – in Haiti, the United States, Cuba, Brazil, Martinique, etc. – that recognized the cultural particularities of Africa?

AC: I believe that at that time in the history of the world there was a coming to consciousness among Negroes, and this manifested itself in movements that had no relationship to each other.

RD: There was the extraordinary phenomenon of jazz.

AC: Yes, there was the phenomenon of jazz. There was the Marcus Garvey movement. I remember very well that even when I was a child I had heard people speak of Garvey.... He inspired a mass movement, and for several years he was a symbol to American Negroes. In France there was a newspaper called *Le Cri des négres*.

RD: I believe that Haitians like Dr. Sajous, Jacques Roumain,[11] and Jean Price-Mars collaborated on that newspaper. There were also six issues of *La Revue du monde noir*, written by René Maran,[12] Claude McKay,[13] Price-Mars, the Achille brothers, Sajous, and others.

AC: I remember very well that around that time we read the poems of Langston Hughes[14] and Claude McKay. I knew very well who McKay was because in 1929 or 1930 an anthology of American Negro poetry appeared in Paris. And McKay's novel, *Banjo* – describing the life of dock workers in Marseilles – was published in 1930. This was really one of the first works in which an author spoke of the Negro and gave him a certain literary dignity. I must say, therefore, that although I was not directly influenced by any American Negroes, at least I felt that the movement in the United States created an atmosphere that was indispensable for a very clear coming to consciousness. During the 1920's and 1930's I came under three main influences, through the works of Mallarmé, Rimbaud, Lautréamont, and Claudel.[15] The second was Africa. I knew very little about Africa, but I deepened my knowledge through ethnographic studies . . . . And as for the third influence, it was the Negro Renaissance Movement in the United States, which did not influence me directly but still created an atmosphere which allowed me to become conscious of the solidarity of the black world.

RD: At that time you were not aware, for example, of developments along the same lines in Haiti, centered around *La Revue indigène* and Jean Price-Mars' book, *Ainsi parla l'oncle*.

AC: No, it was only later that I discovered the Haitian movement and Price-Mars' famous book.

RD: How would you describe your encounter with Senghor, the encounter between Antillean Negritude and African Negritude? Was it the result of a particular event or a parallel development of consciousness?

AC: It was simply that in Paris at that time there were a few dozen Negroes of diverse origins. There were Africans, like Senghor, Guianans, Haitians, North Americans, Antilleans, etc. This was very important for me.

RD: In this circle of Negroes in Paris, was there a consciousness of the importance of African culture?

AC: Yes, as well as an awareness of the solidarity among blacks. We had come from different parts of the world. It was our first meeting. We were discovering ourselves. This was very important.

RD: It was extraordinarily important. How did you come to develop the concept to Negritude?

AC: I have a feeling that it was somewhat of a collective creation. I used the term first, that's true. But it's possible we talked about it in our group. It was really a resistance to the politics of assimilation. Until that time, until my generation, the French and the English – but especially the French – had followed the politics of assimilation unrestrainedly. We didn't know what Africa was. Europeans despised everything about Africa, and in France people spoke of a civilized world and a barbarian world. The barbarian world was Africa, and the civilized world was Europe. Therefore the best thing one could do with an African was to assimilate him: the ideal was to turn him into a Frenchman with black skin.

RD: Haiti experienced a similar phenomenon at the beginning of the nineteenth century. There is an entire Haitian pseudo-literature, created by authors who allowed themselves to be assimilated. The independence of Haiti, our first independence, was a violent attack against the French presence in our country, but our first authors did not attack French cultural values with equal force. They did not proceed toward a decolonization of their consciousness ....

AC: Our struggle was a struggle against alienation. That struggle gave birth to Negritude. Because Antilleans were ashamed of being Negroes, they searched for all sorts of euphemisms for Negro: they would say a man of color, a dark-complexioned man, and other idiocies like that . ...That's when we adopted the word *nègre*, as a term of defiance. It was a defiant name. To some extent it was a reaction of enraged youth. Since there was shame about the word *nègre*, we chose the word *nègre*. I must say that when we founded *L'Etudiant noir*, I really wanted to call it *L'Etudiant nègre*, but there was a great resistance to that among the Antilleans.

RD: Some thought that the word *nègre* was offensive.

AC: Yes, too offensive, too aggressive, and then I took the liberty of speaking of *négritude*. There was in us a defiant will, and we found a violent affirmation in the words *négre* and *négritude*.

RD: In *Return to My Native Land* you have stated that Haiti was the cradle of
      Negritude. In your words, 'Haiti, where Negritude stood on its feet for the
      first time'. Then, in your opinion, the history of our country is in a certain
      sense the prehistory of Negritude. How have you applied the concept of
      Negritude to the history of Haiti?

AC: Well, after my discovery of the North American Negro and my discovery of
      Africa, I went on to explore the totality of the black world, and that is how I
      came upon the history of Haiti. I love Martinique, but it is an alienated land,
      while Haiti represented for me the heroic Antilles, the African Antilles. I
      began to make connections between the Antilles and Africa, and Haiti is the
      most African of the Antilles. It is at the same time a country with a marvelous
      history: the first Negro epic of the New World was written by Haitians,
      people like Toussaint l'Ouverture, Henri Christophe, Jean-Jacques
      Dessalines,[16] etc. Haiti is not very well known in Martinique. I am one of the
      few Martinicans who know and love Haiti.

RD: Then for you the first independence struggle in Haiti was a confirmation, a
      demonstration of the concept of Negritude. Our national history is Negritude
      in action.

AC: Yes, Negritude in action. Haiti is the country where Negro people stood up
      for the first time, affirming their determination to shape a new world, a free
      world ... I would like to say that everyone has his own Negritude. There
      has been too much theorizing about Negritude. I have tried not to overdo it,
      out of a sense of modesty. But if someone asks me what my conception of
      Negritude is, I answer that above all it is a concrete rather than an abstract
      coming to consciousness. What I have been telling you about—the
      atmosphere of assimilation in which Negro people were ashamed of
      themselves – has great importance. We lived in an atmosphere of rejection,
      and we developed an inferiority complex. I have always thought that the
      black man was searching for his identity. And it has seemed to me that if
      what we want is to establish this identity, then we must have a concrete
      consciousness of what we are – that is, of the first fact of our lives: that we
      are black; that we were black and have a history, a history that contains
      certain cultural elements of great value; and that Negroes were not, as you
      put it, born yesterday, because there have been beautiful and important
      black civilizations. At the time we began to write people could write a
      history of world civilization without devoting a single chapter to Africa, as
      if Africa had made no contributions to the world. Therefore we affirmed that
      we were Negroes and that we were proud of it, and that we thought that
      Africa was not some sort of blank page in the history of humanity; in sum,

we asserted that our Negro heritage was worthy of respect, and that this heritage was not relegated to the past, that its values were values that could still make an important contribution to the world.

RD: That is to say, universalizing values ...

AC: Universalizing, living values that had not been exhausted. The field was not dried up: it could still bear fruit, if we made the effort to irrigate it with our sweat and plant new seeds in it. So this was the situation: there were things to tell the world. We were not dazzled by European civilization. We bore the imprint of European civilization but we thought that Africa could make a contribution to Europe. It was also an affirmation of our solidarity. That's the way it was: I have always recognized that what was happening to my brothers in Algeria and the United States had its repercussions in me. I understood that I could not be indifferent to what was happening in Haiti or Africa. Then, in a way, we slowly came to the idea of a sort of black civilization spread throughout the world. And I have come to the realization that there was a 'Negro situation' that existed in different geographical areas, that Africa was also my country. There was the African continent, the Antilles, Haiti; there were Martinicans and Brazilian Negroes, etc. That's what Negritude meant to me .... Our affinities were above all a matter of feeling. You either felt black or did not feel black. But there was also the political aspect. Negritude was, after all, part of the left. I never thought for a moment that our emancipation could come from the right – that's impossible .... I think that the economic question is important, but it is not the only thing.

RD: Certainly, because the relationships between consciousness and reality are extremely complex. That's why it is equally necessary to decolonize our minds, our inner life, at the same time that we decolonize society.

AC: Exactly, and I remember very well having said to the Martinican Communists, in those days, that black people, as you have pointed out, were doubly proletarianized and alienated: in the first place as workers, but also as blacks, because after all we are dealing with the only race which is denied even the notion of humanity.

NOTES

1. Indochina was the name for the French colony in southeast Asia that now consists of the independent states of Cambodia, Laos and Vietnam. After France surrendered to Germany in 1940, Japan took over French Indochina and when France attempted to

regain control at the end of the second world war a national liberation struggle broke out.

2. Madagascar, a large island in the Indian Ocean, 240 miles south-east of the African mainland, was a French colony from 1896 to 1960. There was an armed struggle against colonisation between 1947 and 1949.

3. Algeria, a French colony in north Africa since 1830, rose in rebellion in 1954 and achieved independence in 1962 after a long struggle in which over 250,000 people died.

4. Ernest Renan (1823–92), a French historian and religious scholar, was a professor at the College of France. He is famous for his series of books on the early history of Christianity, the first of which is *Life of Jesus* (1863).

5. Alfred Rosenberg (1893–1946) was the chief philosopher of Hitler's Nazi movement. The author of *Myth of the Twentieth Century* (1930), which argued for 'Aryan' racial superiority, he urged the extermination of the Jews.

6. Friedrich Nietzsche (1844–1900) was a German philosopher, poet and classical scholar who believed that human behaviour is motivated by a 'will to power'. His ideal of the 'superman' has been seen as a precursor of Nazism and other ideologies that promote racism and dictatorships.

7. Walter Hines Page (1855–1918) was an editor, publisher and diplomat, and the US ambassador to Great Britain during the first world war.

8. Woodrow Wilson (1856–1924), the president of the United States from 1913 to 1921, sent troops into Mexico, Nicaragua, Haiti and the Dominican Republic, despite advocating respect for 'political independence and territorial integrity to great and small states alike' (speech to US Congress, 8 Jan. 1918).

9. Harry S. Truman (1884–1972), the president of the United States from 1945 to 1953, presided over the post-war reconstruction of western Europe, the Truman Doctrine to oppose international communism, and the Korean war that began in 1950.

10. Surrealism was an artistic and literary movement that emerged in France in the 1920s. It used a fantastic style or 'super-realism' to criticise the evils and restrictions of society. Surrealists, like the poet André Breton and the painter Salvador Dali, sought to shock the reader or viewer and to show what they thought to be the deeper, more beautiful and true aspects of human nature that were revealed in the unconscious.

11. Jacques Roumain (1907–44) was a founder of the *Revue Indigène* in 1927 that increased awareness of the African roots of Haitian culture. A poet, novelist, ethnologist and diplomat, he was an intense nationalist and champion of the Haitian masses. The founder of the Haitian Bureau of Ethnology, he is best known as the author of *Masters of the Dew*, which was published posthumously and has been praised as Haiti's greatest novel.

12. René Maran (1887–1960), a Martinican, was the author of the novel *Batouala* (1938) which described the life of African people in French Equatorial Africa. It received the prestigious *Prix Goncourt* and influenced the literary revival in Haiti.

13. Claude McKay (1890–1948), a Jamaican poet and novelist, influenced the founders of *négritude* and was a major figure of the Harlem Renaissance. His most famous novel, *Banana Bottom* (1933), is set in rural Jamaica in the early years of the twentieth century.

14. Langston Hughes (1902–67) was a leader of the Harlem Renaissance and one of the most famous African American poets and dramatists.

15. Stéphane Mallarmé (1842–98) and Arthur Rimbaud (1854–91) were leaders of the symbolist movement that sought to convey feelings by means of symbols in poetry. Paul Claudel (1868–1955) was a poet and dramatist who expressed his Catholic belief in the eternal relations between man and woman, and mankind and God.

16. L'Ouverture, Christophe and Dessalines were the chief leaders of the revolution in the French colony of Saint Domingue that ended slavery and founded the independent nation of Haiti in 1804.

Seventeen

Frantz Fanon

Frantz Fanon (1925–61) was born in Martinique and went to France at the age of 22 to study medicine. Although he never returned, the experiences of his youth were crucial to the formulation of his analysis of the black experience in Peau Noire, Masques Blancs *(Black Skin, White Masks), published in Paris in 1952. Fanon, by profession a psychiatrist, did not limit his answer to the question 'Who am I?' to psychoanalysis. On the contrary, he perceived the psychological consequences of the rigid social structures and racist cultures of colonial societies. Fanon understood the mental dangers that resulted from the crippling dependency caused by an internalisation of the colonisers' values and prejudices. In order to succeed, colonised people had to learn to conform to what was defined by the colonisers as 'civilised'. The result was a psycho-pathology that included a horror of blackness – 'negrophobia'. Later, in his study of the colonial world and the process of decolonisation,* Les damnés de la terre *(The Wretched of the Earth), published in Paris in 1961, he indicted those 'Westernised' elites who became not just a replica of Europe but its caricature.*

From 1953 until his resignation in 1956, Fanon worked as a psychiatrist in a hospital in Algeria. The national liberation struggle against France began in 1954 and Fanon witnessed the treatment of Arabs by French doctors. He concluded that French colonial policies ensured that Arabs would feel alienated in their own country and he saw the inadequacy of psychiatric treatment that tried to readjust individuals to this environment. The individual was his starting point in Peau Noire, Masques Blancs *but his experiences in Algeria made him a revolutionary. Two volumes of his essays*, L'an cinq de la Révolution Algérienne *(Paris 1959) and* Pour la Révolution Africaine *(Paris, 1964), were based on these experiences. He became a spokesman for the rebels and a member of the National Liberation Front of Algeria in 1956. Several attempts were made on his life and he was almost killed when the car in which he was travelling was blown up on the Moroccan-Algerian frontier. In 1960, he learned he had leukemia. He completed most of* Les damnés de la terre *between March and May 1961 and he intended to resume psychiatric work in Tunis. However, he went to the United States for treatment when his condition deteriorated and he died in a hospital in Washington on December 6, 1961 at the age of 36. His reputation as a leading revolutionary socialist intellectual of the 'Third World' rose after his death.*

ℬlack Skin, White Masks (excerpts)

I propose nothing short of the liberation of the man of color from himself. We shall go very slowly, for there are two camps: the white and the black . . . .

We shall have no mercy for the former governors, the former missionaries. To us, the man who adores the Negro is as 'sick' as the man who abominates him.

Conversely, the black man who wants to turn his race white is as miserable as he who preaches hatred for the whites . . . .

The white man is sealed in his whiteness.

The black man in his blackness . . . .

Concern with the elimination of a vicious circle has been the only guide-line for my efforts.

There is a fact: White men consider themselves superior to black men.

There is another fact: Black men want to prove to white men, at all costs, the richness of their thought, the equal value of their intellect.

How do we extricate ourselves? . . .

The analysis that I am undertaking is psychological. In spite of this it is apparent to me that the effective disalienation of the black man entails an immediate recognition of social and economic realities. If there is an inferiority complex, it is the outcome of a double process:

– primarily, economic;

– subsequently, the internalization – or, better, the epidermalization – of this inferiority . . . .

It will be seen that the black man's alienation is not an individual question . . .

The black man has two dimensions. One with his fellows, the other with the white man. A Negro behaves differently with a white man and with another Negro.

That this self-division is a direct result of colonialist subjugation is beyond question . . . .

Every colonized people – in other words, every people in whose soul an inferiority complex has been created by the death and burial of its local cultural originality – finds itself face to face with the language of the civilizing nation; that is, with the culture of the mother country . . . .

In any group of young men in the Antilles, the one who expresses himself well, who has mastered the language, is inordinately feared; keep an eye on that one, he is almost white. In France one says, 'He talks like a book'. In Martinique, 'He talks like a white man'. . .

And the fact that the newly returned Negro adopts a language different from that of the group into which he was born is evidence of a dislocation, a separation . . . .

In every country of the world there are climbers, 'the ones who forget who they are', and, in contrast to them, 'the ones who remember where they came from'. The Antilles Negro who goes home from France expresses himself in dialect if he wants to make it plain that nothing has changed . . . .

To speak a language is to take on a world, a culture. The Antilles Negro who wants to be white will be the whiter as he gains greater mastery of the cultural tool that language is . . . .

Historically, it must be understood that the Negro wants to speak French because it is the key that can open doors which were still barred to him fifty years ago . . . .

There was a myth of the Negro that had to be destroyed at all costs . . . .

I was hated, despised, detested, not by the neighbor across the street or my cousin on my mother's side, but by an entire race . . . .

A feeling of inferiority? No, a feeling of nonexistence. Sin is Negro as virtue is white. All those white men in a group, guns in their hands, cannot be wrong. I am guilty. I do not know of what, but I know that I am no good . . . .

The Negro is a toy in the white man's hands; so, in order to shatter the hellish cycle, he explodes . . . .

Nevertheless . . . I feel in myself a soul as immense as the world, truly a soul as deep as the deepest of rivers, my chest has the power to expand without limit. I am a master and I am advised to adopt the humility of the cripple . . . .

The black schoolboy in the Antilles, who in his lessons is forever talking about 'our ancestors, the Gauls', identifies himself with the explorer, the bringer of civilisation, the white man who carries truth to savages – an all-white truth. There is identification – that is, the young Negro subjectively adopts a white man's attitude. He invests the hero, who is white, with all his own aggression . . . .

Little by little, one can observe in the young Antillean the formation and crystallization of an attitude and a way of thinking and seeing that are essentially white. When in school he has to read stories of savages told by white men, he always thinks of the Senegalese. As a schoolboy, I had many occasions to spend whole hours talking about the supposed customs of the savage Senegalese. In what was said there was a lack of awareness that was at the very least paradoxical. Because the Antillean does not think of himself as a black man; he thinks of himself as an Antillean. The Negro lives in Africa. Subjectively, intellectually, the Antillean conducts himself like a white man. But he is a Negro. That he will learn once he goes to Europe; and when he hears Negroes mentioned he will recognize that the word includes himself as well as the Senegalese . . . .

As long as he remains among his own people, the little black follows very nearly the same course as the little white. But if he goes to Europe, he will have to reappraise his lot. For the Negro in France, which is his country, will feel different from other people. One can hear the glib remark: The Negro makes himself inferior. But the truth is that he is made inferior. The young Antillean is a Frenchman called upon constantly to live with white compatriots. Now, the Antillean family has for all practical purposes no connection with the national – that is, the French, or European – structure. The Antillean has therefore to choose between his family and European society; in other words, the individual who *climbs up* into society – white and civilized – tends to reject his family – black and savage – on the plane of imagination . . . .

I have just shown that for the Negro there is a myth to be faced. A solidly established myth. The Negro is unaware of it as long as his existence is limited to his own environment; but the first encounter with a white man oppresses him with the whole weight of his blackness . . . .

The civilized white man retains an irrational longing for unusual eras of sexual license, of orgiastic scenes, of unpunished rapes, of unrepressed incest . . . . Projecting his own desires onto the Negro, the white man behaves 'as if' the Negro really had them. When it is a question of the Jew, the problem is clear: He is suspect because he wants to own the wealth or take over the positions of power. But the Negro is fixated at the genital; or at any rate he has been fixated there. Two realms: the intellectual and the sexual . . . . The Negro symbolizes the biological danger; the Jew, the intellectual danger.

To suffer from a phobia of Negroes is to be afraid of the biological. For the Negro is only biological. The Negroes are animals . . . .

In the beginning I wanted to confine myself to the Antilles. But . . . I was compelled to *see* that the Antillean is first of all a Negro. Nevertheless, it would be impossible to overlook the fact that there are Negroes whose nationality is Belgian, French, English; there are also Negro republics . . . . The truth is that the Negro race has been scattered, that it can no longer claim unity. When Il Duce's troops invaded Ethiopia[1], a movement of solidarity arose among men of color . . . .

Wherever he goes, the Negro remains a Negro . . . .

Is not whiteness in symbols always ascribed in French to Justice, Truth, Virginity? I knew an Antillean who said of another Antillean, 'His body is black, his language is black, his soul must be black too'. This logic is put into daily practice by the white man. The black man is the symbol of Evil and Ugliness . . . .

European civilization is characterized by the presence, at the heart of what Jung[2] calls the collective unconscious, of an archetype: an expression of the bad instincts, of the darkness inherent in every ego, of the uncivilized savage, the Negro who slumbers in every white man. And Jung claims to have found in uncivilized peoples the same psychic structure that his diagram portrays. Personally, I think that Jung has deceived himself . . . .

Jung locates the collective unconscious in the inherited cerebral matter. But the collective unconscious, without our having to fall back on the genes, is purely and simply the sum of prejudices, myths, collective attitudes of a given group . . . .

I hope I have shown that . . . the collective unconscious is cultural, which means acquired . . . . *In Europe, the black man is the symbol of Evil . . . .* Satan is black, one talks of shadows, when one is dirty one is black – whether one is thinking of physical dirtiness or of moral dirtiness. It would be astonishing, if the trouble were taken to bring them all together, to see the vast number of expressions that make the black man the equivalent of sin. In Europe, whether concretely or symbolically, the black man stands for the bad side of the character. As long as one cannot understand this fact, one is doomed to talk in circles about the 'black problem' . . . . In Europe, that is to say, in every civilized and civilizing country, the Negro is the symbol of sin. The archetype of the lowest values is represented by the Negro . . . .

In Europe the Negro has one function: that of symbolizing the lower emotions, the baser inclinations, the dark side of the soul. In the collective unconscious of *homo occidentalis*, the Negro – or, if one prefers, the color black – symbolizes evil, sin, wretchedness, death, war, famine . . . .

The collective unconscious is not dependent on cerebral heredity; it is the result of what I shall call the unreflected imposition of a culture. Hence there is no reason to be surprised when an Antillean exposed to waking-dream therapy relives the same fantasies as a European. It is because the Antillean partakes of the same collective unconscious as the European.

If what has been said thus far is grasped, this conclusion may be stated: It is normal for the Antillean to be anti-Negro. Through the collective unconscious the Antillean has taken over all the archetypes belonging to the European. But I too am guilty, . . . There is no help for it: I am a white man. For unconsciously I distrust what is black in me, that is, the whole of my being . . . .

[W]ithout thinking, the Negro selects himself as an object capable of carrying the burden of original sin. The white man chooses the black man for this function, and the black man who is white also chooses the black man. The black Antillean is the slave of this cultural imposition. After having been the slave of the white man, he enslaves himself. The Negro is in every sense of the word a victim of white civilization . . . .

Hence a Negro is forever in combat with his own image . . . .

[E]ach individual has to charge the blame for his baser drives, his impulses, to the account of an evil genius, which is that of the culture to which he belongs (we have seen that this is the Negro). This collective guilt is borne by what is conventionally called the scapegoat. Now the scapegoat for white society – which is based on myths of progress, civilization, liberalism, education, enlightenment, refinement – will be precisely the force that opposes the expansion and the triumph of these myths. This brutal opposing force is supplied by the Negro.

In the society of the Antilles, where the myths are identical with those of the society of Dijon or Nice, the young Negro, identifying himself with the civilizing power, will make the nigger the scapegoat of his moral life . . . .

As I begin to recognize that the Negro is the symbol of sin, I catch myself hating the Negro. But then I recognize that I am a Negro . . . .

[A]t its extreme, the myth of the Negro, the idea of the Negro, can become the decisive factor of an authentic alienation . . . .

I wonder sometimes whether school inspectors and government functionaries are aware of the role they play in the colonies. For twenty years they poured every effort into programs that would make the Negro a white man. In the end, they dropped him and told him, 'You have an indisputable complex of dependence on the white man' . . . .

I said in my introduction that man is a *yes*. I will never stop reiterating that.

Yes to life. *Yes* to love. *Yes* to generosity.

But man is also a *no*. *No* to scorn of man. *No* to degradation of man. *No* to exploitation of man. *No* to the butchery of what is most human in man: freedom . . .

I do not carry innocence to the point of believing that appeals to reason or to respect for human dignity can alter reality. For the Negro who works on a sugar plantation in Le Robert, there is only one solution: to fight. He will embark on this struggle, and he will pursue it, not as the result of a Marxist or idealistic analysis but quite simply because he cannot conceive of life otherwise than in the form of a battle against exploitation, misery, and hunger . . . .

Those Negroes and white men will be disalienated who refuse to let themselves be sealed away in the materialized Tower of the Past. For many other Negroes, in other ways, disalienation will come into being through their refusal to accept the present as definitive.

I am a man, and what I have to recapture is the whole past of the world. I am not responsible solely for the revolt in Santo Domingo.

Every time a man has contributed to the victory of the dignity of the spirit, every time a man has said no to an attempt to subjugate his fellows, I have felt solidarity with his act.

In no way should I derive my basic purpose from the past of the peoples of color.

In no way should I dedicate myself to the revival of an unjustly unrecognized Negro civilization. I will not make myself the man of any past. I do not want to exalt the past at the expense of my present and of my future . . . .

If the question of practical solidarity with a given past ever arose for me, it did so only to the extent to which I was committed to myself and to my neighbor to fight for all my life and with all my strength so that never again would a people on the earth be subjugated. It was not the black world that laid down my course of conduct. My black skin is not the wrapping of specific values . . . .

I find myself suddenly in the world and I recognize that I have one right alone: That of demanding human behavior from the other.

One duty alone: That of not renouncing my freedom through my choices . . . .

I am a Negro, and tons of chains, storms of blows, rivers of expectoration flow down my shoulders.

But I do not have the right to allow myself to bog down. I do not have the right to allow the slightest fragment to remain in my existence. I do not have the right to allow myself to be mired in what the past has determined.

I am not the slave of the Slavery that dehumanized my ancestors . . . .

Let us be clearly understood. I am convinced that it would be of the greatest interest to be able to have contact with a Negro literature or architecture of the third century before Christ. I should be very happy to know that a correspondence had flourished between some Negro philosopher and Plato. But I can absolutely not see how this fact would change anything in the lives of the eight-year-old children who labor in the cane fields of Martinique or Guadeloupe.

No attempt must be made to encase man, for it is his destiny to be set free.

The body of history does not determine a single one of my actions.

I am my own foundation . . . .

The Negro is not. Any more than the white man.

Both must turn their backs on the inhuman voices which were those of their respective ancestors in order that authentic communication be possible. Before it can adopt a positive voice, freedom requires an effort at disalienation . . . .

It is through the effort to recapture the self and to scrutinize the self, it is through the lasting tension of their freedom that men will be able to create the ideal conditions of existence for a human world.

Superiority? Inferiority?

Why not the quite simple attempt to touch the other, to feel the other, to explain the other to myself?

NOTES

1. Italy, which was led by Benito Mussolini (1883–1945), who took the title Il Duce, invaded Ethiopia in 1935. The emperor Haile Selassie led the resistance and the Italians were defeated in 1941.
2. Carl Gustav Jung (1875–1961) was an influential Swiss psychologist who developed a theory that the human mind, and therefore behaviour, is shaped by instinctive archetypes that bridge our conscious thought and the unconscious by means of symbols and dreams.

Eighteen

René Depestre

René Depestre (born in 1927) is a Haitian poet and intellectual who has lived in Cuba since 1960, and who has written in Spanish as well as French. The child of poor mulatto parents, he was politically active in Haiti, as a leader of the Parti Démocratique Populaire de la Jeunesse Haitienne, *a Marxist group, and also served as editor of the journals* La Ruche *and* La Nouvelle Ruche. *He participated in the* Front Révolutionnaire Haitian *and supported Juste Constant, the secretary-general of the Haitian Communist party (PCH), for president. However, after Dumarsais Estimé won the election and became president in 1946, the PCH dissolved itself the following year, and Depestre took up a government scholarship to study abroad. He became an active opponent of the Duvalier regime in the 1950s.*

Depestre has argued that Haiti's national culture, like any other, has to be understood in its specific historical context and he criticised the conception of a 'black poetry' as mythical, lacking a concrete historical dimension. At the 1968 cultural congress in Havana he denounced négritude *as 'a delirious mystification' that had become exploited by Duvalier and other reactionaries. He condemned as absurd the notion that black people or white people had different natures, or that there was a black culture or a white culture. Though the issue of race and colour was important, he argued, the problem of identity in the Caribbean was rooted in the history of the region's social relations. His essay on this topic,* 'Problemas de la identidad del hombre negro en la literatura antillana', *was originally published in* Casa de las Americas *in 1969.*

Problems of Identity for the Black Man in Caribbean Literatures

The study of the African presence in Caribbean literature poses numerous problems. Among them, there is one which seems to me definitive – 'the problem of the identity of the black man'. I believe that in these islands we are entitled to talk of a 'literature of identification' which expresses itself in French, English and Spanish. I believe that the passionate search for this identification is the first unifying element which presents itself when one compares the major lines of our diverse literatures. The same preoccupation with the idea of coming to terms with oneself is evident in the works of the majority of our 20th century writers – James, Roumain, Césaire, Guillén, Price-Mars, Brierre, Fanon, Damas, Alexis, Lamming, Pedroso, Niger, Tirolien, Glissant, Harris etc.[1]

During the last 30 or 40 years black poets, novelists and essayists in the area have been obsessed by the same theme: to seek and declare our identity as Martinicans, Jamaicans, Cubans, Guadeloupeans, Trinidadians, Haitians, Dominicans, Puerto Ricans, in short as Antilleans, West Indians. Poems, novels, theatrical works, sociological and ethnological essays as well as historical research have all posed the same anguished questions – In what way will the black man of the Caribbean come to terms with himself, convert himself to what he is, find his true self in society and in history? How will he make the synthesis of the diverse historical components of his culture? Under what conditions will he eventually decolonize the socio-economic structures and the psychological structures which have made life in the Caribbean one of the greatest scandals of the 20th century?

These fundamental questions born out of the day to day experiences of our different islands, have so far found effective answers only in Cuba. In fact, in other islands, men and women have not yet been able to recover their social character, their profound personality, their humanity and beauty which colonization has alienated. Literature and the arts, just as science and education do not meet the immediate and future needs of our peoples. Our cultures continue to grow to the rhythm of western neo-colonialism and lack the possibility of advancing in accordance with their own internal dynamism. With the sole exception of Cuba, the development of our nations is not conceived in terms of a decolonization of the alienating structures of the past. Our islands are victims of malnutrition, unemployment, illiteracy, intellectual under-employment and cultural hibernation.

We are in the midst of a divided world, one torn apart by every type of archaism and socio-economic incongruities which freeze the forces of creation and knowledge.

And so, in order to understand the significance and the sociological and anthropological value of the problem of our identity one must place it in the history of social relations in our islands. The struggle for this identity, long before finding expression in our literatures, has had its place in all stages of the history of our societies. This fight has taken many different forms in relation to the historical conditions in each island. The problem of identity is closely linked to a central fact in Caribbean history – Slavery. And what was slavery but anti-identity by definition? Slavery 'depersonalized' the African man who was shipped to the West Indies. The principal object of this means of production was to extract from slave labour the energy to create material riches. The black man was in that way, converted into a coal-man, combustible-man, a nothing-man.

This process of 'cosificacion' (converting a man into a thing), which is inherent to slave labour, involves another complementary process – the cultural assimilation of the colonized West Indian. The colonial system did everything possible to make of us, West Indians, Anglo-Saxons and Latin types with black skins. It was intended to make the West Indian lose not only the worthy use of his human energy in his work, but also his essential truths, his culture, his identity and himself. In our case, just as in the case of any other Negro in America, the famous 'I am another' of Arthur Rimbaud[2] became ' I am a white Anglo-Saxon product, I am a white Latin product'. I am coal, petroleum, prison, ghetto, and the use which was made of my labour force was creating powers such as sugar, coffee, cotton and other products found in abundance in colonial markets, all of which were alien to me. This fantastic process of assimilation and conversion into a thing implied the total loss of my identity as a man, the psychological destruction of my being. It is no mere chance that the myth of the 'Zombi'[3] (jumbee or duppy) was born precisely in the West Indies, since the history of his archipelago is that of a process of the accelerated 'zombificacion' of the black man.

Having robbed me of my creative energy, I was robbed of my past, my history, my psychological integrity, my legends and my most secret beauties as a human being. Subsequently, when slavery had already been abolished, I was still kept, as a West Indian, at the point where it was impossible to work out a synthesis of different African and European components of my culture. By means of a frightening acculturative pressure, everything was done, before my very eyes, to make the African substratum of my life appear unworthy of the human race. I was made to have a terrible opinion of myself. I was forced to deny a decisive part of my social being, to detest my face, my colour, the peculiarities of my culture, the specific reactions of my sensibility in the face of life, love, death and art. And all this was also done so that I might idealize the colour, history and culture of my white masters!

Through alienating work, in colonial society, I was made to be not only a stranger to myself, but hostile to myself, ashamed of myself, enemy of myself.

Alienation was carried to the level of my black skin to which was given a metaphysical, aesthetic and moral significance: in fact, the colour of the black West Indies was changed, as far as the black man was concerned, into a source of permanent frustration, and there was created in our society a real escalade of scorn which showed up its terror between the whites on the one hand, resembling the splendour of day, and the blacks on the other, resembling the shadows of night. Colour became an impassable barrier between the generic character of the West Indian Negro and its realization in history. Whereas the alienation of the white labourer in a capitalist society is linked to the economic and social scheme of work, the alienation of the Negro penetrated into the most intimate structures of his personality. Slavery and the equally oppressive socio-economic structures which have followed it in the West Indies, have been fountains of psychological traumas which have profoundly affected the personality of the West Indian Negro.

How have Caribbean peoples reacted to these totalitarian limitations, so as to avoid the absolute wreck of their identity? How have they resisted this process of depersonalization? As far as possible, they have, like the maroons who fled from the estates, evaded the techniques of total assimilation employed by 'white' powers. The socio-cultural and socio-psychological history of black West Indians (and of the black Americas in general) is largely the history of the ideological 'cimarronaje'[4] (escape) which has allowed the West Indies to not re-interpret the West through an African mentality, as Melville Herskovits[5] has believed, but to adapt itself to the conditions of the class struggle in the region, transforming the popular, Western, cultural schemata into serving our emotional needs which are profoundly tributary of Africa. This cultural escape is an original form of rebellion which has manifested itself in religion, in folklore, in art and singularly in Caribbean literatures.

The major West Indian writers, be they writers in English, French or Spanish (like those who write in our vernacular tongues), are 'cimarrones' (escapees) from western culture. This general escape has not been equally effective in all areas of life. The West Indian Negro has not been able to reject the masters' language, although in some cases, as the existence of creole in Haiti, Guadeloupe and Martinique proves, the linguistic escape has been crowned with success. As is well known, language is an important element in the identity of any man. For us to be fully ourselves, it would be necessary to be able to think and create in languages that are Haitian, Martinician, Jamaican, Barbadian and so on, which would be able to give us a more accurate image of ourselves than that which we have when using instruments such as French, English or Spanish, thinking apparatus which, by force of acculturation, we have had to add to our experience and which we must always conquer, to our own advantage and risk, to express our identity.

It is not always an easy operation, and Léon Laleau[6] was right when he spoke of:

despair unrivalled

trying to conquer with words from France

this heart which I received from Senegal ...

The West Indian Negro's cultural resistance has, on the contrary, won indisputable victories in religion, folklore, music and dance. And yet, except in the case of Haiti, it has failed in regard to economic and political systems. Likewise, African techniques, statuary art, wood and ivory sculpture, fabrics, etc. have not been able to resist the onslaught of European technology. Material expressions of African cultures in the West Indies have been submerged by colonization. In Haiti, the colonial West was, at a given time, resisted and all its values. The Haitian Revolution of 1804 was the only case of a successful rejection recorded in West Indian history, not only on the cultural plane, but also on the political and economic planes.

Nevertheless, it was not able to prevent the myth of assimilation from reestablishing itself later in the society which emerged out of the liberation of the slaves; in fact, it even found indigenous promoters. This demonstrates the great complexity of decolonization, as well as the need to realize, simultaneously, the liberation of the socio-economic structures and the psychological structures of consciousness.

However, apart from the grave limitations which we have just pointed out, the Revolution of the 'Black Jacobins'[7] of Haiti has had some cultural significance and value which have not been sufficiently highlighted. For the first time since the 'Diaspora' of the Negroes in America, the problem of identity was being explored in its theoretical and practical senses. And so, the numerous revolts and uprisings of slaves which spread throughout all our islands were also attempts carried out by our 'negritude' to liberate itself.

This concept of 'negritude', then, explains the operation by which people of black skin in America, in search of their identity, have become aware of the validity of their African heritage latent in our societies, aware of the aesthetic value of the black race, aware of the specific peculiarities of some aspects of our alienation, and aware also of the need to come to a full realization of themselves, in close union and solidarity with the oppressed whites, in a society freed from all the alienating dogmas of capitalism, beginning with the despicable racial dogma.

The social reality which nurtures the concept of 'negritude', just like the struggle for our identification, existed long before the black intellectuals of this century began to express them in literary, historical, sociological and ethnological works. In fact, efforts in the recognition and revaluation of the African heritage date from the years immediately after the victory of the Haitian Revolution of 1804. This successful slave revolution – the only one known in human history – was, in itself, a glorious act of identification for the black man. It showed to the entire world that liberty and human dignity also have a black face in the history of civilizations. It further highlighted in universal life, the personality of the black man, by giving full exposure to great men like Toussaint L'Ouverture[8] and the other heroes of the early independence era in Haiti.

The Haitian Revolution also allowed the Negro, wherever he was in America, to acquire a new vision of himself and to begin to destroy all the cliches and stereotypes of the negro which had been created entirely by colonization. In the Haitian revolutionary context, the psychological mechanisms and motives of self-integration and self-conquest could play an effectual role. In view of this revolutionary experience of the Haitian people, identification manifests itself as a social and a psychological process which allows the Negro to understand that his misfortunes are those of a social class oppressed by capital and that his fight ought to be, above everything else, a national struggle for liberation. Such an awareness, though timid, can be found in the works of some nineteenth century Haitian publicists who are the precursors of the movement of ideas and sensibility which later became known as 'Negritude'. With regard to them, one can speak of a 'pre-negritude' movement just as one would say pre-renaissance, since in the cultural and literary history of the Caribbean, 'negritude' was, at a certain time, regarded as a real Renaissance.

Before analysing the value and significance of the concept of 'negritude' in Caribbean literatures, I would like to deal with another literary phenomenon which is also linked to the problem of the identity of our peoples. It is the question of negrismo. Very often people confuse negrismo and negritude, but, in fact, they are two different cultural entities. Their aesthetic and sociological value is not the same. "Negrismo" in West Indian Literatures has been, primarily, a movement for white intellectuals who, drawing on the works of ethnologists on African survivals in the New World, have used different Afro-Antillean folklores as their source of inspiration. After the first world war, many white poets and artists made use of rhythmic and onomatopoeic elements and sensory factors belonging to the oral literature of the Negro. Some, in search of the picturesque, and out of sympathy, and we might even say humanitarianism, for the Negroes, or – in the worst cases – out of the simple curiosity of a funny tourist. These artists proposed to introduce the 'Negro theme' into their works, so that 'Negrismo' was only a literary fashion.

Its antecedents, on the other hand, date far back into literary history. One can, in fact, find features of 'negrismo' and 'mulatismo' (works about Mulattoes) in the works of Lope, Gongora, Sor Juana Inez de la Cruz,[9] Victor Hugo, Lamartine, Longfellow, Blake, etc. In like manner, in contemporary literature, many famous Europeans and American artists undertook to add a fine 'black cord' to the 'white bow' of the Christian West.

And yet, the works of some white artists in the West Indies, namely, Luis Pales

Matos of Puerto Rico, Ramon Güirao, Emilio Ballagas, Jose Z. Tallet and Aléjo Carpentier of Cuba,[10] acquire, at times, the value of real acculturation of the African heritage. 'Negrismo' is symptomatic of a change in the spiritual state of white, liberal intellectuals. It is a kind of timid recognition, tinged with humour and irony, of the value of the African contribution to our cultures. It represents a real step forward in relation to the 'negrista' literature which appeared in the Southern United States in the last century, or even in the very West Indies, where, under the mask of finding inspiration in Afro-American folklore, they did nothing but insolently glorify all the stereotypes regarding Negro life which, after several centuries of slavery, had been disseminated throughout the continent.

In twentieth century West Indian 'negrismo' the Negro is no longer represented as the clown of universal history; he is no longer an object of denigration and scorn. On the contrary, his specific cultural features are now integrated with an effort to renovate poetry. Nevertheless, the main criticism of the 'negrismo' is that it limited itself to a superficial knowledge of the African heritage and failed to preserve anything more than the formal and folkloric aspects of the Negroes' condition in America. In 'negrismo' there is neither rebellion nor anger.

The historical situation of the West Indian Negro does not emerge in 'negrismo'. This comment is not the result of an internal experience nor even an anthropological notion. For this reason one can justifiably say that between 'negrismo' and 'negritude', there exists every qualitative difference that exists between an ordinary wick and the wick of a dynamite.

On their side, the poets and writers of 'negritude' have tried to take a profound look at the past and at the present of the West Indian Negro. 'Negritude' is, therefore, the fact of an awareness of the historical situation created around Negroes. There is, in 'negritude', a conscious and deliberate pre-occupation with the destruction of the myths and stereotypes of the Negro. And this ontological pre-occupation is present in the works of two or three generations of West Indian authors.

But, admittedly, there are as many forms of 'negritude' as there are varying West Indian societies. This is due to the fact that, the search for identification, of which the 'negritude' movement is the literary and artistic expression, is oriented by different lines of force, as it enters into the concrete conditions of the class struggle in each of our societies. 'Negritude' converts itself into justification when it denies the diversity of the material conditions of evolution of our West Indian societies and it considers the creative sensibility of the Negroes as a homogenous cultural block, interchangeable in its expressive manifestations. The African heritage, after prolonged cohabitation with cultural elements originating in different European countries – France, England, Spain and Holland – and submerged in different realities, has given rise to psychic patterns, psychological peculiarities and states of consciousness which are as different from Africa as from Europe and which, among themselves, are different. In spite of their common source (African-Europe) the cultures of Cuba, Haiti, Jamaica, Martinique, Guadeloupe, Barbados, Trinidad, Puerto Rico, the Dominican Republic as well as Brasil, Rio de la Plata and other Caribbean peoples, present national characteristics of their own because of their historical formation in different territories, in the bosom of an economic and social life which responds to a number of specific factors. This does not deny, however, the existence of numerous common features in the psychology of the different West Indian peoples.

Among the features that establish the cultural unity of the West Indies in history, there are two which seem to me fundamental. In the first place, black West Indian men do not know what is their true identity. In the second place, the history of our diverse and singular cultures follows the same process of a syncretic elaboration of cultural elements taken from Africa and Europe. These two focal points of civilization are present in social consciousness and in the customs and traditions of all West Indian people, like the mixed syncretic expression, in constant change, of diverse conditions of social existence which we have known, from the days of the slave trade to the present. This is why it is an error, when one speaks of 'negritude', to set aside this concept of a socio-economic development peculiar to each of our peoples. Such an error is the result of a false interpretation of the dialectical and internal relations which exist between the many factors and indices which define the historical category called a nation. It becomes evident, after analysis, that belonging to the same race, or the colour of the skin or the shape of the nose or lips, or the 'diaspora' which resulted from the slave trade, are not the factors which determine the national character of each of our islands, but rather, the concrete conditions of life in each island, the conditions of historical development which belong to each West Indian community. I repeat, Africa and Europe manifest their presence through a complex of perceptions, reflections and representations of psychological peculiarities, of specific forms of alienation, and of rhythms, dances and songs which are translated into the manifestations of our sensibility and our psychic life, as the result of a long process of cultural 'mestizaje'[11] (mixing up) and syncretism.

There are, then, various West Indian forms of 'negritude', just as there are various African forms of 'negritude'. In an exhaustive study of 'negritude' it is necessary to distinguish, sometimes in the same country, different currents and various divergent tendencies. The unifying value of 'negritude' lies, not in the colour of the skin, but in a concrete historical situation. 'Negritude' is the modern equivalent of the old 'cimarronaje'.

In several West Indian authors 'negritude' has been – and is still so – a vigorous form of protest which incorporates the revolutionary thought of our era and which completes the articulation of Marxism to our West Indian realities, adding to it the knowledge of our historical uniqueness and, consequently, the traumatic experience of slavery, colonization and racism. There is a right wing 'negritude' and a leftist one. There is a progressive 'negritude' which, taking into account the dual character of alienation among oppressed black peoples, appears in the history of decolonization like the emotional response of the exploited and humiliated black man to the total scorn of the neo-colonial western world. There is a 'negritude' that expounds the need to rise above all the alienations of man by means of a revolutionary praxis. There is a 'negritude' that lives in the socialist experience more intensely than the racial experience and which fights so that everywhere, an end will be put to the epidermal interpretation of the historical situation of men as colonialism has done in the case of the Negroes. There is a 'negritude' that affirms that the skin of all men, no matter what the colour, shares the same privilege of light, because 'all men are men'. There is a 'negritude' which vigorously places itself in the historical context of the Revolution in the Third World[12] grouping and which its human requirements to the immediate facts of the tricontinental and global struggle of underdeveloped peoples against neo-colonialism and imperialism. There is a 'negritude' which outlines to black peoples their duty to carry out the revolution in order to be able to affirm definitively their identity in world history.

However, 'negritude' as a diversified movement of ideas, as an ideology with multiple currents does not always present itself in a progressive and revolutionary form. On the contrary, it can be said that while in Africa and the West Indies a so-called pseudo-decolonization is taking place, 'negritude' tends to be transformed into dangerous dogma, into a new form of mystification and alienation.

There exists an irrational reactionary and mystic version of 'negritude' which evaluates its projects in the sphere of ideological imposture and serves as a cultural base for neo-colonialist penetration into our countries. It has to do with a new myth which deliberately tends to hide the socio-economic factors which have conditioned the situation of Negroes in our societies of alienation and oppression. This 'negritude' does not take into consideration the radical disorder of social relations in the Third World of Africa, Asia, the West Indies and Latin America in general. This 'negritude' has ceased to be a legitimate form of rebellion opposed to the shameful manifestations of racist dogma and has presented itself as a mystic operation which tends to dissimilate the presence, on the historical scene, in Africa and the West Indies, of the black bourgeoisie who, in Haiti for example, long established as a dominant class, try to disguise the real nature of social relations. Those black and mulatto bourgeoisie have perfected the mechanisms of oppression and the alienating networks inherited from the colonial system and cause to fall back on them, all the barbarism which, in the course of the last centuries, dehumanized the history of the peoples of the Third World. They indigenized the violent acts of the old colonizers and practised all the obscene intoxication of tyranny and servitude.

If you want a shocking example of that kind of 'negritude' take a look at the state into which the tyranny of François Duvalier[13] has plunged Haiti. Look at the way in which Negroes are assassinating fellow Negroes! Look at the bloody disasters which take place in Haiti under the mandate of a totalitarian 'negritude' which has nothing for which to envy Hitler's national-socialism. The image which Haitians have of their country today is no longer that of a mythic motherland of 'negritude'. Even if it is true that Haiti was the country 'where 'negritude' first sprang up', it is now the West Indian land where 'negritude' is a sinister mythology which forces our people to live on their knees. What happened to 'negritude' is what happens to any ideology which becomes a dogma used to disguise the real interests and motives of the struggle of the social classes.

In Senghor[14], for example, 'negritude' embraces realities which are very different from those which nourish the work of Damas, Jacques Roumain, Césaire, or Guillén.[15] Far from being a Negro-African humanism as he would like it to be presented, Léopold Sédar Senghor's 'negritude' is a mythology which plays into the hands of neo-colonialism in Africa. In fact, in Senghor's eyes, 'negritude' is an immutable state of the social existence of the Negro; that is to say, it is, in essence, a predetermined substance which 40,000 years ago could have been found in the 'steatopygous statuettes of Grimaldi's negroid women'. With Senghor, 'negritude' ceases to be a historical category, an ideology of decolonization, and becomes an alienating dogma.

Senghor's thought is set in an abstract context, far from the hard realities in which the peoples of Africa are trying, in some cases with arms in hand, to conquer their real personality in history. For Senghor and his African and West Indian disciples, the best defence and illustration of 'negritude' is not social revolution, but a simple recovery of the traditional values that belong to African civilization. We are not facing a mythic Africa where only the exterior signs of the identity of the black man are revealed, so as to conceal the socio-economic and socio-cultural defects of the pseudo-decolonization. Basing his thought on the outstanding Christian figure, Father Teilhard de Chardin[16] and on Bachelard, Senghor, in his essays on 'negritude' has elaborated a kind of cosmological romanticism, neovitalism, a mystic surrealism which he presents as the constant content of 'the inner experiences of the Negro'. Senghor transforms the future into a Senghorian museum! He establishes a complex of metaphysical values which, according to him, he finds in all Negroes, in all parts of the world, and which are independent of class struggle and class structures. His inventory of 'negritude' forms the basis for a pretended Negro-African ontology. According to this Senghorian ontology, black men in their way of life, their way of feeling, in their very being are recognizable anywhere by the following characteristics:

(i)   the natural gift of rhythm, symbol, and image.
(ii)   In them intuitive reason predominates, whereas the whites have the monopoly of discursive reason.
(iii) Negroes would have an innate solidarity, collectivism and spontaneous humanism.

This idyllic picture of the black man does not correspond to historical reality. We know that no race has a monopoly of rhythm, symbol or image. These are attributes of all literatures of the pre-capitalist era. In the same way, one could not, without falling into mystification, subordinate the historical categories of reason to factors in any ethnic order. And if Negroes had, as Senghor claims, a privileged devotion to human solidarity, Haitian people would never have known eleven years of totalitarian Duvalierism, nor would Patrice Lumumba[17] have lost his life at the hands of Negroes in his own country. What comes to Senghor's pen most frequently is the image of Negro-rhythm. In his eyes, the Negro is only rhythm, emotion, intuition. It is a question of a new stereotype of the Negro. Surely, rhythm occupies an important place in the history of our cultures. This is one of the elements of our cultural uniqueness, but thought, reflection and discursive reasoning are values which are seen in the works of the best Negro writers and artists.

On the political plane, Senghor has affirmed finally that 'one has to understand clearly, that if one wishes to speak of twentieth century socialism, that the greatest inequalities are not found among social classes within a particular nation, but among nations, on a world scale'. A quick glance at African and West Indian societies makes it clear that this vision of the contemporary planes, then, Senghor's 'negritude' is a mythology far removed from progressive reality, which could only cover the concept during the period between the two world wars, when Senghor, along with Césaire and Damas, sought an ideology of African values, an ideology of national liberation, against the colonial structures of oppression and alienation.

It has been said that we West Indians, represented the various stages of the same nightmare. In fact, wherever one looks in the West Indies, one sees, not paradise-islands, but peoples frustrated by all sorts of socio-economic and socio-cultural aberrations. We see people stagnating in a hodge-podge of social, technical, demographic, psychological and cultural problems. We see people whose cultural unity is objectively visible in numerous sociological, anthropological and literary realities, and who nevertheless, are still strangers among themselves. Yet, today, it is from London, Paris and Washington – where many of us are still in exile – that we succeed in getting a global vision of the unity of our archipelago. We are Jamaicans, Puerto Ricans, Martinicians, 'West Indians', 'Antilleans' etc., laid aside on the insular frontiers of the human sub-condition. The forces of literature and art in this terrible Caribbean Third World most times remain unproductive because they are dominated by the coercive and violent force of under-development.

The direct, colonial presence, when being wiped out, is inclined to put in its place structures as sterilizing as those of the past. Pseudo-elitist intellectuals, full of cowardice and treachery humiliate national feeling and the dignity of our peoples. Most West Indians continue to be, in the eyes of the rest of humanity, invisible men, without an identity, Zombies who view themselves with shame in their nostalgia for the true human condition.

In this horrible context, there is only one island that offers a different picture – Cuba. Why? The answer is clear: the Cuban people have carried out a Revolution and their life had ceased to be a nightmare. The Cuban people have, by themselves, become the 'bakers of their life' to use an image of Jacques Roumain's. Here, the Revolution simultaneously settled down to the task of transforming their economic and social structures and setting in motion a psychological process of liberation for the mass of the Cuban people. For the first time in the twentieth century, we have in a West Indian island a social force which liberates in the white man, the Negro and the mulatto, their common identity, that is to say, their capacity for creativity and inversion. For the first time, a popular power is vigorously structuring the objective conditions of inter-racial relations based on the equality and dignity of all men. The Cuban man, black, white or mulatto, can be married to the Truth of his life. He has sought and found the process of social liberation and the cognitive process which allows him to transform his life into an explosion of health, creativity and human fraternity. The terrible opinion the Negro had of himself and which the old social system gave him, gives way to an inner life which effectively lives out the unity of the human race. Similarly, the inner life of the white man is enriched by the same liberating joy. All the initiatives of the Cuban Revolution in the various fields of culture and education are also dynamic factors of racial integration. For the first time in the West Indies, since the Haitian Revolution which belongs to another historical era, the struggle for the identification of himself with himself, has become an uninterrupted social creation, a sustained effort, an undertaking carried out in a coherent and reflective manner. For the first time, a group of people in the West Indies knows the foundations of their social being since their history is carried to the highest level of tension and vitality. And so, the writer and poet who integrate themselves into this collective and enriching experience, know right away on what grounds to base the character of their novel or poetry.

The Revolution, in fact, is breaking the emotional alienating circuits of the past, like those relating to racial dogma, and is creating in men reflections of fraternity and solidarity. For the first time in history, not only West Indian history but also in the two black Americas, the descendants of Africans have no need to evade the dominant values since these are universal values which release, in the entire Cuban populace, the forces of imagination and knowledge. The black Orpheus[18] can, today, define himself not by his blackness, but by his objective and subjective human condition, since this West Indian Revolution is ourselves, is our most authentic and profound identity, is a life-giving process of recovery of all the historical components of our personality. The object of this search, that is, our identity, is accessible to us in any society that recognizes the dignity of each human being and where each one recognizes, at the same time, the peculiarity and the universality of his condition. The problem of identity, to be projected in literature and art, must pass through a uniting experience of liberation. This is the joy that I wish for all of the West Indies, so that their dignity and beauty may be restored to our brothers, once and for all, in literature as well as in life.

NOTES

1. These writers are from various parts of the Caribbean, including Trinidad, Haiti, Martinique, Cuba, Cayenne, Barbados and Guyana.
2. Arthur Rimbaud (1854–1891), a French poet, wrote major poems when he was a teenager. The only valid subject of poetry for Rimbaud was the exploration of the self.
3. A *zombie* is a person whose soul has been removed and whose body, disinterred from the grave, is used for slave work.
4. *Cimarrón* may derive from a Taino word meaning fugitive and the Spanish *cimá*, meaning mountaintop. Originally applied to livestock and fugitive Taino slaves in Hispaniola, the word was applied to African fugitive slaves by the 1530s. The French *marron* and the English 'maroon' are derived from the Spanish word.
5. Melville J. Herskovits, an American anthropologist, and his wife, Frances Herskovits, worked in Suriname in 1924, West Africa in 1931, Haiti in 1934, Trinidad in 1939, and Brazil in 1941. Their books include *Life in a Haitian Valley* (1937), *The Myth of the Negro Past* (1941) and *Trinidad Village* (1943). He argued forcefully, and with considerable evidence from their fieldwork, that many elements of African cultures survived in the Americas.
6. Léon Laleau (1892–1979), a Haitian poet and novelist, published *Musique nègre* in 1931. This excerpt is from the poem 'Betrayal' in that collection.
7. The Jacobins were the most radical group in the French Revolution and they were briefly in power from 1793 to 1794, when their leader, Robespierre, was executed. The Haitian revolutionaries became known as the Black Jacobins, as in the title of C.L.R. James's classic study written in 1938.
8. Toussaint L'Ouverture was one of the chief leaders of the revolution in Saint Domingue that resulted in the end of slavery and the independence of Haiti. He became the governor in 1800, but he was captured and taken to France where he died in prison in 1803.
9. Sor Juana Inez de la Cruz (c.1651–95) was a Mexican nun and the author of poems, essays and plays in a baroque and lyrical style, with mystical overtones.
10. Luis Pales Matos (1898–1959), a modernist poet of Puerto Rico, was one of the creators, with Nicolas Guillen of Cuba, of the Afro-Antillean literary movement called

negrismo. Ramon Guirao (1908–49) was a Cuban poet and a founding member of *Sociedad de Estudios Afrocubanos*, who helped to develop Afro-Cuban themes in literature. Emilio Ballagos y Cubeñas (1908–54) was a Cuban poet, essayist and teacher who focussed on Afro-Cuban subjects, including folklore and social conditions. José Zacarías Tallet (1893–1985), a Cuban poet and journalist, a Marxist and member of several left-wing organisations, is best known for his poem, *La rumba*. Alejo Carpentier (1904–80), a prolific Cuban novelist and short story writer, published his first novel, *¡ Ecue-Yamba-o!* in 1933 as part of the Afro-Cuban literary movement.

11. *Mestizaje* refers to a biological process of mixing or miscegenation that produces *mestizos*, people of mixed Indian and European, or in some places, of Indian and African descent.

12. The term 'Third World' was coined in the 1950s, during the cold war, to refer to all those countries, many of which were still in the process of decolonisation, that were not within the First World of the industrialised capitalist countries or the Second World of the communist ones. These countries were very different in their size, history and culture, but it was assumed at the time that they would try to 'develop' along either capitalist or communist lines. With the disintegration of the Second World and the emphasis on the rapid 'globalization' of capitalism in the 1990s the term Third World may have become obsolete, but it does draw attention to the persistent dependency and poverty of many African, Asian and American societies.

13. François Duvalier, known as 'Papa Doc', was elected president of Haiti in 1957. A black physician and folklorist, he claimed he was ending 'mulatto' rule. He rewrote the constitution in 1964, making himself president for life, and again in 1971 to grant himself the power to name his successor. He named his 19 year-old son, Jean-Claude Duvalier, who became president when his father died in 1971. The Duvalier regime, which was maintained by a private army known as the *Tontons Macoutes* as well as the regular army, was ended in 1986 when a popular uprising drove Jean-Claude into exile. When Depestre wrote this essay, François Duvalier was still in power.

14. Léopold Sédar Senghor (1906–2001) was a poet and one of the principal founders of the *négritude* movement in the 1930s. After Senegal became part of the French Union in 1946, Senghor was elected as its representative to the French National Assembly and he was the first African to hold office in the French cabinet. He was elected the first president of Senegal in 1960 when it became independent.

15. Léon-Gontran Damas (1912–78) from Cayenne, Jacques Roumain (1907–44) from Haiti, Aimé Césaire (b. 1913) from Martinique and Nicolas Guillén (1902–89) from Cuba, were leading figures in the development of an Afro-Caribbean literature in the 1930s and 1940s.

16. Pierre Teilhard de Chardin (1881–1955) was a French Jesuit priest and paleontologist. His views on evolution were considered unorthodox by the church authorities who forbade him to continue teaching at the Catholic Institute in Paris. Between 1923 and 1946 he worked in China on fossil research. His writings were so controversial that many were not published until after his death.

17. Patrice Lumumba (1925–61) was the prime minister of Congo after it became independent from Belgium in 1960. After a few months, he was dismissed by President Joseph Kasavubu and he was later arrested. In 1961, he was murdered.

18. Orpheus, in Greek mythology, was a musician who played so beautifully on his lyre that animals, trees and stones followed him, and rivers stopped flowing so they could listen. A film, 'Black Orpheus' (1958), set the tragic story of Orpheus and his wife, Eurydice, in modern Brazil.

Nineteen

Jean Bernabé, Patrick Chamoiseau and Raphaël Confiant

Jean Bernabé (born 1942), Patrick Chamoiseau (born 1953) and Raphaël Confiant (born 1951) published their manifesto of Créolité *(Creoleness) in 1989. These distinguished writers, the first from Guadeloupe and the others from Martinique, have, in their individual works, written about and written in Creole: Bernabé, a linguist, in* Fondal-natal *(1983), a three-volume study of the language of Guadeloupe and Martinique, and* Grammaire créole. Fondas kréyol-la *(1987); Chamoiseau in* Creole Folktales *and the novels* Le quatrième siecle *(1986),* Solibo Magnifique *(1988) and* Texaco *(1992); and Confiant in several novels in the 1980s and a memoir,* Ravines du devant-jour *(1993), as well as Chamoiseau and Confiant's* Lettres créoles *(1991). Like Edouard Glissant, another Martiniquan, they criticise the simplifications of* négritude *while acknowledging Césaire's huge contribution to the search for an authentic culture and identity. Writing three decades after Fanon, they acknowledge that* négritude *was a necessary antithesis to colonialism but argue that the cultural alienation and psychic dispossession caused by colonisation is not transcended by* négritude. *Looking to Africa, like looking to France, is still looking outwards, away from the history and culture of the Caribbean.*

Glissant developed the concept Antillanité *(Caribbeanness), most notably in his* Discours Antillais *(1981), as a way of looking within Martinique and its Antillean surroundings for identity. This concept is developed in* Créolité. *Breaking from the idea that their identity is determined by either their African or their French heritage,* *these theorists emphasise the composite, interactional and synthetic aspects of Caribbean culture, including not only African and European sources but also Carib, Asian and Levantine. 'Our History is a braid (*une tresse*) of histories', they write, and* 'Créolité *is* the world diffracted and then recomposed'. *Unlike* négritude, *which looks outward and backward,* Créolité *looks inward and forward, focusing on the complexity, creativity and open-ended nature of Caribbean culture.* Créolité *is not a defined composite of cultures but rather 'a civilisation in the making'. Moreover, the authors connect Creoleness not only to the cultures of their Anglophone and Hispanophone neighbours, but also to the cultural diversity of the Americas and the multi-vocal and inter-racial world: 'The world is evolving into a state of Creoleness'. Creolisation, then, is global and ceaseless, and* Créolité, *far from being a fixed or final state, is a perpetual process of cultural interaction, exchange and change.*

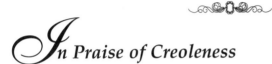

In Praise of Creoleness

Neither Europeans, nor Africans, nor Asians, we proclaim ourselves Creoles. This will be for us an interior attitude – better, a vigilance, or even better, a sort of mental envelope in the middle of which our world will be built in full consciousness of the outer world. These words we are communicating to you do not stem from theory, nor do they stem from any learned principles. They are, rather, akin to testimony. They proceed from a sterile experience which we have known before committing ourselves to reactivate our creative potential, and to set in motion the expression of what we are. They are not merely addressed to writers, but to any person of ideas . . . .

Caribbean literature does not yet exist. We are still in a state of preliterature: that of a written production without a home audience, ignorant of the authors/ readers interaction which is the primary condition of the development of a literature. This situation is not imputable to the mere political domination, it can also be explained by the fact that our truth found itself behind bars, in the deep bottom of ourselves, unknown to our consciousness and to the artistically free reading of the world in which we live. We are fundamentally stricken with exteriority. This from a long time ago to the present day. We have seen the world through the filter of western values, and our foundation was 'exoticized' by the French vision we had to adopt. It is a terrible condition to perceive one's interior architecture, one's world, the instants of one's days, one's own values, with the eyes of the other. All along overdetermined, in history, in thoughts, in daily life, in ideals (even the ideals of progress), caught in the trick of cultural dependence, of political dependence, of economic dependence, we were deported out of ourselves at every moment of our scriptural history. This determined a writing for the Other, a borrowed writing, steeped in French values, or at least unrelated to this land, and which, in spite of a few positive aspects, did nothing else but to maintain in our minds the domination of an elsewhere . . . .

Toward Interior Vision and Self-Acceptance

During the first periods of our writing, this exteriority provoked a mimetic expression, both in the French language and in the Creole language. We unquestionably had our clock-makers of the sonnet and the alexandrine. We had our fabulists, our romantics, our parnassians, our neoparnassians, not to mention the symbolists . . . . This was, said the critics and they had a point, more than secondhand cultural dealing: it was the quasi-complete acquisition of another identity . . . . They saw of their being what France saw through its preachers-travellers, its chroniclers, its visiting painters and poets, or its great tourists . . . .

To a totally racist world, self-mutilated by its own colonial surgeries, Aimé Césaire restored mother Africa, matrix Africa, the black civilisation. He denounced all sorts of dominations in the country, and his writing, which is committed and which derives its energy from the modes of war, gave severe blows to postslavery sluggishness. Césaire's Negritude gave Creole society its African dimension, and put an end to the amputation which generated some of the superficiality of the so called doudouist[1] writing . . . .

Aimé Césaire had exclusively the formidable privilege of symbolically reopening and closing again the circle in which are clasped two incumbent monsters: Europeanness and Africanness, two forms of exteriority which proceed from two opposed logics – one monopolizing our minds submitted to its torture, the other living in our flesh ridden by its scars, each inscribing in us after its own way its keys, its codes, its numbers. No, these two forms of exteriority could not be brought to the same level. Assimilation, through its pomps and works of Europe, tried unrelentingly to portray our lives with the colors of Elsewhere. Negritude imposed itself then as a stubborn will of resistance trying quite plainly to embed our identity in a denied, repudiated, and renounced culture. Césaire, an anti-Creole? Indeed not, but rather an *ante-Creole*. It was Césaire's Negritude that opened to us the path for the actuality of a Caribbeanness which from then on could be postulated, and which itself is leading to another yet unlabelled degree of authenticity. Césairian Negritude is a baptism, the primal act of our restored dignity. We are forever Césaire's sons . . . .

With Césaire and Negritude we were steeped in Surrealism . . . . Indeed,

Surrealism blew to pieces ethnocentrist cocoons, and was in its very foundations the first reevaluation of Africa by Western consciousness. But, that the eyes of Europe should in the final analysis serve as a means for the rising of the buried continent of Africa, such was the reason for fearing risks of reinforced alienation which left few chances to escape from it except by a miracle: Césaire, thanks to his immense genius . . . became one of the most burning figures of this movement . . . .

A violent and paradoxical therapy, Negritude replaced the illusion of Europe by an African illusion. Initially motivated by the wish of embedding us into the actuality of our being, Negritude soon manifested itself in many kinds of exteriority: *the exteriority of aspirations* (to mother Africa, mythical Africa, impossible Africa) and *the exteriority of self-assertion* (we are Africans). It was a necessary dialectical moment, an indispensable development. But it remains a great challenge to step out of it in order to finally build a new yet temporary synthesis on the open path of history, our history . . . .

We were freed on the one hand, and enslaved on the other as we grew more and more involved in French ways. For if during the Negrist rebellion, we protested against French colonization, it was always in the name of universal generalities thought in the Western way of thinking, and with no consideration for our cultural reality. And yet Césairian Negritude allowed for the emergence of those who were to express the envelope of our Caribbean thought: abandoned in a dead end, some had to jump over the barrier (as did Martinican writer Edouard Glissant),[2] others had to stay where they were (as did many), turning around the word Negro, dreaming of a strange black world, . . .

With Edouard Glissant we refused the trap of Negritude, and spelled out Caribbeanness, which was more a matter of vision than a concept. As a project it was not just aimed at abandoning the hypnoses of Europe and Africa. We had yet to keep a clear consciousness of our relations with one and the other: in their specificities, their right proportions, their balances, without obliterating or forgetting anything pertaining to the other sources conjugated with them; thus, to scrutinize the chaos of this new humanity that we are, *to understand* what the Caribbean is; to perceive the meaning of this Caribbean civilisation which is still stammering and immobile; to embrace, like René Depestre,[3] this American dimension, our space in the world; to explore, like Franz Fanon, our reality from a cathartic perspective; to decompose what we are while purifying what we are by fully exhibiting to the *sun of consciousness* the hidden mechanisms of our alienation; to plunge in our singularity, to explore it in a projective way, to reach out for what we are . . . these are Edouard Glissant's words . . . . Somewhat like with the process of archeological excavations: when the field was covered, we had to progress with light strokes of the brush so as not to alter or lose any part of ourselves hidden behind French ways . . . .

To create the conditions of authentic expression meant also to exorcise the old fatality of exteriority. Having only the Other's pupils under one's eyelids invalidated the fairest approaches, processes, and procedures. Opening one's eyes on oneself, like the regionalists, was not enough. Neither was scrutinizing this *'fondal-natal'* culture, as did the Haitian indigenists, in order to keep the essence of our creativity. We had yet to wash our eyes, to turn over the vision we had of our reality in order to grasp its truth: a new look capable of taking away our nature from the secondary or peripheral edge so as to place it again in the center of ourselves, somewhat like the child's look, questioning in front of everything, having yet no postulates of its own, and putting into question even the most obvious facts . . . . This is why interior vision is revealing, therefore revolutionary. To learn again how to visualize our depths. To learn again how to look positively at what revolves around us . . . . It is an inner disruption . . . . a freedom. But, having tried to enjoy it with no success, we realized that there could be no interior vision without a preliminary self-acceptance. We could even go so far as to say that interior vision is a result of self-acceptance.

French ways forced us to denigrate ourselves: the common condition of colonized people. It is often difficult for us to discern what, in us, might be the object of an aesthetic approach. What we accept in us as aesthetic is the little declared by the Other as aesthetic. The noble is generally elsewhere. So is the universal . . . . What good is the creation of an artist who totally refuses his unexplored being? Who does not know who he is? Or who barely accepts it? . . . Our ways of laughing, singing, walking, living death, judging life, considering bad luck, loving and expressing love, were only badly considered in literature, or in the other forms of artistic expression . . . . Some of our traditions disappeared without being questioned by any inquiring mind, and even though we were nationalists, progressivists, independentists, we tried to beg for the universal in the most colorless and scentless way, i.e. refusing the very foundation of our being, a foundation which, today, we declare solemnly as the major aesthetic vector of our knowledge of ourselves and the world: Creoleness.

Creoleness

We cannot reach Caribbeanness without interior vision. And interior vision is nothing without the unconditional acceptance of our Creoleness. We declare ourselves Creoles. We declare that Creoleness is the cement of our culture and that it ought to rule the foundations of our Caribbeanness. Creoleness is the *interactional or transactional aggregate* of Caribbean, European, African, Asian, and Levantine cultural elements, united on the same soil by the yoke of history. For three centuries the islands and parts of continents affected by this phenomenon proved to be the real forges of a new humanity, where languages, races, religions, customs, ways of being from all over the world were brutally uprooted and transplanted in an environment where they had to reinvent life. Our Creoleness was, therefore, born from this extraordinary 'migan',[4] wrongly and hastily reduced to its mere linguistic aspects, or to one single element of its composition. Our cultural character bears both the marks of this world and elements of its negation. We conceived our cultural character as a function of acceptance and denial, therefore permanently questioning, always familiar with the most complex ambiguities, outside all forms of reduction, all forms of purity, all forms of impoverishment. Our history is a braid of histories. We had a taste of all kinds of languages, all kinds of idioms. Afraid of this uncomfortable muddle, we tried in vain to anchor it in mythical shores (exterior vision, Africa, Europe, and still today, India or America), to find shelter in the closed normality of millennial cultures, ignoring that we were the anticipation of the relations of cultures, of the future world whose signs are already showing. We are at once Europe, Africa, and enriched by Asian contributions, we are also Levantine, Indians, as well as pre-Columbian Americans, in some respects. Creoleness is '*the world diffracted but recomposed*' . . . . This new dimension of man, whose prefigured shadow we are, requires notions which undoubtedly we still don't know. So that, concerning Creoleness, of which we have only the deep intuition or the poetic knowledge, and so as not to neglect any one of its many possible ways, we say that it ought to be approached as *a question to be lived*, to be lived obstinately in each light, in each shadow of our mind. To live a question is already to enrich oneself of elements besides the answer. To live the question of Creoleness, at once freely and prudently . . . .

Because of its constituent mosaic, Creoleness is an open specificity. It escapes, therefore, perceptions which are not themselves open. Expressing it is not expressing a synthesis, not just expressing a crossing or any other unicity. It is expressing a kaleidoscopic totality, that is to say: *the nontotalitarian consciousness of a preserved diversity* . . . .

Creoleness is an annihilation of false universality, of monolingualism, and of purity . . . . Creoleness is our primitive soup and our continuation, our primeval chaos and our mangrove swamp of virtualities. We bend toward it, enriched by all kinds of mistakes and confident of the necessity of accepting ourselves as complex. For complexity is the very principle of our identity. Exploring our Creoleness must be done in a thought as complex as Creoleness itself . . . . In multiracial societies, such as ours, it seems urgent to quit using the traditional raciological distinctions and to start again designating the people of our countries, regardless of their complexion, by the only suitable word: *Creole*. Socioethnic relations in our society ought to take place from now on under the seal of a common creoleness, without, not in the least, obliterating class relations of conflicts . . . .

It is necessary to make a distinction between Americanness, Caribbeanness, and Creoleness, all concepts which might at first seem to cover the same realities.

First, the sociohistorical processes which produced Americanization are different in nature from those which were at work in Creolization. Indeed, Americanization and its corollary, the feeling of Americanness, describes the progressive adaptation, and with no real interaction with other cultures, of Western populations in a world they baptized new. Thus, the Anglo-Saxons who formed the thirteen colonies, embryo of the future American state, displayed their culture in a new environment, almost barren, if we consider the fact that the native redskins, who were imprisoned in reservations or massacred, did not virtually influence their initial culture. In the same way, the Boni and Saramak blacks of Guyana,[5] who remained yet relatively closed to the tribes of the Amazonian forest, were Americanized through their interaction with the forest environment. Just as the Italians who emigrated massively to Argentina during the nineteenth century, or the Hindus who replaced the black slaves in the plantations of Trinidad,[6] adapted their original culture to new realities without completely modifying them. *Americanness is, therefore, in many respects, a migrant culture*, in a splendid isolation.

Altogether different is the process of Creolization, which is not limited to the American continent (therefore, it is not a geographic concept) and which refers to the brutal interaction, on either insular or landlocked territories—be it immense territories such as Guyana or Brazil—of culturally different populations: Europeans and Africans in the small Caribbean islands; Europeans, Africans, and Indians in the Mascarene islands;[7] Europeans and Asians in certain areas of the Philippines or in Hawaii; Arabs and black Africans in Zanzibar,[8] etc. Generally resting upon a plantation economy, *these populations are called to invent the new cultural designs allowing for a relative cohabitation between them*. These designs are the result of a nonharmonious (and unfinished therefore nonreductionist) mix of linguistic, religious, cultural, culinary, architectural, medical, etc. practices of the different people in question. Of course there are more or less intense Creolizations depending on whether the peoples in question are exogenous as is the case in the Caribbeans or the Mascarene islands, or whether one of these people is autochthonous as in the island of Cape Verde or in Hawaii. So, Creoleness is the fact of belonging to an original human entity which comes out of these processes in due time. There are a Caribbean Creoleness, a Guyanese Creoleness, a Brazilian Creoleness, an African Creoleness, an Asian Creoleness and a Polynesian Creoleness, which are all very different from one another but which all result from the matrix of the same historical maelstrom. Creoleness encompasses and perfects Americanness because it involves a double process:

  – *the adaption of Europeans, Africans, and Asians to the New World; and*
  – *the cultural confrontation of these peoples within the same space, resulting in a mixed culture called Creole.*

There are obviously no strict frontiers separating zones of Creoleness from zones of Americanness. We might find them juxtaposed or interpenetrated within the same country: thus in the U.S.A., Louisiana and Mississippi are predominantly Creole, whereas New England, which was initially inhabited by Anglo-Saxons only, is just American. After the abolition of slavery, however, and the rise of black people in the North, and during the twentieth century arrival of Italians, Greeks, Chinese, and Puerto Ricans, one might rightly think that the conditions are ripe for a process of Creolization to start presently in New England.

After this distinction between Creoleness and Americanness, what can we say of the relations between Caribbeanness and Creoleness? We consider Caribbeanness to be the only process of Americanization of Europeans, Africans, and Asians in the Caribbean Archipelago. Thus, it is, so to speak, a province of Americanness like Canadianness or Argentineness. Indeed, it leaves out the fact that in certain islands there was, more than mere Americanization, a phenomenon of Creolization (and therefore Creoleness). For example, entire regions in the north of Cuba were affected only by an Americanization of Andalusian colonists, Canarians or Galicians,[9] and knew no Creolization whatsoever. In certain sugar cane areas of Trinidad, Hindu culture adapted itself to the new environment without getting involved in a process of Creolization as opposed to the *bondyékouli* of the small Caribbean islands, which is a Creole cult based in Hinduism. Thus, we believe that Caribbeanness is first of all a geopolitical concept. The word 'Caribbean' says nothing of the human situation of Martinicans, Guadeloupeans, or Haitians. As Creoles, we are as close, if not closer, anthropologically speaking, to the people of the Seychelles,[10] of Mauricius, or the Reunion, than we are to the Puerto Ricans or the Cubans. On the contrary there are little things in common between someone from the Seychelles and a Cuban. We, the Caribbean Creoles, enjoy, therefore, a double solidarity:

   – *a Caribbean solidarity (geopolitical) with all the people of our Archipelago regardless of our cultural differences – our Caribbeanness; and*
   – *a Creole solidarity with all African, Mascarin, Asian, and Polynesian peoples who share the same anthropological affinities as we do – our Creoleness. . . .*

Rootedness in Orality

Our Creole culture was created in the plantation system through questioning dynamics made of acceptances and denials, resignations and assertions. A real galaxy with the Creole language as its core, Creoleness, has, still today, its privileged mode: orality. Provider of tales, proverbs, 'titim',[11] nursery rhymes, songs, etc., orality is our intelligence; it is our reading of this world, the experimentation, still blind, of our complexity. Creole orality, even repressed in its aesthetic expression, contains a whole system of countervalues, a counterculture; it witnesses ordinary genius applied to resistance, devoted to survival. After the failure of the plantation system (sugar crises, abolitions of slavery, etc.), after the destructurings, the restructurings, the consequent conversions and reconversions of all kinds (assimilation, departmentalization), there was no use for this oral force; it was useless to the citizens' lives. Only Frenchness (the adoption of both French language and French values) expressed Man in a society totally alienated. Orality began then to be buried in our collective unconscious (as if in some subterranean transhumance) but not without leaving here and there the scattered fragments of its discontinuous contours . . . .

Here, there was a break, a gap, a deep ravine between a written expression pretending to be universalo-modern and traditional Creole orality enclosing a great part of our being. This nonintegration of oral tradition was one of the forms and one of the dimensions of our alienation. Without the rich compost which could have contributed to a finally sovereign literature and brought it closer to potential readers, our writing . . . remained suspended. Hence the denominative instability of the written production of our countries: *Afro-Caribbean, Negro-Caribbean, Franco-Caribbean, French Speaking Caribbean, Francophone Caribbean Literature . . . etc.,* all qualifiers which from now on are, in our eyes, ineffective.

Fortunately, there were some insignificant reproducers of misunderstood gestures, some modest collectors of useless memories; there were some obscure directors of commercialized culture for tourists more curious about us than we were; there were some dull epigones of a hackneyed speech, some naïve promoters of a trite carnival, some industrious profiteers of a strident, loud *zouk.*[12] They rarely escaped the assertion – shouted or whispered – of doudouism and folklorism. But in the final analysis they were the indispensable links that contributed to save Creoleness from the glorious yet definitive fate of Atlantis.[13] We learned from them that culture is a daily lift and thrust, that ancestors are born everyday and are not fixed in an immemorial past; that tradition takes shape everyday, and that culture is also the link we ought to keep alive between past and present; that taking over oral tradition should not be considered in a backward mode of nostalgic stagnation, through backward leaps. To return to it, yes, first in order to restore this cultural continuity (that we associate with restored historical continuity) without which it is difficult for collective identity to take shape. To return to it, yes, in order to enrich our enunciation, to integrate it, and go beyond it. To return to it, so as simply to invest the primordial expression of our common genius. Knowing this, we may then collect a new harvest of first-hand seeds. We may then, through the marriage of our trained senses, inseminate Creole in the new writing. In short, *we shall create a literature*, which will obey all the demands of modern writing while taking roots in the traditional configurations of our orality.

Updating True Memory

Our history (or more precisely our histories) is shipwrecked in colonial history. Collective memory is the first thing on our agenda. What we believe to be Caribbean history is just the history of the colonization of the Caribbeans. Between the currents of the history of France, between the great dates of the governors' arrivals and departures, between the beautiful white pages of the chronicle (where the bursts of our rebellions appear only as small spots), there was the obstinate progress of ourselves. The opaque resistance of Maroons allied in their disobedience. The new heroism of those who stood up against the hell of slavery, displaying some obscure codes of survival, some indecipherable qualities of resistance, the incomprehensible variety of compromises, the unexpected syntheses of life. They left the fields for the towns, and spread among the colonial community to the point of giving it its strength in all respects, and giving it what we are today. This happened with no witnesses, or rather with no testimonies, leaving us somehow in the same situation as the flower unable to see its stem, unable to feel it. And the history of colonization which we took as ours aggravated our loss, our self-defamation; it favored exteriority and fed the estrangement of the present. Within this false memory we had but a pile of obscurities as our memory . . . . Our chronicle is behind the dates, behind the known facts: *we are Words behind writing*. Only poetic knowledge, fictional knowledge, literary knowledge, in short, artistic knowledge can discover us, understand us and bring us, evanescent, back to the resuscitation of consciousness . . . .

The Thematics of Existence

Here, we do not think that we are outside the world, in the suburb of the universe. Our anchorage in this land is not a dive in a bottomless pit. Once our interior vision is applied, once our Creoleness is placed at the center of our creativity, we will be able to re-examine our existence, to perceive in it the mechanisms of alienation, and, above all, to grasp its beauty. The writer is a detector of existence. More than anyone else, the writer's vocation is to identify what, in our daily lives, determines the patterns and structure of the imaginary. To perceive our existence is to perceive our virtualities. By taking us away from the comfortable gaze of the Other, interior vision compels us to solicit our original chaos. It brings us then to permanent questioning, doubt, and ambiguity. Through this kind of vision, we return to the magma that characterizes us. It also frees us of anticolonialist literary militantism so that we will not examine ourselves in order to find a singular ideology, an apodictic truth, or the ten commandments of a table of laws . . . . The Creole literature we are elaborating takes it as a principle that there is nothing petty, poor, useless, vulgar, or unworthy of a literary project in our world. *We are part and parcel of our world.* We want, thanks to Creoleness, to name each thing in it, and to declare it beautiful. To perceive the human grandeur of the *djobeurs*[14]... To understand the vegetable markets. To elucidate the functioning of the tale tellers. To accept again without any judgment our '*dorlis*', our '*zombis*',[15] our '*chouval-twa-pat*', '*soukliyan*'. To adopt the language of our towns, of our cities. To explore our American Indian, Indian, Chinese, and Levantine origins, and find their poundings in our heartbeats . . . .

Our writing must unreservedly accept our popular beliefs, our magico-religious practices, our magic realism, the '*milan*', '*majò*', '*ladja*', and '*koudmen*' rituals. It must listen to our music and taste our cooking. It must investigate how we live love, hate, die, the spirit we have in melancholy, how we live in happiness and sadness, anxiety and courage. It must look for our truths, and affirm that one of its missions is to present insignificant heroes, anonymous heroes, those who are forgotten by the colonial chronicle, those who resisted indirectly and patiently and who have nothing in common with the Western or French heroes. These realities ought not to be described ethnographically, nor ought there to be a census-taking of Creole practices after the fashion of the Haitian indigenists, instead we ought *to show what, in these practices, bears witness to both Creoleness and the human condition.* We ought to live, relive, and make live all this intensively . . . . There can be no real opening to the world without a prerequisite and absolute apprehension of what we are. Our world, however small it might be, is large in our minds, boundless in our hearts, and for us, will always reflect the human being . . . . It is a question of descending in ourselves, but without the Other, without the alienating logic of his prism. And we must admit that here, we have no indicators, no certainties, no aesthetic criteria, we have nothing but the youth of our eyes, the intuition of our Creoleness which is supposed at every moment to invent every move . . . .

The Burst in Modernity

Despite our youth, we do not have time to live the volutes of a quiet evolution. We now have to live in a contemporary world which is fast. We have to assume order and adventure, as Apollinaire[16] would have put it. Order might be, in this context, that which contributes to the consciousness of our identity, to the development of our nation, to the emergence of our arts and literature: all problems with which we are compelled to deal. As for adventure, it might be the symbol of the modern world and its contemporary progress, which we must not exclude just because we have to put some order in our interior being. Underdeveloped countries today are compelled to this gymnastics. How can we consider the Creole language without touching upon the present problems of linguistics? How can we think of the Caribbean novel without being enriched with all approaches to the novel of all the peoples of the world? How can we consider an artistic expression which, efficient inside the nation, might turn out anachronistic or out-of-date outside the nation? We have, therefore, to do everything at the same time: to place our writing within the progressive forces working at our liberation, and to keep looking for a new aesthetics without which there is no art, much less a literature. We have to be lucid about our neocolonized flaws, and at the same time we have to work at oxygenating our suffocations by a positive vision of our being. We must accept ourselves as we are, completely, and mistrust this uncertain identity still moved by unconscious alienations. We must take root in our country, in its difficulties, in its problems, in its pettiest realities, and yet consider the bubblings where literary modernity is leading the world . . . .

The Choice of One's Speech

Our primary richness, we the Creole writers, is to be able to speak several languages: Creole, French, English, Portuguese, Spanish, etc. Now we must accept this perpetual bilingualism and abandon the old attitude we had toward it. Out of this compost, we must grow our speech. Out of these languages, we must build our own language. Creole, our first language, we the Caribbeans, the Guyanese, the Mascarins, is the initial means of communication of our deep self, or our collective unconscious, of our common genius, and it remains the river of our alluvial Creoleness. We dream in it. In it we resist and accept ourselves. It is our cries, our screams, our excitements . . . . The absence of interest in the Creole language was not a mere mouth silence but a cultural amputation. The Creole tale tellers who no longer exist could have put it better than us. Every time a mother, thinking she is favoring the learning of the French language, represses Creole in a child's throat, is in fact bearing a blow to the latter's imagination, repressing his creativity. School teachers of the great period of French assimilation were the slave traders of our artistic impulse. So that today, it would be an impoverishment not to reinvest this language. Its usage is one of the ways of the submersion in our Creoleness . . . .

The Creole language is not a dying language, it changes continuously . . . . It is comparable to this snake which, though it has been chased around the hills, reappears in our huts without warning, because Creole is linked to our very existence . . . . Hence the need to reinforce its oral density with the contemporary power of writing. And those of our writers who tried to kill it in themselves, or in their writing, lost without their knowing, the best chance for their repressed authenticity: Creoleness. What an aesthetic suicide! Creole literature written in Creole must, before all, build this written language and make it known . . . . The Creole poet writing in Creole, the Creole novelist writing in Creole, will have to be at once the collectors of ancestral speech, the gatherers of new words, and the discoverers of the Creoleness of Creole ....

But our histories, for once generous, gave us a second language. At first, it was not shared by everyone. It was for a long time the language of the oppressors – founders. *We did conquer it, this French language.* If Creole is our legitimate language, we gradually (or at once) were given and captured, legitimated and adopted the French language (the language of the Creole white class). Creoleness left its indelible mark on the French language, as did other cultural entities elsewhere. We made the French language ours. We extended the meaning of some of its words, deviated others. And changed many. We enriched the French language, its vocabulary as well as its syntax. We preserved many of its words which were no longer used. In short, *we inhabited it.* It was alive in us. In it we built our own language, this language which was chased by cultural kapos and viewed as a profanation of the idolized French language. *Our literature must bear witness of this conquest.* We are obviously against the religion of the French language which had spread in our countries since the abolition of slavery, and we completely agree with the Haitian proverb that goes: *"Palé fransé pa vlé di lespri"* (speaking French is no proof of intelligence). Repressing this language amounted, as is the case for Creole, to discouraging our expressiveness, our creative impulse ....

Language will be, therefore, for us, the free, responsible, and creative use of languages. It won't be necessarily a Creolized or reinvented French, nor a Frenchized or reinvented Creole, but our own finally recovered and decisive language .... For the dominant idolized language ignores the personality of the colonized speaker, falsifies his history, denies his freedom, and deports him from himself. Accordingly, the colonized's idolizing of the dominated language, even though it might be beneficial in the early years of the cultural revolution, should absolutely not become the primary or unique objective of Creole writers writing in Creole. Idolized languages function like Nô theatre masks;[17] these masks which endow actors with feelings, with faces, but also with alien personalities. For a Creole poet or novelist, writing in an idolized French or Creole is like remaining motionless in a place of action, not taking a decision in a field of possibilities, being pointless in a place of potentialities .... Aesthetically, it is dying.

Creoleness is not monolingual. Nor is its multilingualism divided into isolated compartments. Its field is language. Its appetite: all the languages of the world ....

Being completely open to the whole linguistic spectrum offered by society, such is the state of mind with which we approached the issue of interlanguage, pedantically called 'interlect' .... His instinctive fear of illegitimacy often dictated to Césaire the use of the most pure and measured French idiom, enhanced by an impossible Creole, impossible because its literary status demanded yet to be invented. Glissant, for his part, never compromised with cliché interlect. Both of them taught us fair patience and the obstinate – though convulsive – quest for words ...

Our aim here is certainly not to prevent writers from exploring the interstices of French and Creole. Better, we believe that creative use of interlect might lead to an order of reality capable of preserving for our Creoleness its fundamental complexity, its diffracted referential space ....

Constant Dynamics

One of the hindrances to our creativity has been the obsessional concern with the Universal. Old syndrome of the colonized: afraid of being merely his depreciated self and ashamed of wanting to be what his master is, the colonized accepts therefore – supreme subtlety – the values of his master as the ideal in the world. Hence exteriority vis-à-vis ourselves. Hence the defamation of the Creole language and the deep mangrove swamp of Creoleness. Hence – except for unique miracles – our aesthetic shipwreck. Creole literature will have nothing to do with the Universal, or this disguised adherence to Western values .... We want to deepen our Creoleness in full consciousness of the world. *It is through Creoleness that we will be Martinicans. Becoming Martinicans, we will be Caribbeans, therefore Americans, in our own way.* It is through Creoleness that we will crystalize Caribbeanness, the ferment of a Caribbean civilization. We want to think the world as a polyphonic harmony: rational/irrational, finished/complex, united/diffracted .... The complex thought of a Creoleness, itself complex, can and should help us in so doing. The Whole-world's life quivers with expressed Creoleness. It is the Whole-world in a particular dimension, and a particular form of the Whole-world.

The world is evolving into a state of Creoleness. The old national immovable organizations are being replaced by federations which in turn might not survive for long. Under the totalitarian universal crust, Diversity maintained itself in small peoples, small languages, small cultures. The world standardized bristles, paradoxically, with Diversity. Everything being in relation with everything, visions embrace more, provoking the paradox of a general consensus around and a celebration of differences .... Cultures melt and spread into subcultures which in turn generate other aggregates. To perceive the world today, a man or woman's identity, the principle of a people or a culture with the values of the eighteenth century or those of the nineteenth century would be an impoverishment. A new humanity will gradually emerge which will have the same characteristics as our Creole humanity: all the complexity of Creoleness. The son or daughter of a German and a Haitian, born and living in Peking, will be torn between several languages, several histories, caught in the torrential ambiguity of a mosaic identity ....

Creoleness liberates us from the ancient world. But, in this new turn, we will look for the maximum of communicability compatible with the extreme expression of a singularity .... One of the conditions of our survival as Creoles (open-complex) is to maintain a consciousness of the world while constructively exploring our initial cultural complexity, and to insure that such a consciousness celebrates and enriches this exploration. Our primary diversity will be part of an integrating process of world diversity, recognized and accepted as permanent. Our Creoleness will have to recover itself, structure itself, and preserve itself, while changing and absorbing. *It will have to survive in Diversity.* Applying this double move will automatically favor our creative vitality. It will also prevent us from returning to the totalitarian order of the old world, fixed by the temptation of the unified and definitive. At the heart of our Creoleness, we will maintain the modulation of new laws, of illicit blendings. For we know that each culture is never a finished product but rather the constant dynamics on the lookout for genuine issues, new possibilities, and interested in relating rather than dominating, in exchanging rather than looting. Respectful. Cultures would have continued living such a dynamics if it wasn't for Western madness. Clinical sign: colonizations. A living culture, and especially Creoleness, is a permanent stimulation of convivial desire. And if we recommend to our artists this exploration of our singularities, that is because it brings back to what is natural in the world, outside the *Same* and the *One*, and because it opposes to Universality the great opportunity of a world diffracted but recomposed, the conscious harmonization of preserved diversities: DIVERSALITY.

Creoleness and Politics

The claims of Creoleness are not just aesthetic in nature, as we saw, they also have important ramifications touching on all fields of activity in our societies and especially the most fundamental ones: politics and economics. Indeed, Creoleness claims a full and entire sovereignty of our peoples without, however, identifying with the different ideologies which have supported this claim to date. This means that it distrusts, in the first place, some sort of primary Marxism which has it that cultural and therefore identity-related issues will find a solution once the revolution is achieved. Thus expressed, often in good faith, this theory, we must insist, has often prevented our political leaders and organizations from thinking seriously about the contents of a true Martinican, Guadeloupean, or Guyanese culture. We also want to distance ourselves from this somewhat narrow nationalism that perceives the Martinican as a stranger to the Guadeloupean, and vice versa. Without denying the differences between our peoples, we would like to say that what unites them is vaster than what opposes them, and that the task of a defender of the Martinican people's sovereignty is also to reconcile his struggle as much as possible with that of the Guadeloupean or Guyanese peoples, and vice versa.

Creoleness sketches the hope for the first possible grouping within the Caribbean Archipelago: that of the Creolophone peoples of Haiti, Martinique, Saint

Lucia, Dominica, Guadeloupe, and Guyana,[18] grouping which is only the prelude of a larger union of our Anglophone and Hispanophone neighbors. This is to say that, for us, the acquisition of an eventual mono-insulary sovereignty will be but a stage (a very brief one, we hope) in the process toward a Caribbean federation or confederation, the only way to stand up efficiently to the different hegemonic blocks that share the planet among them. In this perspective, we maintain our opposition to the present process of integration without popular consultation of the people of the so-called 'départments français d'Amerique' to the European community. Our solidarity is first with our brothers of the neighboring islands and secondly with the nations of South America.

NOTES

1. *Doudouisme* is 'folksiness' or superficial, empty folklorism.
2. Glissant (born in 1928), like his contemporary Frantz Fanon, was influenced by Aimé Césaire. He also met the Cuban painter Wifredo Lam and the Haitian poet René Depestre and became aware of the commonalities among Caribbean cultures. (see chapter 20).
3. René Depestre (b. 1926), a Haitian poet, Marxist and political activist, has criticised Jean Price-Mars and the *négritude* movement for mystifying the culture and history of Haiti by divorcing them from their material basis (see chapter 18).
4. '*Migan*' is an old plantation dish, made with coarsely mashed breadfruit and other vegetables.
5. The Boni (or Aluku) and Saramaka are two of the semi-independent maroon societies that were established in Suriname and French Guiana in the eighteenth century.
6. About 144,000 people, most of them Hindu, came from India to Trinidad between 1845 and 1918.
7. The Mascarene Islands, consisting of Mauritius and Réunion, are in the Indian Ocean east of Madagascar. France colonised Réunion in 1642 and Mauritius in 1715. Réunion became an overseas department of France in 1946 and Mauritius, which was captured by Britain in 1810, became independent in 1968. Both islands, like those in the Caribbean, depended heavily on the sugar industry and have heterogeneous populations, descended from European settlers, enslaved Africans, and Indian and Chinese workers and traders.
8. Zanzibar, an island in the Indian Ocean just off the coast of Africa, was made a British protectorate in 1890 and achieved independence in 1963. The next year, it united with Tanganyika to form the republic of Tanzania. Zanzibar had been an important centre of the slave trade that was run by Arabs in eastern Africa until its market was closed in 1873. About 500,000 people live on the island, most of them Sunni Muslims.
9. Andalucia and Galicia are regions of Spain, in the south and north-west, respectively, and the Canarias (Canary Islands), which lie off the north-west coast of Africa, are also part of Spain.
10. Seychelles consists of about 90 islands in the Indian Ocean, scattered over 400,000 square miles, about 1,000 miles east of Africa. Seychelles was a British colony from 1814 until it became independent in 1976. About 90 per cent of the people are of

African and European ancestry, the remainder including people from China and India. Most people speak a French Creole and are Catholics.

11. *Titim* – a riddle, usually associated with a story.
12. Originally meaning a dance party in Martinique, *zouk* has come to refer to the popular music of the French West Indies, and also Dominica and St Lucia, where there is a strong French Creole culture. *Zouk* was made famous by the group called Kassav, consisting of musicians from Martinique and Guadeloupe, which made over 28 record albums between 1979 and 1989.
13. Atlantis was a mythical island in the Atlantic Ocean that disappeared under the sea after floods and earthquakes.
14. *Djobeurs* are day-labourers or 'odd-jobbers'.
15. *Dorlis* is a frightening nocturnal figure that is believed to rape women and talk with rats. *Zombis* are people whose souls have been removed and whose bodies are made to work, like slaves, without rest.
16. Guillaume Apollinaire (1880–1918) was a French poet who experimented in modern literary styles and coined the word 'surrealism'.
17. In Japanese *No* plays, the actors speak in a stylised way and wear masks, each of which represents a single emotion. Every word and gesture conforms to a set of rules.
18. This refers to French Guiana, not the Cooperative Republic of Guyana.

Twenty

Edouard Glissant

Edouard Glissant, born in 1928 in Martinique, is a poet, playwright, novelist and literary theorist. Glissant and his contemporary, Frantz Fanon, were students at the Lycée Schoelcher in Fort-de-France when Aimé Césaire was appointed to teach modern languages there in 1940. The period between 1940 and 1946, when the French Caribbean colonies experienced hardships under Vichy control and the subsequent blockade by the Allied navies, and then liberation, elections, and the new status of départements d'outre-mer, *was one of 'intellectual and artistic effervescence in Martinique' (Dash 1985, 2). Glissant was influenced by Césaire's radical ideas about poetry and by the* negritude *and surrealist movements. With fellow students, he formed a political and cultural group called* Franc-Jeu *which 'identified itself closely with the desire for change and the political idealism nurtured by the tensions of the war years and the new enthusiasms generated by Césaire's presence'. (ibid., 2) The group supported Césaire when he was elected mayor of Fort-de-France in 1945. Glissant met Wifredo Lam, the Cuban painter, and René Depestre, the Haitian poet, at that time but in 1946 he went to France on a scholarship and* Franc-Jeu *dissolved.*

Some of these events and the political and cultural climate of the period provided the background for Glissant's first novel, La Lezarde *(1958), translated into English as* The Ripening *(1985), which won the Prix Renaudot. In the 1950s and 1960s, Glissant engaged in a variety of activities, as a student of philosophy at the Sorbonne, as a poet who published* Un champ d'îles *(1953),* La terre inquiète *(1954) and* Les Indes *(1955), as a participant in the First Congress of Black Writers and Artists in 1956, and as cofounder of the* Front Antillo-Guyanais *in 1959, 'which called for political liberation for the colonial world and the cultural integration of the French West Indies in the Caribbean region' (Ibid., 3). Officials kept a close watch on Glissant in France and President de Gaulle abolished the* Front *in 1961.*

In many of his poems and in a collection of essays, Soleil de la conscience *(1956), Glissant explored some of the ideas and themes that have persisted through his work: the links between people and particular landscapes, the associations between sensation, symbols, memory and language, and the contrasts between the Caribbean and European civilisations. Glissant returned to Martinique in 1965, founding the* Institut Martiniquais d'Études *in 1967 and the journal* Ancoma *in 1971. His goal was 'to combat the powerful stranglehold that France maintains on Martinique culturally and politically' (Ibid., 4), and Glissant was soon writing of the 'cultural genocide' committed against the French West Indies. Among his literary works of this period are a play,* Monsieur Toussaint *(1961),* Le quatrième siecle *(1964) and* L'intention poétique *(1969). His later work includes the novels* Malemort *(1975) and* Mahogany *(1987), and two important collections of essays on literary theory and Caribbean culture,* Le discours antillais *(1981) and* Poétique de la relation *(1990).*

Glissant's notion of antillanité, *or 'Caribbeanness', is distinct from the more static, essentialist and Afrocentric idea of* négritude. *For Glissant, creolisation or* métissage *is the central and ceaseless cultural process defining the Caribbean. This process is characterized by openness, fragmentation and diversity, and Glissant contrasts the Caribbean experience with the European emphasis on rational progress with its linear and 'totalizing' view of history. 'For Glissant human experience is not to be seen as a tale of inexorable Progress . . . It is precisely such a vision of mankind moving forever upward and onward that fixes the Caribbean on the margins of world history, that dooms the powerless to extinction. Instead, Glissant sees the world, and the Caribbean in particular, in terms of an intricate branching of communities, an infinite wandering across cultures, where triumphs are momentary and where adaptation and* métissage *(creolization) are the prevailing forces' (Dash 1989, xxviii).*

Glissant asserts that creative artists have an important contribution to make in shaping the Caribbean nation:

> When one considers the artist's contribution to the creation of the nation of the French Caribbean, the question is also posed of the possible creation of a Caribbean nation. One can indeed think that the countries of the Caribbean will

develop an original Afro-Caribbean culture whose cultural reality is already in evidence. The problem is that this cultural reality has been activated at the same time it was fragmented, if not totally shattered, by the antagonistic tensions of European nations in the Caribbean. The artist articulates this threatened reality but also explores the often hidden workings of this fragmenting process. If at present Caribbean countries experience or are subjected to social, political, and economic regimes very different from each other, 'artistic vision' creates the possibility of cementing the bonds of unity in the future. The nation does not then appear as the product of divisiveness, but as the promise of a future sharing with others (1989, 235).

losed Place, Open Word

1

The Plantation system spread, following the same structural principles, throughout the southern United States, the Caribbean islands, the Caribbean coast of Latin America, and the northeastern portion of Brazil. It extended throughout the countries (including those in the Indian Ocean), constituting what Patrick Chamoiseau and Raphaël Confiant call the territory of *créolité*.[1] There are grounds for understanding why, despite very different linguistic areas engaged in very divergent political dynamics, the same organization would create a rhythm of economic production and form the basis for a style of life. That takes care of the spatial aspect.

Regarding time, or, if you will, our grasp of the histories that converged in these spaces, two other questions need to be addressed. The first concerns the system's evolution: Why was there no continuation of it anywhere – no social structure organically derived from it, with coherent or contradictory repercussions, inscribed in any enduring aspect? The Plantation system collapsed everywhere, brutally or progressively, without generating its own ways of superseding itself. The second question is even more amazing: How did a system that was so fragile give rise, paradoxically, to what are seen as the modern vectors of civilisation, in the not untolerant sense that this word henceforth holds for us?

Let us sum up in a few connected phrases what we know of the Plantation. It is an organization formed in a social pyramid, confined within an enclosure, functioning apparently as an autarky but actually dependent, and with a technical mode of production that cannot evolve because it is based on a slave structure.

A pyramid organization: everywhere after 1848 the origin of the mass of slaves, then workers, was African – or Hindu in the Caribbean;[2] the middle level, managers, administrators, and overseers, were hired men of European origin, a small number of whom were replaced early in this century by people of color – once again in the Caribbean; at the top of the pyramid were the planters, colonists, or *békés*, as they were called in the Antilles, who strove to constitute a white pseudoaristocracy. I say pseudo because almost nowhere were these attempts at putting down roots within a tradition sanctioned by the stamp of time nor by any legitimacy of absolute filiation. Plantations, despite secreting manners and customs, from which cultures ensued, never established any tradition of great impact.

An enclosed place: each Plantation was defined by boundaries whose crossing was strictly forbidden; impossible to leave without written permission or unless authorized by some ritual exception, such as Carnival time. Chapel or church, stockrooms for distributing supplies or later the grocery store, infirmary or hospital: everything was taken care of within a closed circle. Now the following is what we need to understand: How could a series of autarkies, from one end to the other of the areas involved, from Louisiana to Martinique to Réunion, be capable of kinship? If each Plantation is considered as a closed entity, what is the principle inclining them to function in a similar manner?

Finally, the reality of slavery. It was decisive, of course, in the stagnation of production techniques. An insurmountable tendency toward technical irresponsibility resulted from it, especially among slaveholders. And when technical innovations, mechanization, and industrialization occurred, as they did, for example, in the southern United States, it was already too late. Social dynamics had taken other routes than cane traces, sugarcane alleys, or avenues of magnolias. As for the slaves or their close descendants, who had absolutely no interest in the Plantation's yield, they would be an exception to this technical irresponsibility because of their own need to guarantee daily survival on the edges of the system. This resulted in the widespread development of small occupations, or what is referred to in the Antilles as *djobs,*[3] a habitual economy of bits and scraps. Technical irresponsibility on the one hand and a breakdown into individual operations on the other: immobility and fragmentation lay at the heart of the system eating away at it.

Let us, nonetheless, consult these ruins with their uncertain evidence, their extremely fragile monuments, their frequently incomplete, obliterated, or ambiguous archives. You can guess already what we are to discover: that the Plantation is one of the focal points for the development of present-day modes of Relation.[4] Within this universe of domination and oppression, of silent or professed dehumanization, forms of humanity stubbornly persisted. In this outmoded spot, on the margins of every dynamic, the tendencies of our modernity begin to be detectable. Our first attempt must be to locate just such contradictions.

One of these contradictions contrasts the tidy composition of such a universe – in which social hierarchy corresponds in maniacal, minute detail to a mercilessly maintained racial hierarchy – with the ambiguous complexities otherwise proceeding from it.

Airtight seals were apparently the rule of the Plantation. Not simply the tight social barrier but also an irremediable break between forms of sensibility, despite each one's effects upon the other. Saint-John Perse[5] and Faulkner,[6] two authors born in Plantation regions and to whom I constantly turn, not surprisingly, with my questions, provide us with a chance to assess this split. We recall the famous description, if it is a description, in *Éloges*:

> *but I shall still long remember*
> mute faces, the colour of papaya and of boredom that
> *paused like burnt-out stars behind our chairs . . .*

That papaya and that boredom – seeing people as things – do not so much emphasize the poet's distance as they reveal the radical separation (that impossible apartheid) presiding over the life of the emotions in the Plantation. I have also noted that Faulkner, who spoke so frequently of blacks, never sets out to write one of the interior monologues, of which he is such a master, for one of these characters; whereas he dares do so for some of the mulattoes in his work and even, in a tour de force now classic, for the idiot Benjy at the beginning of his novel *The Sound and the Fury*. Thus Lucas, the black character who is the principal hero of *Intruder in the Dust*, is never interiorized by Faulkner; he is described entirely through postures and gestures, a silhouette filled in against a horizon. *Intruder in the Dust* is not a novel concerning an essence but, rather, an attempt at a phenomenological approach. In the same novel Faulkner, moreover, is explicit about his narrator's understanding – or lack thereof – of the southern black: 'Because he knew Lucas Beauchamp too – as well that is as any white person knew him. Better than any maybe'. As if the novelist, rejected by members of his class and misunderstood by the black Americans who have had access to his work, had premonitions of an impossibility brought to a head by history. The break exerts itself here.

But the break did not form delimited territories, in which the various levels of population were sectioned off. The claim that they were reciprocally extraneous did not prevent contaminations, inevitable within the enclosure of the Plantation. Despite the insistent, cold ferocity of Father Labat's[7] writing, for example, beneath the words of this seventeenth-century chronicler of the Antilles one can feel a curiosity, riveted, anxious, and obsessive, whenever he broaches the subject of these slaves that he struggles so hard to keep calm. Fear, fantasies, and perhaps a barely willing flicker of complicity form the undercurrent of the revolts and repressions. The long list of martyrdoms is also a long *métissage,*[8] whether involuntary or intentional.

A second contradiction contrasts the Plantation's will to autarky with its dependence, in reality, in relation to the external world. The transactions it fostered with this world took place in the elementary form of the exchange of goods, usually at a loss. Payment was in kind, or as an equivalent exchange value, which led to accumulation neither of experience nor of capital. Nowhere did the Planters manage to set up organisms that were sufficiently solid and autonomous to allow them to have access to the control of a market, means of international transportation, an independent system of money, or an efficient and specific representation in foreign markets. The Plantations, entities turned in upon themselves, paradoxically, have all the symptoms of extroversion. They are dependent, by nature, on someplace elsewhere. In their practice of importing and exporting, the established politics is not decided from within. One could say, in fact, that, socially, the Plantation is not the product of a politics but the emanation of a fantasy.

And, if we come even closer to this enclosed place, this Locus Solus,[9] trying to imagine what its inner ramifications may be, auscultating the memory or guts inside it, then the contradictions become madness. I shall not attempt any description here. The current year would not suffice. And we are familiar enough with the countless novels and films inspired by this universe to know already that, from north to south and from west to east, the same conditions of life repeat themselves. Rather, I shall turn to another synthesizing aspect, in this case both oral and written expression – literature – stemming either directly or indirectly from the Plantation.

2

No matter which region we contemplate from among those covered by the system, we find the same trajectory and almost the same forms of expression. We could mark out three moments: literary production – first as an act of survival, then as a dead end or a delusion, finally as an effort or passion of memory.

An act of survival. In the silent universe of the Plantation, oral expression, the only form possible for the slaves, was discontinuously organized. As tales, proverbs, sayings, songs appeared – as much in the Creole-speaking world as elsewhere – they bore the stamp of this discontinuity. The texts seem to neglect the essentials of something that Western realism, from the beginning, had been able to cover so well: the situation of landscapes, the lesson of scenery, the reading of customs, the description of the motives of characters. Almost never does one find in them any concrete relating of daily facts and deeds; what one does find, on the other hand, is a symbolic evocation of situations. As if these texts were striving for disguise beneath the symbol, working to say without saying. This is what I have referred to elsewhere as detour, and this is where discontinuity struggles; the same discontinuity the Maroons created through that other detour called *marronnage*.[10]

Here we have a form of literature striving to express something it is forbidden to refer to and finding risky retorts to this organic censorship every time. The oral literature of the Plantations is consequently akin to other subsistence – survival – techniques set in place by the slaves and their immediate descendants. Everywhere that the obligation to get around the rule of silence existed a literature was created that has no 'natural' continuity, if one may put it that way, but, rather, bursts forth in snatches and fragments. The storyteller is a handyman, the *djobbeur* of the collective soul.

Though this phenomenon is widespread throughout the system, nonetheless, it is within the Creole-speaking realm that it stands out most conspicuously. That is because, in addition to this obligation to get around something, the Creole language has another, internal obligation: to renew itself in every instance on the basis of a series of forgettings. Forgetting, that is, integration, of what it starts from: the multiplicity of African languages on the one hand and European ones on the other, the nostalgia, finally, for the Caribbean remains of these.[11] The linguistic movement of creolization proceeded through very rapid, interrupted, successive settlings of these contributions; the synthesis resulting from this process never became fixed in its terms, despite having asserted from the beginning the durability of its structures. In other words, the Creole text is never presented linguistically as an edict or a relay, on the basis of which some literary progression might be detected, with another text coming along to perfect the former, and so on. I do not know if this diffraction (through which multilingualism is, perhaps, really at work, in an underground way, for one of the first known times in the history of humanities) is indicative of all languages in formation – here, for example, we would have to study the European Middle Ages – or if it is entirely attributable to the particular situation of the Plantation in the Caribbean and the Indian Ocean.

Then delusion. Unlike this oral and popular literature, though equally discontinuous, another, written and elitist literature developed. The colonists and the Planters, as well as the travelers who visited them, were possessed of a real need to justify the system. To fantasize legitimacy. And, of course, this is why, unlike what happened in the oral texts, the description of reality would turn out to be indispensable to them – and irrefutable in their terms. Reality was fantasized here as well, its image the product of a disguised apology rather than that of an austere realism. One condition of the process was that conventional landscape be pushed to extremes – the gentleness and beauty of it – particularly in the islands of the Caribbean. There is something of an involuntary Parnassus[12] in the novels and pamphlets written by colonists of Santo Domingo and Martinique: the same propensity to blot out the shudders of life, that is, the turbulent realities of the Plantation, beneath the conventional splendor of scenery.

Another convention provided the occasion for a specific category of writing.

The supposedly receptive lasciviousness of the slaves, mulatto women and men who were of mixed blood, and the animal savagery with which the Africans were credited, produced an abundant supply for the erotic literature flourishing in the islands from the seventeenth to the end of the nineteenth century. In this manner, from one blind spot to the next, a literature of illusion came into being, one moreover that, every now and then, was not lacking charm or an old-fashioned grace. Lafcadio Hearn,[13] an international reporter and a writer as well, came from Louisiana to the Antilles at the turn of the century, sending us a much embellished report.

Memory. After the System collapsed the literatures that had asserted themselves within its space developed, for the most part, from the general traits so sketchily indicated here, either consenting to them or taking an opposite course. Thus, Caribbean literatures, whether in English, Spanish, or French, tended to introduce obscurities and breaks – like so many detours – into the material they dealt with; putting into practice, like the Plantation tales, processes of intensification, breathlessness, digression, and immersion of individual psychology within the drama of a common destiny. The symbolism of situations prevailed over the refinement of realisms, by encompassing, transcending, and shedding light upon it. This, of course, is equally true of a writer of Creole such as the Haitian Franketienne[14] as of a novelist from the United States such as Toni Morrison.[15]

So, too, the works that appeared in these countries went against the convention of a falsely legitimizing landscape scenery and conceived of landscape as basically implicated in a story, in which it too was a vivid character.

So, finally, historical *marronage* intensified over time to exert a creative *marronage*, whose numerous forms of expression began to form the basis for a continuity. Which made it no longer possible to consider these literatures as exotic appendages of a French, Spanish, or English literary corpus; rather, they entered suddenly, with the force of a tradition that they built themselves, into the relation of cultures.

But the truth is that their concern, its driving force and hidden design, is the derangement of the memory, which determines, along with imagination, our only way to tame time.

Just how were our memory and our time buffeted by the Plantation? Within the space apart that it comprised, the always multilingual and frequently multiracial tangle created inextricable knots within the web of filiations, thereby breaking the clear, linear order to which Western thought had imparted such brilliance. So Alejo Carpentier[16] and Faulkner are of the same mind, Edward Kamau Brathwaite[17] and Lezama Lima[18] go together, I recognize myself in Derek Walcott,[19] we take delight in the coils of time in García Márquez's[20] century of solitude. The ruins of the Plantation have affected American cultures all around.

And, whatever the value of the explanations or the publicity Alex Haley afforded us with *Roots*,[21] we have a strong sense that the overly certain affiliation invoked there does not really suit the vivid genius of our countries. Memory in our works is not a calendar memory; our experience of time does not keep company with the rhythms of month and year alone; it is aggravated by the void, the final sentence of the Plantation; our generations are caught up within an extended family in which our root stocks have diffused and everyone had two names, an official one and an essential one – the nickname given by his community. And when in the end it all began to shift, or rather collapse, when the unstoppable evolution had emptied the enclosure of people to reassemble them in the margins of cities, what remained, what still remains, is the dark side of this impossible memory, which has a louder voice and one that carries farther than any chronicle or census.

The disintegration of the system left its marks. Almost everywhere planter castes degenerated into fixed roles, in which memory no longer functioned except as décor – as landscape had formerly done. Occasionally, they were able to switch to commerce; otherwise, they went to pieces in melancholy. Former employees here and there formed groups of so-called poor whites, who fed the ideologies of racist terror. In the Caribbean and in Latin America the burgeoning shantytowns drew masses of the destitute and transformed the rhythm of their voices. In the islands black and Hindu farmers went to war against arbitrariness and absolute poverty. In the United States southern blacks went up North, following the 'underground railroad', toward cities that were becoming violently dehumanized, where, nonetheless the Harlem writers, for example, wrote their Renaissance[22] upon the walls of solitude. Thus, urban literature made its appearance in Bahia, New York, Jacmel, or Fort-de-France. The Plantation region, having joined with the endless terrain of haciendas or latifundio, spread thin to end up in mazes of sheet metal and concrete in which our common future takes its chances. This second Plantation matrix, after that of the slave ship, is where we must return to track our difficult and opaque sources.

3

It is not just literature. When we examine how speech functions in this Plantation realm, we observe that there are several almost codified types of expression. Direct, elementary speech, articulating the rudimentary language necessary to get work done; stifled speech, corresponding to the silence of this world in which knowing how to read and write is forbidden; deferred or disguised speech, in which men and women who are gagged keep their words close. The Creole language integrated these three modes and made them jazz.

It is understandable that in this universe every cry was an event. Night in the cabins gave birth to this other enormous silence from which music, inescapable, a murmur at first, finally burst out into this long shout – a music of reserved spirituality through which the body suddenly expresses itself. Monotonous chants, syncopated, broken by prohibitions, set free by the entire thrust of bodies, produced their language from one end of this world to the other. These musical expressions born of silence: Negro spirituals and blues, persisting in towns and growing cities; jazz, *biguines*, and calypsos, bursting into barrios and shantytowns; salsas and reggaes, assembled everything blunt and direct, painfully stifled, and patiently differed into this varied speech. This was the cry of the Plantation, transfigured into the speech of the world.

For three centuries of constraint had borne down so hard that, when this speech took root, it sprouted in the very midst of the field of modernity; that is, it grew for everyone. This is the only sort of universality there is: when, from a specific enclosure, the deepest voice cries out.

4

Negative explanations for what is unique to the system are clear: the decisive impact of the African population, but with the horrors of the slave trade as its beginning; the grasping opposition to change inherent in pro-slavery assumptions; the dependent relationship with the outside world that all Plantations had in common.

But one can also see how this monstrously abortive failure, composed of so many solitary instances of sterility, had a positive effect on some portion of contemporary histories. – How? Is your question. How can you claim that such an anomaly could have contributed to what you call modernity? – I believe I have answered this question or at least left clues about how it may be answered.

The Plantation, like a laboratory, displays most clearly the opposed forces of the oral and the written at work – one of the most deep-rooted topics of discussion in our contemporary landscape. It is there that multilingualism, that threatened dimension of our universe, can be observed for one of the first times, organically forming and disintegrating. It is also within the Plantation that the meeting of cultures is most clearly and directly observable, though none of the inhabitants had the slightest hint that this was really about a clash of cultures. Here we are able to discover a few of the formational laws of the cultural *métissage* that concerns us all. It is essential that we investigate historicity – that conjunction of a passion for self-definition and an obsession with time that is also one of the ambitions of contemporary literatures – in the extensions of the Plantation, in the things to which it gave birth at the very instant it vanished as a functional unit. *Baroque*[23] *speech, inspired by all possible speech*, was ardently created in these same extensions and loudly calls out to us from them. The Plantation is one of the bellies of the world, not the only one, one among so many others, but it has the advantage of being able to be studied with the utmost precision. Thus, the boundary, its structural weakness, becomes our advantage. And in the end its seclusion has been conquered. The place was closed, but the word derived from it remains open. This is one.part, a limited part, of the lesson of the world.

NOTES

1. Bernabé, Chamoiseau and Confiant's *Eloge de la Créolité* (1989, see chapter 19) focuses on the concept *créolité* – 'creoleness' – but Glissant prefers the word creolization which he sees as more 'open' and never becoming 'fixed', a 'limitless *métissage*, its elements diffracted and its consequences unforeseeable' (Glissant 1997, 34). The countries in the Indian Ocean they refer to are Mauritius and Réunion, both of which depended heavily on sugar plantations and have ethnically heterogeneous populations.
2. Slavery was abolished in the French colonies in 1848. Between 1852 and 1859, over 6,000 Africans immigrated to Guadeloupe and almost 11,000 to Martinique. Up to 1884, when Indian immigration ceased, about 42,000 Indians entered Guadeloupe and 25,500 entered Martinique. However, of those Indians who entered, about 21 per cent from Guadeloupe and 46 per cent from Martinique were repatriated between 1853 and 1900 (Renard 1993, 161, 166).
3. *Djobs* is derived from the English word job, and *djobeurs* are people who live by doing casual or odd jobs, especially by reusing old materials, in the margins of the economy.
4. Glissant writes of '*Relation*' as a kind of 'shared knowledge' that evolves when people of different cultures are in contact with each other in an open-ended process involving both diversity and unity: 'Not just a specific knowledge, appetite, suffering, and delight of one particular people, not only that, but knowledge of the whole, greater from having been at the abyss, and freeing knowledge of Relation within the Whole' (Glissant 1997, 8).
5. Saint-John (or St John) Perse was the pseudonym of Alexis Saint-Leger Leger (1887–1975), a white Creole from Guadeloupe, who won the Nobel Prize for literature in 1960. His best known collections of poems are *Éloges* (1911) and *Anabase* (1924). The quotation from *Éloges* is from Louise Verese's translation (1956, 17).
6. William Faulkner (1897–1962) was born in Mississippi and was one of the greatest and most prolific US novelists. His complex novels concern the changes and conflicts in the 'Old South' before the civil rights movement. *The Sound and the Fury* (1929) was followed by, among others, *As I Lay Dying* (1930), *Sanctuary* (1931), *Absalom, Absalom!* (1936) and *Intruder in the Dust* (1948).
7. Father Jean-Baptiste Labat (1663–1738) wrote *Nouveaux voyages aux îles des Ameriques* (1722), which includes an account of the customs of French colonists and their slaves in the Caribbean.
8. *Métissage*, or *mestizaje* in Spanish, refers both to the historical process of racial mixture through miscegenation and cultural mixing, or creolisation.
9. Singular place, or isolated location.
10. The Maroons, *marrons*, were slaves who escaped into inaccessible areas of a slave society and formed their own communities. Hence, *marronage* means the political act and form of cultural resistance to the dominant system.

11. Author's note: 'It is the problem of "forgetting" that has made the various Creole dialects so fragile – in comparison to the languages composing them, especially French wherever it is in authority, as in Guadeloupe and Martinique.'

12. Parnassus is a mountain in central Greece, sacred to the god Apollo and the site of worship for the gods Pan and Dionysus, and hence a centre of musical and poetic inspiration.

13. Lafcadio Hearn (1850–1904) was born in Greece, raised in Ireland and France, and migrated to the United States at the age of 19. He became a journalist and travel writer. He lived in Martinique from 1887 to 1889 and wrote *Two Years in the French West Indies* (1890). He moved to Japan, became a Japanese citizen and wrote 12 books about Japanese culture.

14. Frankétienne is the pseudonym of Frank Etienne, a Haitian writer born in 1936, and author of *Dézafi* (1975).

15. Toni Morrison, born in the United States in 1931, has written *The Bluest Eye* (1970), *Sula* (1973), *Song of Solomon* (1977), *Tar Baby* (1981), *Beloved* (1987) and *Jazz* (1992). She won the Pulitzer Prize in 1988 and the Nobel Prize in 1993.

16. Alejo Carpentier (1904–80) was a Cuban novelist, essayist and musicologist who developed the literary style known as magic realism in his novels *El reino de este mundo* (1949), *Los pasos perdidos* (1953) and *El siglo de las luces* (1963).

17. Edward Kamau Brathwaite, see chapter 35.

18. José Lezama Lima (1910–76) was a Cuban poet and novelist, the author of *Paradiso* (1966).

19. Derek Walcott, see chapter 42.

20. Gabriel García Márquez, born in 1928, is from the Caribbean coast of Colombia. He worked as a journalist for many years, but the publication of his novel *Cien años de soledad* in 1967 established him as one of the greatest figures in Latin American literature. He won the Nobel Prize in 1982.

21. Alex Haley (1921–92) was an African-American writer who collaborated with Malcolm X to write *The Autobiography of Malcolm X* (1965) and is best known for his book *Roots: The Saga of an American Family* (1976), for which he received the Pulitzer Prize and which became the basis for a television series in 1977.

22. The Harlem Renaissance was the African-American cultural movement that began in the 1920s. It included the writers Langston Hughes, Countee Cullen, Jean Toomer and the Jamaican Claude McKay, and was associated with the development of jazz in northern cities by Louis Armstrong, Duke Ellington and others.

23. The term 'baroque' is generally used to refer to a particular style and period of art, architecture and music that is distinguished for its elaborate, decorative and dramatic character, in contrast to the more restrained sense of order and balance associated with the 'classical' style and period. Glissant's use of the term emphasises its irregular and even bizarre qualities, resulting from inventiveness and an openness to many and varied influences.

Twenty-One

Maryse Condé

Maryse Condé, an author of poems, plays and novels, was born in 1937 into a black bourgeois family in Guadeloupe. She left for Paris at the age of 16, completed her high school education and achieved a BA in English and Classics. From 1960 until 1966 she lived in Africa, first the Ivory Coast, then Guinea and Ghana. She worked in London for two years and then in Senegal. In 1970 she returned to Paris, received a doctorate in Caribbean literature from the Sorbonne in 1975, and then taught African and West Indian literature at the University of Paris and the University of Nanterre.

Condé's first novel, Heremakhonon *(1976) was published after she had written two plays and several essays on literature and* negritude. *She has taught at many universities in the United States and since the mid-1980s, has divided her time between Guadeloupe and the United States. Her fame is based chiefly on her novels, some of which are set in Africa (*A Season in Rihata, *1981,* Segu, *1984, and* The Children of Segu, *1985). Others are about the experiences of people of African origin and descent in the diaspora, including* I, Tituba, Black Witch of Salem *(1986),* Tree of Life *(1987),* Crossing the Mangrove *(1989),* Colony of the New World *(1993),* Windward Heights *(1995) and* Desirada *(1997).*

In a series of conversations with Françoise Pfaff between 1991 and 1994, Condé indicated her thoughts about negritude, Créolité *and the African diaspora, among other topics.*

C̸onversations with Maryse Condé (excerpts)

MARYSE CONDÉ: I think that for four centuries our people have been victims of political, cultural, and economic domination. Consequently, they are in the process of totally losing their voice. They are threatened. Artists and creators may have the duty to listen to our people before it's too late. In doing this, we may rekindle a pride that they are also about to lose. We may restore their power of speech and imagine what they can be tomorrow. This is the role of creators: not only to preserve the past but also to invent the future ….

FRANÇOISE PFAFF: How did you devise the plot for *Tree of Life*?

MC: The novel is broadly based on the history of my own family. It focuses on the barely fictionalized story of my father's son by a first marriage who left Guadeloupe to study in Saumur, France, right after World War I and began the 'mulatto' branch of the family. However, in the novel, the family account of its origins is interspersed with a great deal of fiction. For instance, I borrowed the forefather, Albert, from a young man I met in Los Angeles. This is a quite an extraordinary story. I went to give a lecture at a university, and a young, light-skinned, red-haired Black man was waiting for me at the entrance. He welcomed me by saying, 'Ka ou fé, Mariz Kondé?' – How are you, Maryse Condé? We went on talking for a few minutes in Creole. His Creole was better than mine, and I asked him where he was from. He laughed and told me he was from Panama. His great-grandfather had emigrated from the French West Indies to work in the Panama Canal construction, and his family stayed there. As a result, this young man spoke Spanish, English, and Creole but no longer had any knowledge of French. This story interested me and we met again. He showed me documents, and I interviewed him about his grandfather and included that information in the novel ….

FP: West Indian participation in the building of the Panama Canal is not well known.

MC: Actually, it is. If you ask four West Indians, at least one of them had a grandfather who went to Panama.[1] The West Indians came mainly from English-speaking islands such as Jamaica, which explains Marcus Garvey's visit to Panama in the novel. It's a historical event . . . . I wanted to show that West Indians move around a lot, though some people incorrectly believe they never leave the islands. In fact, West Indians have gone all over: to Panama, Africa, Europe. I wanted to show that the West Indies is a place of generation and dispersion, not confinement. As I said earlier, some West Indians went to the United States after digging the Panama Canal. The West

Indian community in the United States was very large by the time Marcus Garvey lived in Harlem in the 1920s. It's interesting to see the constant movement of the community to which you belong . . . . I want to stress that the African Diaspora in the West Indies and the Americas has a common history and shares the same heroes, dreams, and aspirations. Members of the African Diaspora should not remain isolated within their national shells. It's not a Pan Africanist ideal per se, but rather a way for diaspora members to claim a common heritage . . . .

FP: In *Lettres Créoles* (Creole letters),[2] Confiant and Chamoiseau state that you begin to question your relationship to the French language in *Crossing the Mangrove*. Is this accurate?

MC: Not quite. I started to call it into question after *Tree of Life*. I had written only part of that book in Guadeloupe, whereas *Crossing the Mangrove*, as I told you before, was entirely conceived here Washington, where people's way of speaking constantly drew my attention. It was not merely the Creole they were using, but their way of deconstructing and reconstructing the French language. I had to rethink the way I wrote in order to be faithful to the community I wanted to describe.

FP: So you incorporated Creole, or rather Creolized French, into your written text. What does Creole represent for you?

MC: This is very complicated. I didn't speak Creole during my childhood, even on the playground at school, where I was surrounded by children raised like me who spoke French. Then I lived abroad for years without speaking Creole to anyone. Consequently, I had barely practiced Creole. Back in Guadeloupe, Creole caught my attention even though it has always been somewhat remote from me. Although I strive to reproduce rhythms and sonorities in what I write, I don't feel any urgency to express myself in Creole . . . . I think I don't live Creole the way other West Indians do.

FP: Does this make you any less West Indian?

MC: The debate on this is endless. I don't think you should make mastery of Creole the key element in West Indian identity, when you take into account the history of exile and displacement of our peoples. When I was at the University of Nanterre, I taught West Indian literature to 'second-generation children', as they are commonly called. They were motivated and very eager to learn but were unable to speak Creole. Where should they be placed? Should they be excluded from the West Indian people? In the United States some of my Haitian students no longer know French, much less Creole. Are they too to be excluded?

FP: So how do you define West Indian identity?

MC: As a matter of fact, I don't. It's not a recipe for cooking. People live a culture, and I believe that there are several ways of living your West Indian identity and your relationship to Creole and popular culture. I think Naipaul is as West Indian as Derek Walcott[3], though one flauntingly denies it and the other celebrates it . . . .

FP: To educate people in terms of 'diaspora literacy'?

MC: I think we don't know ourselves well enough. Someone just called me from Guadeloupe to tell me that a quick survey had been made, asking people, 'Do you know the name Derek Walcott?' This question was asked when he received the Nobel Prize. Three out of four people had never heard the name and did not know who he was. I think that if we are more aware of our heritage and of everything we can share, exchange, and say, we will be stronger in the sort of cultural struggle in which we have been losers so far. Yesterday evening at Chapters Bookstore,[4] a young man was surprised that I had spoken of Malcolm X[5] in *Tree of Life*. I believe we have to get used to sharing our heroes, our creators, our important men and women, so as to have something with which to respond to the White world, which constantly hammers us with its values ....

FP: How do Anglophone and Francophone West Indian literatures compare?

MC: I think this question would require a very long discussion. Let's simply say that Francophone and Anglophone literatures were born in different ways. West Indian Francophone literature emerged from protest engendered by the Négritude movement, while Anglophone literature was born out of an immediate awareness of Otherness. The first Anglophone writers speak about their world, describe their relationship to this world, and make no attempt to define themselves in terms of the White world, the Western world. Obviously the White world is always present, but it is in the background; it is not immediately viewed as the world to which you want to compare yourself or to oppose.

Furthermore, issues of language are different in West Indian Anglophone and Francophone literatures. Problems related to Créolité and to people's relation to Creole languages, which are so acute in the Francophone areas today, are not the same in the Anglophone regions. This is perhaps because the Anglophone West Indies have had more freedom in crafting a language that integrates vestiges of the islands' past linguistic phases and stages. They have never experienced the terribly French exclusion of languages judged to be nonstandard or nonclassic. As a whole, it could be said that there are differences in themes as well as in the linguistic material itself.

FP: You are in the process of preparing an anthology of West Indian literature. Does the book include primarily Francophone and Anglophone literatures, or does it also cover the literatures of former Dutch and Spanish islands?

MC: At first we wanted to write an anthology of all these literatures to show strongly the diversity of the islands as well as their common problems. Unfortunately, this would have been too costly a project, and the publisher limited us to texts in French and English. We saw the differences between the various linguistic zones we've mentioned. We reached the conclusion that within their diversity, unity existed among the Caribbean islands, the affirmation of a personality that was neither African, nor American, nor European, to use the terms of the manifesto *Eloge de la créolité*. This personality was based on a common history and rather similar social and political evolution, an evolution that was more social than political. This year [1992], Anglophone West Indian literature has been crowned in an exceptional way with the awarding of the Nobel Prize to Derek Walcott. But it should be said that Naipaul, who is generally spurned because his work is not a celebration of West Indian culture, is a great writer whose complex books are written in a quite remarkable way. Spanish- and Dutch-speaking West Indian literatures are perhaps less known . . . .

It's a book aimed at the general public, to show that West Indian literature is very dynamic and that in spite of popular beliefs to the contrary, there isn't a wall between America and the West Indies. Certain themes in African-American literature can also be found in the West Indies, similar situations can exist, and the writers' work on language is not drastically different in these literatures. This anthology is a way to link the Americas with the Caribbean, which is so often overlooked, hidden, and forgotten . . . .

FP: In 1978 you ended your book on Césaire with the following words: 'He is unquestionably the foundation of authentic West Indian literature'.[6] What do you think of this sentence in 1992?

MC: I don't know whether I would say that now because I believe that there is no 'authentic West Indian literature'. I wrote these words fifteen years ago, and I have changed a great deal since. I now think that there is no such thing as 'authentic' literature, that all literatures are valid, that everyone can express ideas, and that anyone has a right to express them, even though they may cause shock or displeasure. People who don't want to hear these things can always close the book they are reading. This being said, I would perhaps remove the word 'authentic' from the sentence you quoted and would say that Césaire is the foundation of militant and committed literature, the kind of literature that speaks about the masses. It is in this sense that Césaire is the founder of literature in the French West Indies. His oeuvre is beautiful and eternal. Whatever people may think, no one has yet surpassed him in the West Indies.

FP: But wasn't Césaire inspired by French surrealism?

MC: Yes, but in the journal *Tropiques* he says that he used surrealism as a means rather than an end. He wanted to make use of surrealism to search for his own self and to recover his African essence hidden under the cloak of Western education, the same way surrealists were looking for the primitive man, the child, hidden by education. He has thoroughly explained his relationship with surrealism, which involved a stylistic as well as a political rebellion .... These things are also quite dated. Négritude as a movement is no longer relevant. What is interesting now are other forces such as an Antillanité and Créolité, which are currently at play in the French West Indies. The Négritude movement must be considered primarily from a historical viewpoint. It allowed Black people to assert themselves culturally.... Given the beauty of Césaire's work and its importance in the world, it seems a bit unfair that Césaire has not received any international award consecrating his work.

FP: Why was Derek Walcott awarded the Nobel Prize for literature? Does his work have more international impact than that of Césaire?

MC: I don't have the slightest idea. I can't compare them.

FP: Is Césaire's work as well known by non-Francophone people?

MC: His work has been translated.

FP: What do you think of Derek Walcott's work?

MC: I only know his poem *Omeros*,[7] which I find magnificent.

FP: What will be the impact of Walcott's recognition in terms of the West Indies, West Indian literature, and the Black world?

MC: I am told Walcott will go to Trinidad and Guadeloupe to celebrate his Nobel Prize, which means that West Indian people will perhaps be led to have greater confidence in their writers.

FP: Patrick Chamoiseau, the Martinican writer, has just been awarded the Goncourt Prize for his novel *Texaco*.[8] What do you think about his being selected? What are the characteristics of his work that may have led to the awarding of this highly coveted prize? Will this award result in making Patrick Chamoiseau a full-fledged French writer beyond the frontiers of Créolité?

MC: I don't believe the Goncourt Prize will make a French writer out of Patrick. This award, which was given to him by the French literary world, will modify neither his writing nor his way of life as a Créolité writer. It's an award from the outside over which he has no control and which will not, in my opinion, influence him. His work contains an element that can be seen as 'attractive' by French people: it involves a deconstruction of the French language that may appeal to them and that brings, as they say, spice and a certain zest to French as spoken in France. But I don't believe this is Patrick Chamoiseau's goal. I am convinced that his use of Creole, which is his mother tongue, responds to an inner need.

FP: I found it paradoxical that the Goncourt Prize, which is a French award, was given to a work that tends to move away from standard French in its style.

MC: It's because the French saw a renewal rather than a rejection of the French language in his work . . . .

FP: Chamoiseau is one of the bards of Créolité, a new literary movement extolled by writers from the French West Indies. What importance do you give to such a movement?

MC: Créolité, which is the daughter of Antillanité, has many good points. It has allowed West Indian writers to reevaluate their relationship to the French language. French is not the only language available to us; we also have Creole. However, Créolité should not be transformed into a cultural terrorism within which writers are confined. Créolité should not prevent individuals from having the relationship they wish to have with West Indian reality. To each his or her own Créolité, that is to say, to each his or her own relationship with oral materials and the oral tradition, and to each his or her own way of expressing it in written literature.

NOTES

1. Even before the construction of the Panama canal many workers of African descent, as well as Europeans, Indians and Chinese, migrated to Central America to build a railroad that would provide a link between the oceans. Beginning in 1850, black workers from Cartagena, Colombia, and Jamaica laboured under brutal conditions in tropical swamps and forests. Many of them died, some returned home and others remained on the isthmus, concentrated near Colón and Panama City, on the Caribbean and Pacific coasts, respectively. This early flow primed the flood of migrant workers required to construct the canal. Three-quarters of the 83,000 people who worked on the canal between 1882 and 1914 were from the British and French West Indies. Many thousands of the canal workers died from disease and violence while others became permanently ill or disabled. They all laboured and lived in a strict system of racial segregation and discrimination that resembled a caste society.

2. Patrick Chamoiseau and Raphael Confiant, *Lettres Créoles: Tracées antillaises et continentales de la littérature 1635–1975* (1991).

3. V.S. Naipaul, born in Trinidad in 1932, went to England in 1950 and, apart from travelling (in South Asia, the United States, South America, Iran, Malaysia and Indonesia), has lived in the UK ever since, writing many short stories, novels and reflections on his travels (see chapter 28). Derek Walcott, born in St Lucia in 1930, is a poet, playwright and essayist. He divides his residence between the United States, where he teaches, and St Lucia (see chapter 42). He won the Nobel Prize for literature in 1992 and Naipaul won it in 2001.

4. In Washington, DC, where this particular interview was conducted on November 6, 1992.
5. Malcolm X (1925–65) became a member of the Black Muslims in 1946 while he was in prison for burglary, and he became one of their chief spokesmen after his release in 1952. He broke with them in 1964 and formed his own group, the Organization of Afro-American Unity, but he was assassinated before it was well established.
6. Maryse Condé, *Cahier d'un retour au pays natal - Césaire* (Paris, 1978).
7. *Omeros* (New York, 1990) is Walcott's epic poem, 325 pages long, in which a fisherman, Achille, sets out from St Lucia in a fishing boat and retraces, across the centuries and the ocean, the Middle Passage to his ancestral home in Africa. Like the work of Homer (whose name in Greek is *Omeros*) the epic is about the suffering of people in exile and about great historical events, in this case the effects of colonisation on the Indians of the Americas and the enslavement of Africans.
8. The Goncourt Prize is France's most distinguished award for literature. *Texaco* (Paris, 1992) is a mythic history of the Creole people of Martinique. The central figure, Marie-Sophie Laborieux, is the founder and protector of a shantytown called Texaco, on the edge of Fort-de-France.

Twenty-Two

Edwidge Danticat

Edwidge Danticat, born in Haiti in 1969, is the author of short stories, including the collection Krik? Krak! *(1995) and two novels,* Breath, Eyes, Memory *(1994), which is about four generations of Haitian women, and* The Farming of Bones *(1998), which concerns the massacre of thousands of Haitians that occurred in the Dominican Republic in 1937. Danticat went to the United States when she was 12 and she received degrees from Barnard College and Brown University. In 1996 she was named as one of the 20 'Best Young American Novelists' by Granta.*

In the essay, 'We are Ugly, But we are Here' (1996), Danticat's reference to Anacaona, an Arawak woman who was killed by the first Europeans in the Americas, makes a symbolic link and a shared identity between all the people who have suffered and resisted oppression in the Caribbean. Her emphasis is not so much on nationalism as on the will and ability of people to survive, and particularly on the generations of women who, despite endless abuse, ensure the survival of a people 'against all the odds'.

We Are Ugly, But We Are Here

One of the first people murdered on our land was a queen. Her name was Anacaona and she was an Arawak Indian. She was a poet, dancer, and even a painter. She ruled over the western part of an island so lush and green that the Arawaks called it Ayiti, land of high. When the Spaniards came from across the sea to look for gold, Anacaona was one of their first victims. She was raped and killed and her village pillaged in a tradition of on-going cruelty and atrocity. Anacaona's land is now the poorest country in the Western hemisphere, a place of continuous political unrest. Thus, for some, it is easy to forget that this land was the first Black Republic, home to the first people of African descent to uproot slavery and create an independent nation in 1804.

I was born under Haiti's dictatorial Duvalier regime.[1] When I was four, my parents left Haiti to seek a better life in the United States. I must admit that their motives were more economic than political. But as anyone who knows Haiti will tell you, economics and politics are very intrinsically related in Haiti. Who is in power determines to a great extent whether or not people will eat.

I am twenty six years old now and have spent more than half of my life in the United States. My most vivid memories of Haiti involve incidents that represent the general situation there. In Haiti, there are a lot of 'black-outs', sudden power failures. At those times, you can't read or study or watch TV, so you sit around a candle and listen to stories from the elders in the house. My grand-mother was an old country woman who always felt displaced in the city of Port-au-Prince where we lived and had nothing but her patched-up quilts and her stories to console her. She was the one who told me about Anacaona. I used to share a room with her. I was in the room when she died. She was over a hundred years old. She died with her eyes wide open and I was the one who closed her eyes. I still miss the countless mystical stories that she told us. However, I accepted her death very easily because in Haiti death was always around us.

As a little girl, I attended more than my share of funerals. My uncle and legal guardian was a Baptist minister and his family was expected to attend every funeral he presided over. I went to all the funerals he presided over. I went to all the funerals in the same white lace dress. Perhaps it was because I attended so many funerals that I have such a strong feeling that death is not the end, that the people we bury are going off to live somewhere else. But at the same time, they will always be hovering over us and guide us through our journeys.

When I was eight, my uncle's brother-in-law went on a long journey to cut cane in the Dominican Republic. He came back, deathly ill. I remember his wife twirling feathers inside his nostrils and rubbing black pepper on his upper lip to make him sneeze. She strongly believed that if he sneezed, he would live. At night, it was my job to watch the sky above the house for signs of falling stars. In Haitian folklore, when a star falls out of the sky, it means someone will die. A star did fall out of the sky and he did die.

I have memories of Jean Claude 'Baby Doc' Duvalier and his wife, racing by in their Mercedes Benz and throwing money out of the window to the very poor children in our neighborhood. The children nearly killed each other trying to catch a coin or a glimpse of Baby Doc. One Christmas, they announced on the radio that the first lady, Baby Doc's wife, was giving away free toys at the Palace. My cousins and I went and were nearly killed in the mob of children who flooded the palace lawns.

All of this now brings many questions buzzing to my head. Where was really my place in all of this? What was my grandmother's place? What is the legacy of the daughters of Anacaona? What do we all have left to remember, the daughters of Haiti?

Watching the news reports, it is often hard to tell whether there are real living and breathing women in conflict-stricken places like Haiti. The evening news broadcasts only allow us a brief glimpse of presidential coups, rejected boat people, and sabotaged elections. The women's stories never manage to make the front page. However they do exist.

I know women who, when the soldiers came to their homes in Haiti, would tell their daughters to lie still and play dead. I once met a woman whose sister was shot in her pregnant stomach because she was wearing a t-shirt with an 'anti-military image'. I know a mother who was arrested and beaten for working with a pro-democracy group. Her body remains laced with scars where the soldiers put out their cigarettes on her flesh. At night, this woman still smells the ashes of the cigarette butts that were stuffed lit inside her nostrils. In the same jail cell, she watched as paramilitary 'attachés' raped her fourteen-year-old daughter at gun point. When mother and daughter took a tiny boat to the United States, the mother had no idea that her daughter was pregnant. Nor did she know that the child had gotten the HIV virus from one of the paramilitary men who had raped her. The grandchild the offspring of the rape was named Anacaona, after the queen, because that family of women is from the same region where Anacaona was murdered. The infant Anacaona has a face which no longer shows any trace of indigenous blood; however, her story echoes back to the first flow of blood on a land that has seen much more than its share.

There is a Haitian saying which might upset the aesthetic images of most women. *Nou led, Nou la*, it says. We are ugly, but we are here. Like the modesty that is somewhat common in Haitian culture, this saying makes a deeper claim for poor Haitian women than maintaining beauty, be it skin deep or otherwise. For most of us, what is worth celebrating is the fact that we are here, that we against all the odds exist. To the women who might greet each other with this saying when they meet along the countryside, the very essence of life lies in survival. It is always worth reminding our sisters that we have lived yet another day to answer the roll call of an often painful and very difficult life. It is in this spirit that to this day a woman remembers to name her child Anacaona, a name which resonates both the splendor and agony of a past that haunts so many women.

When they were enslaved, our foremothers believed that when they died their spirits would return to Africa, most specifically to a peaceful land we call Guinin, where gods and goddesses live. The women who came before me were women who spoke half of one language and half another. They spoke the French and Spanish of their captors mixed in with their own African language. These women seemed to be speaking in tongue when they prayed to their old gods, the ancient African spirits. Even though they were afraid that their old deities would no longer understand them, they invented a new language, our Creole patois with which to describe their new surroundings, a language from which colorful phrases blossomed to fit the desperate circumstances. When these women greeted each other, they found themselves speaking in codes.

    – How are we today, Sister?
    – I am ugly, but I am here.

These days, many of the sisters are greeting each other away from the homelands where they first learned to speak in tongues. Many have made it to other shores, after traveling endless miles on the high seas, on rickety boats that almost took their lives. Two years ago, a mother jumped into the sea when she discovered that her baby daughter had died in her arms on a journey which they had hoped would take them to a brighter future. Mother and child, they sank to the bottom of an ocean which already holds millions of souls from the middle passage the holocaust of the slave trade that is our legacy. That woman's sacrifice moved then-deposed Haitian President Jean Bertrand Aristide[2] to the brink of tears. However, like the rest of us, he took comfort in the past sacrifices that were made for all of us, so that we could be here.

The past is full of examples when our foremothers and forefathers showed such deep trust in the sea that they would jump off slave ships and let the waves embrace them. They too believed that the sea was the beginning and the end of all things, the road to freedom and their entrance to Guinin. These women have been part of the very construction of my being ever since I was a little girl. Women like my grandmother who had taught me the story of Anacaona, the queen.

My grandmother believed that if a life is lost, then another one springs up replanted somewhere else, the next life even stronger than the last. She believed that no one really dies as long as someone remembers, someone who will acknowledge that this person had in spite of everything been here. We are part of an endless circle, the daughters of Anacaona. We have stumbled, but have not fallen. We are ill-favored, but we still endure. Every once in a while, we must scream this as far as the wind can carry our voices: We are ugly, but we are here! And here to stay.

NOTES

1. François Duvalier, known as 'Papa Doc', was elected president of Haiti in 1957. A black physician and folklorist, he claimed he was ending 'mulatto' rule. He rewrote the constitution in 1964, making himself president for life, and again in 1971 to grant himself the power to name his successor. He named his son, Jean-Claude, who became known as 'Baby Doc'. The Duvalier regime was maintained by a private army, the *Tonton Macoutes*, as well as the regular army. On his father's death in 1971, Jean-Claude became president and he also claimed to be president for life. A widespread uprising in 1985 to 1986 led him to accept a ride into exile in a US military plane and the army soon established its political power.
2. Jean-Bertrand Aristide, a radical Haitian priest, was a leader first of the revolt against the Duvalier regime and then of resistance to the army. In 1987, the army cancelled elections and installed a president, but he was exiled after four months and replaced by another military regime. When elections were held in December 1990, Aristide was swept in with 67 per cent of the vote and he became president in February 1991. Opposed by the army, the mulatto elite and the conservative church hierarchy, Aristide was forced into exile after only eight months and the army reestablished its power. Widespread terror against Aristide's popular movement led thousands of people to flee Haiti in small boats. In September 1994, 15,000 US troops entered Haiti and Aristide was restored to the presidency in October, for the remainder of his term. He abolished the army but he was forced to accept an unpopular economic programme. In December 1995, he was succeeded by René Préval because he could not succeed himself, but in 2000 Aristide was again elected president by a huge majority.

Part Three
The Anglophone Intellectuals

Twenty-Three

J. J. Thomas

John Jacob Thomas (1841–1889) was born in Trinidad of poor black parents soon after Emancipation, at a time of social and economic crisis. He received enough basic education in one of the new free secular primary schools to enter Woodbrook Normal School, near Port of Spain, as a fee-paying student at the age of 18. Early in 1859, he was awarded a government allowance worth between £20 and £40 a year, in return for teaching in a demonstration school. A year later, he achieved his first job, as the schoolmaster of the Ward School at Savonetta near Point Lisas. The majority of people in the area were illiterate agricultural workers and their families, an increasing number of whom were from India. In 1865, he was transferred to the nearby village of Couva. It was in this context of cultural diversity that Thomas developed a scholarly interest in languages.

According to the Keenan Report on education in Trinidad (1869), 'The operation of the Ward schools has, no doubt, extended the use of English to districts where English has been previously unknown. But the diffusion of the English language has been accomplished by the most irrational process that could possibly be conceived' (Gordon 1968, 73). Children whose first language was Creole, Spanish, French or an Indian language had English forced on them as if by 'a battering-ram', and the textbooks, publications of the Irish National Board, made no reference to anything Trinidadian. Thomas reacted to this situation by studying the languages and cultures of the people around him. Without any formal training, he made a pioneering study of Creole, The Theory and Practice of Creole Grammar, *published in Trinidad in 1869. Thomas showed that Creole was not a debased or formless dialect, as most people persisted in seeing it, but a new language that synthesised elements of African and European languages. His book was favourably received in London and Paris and he was asked to write an essay on Creole and encouraged to publish a collection of folk tales and Creole proverbs. He was promoted in the civil service to Secretary of the Board of Education in 1870 and he produced the first literary journal of the colony,* The Trinidad Monthly, *in 1871 and 1872. He visited England in 1873, where he read his paper, 'On Some Peculiarities of the Creole Language', to the Philological Society, to which he was elected a member.*

About this time, however, Thomas began to suffer from an illness. He was later diagnosed as having rheumatism and he had to retire in 1879. In poor health and near poverty, he continued his study of languages, including Greek and Latin, and Creole culture. In 1887, he lectured on education in Grenada, arguing that the curriculum was 'only a servile imitation of the now almost entirely exploded English fashions of instruction' and should be replaced by West Indian history and geography. While he was in Grenada, Thomas read a new book by James Anthony Froude (1818–94), Regius Professor of Modern History at Oxford University, The English in the West Indies, or the Bow of Ulysses *(London, 1888). On the basis of a short tour of parts of the West Indies, Froude wrote what C.L.R. James has called 'an imperialist attack' on the people of the Caribbean. Most Caribbean colonies, other than the Bahamas and Barbados, had lost their oligarchical assemblies and become Crown colonies, ruled by British governors with autocratic powers. Trinidad, like other colonies Britain acquired in the Napoleonic Wars, had been a Crown colony since 1810. In the 1840s and 1850s, the Colonial Office rejected requests by groups of planters and merchants to have some elected members serve on the legislative council, but a more organised campaign for reform began in 1885, led by a white French Creole journalist, Philip Rostant. A petition, signed by over 5,000 persons, led to the establishment of a Royal Franchise Commission in 1887 to consider the possibility of elected members on the council. Although the majority on the commission recommended that the council should include some elected members, on the basis of a very restricted franchise, the Colonial Office rejected the report and refused to concede to the demands of the reform movement. The debate about constitutional reform was the background for Froude's comments on the West Indies.*

Thomas wrote a series of 15 articles criticising Froude's book in The St. George's Chronicle and Grenada Gazette *between March and July 1888 and these were the basis of his book* Froudacity. *He went to London again to arrange* publication of this book and an enlarged edition of the study of Creole, but his health deteriorated. Soon after Froudacity *was published, Thomas died of tuberculosis at the age of 49. Some English critics commented that he had got the better of Froude, and his arguments continue to ring with passionate conviction more than a century later. Thomas was one of the first of many West Indian intellectuals who studied, understood and proudly defended their culture and people.*

ℱroudacity (excerpts)

Last year had well advanced towards its middle – in fact it was already April, 1888 – before Mr Froude's book of travels in the West Indies became known and generally accessible to readers in those Colonies.

My perusal of it in Grenada about the period above mentioned disclosed, thinly draped with rhetorical flowers, the dark outlines of a scheme to thwart political aspiration in the Antilles. That project is sought to be realised by deterring the home authorities from granting an elective local legislature, however restricted in character, to any of the Colonies not yet enjoying such an advantage. An argument based on the composition of the inhabitants of those Colonies is confidently relied upon to confirm the inexorable mood of Downing Street.[1] Over-large and ever-increasing – so runs the argument – the African element in the population of the West Indies is, from its past history and its actual tendencies, a standing menace to the continuance of civilisation and religion. An immediate catastrophe, social, political, and moral, would most assuredly be brought about by the granting of full elective rights to dependencies thus inhabited. Enlightened statesmanship should at once perceive the immense benefit that would ultimately result from such refusal of the franchise. The cardinal recommendation of that refusal is that it would avert definitively the political domination of the Blacks, which must inevitably be the outcome of any concession of the modicum of right so earnestly desired. The exclusion of the Negro vote being inexpedient, if not impossible, the exercise of electoral powers by the Blacks must lead to their returning candidates of their own race to the local legislatures, and that, too, in numbers preponderating according to the majority of the Negro electors. The Negro legislators thus supreme in the councils of the Colonies would straightway proceed to pass vindictive and retaliatory laws against their white fellow-colonists. For it is only fifty years since the White man and the Black man stood in the reciprocal relations of master and slave. Whilst those relations subsisted, the white masters inflicted, and the black slaves had to endure, the hideous atrocities that are inseparable from the system of slavery. Since Emancipation, the enormous strides made in self-advancement by the ex-slaves have only had the effect of provoking a resentful uneasiness in the bosoms of the ex-masters. The former bondsmen, on their side, and like their brethren of Hayti, are eaten up with implacable, blood-thirsty rancour against their former lords and owners. The annals of Hayti form quite a cabinet of political and social object-lessons which, in the eyes of British statesmen, should be invaluable in showing the true method of dealing with Ethiopic subjects of the Crown . . . . Colonial administrators of the mighty British Empire, the lesson which History has taught and yet continues to teach you in Hayti as to the best mode of dealing with your Ethiopic colonists lies patent, blood-stained and terrible before you, and should be taken definitively to heart. But if you are willing that Civilisation and Religion – in short, all the highest developments of individual and social life – should at once be swept away by a desolating vandalism of African birth; if you do not recoil from the blood-guiltiness that would stain your consciences through the massacre of our fellow-countrymen in the West Indies, on account of their race, complexion and enlightenment; finally, if you desire these modern Hesperides to revert into primeval jungle, horrent lairs wherein the Blacks, who, but a short while before, had been ostensibly civilised, shall be revellers, as high-priests and devotees, in orgies of devil-worship, cannibalism, and obeah – dare to give the franchise to those West Indian Colonies, and then rue the consequences of your infatuation! . . .

Alas, if the foregoing summary of the ghastly imaginings of Mr Froude were true, in what a fool's paradise had the wisest and best amongst us been living, moving, and having our being! Up to the date of the suggestion by him as above of the alleged facts and possibilities of West Indian life, we had believed . . . that to no well-thinking West Indian White, whose ancestors may have, innocently or culpably, participated in the gains as well as the guilt of slavery, would the remembrance of its palmy days be otherwise than one of regret. We Negroes, on the other hand, after a lapse of time extending over nearly two generations, could be indebted only to precarious tradition or scarcely accessible documents for any knowledge we might chance upon of the sufferings endured in these Islands of the West by those of our race who have gone before us . . . .

The following are the words in which our traveller embodies the main motive and purpose of his voyage:

> 'My own chief desire was to see the human inhabitants, to learn what they were doing, how they were living, and what they were thinking about . . . .'

But, alas, with the mercurialism of temperament in which he has thought proper to indulge when only Negroes and Europeans not of 'Anglo-West Indian' tendencies were concerned, he jauntily threw to the winds all the scruples and cautious minuteness which were essential to the proper execution of his project. At Barbados ... he satisfies himself with sitting aloft, at a balcony-window, to contemplate the movements of the sable throng below, of whose character, moral and political, he nevertheless professes to have become a trustworthy delineator . . . . Speaking of St Vincent, where he arrived immediately after leaving Barbados, our author says:

> 'I did not land, for the time was short, and as a beautiful picture the island was best seen from the deck. The characteristics of the people are the same in all the Antilles, and could be studied elsewhere.'

Now, it is a fact, patent and notorious, that 'the characteristics of the people are' *not* 'the same in all the Antilles'. A man of Mr Froude's attainments, whose studies have made him familiar with ethnological facts, must be aware that difference of local surroundings and influences does, in the course of time, inevitably create difference of characteristic and deportment. Hence there is in nearly every Colony a marked dissimilarity of native qualities amongst the Negro inhabitants, arising not only from the causes above indicated, but largely also from the great diversity of their African ancestry . . . .

In Grenada, the next island he arrived at, our traveller's procedure with regard to the inhabitants was very similar. There he landed in the afternoon, drove three or four miles inland to dine at the house of a 'gentleman who was a passing resident', returned in the dark to his ship, and started for Trinidad. In the course of this journey back, however, as he sped along in the carriage, Mr Froude found opportunity to look into the people's houses along the way, where, he tells us, he 'could see and was astonished to observe signs of comfort, and even signs of taste – armchairs, sofas, sideboards with cut-glass upon them, engravings and coloured prints upon the walls'. As a result of this nocturnal examination, *à vol d'oiseau*, he has written paragraph upon paragraph about the people's character and prospects in the island of Grenada. To read the patronising terms in which our historian-traveller has seen fit to comment on Grenada and its people, one would believe that his account is of some half-civilised, out-of-the-way region under British sway, and inhabited chiefly by a horde of semi-barbarian ignoramuses of African descent . . .

Those who know Grenada and its affairs are perfectly familiar with the fact that all of its chief intellectual business, whether official (even in the highest degree, such as temporary administration of the government), legal, commercial, municipal, educational, or journalistic, has been for years upon years carried on by men of colour . . . .

Mr Froude contends, and we heartily coincide with him, that a ruler of high training and noble purposes would, as the embodiment of the administrative authority, be the very best provision for the government of Colonies constituted as ours are. But he has also pointed out, and that in no equivocal terms, that the above are far from having been indispensable qualifications for the patronage of Downing Street. He has shown that the Colonial Office is, more often than otherwise, swayed in the appointment of Colonial Governors by considerations among which the special fitness of the man appointed holds but a secondary place . . . .

After Governor Longden came Sir Henry Turner Irving, a personage who brought to Trinidad a reputation for all the vulgar colonial prejudices which, discreditable enough in ordinary folk, are, in the Governor of a mixed community, nothing less than calamitous. More than amply did he justify the evil reports with which rumour had heralded his coming. Abler, more astute, more daring than Sir James Longden, who was, on the whole, only a constitutionally timid man, Governor Irving threw himself heart and soul into the arms of the Sugar Interest, by whom he had been helped into his high office, and whose belief he evidently shared, that sugar-growers alone should be possessors of the lands of the West Indies. It would be wearisome to detail the methods by which every act of Sir Arthur Gordon's[2] to benefit the whole population was cynically and systematically undone by this his native-hating successor . . . .

In the matter of official appointments, too, Governor Irving was consistent in his ostentatious hostility to Creoles in general, and to coloured Creoles in particular. Of the fifty-six appointments which that model Governor made in 1876, only seven happened to be natives and coloured, out of a population in which the latter element is so preponderant as to excite the fears of Mr Froude. In educational matters, though he could not with any show of sense or decency re-enact the rule which excluded students of illegitimate birth from the advantages of the Royal College,[3] he could, nevertheless, pander to the prejudices of himself and his friends by raising the standard of proficiency while reducing the limit of the age for free admission to that institution – boys of African descent having shown an irrepressible persistency in carrying off prizes . . . .

The Governor was callous. Trinidad was a battening ground for his friends; but she had in her bosom men who were *her* friends, and the struggle began, constitutionally of course, which, under the leadership of the Mayor of San Fernando, has continued up to now, culminating at last in the Reform movement which Mr Froude decries . . . .

Sir Sanford Freeling, by the will and pleasure of Downing Street, was the next successor, after Governor Irving, to the chief ruler-ship of Trinidad. Incredible as it may sound, he was a yet more disadvantageous bargain for the Colony's £4,000 a year. A better man in many respects than his predecessor, he was in many more a much worse Governor . . . .

In evidence of that poor ruler's infirmity of purpose, we would only cite the double fact that, whereas in 1883 he was the first to enter a practical protest against the housing of the diseased and destitute in the then newly finished, but most leaky, House of Refuge on the St Clair Lands, by having the poor saturated inmates carried off in his presence to the Colonial Hospital, yet His Excellency was the very man who, in the very next year, 1884, not only sanctioned the shooting down of Indian immigrants at their festival,[4] but actually directed the use of buck-shot for the purpose! Evidently, if these two foregoing statements are true, Mr Froude must join us in thinking that a man whose mind could be warped by external influences from the softest commiseration for the sufferings of his kind, one year, into being the cold-blooded deviser of the readiest method for slaughtering unarmed holiday-makers, the very next year, is not the kind of ruler whom he and we so cordially desiderate . . . .

Sir Arthur Elibank Havelock next had the privilege of enjoying the paradisiac sojourn at Queen's House, St Anne's, as well as the four thousand pounds a year attached to the right of occupying that princely residence. Save as a dandy, however, and the harrier of subordinate officials, the writer of the annals of Trinidad may well pass him by . . . . That the leading minds of Trinidad should believe in an elective legislature is a logical consequence of the teachings of the past, when the Colony was under the manipulation of the sort of Governors above mentioned as immediately succeeding Sir Arthur Gordon . . . .

The cup of loyal forbearance reached the overflowing point since the trickstering days of Governor Irving, and it is useless now to believe in the possibility of a return of the leading minds of Trinidad to a tame acquiescence as regards the probabilities of their government according to the Crown system. Mr Froude's own remarks point out definitely enough that a community so governed is absolutely at the mercy, for good or for evil, of the man who happens to be invested with the supreme authority. He has also shown that in our case that supreme authority is very often disastrously entrusted. Yet has he nothing but sneers for the efforts of those who strive to be emancipated from liability to such subjection. Mr Froude's deftly-worded sarcasms about 'degrading tyranny', 'the dignity of manhood', etc, are powerless to alter the facts. Crown Colony Government – denying, as it does, to even the wisest and most interested in a community cursed with it all participation in the conduct of their own affairs, while investing irresponsible and uninterested 'birds of passage' (as our author aptly describes them) with the right of making ducks and drakes of the resources wrung from the inhabitants – *is* a degrading tyranny, which the sneers of Mr Froude cannot make otherwise . . . .

We close this part of our review by reiterating our conviction that, come what will, the Crown Colony system, as at present managed, is doomed[5] . . . .

We come now to the ingenious and novel fashion in which Mr Froude carries out his investigations among the black population, and to his dogmatic conclusions concerning them. He says:

'In Trinidad, as everywhere else, my own chief desire was to see the human inhabitants, to learn what they were doing, how they were living, and what they were thinking about, and this could best be done by drives about the town and neighbourhood ....

'Under the rule of England, in these islands, the two millions of these brothers-in-law of ours are the most perfectly contented specimens of the human race to be found upon the planet . . . If happiness be the satisfaction of every conscious desire, theirs is a condition that admits of no improvement . . . [U]nder the beneficent despotism of the English Government, which knows no difference of colour and permits no oppression, they can sleep, lounge, and laugh away their lives as they please, fearing no danger,' etc.

Now, then, let us examine for a while this roseate picture of Arcadian blissfulness said to be enjoyed by British West Indian Negroes in general, and by the Negroes of Trinidad in particular. 'No distinction of colour' under the British rule, and, better still, absolute protection of the weaker against the stronger! This latter consummation especially, Mr Froude tells us, has been happily secured 'under the beneficent despotism' of the Crown Colony system. However, let the above vague hyperboles be submitted to the test of practical experience, and the abstract government analysed in its concrete relations with the people.

Unquestionably the actual and direct interposition of the shielding authority above referred to, between man and man, is the immediate province of the MAGISTRACY. All other branches of the Government, having in themselves no coercive power, must, from the supreme executive downwards, in cases of irreconcilable clashing of interests, have ultimate recourse to the magisterial jurisdiction. Putting aside, then, whatever culpable remissness may have been manifested by magistrates in favour of powerful malfeasants, we would submit that the fact of stipendiary justices converting the tremendous, far-reaching powers which they wield into an engine of systematic oppression, ought to dim by many a shade the glowing lustre of Mr Froude's encomiums. Facts, authentic and notorious, might be adduced in hundreds, especially with respect to the Port of Spain and San Fernando magistracies (both of which, since the administration of Sir J.R. Longden, have been exclusively the prizes of briefless English barristers), to prove that these gentry, far from being bulwarks to the weaker as against the stronger, have, in their own persons, been the direst scourges that the poor, particularly when coloured, have been afflicted by in aggravation of the difficulties of their lot. Only typical examples can here be given out of hundreds upon hundreds which might easily be cited and proved against the incumbents of the above-mentioned chief stipendiary magistracies ....

We now take San Fernando, the next most important magisterial district after

Port of Spain. At the time of Mr Froude's visit, and for some time before, the duties of the magistracy there were discharged by Mr Arthur Child, an 'English barrister' who, of course, had possessed the requisite qualification of being hopelessly briefless. For the ideal justice which Mr Froude would have Britons believe is meted out to the weaker classes by their fellow-countrymen in the West Indies, we may refer the reader to the conduct of the above-named functionary on the memorable occasion of the slaughter of the coolies under Governor Freeling, in October, 1884. Mr Child, as Stipendiary Justice, had the duty of reading the Riot Act to the immigrants, who were marching in procession to the town of San Fernando, contrary, indeed, to the Government proclamation which had forbidden it; and he it was who gave the order to 'fire', which resulted fatally to many of the unfortunate devotees of Hosein.[6] This mandate and its lethal consequences anticipated by some minutes the similar but far more death-dealing action of the Chief of Police, who was stationed at another post in the vicinity of San Fernando. The day after the shooting down of a total of more than one hundred immigrants, the protecting action of this magistrate towards the weaker folk under his jurisdiction had a striking exemplification, to which Mr Froude is hereby made welcome. Of course there was a general cry of horror throughout the Colony, and especially in the San Fernando district, at the fatal outcome of the proclamation, which had mentioned only 'fine' and 'imprisonment', but not Death, as the penalty for disregarding its prohibitions. For nearly forty years, namely from their very first arrival in the Colony, the East Indian immigrants had, according to specific agreement with the Government, invariably been allowed the privilege of celebrating their annual feast of Hosein, by walking in procession with their pagodas through the public roads and streets of the island, without prohibition or hindrance of any kind from the authorities, save and except in cases where rival estate pagodas were in danger of getting into collision on the question of precedence. On such occasions the police, who always attended the processions, usually gave the lead to the pagodas of the labourers of estates according to their seniority as immigrants.

In no case up to 1884, after thirty odd years' inauguration in the Colony, was the Hosein festival ever pretended to be any cause of danger, actual or prospective, to any town or building. On the contrary, business grew brisker and solidly improved at the approach of the commemoration, owing to the very considerable sale of parti-coloured paper, velvet, calico, and similar articles used in the construction of the pagodas. Governor Freeling, however, was, it may be presumed, compelled to see danger in an institution which had had for nearly forty years' trial, without a single accident happening to warrant any sudden interposition of the Government tending to its suppression. At all events, the only action taken in 1884, in prospect of their usual festival, was to notify the immigrants by proclamation, and, it is said, also through authorised agents, that the details of their fête were not to be conducted in the usual manner; and that their appearance with pagodas in any public road or any town, without special license from some competent local authority, would entail the penalty of so many pounds fine, or imprisonment for so many months with hard labour. The immigrants, to whom this unexpected change on the part of the authorities was utterly incomprehensible, both petitioned and sent deputations to the Governor, offering guarantees for the, if possible, more secure celebration of the Hosein, and praying for His Excellency to cancel the prohibition as to use of the roads, inasmuch as it interfered with the essential part of their religious rite, which was the 'drowning', or casting into the sea, of the pagodas. Having utterly failed in their efforts with the Governor, the coolies resolved to carry out their religious duty according to the prescriptive forms, accepting, at the same time, the responsibility in the way of fine or imprisonment which they would thus inevitably incur. A rumour was also current at that time that, pursuant to this resolution, the head men of the various plantations had authorised a general subscription amongst their countrymen, for meeting the contingency of fines in the police courts. All these things were the current talk of the population of San Fernando, in which town the leading immigrants, free as well as indentured, had begun to raise funds for this purpose.

All that the public, therefore, expected would have resulted from the intended infringement of the Proclamation was an enormous influx of money in the shape of fines into the Colonial Treasury; as no one doubted the extreme facility which existed for ascertaining exactly, in the case of persons registered and indentured to specific plantations, the names and abodes of at least the chief offenders against the proclamation. Accordingly, on the occurrence of the bloody catastrophe related above, every one felt that the mere persistence in marching *all unarmed* towards the town, without actually attempting to force their way into it, was exorbitantly visited upon the coolies by a violent death or a life-long mutilation. This sentiment few were at any pains to conceal; but as the poorer and more ignorant classes can be handled with greater impunity than those who are intelligent and have the means of self-defense, Mr Justice Child, the very day after the tragedy, and without waiting for the *pro-formâ* official inquiry into the tragedy in which he bore so conspicuous a part, actually caused to be arrested, sat to try and sent to hard labour, persons whom the police, in obedience to his positive injunctions, had reported to him as having condemned the shooting down of the immigrants! Those who were arrested and thus summarily punished had, of course, no means of self-protection; and as the case is typical of others, as illustrative of 'justice-made law' applied to 'subject races' in a British colony, Mr Froude is free to accept it, or not, in corroboration of his unqualified panegyrics . . . .

It sounds queer, not to say unnatural and scandalous, that Englishmen should in these days of light be the champions of injustice towards their fellow-subjects, not for any intellectual or moral disqualify-cation, but on the simple account of the darker skin of those who are to be assailed and thwarted in their life's career and aspirations. Really, are we to be grateful that the colour difference should be made the basis and justification of the dastardly denials of justice, social, intellectual, and moral, which have characterised the *régime* of those who Mr Froude boasts were left to be the representatives of Britain's morality and fair play? Are the Negroes under the French flag not intensely French? Are the Negroes under the Spanish flag not intensely Spanish? Wherefore are they so? . . . . By Spain and France every loyal and law-abiding subject of the Mother Country has been a citizen deemed worthy if all the rights, immunities, and privileges flowing from good and creditable citizenship. Those meriting such distinction were taken into the bosom of the society which their qualifications recommended them to share, and no office under the Government has been thought too good or too elevated for men of their stamp. No wonder, then, that Mr Froude is silent regarding the scores of brilliant coloured officials who adorn the civil service of France and Spain, and whose appointment, in contrast with what has usually been the case in British Colonies, reflects an abiding lustre on those countries, and establishes their right to a foremost place among nations . . . .

Anyhow, Mr Froude's history of the Emancipation may here be amended for him by a reminder that, in the British Colonies, it was not *Whites* as masters, and *Blacks* as slaves, who were affected by that momentous measure. In fact, 1838 found in the British Colonies very nearly as many Negro and Mulatto slave-owners as there were white. Well then, these black and yellow planters received their quota, it may be presumed, of the £20,000,000 sterling indemnity.[7] They were part and parcel of the proprietary body in the Colonies, and had to meet the crisis like the rest. They were very wealthy, some of these Ethiopic accomplices of the oppressors of their own race. Their sons and daughters were sent, like white planters' children, across the Atlantic for a European education. These young folk returned to their various native Colonies as lawyers and doctors. Many of them were also wealthy planters. The daughters, of course, became in time the mothers of the new generation of prominent inhabitants . . . .

Mr Froude can mention only Mr Justice Reeves[8] in FIFTY years as a sample of the 'exceptional' progress under the British auspices of a man of African descent! Verily, if in fifty long years British policy can recognize only one single exception in a race between which and the white race there is no original or congenital difference of capacity, the inference must be that British policy has been not only systematically, but also too successfully, hostile to the advancements of the Ethiopians subject thereto . . . .

We proceed here another step, and take up a fresh deliverance of our author's in reference to the granting of the franchise to the black population of these Colonies. 'It is', says Mr James Anthony Froude, who is just as prophetic as his prototypes, the slave-owners of the last half-century, 'it is as certain as anything future can be, that *if we give the negroes as a body* the political privileges which *we claim for ourselves*, they will use them only to their own injury'. The forepart of the above citation reads very much as if its author wrote it on the principle of raising a ghost for the mere purpose of laying it. What visionary, what dreamer of impossible dreams, has ever asked for the Negroes *as a body* the same political privileges which are claimed for themselves by Mr Froude and other of his countrymen, who are presumably capable of exercising them? No one in the West Indies has ever done so silly a thing as to ask for the Negroes as a body that which has not, as everybody knows, and never will be, conceded to the people of Great Britain as a body.[9] The demand for Reform in the Crown Colonies – a demand which our author deliberately misrepresents – is made neither by nor for the Negro, Mulatto, White, Chinese, nor East Indian. It is a petition put forward by prominent responsible colonists – the majority of whom are Whites, and mostly Britons besides.

Their prayer, in which the whole population in these Colonies most heartily join in, is simply and most reasonably that we, the said Colonies, being an integral portion of the British Empire, and having, in intelligence and every form of civilised progress, outgrown the stage of political tutelage, should be accorded some measure of emancipation therefrom. And thereby we – White, Black, Mulatto, and all other inhabitants and tax-payers – shall be able to protect ourselves against the self-seeking and bold indifference to our interests which seem to be the most cherished expression of our rulers' official existence . . . .

It behooves us to repeat (for our detractor is a persistent repeater) that the cardinal dodge by which Mr Froude and his few adherents expect to succeed in obtaining the reversal of the progress of the coloured population is by misrepresenting the elements, and their real attitude towards one another, of the sections composing the British West Indian communities. Everybody knows full well that Englishmen, Scotchmen, and Irishmen (who are not officials), as well as Germans, Spaniards, Italians, Portuguese, and other nationalities, work in unbroken harmony and, more or less, prosper in these Islands . . . . These reputable specimens of manhood have created homes dear to them in these favoured climes; and they, at any rate, being on the very best terms with all sections of the community in which their lot is cast, have a common cause as fellow-sufferers under the *régime* of Mr Froude's official 'birds of passage'. The agitation in Trinidad tells its own tale. There is not a single black man – though there should have been many – among the leaders of the movement for Reform. Nevertheless, the honourable and truthful author of *The English in the West Indies,* in order to invent a plausible pretext for his sinister labours of love on behalf of the poor pro-slavery survivals, and despite his knowledge that sturdy Britons are at the head of the agitation, coolly tells the world that it is a struggle to secure 'negro domination'.

The further allegation of our author respecting the black man is curious and, of course, dismally prophetic. As the reader may perhaps recollect, it is to the effect that granting political power to the Negroes as a body, equal in scope 'to that claimed by Us' (*i.e.,* Mr Froude and his friends), would certainly result in the use of these powers by the Negroes to their own injury. And wherefore? If Mr Froude professes to believe – what is a fact – that there is 'no original or congenital difference of capacity' between the white and the African races, where is the consistency of his urging a contention which implies inferiority in natural shrewdness, as regards their own affairs, on the part of black men? Does this blower of the two extremes of temperature in the same breath pretend that the average British voter is better informed, can see more clearly what is for his own advantage, is better able to assess the relative merits of persons to be entrusted with the spending of his taxes, and the general management of his interests? If Mr Froude means all this, he is at issue not only with his own specific declaration to the contrary, but with facts of overwhelming weight and number showing precisely the reverse. We have personally had frequent opportunities of coming into contact, both in and out of England, with natives of Great Britain, not of the agricultural order alone, but very often of the artisan class, whose ignorance of the commonest matters was as dense as it was discreditable to the land of their birth and breeding . . . .

Invested with political power, the Negroes, Mr Froude goes on to assure his readers, 'will slide back into their old condition, and the chance will be gone of lifting them to the level to which we have no right to say they are incapable of rising'. How touchingly sympathetic! . . . The tears of the crocodile are most copious in close view of the banquet on his prey . . . . But, taking it as a serious contention, we find that it involves a suggestion that the according of electoral votes to citizens of a certain complexion would, *per se* and *ipso facto*, produce a revulsion and collapse of the entire prevailing organisation and order of a civilised community.

What talismanic virtue this prophet of evil attributes to a vote in the hand of a Negro out of Barbados, where for years the black man's vote has been operating, harmlessly enough, Heaven knows, we cannot imagine . . . .

With regard to our author's talk about 'the average black nature, such as it now exists, being left free to assert itself', and the dire consequences therefrom to result, we can only feel pity at the desperate straits to which, in his search for a pretext for gratuitous slander, a man of our author's capacity has been so ignominiously reduced. All we can say to him with reference to this portion of his violent suppositions is that 'the average black nature, such as it now exists', should NOT, in a civilised community, be left free to assert itself, any more than the average white, the average brown, the average red, or indeed any average colour of human nature whatsoever. As self-defence is the first law of nature, it has followed that every condition of organised society, however simple or primitive, is furnished with some recognised means of self-protection against the free assertion of itself by the average nature of any of its members . . . .

In heedless formulation of his reasons, if such they should be termed, for urging tooth and nail the non-according of reform to the Crown-governed Colonies, our author puts forth this dogmatic deliverance (p. 123):

'A West Indian self-governing dominion is possible only with a full Negro vote. If the whites are to combine, so will the blacks. It will be a rule by the blacks and for the blacks.'

That a constitution for any of our diversely populated Colonies which may be fit for it is possible only with 'a full Negro vote' (to the extent within the competence of such voting), goes without saying, as must be the case with every section of the Queen's subjects eligible for the franchise. The duly qualified Spaniard, Coolie, Portuguese, or man of any other non-British race, will each thus have a vote, the same as every Englishman or any other Briton. Why, then, should the vote of the Negro be so especially a bugbear? It is because the Negro is the game which our political sportsman is in full chase of, and determined to hunt down at any cost. Granted, however, for the sake of argument, that black voters should preponderate at any election, what then? . . .

Are we to understand him as suggesting that voting by black electors would be synonymous with electing black representatives? If so, he has clearly to learn much more than he has shown that he lacks, in order to understand and appreciate the vital influences at work in West Indian affairs. Undoubtedly, being the spokesman of the few who (secretly) avow themselves to be particularly hostile to Ethiopians, he has done no more than reproduce their sentiments . . . .

White individuals who have part and lot in the various Colonies, with their hearts and feelings swayed by affections natural to their birth and earliest associations; and Whites who have come to think the land of their adoption as dear to themselves as the land of their birth, entertain no such dread of their fellow-citizens of any other section, whom they estimate according to intelligence and probity, and not according to any accident of exterior physique. Every intelligent black is as shrewd regarding his own interests as our author himself would be regarding his . . . . [T]he Negro voter would elect representatives whom he knew he could trust for competency in the management of his affairs, and not persons whose sole recommendation to him would be the possession of the same kind of skin. Nor, from what we know of matters in the West Indies, do we believe that any white man of the class we have eulogised would hesitate to give his warmest suffrage to any black candidate who he knew would be a fitting representative of his interests. We could give examples from almost every West Indian island of white and coloured men who would be indiscriminately chosen as their candidate by either section . . . .

Mr Froude states plainly enough (p.123) that, whereas a whole thousand years were needed to train and discipline the Anglo-Saxon race, yet 'European government, European instruction, continued steadily till his natural tendencies are superseded by a higher instinct, may shorten the probation period of the negro'. Let it be supposed that this period of probation for the Negro should extend, under such exceptionally favourable circumstances, to any period less than that which is alleged to have been needed by the Anglo-Saxon to attain his political manhood – what then are the prospects held out by Mr Froude to us and our posterity on our mastering the training and discipline, which he specially recommends for Blacks? Our author, in view, doubtless, of the rapidity of our onward progress, and indeed our actual advancement in every respect, thus answers (pp. 123-4): 'Let a generation or two pass by *and carry away with them the old traditions*, and an English governor-general will be found presiding over a black council, delivering the speeches made for him by a black prime minister; and how long could this endure? No English gentleman would consent to occupy so absurd a situation.'

And again, more emphatically, on the same point (p. 285): 'No Englishman, not even a bankrupt peer, would consent to occupy such a position; the blacks themselves would despise him if he did; and if the governor is to be one of their own race and colour, how long would such a connection endure?'

It is plainly to be seen from the above two extracts that the political ethics of our author being based on race and colour exclusively, would admit of no conceivable chance of real elevation to any descendant of Africa, who, being Ethiopian, could not possibly change his skin. The 'old traditions' which Mr Froude supposes to be carried away by his hypothetical (white) generations who have 'passed by', we readily infer from his language, rendered impossible such incarnations of political absurdity as those he depicts. But what should be thought of the sense, if not indeed the sanity, of a grave political teacher who prescribes 'European government' and 'European education' as the specifics to qualify the Negro for political emancipation, and who, when these qualifications are conspicuously mastered by the Negro who has undergone the training, refuses him the prize, *because* he is a Negro? We see further that, in spite of being fit for election to council, and even to be prime ministers competent to indite governors' messages, the pigment under our epidermis dooms us to eventual disappointment and a life-long condition of contempt . . . .

As to the dictum that 'the two races are not equal and will not blend', it is open to the fatal objection that, having himself proved, with sympathising pathos, how the West Indies are now well-nigh denuded of their Anglo-Saxon inhabitants, Mr Froude would have us also understand that the miserable remnant who still complainingly inhabit those islands must, by doing violence to the understanding, be taken as the whole of the world-pervading Anglo-Saxon family. The Negroes of the West Indies number a good deal more than two million souls. Does this suggester of extravagances mean that the prejudices and vain conceit of the few dozens whom he champions should be made to override and overbear, in political arangements, the serious and solid interests of so many hundreds of thousands? . . .

Taking our author's 'Anglo-West Indians' and the people of Ethiopian descent respectively, it would not be too much to assert, nor in anywise difficult to prove by facts and figures, that for every competent individual of the former section in active civilized employments, the coloured section can put forward at least twenty thoroughly competent rivals . . . . Referring to his hypothetical confederation with its black office-holders, our author scornfully asks:

'And how long would this endure?'

The answer must be that, granting the existence of such a state of things, its duration would be not more nor less than under white functionaries . . . .

Not content with making himself the mouthpiece of English gentlemen in this manner, our author, with characteristic hardihood, obtrudes himself into the same post on behalf of Negroes; saying that, in the event of even a bankrupt peer accepting the situation of governor-general over them, 'The blacks themselves would despise him!'

Mr Froude may pertinently be asked here the source whence he derived his certainty on this point, inasmuch as it is absolutely at variance with all that is sensible and natural; for surely it is both foolish and monstrous to suppose that educated men would infer the degradation of any one from the fact of such a one consenting to govern and co-operate with themselves for their own welfare. He further asks on the same subject:

'And if the governor is to be one of their own race and colour, how long could such a connection endure?'

Our answer must be the same as with regard to the duration of the black council and black prime minister carrying out the government under the same conditions. . . .

'The exclusive privilege of colour over colour cannot be restored.' Never in the history of the British West Indies – must we again state – was there any law or usage establishing superiority in privileges for any section of the community on account of colour. This statement of fact is also and again an answer to, and refutation of, the succeeding allegation that, 'While slavery continued, the *whites ruled* effectively and economically'. It will be yet more clearly shown in a later part of this essay that during slavery, in fact for upwards of two centuries after its introduction, the West Indies were ruled by *slave-owners,* who happened to be of all colours, the means of purchasing slaves and having a plantation being the one exclusive consideration in the case. It is, therefore, contrary to fact to represent the

Whites exclusively as ruling, and the Blacks indiscriminately as subject.

He goes on to say: 'There are two classes in the community; their interests are opposite as they are now understood.' As regards the above, Mr Froude's attention may be called to the fact that classification in no department of science has ever been based on colour, but on relative affinity in certain salient qualitites. To use his own figure, no horse or dog is more or less a horse or dog because it happens to be white or black. No teacher marshals his pupils into classes according to any outward physical distinction, but according to intellectual approximation. In like manner there has been wealth for hundreds of men of Ethiopic origin, and poverty for hundreds of men of Caucasian origin, and the reverse in both cases. We have, therefore, had hundreds of black as well as white men who, under providential dispensation, belonged to the class, rich men; while, on the other hand, we have had hundreds of white men who, under providential dispensation, belonged to the class, poor men. Similarly, in the composition of a free mixed community, we have hundreds of both races belonging to the class, competent and eligible; and hundreds of both races belonging to the class, incompetent and ineligible: to both of which classes all possible colours might belong. It is from the first mentioned that are selected those who are to bear the rule, to which the latter class is, in the very nature of things, bound to be subject. There is no government by reason merely of skins . . . .

The years of civilised development have dawned in turn on many sections of the human family, and the Anglo-Saxons, who now enjoy preeminence, got their turn only after Egypt, Assyria, Babylon, Greece, Rome, and others had successively held the palm of supremacy. And since these mighty empires have all passed away, may we not then, if the past teaches aught, confidently expect that other racial hegemonies will arise in the future to keep up the ceaseless progression of temporal existence towards the existence that is eternal? What is it in the nature of things that will oust the African race from the right to participate, in times to come, in the high destinies that have been assigned in times past to so many races that have not been in anywise superior to us in the qualifications, physical, moral, and intellectual, that mark out a race for prominence amongst other races? . . .

First, attention must be paid to the patriotic solidarity existing amongst the bondsmen, a solidarity which, in the case of those who had been deported in the same ship, had all the sanctity of blood-relationship. Those who had thus travelled to the 'white man's country' addressed and considered each other as brothers and sisters. Hence their descendants for many generations upheld, as if consanguineous, the modes of address and treatment which became hereditary in families whose originals had travelled in the same ship. These adopted uncles, aunts, nephews, nieces, were so united by common sympathies, that good or ill befalling any one of them intensely affected the whole connection. Mutual support commensurate with the area of their location thus became the order among these people . . . .

The miserable skin and race doctrine we have been discussing does not at all prefigure the destinies at all events of the West Indies, or determine the motives that will affect them. With the exception of those belonging to the Southern States of the Union, the vast body of African descendants now dispersed in various countries of the Western Hemisphere are at sufficient peace to begin occupying themselves, according to some fixed programme, about matters of racial importance. More than ten millions of Africans are scattered over the wide area indicated, and possess amongst them instances of mental and other qualifications which render them remarkable among their fellow-men. But like the essential parts of a complicated albeit perfect machine, these attainments and qualifications so widely dispersed await, it is evident, some potential agency to collect and adjust them into the vast engine essential for executing the true purposes of the civilised African Race. Already, especially since the late Emancipation Jubilee, are signs manifest of a desire for intercommunion and intercomprehension amongst the more distinguished of our people. With intercourse and unity of purpose will be secured the means to carry out the obvious duties which are sure to devolve upon us, especially with reference to the cradle of our Race, which is most probably destined to be the ultimate resting-place and headquarters of millions of our posterity. Within the short time that we had to compass all that we have achieved, there could not have arisen opportunities for doing more than we have effected. Meanwhile our present device is: 'Work, Hope, and Wait!'

NOTES

1. No. 10 Downing Street is the official residence of the British prime minister.
2. Sir Arthur H. Gordon, who was the governor from 1867 to 1870, had encouraged Thomas in his studies and had introduced him to Charles Kingsley, the famous writer, when he visited Trinidad in 1869.
3. Thomas became the secretary to the council of the Queen's Royal College in 1870.
4. This refers to the massacre at the annual Muharram festival in the town of San Fernando.
5. The secretary of state for the colonies, Joseph Chamberlain, rejected the petitions and delegations of the reform movement in 1895. When Trinidad's first elections to the legislative council occurred in 1925, after 128 years of British rule, only about 6 per cent of the population were qualified to vote.
6. The Muslim festival of Muharram, known in Trinidad as Hosein or Hosay, commemorates the deaths of Husain and Hasan, grandsons of the prophet Muhammed. Preceded by a month of fasting, this four-day festival reaches a climax when elaborate *tadjahs*, representations of the brothers' tombs, are carried in processions and cast into the sea.
7. The legislation that was passed in the British parliament in 1833 to end slavery throughout the colonies, replacing it with a period called apprenticeship, gave the slave owners £20 million in compensation for their loss of property. The money was allocated

according to the financial value of each slave. Nothing was given to the former slaves for their years of unremunerated labour and abuse.

8. Sir Conrad Reeves, a prominent Barbadian lawyer of mixed African and European descent, was the chief justice of Barbados from 1882 to 1901.

9. Property qualifications restricted the franchise in Great Britain. After the Second Reform Bill of 1867 the whole electorate in England was less than a tenth of the population. Further reforms in 1884 and 1885 extended the vote to some workers but it was not until 1918 that all adult men, and those women who were over 30 and householders or wives of householders, were eligible to vote. Ten years later all women and men over 21 could vote in the UK.

Twenty-Four

Marcus Mosiah Garvey

Marcus Garvey (1887–1940), who was born in Jamaica, lived in the United States between 1916 and 1927 and in the United Kingdom between 1935 and 1940. Most of the rest of his life he lived in Jamaica but he travelled extensively in Central America and the Caribbean. His Universal Negro Improvement Association (UNIA), an international organisation which he founded in Jamaica in 1914, had a profound impact on racial consciousness, anti-colonialism, and Pan-Africanism among millions of people.

Garvey acknowledged that he learned a great deal about 'race consciousness' from Dr Robert Love (1835–1914), a Bahamian physician who settled in Jamaica in 1894 and who edited the Jamaica Advocate *between 1894 and 1905. As a result of a broadening of the franchise in 1895, which raised the number of eligible voters from 2,000 to 43,266, Love was elected to the Kingston City Council in 1898 and the Legislative Council in 1906. Love advocated land reform, demanded the appointment of black school inspectors and the opening of the colonial bureaucracy to qualified blacks, and urged the elevation of the status of black women in society. In 1901, Love helped to launch the Jamaican branch of the Pan-African Association which had been started in London the previous year by H. Sylvester Williams, a Trinidadian barrister, with delegates from Africa, the Caribbean and the United States. Love and his newspaper played an important part in the rapid expansion of the Pan-African Association in Jamaica. He never had a mass following but his fierce attacks on race and class prejudices and colonialism influenced Garvey.*

A printer by trade, Garvey was elected vice-president of a short-lived printers' union in Jamaica from 1907 to 1909.

He participated in an unsuccessful strike in 1908 but trade unions, which were not then legal in Jamaica, were never the chief arena of his efforts. Garvey became secretary of the National Club, which had been founded the previous year by a barrister, S.A.G. Cox. The club did not last long but Cox's journal, Our Own, *was influential. Cox called for self-government within the empire, the legalisation of trade unions, the distribution of Crown lands to the peasantry, and for an end to racism in the colonial bureaucracy, subsidies for the importation of East Indian workers, and the suppression of the peasants' religious activities. In the final issue of* Our Own *(July 1, 1911) Cox wrote, 'The coloured and black people in Jamaica can only hope to better their condition by uniting with the coloured and black people of the United States of America and with those of other West Indian islands, and indeed with all Negroes in all parts of the world.' This, like many other issues raised by Cox and Love, became a central feature of Garveyism.*

In late 1910 and 1911, Garvey travelled in Central America, observing the exploitation of 'his people', and in 1912, he arrived in England. There, he was influenced by Africans and West Indians among whom he worked and by the Egyptian journalist, Duse Mohammed Ali, who edited a monthly journal, The African Times and Orient Review, *which appeared in 1912 and closed in 1919. Garvey contributed to this journal. His article entitled 'The British West Indies in the Mirror of Civilization', which appeared in the October 1913 issue, shows his anti-colonial position and his belief that West Indian blacks would play a key role in awakening and liberating African peoples in Africa and the diaspora.*

The British West Indies in the Mirror of Civilization. History Making by Colonial Negroes

In these days when democracy is spreading itself over the British Empire, and the peoples under the rule of the Union Jack are freeing themselves from hereditary lordship, and an unjust bureaucracy, it should not be amiss to recount the condition of affairs in the British West Indies, and particularly in the historic island of Jamaica, one of the oldest colonial possessions of the Crown.

It is right that the peoples of the vast Empire to which these colonies belong should be correctly informed on things affecting the welfare of these islands, being a comparatively neglected, if not unknown, region of the Atlantic Archipeligo [sic].

The history of the British possession of these islands is very interesting, as it reveals the many conflicts between the various powers that have been struggling for occupancy and supremacy in the Caribbean waters for three hundred years.

These islands were discovered by Christopher Columbus in the latter part of the fourteenth century,[1] and the major portion of them were handed over to the Spanish throne. England and France laid claim to certain of these colonies, and the former, with her justifiable (?) means of warfare, succeeded in driving the Spaniards from their tropical 'Gold Mines' with much regret on the part of the ejected, who had extinguished the Aborigines, an action quite in keeping with the European custom of depopulating new lands of their aboriginal tribes. The British West Indian Colonies to-day, comprise Jamaica, Trinidad and Tobago, Barbadoes, British Guiana, Grenada, St. Vincent, St. Lucia, Dominica, Antigua and Montserrat, St. Kitts, and Nevis, the Virgin Islands and one or two others, scattered over the groups known as the Greater and Lesser Antilles, with a population of over three million souls.[2]

When the Spaniards took possession of these islands they introduced cotton and sugar growing. To supply the labour that was necessary to make these industries solid and profitable, they started the slave traffic with Africa, from which place they recruited thousands of Negro slaves whom they took from their congenial homes by force. The sugar industry developed wonderfully with Negro labour, and the great output of sugar, as exported to Europe, brought incomputable wealth to the landed proprietors, which they used in gambling and feasting; and for exploration and further development of the veritable 'gold mines' of the Western Hemispheres.

Piratical and buccaneering parties used to frequent the waters of the Caribbean, where they held up on the high sea merchant vessels laden with their rich cargoes bound for Europe and the West Indies. Filibustering[3] was carried on in a daring fashion on land, where a buccaneering invader would hold up one of these islands and force the wealthy landlords to capitulate on conditions suitable to filibustering requirements.

During the sixteenth century England drove the Spaniards from the wealthiest of these islands and established herself in possession. To the Plantations, as they were called, a large proportion of her criminal class was deported, as also a few gentlemen. The new occupiers took over the paying sugar industry, and, with their superior knowledge of agriculture, gave a new impetus to it. These new owners found it necessary to replenish their labourers with new arrivals to foster the industry, hence an agreement was entered into with John Hawkins,[4] of infamous memory, who clandestinely obtained a charter from his sovereign to convey Negroes from Africa to the West Indies, thereby giving new life to the merciless traffic in human souls.

Jamaica was the most flourishing of the British West Indian Islands, and the ancient capital, Port Royal, which has been submerged by earthquake,[5] was said to be the richest spot on the face of the globe. The chief products of this colony were sugar and rum, but its assets were largely added to by its being the headquarters of

European pirates and buccaneers who took their treasures thither, where they gambled and feasted in great luxury. It is amusing to note that many of the pirates who traversed the West Indies had been deprived of their ears as the result of unsuccessful piratical encounters. Some of the early Governors of these islands, such as Sir Henry Morgan,[6] were known as subtle rogues, and were themselves at some time or another, pirates and buccaneers.

Among the many piratical and buccaneering heroes or rogues, whichever you wish to call them, may be mentioned Teach, otherwise known as Blackbeard, Morgan, Hawkins, Rogers, Drake, Raleigh, Preston, Shirley, Jackson and Somers. Such terror did these villains strike in the heart of the people of these islands, that up to the present day their names are held as auguries of fear among the people. It is common to hear a black or coloured mother, in trying to frighten her child, count 'One, two, three, four', and then shout, 'Preston, ah, com!' at which intimation the child runs away in terror.

Owing to the limit of space I shall confine myself to a few facts relating to the island of Jamaica, but I may say that the condition in the various islands are the same, and what is true of one is true of the whole.

Jamaica became a colony of England in 1665, under Oliver Cromwell,[7] and has since remained under her control. The country has passed through many forms of local government; at one time it was self-governing; then it became a Crown Colony. For the last twenty years, it has enjoyed a semi-representative government,[8] with little power of control, the balance of power resting in the hands of the red-tapists, who pull the strings of colonial conservatism from Downing Street,[9] with a reckless disregard of the interests and wishes of the people.

When the English took possession of this island they exploited it agriculturally for all it was worth, which was a great lot. As I have already mentioned they imported Negro slaves from Africa who tilled the soil under the severest torture, and who are the real producers of the wealth that the country has contributed to the coffers of Europe, and the pockets of English adventurers who, in the early days, were men of foul and inhuman characters.

The slaves were inhumanly treated, being beaten, tortured and scourged for the slightest offence. One of the primitive methods of chastisement was to 'dance the treadmill', an instrument that clipped off the toes when not danced to proper motion. In self-defence, and revenge of such treatment, the slaves revolted on several occasions, but with little or no success, as being without arms, they were powerless in the face of the organised military forces of the ruling class. In 1851[10] the Negro slaves in one of the North Western parishes of the island revolted, but were subdued with the loss to the planting proprietors of over three-quarters of a million sterling. They again revolted in 1865 in the East, under the leadership of the Hon. George William Gordon, a member of the Legislative Council, and Paul Bogle.[11]

They sounded the call of unmolested liberty, but owing to the suppression of telegraphic communication, they were handicapped and suppressed, otherwise Jamaica would be as free to-day as Hayti, which threw off the French yoke under the leadership of the famous Negro General, Toussaint L'Ouverture.[12] The Gordon party killed fifteen of the native despots and a savage plutocrat by the name of Baron von Ketelhodt[13] who had great control over the Governor, Edward John Eyre. The victorious party hanged Gordon, Paul Bogle and several hundred negroes, for which crime Governor Eyre was recalled to England and indicted for murder, but escaped by the 'skin of his teeth'.[14]

In 1834[15] a law was passed by the Imperial Parliament declaring all slaves within the British Empire free for ever, with the promise that such slaves should undergo an apprenticeship for a few years. On the 1st August, 1838, the Negro slaves of the West Indies became free. Twenty millions sterling was paid to the planters by the Imperial Government for the emancipation of the people whom they had taken from their sunny homes in Africa. The slaves got nothing; they were liberated without money, proper clothing, food or shelter. But with the characteristic fortitude of the African, they shouldered their burdens and set themselves to work, receiving scanty remuneration for their services. By their industry and thrift they have been able to provide themselves with small holdings which they are improving, greatly to their credit.

Since the abolition of slavery, the Negroes have improved themselves wonderfully, and when the Government twenty or thirty years ago, threw open the doors of the Civil Service to competitive examination, the Negro youths swept the board, and captured every available office, leaving their white competitors far behind. This system went on for a few years, but as the white youths were found to be intellectually inferior to the black, the whites persuaded the Government to abolish the competitive system, and fill vacancies by nomination, and by this means kept out the black youths.[16] The service has long since been recruited from an inferior class of sychophantic weaklings whose brains are exhausted by dissipation and vice before they reach the age of thirty-five.

The population of Jamaica, according to the last census,[17] was 831,383, and is divided as follows:– White, 15,605; Black, 630,181; Coloured, 163,201; East Indian, 17,380; Chinese, 2,111 and 2,905 whose colour is not stated. Thus it can be seen that more than two-thirds of the population of Jamaica (as also of the other West Indian Islands), are descendents of the old African Slaves. The question naturally arises, How comes this hybrid or coloured element? This hybrid population is accountable for by the immoral advantage taken of the Negro women by the whites, who have always been in power and who practice polygamy with black women as an unwritten right. The old slave-owners raped their female slaves, married or unmarried, and compelled them into polygamy much against their will, thus producing the 'coloured' element. The latter day whites, much to their regret, have not the opportunity of compelling black girls to become their mistresses, but they use other means of bewitching these unprotected women whom they keep as concubines; thus perpetuating the evil of which their fathers were guilty. The educated black gentleman, naturally, becomes disgusted with this state of affairs; and in seeking a wife he generally marries a white woman. These are the contributing causes to the negroid or hybrid population of the West Indies. Unlike the whites in the United States the negroes do not lynch white men when they rape and take advantage of black girls; they leave them to the hand of retributive justice.

There have been several movements to federate the British West Indian Islands, but owing to parochial feelings nothing definite has been achieved. Ere long this change is sure to come about because the people of these islands are all one. They live under the same conditions, are of the same race and mind, and have the same feelings and sentiments regarding the things of the world.

As one who knows the people well, I make no apology for prophesying that there will soon be a turning point in the history of the West Indies; and that the people who inhabit that portion of the Western Hemisphere will be the instruments of uniting a scattered race who, before the close of many centuries, will found an Empire on which the sun shall shine as ceaselessly as it shines on the Empire of the North to-day. This may be regarded as a dream, but I would point my critical friends to history and its lessons. Would Caesar have believed that the country he was invading in 55 B.C.[18] be the seat of the greatest Empire of the World? Had it been suggested to him would he not have laughed at it as a huge joke? Yet it has come true. England is the seat of the greatest Empire of the World, and its king is above the rest of monarchs in power and dominion. Laugh then you may, at what I have been bold enough to prophecy [sic], but as surely as there is an evolution in the natural growth of man and nations, so surely will there be a change in the history of these subjected regions.

Garvey returned to Jamaica in 1914 and founded the UNIA and African Communities League (ACL) on July 20. He received an invitation to visit Booker T. Washington's Tuskegee Institute in Alabama, where the curriculum emphasised the need for African Americans to become economically self-sufficient. Garvey was considering the establishment of such a school in Jamaica but Washington died in November 1915 before they could discuss the project. In 1916, Garvey went to the United States and embarked on a year-long speaking tour of 38 states.

Shortly before he left Jamaica, Garvey wrote to Robert R. Moton (1867– 1940), Washington's successor as the principal of the Tuskegee Institute, who was planning to visit Jamaica. In referring to his efforts to develop the UNIA, Garvey wrote,

Whilst we have been encouraged and helped by the cultured whites to do something to help in lifting the masses the so called representative[s] of our own people have sought to draw us down ... I am engaged in fighting a battle with foes of my own all around.

He continued with an interpretation of the 'race question' in Jamaica.

Letter to Major Robert R. Moton, 29 February 1916

You, being a prominent American Negro Leader, coming into a strange country, and I, being a resident here, and one who also claims the distinction of being a race leader, I think it but right that I should try to enlighten you on the conditions existing among our people; hence I now take the opportunity of laying before you my views on the local aspect of Negro life.

Jamaica is unlike the United States where the race question is concerned. We have no open race prejudice here, and we do not openly antagonise one another. The extremes here are not between white and black, hence we have never had a case of lynching or anything so desperate. The black people here form the economic asset of the country, they number 6 to 1 of coloured and white combined and without them in labour or general industry the country would go bankrupt.

The black people have had seventy eight years of Emancipation, but all during that time they have never produced a leader of their own, hence they have never been led to think racially but in common with the destinies of the other people with whom they mix as fellow citizens. After Emancipation, the Negro was unable to cope intellectually with his master, and per-force he had to learn at the knees of his emancipator.

He has, therefore, grown with his master's ideals, and up to today you will find the Jamaica Negro unable to think apart from the customs and ideals of his old time slave masters. Unlike the American Negro, the Jamaican has never thought of race ideals, much to his detriment, as instead of progressing generally, he has become a serf in the bulk, and a gentleman in the few.

Racial ideals do no people harm, therefore, the Jamaica Negro has done himself a harm in not thinking on racial ideals with the scattered Negroes of other climes. The coloured and white population have been thinking and planning on exclusive race ideals – race ideals which are unwritten and unspoken. The diplomacy of one race or class of people is the means by which others are outdone, hence the diplomacy of the other races prevent them leading the race question in Jamaica, a question that could have been understood and regarded without friction.

You will find the Jamaican Negro has been sleeping much to his loss, for others have gained on top of him and are still gaining.

Apparently you will think that the people here mix at the end of a great social question, but in truth it is not so. The mixture is purely circumstancial and not genuine. The people mix in business, but they do not mix in true society. The whites claim superiority, as is done all over the world, and, unlike other parts, the coloured, who ancestrally are the illegitimate off-springs of black and white, claim a positive superiority over the blacks. They train themselves to believe that in the slightest shade the coloured man is above the black man and so it runs right up to white. The black man naturally is kept down at the foot of the ladder and is trampled on by all the shades above. In a small minority he pushes himself up among the others, but when he 'gets there' he too believes himself other than black and he starts out to think from a white and coloured mind much to the detriment of his own people whom he should have turned back to lead out of surrounding darkness.

The black man lives directly under the white man's institutions and the influence over him is so great that he is only a play-thing in the moulder's hand. The blackman of Jamaica cannot think for himself and because of this he remains in the bulk the dissatisfied 'beast of burden'. Look around and see to what proportion the black man appears a gentleman in office. With a small exception the black man is not in office at all. The only sphere that he dominates in is that of the teaching profession and he dominates there because the wage is not encouraging enough for others; and even in this department the Negro has the weapon to liberate himself and make himself a man, for there is no greater weapon than education; but the educated teacher, 'baby-like' in his practice, does not think apart from the written code, hence he, himself, is a slave to what is set down for him to do and no more.

If you were to go into all the offices throughout Jamaica you will not find one per cent of black clerks employed. You will find nearly all white and coloured persons including men and women; for proof please go through our Post Office, Government Offices and stores in Kingston, and you see only white and coloured men and women in positions of importance and trust and you will find the black men and women, as store-men, messengers, attendants & common servants. In the country parts you will find the same order of things. On the Estates and Plantations you will find the black man and woman as the labourer, the coloured man as clerk and sometimes owner and the white man generally as master. White and coloured women are absent from the fields of labour. The professions are generally taken up by the white and coloured men because they have the means to equip themselves.

Whenever a black man enters the professions, he per force, thinks from a white and coloured mind, and for the time being he enjoys the apparent friendship of the classes until he is made a bankrupt or forced into difficulties which naturally causes him to be ostracised.

The entire system here is bad as affecting the Negro and the Negro of education will not do anything honestly and truly to help his brethren in the mass. Black

Ministers and Teachers are moral cowards, they are too much afraid to speak to their people on the pride of race. Whenever the black man gets money and education he thinks himself white and coloured, and he wants a white and coloured wife, and he will spend his all to get this; much to his eternal misery.

Black professionals who have gone abroad have nearly all married white women who on their arrival here leave them and return home. Others marry highly coloured women and others taking in the lessons of others refuse to marry in preference to marrying the black girls. You will find a few educated black men naturally having black wives but these are the sober minded ones who have taken the bad lessons home. Our black girls are taught by observation to despise black men as they are naturally poor and of social discount; hence you will find a black girl willing to give herself up to any immoral suggestion of white or coloured men, and positively refusing the good attentions of a black man at the outset.

Not until when she has been made a fool of by white and coloured before she turns back to the black man and wants him as a companion. Our morality is destroyed this way. Ninety per cent of the coloured people are off-springs of immorality, yet they rule next to the whites over the blacks.

This is shameful, but our men hav'nt the courage to stem the tide. Our ministers are funning at the 'teaching of the gospel' and they have been often criticised for their inactivity in correcting vice and immorality. I am sorry I have to say this; nevertheless it is true.

The black man here is a slave of destiny, and it is only by bold and conscientious leadership that he can emancipate, and I do trust your visit will be one of the means of helping him. I am now talking with you as a man with a mission from the High God. Your education will enable you to understand me clearly. I do not mean literary education alone, for that we have here among a goodly number of Blacks as teachers and ministers. I mean the higher education of man's appreciation for his fellowman; of man's love for his race. Our people here are purely selfish and no man or people can lead if selfishness is the cardinal principle.

One Negro here hates to see the other Negro succeed and for that he will pull him down every time he attempts to climb and defame him. The Negro here will not help one another, and they have no sympathy with one another. Ninety per cent of our people are labourers and serfs, the other ten per cent are mixed up in the professions, trades and small proprietorships. I mean the black people, not coloured or white – you look out for these carefully. We have no social order of our own, we have to flatter ourselves into white and coloured society to our own disgrace and discomfiture, because we are never truly appreciated. Among us we have an excess of crimes and the prison houses, alm houses, and mad houses are over crowded with our people much to the absence of the other classes.[19]

Our prisoners are generally chained and marched through the streets of the city while on their way to the Penitentiary. You should pay a visit to the Prisons, Alms house, and Asylum to test the correctness of my statements. We have a large prison in Kingston and another one at Spanish Town. You will find Alms Houses all over the Island, but the Union Poor House is near to Kingston in St. Andrew.

Our women are prostituted, and if you were to walk the lower sections of Kingston after night fall you will see hundreds of Black prostitutes in the lanes, streets and alleys.

Our people in the bulk do not live in good houses, they live in 'huts' and 'old shanties', and you will see this as you go through the country. If you care to see this in Kingston you can visit places like Smith's Village and Hannah's Town. Our people in the bulk can't afford to wear good clothes and boots. Generally they wear rags and go barefooted in the bulk during the week, and some change their garbs on Sundays when they go to church, but this is not general.

The people have no system of sanitation. They keep themselves dirty and if you were to mix in a crowd on a hot day you would be stifled with the bad odour. You can only see the ragged and dirty masses on alarming occasions when you will see them running from all directions. If a band of music were to parade the city then you would have a fair illustration of what I mean. Our people are not encouraged to be clean and decent because they are kept down on the lowest wage with great expences [sic] hanging over them.

Our labourers get anything from nine pence (eighteen cents) 1/-(25cents) 1/6 (36 cents) to fifty cents a day, on which they have to support a family.

This is the grinding system that keeps the black man down here, hence I personally, have very little in common with the educated class of my own people for they are the bitterest enemies of their own race. Our people have no respect for one another, and all the respect is shown to the white and coloured people.

The reception that will be given you will not be genuine from more than one reason which I may explain later on to you.

Black men here are never truly honoured. Don't you believe like coloured Dr. Du Bois that the 'race problem is at an end here'[20] except you want to admit the utter insignificance of the black man.

It was never started and has not yet begun. It is a paradox. I personally would like to solve the situation on the broadest humanitarian lines. I would like to solve it on the platform of Dr. Booker T. Washington,[21] and I am working on those lines hence you will find that up to now my one true friend as far as you can rely on his friendship, is the whiteman.

I do not mean to bring any estrangement between black and white. I want to have Jamaica a country of 'Black and White' all living in peace and harmony but with equal rights and opportunities.

I would not advise you to give yourself too much away to the desire and wishes of the people who are around you for they are mostly hypocrites. They mean to deceive you on the conditions here because we can never blend under the existing state of affairs – it would not be fair to the black man. –To blend we must all in equal proportion 'show our hands'.

Your intellect, I believe, is too deep to be led away by 'sham sentiment'. Population of Jamaica: white 15,605; coloured 163,201; black *630,181*; East Indian 17,380; Chinese 2,111; 2,905 colour not stated. If you desire to do Jamaica a turn, you might ask those around you on public platforms to explain to what proportion the different people here enjoy the wealth and resources of the country. Impress this, and *let them answer* it *for publication*, and then you will have the whole farce in a *nut shell*. When you are travelling to the mountain parts, stop a while and observe properly the rural life of your people as against the life of others of the classes.

I have much more to say, but I must close for another time.

Garvey lived in the United States for eleven years. His observations of the rigid 'colour line', racial segregation, riots and lynchings radicalised Garvey. The New York branch of the UNIA became the base from which Garvey edited the Negro World, a newspaper with international circulation, and organised the Black Star Line, a steamship line aimed at promoting black pride and self-sufficiency. Garvey was forced to suspend the line in 1922 after he was indicted on mail fraud charges stemming from the sale of its stock. He was convicted and sentenced to five years' imprisonment. Released on bail after three months, his conviction was reaffirmed by the US Court of Appeals and he was imprisoned in the Atlanta Federal Penitentiary from February 8, 1925 until November 1927, when he was deported to Jamaica.

In 1928, Garvey formed the People's Political party and, in 1929, founded the newspaper Black man. The Jamaican and US wings of his UNIA movement split in 1929 and, in 1932, the rival US organisation, led by a Trinidadian physician, Dr Lionel Francis, held a convention. There was a prolonged legal case when the two UNIA wings contested the will of Isaiah Morton, a wealthy Belizean businessman, and Francis was eventually victorious. Meanwhile, Garvey was defeated in 1930 in an election for a seat on Jamaica's Legislative Council because most of his supporters were disenfranchised but he was elected to the Kingston and St Andrew Corporation. Garvey was also the chairman of the Jamaica Workers and Labourers Association but, although he inspired many trade unionists, he did not organise labour. He held international conferences of the UNIA in Jamaica in 1929 and 1934. The UNIA conventions were important occasions for speaking out against racism and colonialism and for defining the future of the movement. In 1934, for example, the convention adopted an ambitious Five-Year Plan to

encourage the 'development of the shipping, manufacturing, mining, agricultural
and other industries which are to affect the Negroes in the United States, the West
Indies, Central and South America and Africa'. However, the split in the movement,
the shortage of funds, and the persistent persecution that Garvey faced in Jamaica
as well as the United States, led to the weakening of the movement.

In 1934, Garvey moved to London where he tried to maintain his international
organisation. At that time there were no black communities in Britain but there
were rival black and Pan-African organisations in London and the United States.
A UNIA conference was held in Toronto in 1937, where Garvey established the
School of African Philosophy. Although the number of branches, the administrative
apparatus and the financial resources of the UNIA had all diminished, Garvey's
influence, in Africa as well as the Caribbean and the United States, persisted.

After Garvey died in London on June 10, 1940, Amy Jacques Garvey (1896–
1973), his second wife, continued to correspond with UNIA members and to spread
his ideas. During her husband's trial and incarceration in 1923–27 she published
two volumes of his speeches and writings in order to raise funds for his defense
and to spread his ideas. In 1963, she published Garvey and Garveyism, an account
of the man and his movement. 'An Appeal to the Conscience of the Black Race to
See Itself' is from the second volume of The Philosophy and Opinions of Marcus
Garvey *(1925), edited by Amy Jacques Garvey.*

An Appeal to the Conscience of the Black Race to See Itself

It is said to be a hard and difficult task to organize and keep together large
numbers of the Negro race for the common good. Many have tried to congregate
us, but have failed, the reason being that our characteristics are such as to keep us
more apart than together.

The evil of internal division is wrecking our existence as a people, and if we do
not seriously and quickly move in the direction of a readjustment it simply means
that our doom becomes imminently conclusive.

For years the Universal Negro Improvement Association has been working for
the unification of our race, not on domestic-national lines only, but universally. The
success which we have met in the course of our effort is rather encouraging,
considering the time consumed and the environment surrounding the object of our
concern.

It seems that the whole world of sentiment is against the Negro, and the difficulty
of our generation is to extricate ourselves from the prejudice that hides itself beneath,
as well as above, the action of an international environment.

Prejudice is conditional on many reasons, and it is apparent that the Negro supplies, consciously or unconsciously, all the reasons by which the world seems to ignore and avoid him. No one cares for a leper, for lepers are infectious persons, and all are afraid of the disease, so, because the Negro keeps himself poor, helpless and undemonstrative, it is natural also that no one wants to be of him or with him.

Progress and Humanity

Progress is the attraction that moves humanity, and to whatever people or race this 'modern virtue' attaches itself, there will you find the splendor of pride and self-esteem that never fail to win the respect and admiration of all.

It is the progress of the Anglo-Saxons that singles them out for the respect of the world. When their race had no progress or achievement to its credit, then, like all other inferior peoples, they paid the price in slavery, bondage, as well as through prejudice. We cannot forget the time when even the ancient Briton was regarded as being too dull to make a good Roman slave, yet today the influence of that race rules the world.

It is the industrial and commercial progress of America that causes Europe and the rest of the world to think appreciatively of the Anglo-American race. It is not because one hundred and ten million people live in the United States that the world is attracted to the republic with so much reverence and respect – a reverence and respect not shown to India with its three hundred millions, or to China with its four hundred millions. Progress of and among any people will advance them in the respect and appreciation of the rest of their fellows. It is to such a progress that the Negro must attach himself if he is to rise above the prejudice of the world.

The reliance of our race upon the progress and achievements of others for a consideration in sympathy, justice and rights is like a dependence upon a broken stick, resting upon which will eventually consign you to the ground.

Self-Reliance and Respect

The Universal Negro Improvement Association teaches our race self-help and self-reliance, not only in one essential, but in all those things that contribute to human happiness and well-being. The disposition of the many to depend upon the other races for a kindly and sympathetic consideration of their needs, without making the effort to do for themselves, has been the race's standing disgrace by which we have been judged and through which we have created the strongest prejudice against ourselves.

There is no force like success, and that is why the individual makes all efforts to surround himself throughout life with the evidence of it. As of the individual, so should it be of the race and nation. The glittering success of Rockefeller makes him a power in the American nation; the success of Henry Ford[22] suggests him as an object of universal respect, but no one knows and cares about the bum or hobo who is Rockefeller's or Ford's neighbor. So, also, is the world attracted by the glittering success of races and nations, and pays absolutely no attention to the bum or hobo race that lingers by the wayside.

The Negro must be up and doing if he will break down the prejudice of the rest of the world. Prayer alone is not going to improve our condition, nor the policy of watchful waiting. We must strike out for ourselves in the course of material achievement, and by our own effort and energy present to the world those forces by which the progress of man is judged.

A Nation and Country

The Negro needs a nation and a country of his own, where he can best show evidence of his own ability in the art of human progress. Scattered as an unmixed and unrecognized part of alien nations and civilizations is but to demonstrate his imbecility, and point him out as an unworthy derelict, fit neither for the society of Greek, Jew nor Gentile.

It is unfortunate that we should so drift apart, as a race, as not to see that we are but perpetuating our own sorrow and disgrace in failing to appreciate the first great requisite of all peoples – organization.

Organization is a great power in directing the affairs of a race or nation toward a given goal. To properly develop the desires that are uppermost, we must first concentrate through some system or method, and there is none better than organization. Hence, the Universal Negro Improvement Association appeals to each and every Negro to throw in his lot with those of us who, through organization, are working for the universal emancipation of our race and the redemption of our common country, Africa.

No Negro, let him be American, European, West Indian or African, shall be truly respected until the race as a whole has emancipated itself, through self-achievement and progress, from universal prejudice. The Negro will have to build his own government, industry, art, science, literature and culture, before the world will stop to consider him. Until then, we are but wards of a superior race and civilization, and the outcasts of a standard social system.

The race needs workers at this time, not plagiarists, copyists and mere imitators; but men and women who are able to create, to originate and improve, and thus make an independent racial contribution to the world and civilization.

Monkey Apings of 'Leaders'

The unfortunate thing about us is that we take the monkey apings of our 'so-called leading men' for progress. There is not progress in Negroes aping white people and telling us that they represent the best in the race, for in that respect any dressed monkey would represent the best of its species, irrespective of the creative matter of the monkey instinct. The best in a race is not reflected through or by the action of its apes, but by its ability to create of and by itself. It is such a creation that the Universal Negro Improvement Association seeks.

Let us not try to be the best or worst of others, but let us make the effort to be the best of ourselves. Our own racial critics criticise us as dreamers and 'fanatics', and call us 'benighted' and 'ignorant', because they lack racial backbone. They are unable to see themselves creators of their own needs. The slave instinct has not yet departed from them. They still believe that they can only live or exist through the good graces of their 'masters'. The good slaves have not yet thrown off their shackles; thus, to them, the Universal Negro Improvement Association is an 'impossibility'.

It is the slave spirit of dependence that causes our 'so-called leading men' (apes) to seek the shelter, leadership, protection and patronage of the 'master' in their organization and so-called advancement work. It is the spirit of feeling secured as good servants of the master, rather than as independents, why our modern Uncle Toms[23] take pride in laboring under alien leadership and becoming surprised at the audacity of the Universal Negro Improvement Association in proclaiming for racial liberty and independence.

But the world of white and other men, deep down in their hearts, have much more respect for those of us who work for our racial salvation under the banner of the Universal Negro Improvement Association, than they could ever have, in all eternity, for a group of helpless apes and beggars who make a monopoly of undermining their own race and belittling themselves in the eyes of self-respecting people, by being 'good boys' rather than able men.

Surely there can be no good will between apes, seasoned beggars and independent minded Negroes who will at least make an effort to do for themselves. Surely, the 'dependants' and 'wards' (and may I not say racial imbeciles?) will rave against and plan the destruction of movements like the Universal Negro Improvement Association that expose them to the liberal white minds of the world as not being representative of the best in the Negro, but, to the contrary, the worst. The best of a race does not live on the patronage and philanthropy of others, but makes an effort to do for itself. The best of the great white race doesn't fawn before and beg black, brown or yellow men; they go out, create for self and thus demonstrate the fitness of the race to survive; and so the white race of America and the world will be informed that the best in the Negro race is not the class of beggars who send out to other races piteous appeals annually for donations to maintain their coterie, but the groups within us that are honestly striving to do for themselves with the voluntary help and appreciation of that class of other races that is reasonable, just and liberal enough to give to each and every one a fair chance in the promotion of those ideals that tend to greater human progress and human love.

The work of the Universal Negro Improvement Association is clear and clean-cut. It is that of inspiring an unfortunate race with pride in self and with the determination of going ahead in the creation of those ideals that will lift them to the unprejudiced company of races and nations. There is no desire for hate or malice, but every wish to see all mankind linked into a common fraternity of progress and achievement that will wipe away the odor of prejudice, and elevate the human race to the height of real godly love and satisfaction.

NOTES

1. Columbus four voyages to the Caribbean took place between 1492 and 1502, not in the 'latter part of the fourteenth century', as Garvey stated.
2. The population of the British West Indies, according to the 1913 *World Almanac* and *Whittaker's Almanacs*, was 1,890,000.
3. Filibusters were people who engaged in unauthorised warfare.
4. Sir John Hawkins, one of the pioneers of the English slave trade, organised four voyages between Africa and the Caribbean, leading three of them himself, between 1562 and 1568.
5. Port Royal, which was on a long spit of sand across the bay from present-day Kingston, was completely destroyed by an earthquake on June 7, 1692.
6. Morgan went to Barbados as an indentured servant, escaped, and became a prominent and bloodthirsty buccaneer. He acquired wealth and large estates, was knighted and appointed lieutenant-governor of Jamaica in 1674, and drank himself to death.
7. Cromwell, who became the ruler of England in 1653, sent a force of about 2,500 men to the Caribbean. Failing to take Hispaniola they moved on to Jamaica, which was captured from Spain in 1655, not in 1665 as Garvey stated.
8. Jamaica, which had been a crown colony since 1865, restored the elective principle in 1884, when nine members of the previously appointed legislative council were elected by a small electorate. In 1895, the elected members were increased to 14, one for each parish.
9. No. 10 Downing Street is the official residence of the British prime minister.
10. This should be 1831 not 1851, by which time slavery had been abolished. In this massive rebellion, led by Sam Sharpe, about a dozen whites and over 400 blacks were killed and many more slaves were executed after courts martial. The rebellion hastened the debate in the British parliament that led, in 1833, to the passage of the law to abolish slavery throughout the colonies.

11. The 1865 rebellion that began at Morant Bay was of former slaves, not slaves as Garvey suggests. Gordon, a coloured planter, businessman and member of the House of Assembly, was an outspoken opponent of the governor, but not the leader of the rebellion. Nevertheless, he was hanged with the leader, Paul Bogle, who was a small landowner and Native Baptist preacher. Both Gordon and Bogle, along with Garvey himself, are now national heroes of Jamaica.

12. Toussaint L'Ouverture (1746–1803) was one of the chief leaders of the revolution that began in the French colony of Saint Domingue in 1791. Captured by the French, he died in captivity in France a year before Haiti became independent.

13. Von Ketelhodt, who was the custos of St Thomas-in-the-East, was beaten to death by the rebels when he fled from the burning courthouse in Morant Bay on October 11, 1865. Although the governor claimed that Gordon was an instigator, there was no 'Gordon party'.

14. Eyre (1815–1901) was commander-in-chief and then governor of Jamaica. When he declared martial law during the rebellion, the troops for whom he was responsible went on a rampage, destroying property and flogging hundreds of innocent people. Almost 500 people were killed, some after brief courts martial but most without any trial. Eyre was charged in England but a grand jury found insufficient evidence to indict him.

15. The Slavery Abolition Act was passed on August 28, 1833, but it was not to come into effect until August 1, 1834 when the apprenticeship system began.

16. Open competitive examinations for the civil service were initiated in 1885 but stopped in 1911 when the governor once again filled vacancies on the recommendation of a department's head.

17. Garvey's figures are from the 1911 census.

18. Julius Caesar invaded Britain twice, in 55 and 54 BC, but it was the emperor Claudius who annexed England to the Roman empire in AD 43 and began Rome's 400-year rule.

19. Garvey wrote from harsh personal experience. In 1915, his father, Maleus Mosiah Garvey, who was a mason and a deacon of the Methodist church, was committed to the St Ann poor house.

20. Dr W.E.B. DuBois (1868–1963), an African-American scholar, editor, civil rights leader, socialist and Pan Africanist, visited Jamaica in 1915. The *Jamaica Times* (May 8, 1915) reported him as saying that Jamaica had 'settled the race question' and that 'there were few places in which that question was so well settled'. DuBois thought that the chief problem facing poor people in Jamaica was economic rather than racial.

21. Washington (1856–1915) was born into slavery and his rise to leadership in black education and politics is told in his autobiography, *Up From Slavery* (1901). He advocated self-help and economic self-sufficiency and his Tuskegee Institute was supported by white northern financiers and southern conservatives who favoured racial segregation. His influence as a racial representative was attacked by DuBois, who considered him to be an accommodationist, but his philosophy inspired Garvey.

22. John D. Rockefeller (1839–1937) was once the world's richest man, his fortune based on the oil business. He achieved this by creating the Standard Oil Company in 1870, a monopoly that controlled oil products from extraction to the consumer. Members of his family became active in politics, including his grandson, Nelson A. Rockefeller, who was the governor of New York (1959–73) and vice-president of the United States (1974–77). Henry Ford (1863–1947) pioneered the use of the assembly-line in the manufacture of automobiles. His company, organised in 1903, sold over 15 million of his 'Model T' automobile between 1908 and 1927, a period when more than half of the

automobiles sold in the United States were Fords. His family retained sole control of the Ford Motor Company until 1956.

23. The anti-slavery novel, *Uncle Tom's Cabin* (1852) by Harriet Beecher Stowe (1811–96), was already famous before the civil war in the United States. The most famous character was popularised in melodramatic 'Tom Shows' in the northern states and in abridged and sentimentalised versions of the novel. In place of the original dignified slave who is beaten to death for refusing to reveal what he knows about two escaped slaves, 'Uncle Tom' came to stand for a black man who humbles himself in order to gain favour with whites.

Twenty-Five

Elma François

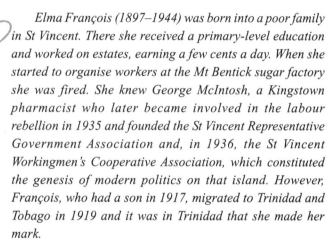

Elma François (1897–1944) was born into a poor family in St Vincent. There she received a primary-level education and worked on estates, earning a few cents a day. When she started to organise workers at the Mt Bentick sugar factory she was fired. She knew George McIntosh, a Kingstown pharmacist who later became involved in the labour rebellion in 1935 and founded the St Vincent Representative Government Association and, in 1936, the St Vincent Workingmen's Cooperative Association, which constituted the genesis of modern politics on that island. However, François, who had a son in 1917, migrated to Trinidad and Tobago in 1919 and it was in Trinidad that she made her mark.

François worked as a domestic servant and a clothes-washer. She joined the Trinidad Workingmen's Association which was led by Captain Arthur Andrew Cipriani, (a Trinidad white) from 1923 until his death in 1945. As trade unions at that time had neither the right to picket nor immunity from legal action for damages arising from strikes, which English unions had enjoyed since 1871, Cipriani transformed the organisation into the Trinidad Labour Party in 1934. There was growing dissatisfaction with his leadership during the Great Depression and more militant members turned to direct action, such as mass demonstrations and hunger marches. François participated in political meetings and became an experienced public speaker which was unusual for women, and especially poor black women. It was at these meetings that she met Jim Barrette, who became her companion, and Jim Headley, a former seaman who had been in contact with George Padmore, the Trinidadian leader of the International Trade Union Committee of Negro Workers. With Dudley Mahon, who was a cook at the Port of Spain hospital, these working people were the leading members of the National Unemployed Movement (NUM), which was formed in 1934. They organised hunger marches and a register of the unemployed which obtained 1,200 names in Port of Spain within two weeks. In 1935, the NUM was joined by Rupert Gittens, a Trinidadian who had just been deported from France for associating with communists. Joined by two other working-class activists, Christina King and Bertie Percival, who had lost his job in the oilfields as the result of a strike, the NUM became the more organised and structured Negro Welfare Cultural and Social Association (NWCSA) in late 1935.

François was the ideological leader of the NWCSA, which included a larger proportion of women than comparable organisations at the time. When other organisations separated women into 'branches' and 'auxiliaries' the NWCSA, with François as the organising secretary, accepted women as equal and integral members. Hunger marches and public meetings were held throughout Trinidad and Tobago in 1935 and 1936 and the Italian invasion of Ethiopia, among other international issues, was a focus of their attention. The NWCSA held a mass meeting on October 10, 1935 at which England was denounced for refusing to sell arms to Ethiopia and the local restrictions of meetings and marches was criticised. The government, the NWCSA said, was curtailing the rights of the working class because it could not solve the unemployment crisis. François and Percival represented the NWCSA in the Friends of Ethiopia Committee which was very active in 1936. François, a chief speaker at a mass meeting in Port of Spain on May 29, 1936, denounced Italy's ruthless assaults on the innocent and largely defenceless people of Ethiopia.

François broke with Cipriani, calling him 'Britain's best policeman in the colonies' because he sought to prevent the NWCSA from holding public meetings in the chief square, and established links through Percival with Cipriani's chief rival, Tubal Uriah Butler, a former oilfield worker who had immigrated from Grenada. However, when their delegation met Governor Sir Murchison Fletcher on November 8, 1936 to protest the impact of the rising cost of living on working people, Butler promptly fell on his knees and begged the governor for assistance. François and others, who had prepared a detailed memorandum on the cost of living, nutrition, health services, school meals and old age pensions, were furious that Butler had preempted their presentation and taken over the proceedings. The NWCSA also took up the issue of the Shop Hours (Opening and Closing) Bill on behalf of small shopkeepers and their customers and, by the end of 1936, its influence was felt around the country. Nevertheless, it was Butler and his British Empire Workers and Citizens' Home Rule party that developed the greater mass following.

In 1937, the NWCSA focused on the workers' struggles, which exploded into an island-wide rebellion and general strike in June. A strike among oilfield workers erupted in violence when police attempted to arrest Butler in Fyzabad on June 19. François investigated the situation on the spot the next day and returned to Port of Spain to urge her comrades in the NWCSA to engage in supportive actions. On June 28, several NWCSA leaders, including François, Barrette and Percival, were arrested and imprisoned. When they were acquitted they continued to organise meetings, collect defense funds and protest against the persecution of strikers. In October, several NWCSA leaders were again arrested, this time for distributing allegedly seditious literature in the oil belt. Percival and Barrette were both convicted.

In February 1938, Percival and François were tried for 'uttering words having a seditious intention' at a public meeting to protest the earlier trial. According to a police informant, François had said on October 13 that Percival and Barrette were being tried on 'framed up charges of Colonial Imperialism to strike terrorism into the hearts of the Negro and East Indian workers. The more prosecutions, the more jail sentences, the more ill-treatment of the workers by the police is the more hatred the workers will have for a British Colonial Imperialism. In the West Indies, the moment you say strike you get jail sentences because you are Negro and East Indian workers .... In Trinidad when the workers ask for bread they get bullets and jail-sentences .... This is what we get for asking for bread – bullets: but war clouds are now hanging over Europe and political howlers will soon be coming to ask you, the same people who when you ask for bread are shot like dogs and given jail sentences, to fight for them. But we will tell them that we will not fight in any war. The only war we will fight is in the fight to better conditions, peace and liberty' (Trinidad Guardian, *Feb. 15, 1938).*

These words are from the policeman's notes and may not be accurate, but they suggest that François was linking labour and human rights issues with British imperialism. At her trial she defended herself aggressively and when she was asked to define what she meant by 'world imperialism and colonialism' she expanded on the relationship between the ruling classes of the world and the exploited workers of the colonies. When the prosecutor, cross-examining her, asked why she persisted in making speeches that were 'causing disaffection among his Majesty's subjects' she replied, 'I don't know that my speeches create disaffection, I know that my speeches create a fire in the minds of the people so as to change the conditions which now exist'. Her speech in self-defense at this trial was printed in the Trinidad Guardian. *The jury found her 'not guilty' but Barrette was imprisoned for nine months.*

The NWCSA, despite persistent harassment by the police, continued with their activities. Several members of the NWCSA, for example, helped form and lead some of Trinidad's first trade unions in 1937 and 1938. In 1939, the NWCSA revived the celebration of Emancipation Day and members spoke publicly about the history of slavery and its abolition. François identified June 19,1937 as the beginning of a 'New Emancipation' because of the growing militancy and organisation of the working people as a class. In 1939 François, as the organising secretary of the NWCSA, sent a memorandum on constitutional reform, proposing the removal of non-elected members of the Legislative Council and the expansion of the franchise, to the secretary of state for the colonies. She expressed the view during the Second World War that the colonised peoples of the Caribbean should not participate in the imperialist war but her son joined the British army and prepared to leave for the front in April 1944. The day after she said goodbye to him, on April 17, François died. The NWCSA did not regain its momentum after her death but some of its members, including Barrette and King, joined the Workers Freedom Movement and Barrette was a founding member of the West Indian Independence party in 1952. François had provided an important ideological influence on the politics of labour in the pre-independence period and on September 25, 1987 she was declared a National Heroine of Trinidad and Tobago.

Elma François' Speech in her Self-Defence at her Sedition Trial

'I am one of the Negro Welfare Cultural and Social Association. The Association was formed about 4 years ago. I am one of the founders. My occupation is clothes-washing. The aims and objectives of the Association are:

1.   To struggle for the development and better welfare of the Negro people.
2.   To develop solidarity with the oppressed Negro people of the West Indies and the entire world.
3.   To make known the conditions of the oppressed Negro people and their struggle against oppression.
4.   To win the masses of oppressed people the world over in a struggle for the better welfare of the Negro people.

'In keeping with the aims and objectives of our Association, we hold meetings. I keep in touch with local affairs, I follow the local politics as best I can. We particularly pay attention to the underdog.

'My organisation expects to achieve our aims and objectives by sending in protest resolutions, petitions and delegations. This is part of my method to achieve my aims. I do not hope to achieve them by violence. We denounce violence at every meeting. On the night of October 13, 1937, we held a meeting on the "Greens" on Piccadilly Street.

'There were three speakers, Bertie Percival, Comrade Peters and myself. We always elected a chairman before going to a meeting. Our meetings are well planned beforehand and we would decide on a chairman. Comrade Percival was chairman that night. I arranged beforehand what subject my address would be based on. The subject of my address was 'World Imperialism and the Colonial Toilers'. The chairman announced the subject and then I commenced. In dealing with my subject I dealt with world conditions linking them up with local conditions; I dealt with land reservations in the Kenya Colony. I explained that a certain amount of land was reserved for the working class and often they were deprived of it and they decided there to organise in order to get their wrongs righted with regard to the question of land reservations, by a Royal Commission. They succeeded in getting a Royal Commission.

'I dealt with Nigeria. I dealt with the natives there protesting against increased taxations. I further told them that only by organised unity can we gain better conditions. I discussed Germany and Russia also. I pointed out the effective method workers in England used by organising and what they gained. I spoke about the Negro and East-Indian workers who sleep under the Town Hall and in the Square through poverty. I wanted their conditions to be bettered. I referred to the struggle my organisation had carried out against the Trade Tax. We sent out a resolution and carried out an island-wide campaign and we collected hundreds of signatures and forwarded them by way of petition to the Governor Claude Hollis. The Tax has since been removed. I then dealt with the Shop Closing Ordinance. My organisation sent a petition with thousands of signatures also to Governor Murchison Fletcher. I produced a copy of the petition. My organisation sent a delegation to Fletcher on the unemployed question. I led the delegation. I handed him a copy of our demands.

'I made an appeal to my audience to assist us financially in aid of the arrested workers. I also reminded them of the charge against Comrade Percival at the "Greens" on the night of the 13th. I was dealing with terror in Germany under the fascist Government and I said that hundreds of workers were being placed in jail. I said that jail sentences and executions do not solve our problems. I discussed the conditions in Soviet Russia. I said workers of the world were not prepared to fight in any way but for bread, peace and liberty.'

Twenty-Six

Eric Williams

Eric Williams (1911–81) was one of the greatest historians and political leaders in the Anglophone Caribbean in the twentieth century, the model of the scholar-statesman. He was the first of 12 children of a poor black Post Office clerk in Port of Spain. His mother, assisted by her eldest son, augmented the family income by baking and selling bread and cakes. He won a competitive scholarship to Queen's Royal College, where one of his teachers was C.L.R. James, and then an Island Scholarship which enabled him to go to England in 1932 to study history at Oxford University. He achieved a first class degree, placing top in his class, and then began the research for his doctoral dissertation that was subsequently expanded into Capitalism and Slavery *(1944), one of the most brilliant and most debated books by a Caribbean scholar. He left England in 1939 to teach social and political science at Howard University in Washington D.C. He created an introductory social science course that surveyed 'the evolution of civilisation and the development of humanity' (Williams 1969: 57). His black students were interested in 'the question of race' and 'the world Negro movement' (Ibid: 59) so Williams taught them something about Africa, the Caribbean and Latin America, but the course, by his own admission, 'was too western in its orientation', meaning too preoccupied with the Greek and Roman heritage that he had been taught in Trinidad and Oxford.*

While Williams taught at Howard, from 1939 to 1948, he continued his research, working in archives in Havana (where he met Fernando Ortiz and Ramiro Guerra y Sánchez), Haiti (where he met Jean Price-Mars), the Dominican Republic and Puerto Rico. He became the senior West Indian staff member of the Anglo-American Commission in 1944. While traveling in connection with this post, he carried out further research in Antigua, Jamaica, Barbados, Curaçao and Guadeloupe. As a result, his knowledge of Caribbean history was probably greater than that of any other scholar at that time.

The arguments in Capitalism and Slavery *are too complex to be briefly summarised, but two major points should be made. First, Williams argued that the triangular trade (in which Britain provided ships and manufactured goods, Africa the enslaved labourers, and the colonies the raw materials from sugar and cotton plantations) made an enormous contribution to Britain's industrial development and the prosperity of the mainland colonies in the eighteenth century. Second, he argued that the revolution in the American colonies, the growth of British interests in Asia, and the demands of the new industrial capitalists in the United Kingdom undermined slavery in the West Indies. As he succinctly expressed it, 'The commercial capitalism of the eighteenth century developed the wealth of Europe by means of slavery and monopoly. But in so doing it helped to create the industrial capitalism of the nineteenth century, which turned round and destroyed the power of commercial capitalism, slavery, and all its works' (Williams 1964, 210). It was his emphasis on the importance of economic forces, and especially on the role of economic interests rather than moral influence in bringing about Emancipation, that was most shocking to the traditional historians of slavery and the West Indies.*

Williams left the Caribbean Commission in 1955 and immediately set about organising a new political party in Trinidad and Tobago. On June 21, he gave a lecture about his relations with the commission in Woodford Square, Port of Spain. It was the beginning of a series of lectures on economic problems, constitutional reform, race relations, party politics and the proposed federation of the West Indies, that became known as the University of Woodford Square. Thousands of people attended these extraordinary lectures which helped establish Williams' reputation as a highly respected and charismatic intellectual leader. Not everyone approved, however, and his analysis of the origins, nature and legacy of slavery, particularly his denunciations of racism and his affirmation of multi-racial politics, disturbed some people. There had been several political parties in Trinidad and Tobago in the 1940s and early 1950s, but none became dominant until the People's National Movement (PNM) was inaugurated on January 15, 1956. Williams led the PNM and was Trinidad and Tobago's first prime minister, from 1956 until his death in 1981.

'Race Relations in Caribbean Society' was Williams' contribution to a symposium on Caribbean studies held by the American Association for the Advancement of Science in December 1956. Among the participants there were other scholars from the Caribbean, including M.G. Smith and Lloyd Braithwaite of

the Institute of Social and Economic Research at what was then called the University College of the West Indies. Frank Tannenbaum, professor of Latin American history at Columbia University, who was the discussant of Williams paper, had argued in his book Slave and Citizen: The Negro in the Americas *(New York, 1947) that there were important differences in the institution of slavery and in race relations between Latin American and Anglo-Saxon societies that derived from their religious and legal traditions, and Williams addressed this question. The second piece, 'The Future of the Caribbean', is taken from the final chapter of Williams'* From Columbus to Castro: The History of the Caribbean, 1492-1969 *(London, 1970).*

$\mathcal{R}$ace Relations in Caribbean Society

Historically, there have been three determinants of the race-relations pattern in the Caribbean area. The first of these has been economic. The distinction between races in the Caribbean area has, for the most part, been a distinction between those who owned property, principally land, and those who did not; between those who lived off the land and those who worked on it. The racial distinction between European and African before emancipation or between European and Asian after emancipation was fundamentally an economic distinction between the slave-owner and the slave before emancipation and between the planter and indentured immigrant after emancipation. The distinction in race or colour was only the superficial visible symbol of a distinction which in reality was based on the ownership of property.

This general truth, which many writers have refused to recognize, can be illustrated for our present purpose in two ways. The first is in the treatment of the slaves, one of the principal forms of property at different periods in the history of the Caribbean. For example, the brutality of the plantation system in Saint Domingue in 1789 was in striking contrast to the relative benevolence of the relations between master and slave at the same time in Trinidad. To give another example, the slave code of Cuba in 1789 was a vastly different thing, so far as its practical operation was concerned, from the slave code of Cuba in 1840.

The attempt has been made to explain these divergencies as a difference between the Latin tradition and the Anglo-Saxon, between Protestantism and Catholicism.[1] This is far too simple. The explanation is rather to be sought in the nature of property in these different countries at different periods. Saint Domingue in 1789 and Cuba in 1840 represented plantation economies producing for the world market, whereas Cuba and Trinidad in 1789 were for the most part subsistence economies which could tolerate the sort of paternal slavery and benevolent despotism that one finds eulogized in the works of Hesiod and the sophistry of Aristotle.[2]

Another illustration of the economic reality behind the superficial racial differences is the fact that while for the most part the slave revolts in the history of the Caribbean were explosions of black men against their white oppressors, many of these revolts hinged around the taking over of the plantations by the slaves and their division into small farms. Peasant proprietorship was fundamentally an economic revolution comparable to the breakup of the feudal regime in the France of 1789. In the case of the Maroons in Jamaica and the Bush Negroes in Surinam,[3] who kept up a permanent revolution against the slave society, the demand went even further than a mere substitution of the peasantry for the plantocracy and resulted in the setting up of an *imperium* (black) in *imperio* (white), anticipating the larger independence movement which ultimately produced the Republic of Haiti.

The second determinant of the race-relations pattern was political, following inevitably from the economic factor. The State existed in Caribbean society to maintain the property relationship. The State became the organ of the plantocracy and the enemy of the people, a tradition which has not completely disappeared from the Caribbean scene even in these days of developing self-government. Thus it was that the *Code Noir,*[4] alleged symbol of metropolitan trusteeship in the age of slavery, merely attempted to rationalize and to legalize the essential aspect of slavery – private jurisdiction of man over man, including the power of life and death. As another example, I cite the Barbados law rejecting the democratic practice of trial by jury on the ground that it was inapplicable to brutish slaves. The French government of the *ancien régime* led the way in the attempt to exclude people of colour from the professions, such as law, and from certain skilled occupations, such as the trade of jeweller. By these means it tried to correct the growing disproportion between the races. A Commission of Enquiry in Antigua openly attributed a slave revolt in 1736 to the tendency to permit slaves to enter occupations from which they should have been excluded. The philosophy behind this policy was very clearly stated in French law – that nothing would ever make the slave the equal of his master. When after emancipation this equality threatened to develop in Jamaica, where the emancipated slaves began not only to qualify for the franchise but to take their seats in the Legislative Assembly, the British government in 1865, under pressure from the planters, formally suspended the Constitution and instituted direct government by the Crown.

The third determinant in the race-relations pattern in the historical sense was the theory of race then prevalent. The objectivity of the scientific approach of Sir Thomas Browne[5] in his discussion of the race question, 'Why are Negroes black'?, stands out like an oasis in the desert of prejudice and emotion which characterized the treatment of the question throughout the slave period. An early example of this was the denunciation of the aboriginal Indians by a Catholic friar, Tomas Ortiz,[6] in 1512. This was the first step in the harnessing of religion to the cause of economics and politics. Bryan Edwards and Edward Long,[7] two planter historians of Jamaica, saw Negroes as inferior in local music and poetry, respectively, and Thomas Jefferson[8] was convinced that they could never understand a proposition of Euclid.

Here and there someone recanted or, like Bartolomé de las Casas,[9] refused to sacrifice the principles of his religion to the expediency of the plantation economy. But these were occasional flashes in the pan until the early nineteenth century when the dissenting religious sects in England openly espoused the cause of the slaves. For the rest, official policy emphasized racial distinctions and officials acted upon them, as in the case of Governor Fénélon of Martinique, who was convinced that the Negroes should be treated like beasts; or Bonaparte's brother-in-law, Leclerc, whose attempt to recapture Saint Domingue from the slaves who revolted was openly based on the policy of terror; or Governor Eyre, who in the Jamaica rebellion of 1865 acted on the view that a rebellion among the Negro peasantry in Jamaica could not possibly be regarded on the same footing as a revolt among the English peasantry in England.

These are the three determinants historically of the race-relations pattern in the Caribbean – the division of property, the use of the State power to maintain this division, and the prevailing theory of race.

Within the past century and a half, this pattern of race relations has not been able to survive the fundamental changes taking place in the world. The first of these has been the bankruptcy of the slave-plantation economy and hence its lesser importance to capitalist society in Europe and America. Side by side with this has gone, ever since the breakdown of feudalism in France in 1789, agricultural developments based not on the plantation but on the small farm or on co-operative methods. These developments are associated with new crops or new enterprises breaking away from the historical domination of sugar in the Caribbean. The positive demands for the development of the peasantry in the Caribbean, which have been endorsed by repeated Commissions of Enquiry in the area, cannot be divorced from agricultural diversification in such small countries of the world as Denmark, Switzerland, New Zealand, and Japan. It is no longer true to say of the Caribbean area that it is a law of nature that Caribbean economy should be based on the plantation unit in which, as a recent historian of sugar eulogizes, Nordic capital directs coloured labour. In our generation, every step that has been taken by the International Labour Organisation[10] to bring contract labour under the control of the law, and to raise the dignity of the plantation worker necessarily has its effect on the race-relations pattern bequeathed to us by the Caribbean slave economy.

Just as the climate of the modern world is hostile to the traditional economic basis of Caribbean society with its racial overtones, so the growth of democracy has necessarily destroyed, at least in the moral sense, the racial foundations on which Caribbean society has been built. The French Revolution was an open attack on the aristocracy of the skin and heralded that sympathy between metropolitan proletariat and colonial labourer, a sympathy which saw its finest hour in the life of Victor Schoelcher[11] and which the Communists today are at pains to exploit. This has not been limited to metropolitan countries. It expresses itself on the Caribbean soil in the fraternization between white and Negro workers and in the revolts against Spanish imperialism in Cuba and in Puerto Rico – which led to the alliance of white planters demanding political independence and Negro slaves demanding social emancipation, and which resulted in the liberation of Cuba by the joint efforts of the white statesman Martí and the Negro soldier Maceo.[12]

This more democratic approach to the Caribbean race-relations pattern was anticipated by Bonaparte, who in exile acknowledged his error in the treatment of Toussaint L'Overture.[13] It was manifested in the intellectual conflict in England over the Jamaica rebellion of 1865, in which John Stuart Mill, the exponent of British democracy at its best, found himself ranged in the opposite camp to Thomas Carlyle,[14] the neo-fascist clamouring for suppression of the Jamaican movement for self-government. The old political attitude to colonies populated mainly by men of colour could not withstand the democratic vistas of Walt Whitman[15] expressed in his 'Salut au Monde'. And what Negro emancipation in the Civil War failed to accomplish in the United States was brought to public attention by the protest of the Jamaican Marcus Garvey, which led up to Myrdal's[16] presentation of the American dilemma in our generation.

The changing pattern of race relations in the Caribbean is nowhere better indicated, in its political aspect at least, than in Puerto Rico. Whereas two hundred years ago racial discrimination was legalized in Jamaica and in Martinique, today racial discrimination is banned by law in Puerto Rico. Some years ago I had the privilege of discussing the question with Muñoz Marín[17], before he became Governor of the island. When I asked him what in his opinion was the solution, he offered the simplest and most meaningful of prescriptions: 'More democracy'.

Of considerable assistance to the Caribbean in this attempt to achieve more democracy, and thereby help to alter its racial pattern, is the repudiation by the modern world of the old theory of race. No credence is attached today to Gobineau's inequality of races,[18] which is associated with the intolerance of fascism, the vapourings of Nietzche,[19] and the indecency of South Africa. Froude[20] would have no respectability today. If he were alive, I would challenge him to repeat the statement, made in 1884, that representative government was not for Negroes and that Trinidad and Jamaica could not govern themselves as well as New Zealand. Macaulay[21] would be stoned to death if he repeated today his infamous dictum that a single shelf of a good European library was worth more than the entire native literature of India; the writings of Gandhi, Nehru, and Tagore[22] cannot be excluded today from the shelves of any good library anywhere in the world. Tennyson[23] would be laughed at for his 'better fifty years of Europe than a cycle of Cathay' – especially after Europe's two world wars in half the period mentioned by Tennyson. Lord Acton's[24] division of the races of mankind into the active, like the Teutons, and the passive, like the Hindus, today stands on its head with Germany divided and Nehru one of the leading world statesmen.

Acton's passive races are today among the principal makers of history and the principle authors of advancement. The Bandung Conference[25] marked the beginning of a new and decisive chapter in human history. The independence of Ghana will destroy the great lie of African history – that Africa has no history before or without Europe. And so with the Caribbean, where the long history of international conflict for the possession of the area, unleashed by the Papal Donation of 1492,[26] has ended up in our time with a new claimant to the inheritance of Columbus – the people of the Caribbean themselves. The object of history for four and a half centuries, the Caribbean people are now and will be hereafter the subject of history; having had history made and written for them, they are today making and writing, and will increasingly make and write their own history.

Look around the Caribbean area today. That Caribbean culture first heralded by the Cuban literary and philosophical movement a century ago is now in full bloom. Poetry, the novel, the drama, painting, music, sculpture – the poetry of Pales Matos of Puerto Rico and Aimé Césaire of Martinique who, in the opinion of a noted French critic, handles the French language better than any white Frenchman, the slavery novel of Zobel and the imaginative novel of Clement Richer in Martinique, the social novels of Jacques Romain in Haiti, the late Roger Mais of Jamaica, George Lamming of Barbados, Edgar Mittelholzer of British Guiana with his emphasis on the historical novel, Samuel Selvon of Trinidad with his concern with race relations; the painting of the Haitian 'primitives', whose work has astonished the Western world; the sculpture of Ramos Blanco of Cuba and Edna Manley of Jamaica; the revival of interest in Caribbean dances which Geoffrey Holder is now popularizing in the U.S.A.; the steel band of Trinidad; the sociological work of Fernando Ortiz, the economic dissertations of Arthur Lewis, the historical research of West Indians in Trinidad, Jamaica, and Puerto Rico – all these are so many signs of a cultural revolution in the Caribbean and the development of an indigenous Caribbean culture.

Against this background there are the day-to-day changes in the Caribbean racial scene. You will see it any night in one of Trinidad's restaurants – a quite astonishing inter-racialism among the cosmopolitan population which would scandalize the generation that thirty years ago permitted an Englishman to lose his job because he married a Chinese girl, the same girl who today would be found working in any bank. The 'black European', at whom we sneered a few years ago – or as the French West Indians put it, *'peau noir, masque blanc'* – is steadily disappearing, except in the French West Indies where the absurd policy of the elite still holds sway (though to a limited extent) among the West Indian population, and in St. Thomas where the former Danish policy of divide and rule still influences a population whose economy is almost entirely geared to that most unstable of revenue earners, the tourist trade. Intermarriage has proceeded in the Caribbean today to a point which earlier generations would have considered inconceivable. Cecilia Vilaverde[27] today would not be, as she was a century ago in Cuba, the subject of a beautiful novel on the tribulations of a quadroon, nor would any poet of mixed ancestry suffer the tortures of Placido,[28] for Cuba prides itself today on being a *mestizo* society. The Caribbean can boast of dozens of Negro lawyers and thousands of white sugar workers, reversing the pattern of Caribbean society of two centuries ago. The rich Negro in Puerto Rico, the wealthy Indian in Trinidad, the opulent Chinese in Cuba, rub shoulders with the poor whites in Grenada, the Red Legs of Barbados, the *jibaros* of Puerto Rico, and the Chachas of St. Thomas.

It is in this framework that the People's National Movement of Trinidad and Tobago, of which I have the honour to be the leader, was born. Its programme, from the outset, was deliberately inter-racial. It is no doubt for this reason that it has been so distorted by some correspondents in the U.S.A., Canada, and the United Kingdom, as well as in the Caribbean. The programme quite naturally placed first emphasis on eliminating the tension which threatened to develop between Negroes and East Indians on the sugar plantations and in ordinary everyday life. Its aim was to cultivate the spirit developed around the conference table in Bandung on the sugar plantation of Trinidad. But it has not been limited to this, and it has sought to bring all racial groups into its nationalist fold, under its four-colour banner of black, brown, yellow, and white, symbolic of the major colour gradations in the country.

The success of the People's National Movement has been very great. In eight months it captured thirteen out of twenty-four seats in the Legislature and is today the government of the island, with two Indians and one European among its eight Ministers and one Chinese among its four Parliamentary Under-secretaries. It proceeded thereafter to win all twelve seats that were being contested in municipal elections, thereby gaining control of two boroughs – one of its mayors is also an East Indian. Facing an opposition in the Legislature of eleven members, seven of whom are Indian, the People's National Movement has publicly declared its intention to make the question of the impending West Indian federation a national rather than a party issue, and has invited the leader of the largest of the several opposition groups, itself Indian, to form part of the country's three-man delegation at federation conferences to ensure representation of the largest minority group in the country. Never in the history of Trinidad and Tobago has racial tension been of so little consequence as under the government of the People's National Movement. Africans, Indians, Chinese, Portuguese, Europeans, Syrians – the Movement includes members of all racial groups and all religious affiliations in one of the most democratic political parties ever established in the Caribbean. The emphasis of the Movement has been principally on political education, the education of the voters, at large mass meetings whose cosmopolitan and inter-racial audiences are a lesson to the world at large.

What is the conclusion to be drawn from all this? One writer, speaking for many of his persuasion, sees the solution of the so-called race problem in the Negro achieving moral status in the eyes of the white world. I see it rather differently from my own intellectual experience, which is now being fortified by my experience in practical politics. I see it rather in the Negro achieving economic and political status in the eyes of the white world – as he is in the C.I.O.[29] in the U.S.A., as he is in the government of the Caribbean. The problem for the future is no longer the transfer of power to local hands but rather the use local hands make of that power. Haiti's permanent revolution is a case in point. The greatest disservice that has been done to the cause of Caribbean self-government and the improvement of race relations is that in its earliest years the self-government movement was associated in many places with declamation, agitation, and demagogy. This was much to the satisfaction, as I saw with my own eyes, of many Europeans and Americans, who were quite content to give up the shadow while they retained the substance of power through the influence they were able to exercise on governments of limited attainments. That tendency has in recent months suffered staggering defeats in Jamaica and in Trinidad and Tobago, as it did in Puerto Rico before them.

The Caribbean is on the road toward responsible self-government with a career open to talent, with talent seeking to render political service to its community, on the basis of inter-racial co-operation and opposition to all forms of discrimination in the community. The last apology or excuse for colonization will have been removed when Caribbean democracy can prove that minority rights are quite safe in its hands and that the imperialist policy of divide and rule, of holding the balance between conflicting interest, was the root cause of racial tension which only a nationalist movement transcending race can contain and ultimately eliminate. It is to that cause that we in Trinidad and Tobago, of the political persuasion to which I belong, have dedicated ourselves. If we succeed, as indeed we shall, it will be our 'Salut au Monde', our democratic vistas for tortured and frustrated humanity.

The Future of the Caribbean

The Caribbean area in 1969 is one of the most unstable areas in our unstable world. A mere catalogue of the instability will suffice: the British invasion of Anguilla (resulting from its secession from the associated state of St. Kitts-Nevis-Anguilla); anti-police rioting in Montserrat; serious labour disturbances in Curaçao; political crises in Surinam; chronic labour unrest in Antigua; endemic racial tension in Jamaica; the secessionist movement in the Rupununi in Guyana; the independence movement in Guadeloupe attended by grave disturbances; the unpopular dictatorship in Haiti; the uncertainties of the democratic movement in the Dominican Republic; the United States blockade of Cuba; and the Castro support for Latin American guerrillas.

The constitutional diversity aggravates the chronic instability – the three Latin American republics of Cuba, Haiti and the Dominican Republic; the four independent Commonwealth states of Jamaica, Trinidad and Tobago, Guyana and Barbados, with Guyana soon to become a republic; associated statehood with Britain of the smaller Commonwealth islands; the departmental status of Martinique, Guadeloupe and Cayenne making them parts of metropolitan France; the peculiar status of Surinam and the Netherlands Antilles in the tripartite kingdom of the Netherlands, which leaves defence and foreign affairs to the Netherlands; the semi-colonial status of the United States Virgin Islands; the Free Associated State relationship with the U.S.A. of Puerto Rico, which since the 1968 elections seems to be heading for statehood within the American Union.

This constitutional diversity is matched by an appalling degree of economic fragmentation –totally absurd for so small an area. Fragmentation goes to such fantastic lengths as would make the angels weep. Fragmentation is reflected both in the politically ordained economic links with different external powers and in the type of development strategy being pursued by individual territories. Thus Puerto Rico (in spite of impressive gains in industrial development and increases in *per capita* income) is being daily ever more closely integrated into the United States economy, enjoying a free flow of its goods and people into the Mainland and receiving vast inflows of both public and private Mainland capital. The traditional agricultural exports – sugar, bananas and citrus – of both the independent and non-independent Commonwealth Caribbean countries still depend on tariff preferences and even more on other forms of special protective arrangements in the United Kingdom market. The French Departments of Martinique and Guadeloupe are economically no less than constitutionally part of metropolitan France. Surinam and the Netherlands Antilles are integrated economically with Holland and the European Common Market and receive unilateral transfers of funds from these two sources. Cuba is heavily dependent for trade and credit on the U.S.S.R. and the Eastern European countries.

Not only do the past and present political links with metropolitan powers determine the pattern of trade and economic alignments and so contribute to fragmentation within the region . . . but . . . the economic policies pursued by the

Governments – both independent and non-independent – also serve to strengthen 'vertical' ties between the individual territories and metropolitan countries and frustrate the creation of 'horizontal' ties between the countries of the region. The individual territories all vie with one another to entice metropolitan firms to establish branches and subsidiaries in the region and to attract tourists from the richer countries. In so vying they pursue competitive rather than co-operative strategies of economic development, competing with one another in the granting of absurdly long tax holidays and in giving concessions such as beach rights, freehold sales of large portions of the areas of their islands to foreign interests, and even in some cases the right to establish casinos. Regional economic disintegration and failure to combine regional markets are further enhanced by the existence of large international corporations exploiting minerals – oil in Trinidad and Tobago, bauxite in Jamaica, Guyana, Surinam, the Dominican Republic and Haiti. The large mineral-producing metropolitan firms are vertically-integrated concerns, with their lines of trade running from the individual Caribbean territory to the metropolis rather than between the Caribbean territories.

Fragmentation is accompanied by massive dependence on the outside world, even in the independent countries of the Commonwealth Caribbean. With the exception of Cuba (the character of whose dependence is different from that of the others), the politically dependent and the politically independent countries of the Caribbean differ only in the latter's possession of formal sovereignty. For the most part, they are all highly dependent on the outside world – for economic aid; for large portions of the capital annually invested in both the traditional and the new manufacturing and tourist sectors of the economy; for sheltered markets for the traditional primary products; and even for emigration outlets for their surplus labour – Puerto Ricans to U.S.A., Jamaicans to Britain, Trinidadians to Canada, Martiniquans to France, Surinamers to Holland. The strategic decisions affecting the economies are made outside the national boundaries – by foreign companies and by large international firms. The original mercantilism of the seventeenth and eighteenth centuries has been replaced by the neo-mercantilism of the second half of the twentieth century. Instead of the British or European merchant firm and the absentee sugar plantation owner, the allocation of resources in the Caribbean is now controlled by the large international corporations. This is the case whether one looks at sugar production and refining; the international marketing of other primary products such as bananas; shipping; banking; insurance; manufacturing industries; hotels; minerals such as oil and bauxite; and even many of the newspapers and mass media. The locus of economic decision-making and the dynamics of economic growth continue to rest well outside the territorial boundaries of the Caribbean territories.

These extensive economic contacts with the outside world do have their positive side. The standard of living and *per capita* incomes of nearly all the Caribbean countries (with the notable exception of Haiti, which has relatively few contacts with the outside world) have been undergoing fairly impressive increases over the last two decades; and social services such as health and education have expanded to some extent. The Caribbean territories (with the exception of Haiti) do not, therefore, face the dismal levels of poverty to be found in Africa and Asia; but dissatisfaction with the standard of living and the level of social services already attained is perhaps greater than in either Africa or Asia. The close proximity to North America; contact with tourists; the high hopes expected of self-government and independence; the existence of strong trade union movements; and the large amount of emigration have fanned the flames of the revolution of rising expectations. Even more critically, deep-seated and rising unemployment, coexisting with the rising levels of *per capita* income and of expectations, aggravate the restlessness. The chronic unemployment and underemployment which emerged after slavery in the nineteenth century have in recent years been intensified by rapid population growth, inappropriate capital intensive technologies imported from abroad, and rising wage rates produced by the activities of the trade unions. Short-term solutions to the unemployment problem continue to be elusive and add to the feeling of helplessness and dependence on the outside world. In the Caribbean, it almost appears as if the growth of *per capita* income and the reduction of unemployment are not only mutually exclusive but also conflicting tendencies.

Dependence on the outside world in the Caribbean in 1969 is not only economic. It is also cultural, institutional, intellectual and psychological. Political forms and social institutions, even in the politically independent countries, were imitated rather than created, borrowed rather than relevant, reflecting the forms existing in the particular metropolitan country from which they were derived. There is still no serious indigenous intellectual life. The ideological formulations for the most part still reflect the concepts and vocabulary of nineteenth-century Europe and, more sinister, of the now almost defunct Cold War. Authentic and relevant indigenous formulations are either ignored or equated with 'subversion'. Legal systems, educational structures and administrative institutions reflect past practices which are now being hastily abandoned in the metropolitan countries where they originated. Even though both in the Commonwealth Caribbean countries and in the French Departments literature of world standard and universal validity has been produced by writers such as Lamming, Naipaul, Brathwaite (from Barbados), Walcott, Aimé Césaire and Frantz Fanon in Martinique, and even though in Trinidad and Tobago the steel band and calypso have emerged, nevertheless artistic, community and individual values are not for the most part authentic but, to borrow the language of the economist, possess a high import content, the vehicles of import being the educational system, the mass media, the films, and the tourists. V. S. Naipaul's description of West Indians as 'mimic men'[30] is harsh, but true. Finally, psychological dependence strongly reinforces the other forms of dependence. For, in the last analysis, dependence is a state of mind. A too-long history of colonialism seems to have crippled Caribbean self-confidence and Caribbean self-reliance, and a vicious circle has been set up; psychological dependence leads to an ever-growing economic and cultural dependence on the outside world. Fragmentation is intensified in the process. And the greater degree of dependence and fragmentation further reduces local self-confidence.

The difficulties multiply. Economic uncertainties are increased by the ever-present danger of Britain joining the European Common Market,[31] with the possibility of its abandonment of the traditional preferential position enjoyed by West Indian exports of primary products in the British market, especially sugar. With respect to these commodities, the West Indies are not free to opt for Latin America as a substitute for Britain and Europe. The Organisation of American States and the Inter-American Development Bank exclude from their purview the non-independent British islands, while Guyana, engaged in a serious boundary dispute with Venezuela, is barred from admission into the Organisation of American States and even from signing the denuclearisation treaty in respect of the Western Hemisphere.

As the Black Power movement makes headway in the United States in its fight for black dignity, there are the obvious repercussions in the Caribbean. Jamaica is seething with racial tension, black versus brown and white. The labour unrest in Antigua and the labour riots of Curaçao were both responses to Black Power propaganda. The large Indian population of Guyana, Surinam and Trinidad and Tobago adds another dimension to the racial disharmony which has already erupted in serious racial riots in Guyana. As the Hindu-Muslim disturbances continue in India, and the Protestant-Catholic disturbances in Northern Ireland, the religious diversity of the Caribbean region raises another cloud over the future. In this bleak picture the only bright spot is the apparent success in Castro's Cuba with the full integration of the black population into his society.

Youth and the students are becoming increasingly restless under the stimulus of world protest, in America, in France, in England, in Mexico and elsewhere. The situation is aggravated by the action of the Government of Jamaica in banning two Guyanese lecturers from the University of the West Indies.[32]

The overshadowing fear and apprehension is the United States of America, which has vowed that it will not tolerate another Cuba in the Western Hemisphere. It was with this motive that the United States intervened in the Dominican Republic in 1965.[33]

To sum up: the contemporary Caribbean is an area characterised by instability; political and economic fragmentation; constitutional diversity; economic, psychological, cultural and in some cases political dependence; large-scale unemployment and underemployment; economic uncertainty; unresolved racial tensions; potential religious conflicts; the restlessness of youth; and an all-pervading fear of the United States.

What then, is the future of the Caribbean?

Given its past history, the future of the Caribbean can only be meaningfully discussed in terms of the possibilities for the emergence of an identity for the region and its peoples. The whole history of the Caribbean so far can be viewed as a conspiracy to block the emergence of a Caribbean identity – in politics, in institutions, in economics, in culture and in values. Viewed in historical perspective, the future way forward for the peoples of the Caribbean must be one which would impel them to start making their own history, to be the subjects rather than the objects of history, to stop being the playthings of other people. In this respect, the Caribbean has so far been the 'outsider' in the New World. The U.S.A. and Canada have emerged as sovereign countries with an identity of their own – even though in recent years Canadians have had reason to be worried about the preservation of their own identity in the face of massive American economic penetration. The countries of Middle and South America (with the exception of the Guyanas) have achieved some small measure of identity – Mexico and Brazil more so than the others. Viewed in this light, the present crisis in Latin America should be seen as a desire on the part of the Latin American countries to complete the process of realising themselves – a process which started with the Wars of Independence against Spain in the nineteenth century. What today appears to the inhabitants of the metropolitan countries to be xenophobia and irrational nationalism in the Third World is more often than not the outward manifestation of this quest for self-realisation. To George III and his Ministry, the leaders of the thirteen American colonies in the 1770s must have appeared to be very bad boys indeed.

In its quest for identity and self-realisation, the Caribbean in 1969 starts with certain favourable conditions – young populations, affected by the world-wide restlessness and idealism of youth; relatively high rates of literacy and education; relatively high levels of *per capita* income; and a long history of contact with the Western World. Indeed, the great Trinidadian, J. J. Thomas,[34] in the course of his brilliant polemic in defence of the West Indian peoples against the calumnies of that nineteenth-century predecessor of Enoch Powell,[35] James Anthony Froude, Regius Professor of History at Oxford, wrote in 1890 of West Indians as 'apt apprentices in every conceivable department of civilised culture'. The task now is to make the West Indian peoples cease being 'apt apprentices' and become ready innovators 'in every conceivable department of civilised culture'. The requirements for this transmutation are twofold—a psychological revolution among the Caribbean peoples themselves and metropolitan empathy with Caribbean aspirations. This revolution and this empathy must rest on a better insight by both the Caribbean and metropolitan peoples of the true meaning of the Caribbean historical experience, an experience which must be set within the wider context of the evolving relations between the advanced countries and the Third World and within the framework of the history of the New World.

It is now being increasingly recognised that in the interests of world peace the relations between the advanced countries and those of the Third World must be put on a new basis. The metropolis and the periphery are not equal in economic power. There cannot therefore be true interdependence between them, as there can be between countries of equal strength. There is only a relationship of dependence. Enlightened economic relationships between centre and periphery must recognise clearly the present inequality and aim at making the periphery less rather than more dependent in the long run. The implementation of this principle will have profound consequences for the future relationship between the U.S.A. and Latin America and indeed between all the developed and all the less developed countries of the world. The Caribbean as a relatively small region with a long historical legacy of heavy dependence on the metropolis will stand to gain more than most other countries of the Third World if and when this new approach is implemented.

The history of the New World represents a still unfinished process of the creation of autonomous, viable societies with equal opportunity for all – free from domination by at first Europe and now by the U.S.A.

In 1776, the thirteen American colonies struck a blow not only for national self-determination but also for liberation of the national economy from its mercantilist shackles. The revolutionary character of the forcible severance of the thirteen colonies from their mercantilist economic past has not been fully appreciated largely because the American Revolution was a 'bourgeois' revolution which left intact – and indeed enshrined in the new Constitution – private property rights.

In the case of Canada, British mercantilism was not killed but died a natural death in the course of the development of economic liberalism in the nineteenth century. Although British investment in Canada in the form of loans was quite heavy, particularly in railways in the last few decades before World War I, it would be true to say that the year 1914 found Canada with an economy controlled by Canadians – although this was an economy heavily dependent for its foreign exchange on exports of wheat. The subjection of Canada to the new American economic imperialism happened almost overnight after World War II – between 1945 and 1955 – when there was a vast inflow of direct investment by U.S. corporations into raw material and manufacturing industries.

Both in the case of Canada and the U.S.A., there was never any real feudalism. In the somewhat pretentious words of the American economic historian, W. W. Rostow, the countries of white settlement were 'born free'. Further, with the two striking exceptions of the Negroes in the U.S.A. and the French in Canada, both the

U.S.A. and Canada evolved after their political independence as relatively equal and open societies.

In the case of continental Latin America, while political independence was in most cases achieved early in the nineteenth century, substantial remnants of feudalism and sharp social inequality within the societies remained. Further, even though the old mercantilist links were broken largely because of Britain's diplomacy (Canning[36] and all that), in the late nineteenth and early twentieth centuries foreign investment flowed in to exploit raw materials and to provide the infrastructure for the export trade in both food and raw materials. A period of highly unbalanced economic growth followed, led by exports of primary products to the industrial countries. But this growth did not spread through the economy, did not stimulate other economic sectors, and did not remove the underlying economic and social inequality. Gradually in the twentieth century, the U.S. corporation increased its relative share of total foreign direct investment in Latin America and spread from the traditional raw material and mining sectors, banks and public utilities to the new industrial sector. This was created in the inter-war period under the protection of the import restrictions imposed to defend the balance of payments which had deteriorated with the collapse in prices of primary products. Unfortunately, the U.S. corporations allied themselves with the privileged landowning and business classes in the Latin American countries to block social change and broadly-based economic development. And to compound the felony, the U.S. Government increasingly tended to support and promote the interest of the U.S. corporations in its diplomacy with the Latin American governments.

To sum up, then, one can say that the achievement of political independence by the continental Latin American countries resulted, internally, in the freezing of already rigid social and economic relationships, and, externally, in very little economic independence because of external economic domination by the U.S. corporations, aided and abetted by the dollar diplomacy of the State Department. The Alliance for Progress[37] sought to promote internal social revolution by non-violent means. But by 1964–65 it had already failed, partly because, when the chips were down, the U.S. Government became afraid of genuine social revolution, fearing that all such revolution would be contaminated by 'communism', and also partly because any thorough-going social revolution had to affect adversely the interests of the large American corporations operating in Latin America. Thus we have the supreme paradox of a nation born in revolution taking a consistent counter-revolutionary stand in the countries in its backyard. At the time of writing, whether the surprisingly mild U.S. reaction to the recent revolution in Peru augurs a permanent change remains to be seen, as will the position she will adopt towards the even more recent Bolivian changes.

The Caribbean differs profoundly from Latin America. It remained the area where both political and economic imperialism had been most deeply entrenched in the New World. In 1958 all the Caribbean islands (and the mainland territories of the three Guianas) were colonies of the European powers, with three exceptions. (Puerto Rico, if not a colony, was certainly not politically independent). The only three independent countries were Haiti, the Dominican Republic and Cuba. Haiti was economically backward and badly misgoverned, but it managed to maintain a certain degree of cultural autonomy and even self-respect. The Dominican Republic presented the spectacle of an unholy tripartite alliance between a ruthless dictator, American business interests and the State Department. In Cuba the same alliance existed, but with the U.S. presence being even more open.

The Caribbean then in 1958 had not even begun to liberate itself from the old dispensation. But in that year and the following year – 1959 – respectively, two important events took place. First, a political Federation was formed in 1958 among the British territories (excluding British Guiana and British Honduras). Second, in 1959 the Cuban Revolution took place.

In 1958 it was hoped that Federation would be the instrument through which the British Caribbean colonies would achieve political independence. Since 1945 Federation had been viewed as a means of permitting the small unviable West Indian islands to group together for the purpose of achieving an independence which West Indian leaders and the United Kingdom Colonial Office alike thought they were incapable of achieving on their own as individual units. But a combination of centuries-old inter-island jealousies, inept Federal leadership and the desire of the units to continue pursuing competitive rather than complementary strategies of economic development conspired to produce an early demise of the Federation. The break-up of the Federation was however followed by the granting of political independence to the three largest islands.

The Federation of the British islands lasted only four years. And by 1966 three of the Federation's constituent units – Jamaica, Trinidad and Tobago and Barbados – together with Guyana, had become politically independent. British Honduras is now on the way to independence[38] and the smaller units of the Leeward and Windward Islands have since achieved full internal self-government, with the United Kingdom responsible for their defence and foreign affairs. The Federal experience as well as the post-independence situation in the Commonwealth Caribbean showed that the quest for identity and solidarity among the ex-British possessions in the Caribbean had to be pursued by other means – namely, the method of regional economic collaboration and the working out of complementary rather than competitive strategies of economic development.

In 1959 Cuba, as the first Caribbean country to challenge successfully the power of the U.S.A. in the hemisphere, sought to establish a regime based on national independence and social justice, including racial equality. To this extent,

Cuba is the first Caribbean country to have attempted a decisive break with the past, (if we exclude the Revolution of the 'Black Jacobins' in Haiti in the 1790's).

Since the Revolution, Cuba has got rid of the traditional curse of the Caribbean – the sugar plantation – and she has got rid of the twentieth-century bane of the Third World – economic domination by metropolitan companies. She is also the first Caribbean country to have got rid of the legacy of slavery – the obsession with race and colour. Even in this respect she has been ahead of Haiti, where, ever since Independence, the mulatto élite has been in a privileged position *vis-à-vis* the black masses. In addition, she is the first Caribbean country (leaving aside the very small tourist economies) to have got rid of unemployment. Finally, whatever her economic mistakes, she is the first Caribbean country to have mobilised the entire population in the task of national reconstruction.

The other side of the coin is that she has the distinction of being the first country to introduce the full-scale apparatus of totalitarianism into the New World – even though the New World has not previously and since been without its perhaps unique collection of nasty and brutal dictatorships.

It is now generally recognised that Cuba is making a genuine attempt to transform her economic and social structure and to achieve a genuine national identity. But it is often said that Cuba has remained a sugar monoculture and that she has changed an American for a Russian master. Both of these propositions are quite misleading, unless properly qualified. Cuba finds that her scarcest resource is foreign exchange which, as a small developing country, she can earn only by exports. Tourist earnings having been lost with the revolution, the only major foreign exchange-earner is sugar, which she must continue to export in large quantities. However, at the same time there has been proceeding a great effort at diversification – the growth of production of poultry, eggs, milk, and vegetables has been phenomenal. And, with the massive new plantings of citrus and with the vast extension of cattle-raising based on Cuba's breakthrough in developing molasses as the basis of a local stockfeed, the composition of exports in the next few years will be profoundly diversified. Moreover, Cuba is the first Caribbean country to have upset the historical pattern and to have become a major fishing nation. She has turned history on its head by sending her trawlers to catch fish off Newfoundland. In education UNESCO[39] recognises Cuba, not only to be the most successful developing country in eliminating illiteracy, but also to be in the leading ranks in general educational development.

The accusation of Russian economic domination is superficially correct. But the essential point is that the heavy dependence on Russia is at least in principle no more than transitional and will last until Cuba removes the foreign exchange constraint to her development, which she is now attempting to do. On the other hand, in the previous situation of domination of the economy by equity investment by American corporations, the dependence on the U.S.A. was a cumulative process rather than a transitional phenomenon. While the present Russian economic domination may in principle be ultimately less deleterious in its effects than the previous American control, Cuba has illustrated the basic weakness of West Indian countries – the tendency to look for external props.

But the real tragedy of Cuba is that she has resorted to a totalitarian framework within which to profoundly transform her economy and society. This is the real point about the essentials of the political system in Cuba today. Perhaps over-simplifying, we may say that Cuba is essentially a highly nationalistic totalitarian society under a form of highly personalised rule, aiming at a complete transformation of previous economic and social structures through centralised planning and mass mobilisation. If in assessing the Cuban achievements, we think too much in terms of Marxism and Communism, we shall have missed the essence of the Cuban Revolution. (To say that Marxism is a veneer, however, is not to deny the reality of the military alliance with Russia and Cuba's consistent efforts to export revolution to Latin America.) Further, even though by all objective standards it is a totalitarian regime, there can be no doubt as to the widespread extent of popular enthusiasm and popular commitment.

The question arises as to whether there are alternative paths in the Caribbean to economic and social transformation and the achievement of a national identity other than the Cuban path.

One path that is being followed by many of the countries of the region is that initiated by Puerto Rico in its 'Operation Bootstrap'. This involves the attraction of U.S. firms to establish branches in Puerto Rico, which offers lower wages and tax holidays and which, as part of the U.S. Customs Union, has free access to the American market. This policy has been successful in that it has led to a high rate of investment, rapid industrial growth and an impressive increase in standards of living and *per capita* incomes in Puerto Rico. Massive transfers of Federal funds for Government development and social welfare activities have also contributed to raise standards of living, as have unrestricted opportunities for emigration to the U.S.A. But, in spite of these advantages, unemployment has remained at a very high level and there is still widespread poverty and much inequality. And any hope of preserving and strengthening the Puerto Rican identity has been destroyed. Puerto Rico has in fact solved its problems of economic and social transformation by incorporating itself into the U.S. economy. The recent election of a pro-Statehood Governor in that island merely reflects a recognition of a *fait accompli* by the Puerto Rican electorate. Economic growth has been achieved, but national identity lost. What shall it profit a country if it gain the whole world and lose its own soul?

Apart from the French Departments of Martinique, Guadeloupe and French Guiana and also possibly of the partner territories of the Netherlands Kingdom –

Surinam and the Netherlands Antilles – there is little hope of the Puerto Rican model achieving what it has in fact achieved in Puerto Rico itself. The Commonwealth Caribbean countries are not in a Customs Union relationship with the United Kingdom, which in any case is much more distant geographically from them than is the U.S.A. from Puerto Rico. Yet, even with these limitations, the offer of fiscal incentives and other concessions (such as beach rights and extensive sales of land) to induce outside investors in industry and tourism to set up shop locally is the main strategy of development being pursued. And, apart from the technical demerits of these policy instruments from the point of view of promoting regional integration and solving the unemployment problem, the result of such a strategy is bound to be the ultimate loss of national identity.

In 1969, with its new Third Five-Year Plan, Trinidad and Tobago adopted a third type of development model which may well be adopted by the other Commonwealth Caribbean countries – a path less revolutionary and more gradualistic, and less totalitarian and more democratic than the Cuban path, but more autonomous and ultimately self-reliant than the Puerto Rican one. It involves continued reliance on outside investment and trade with the outside world; but it also involves steady and increasing assumption of control over the commanding heights of the economy by the Government and nationals, a determined attempt to promote racial harmony and social equality, and the conscious development of a national and cultural identity.

The result of the pursuit of the Puerto Rican model of development is now clear, but only time can show how successful the Cuban and the new Trinidad and Tobago model will be. The success of the new Trinidad and Tobago strategy requires the mobilisation of the population, who will need a greater degree of self-confidence and sense of commitment. In fact, it requires the 'psychological revolution' which has been mentioned earlier – the casting off of the dependent state of mind which their history has bequeathed to the West Indian peoples. The large number of young people in the population of Trinidad and Tobago offers great hope – in fact, the only ray of hope – in this respect.[40] The emergence of a new and more tolerant attitude on the part of the U.S.A. towards Latin American and Caribbean regimes pursuing more autonomous types of social and economic change in their respective countries will also facilitate the success of the new path being followed by Trinidad and Tobago.

Increasingly the Commonwealth Caribbean countries such as Trinidad and Tobago will become aware that the goals of greater economic independence and the development of a cultural identity will involve them in even closer ties one with another – at economic and at other levels. For the present disgraceful state of fragmentation of the Commonwealth Caribbean countries – and the opportunities thereby created for manipulation by outside powers (both from the Old and New

Worlds) and outside business interests – makes it extremely difficult (although not impossible) for a single country to adopt a more independent and less 'open' strategy of development. Moreover, there are obvious limits to the scope for a more independent strategy of development in the Commonwealth Caribbean countries because of their small size.

Already, some slight beginnings have been made towards Commonwealth Caribbean integration. The Caribbean Free Trade Area[41] is now proceeding towards more meaningful integration – the harmonisation of fiscal incentives; the establishment of a common external tariff; agreement on a common policy towards foreign investment; the establishment of regional integrated industries; and the setting up of a Regional Development Bank, primarily in order to redress economic imbalances as between the relatively more and less developed territories. Commonwealth Caribbean integration will also have to be accompanied by sustained efforts to reduce the dependence of the region in the long term on protected external markets for the traditional primary product exports – principally sugar, bananas and citrus. While in the short and medium run, the preferences and special arrangements for these commodities in the United Kingdom market must be maintained – for example, in the eventuality of the United Kingdom's entry into the European Common Market – diversification and cost reduction must be long-run objectives.

Metropolitan economic assistance can serve to promote the objective of Commonwealth Caribbean economic integration, if such assistance is directed towards unifying the region and making it ultimately more independent economically. On the other hand, metropolitan aid designed to protect metropolitan political, diplomatic or commercial interests in the region will not only be a divisive factor but will serve to perpetuate the present deep-seated patterns of dependence.

It is also an imperative of meaningful Commonwealth Caribbean integration that the Associated States should achieve some form of political Independence.[42] For these countries can only participate meaningfully in the Commonwealth Caribbean integration movement if they have the same political status which the four independent countries now have and which British Honduras – soon to join CARIFTA – is on the way to obtaining. Here there are two options. Either the Leeward and Windward Islands must federate and secure political Independence from the United Kingdom – with guarantees of continuing budgetary and development aid from the United Kingdom over a number of years; or they must associate with one or more of the independent Commonwealth Caribbean countries. The former alternative, while clearly preferable, involves the usual West Indian difficulties of inter-island jealousies and the unwillingness of insular political leaders to have the spotlight shifted from them to the Federal leaders. Nevertheless, it should be possible to devise a form of Federalism which leaves the maximum amount of self-determination open to the units, whilst concentrating the power of dealing with the outside world in Federal hands. In fact, this principle may have to be applied in a wider setting should the present economic integration movement in the Commonwealth Caribbean ever develop into a new attempt at political union.

For the real case for unity in Commonwealth Caribbean countries rests on the creation of a more unified front in dealing with the outside world – diplomacy, foreign trade, foreign investment and similar matters. Without such a unified front the territories will continue to be playthings of outside Governments and outside investors. To increase the 'counterveiling power' of the small individual units *vis-à-vis* the strong outside Governments and outside companies requires that they should aim at nothing less than the creation of a single centre of decision-making *vis-à-vis* the outside world. Everything other than external contacts can and should be left to the individual units which should be given the maximum autonomy and power of self-determination. Herein lies the resolution of the problem which plagued the former Federation so much – the division of powers between the centre and the units.

Once the movement towards economic integration and political Independence of all the units begins to gather momentum in the Commonwealth Caribbean, it will be necessary to establish closer economic relationships with the non-Commonwealth countries – the French and Dutch territories and the independent countries of the Dominican Republic, Haiti and Cuba, which must be reincorporated into the inter-American family. (Puerto Rico, as we have seen, seems to be now drifting slowly but surely into Statehood as part of the American Union.)

A pre-condition of closer economic ties between the French territories and the other Caribbean countries would be an ending – or at least a considerable loosening – of the close ties with metropolitan France. While at present majority sentiment in Martinique and Guadeloupe favours the retention of the close links with France, it is reasonably certain that time will show that the present arrangements do not present a final solution to the problem of these territories.

It is not possible at this stage to sketch out precisely the type of relationship which might be established between the Commonwealth and non-Commonwealth Caribbean. Suffice it to say that there is a great scope for functional collaboration in respect of the production, processing and marketing of commodities such as sugar and minerals such as bauxite; for the exchange of technological and scientific knowledge; for the rationalisation of regional agriculture; and, not least, for the establishment of regional integrated industries in specific sectors, drawing their raw materials either from regional or extra-regional sources and serving both regional and non-regional markets.

Once there is true integration among all the units of the Caribbean (excluding Puerto Rico for reasons mentioned above), and once all the vestiges of political, economic, cultural and psychological dependence and of racism have been removed from the Caribbean, then and only then can the Caribbean take its true place in Latin America and the New World and put an end to the international wars and inter-regional squabbles which, from Columbus to Castro, have marked the disposition of Adam's will.

NOTES

1. Williams was referring to Frank Tannenbaum's book, *Slave and Citizen* (1947).
2. Hesiod (700s BC) was a Greek poet, the author of *Works and Days*, and Aristotle (384–322 BC) was a Greek philosopher and educator, one of the most influential thinkers of European culture. One of Aristotle's arguments was that people would achieve happiness when they fulfilled their own function, doing what they could do best, and it was therefore necessary to ascertain what each person's function was. Some people, he believed, were slaves by nature and so they should be enslaved for their own good and for the good of society.
3. These maroon communities in Jamaica and Suriname, which symbolised the struggle for freedom in the slave societies, persist to the present day and are proud of the independence that they negotiated. Maroons in other countries, for example Brazil, Colombia, Cuba, Ecuador, Hispaniola and Mexico, also succeeded in negotiating treaties granting them freedom and territorial integrity.
4. The *Code Noir*, formulated in France in 1685, was the most comprehensive attempt by a European state to regulate slavery in its colonies. Following Roman law, the slaves were defined as chattel, that is, moveable property, that could be sold, bequeathed, mortgaged or seized for debt.
5. Sir Thomas Browne (1605–82), an author and physician, wrote in *Pseudodoxia Epidemica* (1646) –Vulgar Errors – that the generally accepted explanations of black skin, the heat of the sun and God's curse on Ham and his descendants, were false. Although he did not claim to know the true cause he concluded that beauty was simply a matter of opinion and that black people were content to be black and tended to think that other colours were strange.
6. Tomas de Ortiz, a Dominican friar, wrote to the Council of the Indies, 'On the mainland [the Indians] eat human flesh. They are more given to sodomy than any other nation. There is no justice among them. They go naked. They have no respect either for love or for virginity. They are stupid and silly. They have no respect for truth …. They are unstable … ungrateful and changeable …. They are brutal …. They are incapable of learning …. They eat fleas, spiders and worms raw, whenever they find them. They exercise none of the human arts or industries …. They are beardless …. The older they get the worse they become … like real brute beasts …. The Indians are more stupid than asses', and so on (quoted in Todorov 1985, 150-51).
7. Bryan Edwards (1743–1800) and Edward Long (1734–1813) wrote the best-known early histories of the British West Indies, respectively *History, Civil and Commercial, of the British Colonies in the West Indies* (1793) and *History of Jamaica* (1774).
8. Thomas Jefferson (1743–1826) was the author of the Declaration of Independence and the third president of the United States (1801–9). He was born and grew up in the colony of Virginia where he inherited an estate of over 2,500 acres and 30 slaves.

9. Bartolomé de Las Casas (1474–1566) was born in Seville, arrived in Hispaniola in 1502 and in 1510 was the first Roman Catholic priest to be ordained in the Americas. He protested the enslavement and ill treatment of Indians. He wrote the *Historia de las Indias*, which was first published in Madrid in 1875.

10. The International Labour Organisation (ILO), founded in 1919, became an agency of the United Nations with its headquarters in Switzerland. Its mission is to improve the conditions of workers throughout the world. In 1969, the ILO was awarded the Nobel Peace Prize for its work.

11. Victor Schoelcher (1804–93) was the leading French abolitionist. As the under secretary of state for the navy with jurisdiction over the colonies, he prepared the report that led to emancipation in 1848.

12. General Antonio Maceo (1845–96) fought in Cuba's Ten Years War and repudiated the protocol that ended it. He led the war against Spain from 1895 until his death in battle in 1896. There is a statue of him, mounted on a horse and wielding a machete, in Maceo Park, Havana.

13. Toussaint L'Ouverture, the chief leader of the revolution that resulted in the end of slavery and the independence of Haiti, died of pneumonia in 1803, as a result of prolonged ill-treatment in a cell in a fortress 3,000 feet high in the Jura mountains in France.

14. John Stuart Mill (1806–73), a liberal philosopher and political economist, was the author of *On Liberty* (1859) and *The Subjection of Women* (1869). Thomas Carlyle (1795-1881) was an essayist and historian who wrote the notorious *Occasional Discourse upon the Nigger Question* (1849), in which he claimed that emancipation had encouraged idleness because Africans and people of African descent had to be compelled to work.

15. Walt Whitman (1819–92) was one of the greatest poets of the United States.

16. Gunnar Myrdal (1898–1987), a Swedish social scientist, wrote *An American Dilemma: The Negro Problem and Modern Democracy* (1944) that drew attention to contradictions in the United States between the status of African-Americans and the principles of democracy.

17. Luis Muñoz Marín (1898–1980) was the dominant politician in Puerto Rico for 40 years. He founded the Popular Democratic Party in 1938 and was the first elected governor in the colony from 1948 until 1964 (see chapter 7 in this volume).

18. Comte Joseph Arthur de Gobineau (1816–82) published *The Inequality of Human Races* in 1854, in which he wrote, 'The Negroid variety is the lowest, and stands at the foot of the ladder'.

19. Friedrich Nietzche (1844–1900), a German poet and philosopher, argued that human behaviour was motivated by the 'will to power'. It has been said that he was a precursor of Nazism, which claimed that Germans belonged to a 'superior Nordic race'.

20. James Anthony Froude (1818–94), Regius Professor of Modern History at Oxford University, wrote *The English in the West Indies, or the Bow of Ulysses* (1888) in which he claimed that the blacks of the West Indies were incapable of governing themselves. (For J.J. Thomas' critique of Froude's book see chapter 23 in this volume).

21. Thomas Babington (Lord) Macaulay (1800–59), an essayist, poet, historian and statesman, wrote a *History of England* which portrayed English history as a march of progress and the British empire as the most natural thing in the world. His infamous

Minute (1835) provided a rationale for an entirely English system of education for the few Indians who would become administrators in the Indian civil service. The result was the creation of a small anglicised elite of Indians who despite their cultural assimilation would never be treated as English by the English.

22. Mohandas Gandhi (1869–1948) developed a method of non-violent direct action that helped India achieve its independence in 1947. His autobiography, called *My Experiments With Truth*, inspired Martin Luther King, among others. His political heir, Jawaharlal Nehru (1889–1964), was leader of the Indian National Congress and the prime minister of India from 1947 until his death. *Towards Freedom*, his autobiography, inspired nationalists, including Cheddi Jagan of Guyana (see chapter 31 in this volume). Sir Rabindranath Tagore (1861–1941) was an Indian poet and philosopher who supported the independence movement. He won the Nobel Prize for literature in 1913 for his mystical poems, written in Bengali.

23. Lord Alfred Tennyson (1809–92) was a popular English poet. He succeeded William Wordsworth as poet laureate in 1850 and many of his poems are highly patriotic.

24. Lord Acton (1843–1902), the Regius Professor of Modern History at Cambridge University from 1895 until his death, is famous for having said, 'All power tends to corrupt, and absolute power corrupts absolutely'.

25. An international conference held at Bandung, Indonesia, in 1955, attended by nationalists like Jawaharlal Nehru of India, President Sukarno of Indonesia, Gamal Abdel Nasser of Egypt, and President Tito of Yugoslavia, sought to find political space between the world's superpowers, the USA and the USSR. This was the beginning of a 'non-aligned' movement.

26. The Pope's division of the world between Spain, to the west of an imagined line, and Portugal, to the east of the line, culminated in the Treaty of Tordesillas in 1494. This gave all the Caribbean and most of the mainland, which was then unknown to Europeans, to Spain and Brazil to Portugal.

27. *Cecilia Valdes* (1839) by Cirilo Villaverde is a classic novel of slavery in Cuba.

28. Gabriel de la Concepcion Valdes, known as Placido, was a free coloured poet and Cuba's most famous person of colour by 1840. He was accused of leading a conspiracy in 1843 and executed in 1844.

29. C.I.O is the Congress of Industrial Organizations, a federation of US trade unions created in 1938. Unions that were associated with communists were expelled in 1949 and 1950 and the CIO merged with the American Federation of Labor in 1955, forming the AFL-CIO.

30. V.S. Naipaul, born in Trinidad in 1932, is one of the most prolific and famous Caribbean authors. His novel *The Mimic Men* (London, 1967) won the W.H. Smith award in 1968 and Naipaul won the Nobel Prize for literature in 2001 (see chapter 28 in this volume).

31. The European Economic Community was formed in 1957, with six member nations, Belgium, France, Italy, Luxembourg, the Netherlands and West Germany. It became known as the European Common Market and Britain's efforts to join were blocked by French President Charles de Gaulle in 1963 and 1967. De Gaulle resigned in 1969 and Britain, along with Denmark and Ireland, joined the EEC in 1973. These nations became the core of the emerging European Union.

32. These were the historian Walter Rodney (see chapter 33 in this volume) and the economist Clive Thomas (see chapter 40 in this volume).

33. The United States had occupied the Dominican Republic from 1916 to 1924 and continued to control the customs until 1941. The National Guard, led by Rafael Leonidas Trujillo Molina (1891–1961), overthrew the elected president in 1930. Trujillo ruled with an iron fist until he was assassinated. Juan Bosch, elected president in 1963, was overthrown by the military after only seven months in office. When his supporters took to the streets in 1965, demanding a return to constitutional rule, the United States invaded with 23,000 troops, on the pretense that the republic was about to be overrun by communists. Thousands of Bosch's supporters fled and, in 1966, Joaquin Balaguer (1906-2002), one of Trujillo's henchmen, was elected president. He dominated politics in the Dominican Republic for 30 years, with support from the United States.
34. See chapter 23 in this volume.
35. Enoch Powell, a Conservative politician in England, became infamous in 1968 for a speech in which he claimed that the British way of life was threatened by an invasion of coloured people. He provocatively made a classical reference to 'the River Tiber foaming with much blood', and suggested that, in order to avoid violence, the immigrants should be encouraged to go back to wherever they had come from.
36. George Canning (1770–1827) was the British foreign secretary from 1822 to 1827 and then, briefly, the prime minister. He led the more liberal branch of the Tories.
37. The Alliance for Progress was created in 1961 by President John F. Kennedy as a way to channel funds and technical assistance into a variety of development projects in Latin America through the Agency for International Development of the US Department of State.
38. The independence of Belize was delayed until 1981 because Guatemala persisted in claiming the territory.
39. The United Nations Educational, Scientific, and Cultural Organization is one of the specialised agencies of the United Nations.
40. In 1970, the year in which Williams' book *From Columbus to Castro* was published, thousands of young Trinidadians protested the lack of progress made by Williams' government in cultural and institutional decolonisation and demanded political reforms and the redistribution of wealth.
41. The Caribbean Free Trade Association (CARIFTA), established in 1968, became the Caribbean Community and Common Market (CARICOM) in 1973.
42. By the end of the twentieth century all the British Caribbean colonies had become independent except for Anguilla, Montserrat, the British Virgin Islands, the Cayman Islands and the Turks and Caicos Islands.

Twenty-Seven

M.G. Smith

Michael Garfield Smith (1921–93) was an internationally respected anthropologist from Jamaica. His professional career was built mostly in England and the United States but his reputation was established by the work he did in Nigeria and the West Indies in the 1950s and 1960s.

Smith entered Jamaica College in 1929 and won the Jamaica Scholarship ten years later, achieving the highest grades in the Higher School Certificate examinations of any candidate in the British empire. Smith entered McGill University in Montreal in 1941 to study English (he was already a fine poet) but interrupted his studies to join the Canadian army in 1942 to fight in Europe during the Second World War. He demobilised in 1945 and entered University College, London, to study law. After one year he switched to read for a first degree in Anthropology, Psychology and Ethics, and took his final examinations in 1948. He then studied to work in northern Nigeria, a predominantly Hausa-Fulani region, and arrived there in 1949. He did fieldwork in northern Nigeria for 18 months before returning to London and completing his doctorate in 1951.

In 1952, Smith returned to Jamaica where he was a research fellow at the Institute of Social and Economic Research (ISER) of what was then the University College of the West Indies. He was one of a group of distinguished scholars that included the West Indians William Demas, Roy Augier and Lloyd Brathwaite, and the English anthropologist Raymond T. Smith. During his six years at ISER, he published many articles based on his African research and started the series of essays that was later collected into a book, The Plural Society of the British West Indies *(Berkeley, 1965). In 1958 and 1959, he worked as a senior research fellow at the Nigerian Institute of Social and Economic Research in Ibadan before returning to Jamaica for a brief period as senior lecturer in sociology. He left Jamaica and went to the University of California at Los Angeles as a professor of anthropology. In 1965, he moved back to University College, London, where he was professor and head of the Department of Anthropology until 1975.*

From 1972 until 1977 Smith served as a special advisor to Michael Manley, an old friend who had become the prime minister of Jamaica. He advised the government on a variety of topics, including youth and community development, local government, the wages and incomes policy, the crime wave and the reorganisation of the civil service. He continued to write and publish academic studies, including the book Corporations and Society *(London, 1974). In 1975, at the age of 54, he gave up his position at University College, London, and moved back to Jamaica to work full-time for the government. He left Jamaica in 1977 to do six months of research in Nigeria before he took up his last academic post, as the Franklin M. Crosby Professor of the Human Environment at Yale University, in 1978. Smith continued writing about Africa and the Caribbean, including* Culture, Race and Class in the Commonwealth Caribbean *(Kingston, 1984) and* Pluralism, Politics and Ideology in the Creole Caribbean *(New York, 1991). When he retired in 1986, he returned to England, where he died in 1993.*

Smith is best known for his characterisation of the West Indies as plural societies. He focused his analysis on institutions such as kinship and religion, and argued that the diverse peoples of the Caribbean, beginning with the Europeans and enslaved Africans and then including the free people of colour and indentured Indians and Chinese, constituted various social sections, each of which practiced different cultures. His essay 'West Indian Culture' was written in 1960 during the brief life of the Federation of the West Indies. His answers to such questions as 'Is there a West Indian culture?' and 'Who is a West Indian?' lie in the 'multiracial Creole complex'. Smith concludes, paradoxically, 'the Creole culture which West Indians share is the basis of their division.'

West Indian Culture

When people ask 'Is there a West Indian culture?' a monosyllabic answer is rarely adequate. If there is a West Indian culture, we can surely define or at least identify it; if there is not, we should at least say what sort of culture West Indians have. It is also worth understanding why the question is raised at all, and what functions answers of either sort may serve. Instead of presenting a cultural inventory stressing provenience of cultural traits, I shall therefore discuss the factors that underlie this question of cultural identity, as well as the nature of this identity itself.

Alfred Mayer has shown that the culture concept first emerged in Germany and Russia as 'a typical ideological expression of the rise of backward societies against the encroachments of the West on their traditional culture'.[1] Thus the connection between cultural and political nationalism is evident in the history of this idea. After several decades, Sir Edward Tylor adopted the term culture to denote 'that complex whole which includes knowledge, belief, art, law, morals, custom, and any other capabilities and habits acquired by man as a member of society'.[2] Fifty years later English-speaking anthropologists defined their discipline as the study of culture. Since then, cultural theories and definitions have developed apace. In their recent review of these concepts, A. L. Kroeber and C. Kluckhohn cite 164 statements of somewhat differing emphases, content, and organization. After analyzing these formulas, they conclude that "culture is a product; is historical; includes ideas, patterns, and values; is selective; is learned; is based upon symbols; and is an abstraction from behaviour and the products of behaviour'.[3]

There is then no single correct definition of culture, although there is an impressive correspondence among the many academic definitions. The culture concept moreover has two quite distinct functions, each dominant in its own sphere: the ideological and the analytic. Since anthropologists have developed a specialized concept of culture, its meaning for them differs from that generally current; but since social ideas form part of the culture which anthropologists study, they are also concerned with the content, context, and functions of cultural ideologies.

As colonial peoples move to freedom, the connections between their culture and nationalism are important but various. Questions of cultural unity and distinctiveness typically emerge within contexts of nationalist action seeking autonomy. Where cultural diversity within the emerging group is too great to be ignored, several alternatives are available. The nationalist movement may claim the people's loyalty for itself on behalf of the state, as in Ghana; or the major cultural divisions within the emerging group may be given important margins of local autonomy, as in Nigeria. Where the 'movement' is interterritorial and the range of cultural diversity is greatest, solidarity may be invoked in racial or metacultural terms. Thus, Pan-Africanism presently pursues African political unity to fulfill 'the African personality'. Although an important basis for nationalism, cultural unity is not indispensable after all. Race and communism offer adequate ideological alternatives.

Nonetheless, cultural distinctiveness has great values for nationalist movements. For a people emerging from tutelage, cultural distinctiveness may be used to justify demands for independence. Cultural homogeneity may also be used to promote political unity. For these reasons, nationalists often employ an ideology of culture to legitimate their movement – its methods and aims. Critics may make counter-charges of cultural diversity and unrepresentative leadership. The uncommitted public is then caught between two sets of conflicting assertions, and their political adherence depends on the answers they adopt to such questions as 'Have we a separate culture? Are we a distinct nation or people?'

These questions are very much in people's minds in the British West Indies today (1960). Their principal spokesmen are politicians, educators, and journalists. 'Before the West Indies can emerge as a nation, there must be a common culture. We must be West Indians first, and anything else afterwards'. [4] Chaguaramas, selected as the site of the capital of the West Indies Federation, has often been cited as symbolic of West Indian and Trinidadian nationalism. Nationalism itself has few public critics in the West Indies; but the problems that beset federation indicate the uncertainty of many West Indians. Within the federated territories themselves, parallel cleavages are often present. To cite a recent article, 'The two leading political parties of Trinidad – the People's National Movement and the Democratic Labour Party–are accusing each other of preaching and practicing racialism in Trinidad'. [5] A nationalist movement may therefore flourish amid conditions of racial tension. Since race and nationalism are ideologies, consistency is essential to neither. The nationalist may invoke the nation during racial strife; the racialist may invoke race solidarity on cultural or other grounds.

For many West Indians, the problem of cultural identity is unusually acute. As our poets show, the question is often primarily personal. 'What are we?' and 'Who am I?' go together in this uncertain context. West Indians may intuitively sense something distinctive about themselves and their culture, without being able to define either satisfactorily. Especially because of their political implications, such definitions are unlikely to win a general consensus. West Indians also recognize the cultural diversity within their own and neighboring territories, without being clear how these differences fit into the larger schemes of national or cultural unity and distinctiveness.

When people ask 'Is there a West Indian culture?' the short answer must always be positive. Since culture is a universal human attribute, every local group has a culture. If the group is fairly distinct or has a peculiar habitat, its culture will almost certainly reflect this in some particulars, and even if the group is part of a larger cultural and social unit, it may still be sufficiently distinctive to have its own subculture. Thus we can recognize subcultural variants of the more general British Caribbean culture in St. Kitt's, Barbuda, or Trinidad.

Culture is an abstraction from people's behavior. As an abstraction, the concept is serviceable to anthropologists and ideologues alike. For the anthropologist, its special importance lies in its patterning or regular standardized forms, its transmissibility as a tradition acquired by learning, and its intimate connections with society. As Nadel says, 'Society means the totality of social facts projected onto the dimension of relationships and groupings; culture, the same totality in the dimension of action'.[6] Like Nadel, Sir Edward Tylor also defined culture in terms of society.

The West Indies now (1960) has a common federal government, and so by one definition the component units form a single society. Yet it is clear that British Guiana and British Honduras, which do not belong to this polity, are culturally West Indian as much as those units that do. The prospect of Jamaica's forthcoming referendum on its federal association underlines this point. Should the Jamaicans vote for withdrawal from the Federation, will they cease to be West Indian?

Within the Caribbean, differences of history and metropolitan affiliation intensify local divisions; Guadeloupe and Martinique are no less West Indian than Barbados and Montserrat, but the two groups differ so sharply in consequence of their historical metropolitan affiliations that it is illusory at this stage to postulate their common cultural or national identity. Even within the British West Indies – to which I shall limit this discussion – important territorial differences reflect the course of history. Jamaica, St. Kitts, Antigua, and Barbados are predominantly Protestant by virtue of unbroken British rule; St. Lucia, Grenada, Dominica, and Trinidad remain Catholic as their original rulers left them. In Grenada, St. Lucia, and Trinidad the popular dialect is patois intelligible to Haitians or Martiniquans but quite beyond the Antiguan or Jamaican. The Shango cult is prevalent in some units, absent from others. The same staples, such as breadfruit, are cooked differently in different areas. In a sense, the large East Indian populations which differentiate British Guiana and Trinidad from other British Caribbean units are also historical accidents. Perhaps the specially dense population of Barbados is another.

Being learned, culture is derivative as well as transmissible; being transmitted, it is liable to change, even if this is selective rather than random. Being transmissible, it is not bound to particular society, although intimately involved in social life. Being an abstraction from behavior, it has an elastic reference according to problem and interest. Thus we may speak of West Indian or Trinidadian culture with equal relevance; the greater does not preclude the less, but rather assumes it. Moreover, although a system of patterns, cultures are in the process of change. Contemporary West Indian culture certainly differs from its future as well as its past condition. Its derivation from an earlier phase directs our attention to the history and composition of these societies. The intimate relations between culture as a way of life, and society as the people who live that way, indicate that West Indian culture at any moment is the sum of patterns, behaviors, ideas, and customs characteristic of West Indian societies.

I have already shown that the West Indian Federation in its present form does not correspond with the West Indian area whose common culture is my concern. This illustrates the distinctions between nationalism, political union, and cultural community. Despite the cultural continuities across imperial frontiers, I have also excluded the French, Dutch, American, and Latin units from my present field of interest. Political differences underlie and express the differences of language, history, economic, and social orientation which characterize the Caribbean dependencies of different metropolitan powers. Despite the best will in the world, these factors take precedence over regional coexistence and cooperation. British Guiana and Honduras were both invited to join the West Indies Federation; not so Martinique, Surinam, or Puerto Rico. If we are to answer that thorny question, 'Who [or sometimes What] is a West Indian'? without setting any political restriction on the reply, it may well be 'Anyone born in the West Indies or adopting it as his home'. Beyond this point we run into differences of citizenship and cultural model.

Properly speaking, we should distinguish here between British, Dutch, French, and other West Indians. It is an unhappy feature of the West Indies Federation that its name suggests it includes all West Indians; no doubt this is an effect of nationalism. By limiting the definition above to British West Indians, I include everyone native to this group of territories who has not transferred allegiance, as by naturalization in the United States, or by permanent emigration. I also include all immigrants who have adopted these territories as their home, whether formally or informally, provided they have developed local loyalties and attachments which take precedence over others elsewhere. These immigrants are subject to no racial restriction. In itself, this is a notable fact. But my definition excludes those immigrants whose primary loyalties to their homelands and native cultures undergo no major change. Such people may be described as expatriates; and within the British West Indies itself there is a sense in which Jamaicans in Trinidad, or Barbadians in Jamaica, may be expatriates; but this is subcultural. Once we have abstracted the distinctive West Indian pattern from their behavior, such intra-Caribbean migrants are distinguished mainly by in-group rather than cultural features.

The British Caribbean culture is one form of Creole culture; the French or Dutch West Indian cultures are other forms. Creoles are natives of the Caribbean; formerly, people born in Louisiana were Creoles also. Creole cultures vary a good deal, but all are sharply distinct from the mestizo cultures of Spanish-Amerindian derivation which dominate Middle America. The Creole complex has its historical base in slavery, plantation systems, and colonialism. Its cultural composition mirrors its racial mixture. European and African elements predominate in fairly standard combinations and relationships. The ideal forms of institutional life, such as government, religion, family and kinship, law, property, education, economy, and language are of European derivation; in consequence, differing metropolitan affiliations produce differing versions of Creole culture. But in their Creole contexts, these institutional forms diverge from their metropolitan models in greater or less degree to fit local conditions.[7] This local adaptation produces a Creole institutional complex which differs from the metropolitan model. Similar institutions function differently in Creole and metropolitan areas. In consequence, despite their shared traditions, Creoles and metropolitans differ culturally in orientations, values, habits and modes of activity. These differences alone would be quite sufficient to distinguish the Creole culture from its metropolitan model. The immigrant who adopts West Indian culture as a way of life 'creolizes' in doing so.

The Creole culture, however, also contains many elements in African and slave derivation which are absent from metropolitan models. Perhaps this combination of European and African traditions is the most important feature of Creole life. As we know, slavery defined the initial circumstances of this cultural accommodation. European interests and institutions then predominated, but the functional problems of the slave society required adaptations which promoted a distinctive Creole version of the European parent culture. The African slaves made their own adaptations also, often in contraposition to those slaves born and reared as Creoles. Within this structural complex, the Creole society and culture emerged together, its white rulers having the highest status and their culture the greatest prestige. Things African were correspondingly devalued, including African racial traits. The basis of the 'white bias' which characterizes West Indian society is thus cultural rather than racial.

Miscegenation complicated the picture, producing hybrids, some of whom were free and predominantly European in culture, while others were slave, acculturated to the Creole 'African' complex. Emancipation removed the legal basis for this extreme form of racial domination; it neither could nor did establish social and cultural homogeneity. The Creole ruling class adapted to the changing conditions as best they could; so did the ex-slaves. The Creole culture area remained defined by the formative situation of African plantation slavery. Within this New World context, Old World cultural forms assumed new features and functions.

Professor and Mrs. Herskovits have shown the importance of African contributions to the Creole cultural complex.[8] 'African' elements are observable in language, diet, folklore, family and kinship, property, marketing, medicine, magic and religion, exchange-labor, economic organizations such as the *susu*[9] or 'partners'.[10] In music, dress, dancing, and domestic life the African contribution is unmistakable. Only rarely however do we find African traits persisting in a pure form; more generally they are overlaid with Creole influences and situations, or they are associated with elements of European origin. Thus, the Shango cult is identified with Christian saints, 'African' syntax underlies Creole dialects, and the Sixth and Seventh Books of Moses belong with herbal and animal medicines in the local obeah complex. The complex historical factors involved in this cultural accommodation are illustrated in the long debate about the derivation of Creole Negro family forms. Some scholars argue that the 'matrifocal' New World Negro family is traceable to slavery; others admit the influence of slavery on its formation, but point to West African structural parallels. While I recognize the importance of both these historical influences, it seems clear that if we are to understand the persistence of these mating and kinship forms, we have to study them in their present context to determine their structural variability and functional correlates.[11] One reasonable hypothesis is that the structure of Creole society and culture is still sufficiently similar to that of its slave period for many old customs to retain functional value.

Without explicit recognition of this fundamental Negro-white combination within the Creole complex, it is difficult either to specify the distinctive features of West Indian life and culture, or to understand how other ethnic groups and traditions fit into it. This Negro-white complex which has been formative for the West Indies diverges sharply in its racial and cultural components. In this area Negroes outnumber whites markedly, and have done so for centuries; but European institutions and cultural models predominate. The Creole configuration which reflects the particulars of this association is unique because of this imbalance and historical depth. The West Indian-bred white is not culturally European, nor is the West Indian-bred black culturally African. Naturally, in view of its predominance, the European component in Creole culture has undergone less obvious modification than its African counterpart; but that it has been modified, there can be no doubt.

By 1838 the basic framework of West Indian society and culture was fully established. In Jamaica some Jewish elements had been partly assimilated to the British. After Emancipation, planters short of labor sought to import supplies. The greater their scope for economic expansion and their sense of labor shortage, the greater was their demand. Germans, Portuguese, Britons, Chinese, and Indians were imported. A certain number of African slaves liberated by the Royal Navy were also brought in at this time. The greatest scope for plantation operations then lay in Trinidad and British Guiana, and there the immigration was heavy and continuous. A few Indians came to Grenada but no Chinese. Barbados and Carriacou, already overpopulated, exported surplus workers instead of importing them. The economic depression in Jamaica discouraged immigration there, and the few Indians, Chinese, or Europeans brought in as workers presented no major problems. Naturally the immigrants sought to withdraw from their onerous situation as best they could. In Jamaica the Chinese rapidly acquired control of the grocery trade; the East Indians, although more numerous, have been less successful; the white immigrant laborers withdrew into rural enclaves, closed endogamous units, or, if Portuguese, into commercial urban activities. In Trinidad and British Guiana, where Indian immigration continued for decades on a substantial scale, the immigrants were concentrated on plantations in conditions which ensured social and ethnic isolation.

The cultural framework of Creole society governed the accommodation of these immigrant groups. The Creole cultural and social organization was a graduated hierarchy of European and African elements, crudely visualized in a white-black color scale. To participate adequately in this system, immigrants had to learn the elements of Creole life. This degree to which they adopted European cultural forms set the upper limits of their place in the social hierarchy. On their arrival, the indentured workers were therefore marginal to Creole society in much the same way as the Dominican Caribs, Honduran Maya, and Guianese Amerindians are marginal today. Being marginal, the immigrants were free to abstain from Creole activities or to take part in them. If participating, they were also theoretically free to enter the Creole hierarchy at points of their own choice, providing only that they manipulated the requisite cultural skills and had the necessary economic backing. Being neither white nor black, both the Indians and the Chinese escaped placement in the Creole color scale which crudely equated race and culture. This position itself indicates their marginal status in the Creole society not so long ago. Being white, the European indentured laborers found themselves in an especially difficult situation, equated with Negro peasants economically and socially, but with the white planter class in race and culture. It is therefore quite understandable that they withdrew from this contradictory structural context into the closed communities in which they presently live. The variable degrees of acculturation and assimilation among Chinese and Indian immigrants illustrate their opportunities and attendant problems. The Jamaican Chinese exhibit different patterns of assimilation from those in British Guiana.[12] For the large Indian populations of British Guiana and Trinidad, the prospect of creolization – that is, the adoption of Creole culture and assimilation to Creole society – still presents a number of problems, including the probable loss of their Indian heritage and group solidarity. In British Guiana the Indian population occupies an especially difficult position; although the largest racial group, it had no clear alternative to becoming Creole. Under slavery the African majority were in a somewhat similar situation. The current racial tensions of Guiana or Trinidad may thus express changes presently under way as the Indians resolve the problems presented by creolization, while the Creoles resolve the problems of accommodating these Indian groups.

It is only with this multiracial Creole complex that West Indians can identify as West Indians. Whatever their racial affiliation, self-declared West Indians implicitly refer to this amalgam in which the basic racial and cultural elements are white and Negro, and society is that mode of their association to which important elements from other traditions are selectively accommodated. The Lebanese colony in Jamaica merely demonstrates this analysis; arriving late, they rapidly won a major share of the trade in consumer goods. A generation ago, this group was distinguished from others as 'Syrian'; today they are simply 'Jamaican', partly assimilated to the urban upper class while remaining mainly endogamous. As indicated above, the Jamaican Jews went through a similar process long ago.

If my argument is correct, the characteristic West Indian complex combines two basic traditions, each of which is quite distinct and may persist more or less separately within the population. This is another way of saying that acculturation to the dominant Creole-European tradition varies widely among Creoles as well as immigrant groups. The problems presented by this cultural diversity are of special importance to student and nationalist alike, especially because the subordinate cultural tradition is that of the majority of the population whose social status and life chances differ radically from the minority acculturated to Creole 'Europeanism'. For the student, the demographic disbalance coupled with this cultural division presents important problems and conditions. For the nationalist, who is usually a member of the numerical minority, the issues are immediate and compelling.

People who are uncertain of their cultural or national status are unlikely to be clear about 'national' cultural goals. To many West Indians of low status and predominantly 'African' Creole culture, nationalism may have the initial appeal of promising full citizenship; if it does not deliver this, it will cease to retain their support and may be cynically regarded as of benefit primarily to the 'middle class'. Granted the social and cultural cleavages that are characteristic of Creole society, and the numerous factors that continuously reinforce them, 'national' unity may be scarce, even within the Negro-white population, much less between this group and later immigrants. If this is so within separate territories, difficulties at the regional level can be expected. The common culture, without which West Indian nationalism cannot develop the dynamic to create a West Indian nation, may by its very nature and composition preclude the nationalism that invokes it. This is merely another way of saying that the Creole culture which West Indians share is the basis of their division. Hence present interest in the questions: 'Is there a West Indian culture? What is it?'

NOTES *(Author's endnotes as they appear in the original essay)*

1. Alfred G. Mayer, 'Historical Notes on Ideological Aspects of the Concept of Culture in Germany and Russia' in A.L. Kroeber and Clyde Kluckhohn, *Culture: A Critical Review of Concepts and Definitions* (Cambridge, Mass.: Peabody Museum Papers, Vol. 47, No. 1, 1952).
2. Sir E.B. Taylor, *Primitive Culture* (1871), Vol. I (New York: Harpers, 1958).
3. A.L. Kroeber and Clyde Kluckhohn, *op. cit.*, p. 157.

4. John H. Pilgrim, 'West Indian Digest', *The Sunday Gleaner* (Kingston, Jamaica), June 5, 1960, p. 7.

5. *Ibid.*

6. S.F. Nadel, *The Foundations of Social Anthropology* (London: Cohen & West, 1951), pp. 79-80.

7. Lambros Comitas, 'Metropolitan Influences in the Caribbean: The West Indies', in Vera Rubin, *Social and Cultural Pluralism in the Caribbean*, Annals of The New York Academy of Sciences, Vol. 83, Art. 5 (1960), pp. 809-815.

8. M.J. Herskovits, *The Myth of the Negro Past* (New York: Harpers, 1941); M.J. and F.S. Herskovits, *Trinidad Village* (New York: Knopf, 1947).

9. W.R. Bascom, 'The Esusu: A Credit Institution among the Yoruba', *Journal of the Royal Anthropological Institute*, Vol. 72 (London, 1952), pp. 63-70.

10. Margaret Katzin, 'The Jamaican Country Higgler', *Social and Economic Studies*, Vol. 8, No. 4 (Jamaica: University College of the West Indies, 1959).

11. Raymond T. Smith, *The Negro Family in British Guiana* (London: Routledge & Kegan Paul, 1956).

12. Morton Fried, 'The Chinese in British Guiana', *Social and Economic Studies*, Vol. 5, No. 1 (1956), pp. 54-73.

Twenty-Eight

V.S. Naipaul

Vidiadhar Surajprasad Naipaul, who was born in rural Chaguanas, Trinidad, in 1932, is the author of over 20 books, including non-fiction as well as fiction. He is best known for his novels and volumes of short stories, which include The Mystic Masseur *(1957),* A House for Mr Biswas *(1961),* The Mimic Men *(1967),* A Bend in the River *(1979),* The Enigma of Arrival *(1987),* A Way in the World *(1994) and* Half a Life *(2001). Among his volumes of non-fiction are* An Area of Darkness *(1964),* The Loss of El Dorado *(1969),* India: A Wounded Civilization *(1977),* Among the Believers *(1981),* A Turn in the South *(1989) and* India: A Million Mutinies *(1990). Naipaul was knighted in 1990 for his contributions to literature and won the Nobel Prize for literature in 2001.*

Although Naipaul's mother's family, the Capildeos, were important members of Trinidad's Hindu community, his father, Seepersad Naipaul (1906–53) was a poor journalist and aspiring but unsuccessful writer. In 1943 Seepersad published at his own expense a small collection of short stories, which were republished by his son in 1976 as The Adventures of Gurudeva and Other Stories. *These, one of the first literary efforts by an Indo-Trinidadian to focus on his own community, influenced the son to become a writer. (Another son, Shiva Naipaul [1945–85] also became a successful writer, as has V.S. Naipaul's nephew, Neil Bissoondath, in Canada). The 1940s were a particularly difficult time for the East Indians of the West Indies. While India itself was a leader of the anti-colonial struggle, and hence a source of pride for many people of Indian descent throughout the diaspora, nationalism in the West Indies was largely a movement of Creoles of predominantly African descent. The problem of being marginalised in the political culture was compounded by the fact that most Trinidadian Indians, like those in Guyana, lived in rural areas when the centres of political activity were generally the towns, and especially the capital city. Naipaul grew up in a situation where most Indians lived in their own social world which, although (and perhaps because) they were proud of it, kept them quite isolated from the rest of the society. When Naipaul won a scholarship and attended Queen's Royal College in Port of Spain he must have felt like an outsider in a milieu that was dominated by the black-white Creole culture.*

In 1950, Naipaul went to Oxford University on a government scholarship. There, too, he was an outsider, this time in the heart of the imperial culture, and he suffered for a while from mental illness. Soon after graduating in 1953, he became a writer and editor, working for the BBC programme Caribbean Voices, which was so influential by providing opportunities for new writers. At this time he began writing the short stories that were later collected as Miguel Street *(1959). In 1957 his first novel,* The Mystic Masseur, *was published and this was soon followed by the second,* The Suffrage of Elvira *(1958). His next novel,* A House for Mr Biswas *(1961), confirmed his reputation as a major West Indian writer. In all these works Naipaul explored, with a comic touch and a serious undertone, the Indian experience in Trinidad.*

With the support of a grant from Trinidad and Tobago's PNM government, Naipaul returned to his country in 1960 and travelled through the Caribbean, on Eric Williams's suggestion, to gather material for a book. The result was The Middle Passage: The Caribbean Revisited *(1962). Williams had the support of some Muslim and Christian Indians, such as Kamaluddin Mohammed and Winston Mahabir, but the PNM was largely a Creole party and the majority of Hindus supported the opposition, the Democratic Labour party (DLP). A growing tendency towards ethnic chauvinism had been strengthened in the federal elections in 1958. Naipaul's uncle, Dr Rudranath Capildeo, became the leader of the DLP in 1960, when the Federation of the West Indies appeared to be poised on the edge of independence. The increasing political polarisation between Creoles and Indians had gone even further in Guyana than in Trinidad. Naipaul saw 'racial rivalry, factional strife' as a threat to nationalism, which was 'the only revitalizing force' in the West Indies. Naipaul is said to regard himself 'as a former colonial who has become a homeless cosmopolitan' and has been described as 'a nationalist who feels humiliated by the weakness and exploitation of the colonized' (King 1993, 2). Although he adopted the manner of a Victorian traveller, his observations and writing reveal far more of the region's social complexity than most travel writers ever achieve.*

The Middle Passage (excerpts)

There was such a crowd of immigrant-type West Indians on the boat-train platform at Waterloo that I was glad I was travelling first class to the West Indies. It wasn't an expensive first class. Ninety-four pounds, which might have bought cabin-class accommodation on one of the ships of the French Line, had got me a cabin to myself on the Spanish immigrant ship *Francisco Bobadilla*. . . .

We were directed to one of the ocean terminal's less luxurious waiting rooms, next to the railway sheds, in the gloomy recesses of which we could see the immigrants who had arrived that morning on the *Francisco Bobadilla*: a thick, multi-coloured mass herded behind wooden rails, and as silent as though they were behind glass. We stood at the doors and watched. No one stepped out of the travellers' waiting room into the immigrants' shed. There was interest, disapproval, pity and mockery in the gazes, the old hands sizing up the clothes of the new arrivals, clothes like those in which they had themselves landed some time before: thin white flannel trousers, sky-blue tropical suits, jackets with wide shoulders and long skirts, and those broad-brimmed felt hats, unknown in the West Indies yet *de rigueur* for the West Indian immigrant to Britain. Cheap cardboard suitcases were marked with complete addresses, all ending with ENGLAND in large letters. They stood motionless in the gloom; about them bustled dark-coated porters and railway officials; and there was silence . . . .

As yet we were subdued, as silent as the immigrants outside. But whispered rumours were beginning to circulate. Seven hundred, a thousand, twelve hundred immigrants had come on the *Francisco Bobadilla*. Two trains were taking them to London, from where they would make for those destinations written so proudly in those illiterate hands on their suitcases.

'You wouldn't want to travel with all them West Indians,' the man at the travel agency had said. 'Even the dockers are sick when they come off those ships.'

The *Francisco Bobadilla* was indeed in an appalling condition. The crew had not had time to clean up after the seven hundred immigrants. Paintwork was tarnished, metal rusting. In my first-class cabin, so cramped that I could open my suitcase only on my bunk, there was dust and fluff everywhere. The water carafe was hazy with dirt; the hot water didn't run; the lights didn't work . . . .

But there was an advantage. On this outward journey there were few passengers, and most of those who lined the deck rails as we moved down the Solent were travelling tourist. When the dinner gong went they disappeared to their canteen below decks. There were only nine first-class passengers, and we sat at three tables in one corner of the large shabby dining room.

As he sat down, an elderly coloured man said, just to open the conversation, 'A lot of these black fellers in Tobago are damn intelligent, you know.'

We were in the West Indies. Black had a precise meaning; I was among people who had a nice eye for shades of black. And the elderly coloured man – a man, that is, of mixed European and African descent, with features and skin-colour closer to the European – was safe. There were no black men or women at the table. The coloured man's wife was, we were told, Spanish. Correia was a Portuguese from British Guiana. And Philip, who came from Trinidad, where he had 'a little business', could have been white or Portuguese or coloured or Jewish.

'A lot of those black fellers in B.G. ain't no fools either,' Correia said.

The intelligence of black fellers in Trinidad and Jamaica and Barbados was assessed; and then they started groping for common acquaintances. It turned out that Correia and Philip had some, in a football team that had toured the West Indies in the 1920s.

Correia was a small, bald man. He wore spectacles, had a sharp hooked nose and had lost his teeth. But he was once a goalkeeper. He had a booming voice.

'You remember Skippy?' he asked.

'I can't remember when last I see Skippy,' Philip said.

'Well, you not going to see him again. Son of a bitch catch a pleurisy and dead. Frankie and Bertie and Roy Williams. All of them dead like hell.'

The waiter, middle-aged and mournful, couldn't speak English.

'But look at this, nuh,' Correia boomed. 'And I got to spend fo'teen days on this ship. Look here, man, look here. I want some tomatoes. You got that? Tomatoes. Having a lil trouble with the stomach,' he explained to us. 'Tomatoes. You got that? Me. Wantee. Tomatee. Me wantee tomatee. I don't know where they pick up these people who can't talk English.'

The Spanish lady couldn't talk Spanish; Correia himself couldn't talk Portuguese. West Indians are English-speaking and when confronted with the foreigner display the language arrogance of all English-speaking people.

A young couple from Northern Ireland and an English librarian sat at the next table. The librarian was distressed. She had been under the impression that the *Francisco Bobadilla* was a cruise ship and had booked for the round trip. She had just learned that we were going to the West Indies to pick up another seven hundred immigrants . . . .

Early next morning I was awakened by Correia. He had the cabin across the corridor from mine. He came into my cabin naked except for a pair of pants. He was without his spectacles; his little face was haggard; his beard had begun to sprout; his thin hair was disarrayed; and he was hugging himself.

'Hi there, man. How you sleep? Lemme see a cigarette, nuh.' He took one of mine and lit it. 'You look as if you sleep well, you know. I had a hell of a night, boy. Didn't want to wake you up earlier. Thought you would be sleeping. But I can't open my suitcase. The one with pyjamas and soap and razor and Eno's and every blasted thing in. You want to try it?'

The canvas suitcase was bulging and taut; it was a wonder that Correia had managed to close it.

'I try those blasted keys all how,' he said, sitting on his bunk, while I tried.

Eventually we opened it, Correia jumping on the suitcase, I turning the key.

'Thanks, thanks, man. I hope I ain't catch a cold, boy. You ain't have a lil Eno's or Andrews with you? Stomach giving me hell, boy. Went three times already this morning. Not one blasted thing. Is this damn *mañana* food. First and last Spanish ship you catch *me* on.'

And all that morning he padded up and down outside the lavatories, smoking, head bowed as if in meditation, tie slackened, spectacles half-way down his nose, hands in pockets. Whenever I went down he gave me a progress report.

'It coming, it coming. I feel it coming.'

By lunchtime, to add to his troubles, he was sea-sick.

I reported this to the table.

'He wake me up at five this morning asking for Eno's,' Philip said.

The coloured man, Mr Mackay, said, 'We have two madmen with us this trip. Black fellers. I was talking to their keepers this morning. White fellers. The British Government paying for them going out and coming back.'

'I see them walking up and down,' Philip said. 'Is a funny thing. But you could always tell people who make it their business to keep other people lock up. They have this walk. You ever notice?'

'You see how these black fellers going to England and stinking up the country,' Mr Mackay said. 'I mean, if a black feller want to get mad, he could stay home and get mad there.'

They spoke of the telephone strike in Trinidad, which had been going on for some time. Mr Mackay said that the strike was a racial one. He spoke of this with feeling. Quite suddenly he was identifying himself with the black fellers. He was an old man; he had never risen to the top; superiors had always been imported from England.

'Is these Potogees who cause the trouble, you know,' he said. 'They have their hands in the stinking salt-fish barrel and they are still the first to talk of nigger this and coolie that.'

'I believe the ship has a list,' Philip said. 'Go up on the sun deck and see.'

'I must say I don't care for the look of those lifeboats. If anything happen we drowning like hell. As soon as we get to the Azores I am going to try to insure Mrs Mackay and myself against accident. I suppose you could do that sort of thing in the Azores?'

'But you don't know the language, Daddy,' Mrs Mackay said.

'Why, what they talk there? A sort of Potogee *patois*?'

'Something like that,' Philip said. 'But I could help you with it.'

'What, you know Potogee?'

'We used to speak it at home,' Philip said.

So Philip was Portuguese.

Mr Mackay fell silent. He stared at his plateful of Spanish food and looked unwell.

Philip said briskly, 'This Trinidad coming like a little America. All these strikes. All these hold-ups. You hear about that man the police catch with eighty-three thousand dollars in notes stuff up in a chest-of-drawers?'

Mr Mackay spoke at length about getting insured at the Azores. And for the rest of the journey he was silent about Portuguese and others and spoke only of black fellers. It was a cramping of his style; but in the West Indies, as in the upper reaches of society, you must be absolutely sure of your company before you speak: you never know who is what or, more important, who is related to what.

It was warm. The tourist-class passengers, who had for a day or two been battened down, it seemed, on the lower decks, emerged singly and in pairs and sunned themselves. The two lunatics came out with their keepers. The young Baptist missionary from the North of England, off to the West Indies on his first posting and travelling tourist out of a sense of duty, read large theological works and made notes. A Negro woman of about eighty, wearing sensationally old clothes, wandered about with cheerful inquisitiveness. She had left St Kitts to look for work in England; the rumour went round that the British Government was paying for her passage back.

Because there were so few passengers the class divisions on the ship were ignored. An Indian butcher from British Guiana trotted round the first-class deck morning and afternoon. A tall handsome Negro, who spoke to no one, walked around the deck as well, for hours at a time, smoking a tiny pipe and holding a paperback called *The Ten Commandments*, the book of the film. This man, according to Mr Mackay, had had some mental trouble in England and was being sent back, at his own request, at the expense of the British Government.

We all rooted among the tourist-class passengers and brought back stories.

Miss Tull, the librarian, came back distressed. She had met a woman who had left England because she couldn't get a room for her baby and herself. 'The landlord just threw them out when the baby came,' Miss Tull said, 'and put up a big sign in green paint. No Coloured Please. Do you mean that in the whole of Britain they couldn't find room for one woman and her baby?'

'They've found room for quite a lot,' Mr Mackay said.

'I can't understand it. You West Indians don't seem to care at all.'

'All this talk about tolerance is all right,' Mr Mackay said. 'But a lot of you English people forget that there is a type of black man – like the Jamaican – who is an animal.'

'But this woman isn't Jamaican,' Miss Tull said, conceding the point.

'A lot of these black fellers provoke the English people,' Mr Mackay said, putting an end to the discussion. Like all good West Indians, he was unwilling to hear anything against England.

My own encounter had been with a fat brown-skinned Grenadian of thirty-three. He said he had ten children, in Grenada, in various parishes and by various women. He had gone to England to get away from them all, but then had begun to feel that he should go back and face his responsibilities. He thought he might even get married. He hadn't yet decided who to, but it probably would be the mother of his last child. He loved this child; he didn't care for the others. I asked why, then, he had had so many. Didn't they have contraceptives in Grenada? He said with some indignation that he was a Roman Catholic; and for the rest of the journey never spoke to me.

From our ventures among the tourist class we came back with stories, and sometimes with captives. Correia's captive was an Indian boy called Kripal Singh from British Guiana, who so endeared himself to the company that he was invited to tea.

'So handsome,' Mrs Mackay said over and over. 'So fair.'

'This boy,' Correia said, 'comes from one of the best families in B.G. You never hear of them? Biggest people in the ground provision business. Singh Brothers, man. Singh, Singh, and Singh.'

Kripal Singh looked correctly modest, his manners suggesting that what Correia said was true but that he didn't want to boast. He was tall and slender; his features were fine, his mouth as delicate as a girl's. He smoked with nervous elegance.

'Tell them about your family, Kripal,' Correia said.

Kripal, bowing slightly, offered cigarettes. He was a little drunk. So was Correia.

'They don't *grow* the ground provisions, you know,' Correia said, taking one of Kripal's cigarettes. 'They does only buy and sell. Tell them, Kripal.'

'So fair,' Mrs Mackay said.

For the rest of the voyage Kripal remained attached to the first class, only sleeping with the tourists and eating with them. He could find no suitable drinking companions among them; and he shared a cabin with the British Guianese butcher, whom he detested.

'The man s-say he went to England for holiday,' Kripal said, recalled to the subject by the sight of the butcher running around the deck. 'And he s-spend all s-seven weeks drawing dole.'

Kripal himself had gone to England to study. This studying in England is one of the strange activities of West Indian youth, of well-to-do Indians in particular. It can last until early middle age. Kripal had studied deeply in England and the Continent until his father, alarmed at the expense, had summoned him home to the business and marriage. By travelling tourist Kripal was having his last subsidized fling; his studies were almost over.

One morning, not long after we had left the Azores, I found Correia in a sparkling mood.

'How, how, man? You is a son of a bitch, you know. You never tell me you was a educated man. Let we go and have a drink, nuh.'

Correia had been lucky in me. He became sea-sick: I had Marzine pills. He had headaches: I had Disprin tablets. He developed a corn: I had Dr Scholl's corn-plasters. When he wanted to drink and couldn't find Kripal Singh, he came to me. Drinking with him had its dangers. He drank rapidly and became drunk in a matter of minutes. And he seldom had money on him: he preferred to settle later.

'You know,' he said at the bar, 'I had a damn good wash-out this morning. First try.' This explained his mood. 'You are a damn good writer, boy. Yes, man. I watch you at the post office in the Azores. Writing off those cards so damn fast I couldn't even read what you was writing.'

Philip joined us. He had been reading the *Kama Kalpa* in his cabin. I thought he had been reading the wrong book, but he said, 'This Indian philosophy is a great thing.'

'It *is* a great thing,' Correia said, drunk already. 'What is the first thing you going to do when you get back home, Philip?'

'I think I have to see about insuring the car, first of all.'

'I'm going to have a damn good purge-out with some Epsom Salts, boy.'

Both Correia and Philip had married daughters in England. Correia's daughter had been married not long before; Philip had just attended his daughter's wedding.

'You know what it make a father feel to lose his daughter, Naipaul?' Correia asked. 'You know how he does feel when she cry out at the train, "Don't go, Pa"? You don't know, Naipul. *"Don't go, Pa. Don't leave me."* His one and only daughter.' He beat his feet on the rung of his stool and burst into tears. 'He don't know, Philip.'

'No, old man. He don't know.'

'Where your daughter living, Philip? Mine living in a kiss-me-arse place called Dudley.'

Philip didn't answer. He left the bar and came back some moments later with an album stamped on the white leather cover: The Wedding of Our Daughter. Philip was anxious about his daughter and now, looking through the album, recognizing the working-class faces, clothes and backgrounds, I understood why. What had been desirable in the West Indies appeared differently in England.

Everyone seemed to be thinking about his children that day. The Mackays had left their son in England. Mr Mackay had made his last voyage; he would never see his son again.

'He's picking up all sorts of English habits.' Mrs Mackay said with pride.

'Everything for him is a "flipping" this and a "flipping" that. I just can't keep up with his English slang and English accent.'

Mr Mackay smiled, remembering.

It is possible for an escaped English convict to be welcomed by the white community in Trinidad and set up in business. And the West Indian, knowing only the value of money and race, is lost as soon as he steps out of his own society into one with more complex criteria . . . .

As England receded, people prepared more actively for the West Indies. They formed colour groups, race groups, territory groups, money groups. The West Indies being what they are, no group was fixed; one man could belong to all. A small group of Indians, dropping the competitive talk of London and Paris and Dublin and brilliant children studying in England, Canada and America, discussed the political situation in Trinidad. They spoke of Negro racism, and on the subject of miscegenation repeatedly wound themselves up to hysteria. The British Guianese Indians, among them a man who spent much of the voyage playing Monopoly and reading the first volume of Radhakrishnan's *Indian Philosophy*, were less impassioned. Believing that racial coexistence, if not cooperation, is of urgent importance to the West Indies, I was disturbed by these Indian views and wanted to explore them further. But I had to drop out of the group because of the unpleasantness with Mr Hassan.

Mr Hassan had lent me a copy of *Time* magazine. I had lent it to Philip (in exchange for his *Kama Kalpa*), and when on the following day Mr Hassan asked for his magazine, it couldn't be found. Thereafter, four, five, six times a day, Mr Hassan asked for his magazine. He waited for me on deck. He waited for me before and after the film show. He waited for me outside the dining room. He waited for me in the bar. I bought him drink after drink. But he never relented. I promised to buy him a copy in Trinidad. But he wanted his particular copy of *Time*. I told him it was lost. That didn't matter. He wanted his *Time*. After three days of this persecution I burrowed deep down into the tourist class and, miraculously, found someone who had a copy of the magazine. It was then, needless to say, that Mr Hassan's own copy turned up. Mr Hassan's main subject of conversation had been his wealth and his persecution, at the hands of government departments, customs officials, shipping companies, his wife's family, his children's teachers. From the depths of my heart I wished his persecutors greater strength and a long life.

And one day there was very nearly a racial incident in the bar. It seemed that a group of tourist-class passengers, made restless by the long journey and the approach of their various native lands, and provoked by the comparative emptiness of the first-class bar, had decided to rush it. A group burst in that evening, singing. They came running in and bobbed up and down before the bar. They called loudly for drinks. The barman refused to serve them. The group, their bouncing abruptly stilled, their high spirits gone, stood silently in front of the bar for a few seconds. One man withdrew. The others followed him. They walked in a body down the deck, then back again. They stood in the doorway and muttered. At length one man left the group and, buttoning his jacket, walked up to the bar and said, 'Gimme a pack of cigarettes, please.' The barman handed over the cigarettes. The man looked at the cigarettes, surprised. For a second he hesitated. Then, with careless swinging steps, he strode out. The group, moral victory theirs, went running off to the tourist bar, singing loudly.

And poor Miss Tull became more and more worried about her return journey. No one could console her. Philip suggested that she should abandon her sunshine cruise at Trinidad and fly back to England.

'I'm not going to lie to you,' Mr Mackay said. 'When I saw that pack of orang-outangs getting off the ship at Southampton, I didn't feel good. It was a damn frightening thing to see. You can't blame some people for not wanting to call themselves West Indians.'

'Angus always tells people he's Brazilian,' Mrs Mackay said. 'He could pass for one too.' Angus was her son, who spoke English slang with an English accent.

We were near St Kitts. A drink, a sunset as flamboyant as one could have wished, the Caribbees pastel-grey outlines around us, the waters where the navies of Europe acquired their skills in the seventeenth and eighteenth centuries: it wasn't enough to take our minds off the horror that was nearly upon us. That evening we would take on our first load of emigrants. St Kitts, the mother colony of the British West Indies, 'the first and best earth' (according to an inhabitant of 1667) 'that ever was inhabited by Englishmen amongst the heathen cannibals in America', today an overpopulated island of sixty-eight square miles, producing a little sea-island cotton, having trouble to sell its sugar, and no longer growing the tobacco, the first crop of the settlers, which Thomas Warner[1] took back to England in 1625 to prove the success of his enterprise. The romance of its history – Warner and his Amerindian mistress, their son 'Indian' Warner – is buried. There are reminders only of the brutality of that history: the slaves shanghaied there, their descendants abandoned when prosperity went, and now *their* descendents, their belongings packed, their good-byes said, searching the sea for the black smoke-stack of the *Francisco Bobadilla*, prepared for another middle passage.

It was night when we anchored, far out at sea. We saw nothing of St Kitts except the scattered lights of its capital. We looked for tenders; several lights deceived us. Nothing moved, except the headlamps of motor-cars.

'Eh!' Mr Mackay said. 'They have motor cars here too?'

Tourist class, first class, we were one now, lining the rail, watching the lights of the toy capital where people took themselves seriously enough to drive cars from one point to another.

Mr Mackay, joining us later in the bar, reported that one of the lunatics had been taken off. A launch had taken him away with his keeper; the keeper had returned alone. Presently the keeper himself turned up in the bar. In spite of the gravity of his charge, he had come prepared for the tropical climate, and we had observed his degeneration from grey-flannelled, soft-soled official into red-shirted, sandalled cruise passenger.

A commotion, and some shouts, told us that the emigrants had arrived.

Part of the port deck had been roped off; the companion-way had been lowered. Bright lights made the deck dazzle, bright lights played on the black water. There they were, rocking in the water, in three large rowing-boats. Men sat on the gunwales and with long oars steadied the boats. Policemen had already come aboard. Tables had been placed just in front of the companion-way, and there the purser and his officials sat, consulting long typewritten sheets. Below, the boats rocked. We could see only white shirts, black faces, hats of many colours, parcels, suitcases, baskets. The men with the oars shouted occasionally, their voices dying quickly in the darkness. But from the passengers we heard no sound. Sometimes, for a second or two, a face was upturned, examining the white ship. We saw women and children, dressed as for church. They all looked a little limp; they had been dressed for some time. The lights played on them, as if for their inspection. Beyond there was darkness. We picked out suits, new broad-brimmed felt hats, ties whose knots had slipped, shining faces.

'They could at least have brought them out in launches,' Miss Tull said. 'At least in launches!'

The tourist class looked down, chattering, laughing whenever a rowing-boat struck the side of the ship or when an emigrant tried to get on to the companion-way and was turned back.

Presently they started coming up. The companion-way quickly became packed, a line of people from ship to boat. They looked tired; their clothes were sweated, their faces blank and shining. With policemen on either side, they produced tickets and brand-new passports. Separated from them by ropes, we stood and watched. The blue-dungareed crew leaned over the rails, exclaiming at the beauty of black women and pointing; we had never seen them so animated.

The deck became crowded. Passengers recognized an emigrant here and there.

'What, you come back already?'

'I just went up on a lil holiday, man.'

'I think I would go up and try my luck. You see Ferdie or Wallace or any of them up there?'

But most of them were subdued. One or two tried to duck under the ropes before presenting their papers. The tourist class, with sudden authority, bullied them back. The deck was choked with plastic bags in plaid patterns, brown paper parcels, cardboard boxes tied with string. The crowd grew. We lost sight of the purser and his table. The crowd pressed against the rope. One man with a blue suit, a slipped tie and a hat was jammed against me. He pushed his frightened, red-eyed face close to mine. He said hoarsely, anxiously, 'Mister, this is the ship that going to England?' Sweat was running down his face; his shirt stuck to his chest. 'It all right? It does go straight?'

I broke away from the group behind the rope and walked round to the starboard deck, where it was still and dark and silent, and looked at the lights of the island.

'Well!' someone said loudly.

I turned to see a tourist. We had not spoken during the voyage.

'The holiday is over,' he said. 'The wild cows are coming on board.'

He spoke in earnest. And what was he, this tourist? A petty official perhaps, an elementary school teacher. *The wild cows are coming on board.* No attitude in the West Indies is new. Two hundred years before, when he would have been a slave, the tourist would have said the same. 'The creole slaves,' says a writer of 1805, 'looked upon the newly imported Africans with scorn, and sustained in their turn that of the mulattoes, whose complexions were browner; while all were kept at a distance from the intercourse of the whites.' On this ship only the Portuguese and the Indians were alien elements. Mr Mackay and his black fellers, the tourist and the wild cows: these relationships had been fixed centuries before.

The emigrants were running all over the ship. They peered in at the window of the bar, stood in the doorway. The ship was suddenly crowded. The first-class bar was the only place of refuge, and to it now came many of the tourists who had come with us from Southampton. No one objected. There were now only two classes: travellers and emigrants.

The barman vented his rage on two small emigrant children who had drifted into the bar, still in their fussy emigrant clothes. He lifted the counter flap, shooed the young emigrants to the door, and, blind to their charm, lifted them firmly and with an expression of distaste out on to the deck.

Sometimes for as much as three months at a time a slave ship would move from anchorage to anchorage on the West African coast, picking up its cargo. The *Francisco Bobadilla* would be only five days. It would go from St Kitts to Grenada to Trinidad to Barbados: one journey answering another: the climax and futility of the West Indian adventure. For nothing was created in the British West Indies, no civilisation as in Spanish America, no great revolution as in Haiti or the American colonies. There were only plantations, prosperity, decline, neglect: the size of the islands called for nothing else.

What are the points in the history of an island like Jamaica? 'This isle,' we are told in 1597, in *A true Relation of the Voyage Undertaken by Sir Anthony Shirley,* 'is a marvellous fertil Isle, & is as a garden or store house for divers parts of the maine. We have not found in the Indies a more pleasant and holsome place.' From that, to Trollope in 1859: 'If we could, we would fain forget Jamaica altogether. But there it is; a spot on the earth not to be lost sight of or forgotten altogether, let us wish it ever so much.' From Trollope in 1859 to the Ras Tafarian of 1959, who rejects Jamaica entirely and wishes to return to Africa, to a heaven called Ethiopia: 'Jamaica was a nice island, but the land has been polluted by centuries of crime.'

When Columbus put his ideas to King John II of Portugal in 1483, King John, telling Columbus nothing, sent a ship out into the Atlantic. Within weeks of the discovery of the New World in 1492, Columbus's companion Pinzón, deserting, took the *Pinta* off on his own to look for gold in an unknown sea. And there, in the treachery of the Portuguese king, in Pinzón's courage, treachery and greed, are all the elements of the European adventure in this part of the New World.

There is a myth, derived from the Southern states of America, of the gracious culture of the slave society. In the West Indian islands slavery and the latifundia created only grossness, men who ate 'like cormorants' and drank 'like porposes'; a society without standards, without noble aspirations, nourished by greed and cruelty; a society of whose illiteracy metropolitan administrators continued to complain right until the middle of the last century; illiteracy which encouraged Governor Vaughan of Jamaica to suggest the placing of a collection of books in the English language 'in the most conspicuous places where such of the gentry as are studious may always resort, since there is nothing more ridiculous than ignorance in a person of quality'; grossness to which traveller after traveller testifies and which made a seventeenth-century observer say of Barbados: 'This Iland is the Dunghill whareone England doth cast forth its rubidg: Rodgs and hors and such like peopel are those which are gennerally Broght heare. A rodge in England will hardly make a cheater heare; a Baud brought over puts one a demuor comportment, a whore if hansume makes a wife for sume rich planter.'

How can the history of this West Indian futility be written? What tone shall the historian adopt? Shall he be as academic as Sir Alan Burns,[2] protesting from time to time at some brutality, and setting West Indian brutality in the context of European brutality? Shall he, like Salvador de Madariaga,[3] weigh one set of brutalities against another, and conclude that one has not been described in all its foulness and that this is unfair to Spain? Shall he, like the West Indian historians, who can only now begin to face their history, be icily detached and tell the story of the slave trade as if it were just another aspect of mercantilism? The history of the islands can never be satisfactorily told. Brutality is not the only difficulty. History is built around achievement and creation; and nothing was created in the West Indies . . .

Twenty million Africans made the middle passage, and scarcely an African name remains in the New World. Until the other day African tribesmen on the screen excited derisive West Indian laughter; the darkie comic (whose values were the values of the Christian-Hellenic tradition) was more admired. In the pursuit of the Christian-Hellenic tradition, which some might see as a paraphrase for whiteness, the past has to be denied, the self despised. Black will be made white. It has been said that in concentration camps the inmates began after a time to believe that they were genuinely guilty. Pursuing the Christian-Hellenic tradition, the West Indian accepted his blackness as his guilt, and divided people into the white, fusty, musty, dusty, tea, coffee, cocoa, light black, dark black. He never seriously doubted the validity of the prejudices of the culture to which he aspired. In the French territories he aimed at Frenchness, in the Dutch territories at Dutchness; in the English territories he aimed at simple whiteness and modernity, Englishness being impossible.

Living in a borrowed culture, the West Indian, more than most, needs writers to tell him who he is and where he stands. Here the West Indian writers have failed. Most have so far only reflected and flattered the prejudices of their race or colour groups. Many a writer has displayed a concern, visible perhaps only to the West Indian, to show how removed his group is from blackness, how close to whiteness. The limits of this absurdity were reached in one novel when a light-skinned Negro (or, as the writer prefers to call people of this group, a 'good-class coloured') made a plea for tolerance towards black Negroes. In the context it was not the plea that mattered, but the behaviour: light-skinned Negroes, it was implied, have the same feelings as white people and the same prejudices, and behave just like white people in a certain type of novel. So the brown writer will have his brown heroes who behave whitely, if not well; they will further establish their position by being permitted to speak as abusively as possible of other groups. This yearning to be thought different and worthy is not a new thing. A hundred years ago Trollope[4] found that 'coloured girls of insecure class' delighted in speaking contemptuously of Negroes to him. 'I have heard this done by one whom I had absolutely taken for a Negro, and who was not using loud abusive language, but gently speaking of an inferior class.' The black writer is now, of course, able to retaliate; he might speak, as one writer has done, of 'English soldiers smelling of khaki and their race'. To the initiated one whole side of West Indian writing has little to do with literature, and much to do with the race war.

The insecure wish to be heroically portrayed. Irony and satire, which might help more, are not acceptable; and no writer wishes to let down his group. For this reason the lively and inventive Trinidad dialect, which has won West Indian writing many friends and as many enemies abroad, is disliked by some West Indians. They do not object to its use locally; the most popular column in Trinidad is a dialect column in the *Evening News* by the talented and witty person known as Macaw. But they object to its use in books which are read abroad. 'They must be does talk so by you,' one woman said to me. 'They don't talk so by me.' The Trinidadian expects his novels, like his advertisements, to have a detergent purpose, and it is largely for this reason that there are complaints about the scarcity of writing about what is called the middle class.

In fact there is a good deal of West Indian writing about the middle class, but the people tend to be so indistinguishable from white and are indeed so often genuinely white that the middle class cannot recognize itself. It is not easy to write about the West Indian middle class. The most exquisite gifts of irony and perhaps malice would be required to keep the characters from slipping into an unremarkable mid-Atlantic whiteness. They would have to be treated as real people with real problems and responsibilities and affections – and this has been done – but they would also have to be treated as people whose lives have been corrupted by a fantasy which is their own cross. Whether an honest exploration of this class will ever be attempted is doubtful. The gifts required, of subtlety and brutality, can grow only out of mature literature; and there can be advance towards this only when writers cease to think about letting down their sides . . . .

No writer can be blamed for reflecting his society. If the West Indian writer is to be blamed, it is because, by accepting and promoting the unimpressive race-and-colour values of his group, he has not only failed to diagnose the sickness of his society but has aggravated it . . . .

As the Trinidadian becomes a more reliable and efficient citizen, he will cease to be what he is. Already the gap between rich and poor – between the civil servant, the professional man, and the labourer – is widening. Class divisions are hardening and, in a land where no one can look back too far without finding a labourer or a crook, and sometimes a labourer who became a crook, members of the embryonic middle class are talking of their antecedents. Standards are being established by this class, and the fluidity of the society has diminished. With commercial radio and advertising agencies has also come all the apparatus of the modern society for joylessness, for the killing of the community spirit and the shutting up of people in their separate prisons of similar ambitions and tastes and selfishness: the class struggle, the political struggle, the race struggle.

When people speak of the race problem in Trinidad they do not mean the Negro-white problem. They mean the Negro-Indian rivalry. This will be denied by the whites, who will insist that the basic problem remains the contempt of their group for the non-white. Now that complaints about white prejudice are rarely heard, it is not uncommon to find whites scourging themselves for the prejudices of their group before black audiences. This they do by reporting outrageous statements made by members of their group and dissociating themselves from the sentiments.

The fact is that in Trinidad power is so evenly distributed – whites in business, Indians in business and the professions, Negroes in the professions and the civil service – that racial abuse is without meaning. . . .

The virtual by-passing of white prejudice was inevitable. The cultural involvement of the Negro was with the white world in general and not so much with the local whites, who had shown little interest in education and who rarely entered the professions. The break-up of the colonial system made plain their inaptitudes at the same time that it released the pent-up ambitions of the better equipped non-white. The chaotic social divisions also help. Each of the island's many cliques believes that it is the true élite. The expatriates believe they are the élite; so do the local whites, the businessmen, the professional men, the higher civil servants, the politicians, the sportsmen. This arrangement, whereby most people don't even know when they are being excluded, leaves everyone reasonably happy. And most important of all, the animosity that might have been directed against the whites has been channelled off against the Indians.

Throughout the Caribbean today the Negro's desire to assert himself is a constant quantity. This brings him in collision with white, coloured, Chinese, Syrians and Jews in Jamaica, white and coloured in Martinique, Indians in Trinidad. The animosity between Negroes and Indians is, at first sight, puzzling. At all levels they share the same language, the same ambitions – *My Mummy has a lovely Valor*[5] – and increasingly, the same pleasures. Their interests don't clash. The Negro is a town-dweller; the Indian is an agriculturist. The Negro with a good hand-writing and a head for intrigue goes into the civil service; the Indian similarly equipped goes into business. Both go into the professions.

Of late, with Indians entering the civil service and small-island Negroes muscling in on the taxi business, there has been a certain direct rivalry; but this is out-weighed by a long-standing division of labour which is taken so much for granted that Trinidadians are hardly aware of it. Coconut-sellers, for instance, are Indian; it would be unnatural and perhaps unwise to receive a coconut from a black hand. No one, not even an Indian, will employ a mason or a carpenter who is not a Negro. The lower down the scale one goes, the nicer the divisions of labour become. Negroes sell ice and its immediate by-products: shaved ice, 'presses', snowballs. Indians sell iced lollies. Before the war Indians swept the streets of Port of Spain; Negroes emptied the cesspits. Each felt a hearty contempt for the other; and when, during the war, Negroes from the smaller islands began sweeping the streets, it was felt by some Indians that this was another example of Indians losing their grip, the virtues of their fathers . . . .

All this speaks of accord. But Trinidad in fact teeters on the brink of racial war. Politics must be blamed; but there must have been an original antipathy for the politicians to work on. Matters are not helped by the fierce rivalry between Indians and Negroes as to who despises the other more. This particular rivalry is conducted by the liberal-minded, who will not be denied the pleasure of appealing to their group to show more tolerance towards the other group, and who are deeply annoyed when it is claimed by liberals of the other party that it is the other group which has to do the tolerating. There is also considerable rivalry as to who started the despising.

It is sufficient to state that the antipathy exists. The Negro has a deep contempt, as has been said, for all that is not white; his values are the values of white imperialism at its most bigoted. The Indian despises the Negro for not being an Indian; he has, in addition, taken over all the white prejudices against the Negro and with the convert's zeal regards as Negro everyone who has any tincture of Negro blood. 'The two races,' Froude[6] observed in 1887, 'are more absolutely apart than the white and the black. The Asiatic insists the more on his superiority in the fear perhaps that if he did not the white might forget it.' Like monkeys pleading for evolution, each claiming to be whiter than the other, Indians and Negroes appeal to the unacknowledged white audience to see how much they despise one another. They despise one another by reference to the whites; and the irony is that their antagonism should have reached its peak today, when white prejudices have ceased to matter.

Few non-Indians know much about the Indians, except that they live in the country, work on the land, are rich, fond of litigation and violence . . . . Nothing is known about Hinduism or Islam. The Muslim festival of Hosein, with its drum-beating and in the old days stick-fighting, is the only Indian festival which is known; Negroes sometimes beat the drums. Indian weddings are also known. There is little interest in the ritual; it is known only that at these weddings food is given to all comers. Even the simple distinction between Hindu and Muslim names is not known; and the Negro makes less effort than the average English person to pronounce Indian names correctly. This is partly because of the attitude that nothing which is not white is worth bothering about; partly because Indians are difficult to know; and partly because so many Indians have been modernizing themselves at such a rate that Indian customs have come to be regarded as things out of which people grow. So although Indians make up more than one-third of the population, their customs and ceremonies remain quaint and even exotic.

Everything which made the Indian alien in the society gave him strength. His alienness insulated him from the black-white struggle. He was taboo-ridden as no other person on the island; he had complicated rules about food and about what was unclean. His religion gave him values which were not the white values of the rest of the community, and preserved him from self-contempt; he never lost pride in his origins. More important than religion was his family organization, an enclosing self-sufficient world absorbed with its quarrels and jealousies, as difficult for the outsider to penetrate as for one of its members to escape. It protected and imprisoned, a static world, awaiting decay.

Islam is a static religion. Hinduism is not organized; it has no fixed articles, no hierarchy; it is constantly renewing itself and depends on the regular emergence of teachers and holy men. In Trinidad it could only wither; but its restrictions were tenacious. Marriage between unequal castes has only just ceased to cause trouble; marriage between Hindu and Muslim can still split a family; marriage outside the race is unthinkable. Only the urban Indian, the Indian of the middle class, and the Christian convert were able to move easily out of the Indian framework. The Indian Christian was more liberal and adaptable in every way; but, following far behind the Negro on the weary road to whiteness, he was more insecure.

Living by themselves in villages, the Indians were able to have a complete community life. It was a world eaten up with jealousies and family feuds and village feuds; but it was a world of its own, a community within the colonial society, without responsibility, with authority doubly and trebly removed. Loyalties were narrow: to the family, the village. This has been responsible for the village-headman type of politician the Indian favours, and explains why Indian leadership has been so deplorable, so unfitted to handle the mechanics of party and policy.

A peasant-minded, money-minded community, spiritually static because cut off from its roots, its religion reduced to rites without philosophy, set in a materialist colonial society: a combination of historical accidents and national temperament has turned the Trinidad Indian into the complete colonial, even more philistine than the white.

Much of the West Indian Negro's drive arises out of his desire to define his position in the world. The Indian, with no such problem, was content with his narrow loyalties. Whether he knew his language or practised his religion, the knowledge that a country called India existed was to him a pole. He felt no particular attachment to this country. It is said that Indian Independence in 1947 encouraged Indian racialism in Trinidad; but the explanation is too simple . . . . 1947 is not the date. 1946 is the date, when the first elections were held under universal adult suffrage in Trinidad. Then the bush lawyers and the village headmen came into their own, not only in the Indian areas but throughout the island. Then the loudspeaker van reminded people that they were of Aryan blood. Then, as was reported, the politician, soon to be rewarded by great wealth, bared his pale chest and shouted, 'I is a nigger too!'

Though now one racialism seems to be reacting on the other, each has different roots. Indian politicians have created Indian racialism out of a harmless egoism. Negro racialism is more complex. It is an overdue assertion of dignity; it has elements of bitterness; it has something of the urban mob requiring to be satisfied with bread and circuses. It has profound intellectual promptings as well, in the realization that the Negro problem lies not simply in the attitude of others to the Negro, but in the Negro's attitude to himself. It is as yet confused, for the Negro, while rejecting the guilt imposed on him by the white man, is not able to shake off the prejudices he has inherited from the white man . . . .

In the Negro-Indian conflict each side believes it can win. Neither sees that this rivalry threatens to destroy the Land of the Calypso . . . .

The West Indian colonial situation is unique because the West Indies, in all their racial and social complexity, are so completely a creation of Empire that the withdrawal of Empire is almost without meaning. In such a situation nationalism is the only revitalizing force. I believe that, below the ebullience and bravado, a positive nationalism existed in British Guiana in 1953. This was the achievement of the Jagans and Mr Burnham[7] and their colleagues, and it was destroyed by the suspension of the constitution in that year and – gratuitous humiliation – by the dispatch of troops. Colonial attitudes, so recently overcome, easily reasserted themselves. Under pressure, like the West Indians in London during the Notting Hill riots,[8] the country split into its component parts; and the energy which, already gathered, ought to have gone towards an ordered and overdue social revolution was dissipated in racial rivalry, factional strife and simple fear, creating the confusion which is today more dangerous to Guiana than the alleged plot of 1953 ....

[In Surinam] a nationalism has arisen which is unsettling the established order, proving that the objection to colonialism in the West Indies is not only economic or political or, as many believe, simply racial. Colonialism distorts the identity of the subject people, and the Negro in particular is bewildered and irritable. Racial equality and assimilation are attractive but only underline the loss, since to accept assimilation is in a way to accept a permanent inferiority. Nationalism in Surinam, feeding on no racial or economic resentments, is the profoundest anti-colonial movement in the West Indies. It is an idealist movement, and a rather sad one, for it shows how imprisoning for the West Indian his colonial culture is. Europe, the Surinam Nationalist says, is to be rejected as the sole source of enlightenment; Africa and Asia are to be brought in as well. But Europe is in the Nationalist's bones and he feels that Africa and Asia are contemptible and ridiculous . . . .

For seven months I had been travelling through territories which, unimportant except to themselves, and faced with every sort of problem, were exhausting their energies in petty power squabbles and the maintaining of the petty prejudices of petty societies. I had seen how deep in nearly every West Indian, high and low, were the prejudices of race; how often these prejudices were rooted in self-contempt; and how much important action they prompted. Everyone spoke of nation and nationalism but no one was willing to surrender the privileges or even the separateness of his group. Nowhere, except perhaps in British Guiana, was there any binding philosophy: there were only competing sectional interests. With an absence of a feeling of community, there was an absence of pride, and there was even cynicism. There was, for instance, little concern about West Indian emigration to Britain. It was a lower-class thing; it was a black thing; it was a Jamaican thing. At another level, it was regarded with malicious pleasure as a means of embarrassing the British people, a form of revenge; and in this pleasure there was no thought for the emigrants or the dignity of the nation about which so much was being said and which on every side was said to be 'emergent'. And the population was soaring – in thirty years Trinidad has more than doubled its population – and the race conflicts of every territory were growing sharper.

Dr Arthur Lewis[9] has drawn the distinction between 'protest' leaders and 'creative' leaders in colonial societies. It is a distinction of which the West Indies are yet scarcely aware. In the West Indies, with its large middle class and its abundance of talent, the protest leader is an anachronism, and a dangerous anachronism. For the uneducated masses, quick to respond to racial stirrings and childishly pleased with destructive gestures, the protest leader will always be a hero. The West Indies will never have a shortage of such leaders, and the danger of mob rule and authoritarianism will never cease to be real. The paternalism of colonial rule will have been replaced by the jungle politics of rewards and revenge, the text-book conditions for chaos.

NOTES

1. Thomas Warner landed on St Kitts in 1622. Having obtained wealthy backing, he returned in 1624 with some 40 or 50 settlers and he was later made the governor.
2. Sir Alan Burns (1887-1980) was born in St Kitts and was the governor of Belize, then British Honduras, from 1934 to 1940. He wrote *Colonial Civil Servant* (1949) and *History of the British West Indies* (1954), from which Naipaul took many quotations in *The Middle Passage*.
3. Salvador de Madariaga y Rojo (1886–1978) was a Spanish diplomat and historian who wrote about Spain and its colonial empire, as well as essays about literature and political philosophy.
4. Anthony Trollope (1815–82), an English novelist, travelled in the West Indies and wrote *The West Indies and the Spanish Main* (1860).
5. 'My Mummy has a lovely Valor. How do you manage to look so cool...cooking?' is from Trollope's *The West Indies and the Spanish Main* (1860).
6. James Anthony Froude (1818–94) was the Regius Professor of Modern History at Oxford University who travelled through the Caribbean and wrote *The English and the West Indies or the Bow of Ulysses* (1888). For J.J. Thomas' critique of this book see chapter 23 in this volume.
7. The People's Progressive party (PPP), led by Cheddi and Janet Jagan and Forbes Burnham, won the first election under universal adult suffrage in 1953 but the British government suspended the constitution. The PPP had achieved considerable inter-racial cooperation but politics soon polarised sharply along racial lines between Jagan's PPP and Burnham's People's National Congress.
8. There were 'race riots' in Notting Hill, an area of London in which many West Indians had settled, in 1958. In fact, these riots really consisted of groups of whites attacking black people, and West Indians organised to defend themselves.
9. Sir W. Arthur Lewis (1915–91), from St Lucia, won the Nobel Prize for economics in 1979 for his research on economic development. His best known book is *The Theory*

of Economic Growth (1954). He taught at the Universities of London and Manchester, was the Vice Chancellor of the University of the West Indies from 1959 to 1963, and then the James Madison Professor of Political Economy at Princeton University until he retired in 1983 (see chapter 36 in this volume).

❧ Twenty-Nine ❧

C.L.R. James

Cyril Lionel Robert James (1901–89) grew up in the small town of Tunapuna in Trinidad, the eldest child in a middle-class black family. His father was a school teacher and James studied in his father's classroom before going, at the age of ten, to Queen's Royal College (QRC), the colony's most prestigious secondary school in Port of Spain. In the 1920s, James taught at QRC and the Government Teachers' College and participated in a literary group that produced two issues of a journal called Trinidad *and then* The Beacon. *James and Alfred Mendes (1897–1991), a Portuguese Creole Trinidadian, pioneered social realism in West Indian literature. When James went to England in 1932, he had manuscripts of a novel and a study of Captain Arthur A. Cipriani, the politician and labour leader, in his luggage:* Minty Alley *(London, 1936) and* The Life of Captain Cipriani: An Account of British Government in the West Indies *(London, 1932). A shortened version of the latter, titled* The Case for West Indian Self-Government, *was published in 1933.*

While he earned his living reporting on cricket for the Manchester Guardian, *James moved in radical anti-imperialist circles. He joined with an old Trinidadian childhood friend, Malcolm Nurse (1903–59) who had changed his name to George Padmore and become a member of the Communist International (Comintern). James was then a Trotskyist and so opposed the 'Moscow line' and Padmore left the Comintern when it changed its policy regarding national liberation movements in Africa and Asia in 1933. After Padmore moved to London in 1935, the two Trinidadians worked, together with other West Indians and Africans, in support of Ethiopia and Pan-Africanism. During this period James wrote* World Revolution *(London, 1938) and his masterpiece,* The Black Jacobins: Toussaint L'Ouverture and the San Domingo Revolution *(London, 1938). Based on considerable research and written with the excitement of a novel,* The Black Jacobins *identified the enslaved masses of Haiti as the makers of their own, and indeed of world, history. James discredited the old claim that slavery had been brought to an end simply by the philanthropy of the abolitionists and analysed the relationship between leaders and masses in a revolution. So that nobody could miss the point, he stated in his conclusion that the Black Jacobins of Haiti offered an example to the people of Africa in their struggle against imperialism.*

In 1938, when James went to the United States, he was a Pan-African Trotskyist. For the next 15 years, working and writing often under assumed names, he was the most intellectual revolutionary and the most revolutionary intellectual in the United States. He broke away from Trotskyism and developed his own theory of revolution. Under the name J.R. Johnson he was a leader of the 'Johnson-Forest Tendency' (Forest was a Russian immigrant, Raya Dunayevskaya), a small group of revolutionaries that struggled through the Cold War. James elaborated his theories in State Capitalism and World Revolution *(1950) and his principal philosophical document,* Notes on Dialectics: Hegel, Marx, Lenin *(1948). In 1952, while harassed by the FBI and interned on Ellis Island prior to his deportation to England, he wrote a study of Herman Melville and American civilisation,* Mariners, Renegades and Castaways *(1953).*

James returned to Trinidad in 1958 and found a different political situation than the one he had left 26 years before. He participated in the People's National Movement (PNM) as the editor of The Nation *and his commitment to the ideal of federation is reflected in his becoming the secretary of the West Indian Federal Labour Party. He told an audience in Guyana in 1958, 'Federation is the means, and the only means, whereby the West Indies and British Guiana can accomplish the transition from colonialism to national independence, can create the basis for a new nation; and by reorganizing the economic system and the national life give us our place in the modern community of nations' ('Lecture on Federation,' in* At the Rendezvous of Victory: Selected Writings *[London, 1986], 60).*

In 1960, James resigned as editor of The Nation *and broke with the PNM. A series of lectures he gave at the public library in Port of Spain was published as* Modern Politics *(1960) but Eric Williams ordered it to be seized and held. In 1962, after recovering from a serious automobile accident in Jamaica, James went back to England. He published* Party Politics in the West Indies *(1962) and* Beyond a Boundary *(1963), an extraordinary book that is partly autobiography and partly about cricket, but is all about the changing West Indian political culture.*

When James returned to Trinidad in 1965, ostensibly to report on the tour of England's cricket team in the West Indies, he was briefly placed under house arrest for fear that he would become involved in the current labour unrest and become a radical opposition leader. He helped create the Workers' and Farmers' party but in the 1966 elections all its candidates lost their deposits and James left Trinidad again. In the late 1960s and the 1970s, James lectured at universities in Africa and the United States, becoming an intellectual guide and model for a new generation of scholars including Walter Rodney, Orlando Patterson, Paget Henry and Manning Marable. In 1980, he returned to Trinidad as an honoured guest of the Oilfield Workers' Trade Union (OWTU) which created an institute named after him in San Fernando. Three volumes of his essays were published in London, where James lived his last years. In 1983, he was awarded an honorary doctorate by the University of the West Indies and, in 1986, received the Trinity Cross, Trinidad and Tobago's highest national honour. He died in London at the age of 88 and was buried in Tunapuna after a huge 'Celebration of a Life' organised by the OWTU.

James wrote the essay 'From Toussaint L'Ouverture to Fidel Castro' as an appendix for a new edition of The Black Jacobins *that was published in 1963, in order to do for the future of the Caribbean what he had done for Africa in 1938. In his preface to this edition, written in 1962, he wrote, 'Writers on the West Indies always relate them to their approximation to Britain, France, Spain and America, that is to say, to Western civilisation, never in relation to their own history. This is here attempted for the first time.'*

From Toussaint L'Ouverture to Fidel Castro

Toussaint L'Ouverture is not here linked to Fidel Castro because both led revolutions in the West Indies. Nor is the link a convenient or journalistic demarcation of historical time. What took place in French San Domingo in 1792–1804 reappeared in Cuba in 1958. The slave revolution of French San Domingo managed to emerge from

> ... The pass and fell incensed points
> Of mighty opposites.[1]

Five years later the people of Cuba are still struggling in the same toils.

Castro's revolution is of the twentieth century as much as Toussaint's was of the eighteenth. But despite the distance of over a century and a half, both are West

Indian. The people who made them, the problems and the attempts to solve them, are peculiarly West Indian, the product of a peculiar origin and a peculiar history. West Indians first became aware of themselves as a people in the Haitian Revolution. Whatever its ultimate fate, the Cuban Revolution marks the ultimate stage of a Caribbean quest for national identity. In a scattered series of disparate islands the process consists of a series of unco-ordinated periods of drift, punctuated by spurts, leaps and catastrophes. But the inherent movement is clear and strong.

The history of the West Indies is governed by two factors, the sugar plantation and Negro slavery. That the majority of the population in Cuba was never slave does not affect the underlying social identity. Wherever the sugar plantation and slavery existed, they imposed a pattern. It is an original pattern, not European, not African, not a part of the American main, not native in any conceivable sense of that word, but West Indian, *sui generis*, with no parallel anywhere else.

The sugar plantation has been the most civilising as well as the most demoralising influence in West Indian development. When three centuries ago the slaves came to the West Indies, they entered directly into the large-scale agriculture of the sugar plantation, which was a modern system. It further required that the slaves live together in a social relation far closer than any proletariat of the time. The cane when reaped had to be rapidly transported to what was factory production. The product was shipped abroad for sale. Even the cloth the slaves wore and the food they ate was imported. The Negroes, therefore, from the very start lived a life that was in its essence a modern life. That is their history – as far as I have been able to discover, a unique history.

In the first part of the seventeenth century, early settlers from Europe had made quite a success of individual production. The sugar plantation drove them out. The slaves saw around them a social life of a certain material culture and ease, the life of the sugar-plantation owners. The clever, the lucky and the illegitimate became domestics or artisans attached to the plantation or the factory. Long before the bus and the taxi, the small size of the islands made communication between the rural areas and the urban quick and easy. The plantation owners and the merchants lived an intense political life in which the ups and downs of sugar and in time the treatment and destiny of the slaves played a crucial and continuous role. The sugar plantation dominated the lives of the islands to such a degree that the white skin alone saved those who were not plantation owners or bureaucrats from the humiliations and hopelessness of the life of the slave. That was and is the pattern of West Indian life.

The West Indies between Toussaint L'Ouverture and Fidel Castro falls naturally into three periods: I. The Nineteenth Century; II. Between the Wars; III. After World War II.

I.   THE NINETEENTH CENTURY

The nineteenth century in the Caribbean is the century of the abolition of slavery. But the passing of the years shows that the decisive patterns of Caribbean development took form in Haiti.

Toussaint could see no road for the Haitian economy but the sugar plantation. Dessalines was a barbarian. After Dessalines came Christophe, a man of conspicuous ability and within his circumstances an enlightened ruler. He also did his best (a cruel best) with the plantation. But with the abolition of slavery and the achievement of independence the plantation, indelibly associated with slavery, became unbearable. Pétion[2] acquiesced in substituting subsistence production for the sugar plantation.

For the first century and a half of Haiti's existence there was no international opinion jealous of the independence of small nations; no body of similar states, ready to raise a hue and cry at any threat to one of their number; no theory of aid from the wealthy countries to the poorer ones. Subsistence production resulted in economic decay and every variety of political disorder. Yet it has preserved the national independence, and out of this has come something new which has captured a continent and holds its place in the institutions of the world.

This is what has happened. For over a century after independence the Haitians attempted to form a replica of European, i.e., French civilisation in the West Indies. Listen to the Haitian Ambassador, M. Constantin Mayard, in Paris in 1938:

> French our institutions, French our public and civil legislation, French our literature, French our university, French the curriculum of our schools ...
>
> Today when one of us [a Haitian] appears in a circle of Frenchmen, 'welcome smiles at him in every eye'. The reason is without doubt that your nation, ladies and gentlemen, knows that within the scope of its colonial expansion it has given to the Antilles and above all to San Domingo all that it could give of itself and its substance... It has founded there, in the mould of its own national type, with its blood, with its language, its institutions, its spirit and its soil, a local type, an historic race, in which its sap still runs and where it is remade complete.

Generation after generation the best sons of the Haitian élite were educated in Paris. They won distinctions in the intellectual life of France. The burning race hatred of pre-independence days had vanished. But a line of investigators and travellers had held up to international ridicule the hollow pretensions of Haitian civilisation. In 1913 the ceaseless battering from foreign pens was re-enforced by the bayonets of American Marines.[3] Haiti had to find a national rallying-point. They looked for it where it can only be found, at home, more precisely, in their own backyard. They discovered what is known today as Negritude. It is the prevailing social ideology among politicians and intellectuals in every part of Africa. It is the subject of heated elaboration and disputation wherever Africa and Africans are discussed. But in its origin and development it is West Indian, and could not have been anything else but West Indian, the peculiar product of their peculiar history.

The Haitians did not know it as Negritude. To them it seemed purely Haitian. Two-thirds of the population of French San Domingo in Toussaint's time had made the Middle Passage. The whites had emigrated or been exterminated. The Mulattoes who were masters had their eyes fixed on Paris. Left to themselves, the Haitian peasantry resuscitated to a remarkable degree the lives they had lived in Africa. Their method of cultivation, their family relations and social practices, their drums, songs and music, such art as they practised and above all their religion which became famous, Vodun – all this was Africa in the West Indies. But it was Haitian, and the Haitian élite leapt at it. In 1926 Dr. Price Mars in his famous book, *Ainsi Parla L'Oncle*[4] (This is What Uncle Said), described with loving care the way of life of the Haitian peasant. Rapidly, learned and scientific societies were formed. The African way of life of the Haitian peasant became the axis of Haitian literary creation. No plantation labourer, with free land to defend, rallied to the cause.

The Caribbean territories drifted along. At the end of the nineteenth century, Cuba produced a great revolution which bears the name 'The Ten Years' War'. It produced prodigies – no West Indian pantheon but will have among its most resplendent stars the names of José Martí the political leader and Maceo the soldier.[5] They were men in the full tradition of Jefferson, Washington and Bolivar. That was their strength and that was their weakness. They were leaders of a national revolutionary party and a national revolutionary army. Toussaint L'Ouverture and Fidel Castro led a revolutionary people. The war for independence began again and ended in the Platt Amendment of 1904.[6]

It was just one year after the Platt Amendment that there first appeared what has turned out to be a particular feature of West Indian life–the non-political writer devoted to the analysis and expression of West Indian society. The first was the greatest of them all, Fernando Ortiz. For over half a century, at home or in exile, he has been the tireless exponent of Cuban life and *Cubinidad*, the spirit of Cuba. The history of Spanish imperialism, sociology, anthropology, ethnology, all the related sciences are his medium of investigation into Cuban life, folklore, literature, music, art, education, criminality, everything Cuban. A most distinctive feature of his work is the number of solid volumes he has devoted to Negro and Mulatto life in Cuba. A quarter of a century before the Writers' Project of the New Deal began the discovery of the United States, Ortiz set out to discover his native land, a West Indian island. In essence it is the first and only comprehensive study of the West Indian people. Ortiz ushered the Caribbean into the thought of the twentieth century and kept it there.

II. BETWEEN THE WARS

Before World War I Haiti began to write another chapter in the record of the West Indian struggle for national independence. Claiming the need to recover debts and restore order, the Marines, as we have seen, invaded Haiti in 1913. The whole nation resisted. A general strike was organized and led by the literary intellectuals who had discovered the Africanism of their peasants as a means of national identity. The Marines left, and Negroes and Mulattoes resumed their fratricidal conflicts. But Haiti's image of itself had changed. 'Goodbye to the Marseillaise', a famous phrase by one of the best-known of Haitian writers, signifies the substitution of Africa for France in the first independent West Indian state. Africa in the West Indies would seem to have been evoked by an empirical need and accidental circumstance. It was not so. Long before the Marines left Haiti, the role of Africa in the consciousness of the West Indies people had proved itself to be a stage in the development of the West Indian quest for a national identity.

The story is one of the strangest stories in any period of history. The individual facts are known. But no one has ever put them together and drawn to them the attention they deserve. Today the emancipation of Africa is one of the outstanding events of contemporary history. Between the wars when this emancipation was being prepared, the unquestioned leaders of the movement in every public sphere, in Africa itself, in Europe and in the United States, were not Africans but West Indians. First the unquestioned facts.

Two black West Indians using the ink of Negritude wrote their names imperishably on the front pages of the history of our time. Standing at the head is Marcus Garvey. Garvey, an immigrant from Jamaica, is the only Negro who has succeeded in building a mass movement among American Negroes. Arguments about the number of his followers dispute the number of millions. Garvey advocated the return of Africa to the Africans and people of African descent. He organised, very rashly and incompetently, the Black Star Line, a steamship company for transporting people of African descent from the New World back to Africa. Garvey did not last long. His movement took really effective form in about 1921, and by 1926 he was in a United States prison (some charge about misusing the mails); from prison he was deported home to Jamaica. But all this is only the frame and scaffolding. Garvey never set foot in Africa. He spoke no African language. His conceptions of Africa seemed to be a West Indian island and West Indian people multiplied a thousand times over. But Garvey managed to convey to Negroes everywhere (and to the rest of the world) his passionate belief that Africa was the home of a civilisation which had once been great and would be great again. When you bear in mind the slenderness of his resources, the vast material forces and the pervading social conceptions which automatically sought to destroy him, his achievement remains one of the propagandistic miracles of this century.

Garvey's voice reverberated inside Africa itself. The King of Swaziland told Mrs. Marcus Garvey that he knew the name of only two black men in the Western world: Jack Johnson, the boxer who defeated the white man Jim Jeffries, and Marcus Garvey. Jomo Kenyatta[7] has related to this writer how in 1921 Kenya nationalists, unable to read, would gather round a reader of Garvey's newspaper, the *Negro World*, and listen to an article two or three times. Then they would run various ways through the forest, carefully to repeat the whole, which they had memorised, to Africans hungry for some doctrine which lifted them from the servile consciousness in which Africans lived. Dr. Nkrumah,[8] a graduate student of history and philosophy at two American universities, has placed it on record that of all the writers who educated and influenced him, Marcus Garvey stands first. Garvey found the cause of Africans and of people of African descent not so much neglected as unworthy of consideration. In little more than half of ten years he had made it a part of the political consciousness of the world. He did not know the word Negritude but he knew the thing. With enthusiasm he would have welcomed the nomenclature, with justice claimed paternity.

The other British West Indian was from Trinidad, George Padmore.[9] Padmore shook the dust of the cramping West Indies from his feet in the early 1920's and went to the United States. When he died in 1959, eight countries sent representatives to his funeral, which was held in London. His ashes were interred in Ghana; and all assert that in that country of political demonstrations, there never has been a political demonstration such as was evoked by these obsequies of Padmore. Peasants from remote areas who, it could have been thought, had never heard his name, found their way to Accra to pay the last tribute to this West Indian who had spent his life in their service.

Once in America he became an active Communist. He was moved to Moscow to head their Negro department of propaganda and organisation. In that post he became the best known and most trusted of agitators for African independence. In 1935, seeking alliances, the Kremlin separated Britain and France as 'democratic imperialisms' from Germany and Japan, making the 'Fascist imperialisms' the main target of Russian and Communist propaganda. This reduced activity for African emancipation to a farce: Germany and Japan had no colonies in Africa. Padmore broke instantly with the Kremlin. He went to London where, in a single room, he earned a meagre living by journalism, to be able to continue the work he had done in the Kremlin. He wrote books and pamphlets, attended all anti-imperialist meetings and spoke and moved resolutions wherever possible. He made and maintained an ever-increasing range of nationalist contacts in all sections of African society and the colonial world. He preached and taught Pan-Africanism and organised an African Bureau. He published a journal devoted to African emancipation (the present writer was its editor).

This is no place to attempt even a summary of the work and influence of the most striking West Indian creation between the wars, Padmore's African Bureau. Between the wars it was the only African organisation of its kind in existence. Of the seven members of the committee, five were West Indians, and they ran the organisation. Of them, only Padmore had ever visited Africa. It could not have been accidental that this West Indian attracted two of the most remarkable Africans of this or any other time. A founder-member and a simmering volcano of African nationalism was Jomo Kenyatta. But even better fortune was in store for us.

The present writer met Nkrumah, then a student at the University of Pennsylvania, and wrote to Padmore about him. Nkrumah came to England to study law and there formed an association with Padmore; they worked at the doctrines and premises of Pan-Africanism and elaborated the plans which culminated in Nkrumah's leading the people of the Gold Coast to the independence of Ghana. This revolution by the Gold Coast was the blow which made so many cracks in the piece of African colonialism that it proved impossible ever to stick them together again. With Nkrumah's victory the association did not cease. After independence was signed and sealed, Nkrumah sent for Padmore, installed him once more in an office devoted to African emancipation and, under the auspices of an African government, this West Indian, as he had done in 1931 under the auspices of the Kremlin, organised in Accra the first conference of independent African states, followed, twenty-five years after the first, by the second world conference of fighters for African freedom. Dr. Banda, Patrice Lumumba, Nyerere, Tom Mboya,[10] were some of those who attended the conference. Jomo Kenyatta was not there only because he was in jail. NBC made a national telecast of the interment of his ashes in Christiansborg Castle, at which Padmore was designated the Father of African Emancipation, a distinction challenged by no one. To the degree that they had to deal with us in the period between the wars, many learned and important persons and institutions looked upon us and our plans and hopes for Africa as the fantasies of some politically illiterate West Indians. It was they who completely misconceived a continent, not we. They should have learned from that experience. They have not. The same myopic vision which failed to focus Africa is now peering at the West Indies.

The place of Africa in the West Indian development is documented as few historical visions are documented.

In 1939 a black West Indian from the French colony of Martinique published in Paris the finest and most famous poem ever written about Africa, *Cahier d'un retour au pays natal* (Statement of a Return to the Country Where I was Born). Aimé Césaire first describes Martinique, the poverty, misery and vices of the masses of the people, the lickspittle subservience of the coloured middle classes. But the poet's education has been consummated in Paris. As a West Indian he has nothing national to be aware of. He is overwhelmed by the gulf that separates him from the people where he was born. He feels that he must go there. He does so and discovers a new version of what the Haitians, as had Garvey and Padmore, had discovered: that salvation for the West Indies lies in Africa, the original home and ancestry of the West Indian people.

The poet gives us a view of Africans as he sees them.

> . . . *my Negritude is not a stone, its*
> *deafness a sounding board for*
> *the noises of the day*
> *my Negritude is not a mere spot of*
> *dead water on the dead eye of*
> *the earth*
> *my Negritude is no tower, no cathedral*
> *it cleaves into the red flesh of the*
> *teeming earth*
> *it cleaves into the glowing flesh of*
> *the heavens*
> *it penetrates the seamless bondage of*
> *my unbending patience*
> *Hoorah for those who never invented*
> *anything*
> *for those who never explored anything*
> *for those who never mastered anything*
> *but who, possessed, give themselves up*
> *to the essence of each thing*
> *ignorant of the coverings but possessed*
> *by the pulse of things*
> *indifferent to mastering but taking the*
> *chances of the world . . .*

In contrast to this vision of the African unseparated from the world, from Nature, a living part of all that lives, Césaire immediately places the civilisation that has scorned and persecuted Africa and Africans.

> *Listen to the white world*
> *its horrible exhaustion from its*
> *immense labours*
> *its rebellious joints cracking under*
> *the pitiless stars*
> *its blue steel rigidities, cutting*

> *through the mysteries of the*
> *flesh*
> *listen to their vainglorious conquests*
> *trumpeting their defeats*
> *listen to the grandiose alibis of their*
> *pitiful floundering*

The poet wants to be an architect of this unique civilisation, a commissioner of its blood, a guardian of its refusal to accept.

> *But in so doing, my heart, preserve*
> *me from all hate*
> *do not turn me into a man of hate of*
> *whom I think only with hate*
> *for in order to project myself into*
> *this unique race*
> *you know the extent of my boundless*
> *love*
> *you know that it is not from hatred*
> *of other races*
> *that I seek to be cultivator of this*
> *unique race . . .*

He returns once more to the pitiful spectre of West Indian life, but now with hope.

> *for it is not true that the work of man*
> *is finished*
> *that man has nothing more to do in the*
> *world but be a parasite in the world*
> *that all we now need is to keep in step*
> *with the world*
> *but the work of man is only just beginning*
> *and it remains to man to conquer all*
> *the violence entrenched in the recesses*
> *of his passion*
> *and no race possesses the monopoly of beauty,*
> *of intelligence, of force, and there*
> *is a place for all at the rendezvous*
> *of victory . . .*

Here is the centre of Césaire's poem. By neglecting it, Africans and the sympathetic of other races utter loud hurrahs that drown out common sense and reason. The work of man is not finished. Therefore the future of the African is not to continue not discovering anything. The monopoly of beauty, of intelligence, of force, is possessed by no race, certainly not by those who possess Negritude. Negritude is what one race brings to the common rendezvous where all will strive for the new world of the poet's vision. The vision of the poet is not economics or politics, it is poetic, *sui generis*, true unto itself and needing no other truth. But it would be the most vulgar racism not to see here a poetic incarnation of Marx's famous sentence, 'The real history of humanity will begin'.

From Césaire's strictly poetic affinities we have to turn our faces if even with distinct loss to our larger general purpose. But *Cahier* has united elements in modern thought which seemed destined to remain asunder. These had better be enumerated.

1. He has made a union of the African sphere of existence with existence in the Western world.
2. The past of mankind and the future of mankind are historically and logically linked.
3. No longer from external stimulus but from their own self-generated and independent being and motion will Africa and Africans move towards an integrated humanity.

It is the Anglo-Saxon poet who has seen for the world in general what the West Indian has seen concretely for Africa.

> Here the impossible union
> Of spheres of existence is actual,
> Here the past and future
> Are conquered, and reconciled,
> Where action were otherwise movement
> Of that which is only moved
> And has in it no source of movement–

Mr. Eliot's[11] conclusion is 'Incarnation'; Césaire's, Negritude.

Cahier appeared in 1938 in Paris. A year before that *The Black Jacobins* had appeared in London. The writer had made the forward step of resurrecting not the decadence but the grandeur of the West Indian people. But as is obvious all through the book and particularly in the last pages, it is Africa and African emancipation that he has in mind.

Today (but only today) we can define what motivated this West Indian preoccupation with Africa between the wars. The West Indians were and had always been Western-educated. West Indian society confined black men to a very narrow strip of social territory. The first step to freedom was to go abroad. *Before they could begin to see themselves as a free and independent people they had to clear from minds the stigma that anything African was inherently inferior and degraded.* The road to West Indian national identity lay through Africa.

The West Indian national community constantly evades racial categorisation. After Ortiz, it was another white West Indian who in the same period proved himself to be the greatest politician in the democratic tradition whom the West Indies has ever known.

Arthur Andrew Cipriani was a French Creole in the island of Trinidad who came into public life as an officer in a West Indian contingent in World War I. It was in the army that many of the soldiers, a medley from all the British West Indian islands, for the first time wore shoes consistently. But they were the product of their peculiar history. The speed with which they adjusted themselves to the spiritual and material requirements of a modern war amazed all observers, from General Allenby down. Cipriani made a reputation for himself by his militant defence of the regiment against all prejudice, official and unofficial. To the end of his days he spoke constantly of the recognition they had won. By profession a trainer of horses, it was only after much persuasion that, on his return home after the war, already a man over forty, he entered politics. He at once put himself forward as the champion of the common people, in his own phrase, 'the barefooted man'. Before very long this white man was acknowledged as leader by hundreds of thousands of black people and East Indians. An utterly fearless man, he never left the colonial government in any doubt as to what it was up against. All who ever heard him speak remember his raising of his right hand and his slow enunciation of the phrase, 'If I raise my little finger . . .' Against tremendous odds he forced the government to capitulate on workmen's compensation, the eight-hour day, trade union legislation and other elementary constituents of democracy. Year after year he was elected mayor of the capital city. He made the mayoralty a centre of opposition to the British Colonial Office and all its works.

Cipriani always treated West Indians as a modern contemporary people. He declared himself to be a socialist and day in and day out, inside and outside of the legislature, he attacked capitalists and capitalism. He attached his party to the British Labour Party and scrupulously kept his followers aware of their privileges and responsibilities as members of the international labour movement. Cipriani was that rare type of politician to whom words expressed realities. Long before any of the other territories of the colonial empires, he not only raised the slogans of national independence and federation of the British West Indian territories, he went tirelessly from island to island mobilising public opinion in general and the labour movement in particular in support of these slogans. He died in 1945. The islands had never seen before and have not seen since anything or anybody like him.

The West Indian masses jumped ahead even of Cipriani. In 1937, among the oil field workers in Trinidad, the largest proletarian grouping in the West Indies, a strike began. Like a fire along a tinder track, it spread to the entire island, then from island to island, ending in an upheaval at the other end of the curve, in Jamaica, thousands of miles away. The colonial government in Jamaica collapsed completely and two local popular leaders had to take over the responsibility of restoring some sort of social order.[12] The heads of the government in Trinidad and Tobago saved their administrations (but earned the wrath of the imperial government) by expressing sympathy with the revolt.[13] The British Government sent a Royal Commission, which took much evidence, discovered long-standing evils, and made proposals by no means unintelligent or reactionary.[14] As usual they were late, they were slow. Had Cipriani been the man he was ten years earlier, self-government, federation and economic regeneration, which he had advocated so strenuously and so long, could have been initiated then. But the old warrior was nearly seventy. He flinched at the mass upheavals which he more than anyone else had prepared, and the opportunity was lost. But he had destroyed a legend and established once and for all that the West Indian people were ready to follow the most advanced theories of an uncomprising leadership.

III.   AFTER WORLD WAR II

Cipriani had built soundly and he left behind a Caribbean Labour Congress devoted to federation, independence and the creation of an enlightened peasantry. But what has happened to Castro's Cuba is inherent in these unfortunate islands. In 1945 the Congress, genuinely West Indian, joined the World Federation of Trade Unions. But in 1948 that body split into the World Federation of Trade Unions of the East and the International Confederation of Free Trade Unions of the West. The split in the international split the Caribbean Labour Congress and it lost its place as the leader and inspirer of a genuinely West Indian movement. The British Colonial Office took the coloured middle class under its wing. These gradually filled the Civil Service and related organisations; they took over the political parties, and with the parties, the old colonial system.

What is this old colonial system? It is the oldest Western relic of the seventeenth century still alive in the world today, surrounded on all sides by a modern population.

The West Indies has never been a traditional colonial territory with clearly distinguished economic and political relations between two different cultures. Native culture there was none. The aboriginal Amerindian civilisation had been destroyed.

Every succeeding year, therefore, saw the labouring population, slave or free, incorporating into itself more and more of the language, customs, aims and outlook of its masters. It steadily grew in numbers until it became a terrifying majority of the total population. The ruling minority therefore was in the position of the father who produced children and had to guard against being supplanted by them. There was only one way out, to seek strength abroad. This beginning has lasted unchanged to this very day.

The dominant industrial structure has been the sugar plantation. For over two hundred years the sugar industry has tottered on the brink of disaster, remaining alive by an unending succession of last-minute rescues by gifts, concessions, quotas from the metropolitan power or powers.

SUGAR MANUFACTURERS' 'GRIM FUTURE'
From our Correspondent

Georgetown, Sept.3

The British West Indies Sugar Association's chairman, Sir Robert
Kirkwood, has stated here that cane sugar manufacturers were facing
a grim future and the position was reaching a stage where beet sugar
production should be restricted to provide cane manufacturers with
an enlarged market. Sir Robert pointed out that Britain's
participation in the European Common Market should be no threat
to sugar manufacturers in the region provided preferences under the
Commonwealth sugar agreement were preserved .

You would be able to read the same in any European newspaper at regular intervals during the last two hundred years. Recent official reports on the life and labour of the plantation labourer are moved to language remarkably similar to that of the non-conformist agitators against plantation slavery. There are economists and scientists today in the West Indies who believe that the most fortunate economic occurrence would be a blight that would destroy the sugar cane completely and thus compel some new type of economic development.

As they have been from the first days of slavery, financial power and its mechanism are today entirely in the hands of metropolitan organisations and their agents.

Such a Westernized population needs quantities of pots, pans, plates, spoons, knives, forks, paper, pencils, pens, cloth, bicycles, buses for public transport, automobiles, all the elementary appurtenances of civilisation which the islands do not manufacture, not forgetting Mercedes-Benzes, Bentleys, Jaguars and Lincolns.

In this type of commerce the dominating elements are the foreign manufacturers and the foreign banks. The most revealing feature of this trade and the oldest is the still massive importation of food, including fresh vegetables.

The few industries of importance, such as oil and bauxite, are completely in the hands of foreign firms, and the local politicians run a ferocious competition with each other in offering inducements to similar firms to establish new industries here and not there.

As with material, so with intellectual necessities. In island after island the daily newspaper is entirely in the hands of foreign firms. Radio and television cannot evade the fate of newspapers.

In 1963 the old colonial system is not what it was in 1863; in 1863 it was not what it had been in 1763 or 1663. The fundamentals outlined above, however, have not changed. But for the first time the system is now threatened, not from without but from within, not by communism, not by socialism, but by plain, simple parliamentary democracy. The old colonial system in the West Indies was not a democratic system, was not born as such. It cannot live with democracy. Within a West Indian island the old colonial system and democracy are incompatible. One has to go. That is the logic of development of every West Indian territory, Cuba, the Dominican Republic, Haiti, the former British colonies, the former French colonies, and even Puerto Rico, the poor relation of the wealthy United States.

The supreme wrong of West Indian politics is that the old colonial system has so isolated the ruling classes from the national community that plain, ordinary parliamentary democracy, *suffused with a sense of national identity*, can remake the islands.

Statistics of production and the calculations of votes together form the surest road towards misunderstanding the West Indies. To which for good measure add the antagonism of races. The people of the West Indies were born in the seventeenth century, in a Westernized productive and social system. Members of different African tribes were carefully split up to lessen conspiracy, and they were therefore compelled to master the European languages, highly complex products of centuries of civilisation. From the start there had been the gap, constantly growing, between the rudimentary conditions of the life of the slave and the language he used. There was therefore in West Indian society an inherent antagonism between the consciousness of the black masses and the reality of their lives, inherent in that it was constantly produced and reproduced not by agitators but by the very conditions of the society itself. It is the modern media of mass communication which have made essence into existence. For an insignificant sum per month, the black masses can hear on the radio news of Dr. Nkrumah, Jomo Kenyatta, Dr. Julius Banda,[15] Prime Minister Nehru,[16] events and personalities of the United Nations and all the capitals of the world. They can wrestle with what the West thinks of the East and what the East thinks of the West. The cinema presents actualities and not infrequently stirs the imagination with the cinematic masterpieces of the world. Every hour on the hour all variations of food, clothing, household necessities and luxuries are presented as absolutely essential to a civilised existence. All this to a population which over large areas still lives in conditions little removed from slavery.

The high material civilisation of the white minority is now fortified by the concentration of the coloured middle classes on making salaries and fees do the work of incomes. Sometimes a quarter of the population is crowded into the capital city, the masses irresistibly attracted by the contrast between what they see and hear and the lives they live. This was the tinder to which Castro placed a match. Historical tradition, education in the sense of grappling with the national past, there is none. History as taught is what it always has been, propaganda for those, whoever they may be, who administer the old colonial system. Power here is more naked than in any other part of the world. Hence the brutality, savagery, even personal cruelties of the régimes of Trujillo and Duvalier,[17] and the power of the Cuban Revolution.

This is the instrument on which perform all West Indian soloists, foreign or native. Take the French West Indian islands of Martinique and Guadeloupe. The colonial administration declared and acted for Vichy,[18] the mass of the population for the Resistance. Vichy defeated, the islands whole-heartedly became departments of France,[19] anxious to be assimilated into French civilisation. But the hand of the Paris administration, notoriously heavy in the provincial administrations of France itself, is a crushing weight on any attempt to change the old colonial system. To-day the mass of the population, disillusioned, is demanding independence. Their students in Paris are leading the struggle with blood, with boldness and with brilliance available to all who use the French language.

The British system, unlike the French, does not crush the quest for a national identity. Instead, it stifles it. It formed a federation of its Caribbean colonies. But the old colonial system consisted of insular economies, each with its financial and economic capital in London. A federation meant that the economic line of direction should no longer be from island to London, but from island to island. But that involved the break-up of the old colonial system. The West Indian politicians preferred the break-up of the Federation. Two of the islands have actually been granted independence.[20] The Queen of England is their queen. They receive royal visits; their legislatures begin with prayers; their legislative bills are read three times; a mace has been presented to each of these distant infants by the Mother of Parliaments; their prominent citizens can receive an assortment of letters after their names, and in time the prefix 'Sir'. This no longer lessens but intensifies the battle between the old colonial system and democracy. Long before the actual independence was granted, large numbers of the middle classes, including their politicians, wanted it put off as far into the distance as possible. For the cruiser in the offing and the prospect of financial gifts and loans, they turn longing eyes and itching feet towards the United States.

The Caribbean is now an American sea. Puerto Rico is its show piece. Puerto Rican society has the near-celestial privilege of free entry into the United States for their unemployed and their ambitious. The United States returns to the Puerto Rican Government all duty collected on such staple imports as rum and cigars. American money for investment and American loans and gifts should create the Caribbean paradise. But if the United States had the Puerto Rican density of population, it would contain all the people in the world. Puerto Rico is just another West Indian island.

In the Dominican Republic there is no need to go beyond saying that Trujillo had gained power by the help of the United States Marines and all through the more than quarter-century of his infamous dictatorship he was understood to enjoy the friendship of Washington. Before the recent election of his successor, Sr. Juan Bosch, [21] the French newspapers stated as an item of news that members of the left in the Dominican Republic (names were given) were deported to Paris by the local police, who were assisted in this operation by members of the FBI. Trujillo gone, Duvalier of Haiti is the uncrowned king of Latin American barbarism. It is widely believed that despite the corruption and impertinence of his régime, it is American support which keeps him in power: better Duvalier than another Castro.

Such a mass of ignorance and falsehood has surrounded these islands for so many centuries that obvious truths sound like revelations. Contrary to the general belief, the Caribbean territories taken as a whole are not sunk in irremediable poverty. When he was Principal of the University of the West Indies in Jamaica, Professor Arthur Lewis, [22] former head of the faculty of economics at Manchester University and at the time of writing due to head the same faculty at Princeton, tried to remove some cobwebs from the eyes of his fellow West Indians:

> This opinion that the West Indies can raise all the capital it needs from its own resources is bound to shock many people, because West Indians like to feel that ours is a poor community. But the fact of the matter is that at least half of the people in the world are poorer than we are. The standard of living in the West Indies is higher than the standard of living in India, or China, in most of the countries of Asia, and in most of the countries of Africa. The West Indies is not a poor community; it is in the upper bracket of world income. It is capable of producing the extra 5 or 6 per cent of resources which is required for this job, just as Ceylon and Ghana are finding the money they need for development by taxing themselves. It is not necessary for us to send our statesmen around the world begging for help. If help is given to us let us accept it, but let us not sit down and say nothing can be done until the rest of the world out of its goodness of heart is willing to grant us charity.

The economic road they have to travel is a broad highway on which the sign posts have long been erected. Sr. Juan Bosch began his campaign by promising to distribute the land confiscated from the baronial plunder of the Trujillo family. His supporters rapidly transformed this into: 'A house and land for every Dominican'. Not only popular demand and modern economists, but British Royal Commissions during the last sixty years, have indicated (cautiously but clearly enough) that the way out of the West Indian morass is the abolition of the plantation labourer and the substitution, instead, of individual landowning peasants. Scientists and economists have indicated that an effective industry is possible, based on the scientific and planned use of raw material produced on the islands. I have written in vain if I have not made it clear that of all formerly colonial coloured peoples, the West Indian masses are the most highly experienced in the ways of Western civilisation and most receptive to its requirements in the twentieth century. To realise themselves they will have to break out of the shackles of the old colonial system.

I do not propose to plunge this appendix into the turbulent waters of controversy about Cuba. I have written about the West Indies in general and Cuba is the most West Indian island in the West Indies. That suffices.

One more question remains – the most realistic and most pregnant question of all. Toussaint L'Ouverture and the Haitian slaves brought into the world more than the abolition of slavery. When Latin Americans saw that small and insignificant Haiti could win and keep independence they began to think that they ought to be able to do the same. Pétion, the ruler of Haiti, nursed back to health the sick and defeated Bolivar, [23] gave him money, arms and a printing press to help in the campaign which ended in the freedom of the Five States. What will happen to what Fidel Castro has brought new to the world no one can say. But what is waiting in the West Indies to be born, what emerged from the womb in July 1958, is to be seen elsewhere in the West Indies, not so confused with the pass and fell incensed points of mighty opposites. I speak now of a section of the West Indies of which I have had during the past five years intimate and personal experience of the writers and the people. But this time the people first, for if the ideologists have moved closer towards the people, the people have caught up with the ideologists and the national identity is a national fact.

In Trinidad in 1957, before there was any hint of a revolution in Cuba, the ruling political party[24] suddenly declared, contrary to the declaration of policy with which it had won the election, that during the war the British Government of Sir Winston Churchill had given away Trinidad property and it should be returned. What happened is one of the greatest events in the history of the West Indies. The people rose to the call. Mass meetings and mass demonstrations, political passion such as the island had never known, swept through the population. Inside the chains of the old colonial system, the people of the West Indies are a national community. The middle classes looked on with some uncertainty but with a growing approval. The local whites are not like whites in a foreign civilisation. They are West Indians and, under a strong impulse, think of themselves as such. Many of them quietly made known their sympathy with the cause. The political leader was uncompromising in his demand for the return. 'I shall break Chaguaramas or it will break me', he declared, and the words sprouted wings. He publicly asserted to mass meetings of many thousands that if the State Department, backed by the Colonial Office, continued to refuse to discuss the return of the base, he would take Trinidad not only out of the West Indian Federation but out of the British association altogether: he would establish the independence of the island, all previous treaties entered into under the colonial régime would automatically become null and void, and thus he would deal with the Americans. He forbade them to use the Trinidad airport for their military planes. In a magnificent address, 'From Slavery to Chaguaramas', he said that for centuries the West Indies had been bases, military footballs of warring imperialist powers, and the time had come to finish with it. It is the present writer's opinion (he was for the crucial period editor of the party journal) that it was the response of the population which sent the political leader so far upon a perilous road. They showed simply that they thought the Americans should quit the base and return it to the people. This was all the more remarkable in that the Trinidad people freely admitted that Trinidad had never enjoyed such financial opulence as when the Americans were there during the war. America was undoubtedly the potential source of economic and financial aid. But they were ready for any sacrifices needed for the return of the base. They were indeed ready for anything, and the political leadership had to take great care to do or say nothing which would precipitate any untoward mass intervention.

What was perhaps the most striking feature of this powerful national upheaval was its concentration on the national issue and its disregard for all others. There was not the slightest trace of anti-American feeling; though the British Colonial Office was portrayed as the ally of the State Department and the demand for political independence was well on the way, there was equally no trace of anti-British feeling. There was no inclination towards non-alignment, not even, despite the pressure for independence, anti-imperialism. The masses of the people of Trinidad and Tobago looked upon the return of the base as the first and primary stage in their quest for national identity. That they were prepared to suffer for, if need be (of this I am as certain as one can be of such things) to fight and die for. But in the usual accompaniments of a struggle against a foreign base, they were not in any way concerned. Not that they did not know. They most certainly knew. But they had had a long experience of international relations and they knew precisely what they wanted. Right up the islands, the population responded in the same way to what they felt was a West Indian matter. The press conference of the political leader was the most popular radio programme in the West Indian islands. It was 1937–38 all over again. 'Free is how you is from the start, an' when it look different you got to move, just move, an' when you movin' say that is a natural freedom make you move'. [25] Though the British flag still blew above them, in their demands and demonstrations for Chaguaramas they were free, freer than they might be for a long time.

The West Indian national identity is more easily to be glimpsed in the published writings of West Indian authors.

Vic Reid[26] of Jamaica is the only West Indian novelist who lives in the West Indies. That presumably is why he sets his scene in Africa. An African who knows the West Indies well assures me that there is nothing African about Reid's story. It is the West Indies in African dress. Whatever it is, the novel is a *tour-de-force*. African or West Indian, it reduces the human problems of under-developed countries to a common denominator. The distinctive tone of the new West Indian orchestra is not loud but it is clear. Reid is not unconcerned about the fate of his characters. The political passions are sharp and locked in murderous conflict. But Reid is detached as no European or African writer is or can be detached, as Garvey, Padmore, Césaire were not and could not be detached. The origin of his detachment appears very clearly in the most powerful and far-ranging of the West Indian school, George Lamming[27] of Barbados.

Confining ourselves strictly to our purpose, we shall limit ourselves to citing only one episode from the latest of his four powerful novels.

Powell, a character in *Season of Adventure*, is a murderer, rapist and altogether criminal member of West Indian society. Suddenly, after nine-tenths of the book, the author injects three pages headed 'Author's Note'. Writing in the first person he accounts for Powell.

> *Until the age of ten Powell and I had lived together, equal in the affection of two mothers. Powell had made my dreams; and I had lived his passions. Identical in years, and stage by stage, Powell and I were taught in the same primary school.*
>
> *And then the division came. I got a public scholarship which started my migration into another world, a world whose roots were the same, but whose style of living was entirely different from what my childhood knew. It had earned me a privilege which now shut Powell and the whole* tonelle *right out of my future. I had lived as near to Powell as my skin to the hand it darkens. And yet! Yet I forgot the* tonelle *as men forget a war, and attached myself to that new world which was so recent and so slight beside the weight of what had gone before. Instinctively I attached myself to that new privilege; and in spite of all my effort, I am not free of its embrace to this day.*

> *I believe deep in my bones that the mad impulse which drove Powell to his criminal defeat was largely my doing. I will not have this explained away by talk about environment; nor can I allow my own moral infirmity to be transferred to a foreign conscience, labelled imperialist. I shall go beyond my grave in the knowledge that I am responsible for what happened to my brother.*
>
> *Powell still resides somewhere in my heart, with a dubious love, some strange, nameless shadow of regret; and yet with the deepest, deepest nostalgia. For I have never felt myself to be an honest part of anything since the world of his childhood deserted me.*

This is something new in the voluminous literature of anti-colonialism. The West Indian of this generation accepts complete responsibility for the West Indies.

Vidia Naipaul[28] of Trinidad does the same. His Mr. Biswas writes his first article for a newspaper.

DADDY COMES HOME IN A COFFIN
U.S. Explorer's Last Journey
On Ice by M. Biswas

> *... Less than a year ago Daddy – George Elmer Edman, the celebrated traveller and explorer – left home to explore the Amazon.*
> *Well, I have news for you, kiddies.*
> *Daddy is on his way home.*
> *Yesterday he passed through Trinidad.*
> *In a coffin.*

This earns Mr. Biswas, former agricultural labourer and keeper of a small shop, a job on the staff of this paper.

Mr. Biswas wrote a letter of protest. It took him two weeks. It was eight typewritten pages long. After many re-writings the letter developed into a broad philosophical essay on the nature of man; his son goes to a secondary school and together they hunt through Shakespeare for quotations and find a rich harvest in *Measure for Measure*. The foreigner may miss this bland reproduction of the *modus operandi* of the well-greased West Indian journalist, politician, prime minister.

Mr. Biswas is now a man of letters. He is invited to a session of local literati. Mr. Biswas, whose poetic peak is Ella Wheeler Wilcox, is bewildered by whisky and talk about Lorca, Eliot, Auden. Every member of the group must submit a poem. One night after looking at the sky through the window Mr. Biswas finds his theme.

> He addressed his mother. He did not think of rhythm; he used no cheating abstract words. He wrote of coming up to the brow of the hill, seeing the black,

forked earth, the marks of the spade, the indentations of the fork prongs. He wrote of the journey he had made a long time before. He was tired; she made him rest. He was hungry; she gave him food. He had nowhere to go; she welcomed him ...

'It is a poem', Mr. Biswas announced. 'In prose'.

... 'There is no title', he said. And, as he had expected, this was received with satisfaction.

Then he disgraced himself. Thinking himself free of what he had written, he ventured on his poem boldly, and even with a touch of self-mockery. But as he read, his hands began to shake, the paper rustled; and when he spoke of the journey his voice failed. It cracked and kept on cracking; his eyes tickled. But he went on, and his emotion was such that at the end no one said a word ...

The West Indian had made a fool of himself imitating American journalism, Shakespeare, T.S. Eliot, Lorca. He had arrived at truth when he wrote about his own West Indian childhood, his West Indian mother and the West Indian landscape. Naipaul is an East Indian. Mr. Biswas is an East Indian. But the East Indian problem with the West Indies is a creation of politicians of both races, seeking means to avoid attacking the old colonial system. The East Indian has become as West Indian as all the other expatriates.

The latest West Indian novelist is one of the strangest living novelists. Beginning in 1958 he has just concluded a quartet of novels. He is from British Guiana, which is a part of the South American continent. There are nearly 40,000 square miles of mountains, plateaux, forest, jungle, savannah, the highest waterfalls in the world, native Amerindians, settled communities of escaped African slaves – all largely unexplored. For fifteen years, over this new territory, Wilson Harris [29] worked as a land surveyor. He is a member of a typical West Indian society of 600,000 people which inhabits a thin strip of coastline. Harris sets the final seal on the West Indian conception of itself as a national identity. On the run from the police a young Guianese, half-Chinese, half-Negro, discovers that all previous generations, Dutch, English, French, capitalists, slaves, freed slaves, white and black, were expatriates.

> ... All the restless wayward spirits of all the aeons (who it was thought had been embalmed for good) are returning to roost in our blood. And we have to start all over again where they began to explore. We've got to pick up the seeds again where they left off. It's no use worshipping the rottenest tacouba and tree-trunk in the historic topsoil. There's a whole world of branches and sensations we've missed, and we've got to start again from the roots up even if they look like nothing. Blood, sap, flesh, veins, arteries, lungs, the heartland, Sharon. *We're the first potential parents who can contain the ancestral house.* Too young? I don't

know. Too much responsibility? Time will tell. We've got to face it. Or else it will be too late to stop everything and everyone from running away and tumbling down. And then All the King's Horses and all the King's Men won't be able to put us together again. Like all the bananas and the plantains and the coffee trees near Charity. Not far from here, you know. A small wind comes and everything comes out of the ground. Because the soil is unstable. Just pegasse. Looks rich on top but that's about all. What do you think they say when it happens, when the crops run away? They shrug and say they're expendable crops. They can't begin to see that it's *us*, our blood, running away all the time, in the river and in the sea, everywhere, staining the bush. *Now* is the time to make a newborn stand, Sharon; you and me; it's up to us, even if we fall on our knees and *creep* to anchor ourselves before we get up.

There is no space here to deal with the poet in the literary tradition, or the ballad singer. In dance, in the innovation in musical instruments, in popular ballad singing unrivalled anywhere in the world, the mass of the people are not seeking a national identity, they are expressing one. The West Indian writers have discovered the West Indies and West Indians, a people of the middle of our disturbed century, concerned with the discovery of themselves, determined to discover themselves, but without hatred or malice against the foreigner, even the bitter imperialist past. To be welcomed into the comity of nations a new nation must bring something new. Otherwise it is a mere administrative convenience or necessity. The West Indians have brought something new.

> *Albion too was once*
> *a colony like ours ...*
> *... deranged*
> *By foaming channels, and the vain expense*
> *Of bitter faction.*
> *All in compassion ends.*
> *So differently from what the heart arranged.*[30]

Passion not spent but turned inward. Toussaint tried and paid for it with his life. Torn, twisted, stretched to the limits of agony, injected with poisonous patent medicines, it lives in the state which Fidel started. It is of the West Indies West Indian. For it, Toussaint, the first and greatest of West Indians, paid with his life.

NOTES

1. 'Tis dangerous when the baser nature comes
   Between the pass and fell incensed points
   Of mighty opposites'
   William Shakespeare, *Hamlet,* Act. V, scene 2.
2. Jean Jacques Dessalines (1758–1806), who rose from slave to general, was the man who proclaimed Haiti's independence on January 1, 1804. He was soon proclaimed emperor he ruled the nation until he was assassinated. His successor, Henri Christophe (1767–1820), who was born in Grenada, was president from 1806 to 1811 and then king from 1811 until his suicide in 1820. Alexandre Pétion (1770–1818) was another revolutionary general and the leader of the mulattos in southern Haiti. While Christophe was president, Pétion was elected president of the southern Republic of Haiti in 1807. He made himself president for life in 1816 but died two years later.
3. The United States, in fact, invaded Haiti in 1915 and stayed until 1934.
4. *Ainsi Parla L'Oncle* was first published in 1928 (see chapter 15 in this volume).
5. The Ten Years' War, from 1868 to 1878, ended with a truce, the Pact of Zanjón, and the Cuban war of independence recommenced in 1895, ending with the US occupation in 1898. José Martí (1835–95), a poet and philosopher, organised the broad national coalition that started the second phase of the war of independence, in which he was killed (see chapter 1 in this volume). General Antonio Maceo (1845–96), who had refused to accept the terms of the truce in 1878, was killed in action a year after Martí. Both Martí and Maceo, a white and a black Cuban, respectively, are revered as leaders and martyrs in the struggle for national liberation.
6. In 1901, while Cuba was under the military occupation of the United States, the Cuban constituent assembly was required to incorporate the Platt Amendment into the nation's constitution and, in 1903, after the inauguration of the Cuban republic, the Platt Amendment was incorporated into a formal treaty between the two countries. Among other restrictions on Cuban sovereignty, this amendment restricted Cuba's authority in foreign relations and permitted the United States to intervene, with military force if it wanted, in Cuba's internal affairs. In 1933, a revolutionary Cuban government repudiated the Platt Amendment.
7. Jomo Kenyatta (1889–1978), an early spokesman of African independence, was the secretary of the International African Friends of Abyssinia when James was its chairman. He lived in Europe from 1931 until he returned to Kenya in 1946 to become the leader of his country's independence movement. In 1963, he became the first prime minister of independent Kenya and then its first president when it became a republic in 1964. He held that post until his death.
8. Kwame Nkrumah (1909–72), a leading Pan-Africanist, led Ghana's movement for independence in the 1950s and became its first prime minister in 1952. Ghana became independent in 1957 and, when it became a republic in 1960, Nkrumah was its first president. He was ousted by a military coup in 1966 and he went into exile in Guinea.
9. George Padmore (1903–59) was born in Trinidad, as Malcolm Nurse, and he was one of James' childhood friends. He assumed his cover name when he joined the Communist party in the United States. He travelled extensively on Party business and on behalf of the American Negro Labor Congress and the League Against Imperialism and for National Independence. He became the head of the Negro Bureau of the Red International of

Labour Unions in Moscow and was elected to the Moscow City Soviet. He helped plan the First International Conference of Negro Workers, held in Hamburg in 1930, and was a member of the Communist International (Comintern) until he resigned in 1933 when its policy toward the national liberation movements of Africa and Asia changed. Padmore concentrated increasingly on African affairs and, with James's introduction, became a close associate of Kwame Nkrumah. He left London in 1957 and became Nkrumah's advisor on African affairs, but he died two years later.

10. Dr Hastings Banda (c. 1906–97) became the first prime minister (1964-66) and then president (1966-94) of Malawi. Patrice Lumumba (1925–61) was the first prime minister of the independent Congo in 1960 until he was imprisoned and then assassinated. Julius Nyerere (1922–99) led Tanganyika to independence in 1961 and was president of Tanzania from 1964 to 1985. Tom Mboya (1930–69) was secretary-general of the Kenya African National Union until his assassination.

11. T.S. Eliot (1888–1965) was an American-born English poet and dramatist who won the Nobel Prize for literature in 1948. James quotes from Eliot's 'The Dry Salvages' in *Four Quartets* (1943).

12. These leaders were the cousins Alexander Bustamante (1884-1977) of the Jamaica Labour party and Norman Washington Manley (1893–1969) of the People's National party.

13. James refers to the governor, Sir Murchison Fletcher, and the colonial secretary, Howard Nankivell.

14. The West India Royal Commission (1938–39), usually known as the Moyne Commission after its chairman, Lord Moyne, was sent to investigate the causes of the labour rebellions and to make recommendations. The British government, fearing that its descriptions of the terrible conditions in which West Indians lived and worked could be used as propaganda by the enemy in the Second World War, did not allow the report to be published until 1945.

15. Presumably, this should be either Dr Hastings Banda or Julius Nyerere (see note 10 above).

16. Jawaharlal Nehru (1889–1964) was the first prime minister of independent India, from 1947 until his death, and an influential statesman in the Nonaligned Nations.

17. Rafael Leonidas Trujillo Molina (1891–1961) was head of the army and, from 1930 until his assassination in 1961, the dictator of the Dominican Republic. Dr François Duvalier (1907–71) was elected president of Haiti in 1957 and in 1964 declared himself president for life.

18. When Germany defeated France in 1940, during the Second World War, the town of Vichy in central France became the seat of a government that collaborated with the Germans. This Vichy government lasted until 1945.

19. They became overseas departments of France in 1946, electing their own senators and deputies to the National Assembly in Paris.

20. The West Indies Federation lasted from 1958 until 1962, when first Jamaica and then Trinidad and Tobago became independent. In 1976, Trinidad and Tobago became a republic, so the queen of England was no longer its head of state.

21. Juan Domingo Bosch (b.1909) was elected president of the Dominican Republic in 1962 but he was overthrown seven months later by the army. When his supporters rose up to restore him in 1965, the United States invaded under the pretense that there was a communist threat.

22. W. Arthur Lewis (1915–91), an economist from St Lucia, won the Nobel Prize for economics in 1979 (see chapter 36 in this volume).

23. Simón Bolívar (1783–1830) was called the Liberator because he led the struggle of the Spanish American colonies for independence from 1810.

24. The ruling party in 1957 was the People's National Movement (PNM), led by Dr Eric Williams, who James actively supported between 1958 and 1960 but whom he refers to here as 'the political leader'.

25. From George Lamming's *Season of Adventure* (1960).

26. Vic (Victor Stafford) Reid (1913–87) was the author of *New Day* (1949), a historical novel about Jamaica's struggle for independence, and *The Leopard* (1958), which is set in Kenya during the Mau Mau rebellion (1952-56) against British colonialism.

27. George Lamming, born in Barbados in 1927, is the author of many novels, including *In the Castle of My Skin* (1953), *Of Age and Innocence* (1958) and *Natives of My Person* (1972); (see chapter 44 in this volume).

28. Vidia (V.S.) Naipaul, born in Trinidad in 1932, has written many novels and works of non-fiction. He won the Nobel Prize for literature in 2001 (see chapter 28 in this volume).

29. Wilson Harris, born in Guyana in 1921, has written many novels in addition to the four James mentions. *Palace of the Peacock* (1960) was his first, followed by *The Far Journey of Oudin* (1961), *The Whole Armour* (1962) and *The Secret Ladder* (1963).

30. 'That Albion too, was once

    A colony like ours, 'Part of the continent, piece of the main'

    Nook-shotten, rook o'er blown, deranged

    By foaming channels, and the vain expense

    Of bitter faction.

    All in compassion ends

    So differently from what the heart arranged:

    'as well as if a manor of thy friend's…'

    From 'Ruins of a Great House' in *In a Green Night* (1962) by Derek Walcott. Born in St Lucia in 1930, Walcott is a prolific poet and dramatist, and winner of the Nobel Prize for literature in 1992 (see chapter 42 in this volume).

Thirty

Elsa Goveia

Elsa Vesta Goveia (1925–80), born in what is now Guyana, won the British Guiana Scholarship in a competitive examination and entered University College, London, in 1945. While she studied the social and economic history of Tudor England she became active in the West Indian Students' Union (WISU), of which she became the assistant secretary by 1946. She also participated in a study group on West Indian history led by W. Arthur Lewis, the St Lucian economist, at the London School of Economics. This was 'a field study entirely new to most of us' and she became 'more than ever convinced that a people must know something of its past in order to plan for the future' (WISU Newsletter Dec. 1, 1946, quoted in Higman 1999: 101).

After she graduated with first class honours in 1948, Goveia began work on her doctorate. The dissertation, submitted to the University of London in 1952, was the basis of her book Slave Society in the British Leeward Islands at the End of the Eighteenth Century *(New Haven, 1965). In the meantime, she became an assistant lecturer in history at the recently created University College of the West Indies (UCWI) in 1952. There, in Jamaica, she pioneered the development of courses on West Indian history and published* A Study on the Historiography of the British West Indies to the End of the Nineteenth Century *(Mexico, 1956) and a study of the slave laws in the eighteenth century.*

The 1950s was a watershed in the development and institutionalisation of the history of the Anglophone Caribbean. The UCWI, established in 1948 at Mona in Jamaica, included four West Indian historians by 1960. Goveia was joined by Fitzroy R. Augier (born in 1924) from

St Lucia, Douglas G. Hall (1920–99) from Jamaica, and Keith Laurence (born in 1933) from Trinidad. By 1960, also, there were two general histories of the Caribbean, J.H. Parry and P.M. Sherlock's A Short History of the West Indies *(1956) and F.R. Augier, S.C. Gordon, D.G. Hall and M. Reckord's* The Making of the West Indies *(1960). Their publications coincided with the development and initiation of the Federation of the West Indies (1958–62). They were written for West Indian students so it is not surprising that they emphasised the Anglophone Caribbean at the expense of a pan-Caribbean perspective. In 1961, Goveia was appointed Professor of West Indian History, the only person to date with this title, and the next year, when the Federation disintegrated and Jamaica and Trinidad and Tobago became independent, the UCWI became the University of the West Indies (UWI).*

Goveia's study of the slave society of the Leeward Islands is one of a series of excellent monographs about a particular part or territory of the West Indies and it is one of the few in which the author wrote about a territory other than her own. The UWI's Department of History has generally espoused a pan-Caribbean perspective and most of the first West Indian historians supported the Federation, but research has most often been on the researchers' home territories or territories of residence. Goveia, however, made it clear that she was concerned with understanding not only the 'grim logic' of the system of slavery in the Leeward Islands but also the contemporary relevance of the struggle against 'the form of society which slavery had created' and the urgent need to develop 'a new sense of community' in the West Indies. Her teaching and writing exerted a powerful influence upon members of the next generation of West Indian scholars, including such distinguished historians as Franklin Knight and Walter Rodney.

✧❋✧

Slave Society in the British Leeward Islands at the End of the Eighteenth Century (excerpts)

The Ranks of Society

At the end of the eighteenth century the slave system in the Leeward Islands[1] was neither static nor uniform, and its effects upon the society within which it had developed were profound. Throughout the islands the maintenance of the established order depended on the strict subordination of the numerous labouring class of Negro slaves to the control of the small group of white masters and their representatives. The whites were afraid that without slavery the Negroes could not be made to accept their inferior position in the society of the islands. Though it was becoming unprofitable, the slave system appeared to them to be indispensable, since it was the one sure means of maintaining the existing social structure and their own control of it. The economic, legal, and social inequalities between masters and slaves preserved and reinforced the economic, legal, and social inequalities between whites and Negroes, which the slave system itself had engendered. At the end of the eighteenth century, slavery was more than an economic institution. It had become the basis of the social system, regulating the whole social organisation of each of the insular communities of the Leeward Islands government . . . .

The whites knew that the acquiescence of the slaves in the slave system did not signify a real consent to the government under which they lived. They knew that, in the last analysis, slavery was a system of compulsion. They were not hostile to amelioration but they accepted it only on condition that it did not interfere with the subordination of their slaves, which was held to be essential to their own survival and the survival of the slave system. At the end of the eighteenth century, the elements of force and fear were still the indispensable basis of slavery, and most of the whites were determined to maintain them in face of all pressure for change. They evidently believed, as Bryan Edwards did, that 'in countries where slavery is established, the leading principle on which the government is supported, is *fear*; or a sense of that absolute coercive necessity, which, leaving no choice of action, supersedes all questions of right'[2] . . . .

Towards the end of the eighteenth century the total population of the British Leeward Islands was probably more than 94,000 persons. Of this number 300 to 400 whites and 2,000 Negroes lived in Anguilla, and there were 2 whites and 290 slaves in Barbuda. The rest of the population lived in Antigua, St. Kitts, Nevis, Montserrat, and the Virgin Islands. In these islands there were about 8,000 whites and over 81,000 slaves, and their total free coloured population can be estimated at about 2,600 persons . . . .

The relationships of the groups of whites, free persons of colour, and Negro slaves who made up the population were largely determined by colour and legal status. The whites, who were all free, were the leaders of the whole community in town and country. The class of free persons of colour, which included a majority of persons of mixed blood, was made up of freed slaves and their descendents, and occupied a marginal position between the whites and the slaves. The slaves, a predominantly black group, had the lowest status of any group in the community, of which they were both the most numerous and the poorest members.

There were, of course, differences within each group, as well as between the separate groups in the community. There were differences of privilege, wealth, and status within the white group, for instance, and, although the whites were the effective ruling class of the islands and dominated the economic and social life, there were still some whites who were excluded from the society of the white elite by their poverty and inferior status, and there were still some whites who were without political rights either because of their lack of property or because of their religious affiliations.

The leading inhabitants among the whites included planters, merchants, and professional men, who were all usually substantial property owners. The planters had large holdings of land and slaves. The merchants owned stores, town-houses, and domestic slaves, as well as many of the small vessels and seamen slaves engaged in the coastal trade of the islands. The professional men frequently held property and slaves in the towns; and both they and the merchants often invested their capital in sugar estates. Because of their property and position these men generally had easy access to the political power which was denied to poorer members of the white group. By the end of the eighteenth century, however, absenteeism had reduced the number of the leading whites still living in the islands. The wealthier planters took up residence in England, and the more affluent of the merchants and professional men also retired there either permanently or for long periods.

The result was a 'leveling down' of the white upper class that remained. By the end of the eighteenth century this group included government officials, planters and merchants of middling wealth, and professional men who were still making their fortunes. Its ranks had been opened to admit the absentees' managers and attorneys, whose numbers steadily increased as those of the resident proprietors declined. The members of this new group were generally less wealthy than the planters, merchants, and professional men, and their property consisted chiefly of slaves. But, like many of the professionals working in the islands, they were men on the make, and they proved eager to take advantage of the opportunities opened up to them by their acceptance into the white elite. They lived like gentlemen and did their best to accumulate wealth and influence, and by the end of the eighteenth century they were playing an active and important part in the political and social life of the Leeward Islands.

The inclusion of the managers and attorneys in the white elite, however, still left a considerable number of whites outside the white upper class. Overseers, small shopkeepers and hucksters, clerks, and artisans were among the second rank of whites who remained excluded from the society of the leading inhabitants . . . .

But there were forces at work that emphasised the solidarity of the white group in spite of the considerable differences among its members. Most important of all, perhaps, was the existence of economic opportunities for individuals among the group of poorer whites. For wealth was the great distinguishing factor between the leading whites and the whites of second-rate status in the islands, and the acquisition of wealth enabled poorer whites to gain admittance into the dominant upper class of whites. At the end of the eighteenth century the way up to fortune and distinction in planting and the professions was still open to whites who had begun life in poverty . . . .

In their efforts to rise in society these whites were greatly helped by the existence of the institution of Negro slavery, which had produced a considerable 'leveling up' among the white population, parallel to the 'leveling down' of the upper class resulting from absenteeism.

Generally speaking, the whites of the Leeward Islands no longer did manual work. The Leewards had no permanent group of poor white peasants, like those of Barbados, ... and the white field labourer had long since disappeared from the slave plantations. At the end of the eighteenth century the lowest starting point for the whites in agriculture was the supervisory position of overseer. White domestic servants were rarely employed in town or country. Their place was filled by the numerous Negro attendants who waited on white families.

As for the white artisans, they had found that independence could be purchased for the price of a few slaves, to be employed in the manual work of the trade under white supervision. They had therefore ceased to be labourers themselves and had become employers and owners of labour . . . . The aim of every white artisan was to become as soon as possible a master of working slaves.

At the end of the eighteenth century the distance between the lower ranks of whites and the white elite was much narrower than it had been in the later seventeenth and early eighteenth centuries, when the slave system was establishing itself. The absenteeism of the richer whites and the improved position of the poorer whites combined to reduce the extremes of wealth and poverty which had once been evident among the white population . . . .

With its numbers decreasing, the white population was tending to become more homogeneous in its composition. Differences of class still persisted among the whites. But the way up from one class to another was shorter, and the prospects of rising were more encouraging than they had been earlier . . . .

Whites of all ranks were enabled to earn a livelihood by purchasing and hiring out the labour of slaves . . . .

As the poorer whites acquired property they became entitled to take part in the political life of the islands. They served as jurors, voted in elections, and sometimes even held public office . . . . This process of assimilation was greatly speeded up in the Leeward Islands towards the end of the eighteenth century, when there was a growing tendency to admit as many whites as possible to the ruling group . . . . With the numbers of the resident white population in decline, the solidarity of the whites as a racial group was beginning to outweigh the differences of class and privilege among them.

The small numbers of the whites, and their racial pride, encouraged among them a willingness to help the more unfortunate of their own group . . . .

So long as a man was white he could hope to rise to wealth and leadership in the islands, and, though his origins might be humble, his possession of wealth would gain him admittance into the society of the white upper class, which already included many new men who were rising in the world . . . .

All the whites, whatever their station in society, were united by their superiority to the other groups in the community. In the West Indies, this was generally interpreted as a superiority of race. The West Indian whites believed that the Negroes were either an inherently inferior race, or, at the very least, culturally backward in comparison with Europeans . . . .

The racial prejudice of the whites extended to the free coloured as well as the slaves . . . . As a result, the free people of colour were rigidly excluded from all ranks of society among the whites, and this racial separation was maintained even in death . . . .

There was, however, a major exception to the social separation of the races in the West Indian community, and this exception was the prevalence of sexual relationships between white men and women of African descent. Not that the whites generally married women of colour – that would have been too much out of keeping with their racial and social exclusiveness . . . . Instead of white wives, many of the whites in the islands had mistresses among the women of colour, both slave and free; and the system of concubinage was so well established that even the married men among the whites frequently had coloured mistresses . . . .

Since white women were often outnumbered by the men of their own group and married only white men, the free men of colour were forced to find mates among the slave population. As the child took the status of the mother, these children remained slaves, unless their freedom could be purchased by the father. By the effect of free births alone, therefore, the free coloured group came to include a steadily increasing proportion of persons of mixed blood.

Female slaves as well as free coloured women were used as concubines by the whites, and the result of these contacts was a growing minority of slaves of mixed blood . . . . The white fathers of these slaves sometimes felt obliged to arrange for the freedom of their concubines and children, which further increased the proportion of persons of mixed blood among the free people of colour.

The system of concubinage was accepted by the women of colour, because association with the whites, even on terms of inequality, enabled them to improve their standing within their own groups. To the slave woman association with a white man was likely to bring increased privileges and possibly even manumission for the woman and her children. To the free woman of colour it meant an improvement of personal status and usually also of material conditions, and it was one more step in the long struggle to efface the humiliating links between the free people of colour and the slaves and to replace them by a relationship of attachment to the superior class of whites. But, though it conferred these benefits on the coloured women who were mistresses to white men, the system of concubinage was itself a direct result of the social inferiority of the coloured population under the slave system. Although it permitted intimate relations between white men and coloured women, it nevertheless reflected and preserved the exclusion of persons of colour, even when born free, from white society in all the Leeward Islands.

It was fully accepted that individuals within the white group should move freely from the lower to the upper class. But a sharp line of division separated members of the free coloured group from the whites . . . .

Among the free people of colour, therefore, the only real prospect of sharing in the privileges of the class above them seemed to lie in the slow progression of increasing whiteness, which led from 'Negro' to mulatto, from mulatto to quadroon, from quadroon to mestee, and from mestee to 'white'. With the exception of those who succeeded in crossing this racial line, the free coloured were usually regarded as an inferior class, without legal claim to political or civil rights . . . .

To preserve the property of masters in their slaves, the island legislatures were willing to risk the freedom of the people of colour. To preserve the subordination of their slaves, the white inhabitants generally were determined to continue the subjection of the whole coloured population under their control. The social and political inferiority of free persons of colour was considered to be a necessary bulwark of the slave system . . . .

Fortunately for the whites, the number of free people of colour in the Leeward Islands at this time was small, and it was very unlikely that they would combine with the slaves to overthrow the slave system. The free coloured generally accepted slavery and owned and used slaves themselves. There was little sympathy between them and the enslaved Negroes . . . . Instead of strengthening the relationship between the free people of colour and the Negro slaves, their common origin served only to embitter it . . . .

The free coloured group would have been glad to detach themselves from their relation to the slaves and to identify themselves with the dominant class of whites. But there was no welcome for them in the white world . . . . Like the many poor whites who had been driven from the islands by the pressure of slave labour, the free coloured found their economic opportunities seriously limited by the ever-increasing spread of the slave system. But, unlike the whites who emigrated, the free coloured could not leave the islands, since there was nowhere else for them to go. They had therefore to compete with the slaves for employment or attempt to penetrate occupations in which the whites had established themselves. In their efforts to find a place in the economic life of the islands, the free coloured were under even greater disadvantages than the poorer whites, since they were hindered rather than helped by the white group, which effectively controlled most economic activities . . . .

The economic activities of the free people of colour, like their social and political status, were marginal . . . . Like the whites, they engaged in huckstering and shopkeeping, and, like the slaves, they worked as servants and as porters. They also mingled with the slaves as sailors and boatmen and in a variety of trades, such as caulking and sailmaking, which arose directly from the activity of the towns as ports. In these trades, and in the other trades of the towns, the position of the free coloured artisans might approximate that of the slaves who worked under white supervision, or they might be able to establish themselves as independent tradesmen, in a position more nearly resembling that of the white artisans who made a living by directing the labour of slaves. In the artisan trades, therefore, as in their other occupations, generally, the free coloured stood on the borderline between the lower ranks of the whites and the upper ranks of the slaves.

The occupations in which the free coloured were willing to work with slaves were better paid than field labour, and they were not regarded as being definitively servile. The superior status and opportunities of these occupations, as compared with field labour, enabled the free people of colour to engage in them without losing caste. The skilled slave artisans, with whom the free coloured competed, enjoyed the privileges attached to this status in a society where such workers were few and their labour at a premium. While the domestic slaves of the plantations were favoured, rather than skilled workers, the towns offered opportunities for a class of skilled domestics, who could be rented out for a good return . . . .

Generally speaking, the slaves of the towns were able to achieve a much greater independence and freedom of movement than the plantation slaves. . . . [T]he nature of the work done by many town slaves made it essential to give them a degree of freedom and mobility that would never have been allowed to the ordinary field slave.

The movements of porters and boatmen could not be rigidly controlled, even though their occupations were regulated by law; and there can have been little difference between the slave and free coloured tailors, or carpenters, or sailmakers, in their daily occupations in the towns. All these employments were governed by the conditions which were necessary for the work, rather than by the legal status of the worker . . . .

The slaves following occupations in which the free coloured sought employment were also generally distinguished from the ordinary field slaves by their higher standard of living and by their greater opportunities for earning the price of their freedom . . . . A high proportion of the slaves manumitted, whether by purchase or by gift, belonged to the privileged group of slaves which included artisans, domestics, and the 'wage-earning' slaves of the towns. It was from among the elite of the slave class, therefore, that the free coloured class was itself generally recruited.

At the end of the eighteenth century this elite already included a significant proportion of slaves of mixed blood. There was a strong social prejudice against employing these slaves in field work; and no master would normally send a mulatto into the field, except as a driver . . . . The slaves of mixed blood were therefore concentrated in employments held to be less laborious and less servile than field work. Their occupations were those of the more privileged slaves, and, like them, the slaves of mixed blood found opportunities to free themselves and to enter the free coloured class, some of whose occupations they already followed . . . .

The line of differentiation by colour was thus being advanced one stage further, by the emergence of a group of people of mixed blood following marginal occupations above and below the line of slavery. This group, which was distinguished from the ordinary field slaves by differences of occupation and living standards, as well as of colour, provided an intermediate mulatto class of skilled and semi-skilled labour between the proprietary and managerial class of whites and the great mass of unskilled black labourers who did the field work of the plantations.

The privileged slaves of mixed blood shared not only the occupations but also the general outlook of the free coloured group. Their advancement depended, to a very large extent, on the favour and patronage of the whites, and, like the free people of colour, they wished to identify themselves with the superior class of whites rather than with the inferior class of blacks. Most of their women were attached to the whites by the system of concubinage, and the group as a whole was linked to the whites by the ties of blood. Though they were treated as inferiors their connections with the white group led them to claim superiority over the blacks and to dissociate themselves as far as possible from them . . . . Like the free coloured, the slaves of mixed blood avoided field labour and despised the ordinary field slave . . . .

These ordinary field slaves were the backbone of the economy of the Leeward Islands at the end of the eighteenth century, but they suffered rather than benefited from the importance of their role. No other group of slaves was so completely subject to the harsh necessities of slavery as an industrial system. The life of the ordinary field slave was characterised by coercion and dependence. Forced labour was the basis of all agricultural production on the plantations, where the whole routine of field work had been moulded by the habitual use of compulsion and regimentation. The gangs of field slaves were worked for long hours under the discipline of the whip; their enslavement compelled them to submit to these rigorous working conditions and kept them dependent on the meagre allowances that they received from their masters in return for their labour.

Since the field slaves had fewer opportunities for earning a cash income than most other slaves, they relied heavily on the master for the necessities of life. But the need to safeguard their profits by keeping recurrent expenditure as low as possible led the planters to limit very strictly the quantity and quality of food, clothing, housing, and land made available to the numerous population of field labourers. With the exception of the drivers, who received the extra allowances given to 'Principal Negroes', the field slaves were maintained by their owners on the bare margin of subsistence . . . .

The inevitable results were ill health and a high death rate. The field slaves suffered from all the diseases which afflicted the slave population generally, including scurvy, dysentery, leprosy, yaws, smallpox, tetanus, worms, dropsy, venereal diseases, a variety of fevers, and the disease of dirt-eating or mal d'estomach, which appears to have been a result of malnutrition . . . . As a group they were more unhealthy than the artisans and domestic servants, who enjoyed a better standard [of] living . . . .

The 'husband' was not an essential part of the slave family. It made little difference whether he was a free man or a slave of the same or of another plantation. As long as his 'wife' and children were the property of another, he had no legal rights over them, and they were not even dependent on him for their maintenance, since they received their allowances directly from the master . . . . It was the relationship between the slave mother and her children which was fundamental, because the status and ownership of the mother determined the status and ownership of her children.

The slave family consisted effectively of the mother and her children, who all belonged to the mother's owner though they might be born of different fathers . . .

It was the influence of slavery which ensured that the matrifocal family would become the dominant family type among the Negro slaves and which gave slave 'marriage' its typical character of informality and instability. For it was the claims of slave ownership which made the slave mother the essential link in the chain of descent and reduced marriage to the status of a personal arrangement between the two partners which could be terminated at will, and it was the influence of these claims, reinforced by the system of slave allowances, which tended to deprive the male of all but a physical function in the creation of the slave family and enabled the slave woman, if she so wished, to dispense with a recognised 'husband and father' for herself and her children . . . .

Plantation slavery had a profound, pervasive effect on the life of the field slave. It determined his conditions of labour, his standard of living, and the pattern of his family life; and it denied him the relative independence and mobility enjoyed by many of the slaves of the towns. At the end of the eighteenth century each of the plantations that covered the countryside in the Leeward Islands was itself a small world, and the field slave was trapped in this world, like a fly in a spider's web. He was bound by the routine, the customs, and the fortune of his own plantation, and surrounded by an ever-widening circle of police laws and economic regulations, designed to prevent his escape from it. The plantation was completely dependent on the institution of slavery, which ensured the subordination of its labour force. The whole life of the field slave was built up within the limits imposed by the slave plantation and by the political and social conditions required for its preservation. His poverty and subjection were necessary features of the plantation system, which rested on the planters' ability to exploit for commercial profit the labour of a numerous and dependent population of workers.

Sunday, with perhaps an extra day or half-day out of crop, was the only time allowed to the field slave to work on his own account. On that day he could cultivate his allotment or attend the Sunday market to dispose of his surplus produce . . . .

The growth of provisions and small stock and their sale in the Sunday market provided the field slave with his most important opportunity to earn a cash income. The small profits of his trade might possibly be saved in the hope of buying a manumission after many years. But few field slaves were able to save enough for this purpose . . . .

Whether the field slave wasted his earnings, or spent them on necessities, or saved them, the Sunday market was of unique economic and social importance in his life. It was the one occasion on which he was permitted to share in the greater freedom of the town slaves; and it enabled him to modify, in some degree, his heavy dependence on the master, by acquiring a little money of his own to use as he wished. The participation of the field slaves in the Sunday market released them temporarily from the isolation and confinement of the plantations, and helped to make their hard life more tolerable.

Except for the Sunday market, where they joined with the hucksters and slaves of the town in buying and selling, the field slaves had only the most limited contact with other groups in the community. Normally, the pass laws and the demands of their daily work made it difficult for them to leave their plantations . . . .

Even within the plantations, however, there were barriers to close contacts between the field slaves and other groups. The artisans and domestics were privileged slaves and considered themselves superior to the field labourers. The contacts between the whites and the field slaves were largely confined to the field . . . .

The concentration of whites in the towns combined with the concentration of slaves on the plantations to produce a low ratio of whites to slaves throughout the rural areas. By their numbers the whites in the country were far less capable than the whites of the towns of exercising a direct personal influence over the lives of their slaves. They had, therefore, to rely on the sanctions of force and fear in the task of governing them.

The control of the large numbers of slaves in the rural areas was a more urgent problem than their control in the towns. This helps to account for the strict discipline imposed on the field slaves . . . . The field slaves were the most systematically oppressed section of the whole slave population, because their subordination was more necessary and more difficult to achieve than that of other less numerous groups of slaves.

The whites showed great determination in keeping the mass of the slaves under control politically. However, they did not consider it part of their business to attempt to 'civilise' the slaves, and, in any case, the lack of social contact made it impossible for them to assimilate the field slaves culturally. These slaves therefore remained the most isolated and the most 'African' group in a society where the words Negro and slave were almost synonymous and everything African was held to be, by definition, inferior.

Though the whites had little respect for African culture, they welcomed the fact that 'in general the Negroes are obstinately wedded to their own customs'. [3] For they wished to maintain the social and cultural distance separating the slave from his master . . . . The marked cultural difference of the field slaves from their masters was regarded as a fitting symbol of their subjection in the slave society, and it helped to confirm the whites in their belief that the Negroes were really a separate and inferior species of men.

The African origins of the West Indian slaves were very diverse. During the eighteenth century, slaves were brought to the islands from all parts of the West African coast between Senegambia in the Northwest and Angola in the Southeast . . . .

In spite of their diversity of origin, however, all the different groups of Negroes brought to the West Indies as slaves shared a considerable basic community of beliefs and practices, based upon their African cultural traditions. In any case, they tended, after a time, to lose those special characteristics which originally distinguished them and became merged in the mass of the slave population . . . . The influence of slavery made for 'a similitude of manners, and a uniformity of character throughout the whole body',[4] and this tendency became stronger as the proportion of Creoles, or persons born in the islands, increased among the slave population.

By the 1780's the slave trade to the Leeward Islands had greatly decreased, and a slave population composed predominantly of Creoles was developing in all the islands. It seems likely that most of the Negroes in the Leeward Islands at the end of the eighteenth century were descended from slaves brought from the Windward Coast and the Gold and Slave Coasts, and from the Bight of Benin and the Niger Delta, since these had been the most important suppliers of slaves to the British West Indies during the period of the eighteenth century when the slave trade of the Leeward Islands was most active. But the pressures of slavery and the emergence of a Creole population had largely effaced the original differences among them and had produced instead a certain homogeneity of culture, common to the majority of the slaves, and shared by the long-resident Africans as well as by the slaves born in the islands.

This common culture of the slave population was shaped primarily by their conditions of enslavement. But the new culture also retained a very considerable African element, based chiefly on those features of the African cultural heritage which were able to survive, not only because they were often common to the different 'tribes' of the slaves but also because they did not conflict with the requirements of the slave system. It was based, in fact, on a combination of these surviving African customs with patterns of behaviour derived from slavery; the resulting mixture was not African but 'Creole' . . . .

The association of African customs with slave behaviour generally tended to debase their value in the eyes of the community, and few Africanisms gained general acceptance among the higher ranks in the established society. The use of foods which were highly seasoned, especially with pepper, seems to have been carried by Negro domestics into the homes even of the white upper class; and the children, who were almost universally reared by Negro nurses, became acquainted with some elements of African folklore, such as the riddles, proverbs, and dramatic folk tales, which were kept alive by their currency among the slave population. Many of the free women of colour also customarily wore head ties, which were of African origin. But, in general, the prominence of African traits in the culture of the majority of the slave population caused the surviving African cultural heritage to be regarded as belonging peculiarly to the slaves, and led the whites and free coloured to reject it as part of their own official culture. The fact that many of the privileged slaves, as well as the free coloured, were more Europeanised than the isolated and lowly field slaves tended to confirm the inferior status of the African cultural tradition Because it survived most strongly among the lowest class of the slave population, attachment to the African tradition was regarded as a symptom of cultural backwardness and a symbol of social inferiority.

The mass of ordinary slaves in the Leeward Islands at the end of the eighteenth century were divided from their masters by a wide difference of culture as well as by their race and status. Like the majority of the West Indian slave population, they had preserved in their culture an important element of African practices and beliefs, which distinguished them from other groups in the slave society. The influence of Africa could be traced, not only in their cooking and folklore, which were to some extent shared by other classes, but also in the cultural features which were more peculiar to the slave group – in their dress, their speech and songs, their music and dancing, in their respect for age, and in the survival of religious beliefs and ceremonies, magical rites, and herbal lore of African origin, under the general appelations of Confu and Obeah.

The slaves in the Leeward Islands often used African-style clothing, including not only the head tie for women but also the garb of flowing cloths for men . . . . Their language was Creole, which combined the English of the masters with the African speech patterns of the slaves. In this dialect, they were fluent and dramatic speakers . . . . Their vivacity and verbal agility were well demonstrated in their songs, made up of improvised verses with a chorus . . . .

The music and dancing of the slaves were very African in character . . . .

The African respect for age . . . . was reflected in the Creole dialect of the Leeward Islands, where the terms 'daddy or uncle' and 'mammy or aunty' were used to address older men and women . . . .

The persistence of the African tradition was also reflected in the religious and magical beliefs and rituals of the Negro slaves in the Leeward Islands . . . .

While the majority of the slaves in the Leeward Islands at the end of the eighteenth century retained a very strong African element in their culture, the culture of their masters, the whites, was greatly influenced by their own European background. In contrast to the slaves, the whites of the Leeward Islands usually wore European-style clothing. They spoke English as their mother tongue, and their folk-lore, music, songs, and dances were derived chiefly from Great Britain. Their official religion was Christianity. However, the culture of the whites was no more wholly European than the culture of the slaves was wholly African. Like the culture of the slaves, the culture of the whites had been shaped by the powerful pressures of the slave society in which they lived . . . .

The culture of the whites was as much a Creole culture as the culture of their slaves, though it substituted European influences for the African influences that prevailed among the slave population.

The culture of the Leeward Islands, like their social organisation, was segmentary. The highest ranks in the community, consisting of whites, had a European-based Creolised culture, while the lowest rank of black field slaves had an African-based Creolised culture. The intermediate groups of privileged slaves and free people of colour, combining elements derived from the culture of the whites and the culture of the blacks, generally strove to 'Europeanise' themselves. But their striving was due to their desire to improve their status in the slave society by identifying, as far as possible, with its dominant class. In spite of its segmentation, the culture of the Leeward Islands formed a coherent whole, faithfully reflecting the social structure of the Creole society of the islands.

The slave society of the Leeward Islands at the end of the eighteenth century was divided into separate groups, clearly marked off from each other by their differences of legal and social status, of political rights and economic opportunity, and of racial origin and culture. The existence of these separate groups is so striking that it tends to obscure the existence of the community of which they were all a part. But this community did exist, and its fundamental principles of inequality and subordination based on race and status were firmly impressed upon the lives of all its members. It was these basic principles, embodying the necessities of the West Indian slave system, which determined the ordering of the separate groups as parts of the community and held them all together within a single social structure.

This social structure was headed by the groups of free-born whites, who had a social status superior to that of all other groups and almost exclusive access to political and economic power in the community. Although there were some class divisions among the whites, communications between their upper and lower ranks were kept open and friendly, and their relations were characterised by racial solidarity and a considerable degree of social mobility.

The line of exclusion in the free community was drawn between the whites and the free-born or manumitted people of colour, who were almost universally treated as a class of freedmen, without claim to political rights. The free coloured, who were often related to the whites by ties of blood, would gladly have identified themselves with this superior class, but their social and legal status placed them below even the poorest whites in the social hierarchy. They formed, therefore, a marginal class between the whites and the slaves, and, since their economic opportunities were limited both by law and by convention, they usually followed occupations common to the poorer whites or to the more privileged slaves. In colour and culture, as well as in status and opportunity, the free coloured were a middle group, because they were usually of mixed blood and more Europeanised than the ordinary slaves.

Immediately below the free coloured in the social structure came the minority of privileged slaves, which generally included all slaves of mixed blood, as well as some of the blacks. Like all the slaves, the privileged slaves were without political rights. But their status and standard of life were higher than those of the rest of the slave population, and their better economic opportunities and more direct personal contacts with the whites frequently enabled them to gain their manumission and to move into the class above them, which they often already resembled in social ambitions and outlook.

The last group in the community was made up almost exclusively of ordinary field slaves, who were all black. The life of the community largely depended on their labour. But they received little benefit in return for their major contribution to the wealth of the society. Their group, which included the overwhelming majority of the slave population, was allowed no political rights and very few economic opportunities. They had the lowest status, the lowest standard of living, and the lowest expectation of life or of freedom, and they lived under conditions of dependence and subjection which were generally harsher than those imposed on any other group among their fellow slaves. They were treated by all other classes as their social inferiors, and, except for their usefulness in underlining the differences between the masters and their slaves, their cultural traditions were generally regarded as worthless. In the midst of so much contempt they had even been persuaded . . . . to despise themselves.

In the social structure of the Leeward Islands at the end of the eighteenth century, colour and status were most significantly linked. A small ruling class, which was almost exclusively white, held in subordination a predominantly brown middle class of free people of colour, a mixed group of brown and black privileged slaves, and a dispossessed labouring population of field slaves, who were almost all black. The Negroes made up the great majority of the population of the islands, but the principles of racial inequality on which the slave society rested were hostile to their dignity and interests.

In such a society, where the law itself enforced the inequality of the races, the doctrines of human rights and the equality of men were potentially inflammatory and dangerous, since anything which weakened the principles of inequality and subordination threatened the existence of the whole society. For this reason the West Indians found the humanitarian attack sufficiently disturbing, because it called in question the basic principles of their social organisation. But their greatest fear was always the fear of revolt from below, and in the late eighteenth century the circumstances of the West Indies made this fear seem particularly real. The rebellions of the free coloured and the slaves, which followed the spread of the French Revolution in the French islands, and especially in the great colony of St. Domingue, were horrifying to the West Indians in the British islands, who feared for the survival of their own society when they saw the revolutionary assault launched against the barriers of colour elsewhere. When the system of legally enforced inequality between the races was challenged and even overthrown in some of the islands, the whites foresaw a dissolution of their society and trembled for their safety . . . .

The experiences of revolutionary war in the West Indies served to emphasise that the preservation of the slave society depended not only on the availability of imperial force but also on the success achieved in insulating it from egalitarian ideas. To preserve the society it appeared vitally necessary to preserve its racial stratification. But this, in turn, depended on preserving the acquiescence of the majority of the Negroes in their subjection to the control of the whites . . . .

Force, law, and habit supported the existing social structure in the Leeward Islands. But by the end of the eighteenth century the general acceptance of Negro inferiority, inculcated even among the Negroes themselves by the harsh realities of their status and conditions of life, had become a very significant factor in maintaining its stability . . . .

In the midst of the social conflicts fought out elsewhere in the West Indies during the course of the revolutionary wars, the Negro population of the Leeward Islands remained quiet. The slave revolt of 1790 in the Virgin Islands appears to have been the last major rebellion to take place in the whole government during the eighteenth century.

This was not because resistance to slavery had ceased among the slaves, but because their resistance tended to be individual and peaceful rather than concerted and violent. Running away, for instance, was always a great deal more common than insurrection, and by the late eighteenth century runaway slaves were increasingly seeking escape by gaining employment in the towns or by deserting the island altogether, and even the problem of rebellious bands of runaways had largely disappeared.

Running away was not only a more frequent and more peaceful form of resistance but it also offered more hope of successful escape from enslavement . . . .

The runaways who escaped into the towns or abroad represented a loss of property, but they did not threaten social stability. Those who managed to escape the net of the slave laws and find employment in the towns sought their opportunities within the existing structure of society, and those who deserted the islands completely were in no position to disturb their internal tranquility. Running away was often an effective form of individual resistance to slavery, but it left the slave system and the slave society quite intact.

The two attempts to organise slave revolts in the Leeward Islands in 1778 and 1790 were potentially more dangerous, because they were directed against slavery itself. But the slaves lacked both the organisation and the opportunities which were necessary to sustain a successful resistance, and both attempts were defeated. In the end, though their resistance gained strength only in the nineteenth century, it was the free coloured, rather than the slaves, who successfully challenged the exclusive control of the whites in the slave society . . . .

The exclusiveness of the whites towards them had eventually forced the free people of colour to attack the principles of inequality and subordination based on race ... But, in spite of their challenge to the established order, the free coloured in the Leeward Islands were not social revolutionaries. Their methods of protest were entirely peaceful, and they based their claims to political rights on the fact that they had acquired property and education as well as freedom and generally resembled the whites in most things, except for their colour. The free coloured wanted to end the system of subordination based on race, but they supported a system of subordination based on other qualifications, which were not effectively available to the mass of the population. Although they were instrumental in securing the equality without regard to race which made the emancipated slaves legally equal to all other inhabitants, the free people of colour continued to regard the social subordination of the lower classes as natural and necessary.

Because the legal change of principle which they sought was peacefully conceded by the whites, the free coloured attack on the organisation of the society soon lost most of its momentum, and the fact that the social revolution in the islands was carried a stage further by the achievement of the emancipation of the slaves was largely due to the determination of the humanitarians in England, who were successful in forcing the British Government into decisive action at a time when the West Indian whites were politically isolated and almost overwhelmed by their economic difficulties . . . .

Since they could not afford to break the military and economic ties with Britain or to reject the British offer of compensation for the loss of their slaves, the West Indians found themselves compelled to accept the emancipation of the slaves, as they had already accepted the enfranchisement of the free coloured. The slave system with its basic inequalities of legal status, which the British had fought to preserve during the War of the French Revolution, was finally destroyed in the British West Indies by decree of the British Parliament, peacefully imposed on the white minority of the population, who had come to the reluctant conclusion that a violent struggle over emancipation would be more dangerous to their lives, their property, and their social position than emancipation itself.

When the whites in the West Indies accepted emancipation and carried it fully into effect, the legal basis of their society was transformed. The slaves ceased to be a form of property and became free persons, equal to all others in the eyes of the law, and it was at last possible for them to attempt to bring about changes in the economic and social organisation of the islands without breaking the law or threatening to overthrow the whole society. This made for the acceptance of a peaceful process of social development by the emancipated population and greatly increased the social stability of the islands. As they had proved by their concessions to the free coloured, the whites were able to moderate the force of the demand for change by moderating their own resistance to change. By conceding emancipation and legal equality, without a recourse to violence, they ensured that the effects of these changes would be essentially peaceful and slow. Because the legal and political status of the coloured population had been radically altered, it was possible to argue that every member of the society was now free to advance himself as far as he was able.

But, though it opened the way to a gradual erosion of the old economic and social structure, legal equality was not, by itself, enough to obliterate the differences of social status and economic opportunity, and of colour and cultural tradition, which had divided the racial groups under the slave system. So long as the plantation system remained the basis of economic organisation, the whites were likely to maintain their hold on the economies of the islands, and the social structure derived from the requirements of plantation slavery was likely to persist.

The economic decline leading to emancipation had seemed to presage an imminent collapse of the whole plantation economy, and this was a matter of urgent concern to the whites when they opposed emancipation. But, in fact, the emancipation of the slaves, with its accompanying grant of compensation to the slave owners, actually had the effect of reviving the flagging sugar industry in some of the islands, by liquidating old debts and cutting the costs of production in densely populated territories like the Leeward Islands, where many of the former slaves were forced to seek work on the plantations, even at very low wages.

Wherever it occurred, and it occurred among the Leeward Islands, the revival of sugar and the plantation system enabled the whites to salvage much of their old pre-eminence in the society of the islands. Even after the profound crisis of emancipation, therefore, the social structure which had been characteristic of the slave society in the Leeward Islands at the end of the eighteenth century was still, in large measure, preserved . . . .

At a time when a diversification of ownership and of economic activities was becoming vitally important to the development of the new free society in the Leeward Islands, the attention of the ruling classes was concentrated on the task of salvaging the plantation economy, and the bulk of the emancipated population had little effective alternative to earning a poor livelihood by plantation labour . . . .

The emancipation of the slaves in the Leeward Islands in the nineteenth century was the beginning of a social revolution which is still working itself out at the present day. But because of the relative peacefulness and continuity of social development in these islands, even at the time of emancipation, the foundations of the free society were built upon a social structure which had been shaped by the necessities of the slave system, with its basic principles of racial inequality and subordination. When the social structure of the Creole society of the eighteenth century was incorporated in the new, free society of the nineteenth century, many of the values of the old slave society were inevitably carried over into the era of freedom . . . .

Change and Stability

In the slave society of the Leeward Islands at the end of the eighteenth century, the white minority had successfully imposed its claims to superior status upon the overwhelming black majority of the population, who were generally immobilised without hope of escape in the lowest ranks of the social structure, and upon the growing proportion of people of mixed blood making up the groups of coloured freedmen and privileged slaves, who were already occupying the marginal position of a middle class, between the depressed lower class of blacks and the dominant upper class of whites. The social order of the whole community hung upon the distinctions established between its constituent races.

This is a pattern of social subordination which has been extremely influential and persistent in the historical development of the West Indies. . . . Shortly before emancipation came in the nineteenth century, the social structure in the British Caribbean, as M.G. Smith has briefly outlined it, consisted of 'three main social sections defined primarily by legal status . . . . [and] composed in the main, but not universally, of persons who differed also in race and colour',[5] and it was the desire of the whites to maintain their status in this structure which led them to resist the movement towards freedom. But, even after this movement had succeeded, the demise of the slave society did not mean the automatic disappearance of the forms of social stratification to which it had given birth. For, to cite only one more example out of several possible illustrations, Lloyd Braithwaite's analysis of Trinidadian society in the middle of the twentieth century proves, with a wealth of graphic detail, that the relationships between colour and class inherited from the nineteenth century have not been basically transformed, though they have certainly been modified, by the immigration which has introduced new groups and the increased mobility which has affected old ones in the free society of that island. The findings of this excellent study also demonstrate very clearly that the survival of a system of social stratification in which colour is still a basic factor has entailed the survival of many of the particularistic and ascriptive values which originally served to maintain the characteristic inequalities of status and opportunity between the races in the West Indian slave society[6]. . . .

The myth of Negro inferiority was the creature of the slave system as well as its most influential ethical defence.[7] It was made inevitable, and plausible, by the rigid distinctions separating Negroes from whites in the racially graded system of social subordination which the growth of Negro slavery had engendered in the West Indies. By the end of the eighteenth century a great gulf had become fixed between the races in consequence of the privileges and protection customarily enjoyed by the whites and the subjection and deprivation customarily suffered by the blacks, and gross inequalities of status and opportunities, of material condition and social aspirations, emphasised their differences of racial origin. This legal and social division of the races was reinforced by the survival of African cultural traditions among the blacks which contrasted with the European cultural traditions preserved among the whites.

The combination of so many distinctive differences between the races made their separation seem not only complete but natural and right. Thus the sanction of racialist beliefs was added to the sanctions of force, law, and habit which supported the slave system. The brutal contrasts created by enslavement could then be interpreted as proof of the essential racial inferiority of Negroes and the intrinsic racial superiority of whites. The influence of these ascriptive values made it impossible for the small intermediate group of people of mixed blood to bridge the social distance between the classes above and below them, because they were too alienated, both from the blacks and from the whites, by the inescapable significance attached to colour in the communal life of the slave society.

The Christian missionaries engaged in converting the Negroes in the West Indies at the end of the eighteenth century were among the very few whites then resident in the islands who were not committed to the most characteristic racial assumptions of the community within which their work was proceeding. For this reason their activities among the slaves were frequently regarded with suspicion by the ruling class, who were inclined to distrust the religious universalism of missionary Christianity. But though the missionaries deliberately stood somewhat apart from local white society at the end of the eighteenth century, they were nevertheless contributing an active and powerful reinforcement to the many sanctions already making for the internal stability of the slave system. In spite of the fears of the whites, the growing success of the missions was of more practical value to them than the neglect of the work of conversion which was usual among the regular clergy of the Established Church, who were very closely identified with the ruling class of the islands. For, far from being a threat to the social order, the increase of the Christian missions was calculated to maintain and strengthen the slave society.

After only about twenty-five years of work in the Leeward Islands, the missions had converted about one-fourth of the Negro population, and their converts were organised in predominantly Negro churches under the strict supervision of white leaders who carefully inculcated the morality of resignation and submission among the Negroes. The establishment of these churches gave the slaves forms of social organisation and expression, and even opportunities for leadership, which they had previously lacked. But the extensive moral influence and intensive religious discipline which the missionaries were enabled to build up among their converts were consistently used to enjoin on them the practice of Christian virtues, such as diligence, honesty, obedience, and fidelity, which would make the converted Negro a better slave, and every possible effort was devoted to the task of convincing him that it was an essential testimony of conscientious faith to accept and obey the rule of the master, whose authority over him had previously depended upon sanctions which were almost entirely external . . . .

The case of the missionaries, who only began their work in the British West Indies during the later eighteenth century, readily illustrates that a number of the changes taking place in the islands at the end of the eighteenth century were of a kind adapted to confirm and perpetuate the established social order. Similar elements of change were embodied in the new willingness to reduce or neglect property qualifications, and even to abandon the religious qualifications still considered essential by the imperial government, so as to recruit more whites into the ranks of the ruling class; in the growing importance of racialism as a basic principle of the social as well as the political organisation of the slave society; in the rapid spread of slaves into non-agricultural employment, especially in the towns; in the increased emphasis consequently placed on the provision of economic regulations covering their activities as well as those of the free coloured; and even in the carefully guarded concessions made in the island laws to meet the rising humanitarian pressure for an amelioration of slave conditions. The distinguishing feature common to all these changes was their tendency to strengthen the hold of slavery on the life of the community and thus to strengthen the foundations supporting the system of racial inequality and subordination prevailing in the islands. They were essentially 'conservative' changes, confined within the limits set by the existing organisation of the slave society, which was neither endangered nor fundamentally contradicted by them.

Towards the end of the eighteenth century, however, there were other changes at work which were more likely to destroy the slave system than to stabilise it. These challenging new forces could not be contained within the existing structure as conservative change was, because they were directly opposed to its continuance and implied the necessity for basic or 'radical' change in its organisation. Among these changes, the most immediately alarming to the West Indian whites was the spread of ideas of human rights and of social and political reform both in Europe and in the islands. For it intensified their chronic fear that the slave society might be overthrown from below, and it also led their humanitarian critics to insist that abolition of the slave trade was the only secure means of avoiding the disastrous social conflicts which must inevitably follow unless the slave owners were forced to ameliorate the deplorable conditions of life among the slaves and to pay some respect to their neglected human claims.

Equally dangerous currents of economic change were, by the end of the century, also threatening to undermine the basis of the social structure in the British West Indies, where the plantation economy was beginning to show warning symptoms of distress and decline. When these two streams of political and economic change flowed together, as they did early in the nineteenth century, the West Indians soon found themselves facing a situation of acute crisis in which they were exposed to the full impact of radical change because they could no longer preserve the favourable balance of influence and interests which had protected them before . . .

The struggle over emancipation, like that over abolition of the slave trade, was a tragi-comedy of errors of miscalculation. The Leeward Islands joined the rest of the British West Indies in opposing it, as they had opposed abolition. For their planters, like those of the other colonies, believed that freedom would be their ruin. But, in fact, the very density of population which was ruining them under the declining system of slave agriculture ensured them a cheap and numerous working population under the system of free labour. It was emancipation which finally revived their failing sugar industry, both by bringing in compensation money[8] which paid off many of the planters' longstanding debts and by making their dense populations an asset rather than a liability so long as enough capital could be found to finance the continued operation of the sugar estates after emancipation. The final irony of these results was that the revival of the sugar industry in many of the British West Indian territories, particularly in densely populated islands like Antigua and St. Kitts, under the regime of free labour, also preserved the economic foundation of plantation agriculture on which it had been built.

Emancipation was a legal revolution of fundamental significance for the future of the West Indies. For it set the mass of the population free from the legally enforced subordination to which they had been subjected in the days of slavery. But civil equality was not practical equality, which depended upon such factors as the distribution of wealth and opportunity and the exercise of political rights. Upon emancipation the Negroes started from a position of practical inequality, and the peacefulness of the process by which their freedom was achieved ensured that the consequences of the legal revolution would be felt only slowly and as a result of the efforts of particular individuals to improve their status and opportunities. These efforts were, however, least likely to succeed where the great plantation, with its industrial need to guarantee profits by exploiting poverty and dependence, continued to be the dominant form of economic organisation.

Among the Leeward Islands this dominance was often made less insecure by the adoption of free labour, and the immediate results of emancipation were therefore in many respects conservative. The legal status of the mass of the population was radically changed. But, though they were now less physically oppressed, their life chances in the free society, as compared with those of other groups, were not very substantially different from what they had been before. The old community based on slavery had been destroyed. But the emergent free society could only offer them a confused amalgam of opposing social values – on the one hand, practical subordination in a particularistic social structure still based on racial inequality, and on the other, universalist claims to equal status before the law without regard to class or race. As Lord Harris said in 1848, the effect of emancipation was that 'a race has been freed but a society has not been formed'.[9] New guiding principles of order and coherence had still to be decided on . . . .

In their struggles to preserve the slave system the whites of all the islands were bitterly opposed to the recognition that the Negro population had inalienable human rights which the law should protect. They were even more opposed to the acceptance of changes by which the coloured majority of the population would be allowed to escape from their enforced subordinate status by being granted legal equality with all other inhabitants. This was because they believed that their very survival depended on keeping the Negroes 'in their place' at the bottom of the social structure, where slavery had held them, more or less securely, for more than a century. But because they were too weak and too isolated institutionally to resist Britain or even to defend themselves by force of arms, they had in the end to take the consequences of their own subordination to the will of the metropolis. The whites paid the price of their dependence by abandoning slavery, because the only alternative to this surrender was a rebellion in which defeat appeared to be the only possible outcome . . . .

The era of moral crisis which was signalled by the widespread unrest and political agitation of the late eighteenth century is not yet over, and there is much to be learnt from the experience of those who took part in these struggles for reform. Our conception of human rights is inevitably somewhat different from theirs, since we are now working within a democratic political system that is very different from the limited representative system of government which they knew. But the fundamental question then raised as to whether the 'rights of man' should be recognised and respected in the West Indies has not yet been given an unequivocal answer by our free but disunited society. The universalist tenets of liberty and equality still present to the troubled conscience of the contemporary West Indies a problem of choice which it is becoming more and more urgent to resolve.

Ever since the time of emancipation we have been trying to combine quite opposite principles in our social system. But sooner or later we shall have to face the fact that we are courting defeat when we attempt to build a new heritage of freedom upon a structure of society which binds us all too closely to the old heritage of slavery. Liberty and equality are good consorts, for, though their claims sometimes conflict, they rest upon a common basis of ideas which makes them reconcilable. But a most profound incompatibility necessarily results from the uneasy union which joins democracy with the accumulated remains of enslavement. In the end, either one or the other must be undermined by the constant antagonism of mutually intolerant elements.

Perhaps, however, there is still good reason to believe that the forces of radicalism will prevail. For now that a democratic suffrage has been established in many parts of the West Indies as well as elsewhere in the world, the time may be ripening for the emergence and success of renewed movements of protest. The existence of political democracy gives the partisans of radical change the hope of appealing to the large majorities still suffering from the effects of poverty and lack of opportunity to vote for effective reforming policies based on universalist social values. If they persuade the people to accept a fundamental commitment to these values, the fragmented territories of the West Indies may be enabled to develop at last a new sense of community, transcending the geographical and political divisions and the alienations of caste and race that have so far marked their common history.

NOTES

1. The British Leeward Islands included the colonies of Antigua, St Kitts, Nevis, Montserrat, Barbuda, Anguilla and the British Virgin Islands.
2. Bryan Edwards, *History, Civil and Commercial, of the British Colonies in the West Indies* vol.3 (London, 1793).13. Edwards (1743–1800) was born in England but Goveia wrote that 'he saw with the eyes of a "Creole" ' (1956, 80).
3. Author's note: The words quoted are taken from James Tobin's evidence in *House of Commons Accounts and Papers*, vol. XXIX (1790), No. 698(5), p.278.

4. Edwards, op. cit., vol.2, p.93.
5. M.G. Smith, 'Social Structure in the British Caribbean,' *Social and Economic Studies* 1 (1953): 75. Smith (1921–93), a Jamaican anthropologist, was a Research Fellow of the Institute of Social and Economic Research (ISER) of the University College of the West Indies in Jamaica between 1952 and 1961 (see chapter 27), and a colleague of Goveia.
6. Lloyd Braithwaite, 'Social Stratification in Trinidad,' *Social and Economic Studies* 2 (1953): 5–175. Braithwaite (1919–95), a Trinidadian sociologist, began his career as a Research Fellow in the ISER in Jamaica in the 1950s, became Professor of Sociology and then the Principal and Pro-Vice Chancellor of the UWI at St Augustine in Trinidad.
7. Author's note: E.V. Goveia, *A Study of the Historiography of the British West Indies* (Mexico, 1956) has shown that the historians of the British West Indies, who generally reflected the prevailing ideas of their time, did not begin to justify the slavery of the Negroes by this form of reasoning until after the start of the eighteenth century, when this racialist argument emerged as 'a by-product of the institution of Negro slavery' and became the dominant historical explanation among the pro-slavery historians.
8. Prolonged negotiations resulted in an award of £20 million to the slave owners when slavery was abolished in 1834, in compensation for their loss of property. The British government thought that this generous award was necessary in order to pacify the slave owners and to avoid setting a dangerous precedent by appropriating private property without compensation. All slave owners were eligible for compensation, which was given according to the estimated value of each slave, but a lot of capital accrued to their British creditors.
9. Lord Harris was the governor of Trinidad from 1846 to 1854, a time of crisis in the island's sugar industry.

Thirty-One

Cheddi Jagan

Cheddi Jagan (1918–97), the grandchild of indentured Indian immigrants to what was then British Guiana, was the leader of his country's first modern political party, the first prime minister and later the president of Guyana. He was the first Marxist political leader in the Caribbean. He and his party won the first three elections held under universal adult suffrage in Guyana but his government was twice overthrown and the constitution suspended and changed to ensure that he would not lead his country into independence.

Jagan's father was a cane cutter, with only three years of schooling, who became the foreman of a gang. His mother, who never went to school, kept their home, a two-room house with a dirt floor and thatched roof. They were Hindu and Jagan was brought up in the Hindu tradition but he recalled that the religious significance of the festivals was lost on him. The social life of his childhood revolved around the plantation but his parents kept him in school and paid for him to go to secondary school in Port Mourant. In 1933, at the age of 15, he went to Queen's College in Georgetown. He passed his exams after spending two years there. Unable to find a job, he went to the United States where he studied dentistry in Washington and Chicago, qualifying in 1942. He experienced the crude reality of racism and segregation in the United States but he also encountered socialist literature and met Janet Rosenberg, whom he married shortly before he returned to Guyana in 1943. He described the social and cultural influences on his early life in one of his books, The West on Trial, *which was first published in 1966.*

Jagan became the treasurer of the Man-Power Citizens' Association (MPCA), a trade union of the largely Indian sugar estate workers. His desire for more political involvement led to the creation, with his wife and two trade unionists, Ashton Chase and Jocelyn Hubbard, of the Political Affairs Committee in 1946. The next year, despite a very limited suffrage, he was elected to the Legislative Council where, at the age of 29, he was the youngest member. In 1950, he formed the People's Progressive party (PPP), the first mass party in the country. The PPP brought together people of African and Indian descent, along with whites, Chinese and others, in a radical anti-colonial movement. Jagan was the leader and Forbes Burnham, an Afro-Guyanese lawyer who had returned from studies in England, became the party chairman.

In 1953, in the first elections under universal adult suffrage, the PPP won easily. About 75 per cent of the electorate voted and the PPP received 51 per cent of the votes, winning 18 of the 24 seats, in a demonstration of inter-racial cooperation. The PPP's agenda of radical reform, coupled with Marxist rhetoric, upset the British government which was determined to control the decolonisation process in Guyana as it did elsewhere in the West Indies. Only 133 days after their triumphant entry into the legislature, Britain sent troops to occupy the colony and suspended the constitution. Burnham was encouraged by the British government, which considered him more moderate than Jagan, to split the PPP and, in 1957, he founded the People's National Congress (PNC).

Jagan's PPP won the elections in 1957 and 1961, with 47 and 43 per cent of the vote, respectively. The PPP lacked a majority of the popular vote but, in 1961, won 20 seats to 11 for the PNC and four for the business-oriented United Force (UF). Jagan's administration undertook a programme of reforms in education, health and housing, and he expected to lead Guyana into independence. However, the United States had identified Jagan and his party as communist and was concerned, after Castro's revolution in 1959, not to allow 'another Cuba' in the hemisphere. With extensive US involvement and British connivance, a series of strikes and riots between 1962 and 1964 fomented ethnic conflict and the further racialisation of Guyana's politics. British troops returned and Britain, with US support, imposed a system of proportional representation, though neither of these metropolitan powers accepted this in their own political systems. They had calculated that Jagan would lose under this system, although the Indo-Guyanese were about half the population.

In 1964, under the new system, the PPP won 46 per cent of the votes and 24 seats, the PNC won 40.5 per cent of the votes and 22 seats, and the UF won 12.4 per cent of the votes and 7 seats. Although the PNC had won fewer votes and seats than the PPP, Burnham was able to form a coalition government with the

UF and he led Guyana to independence in 1966. In subsequent elections, from 1968 until his death in 1985, massive fraud and violence kept Burnham and his PNC in power. Guyana, meanwhile, became a republic and in 1992, in the first fair elections since 1964, Jagan was elected president.

An unusually modest and approachable man, Jagan inherited a country that had suffered from years of corruption and mismanagement, massive emigration, a huge international debt, and widespread cynicism about politics. He died in 1997 at the age of 78 and was succeeded by his wife, Janet Jagan, a Jewish-American grandmother, who became the first woman elected president of a South American country. In 1999 she stepped down for health reasons.

Jagan's account of some of these events, excerpted from The West on Trial, *reveals his analysis and understanding of his society and its problems in the process of decolonisation.*

$\mathcal{T}$he West on Trial (excerpts)

Growing Up

The plantation appeared to me as the hub of life. Everything revolved around sugar, and the sugar planters seemed to own the world. They owned the canefields and the factories; even the small pieces of land rented to some of the workers for family food production belonged to them. They owned the mansions occupied by the senior staff, and the cottages occupied by dispensers, chemists, engineers, bookkeepers and drivers. They owned the logies (ranges) and huts where the labourers lived, the hospitals and every other important building. At one time they also owned and operated a rice mill. Even the churches and schools came within their patronage and control.

The plantation was indeed a world of its own. Or rather it was two worlds: the world of exploiters and the world of the exploited; the world of whites and the world of non-whites. One was the world of managers and the European staff in their splendid mansions; the other the world of the labourers in their logies in the 'niggeryard' and the 'bound-coolie-yard'. The mansions were electrically lit; the logies had kerosene lamps. It was not unusual to hear it said that the mules were better treated than human beings, for the stables had electric light. It was not that electricity could not have been taken to the workers' quarters and residences. The owners could easily have generated more electricity at very little extra cost to satisfy the needs of all. But electricity, like so many other things, was a status symbol . . . .

Sitting at the apex of this world was the plantation manager. At Port Mourant, the premier plantation in Berbice, the manager during my boyhood was J.C. Gibson. His reputation extended far and wide; he was czar, king, prosecutor, and judge, all in one. Almost everyone looked upon him with awe and fear . . . .

Between these white and non-white worlds there were distances – social (inhabitants of these two worlds did not associate) and physical (the mansions were out of bounds). There was also a psychological distance. I recall vividly my great curiosity about the manager's mansion. I wanted to know what it felt like to be inside the gate. I wanted to know what was going on inside. The opportunity came one Christmas when I must have been about eight or nine years old. I joined the creole gang and went to share in the largesse of the manager. The manager's wife, Mrs. Gibson, stood at the window of the top floor of this imposing mansion. She threw coins down to us and enjoyed seeing the wild scramble for the pennies.

The plantation hierarchy had an unwritten but nevertheless rigid code. Managers and overseers could have sex relations with non-white women, but intermarriage was strictly forbidden. These women were not considered good enough to be wives of whites. Although sexual intercourse between white members of the staff and non-white women was looked upon with disfavour by the Immigration Department, in practice the plantation system was so organised that nothing could be done to prevent it . . . .

Plantation life gave me the opportunity of seeing at first hand the raw deal which the labourers received. No doubt these experiences were the factors which led to my early interest in social and economic questions.

Between the worlds of employers and employees was the middle stratum of shopkeepers, pandits, parsons, teachers, dispensers, bookkeepers and drivers, all of whom depended for their status and social position on the patronage of the manager. They could be penalised at any time if they lost favour with him.

My father was at the lowest level of the middle stratum. His position was the source of a real dilemma to him. He felt himself one of the exploited, but as a driver had to carry out the orders of his exploiters. I recall how this grieved him. His way out was publicly to carry out his duties while privately advising and urging the workers on the courses of action open to them.

Having attained the position of driver, my father had no further avenue of promotion, for the unwritten law was that none other than a white man could hold the post of overseer. This was a cause of frustration and bitterness as he had to train white men who did not know the difference between young sugarcane plants and grass.

My father proved his competence at work and at play. In many ways he demonstrated that he was a man equal to, and sometimes better than, those placed above him because of their white skins . . . .

Like most people of the labouring class whose privations began in infancy, disease began to affect my father's health when he was about fifty. However, because he was a man of fine and indomitable spirit, he died fighting to the very end. He refused to agree with the surgeon's decision that his gangrenous foot should be amputated. This might save his life, he was told, but this argument was of no avail; he did not wish to live as a cripple . . . .

If my father could not break out of his environment himself, he sought to do so through me. He saw to it that the opportunities of which he had been deprived were made available to me. He well knew what the lack of formal education meant, so he made sure that I attended school . . . .

In 1933, at the age of fifteen, my father decided to send me to Queen's College, the government secondary school for boys in the capital city of Georgetown, about a hundred miles away from home, a great distance in those days of very poor roads and slow transport.

My self-confidence was to receive a sharp blow on my arrival in Georgetown. At Port Mourant I had been a big fish in a small pond, a king in my own kingdom. Georgetown was different. There I was a country boy in a big city, a tiny 'patwa'[1] in a big pond. At home I had felt the social distance between my parents and even shopkeepers. Here I was suddenly thrown among the sons of 'famous' people . . .

Though Queen's College was a challenge, in many respects it was a disappointment. On the one hand, it was very remote from the life and experience of a boy such as myself; and on the other, it was involved in training a fortunate few, quite without relation to Guiana and realities.

I soon found myself in conflict with the ways in which I had been brought up and with the kind of things I had been doing. At Port Mourant, poverty was intense – I didn't wear shoes until I was about twelve. From an early age I had to undertake various jobs to supplement the family income. As the combined income of my parents from work in the fields was inadequate even to meet the barest necessities of life, our family diet was not only very simple and modest but also monotonous, consisting of the same items over and over again. Rice and dhal (split peas), occasionally roti (a form of bread) and fish were the principal items . . . .

Additional income for the family came from three sources – five acres of rice, a few head of cattle and a kitchen garden at the rear of our home. I often had to take time off from school to work in the rice fields at both planting and harvest, and on Saturdays to help my father cut and fetch canes. Cutting grass for our cows, helping with the kitchen garden and at times even selling produce from the latter in the open-air plantation market, became part of my routine . . . .

In Georgetown and at Queen's College, however, values were different. Here I began to develop a kind of snobbery, entangling myself in the problem of adjustment arising from the process of cultural integration and assimilation that was taking place. For Indians, urbanisation had a Western and Christian influence, particularly among the second and third generations, who were torn between the new and dominant mores of the city and the older customs and habits of home, based originally on an oriental way of life, but somewhat modified by time . . . .

The 'clash of cultures' was particularly evident in two of the three families with whom I boarded in Georgetown. In the first family, a beautiful daughter resented the old-fashioned restrictions her father imposed upon her. I became the victim not only of his rigid discipline, but also of his frugality. To compensate him for the small amount of money my father paid for my board and lodging, I had to do many chores such as washing his car, carrying his lunch on my bicycle, going to market, and cutting grass for his goats. I particularly resented the latter. Cutting and fetching grass in the country was one thing; doing so in Georgetown as a Queen's College student was quite another. Georgetown middle-class snobbery had so influenced me that I soon found some pretext to persuade my father to find me other lodgings.

But this change was a case of out of the frying pan into the fire. The new family with whom I stayed belonged to the Kshatriya caste. One of the daughters had married a Brahmin and had three sons and one daughter. So strait-laced were the family elders that the three boys, who also went to Queen's College, became pale imitations of robust boyhood. Two things particularly irked me about my position in this household: firstly, I was singled out to go occasionally to the market; secondly, I had to sleep on the floor, although there was an empty room with a vacant bed. Apparently this was for reasons of status, based on caste – my family caste was Kurmi, lower in status than a Kshatriya or a Brahmin. Until then, although I had heard my mother occasionally mention caste, I had never really encountered it, so I deeply resented this treatment and rebelled against it in many ways.

It was not long before I moved to a third family, who were not Hindus but Catholic converts, and it was here, ironically enough, that I felt really free. This was largely due to the fact that the head of the family was not only a relatively young man, but he had also come up the hard way, from chauffeur to an estate manager to customs clerk in the office of one of the three foreign-owned sugar companies. I suppose, too, that I was growing up . . . .

Victory and 133 Days in Office

The 1953 election campaign roused unprecedented enthusiasm throughout the country. For the first time in our history the people were really involved; it was their first election under universal adult suffrage. So great was interest that the percentage (74.8 percent) who turned out to vote was higher than in Jamaica, Barbados and Trinidad, where the figures ranged between 53 and 65 percent . . . .

Our campaigning in 1953 brought us into contact with working people all over the country, with the exception of the Interior. We did not have enough funds to make expensive trips to the remote areas. That was why we contested only 22 of the 24 seats. My wife was in charge of Essequibo and West Demerara. I was responsible for the East Coast of Demerara and Berbice while Burnham[2] conducted the campaign in Georgetown. This division was forced upon us for we had soon discovered that Burnham was not one of those who was prepared to undertake arduous work. He had never ventured very far away from Georgetown and had made few contributions to the party newspaper.

One of the major charges against us during the campaign was that we were getting 'red gold' from Moscow. This was a fantasy. Actually our campaign was run on a shoestring . . . .

In this campaign, the Opposition had the support of big business with the press as its powerful weapon. On two Sundays prior to voting day, the MPCA[3] circulated in the three daily newspapers a four-page supplement which viciously attacked us and laid great stress on my wife being Jewish . . . .

The churches, too, played a big role in opposition to us. In our colonial society, the hierarchy of the Anglican Church was closely identified with the ruling class; the planters and their supporters and high Anglicanism were inseparable, with deep commitment to the preservation of the *status quo*. A similar role was played by the powerful Roman Catholic Church, controlled by the small but wealthy Portuguese group who, next to the ruling British-European group, dominated the social and economic life of the country . . . .

The Churches' hostility to us was mainly due to our policy with respect to the control of schools. We had stated categorically that we were in favour of the abolition of the system of dual (church-state) control of schools. The organised Hindu and Muslim groups – the Hindu Maha Sabha, the Pandits' Council, the United Sad'r Islamic Anjuman and the Muslim League – also attacked us.

What was more alarming was the cross fire of racism in which we were caught. The NDP[4] and the League of Coloured People attempted to woo support away from us by appealing to African racism. Their propaganda line was simple enough – the PPP was Indian-dominated, and Burnham, an African, was only being used. On the other hand, in the countryside, the Indian voters were told that I was sacrificing the interests of the Indians and selling out to the Africans. Crude religious and racist appeals were made by the Hindu Pandits and Debidin's United Farmers' and Workers' Party respectively. They exploited the issue of the West Indies Federation which the PPP strongly supported. We were attacked by Indian racist leaders like Daniel P. Debidin who argued that Indian interests in Guiana would be lost and submerged in an African-dominated Federation. And so it originated the slogan 'Apan Jhaat' (literall y, own race) – the use of racist emotionalism to frighten the Indians away from the PPP. This was what led the PPP at the 1953 general election to include in its manifesto the call for a referendum on the question whether or not Guiana should enter the Federation . . . .

In spite of the tremendous excitement generated by the election, it all went off quite smoothly. The campaign was orderly with hardly any incidents. The Commissioner of Police kept the Volunteer Force in reserve but did not have to call it out. When the count was finally made, the PPP won 18 seats, the NDP 2 and the independents 4 . . . .

But the most significant outcome of the election was the complete rout of the racists – the League of Coloured People and the East Indian Association. We won all the 5 seats in Georgetown which at the 1947 election had been the stronghold of the LCP and all the 8 seats in the 'sugar belt' . . . .

Winning the election was only the first phase of the battle . . . .

We took our seats feeling very proud of ourselves and all too aware of our constitutional limitations. We told our supporters that even though we had won the election, we were really Her Majesty's Government's loyal Opposition. In our policy statement, we pointed out that even if we were elected we would be dependent on, and subordinate to the metropolitan power and we had offered only such proposals as could be realised within the limitation of our colonial position.

The changes we began to introduce now seem quite modest . . . .

On the very day British troops entered Guiana, we passed in the House of Assembly our Labour Relations Bill. Employers were to be required by law to negotiate with the trade unions enjoying majority support; this support was to be determined by a procedure modelled upon that of the U.S. National Labor Relations Act, and similar legislation in Canada. The bill was aimed at minimising inter-union rivalry and preventing jurisdictional disputes. It included two other important provisions – one seeking to prohibit victimisation of workers and the other seeking the right of trade union officials to visit the place at which their members were employed.

This Bill touched 'King Sugar'. The recognition of the Guiana Industrial Workers' Union, then the unrecognised sugar union, would have meant better wages and proper working conditions for the sugar workers and reduced profit for the sugar planters.

The legislation had become necessary because the sugar industry had been paralysed by a 25-day strike called by the GIWU and a sympathy strike on the part of practically the whole trade union movement.

The response of the enemies of the PPP was true to form: 'another communist measure', they howled.

The bill 'brought down the clouds'. On Thursday, October 8, 1953, British troops were hurried across the Atlantic in warships and aircraft to Georgetown.

They had been given to understand that they were being sent to put down a Communist coup. The troops arrived asking: 'Where is the war?' Guyanese women in the markets rocked with laughter. Then the people were puzzled. Finally, as the hours went by, it became clear that this was no passing visit; the country was occupied.

Our 133 days in office had demonstrated our concept of democracy. Now the British and our opponents in Guiana demonstrated theirs . . . .

In Office but Not in Power

If the years of the suspended constitution, 1953 to 1957, were a period of colonial dictatorship, the years 1957 to 1964 were the period of the People's Progressive Party in office but not in power. The first four of these years were tantamount to a coalition of the People's Progressive Party and the Colonial Office; towards the end of this first term I was dubbed Chief Minister. Then in 1961 after we were re-elected, my title changed to Premier under 'internal self-government'. But real power to govern, to carry out our programme fully, was withheld from us throughout.

The government was deemed PPP, but in fact real power remained in the hands of the Governor; constitutionally, we were merely his advisers. With him in the Executive Council were 3 other Englishmen who held the most important portfolios. Apart from their support, he also had the right to appoint if necessary additional ministers – 1 *ex officio* and 1 nominated to counter the influence of the 5 elected ministers ...

In 1962, the dissentient elements had used the budget to start trouble. In 1963, their pretext for the strife was the Labour Relations Bill.

This Bill introduced in March, was essentially similar to the one which we had introduced in 1953 when Burnham was a member of the government. It provided for a secret poll of workers by which the union securing the majority of votes would become the recognised union.

Actually, we had a mandate to enact such a law by virtue of three successive general elections which we had won on the basis of a platform which emphasized this measure . . . .

The question might well be asked, what accounted for the changed attitude to the Labour Relations Bill by the TUC[5] leadership and Burnham in 1963, as compared with that in 1953, a decade earlier? Firstly, a poll would have ended the power of the MPCA in the sugar industry and elsewhere by the election of trade union leaders who were sympathetic with the aims and objectives of the People's Progressive Party. Secondly, the strike was the only means of forestalling independence and of putting back into power reactionary and opportunistic politicians. Burnham, after losing two successive elections, saw no other way to satisfy his personal ambitions. Thirdly, the poll would have removed the bureaucratic TUC leadership and the reactionary U.S. influence on the trade-union movement.

The violence and disturbances of 1962 and 1963 did not succeed in their immediate objective of bringing about the fall of the government or the suspension of the constitution. But they did result, as we shall see, in the delay of independence and the imposition of a constitutional and electoral formula designed to bring the opposition to power. It was a major tragedy for Guyana that a section of the working class was deluded into forging its own chains by directing its attacks not, as previously, against the capitalists and landlords but against a national, pro-working class, socialist-oriented government . . . .

The governments of the United States and Britain were deeply involved in the disturbances of 1962 and 1963 . . . .

[T]he strike was inspired by a combination of U.S. Central Intelligence Agency money and British Intelligence. The Anglo-American conspiracy of 1962 and 1963 failed to bring down the government. But it undermined confidence in it and encouraged and emboldened the opposition. The PNC and UF leaders[6] were encouraged to feel that no matter how irresponsible, illegal and violent were their acts, no effective counter action would be taken against them. This led to their rejection of every reasonable proposal we made for a political and constitutional settlement and ultimately to the rape of our constitution in 1963 . . . .

Race, Class, Colour and Religion

British and American rulers deliberately fomented racial disturbances in order to prevent the transfer of full powers to us . . . . The fact is that race and religion have been used by the colonialists to divide and rule and to blur the basic issues, which include the struggle for national liberation from colonialism and imperialism and the struggle of the workers and farmers for freedom from exploitation. These struggles sharpened with the advent of the People's Progressive Party . . . .

During the course of our history, there occurred almost a racial division of labour. After the abolition of slavery, Portuguese immigrants first replaced the freed African slaves. Their numbers, however, were small. Then followed Indians and Chinese.[7] The freed Africans in the meantime moved away to the city and to village settlements adjoining sugar plantations. In the city, they filled the lowest positions in the administration and other unskilled jobs in the government services such as transport, postal, medical, telecommunications. Those who could not find employment in government services provided unskilled wage labour for private enterprise in the city, and for sawmills, wood grants, mines and quarries in the Interior. Generally, the Africans shunned the land, especially after the failures of the early cooperative land settlements largely because of inadequate water control.

The Portuguese and Chinese immigrants also followed the example of the Africans. Some of the Portuguese, mainly because of their colour, took their position side by side with the small but powerful British European community in the administrative and technical branches of the civil service. The rest of the Portuguese and the Chinese went into commerce, the Chinese in particular specialising in the grocery trade.

The bulk of the Indians remained in the countryside, mostly in the sugar plantations and in the rice fields. Even up to 1960, they constituted only 22 percent of the urban population as compared with African – 48.5 percent, and Mixed – 22 percent.[8]

This early division of labour occupationally and geographically according to race tended to prevent integration and to arouse racial hostility. Undercutting of wages and of the emancipated Africans by cheap Indian immigrant workers was the source of early conflict. So was the division of plantation labour into 'field' and 'factory'. The Indians, the 'field slaves', were the least favoured and lowest paid; the Africans, the 'house slaves', who provided the factory labour and domestic retinue were more favoured and better paid. The 'mixed' races were the best treated and the best paid, and constituted the bulk of the emerging middle class.

Whatever hostility existed, however, was generally contained except on a few occasions when economic conditions badly deteriorated . . . .

The social hierarchy was built on 'colour'. The colour of the person generally determined his social status – the whiter the colour of skin, the higher the social status. At the top were the white planters; at the bottom were the African slaves; in the middle were the 'men of colour' who, originally the offspring of the white planters and their African slave concubines, were freed, educated and favoured.

The mystique was built up that everything 'white' was good; everything 'black' was bad. Soon everyone was aspiring to 'whiteness', adopting Western cultural characteristics and traits – personal features, dress, music, song. The African was made to despise his own cultural background. With the help of Christian missionaries, the process of de-Africanisation began; the African was educated and anglicised. Soon opportunism developed and even 'black' men by their accommodation, behaviour and performance were accepted into the 'white' hierarchy of Guyanese 'creole' society.

The Indians, although 'brown' in colour, were not accommodated within the social hierarchy. They were regarded as outcasts, and despised by the creole society as 'coolies', as being culturally different and economically subservient. They were generally illiterate and stuck to Hinduism and Islam despite the efforts of Christian missionaries to proselytise them.

In the early period, there was no real conflict between Africans and Indians; the latter, despised and downtrodden, concentrated on survival. Up to the mid-

1920s, they had a common enemy – the white planters. At that stage, the Indian sugar workers accepted the African militant trade union leader, Hubert N. Critchlow,[9] as their 'Black Crosby';[10] the class struggle then tended to take on the racial appearance of black against white, and African and Indian against European. It was only when the Indians began to climb out of their 'logie'[11] environment and to compete at the middle-class level for jobs and positions of prestige that conflict began, clearly indicating the economic basis of racism.

Racial consciousness first developed in an organised manner in 1919 with the formation of the British Guiana East Indian Association (BGEIA). The Africans founded the Georgetown Branch of the Universal Negro Improvement Association (Marcus Garvey's), the African Communities League and the Negro Progress Convention. The small Portuguese community organised itself around the Portuguese Benevolent Society, which talked of the need to preserve the Portuguese language and to form a Portuguese political party.

But racial consciousness did not act as a barrier to common action on the political and industrial front. Indians and Africans were aware of the peculiar disadvantages under which their own races lived. This led to a common assault against the colonial society. And the more moderate leaders were propelled forward by the militant struggles waged on the political and industrial fronts; Indian and African workers rallied together under the leadership of Critchlow in the industrial battles from 1906 to the 1920's for better wages, improved working conditions and the 8-hour day.

On the political front, too, various measures were effected. Even though some were taken in the context and process of racial self-realisation, they did not result in racial conflict. Indeed, they helped to further the common struggle against imperialism.

The ending of indentureship in 1917, which was resisted by the sugar planters, was seen by the Indians as an end to their bondage; the Africans saw it as an end to cheap labour and potential strikebreaking . . . .

These industrial and political struggles united the working people of the various ethnic groups in spite of the wishes of the more moderate communal leaders . . . .

However, this unity and racial harmony were soon to be destroyed. In 1928, the British government smashed the constitution. It decided that for the 'good' of Guiana, the constitution should be amended to give the Governor power to create a legislature which he could control. But the real reason was to re-establish power in the hands of the planters from which it had passed to Guyanese . . . .

After the introduction of the new Crown Colony constitution in 1928, the 'European class' regained and maintained control of the legislature, the executive, and the civil service.

The interval between 1928 and 1953 was disastrous for Guyanese unity and nationhood; British divide-and-rule techniques and the competition for jobs and positions of prestige and power at the middle-class level between Indians and Africans led to racial alignments and divisions among the working class.

In this period, a pronounced differentiation took place in the Indian population. Although 90 to 95 percent still battled for survival on the sugar plantations and rice fields, a small group of landlords, moneylenders, shopkeepers and rice millers emerged. These could now afford the 'luxury' of secondary education for their children; they also wanted positions of power and prestige in the legislature and jobs in the civil service for their children. They wished to establish themselves in the creole hierarchy then occupied by the Europeans, Portuguese, Coloured or Mixed, and Africans (in descending order of importance) . . . .

Indians had found closed doors wherever they went, even though they were qualified. This was also my experience in 1938. Discrimination, nepotism and favouritism were widely practiced . . . .

The Indians, finding themselves obstructed and rebuffed, concentrated in the only fields open to them – business and the professions – where they could earn an independent livelihood. Later, in the 1960's, this proved a source of conflict. Portuguese and European businessmen feared competition from the rising but aggressive Indian commercial and industrial bourgeoisie; Africans feared that Indians armed with high qualifications would supersede them in the public service.

The middle-class Indians also sought to attain their ends by political action. This led the BGEIA to become more and more the political and racial sounding board of the new rising middle-class Indians.

It was in this narrow context that the struggle prevailed before the formation of the People's Progressive Party in 1950. The BGEIA had fought for limited reforms such as universal adult suffrage. Property, income and literacy qualifications disenfranchised the great majority of the working class. The large majority of Indians were illiterate . . . .

Indians, however, achieved constitutional equality with other Guyanese when the discriminatory and limited franchise was extended after much agitation by the PPP and other organisations, to universal adult suffrage in 1953 . . . . This was the culmination of united working-class struggles into which I had entered in 1945 and which had been led by the PPP . . . .

But this racial unity was to be short-lived. As in the post-1928 period, the British government, after the second suspension of the constitution in 1953, set about to create a rift between the Indians and Africans . . . .

Notable British ecclesiastical and political figures were sent to Guiana to persuade African and 'moderate' elements to split the PPP.

The split in 1955 did not bring about our defeat at the 1957 election, even though there were, in addition, electoral boundary manipulations. But it did succeed in causing a resurgence of racism; it led to the opposition pursuing party politics along racial lines . . . .

Burnham's alliances with conservative and racist elements resulted in the class struggle appearing as Indians against Africans and Mixed and not as Coloured (Indians, Africans, Mixed) against White, as it had in the 1920's. Fears of one kind or another, whether real or imagined, were generated against the PPP and expressed in racial and anti-Communist terms.

The People's Progressive Party and the various governments were dubbed Indian. Our 1960–64 development programme, which was heavily weighted toward agriculture and drainage and irrigation, was deemed to be essentially designed to help Indians . . . .

The PNC's defeat in the 1961 election caused it to move further in the direction of African racism; its leadership launched a racist campaign at home and abroad . . . .

The European ruling class and their local big-business supporters, through their control of the press and radio, joined in the campaign to foment racial feelings between Indians and Africans. This was for them a better means of directing their class hostility against the PPP government . . . .

The British government also joined in the campaign of distortion. Duncan Sandys,[12] on his return to London from Guiana in June 1963, referred to 'racial leaders' and 'racial parties' . . . .

Whatever may be said of the People's Progressive Party, it is not racial. Before the 1962-64 disturbances, it drew, in spite of the 1955 split, from between 15 percent to 20 percent of its support from the African working class . . . .

Sandys' concluding remark at the 1963 Conference that 'both parties have, for their political ends, fanned the racial emotions of their followers, with the result that each has come to be regarded as the champion of one race and the enemy of the other', was thus aimed at deliberately misleading the British public and the world and justifying his imposition of proportional representation (PR). His conclusion that PR was the way to solve the racial problem was far from the truth; PR was introduced not to heal but to crystallise and further widen the racial breach. As Eric Lubbock, M.P., wrote in the *Guardian*: 'Far from eliminating the poison of racial violence, Mr. Sandys' proposal will inject it into the constitution itself ' . . . .

In Guiana, a multiracial and multireligious society, Proportional Representation was the most effective weapon to keep the working class divided, ruled and exploited. It was precisely with these ends in mind that the British government set its course in 1964 . . . .

The toll for the 1964 disturbances was heavy. About 2,668 families involving approximately 15,000 persons were forced to move their houses and settle in communities of their own ethnic group. The large majority were Indians. Over 1,400 homes were destroyed by fire. A total of 176 people were killed and 920 injured.

Damage to property was estimated at about $4.3 million and the number of displaced persons who became unemployed reached 1,342 . . . .

Full responsibility for the carnage must be placed at the door of the Colonial Office . . . .

In my country, a microcosm of today's world, successive U.S. and U.K. governments have achieved their purpose by force, fraud and rigged elections . . . .

In this part of the world, the situation is becoming more and more unstable and explosive. An independent Guyana will be subject to the same economic and cultural forces of Western imperialism that are today causing poverty, disease, illiteracy and insecurity on a worldwide scale. The stark reality of the second half of the 20th century is the growing impoverishment of the people in Asia, Africa, Latin America and the Caribbean . . . .

NOTES

1. Patwa is a small fresh-water fish.
2. Forbes Burnham (1923–85), an Afro-Guyanese lawyer, was chairman of the PPP.
3. Man-Power Citizens' Association.
4. The National Democratic Party.
5. Trades Union Council.
6. The People's National Congress and the United Force were led by Forbes Burnham and Peter d'Aguiar, respectively.
7. Between 1834 and 1918, over 300,000 immigrants, most of them indentured workers, entered Guyana. Among them were 238,909 Indians, 32,216 Portuguese, 14,060 Africans, and 13,533 Chinese.
8. In the 1960s about 50 per cent of the Guyanese population was Indian, 30 per cent African, 12 per cent Mixed, and 5 per cent Amerindian.
9. Critchlow (1884–1958), a waterfront worker, launched the British Guiana Labour Union in 1919. He was the general secretary and chief organiser.
10. James Crosby was an Immigration Agent General who was trusted by many indentured workers. Subsequent immigration agents became known as 'Crosby', a man to whom the workers could take their grievances.
11. Barrack housing on the estates.
12. Sandys was the colonial secretary in the Conservative government.

Thirty-Two

Rex M. Nettleford

Rex M. Nettleford, born in 1933, is a Jamaican of many talents and achievements. After earning an honours degree in history at the University of the West Indies in Jamaica he did graduate work in politics at Oriel College, Oxford, as a Rhodes scholar. He was a co-founder, principal dancer and choreographer, and the artistic director of the Jamaican National Dance Theatre Company, formed in 1962. Nettleford has served the University of the West Indies as the director of the School of Continuing Studies, head of the Trade Union Education Institute, and Vice-Chancellor. He has taught on West Indian politics and industrial relations, and has been the cultural advisor to the prime minister of Jamaica, and chairman of the Institute of Jamaica. He has led numerous cultural missions on behalf of Jamaica in North and South America, Africa, Europe and Australia, has been a consultant to the Caribbean Festival of Arts and UNESCO, and a member of the Inter-American Committee on Culture of the Organization of American States. He is the editor of the journal Caribbean Quarterly *and author of many works, including the books* Mirror Mirror: Identity, Race and Protest in Jamaica *(1970),* Caribbean Cultural Identity: The Case of Jamaica *(1979) and* Inward Stretch, Outward Reach: A Voice From the Caribbean *(1993).*

'National Identity and Attitudes to Race in Jamaica' was first published in Race, *Vol. 7. No 1, in 1965 and reprinted by the Bolivar Bookshop in Jamaica in 1966.*

$\mathcal{N}$ational Identity and Attitudes to Race in Jamaica

The need for roots and the attendant quest for identity are said to be natural to peoples everywhere. The phenomenon may be said to inhere in a people's desire to collate and codify their past collective experience as well as to lay foundations for the realization of future aspirations. New nations usually give large portions of their creative energy to what may be termed the 'identity problem' and the mid twentieth-century with its flux of emergent countries in Africa, Asia and the Caribbean is particularly noted for this aspect of nation-building. In Jamaica, a Caribbean country which attained independence from Great Britain in August, 1962, the search for identity has been the focus of attention for some time. It is indeed difficult to determine what exactly is meant by the term 'the Jamaican identity'. It is variously expressed as 'things Jamaican' or the 'Jamaican image'.

There are, however, ways of approaching the problem. The question 'What *are* we?' entails the desire of 'What we *want* to be'. And if what we want to be is to have any practical significance for Jamaica, there should be some concordance between the *external conception* of the island's almost two million people on the one hand, and Jamaicans' own *internal perception* of themselves as a national entity on the other. This is presumably one certain way of being saved from a schizoid state of existence. The postulate seems more reasonable when one remembers that Jamaicans are a people who are constantly exposed to external influences, whose economic system traditionally depends on the caprice of other people's palates, whose values are largely imported from an alien set of experiences, and whose dreams and hopes have, at one time or another, been rooted either in a neighboring Panama, Cuba or Costa Rica, in big brother America and sometimes in Canada, a Commonwealth cousin. Of late, they tend to be rooted in father Africa and more so in mother England. The multi-focal nature of Jamaican life and history is often said to be the greatest obstacle to a real national identity. And the object of this essay is to relate the resulting quest to Jamaicans' attitudes towards race.

There are obvious difficulties in any such task. For one thing, data drawn from attitudes, revealed or scientifically observed, do not usually solve the problem of the transition from attitude to behaviour. For another, there is need for a social psychology of West Indian race relations. What is more, race presupposes a biological purity which is difficult to justify. This makes the concept an extremely difficult one with which to work. The fact is that claims to such biological purity are not absent from Jamaican society and these claims have traditionally served to underline, rather boldly, the social stratification, thus making the matter of race more than yeast for the dough. If one assumes that the Jamaican identity must entail a measure of national unity, though not uniformity, among all the differentiated sectors of the society, then one can pose the question of whether the phenomenon of racial consciousness or non-consciousness is an obstacle to national unity. This is the measure of the internal problem. Since race is an important determinant in people's assessment of each other in the outside world, it is of particular relevance to know if what we think of ourselves racially as a nation coincides with what others think of us in this particular. Racial attitudes, especially when they are accompanied by national or individual schizophrenia, are therefore important. The Jamaican Mental Health Association could well do a serious study of the factor of race attitudes in its records of mental illness. Paranoiac experiences sometimes turn on a patient's frustrated aspirations of being 'white'. In this context being 'white' means little more than being privileged and rich. But the fact remains that even today one is still able to have 'whiteness' connote privilege, position, wealth and, of course, purity which is ingrained in Christian mythology. This attitude is particularly evident among many who form the large majority of the population and who happened to wear that colour of skin long associated with poverty, manual labour, low status and ignorance. The *in-betweenness* and *half-identification* resulting from these attitudes is probably one of the positively distinctive features of Caribbean communities emerging from a plantation and colonial system. It does mark us off from many of the developing countries of Asia and Africa, as can be seen in fundamental differences in attitudes to certain aspects of social and political organization.

For example, it is difficult to find the kind of logic that would justify the renunciation of the Queen of England, as the head of the Jamaican State, in favour of a 'son of the soil'. Quite apart from the fact that any such suggestion would be confronted with letters of horror from conscientious Jamaican 'monarchists', one would have to ask who are the real sons of the Jamaican soil. Is it Sir Clifford Campbell, Sir John Mordecai, Hubert Tai Tenn Quee, Dr. Varma, Edward Seaga or Bruce Barker?[1] In fact they are none of them 'sons of the soil' in the sense that Tunku Abdul Rahman is of Malaya, Jomo Kenyatta is of Kenya, Nkrumah was of Ghana or Nehru of India. No Jamaican can seriously make claims to Arawak ancestry. In a real sense, we are all of us immigrants – most of us of long-standing, but immigrants, nevertheless! We have had to work out ways and means of distributing power internally as a result of our uprootedness. Over the centuries this has been done by a certain amount of piecemeal political engineering. One significant thing about the progressive assumption of civic status is that the people receiving their share of power at the different stages of development came from groups distinguishable largely by their racial origin and were in fact so described. So, if it were the white planters and their managerial aides who first received control of representative government in the late seventeenth century, it was the 'free coloureds' who next shared in the citizenship rights in 1832; and although they both joined with the blacks to encourage the takeover of the Constitution by white honest brokers at the Colonial Office after the chaos of 1865,[2] it was the whites and free coloureds whose wealth, influence and social position qualified them for participating in the nominated legislatures of the Crown Colony system. It was not until 1944, following the disturbances of the late thirties, that the blacks who form the vast majority of the populace were given the right to share in the political cake. Despite the potential power of the black vote which followed universal adult suffrage, one still hears that the upper echelons of governments and the centres of influence do not reflect the racial composition of the country. The Queen, despite the way she looks, therefore fits into the landscape as head of state. It is fair to say that she is generally preferred to a black President, though a black representative of the Queen manages to hit a very comfortable medium. The feature makes Jamaica an autonomous Commonwealth entity resembling Canada, Australia and New Zealand inhabited by Britons overseas, more than Ghana, India, Nigeria, Malaya or Tanzania which are autochthonous entities. Jamaicans have earned the name, understandably, of 'Afro-Saxons' among some Africans at the United Nations.

Jamaica's apparently peculiar position is usually explained along lines somewhat like this: 'We are neither Africans though we are most of us black, nor are we Anglo-Saxon though some of us would have others to believe this. We are *Jamaicans*! And what does this mean? We are a mixture of races living in perfect harmony and as such provide a useful lesson to a world torn apart by race prejudice.' The harmony based on tolerance is the thing which is supposed to make Jamaicans distinct from such countries as Rhodesia, South Africa, and parts of the United States of America. In other words, Jamaica is a non-racial nation and non-racialism, besides being a distinctive feature, is an essence of the Jamaican identity. Jamaican leaders make non-racialism into an important national symbol by declaring at home and abroad that Jamaica and the West Indies are 'made up of peoples drawn from all over the world, predominantly Negro or of mixed blood, but also with large numbers of others, and nowhere in the world has more progress been made in developing a non-racial society in which also colour is not psychologically significant'.[3] This was a report of a speech made by a prominent Jamaican leader in April, 1961, to an American audience. It was, therefore, somewhat reassuring to read subsequently in a Jamaican newspaper that the Jamaican Government had admitted to the Secretary General of the United Nations that 'racial discrimination has yet to be entirely eliminated from the island'.[4] The Report was, however, soon marred by the assertion that any problem of racial discrimination still existing in Jamaica was due in part to the fact that Jamaica was a small country which received large numbers of visitors from abroad and that some 'of these visitors bring with them prejudices they acquired in societies less tolerant than Jamaica's'.[5] This betrays a somewhat smug pride in what is assumed to be tolerance and we still look outside ourselves for the foreign bogey which should take some, if not all, of the blame. One has cause to wonder how it is that visitors find it so easy to practise discrimination when they visit Jamaica. The question could be asked whether there is a cradle ready and waiting to receive the bad seed? Or, is it that there are certain visitors who believe in the old injunction – when in Rome, do as the Romans do?

With a bit of charity one could assert that the tendency of Jamaicans to deny their own shortcomings in the matter may indeed stem from a genuine desire to free our national unity and identity of a disruptive racial differentiation. The motto ['Out of Many One People'] is almost daily invoked in sermons – secular and religious – to make into a fact what is as yet an aspiration. Unfortunately, it is the 'many' in the motto and not the 'one' which tends to get the emphasis. So against a background of unemployment, and disparities of economic wealth and educational opportunities, the 'many' too often connotes a differentiation according to how people look. In the minds of many Jamaicans, it is still a poor-black, a middle-class and privileged brown man, and a rich or wealthy white man. This is the traditional colour/class correlation. Chinese and East Indian Jamaicans are marginal to this structure, having come to Jamaica after the classifications were long determined in society. They tend to be assessed by the mass of Jamaicans largely on their economic position rather than on their racial origin. The peasant Indian hardly has significance outside of his membership of the lower class where he marries and still lives and has his being. Significantly, no one makes a mistake about to what section of the society the Bombay merchants and their sari-clad wives belong. The Chinese have grown in stature since the early days when terms like 'Madam' and 'John' expressed attitudes of disrespect or even contempt for the men and women in what has always proved to be a self-contained and restrained minority group. They, the Chinese, chose to stay out of the society as long as they could and now enter it at the top on the basis of their wealth and education. When the commercial banks yielded to pressure to employ Jamaicans of colour the Chinese were among the first to be used to break tradition. They provided a gradual and smooth transition for the more recent developments in those very commercial banks.

Yet both the Indians and the Chinese intermarried, or rather cohabited, with the blacks quite extensively to produce a new group of Jamaicans numbering some thirty-six thousand.[6] This new development bolstered an attitude long evident among the middle-class people of mixed African and European blood. This attitude is expressed in the idealization of mixed blood. As an integrating force in the national life of Brazil this phenomenon has reputedly helped that country to find and project an identity generally accepted at home and abroad. Indeed, it can probably be said that the objective norm in the minds of many Jamaicans (both black and coloured) who choose beauty queens is the hybrid or the miscegenated person.[7] The trouble with this solution to our race differentiation problems is that if the hybrid is the norm, then the vast majority of pure blacks must be the aberration. It therefore invests the mixed-blood idealization with a middle-class unction which is unacceptable to the lower-class blacks. The implications are also a source of great irritation to a growing body of middle-class black opinion which insists that, despite the virtues of a mixed-blood ideal in Jamaica, it is the 'African' which is the constant in the racial complex and all the other racial strains are variables among the majority of the people.

The 1960 census bears this out by padding the categories into which people are placed. These are African, European, East Indian, Chinese or Japanese, Syrian, Afro-European, Afro-East Indian, Afro-Chinese, and Other (meaning, no doubt, odd admixtures). The prefatory remarks in the provisional report give something of a clue to our racial attitudes. For it declares that it is the 'intention that the first five categories should contain persons who appeared to be racially pure and the following three, various mixtures'. This betrays a certain sensitivity to universally accepted norms which classify races into Caucasoids, Mongoloids and Negroids, usually in that order. But the Jamaican classification betrays also a sensitivity to the realities of the local situation. It not only puts the Negroid group first, it gives a detailed breakdown of groups of persons who in the wider world would be termed simply 'coloured'. The preface further informs us that enumerators were 'instructed to include in the "African" group persons of pure African descent, that is those who were classified as "black" in 1943'.[8] This is a clear indication of the growing refinement in attitudes since the term 'black' had long been considered an epithet of opprobrium in the country and not suitable for use in official circles. It had in a sense changed places with the term 'African' which once meant 'primitive' and 'uncivilized' in the vocabulary of Jamaicans. The enumerators were also instructed to include in the term 'European' persons usually listed as English, French, Spanish, German, etc. Could this mean that attitudes which once marked off the English as a privileged group among whites had changed? It certainly makes for easier census-taking, if nothing else. The same cannot be said, however, of the group that used to be classified as 'coloured' in previous censuses. The Jamaican census restricts the term to Afro-European though the outside world would include Afro-Asians as well. Small wonder, then, that the resultant large areas of doubt as to people's descriptions of themselves led the census organizers to omit the racial classification of Jamaicans from the final census reports.

This does not, however, prevent racially conscious black Jamaicans from keeping their eyes glued to the census figures. For although the blacks cannot claim prior discovery of Jamaica (the Jews were here before) nor effective occupation (the economy is still said to be in the hands of the white and half-white groups) they make strong claims for more influence on the basis of their numbers. For of every

100 Jamaicans, 76.8 are of pure African descent, 0.8 are pure European or White, 1.7 are East Indian, 0.6 are Chinese, 0.1 are Syrian, 14.6 are Afro-European, 1.7 are Afro-East Indian, 0.6 are Afro-Chinese, and other mixtures add up to 3.1. If we add together all the persons of obvious African descent (pure or mixed) we get some ninety-one persons out of every hundred with the 'tarbrush'. It is this obvious fact which apparently leads to the external conception of Jamaica as a *coloured country* – a conception which does not coincide with the current internal perception which is one described usually in terms of *multi-racialism*. Now this implies a number of things. It gives to the hybrid groups a positive racial quality which in terms of external classifications they should not have. There is nothing necessarily wrong with the claim, however, since it further implies a robust and even healthy refusal on the part of some Jamaicans to bow to the rather arbitrary and crude classification of human beings into coloured and white. Such Jamaicans prefer to see the world in terms of greys and 'in-between colours', each shade and hue deserving of its own individual identity. This, taken to its logical conclusion, produces in practice a denial of that half of the racial ancestry which is regarded as inferior and a corresponding exaltation of the other half which happens to be respectable in the sight of the world at this particular time. This comes out in many Jamaicans' attitudes towards Great Britain and the white world in general and to the black world and emergent Africa in particular.

The historical antecedents of slavery, the plantation system, and colonialism which are responsible for this, are too well known for detailed recapitulation. But the conscious choice by some Jamaicans and the projection by those Jamaicans of civilized 'whitedom' over primitive 'blackdom' result from the firmly rooted attitudes of a plantation society of a perfect pyramid with white masters at the apex and black labour at the base. The free coloured buffer between the two extremities developed out of widespread miscegenation and formed a natural middle class. This middle class became the target as well as the expression of all the pressures and psychological problems of a society that depended for its rationale in the long run on theories and attitudes of superiority on the part of a white governing and ruling class over an inferior black labouring group. The free coloureds had to pay for their African taint by suffering indignities in the early stages but they were later to benefit from their European blood-stain through the acquisition of wealth and inheritances and from culture through exposure to tolerably good education both in Jamaica and in England. As the pure white population dwindled, the free coloureds became the heirs to the European position and power and regarded themselves as the rightful sons of the Jamaican soil since they, of all groups in Jamaica, were the ones that came directly out of the peculiar circumstances and conditions of early Jamaican society. After all, the argument seemed to go, the blacks can look to Africa, the whites to England, the Chinese to Formosa or Hong Kong, the Indian to

India and the Syrians to Lebanon. But they, the coloureds (*mulatos*), must look to Jamaica. This 15 per cent of Afro-Europeans form the core of the middle class and persist in attitudes which bolster the motto, reprimand the Rastas[9] for turning the clock back, and indulge in a strange love-hate relationship with the whites of both local and expatriate vintage who threaten their claim to the inheritance from Britain. They regard themselves as the true heirs to the governing class despite their small numbers if only because they were the first to display a capacity to assimilate completely the ideals of the masters. They could be as good as, if not better than, the whites. John Hearne in his essay on 'The European Heritage' discusses this group's striving towards the European image – an effort which was further aided by the system of boarding and grammar schools in which some 'five generations of this new brown ruling middle class learned by rote all the attitudes, patterns of behaviour and values taught to English contemporaries'.[10] These are the people who dominate the trading classes and exert influence in the taking of decisions of national moment.

The assertion by Rastafari cultists that since 1938 there has been a series of 'brown-man governments' therefore makes sense in the light of Jamaican history. And the further assertion that these people are really white in attitude is merely another way of describing what the sociologists call the 'white bias' in a society with a population of which 76 per cent is black. The incongruity has led Jamaican commentators to declare that Jamaica will never know what she really is until she accepts the fact that she is a *black country* and projects a black personality. This is a counter-claim to the unspoken but eloquent claim by the brown middle classes that the Jamaican image should root itself in that group of Jamaicans to which they belong since they are the very embodiment of the tensions set up by the counterpoint relationships in the twin heritage from Europe and Africa. A well-known Jamaican journalist and political commentator once said that 'the most obvious bar to integration of our society is the white bias that assaults and degrades the sense of self-respect of the vast majority of the Jamaican people. If everything worthwhile is to be associated with white – goodness, beauty, even God – and if the society as a whole accepts these standards without question, then you are condemning the non-white groups in our society to a permanent and perpetual inferiority since they are inexorably outside the pale of whiteness'.[11]

This plea for a fundamental change will have to be seen in a wider context. The Jamaican's conception of his own racial rank is going to be determined partly by the conception of racial segmentation in the world at large. It is significant that with the rise of black Africa, greater confidence has developed among the black people of the society. And many a black middle-class professional need no longer carry around with him a protective hostility to the group he has left behind. He can even marry a black woman of class and thus save her from life-long spinsterhood in the confines of the teaching, social welfare or nursing professions which Professor Fernando Henriques once observed to be havens of black unmarryable spinsters.[12] Many Afro-Europeans of the middle class are even now discovering the beauty of the blacks among them and there are now several places in the sun for Jamaican young women of all shades through the fetish of the beauty contest. These have even received Ministerial blessing. Such harmless terms as 'bad hair' and 'good hair', meaning African kink and European straight respectively, are still being used and one can still hazard the guess that certain mothers will prefer a white Glasgow carpenter to a Jamaican flag-black civil servant for their daughter.[13] The latter alternative might just mean hardships for everybody concerned. In 1964, the *Daily Gleaner*, Jamaica's only daily newspaper, could carry without fear of contradiction a leader, the first paragraph of which read: 'Many people in Jamaica still boast that they have never entertained a negroid person in their homes. They do not say it openly but that is their boast nevertheless. Every change in our society that has enabled the people really to live like the nation's motto is pain and distress and "disaster" to them'.[14] A letter to the editor published subsequently commented on the inconsistency between the view and what is often proclaimed as the island's attainment of racial harmony.[15]

If we look at the expressed attitudes of people on the Jamaican Government's plans to make a national hero out of the late Marcus Garvey, we find the anxieties and emotionalism that exist among many Jamaicans on the matter of race.[16] It is more than coincidental that it should be a white Jamaican who took the trouble to chronicle the misdemeanours which Garvey reputedly committed during his lifetime.[17] One could indeed have predicted the sharpness of the replies in the Press. They all expressed people's belief in the importance of African consciousness in Jamaican development. Here is a typical argument against the fuss that was made over Garvey: it is in a letter to the *Daily Gleaner*: 'Certainly, transporting of Negroes from America to Africa does not in the least affect the welfare of Jamaica. To my way of thinking we do not have in Jamaica any Negroes, Chinese, Syrians or English; we have Jamaicans and certainly if we are to spend thousands of pounds on a monument to honour someone, let it be spent to honour a Jamaican who has contributed tangibly to the development of the nation'.[18] This was doubtless written with the best intentions, but this may well be mistaking a wish for the facts! There are indeed all the racial groups which the writers claimed not to exist. There are people 'negro' enough to feel a sense of personal affront when reports of discriminatory acts against a black American college student are reported in the local press. There can hardly be any difficulties of identification. There are people 'Syrian' enough to want to return to Lebanon for a spouse. The bond among the Chinese of Jamaica may be said to be a racial Chinese one and not a sophisticated *Jamaican* one. And there are 'English' or white people who are English or white enough to want to help out people who look like themselves when it comes to the matter of a job. Whether this kind of differentiation is strong enough to rend the society apart is doubtful outside the framework of purely private individual relationships. But this is where the shoe pinches, and a localized pain can affect the entire body. The scores of letters from middle-class citizens clearly indicated further that Garvey's championing of the dignity and self-respect of the black man is a very tangible contribution to the development of a nation which is 91 per cent of African descent.

Yet for all Garvey's work, one might say that attitudes among the black-skinned masses still exist which betray a self-contempt and a lack of self-confidence. Herein lies the greatest danger to attempts at finding an identity in terms of race. For a people who do not believe in themselves cannot hope to have others believing in them. The insecurities of this important racial grouping persist with a vengeance. A poor peasant is indeed glad to have her children rise above the peasantry, marry brown, and forget the roots. A bright young university graduate must suffer praise for a barely tolerably competent speech because of no other reason than he 'use the white people dem word good good'. People like the Rastafari and their neighbours in West Kingston are still convinced that there is some dark conspiracy to keep 'black people down' and although Millard Johnson's coarse *negritude*[19] was rejected the leadership of two bona fide political parties are sometimes identified with the brown middle-class. A maid insists that she would never work 'for black people'; and well she might not, for the bad treatment meted out to servants by coloured and black middle-class housewives is usually a topic for conversation among some visitors to the island. A watchman in a private compound coldly informs a black-skinned university student that he cannot proceed on the compound for the authorities have instructed him (the watchman) not to let 'any black people pass there after six o'clock'. A black doctor goes into stores in Kingston and fails to receive the civil attention due to every citizen until he pulls rank and invokes his status. A worker in an industrial plant finds it impossible to have any interest in the plant because 'there's no hope for the black man' and he resents the black supervisor in authority. The black supervisor in turn abuses his unaccustomed power in dealing with his own and toadies to the white boss. A young black woman destroys a photographic print of herself because it is printed too black; and an older black woman insists that she is giving her vote to a white candidate 'for no black man can help me in this yah country these days'. The examples just cited are based on actual occurrences and betray an interesting ambivalence on the part of these people in their attitudes to race. They also betray a signal lack of self-confidence.

This happens to coincide with coloured and near-white Jamaican group-attitudes towards the blacks. So when a black-skinned official replaces the white official at the old colonial governor's mansion some middle-class verandahs sigh sighs of disapproval and even apprehension. The Afro-European middle classes seem to be fighting on two fronts. For they are beginning to experience competition from a growing group of newer white expatriates who are felt to be without caste since they speak with the wrong accents and betray no sensitivity for the finer things.[20] The trouble is that these people come in and take their traditional place of privilege in the white bias structure. They drink in the right bars and hotels and even get into the right kind of brawls. The coloured middle class resent their pretensions and even object to their own children 'picking up cockney intonations from certain expatriate children'.[21] It might very well turn out that the coloured middle class will be the ones to find greatest satisfaction in the new act designed to limit the employment of expatriates.[22] The resentment of the Jamaican blacks to this group of people and indeed to white visitors in places like hotels may very well be an extension of their dislike for the Jamaican high browns who have long been the symbols of wealth, influence and privilege in the society.

The important thing about all this is that the black-skinned Jamaican senses that he must compete on the same ground as his brown, Chinese and white compatriots. In many a case he has to work twice as hard because of the handicap of being years at the base of the social pyramid. Psychologically, he does not possess such a strong racial memory of great cultural achievements as these European, Chinese and Indian compatriots. The Africans, of all the groups which came to the New World, came as individuals and not as part of a group which maintained identity through some great religion, or activity through age-old recognizable customs. The obvious answer for the African or black Jamaican is to sink his racial consciousness in the wider, greater aspirations to acquire education and other means of making himself economically viable. Of course, if he sees no chance of doing this he is bound to fall back on the religion of race which is the one thing which he will feel makes him distinctive and which is aided and abetted by the rise of black Africa and the increased stature of the black man in the world at large.

It could indeed be argued that there is nothing necessarily wrong with stratification based on racial consciousness *per se*. But there is everything wrong with racial stratification which has no compensatory responsibilities to complement it. In other words, each racial group must be assured of such things as adequate educational opportunities, of accessibility to rewards for efforts and of an environment which provides incentives to even greater efforts. Only with these will there follow an accelerated social mobility, which is yet another compensatory responsibility. Such compensatory responsibilities do indeed exist in Jamaica and this is frequently the cause of the hyperbolic expressions of the virtue of racial harmony in Jamaica, but in fact they are extremely limited. However, where attempts might be made to plough more money and planning into the black groups, as the Malayan people did among the Malays, there is fear that accusations will be made that blacks are being favoured at the expense of other racial groups in the society –

colour prejudice in reverse. And this is so even if politicians are able to justify their actions with the democratic argument of the greatest good for the greatest number.

The truth of the matter is that while in Malaya the Malays are the accepted indigenous sons of the soil and the foundation of the Malayan image, in Jamaica the blacks are not regarded as the desirable symbol for national identity. The fact is that we are still enslaved in the social structure born of the plantation system in which things African, including African traits, have been devalued and primacy is still given to European values in the scheme of things. The developments of the twentieth century are putting pressures on the structure but most people seem to prefer to remain with the known evil rather than accept the uncertain good. As I have said elsewhere, the parboiled state of our national identity will continue to be just this until adjustments are made in the society in bold economic and social terms.[23] People who look like Africans will then no longer have evidence to support their much-repeated claim that their poverty, destitution and loss of hope is somehow organically linked with the fact that they are of a certain ethnic origin in a country controlled by people of another ethnic origin who think themselves superior.

NOTES

1. Nettleford notes that these are 'well-known Jamaicans of different racial origin', in his terms, African, Afro-European, Chinese, East Indian, Syrian and European, respectively.
2. A local peasant uprising in 1865, the Morant Bay rebellion, led to the declaration of martial law and the execution and flogging of hundreds of Jamaicans and the destruction of over a thousand homes. In the aftermath, the oligarchic Legislative Assembly was abolished and the Crown Colony system of government was imposed.
3. Norman W. Manley, speech to the National Press Club, USA, April 1961. Founder of the People's National party in 1938, Manley (1893-1969) was the premier of Jamaica from 1955 to 1961.
4. Reported in the *Daily Gleaner,* Oct 4. 1964.
5. Ibid.
6. *West Indies Population Census (Jamaica),* 1960.
7. Author's note: Beauty contests are held frequently for the selection of 'queens' from all sections of the community. Traditionally 'Miss Jamaica' tended to be either near-white or with coffee-coloured European features and straight ('good') hair. This fact sparked off controversy in the Press from time to time until in 1955 the island's evening newspaper – *The Star* – sponsored a 'Ten Types One People' contest giving the titles to Jamaican women who span the colour spectrum from 'Ebony' (black) through 'Mahogany' (coloured), 'Lotus' and 'Satinwood' (Chinese and East Indian), and 'Pomegranate' (Mediterranean type, Syrian-Jewish), to 'Appleblossom' (Caucasian). The event received wide international Press coverage.
8. *West Indies Population Census (Jamaica)*, 1960.
9. Rastafarians, known colloquially as Rastas, emerged in the 1930s as a distinct religious group in Jamaica.

10. John Hearne, 'The European Heritage and Asian Influence', in *Our Heritage* (University of the West Indies, 1963). Hearne (1926-94) wrote many novels, including *Voices Under the Window* (1955), *Land of the Living* (1961), and *The Sure Salvation* (1981).

11. Frank Hill, lecture entitled 'Racial Integration in Jamaica', delivered at the University of the West Indies, Feb 10. 1963.

12. Fernando Henriques, *Family and Colour in Jamaica* (London, 1953), 62.

13. Author's note: 'Flag-black' alludes to the symbolism behind the colours in the Jamaican flag, which are green, gold and black. The black symbolises 'hardships' and this was criticised as a further example of Jamaican attitudes to that colour.

14. Editorial, *Daily Gleaner,* May 6, 1964.

15. Letter to the editor, *Daily Gleaner*, June 24, 1964.

16. Garvey died in England in 1940. His remains were brought back to Jamaica in 1965 and placed in a shrine, and he was declared Jamaica's first National Hero.

17. Letter to the editor, *Daily Gleaner,* Sept. 10, 1964.

18. Letter to the editor, *Daily Gleaner*, Sept. 22 , 1964.

19. Author's note: Millard Johnson, a Jamaican barrister, attempted to base his campaign on racism by invoking the name of Garvey during the 1962 (April) General Elections. His People's Progressive Party (PPP) polled 12,616 votes with no seats while the People's National Party (PNP) now in opposition polled 279,771 votes and the ruling party, the Jamaica Labour Party (JLP) polled 288,130 votes out of a total of 580,517 votes cast (i.e. 72.88 per cent of registered voters).

20. Shirley Maynier-Burke, 'The Jamaican Civil Rights Dilemma', *Daily Gleaner*, Oct. 2, 1964.

21. Author's note: The view of a coloured Jamaican housewife in an interview with the author.

22. Author's note: The Foreign Nationals and Commonwealth Citizens (Employment) Act, commonly called the Work Permits Act, came into force in Jamaica on April 1, 1965, limiting the employment of aliens only to those jobs which cannot be suitably filled by Jamaicans.

23. Rex Nettleford, 'The African Connexion', in *Our Heritage* (University of the West Indies, 1963).

Thirty-Three

Walter Rodney

Walter Rodney (1942–80) was a historian from Guyana who worked and wrote in the radical scholarly tradition of C.L.R. James, Eric Williams, and Frantz Fanon. Among his many publications, which include a revision of his doctoral dissertation, A History of the Upper Guinea Coast 1545-1800 *(1970), the most influential have been* How Europe Underdeveloped Africa *(1972), which examines the dialectical relationship between the development of Europe and the underdevelopment of Africa, and* A History of the Guyanese Working People, 1881–1905 *(1981), which he completed shortly before his death.*

The son of a tailor and seamstress, Rodney was born in Georgetown, the capital of Guyana. After primary school, he won a scholarship to Queen's College in 1953, a beneficiary of the expanding educational opportunities created in the early 1950s. He excelled academically and won a scholarship to study at the University of the West Indies (UWI) in Jamaica, from which he graduated with first class honours in history in 1963. Another scholarship enabled him to study at the School of Oriental and African Studies at the University of London where he received his PhD in 1966, at the age of 24. While studying African history in London, Rodney participated in discussion groups with C.L.R. James, the Marxist theoretician from Trinidad. Rodney had grown up in the years of radical nationalism in Guyana, when his parents were active in the People's Progressive party (PPP), and had taken a course in the History of Political Thought as an undergraduate, but James' influence on his intellectual and political development was decisive. Rodney came to share James' independent thinking, based on Marxist theory and 'belief in the transformatory powers of the ordinary people and the necessity of democracy in effecting real change' (Lewis 1998, 35).

Rodney's first academic post was at the University College of Dar es Salaam in Tanzania, where he taught from 1966 until January 1968 when he returned to the UWI in Jamaica as a lecturer in African history. He was a popular and eloquent lecturer both on and off the campus. His involvement with Rastafarians and political activists, high school students and community groups with whom he discussed African and Caribbean history, Marcus Garvey and the politics of Black Power, led to the Jamaican government expelling him after nine months. His talks on Black Power, first published in Jamaica in Bongo-man, *became chapters 2 and 3 of* The Groundings with My Brothers *(1969). 'Groundings' means an informal, grassroots discussion which could take place in a yard or at a street corner. The Jamaican government, led by Hugh Shearer, felt threatened by the meetings and thought Rodney was a dangerous influence as he linked race and class issues in a radical and regional black nationalist ideology.*

Rodney, like James, was developing an unorthodox and non-dogmatic Marxist analysis with revolutionary implications. A protest march by UWI students on October 16, 1968, in response to the banning of this popular lecturer, exploded into widespread rioting in Kingston and the government temporarily closed the university. A variety of economic, social and cultural issues that the independence movement had not resolved, or even addressed, were emerging at this time. Rodney's influence, and the publicity created by his expulsion and the resulting demonstrations, stimulated the development of newspapers, such as Abeng *in Jamaica,* Moko *in Trinidad,* Ratoon *in Guyana and* Amandala *in Belize. African-oriented cultural and political groups emerged around the region, promoting Black Power ideas and criticising governments, most of which were led by black politicians. The 'February Revolution' in Trinidad in 1970, which briefly threatened the Eric Williams government, and the New Jewel Movement which overthrew Eric Gairy in Grenada in 1979, were influenced by these developments.*

Rodney returned to Tanzania where he taught from 1968 to 1974. He accepted an appointment as professor of history at the University of Guyana in 1974, but President Burnham's supporters overturned the offer. Rodney became a leader of the Working People's Alliance (WPA), which was founded in Guyana in 1974 and became a political party in 1979. As an independent scholar, Rodney obtained a Canadian research grant to work on Guyanese history, he taught at a US university, and gave papers at academic conferences. He remained a political activist while Guyana descended into an oppressive and violent state. He was jailed in 1979 and, on June 13, 1980, government agents assassinated him with a small but sophisticated bomb. Scholars and political leaders, including Kamau Brathwaite, Martin Carter, Fidel Castro, George Lamming and Michael Manley expressed outrage over this ruthless murder. In 1994, Rodney was posthumously awarded his country's highest honour, the Order of Excellence.

❦

*B*lack Power in the West Indies

Black Power is a doctrine about black people, for black people, preached by black people. I'm putting it to my black brothers and sisters that the colour of our skins is the most fundamental thing about us. I could have chosen to talk about people of the same island, or the same religion, or the same class – but instead I have chosen skin colour as essentially the most binding factor in our world. In so doing, I am not saying that is the way things ought to be. I am simply recognising the real world – that is the way things are. Under different circumstances, it would have been nice to be colour blind, to choose my friends solely because their social interests coincided with mine – but no conscious black man can allow himself such luxuries in the contemporary world.

Let me emphasise that the situation is not of our making. To begin with, the white world defines who is white and who is black. In the U.S.A. if one is not white, then one is black; in Britain, if one is not white then one is coloured; in South Africa, one can be white, coloured, or black depending upon how white people classify you. There was a South African boxer who was white all his life, until all the other whites decided that he was really coloured. Even the fact of whether you are black or not is to be decided by white people – by White Power. If a Jamaican black man tried to get a room from a landlady in London, who said 'No Coloureds', it would not impress her if he said he was West Indian, quite apart from the fact that she would already have closed the door in his black face. When a Pakistani goes to the Midlands he is as coloured as a Nigerian. The Indonesian is the same as a Surinamer in Holland, the Chinese and New Guineans have as little chance of becoming residents and citizens in Australia as do you and I. The definition which is most widely used the world over is that once you are not obviously white then you are black, and are excluded from power – Power is kept pure milky white.

The black people of whom I speak, therefore, are non-whites – the hundreds of millions of people whose homelands are in Asia and Africa, with another few millions in the Americas. A further subdivision can be made with reference to all people of African descent whose position is clearly more acute than that of most non-white groups. It must be noted that once a person is said to be black by the white world, then that is usually the most important thing about him; fat or thin, intelligent or stupid, criminal or sportsman – these things pale into insignificance. Actually I've found out that a lot of whites literally cannot tell one black from another. Partly this may be due to the fact that they do not personally know many black people, but it reflects a psychological tendency to deny our individuality by refusing to consider us as individual human beings.

Having said a few things about black and white, I will try to point out the power relations between them. By the outbreak of the First World War in 1914, the capitalist division of the world was complete. It was a division which made capitalists dominant over workers and white people dominant over black. At that point, everywhere in the world white people held power in all its aspects – political, economic, military and even cultural. In Europe, the whites held power – this goes without saying. In the Americas the whites had committed mass murder as far as many 'Red Indian' tribes were concerned and they herded the rest into reservations like animals or forced them into the disadvantageous positions, geographically and economically, in Central and South America. In Australia and New Zealand, a similar thing had occurred on a much smaller scale. In Africa, European power reigned supreme except in a few isolated spots like Ethiopia; and where whites were actually settled the Africans were reduced to the status of second-class citizens in their own country. All this was following upon a historical experience of 400 years of slavery, which had transferred millions of Africans to work and die in the New World. In Asia, Europe's power was felt everywhere except in Japan and areas controlled by Japan. The essence of White Power is that it is exercised over black peoples – whether or not they are minority or majority, whether it was a country belonging originally to whites or to blacks. It is exercised in such a way that black people have no share in that power and are, therefore, denied any say in their own destinies.

Since 1911, White Power has been slowly reduced. The Russian Revolution put an end to Russian imperialism in the Far East, and the Chinese Revolution by 1949 had emancipated the world's largest single ethnic group from the white power complex. The rest of Asia, Africa and Latin America (with minor exceptions such as North Korea, North Vietnam and Cuba) have remained within the white power network to this day. We live in the section of the world under white domination – the imperialist world. The Russians are white and have power but they are not a colonial power oppressing black peoples. The white power which is our enemy is that which is exercised over black peoples, irrespective of which group is in the majority and irrespective of whether the particular country belonged originally to whites or blacks.

We need to look very carefully at the nature of the relationships between colour and power in the imperialist world. There are two basic sections in the imperialist world – one that is dominated and one that is dominant. Every country in the dominant metropolitan area has a large majority of whites – U.S.A., Britain, France, etc. Every country in the dominated colonial areas has an overwhelming majority of non-whites, as in most of Asia, Africa and the West Indies. Power, therefore, resides in the white countries and is exercised over blacks. There is the mistaken belief that black people achieved power with independence, e.g. Malaya, Jamaica, Kenya, but a black man ruling a dependent State within the imperialist system has no power. He is simply an agent of the whites in the metropolis, with an army and a police force designed to maintain the imperialist way of things in that particular colonial area.

When Britain announced recently that it was withdrawing troops from East of Suez, the American Secretary of State remarked that something would have to be done to fill the 'power vacuum'. This involved Saudi Arabia, India, Pakistan, Ceylon and Malaysia. The white world in …[its] … own way …[was]… saying that all these blacks amounted to nothing, for power was white and when white power is withdrawn, a vacuum is created, which could only be filled by another white power.

By being made into colonials, black people lost the power which we previously had of governing our own affairs, and the aim of the white imperialist world is to see that we never regain this power. The Congo provides an example of this situation. There was a large and well-developed Congolese empire before the white man reached Africa. The large Congolese empire of the 15th century was torn apart by Portuguese slave-traders and what remained of the Congo came to be regarded as one of the darkest spots in dark Africa. After regaining political independence the Congolese people settled down to reorganise their lives, but white power intervened, set up the black stooge Tshombe[1], and murdered both Lumumba[2] and the aspirations of the Congolese people. Since then, paid white mercenaries have harassed the Congo. Late last year, 130 of these hired white killers were chased out of the Congo and cornered in the neighboring African State of Burundi. The white world intervened and they have all been set free. These are men who for months were murdering, raping, pillaging, disrupting economic production, and making a mockery of black life and black society. Yet white power said not a hair on their heads was to be touched. They did not even have to stand trial or reveal their names. Conscious blacks cannot possibly fail to realise that in our own homelands we have no power, abroad we are discriminated against, and everywhere the black masses suffer from poverty. You can put together in your own mind a picture of the whole world, with the white imperialist beast crouched over miserable blacks. And don't forget to label us poor. There is nothing with which poverty coincides so absolutely as with the colour black – small or large population, hot or cold climates, rich or poor in natural resources – poverty cuts across all of these factors in order to find black people.

That association of wealth with whites and poverty with blacks is not accidental. It is the nature of the imperialist relationship that enriches the metropolis at the expense of the colony, i.e. it makes the whites richer and the blacks poorer.

The Spaniards went to Central and South America, and robbed thousands of tons of silver and gold from Indians. The whole of Europe developed on the basis of that wealth, while millions of Indian lives were lost and the societies and cultures of Central and South America were seriously dislocated. Europeans used their guns in Asia to force Asians to trade at huge profits to Europe, and in India the British grew fat while at the same time destroying Indian irrigation. Africa and Africans suffered from the greatest crimes at the hands of Europeans through the Slave Trade and Slavery in the West Indies and the Americas. In all those centuries of exploitation, Europeans have climbed higher on our backs and pushed us down into the dirt. White power has, therefore, used black people to make whites stronger and richer and to make blacks relatively, and sometimes absolutely, weaker and poorer.

'Black Power' as a movement has been most clearly defined in the U.S.A. Slavery in the U.S. helped create the capital for the development of the U.S. as the foremost capitalist power, and the blacks have subsequently been the most exploited sector of labour. Many blacks live in that supposedly great society at a level of existence comparable to blacks in the poorest section of the colonial world. The blacks in the U.S. have no power. They have achieved prominence in a number of ways – they can sing, they can run, they can box, play baseball, etc., but they have no power. Even in the fields where they excel, they are straws in the hands of whites. The entertainment world, the record-manufacturing business, sport as a commercial enterprise are all controlled by whites – blacks simply perform. They have no power in the areas where they are overwhelming majorities, such as the city slums and certain parts of the Southern United States, for the local governments and law-enforcement agencies are all white controlled. This was not always so. For one brief period after the Civil War in the 1860s, blacks in the U.S.A. held power. In that period (from 1865 to 1875)[3] slavery had just ended, and the blacks were entitled to the vote as free citizens. Being in the majority in several parts of the southern United States, they elected a majority of their own black representatives and helped to rebuild the South, introducing advanced ideas such as education for all (blacks as well as whites, rich and poor). The blacks did not rule the United States, but they were able to put forward their own viewpoints and to impose their will over the white racist minority in several states. This is a concrete historical example of Black Power in the United States, but the whites changed all that, and they have seen to it that such progress was never again achieved by blacks. With massive white immigration, the blacks became a smaller minority within the United States as a whole and even in the South, so that a feeling of hopelessness grew up.

The present Black Power movement in the United States is a rejection of hopelessness and the policy of doing nothing to halt the oppression of blacks by whites. It recognises the absence of black power, but is confident of the potential of black power on this globe. Marcus Garvey was one of the first advocates of Black Power, and is still today the greatest spokesman ever to have been produced by the movement of black consciousness. 'A race without power and authority is a race without respect', wrote Garvey. He spoke to all Africans on the earth, whether they lived in Africa, South America, the West Indies or North America, and he made blacks aware of their strength when united. The U.S.A. was his main field of operation, after he had been chased out of Jamaica by the sort of people who today pretend to have made him a hero. All of the black leaders who have advanced the cause in the U.S.A. since Garvey's time have recognised the international nature of the struggle against White Power. Malcolm X, [4] our martyred brother, became the greatest threat to White Power in the U.S.A. because he began to seek a broader basis for his efforts in Africa and Asia, and he was probably the first individual who was prepared to bring the race question in the U.S. up before the U.N. as an issue of international importance. S.N.C.C.,[5] the important Black Power organisation, developed along the same lines; and at about the same time that the slogan Black Power came into existence a few years ago, S.N.C.C. was setting up a foreign affairs department, headed by James Foreman, who afterwards travelled widely in Africa. Stokely Carmichael has held serious discussions in Vietnam, Cuba and the progressive African countries, such as Tanzania and Guinea. These are all steps to tap the vast potential of power among the hundreds of millions of oppressed black peoples.

Meanwhile, one significant change had occurred since Garvey. The emphasis within the U.S. is that black people there have a stake in that land, which they have watered with their sweat, tears, and blood, and black leadership is aware of the necessity and the desirability of fighting white power simultaneously at home and abroad. Certain issues are not yet clear about the final shape of society in America. Some form of co-existence with whites is the desired goal of virtually all black leaders, but it must be a society which blacks have a hand in shaping, and blacks should have power commensurate with their numbers and contribution to U.S. development. To get that, they have to fight.

Black Power as a slogan is new, but it is really an ideology and a movement of historical depth. The one feature that is new about it as it is currently exercised in the U.S. is the advocacy of violence. Previously, black people prayed, we were on our best behaviour, we asked the whites 'please', we smiled so that our white teeth illuminated our black faces. Now it is time to show our teeth in a snarl rather than a smile. The death of Martin Luther King[6] gave several hypocritical persons the opportunity to make stupid remarks about the virtues of non-violence. Some of the statements made in the Jamaica press and on the radio and TV were made by individuals who probably think that the Jamaican black man is completely daft. We were told that violence in itself is evil, and that, whatever the cause, it is unjustified morally. By what standard of morality can the violence used by a slave to break his chains be considered the same as the violence of a slave master? By what standards can we equate the violence of blacks who have been oppressed, suppressed, depressed and repressed for four centuries with the violence of white fascists? Violence aimed at the recovery of human dignity and at equality cannot be judged by the same yardstick as violence aimed at maintenance of discrimination and oppression.

White Americans would certainly argue the moral and practical necessity of their participation in the First and particularly the Second World War. What is curious is that thousands of black people fought and died in these wars entirely in the interest of the white man. Colonialism is the opposite of freedom and democracy and yet black colonials fought for this against the Fascism of Hitler – it was purely in the interests of the white 'Mother Countries'. Slaves fought for American Independence and for the North in the American Civil War. Black oppressed Americans went in thousands to fight for justice in the world wars, in Korea and in Vietnam. We have fought heroically in the white men's cause. It is time to fight in our own.

Violence in the American situation is inescapable. White society is violent, white American society is particularly violent, and white American society is especially violent towards blacks.

Slavery was founded and maintained by violence and in the 100 years since the 'Emancipation' of slaves in the U.S. the society has continued to do black people violence by denying them any power or influence (except for the occasional individual). Their interests are therefore ignored, so that thousands of black babies die each year because of lack of proper food, shelter and medicine; while hundreds of thousands are destroyed emotionally and intellectually because of conditions of poverty and discrimination. This is the worst sort of violence, and it is accompanied by many acts of individual violence carried out by white citizens, police and sheriffs against blacks. Most incidents of rioting in recent years arose spontaneously out of self-defense and out of anger against brutality. When black Americans react to meet force with force this should surprise nobody, because even the most harmless animal will finally turn in desperation against its hunters. It is useful to know that this is the conclusion arrived at not only by Black Power leaders, but also by the official committee of the U.S. Senate which was appointed to investigate the racial situation.

Apart from local violent protests (riots), U.S. society faces the possibility of large-scale racial war. The book *Black Power*, written by Stokely Carmichael and Charles Hamilton (and now banned by 'White Power' Jamaican government) stresses that its aim was to present an opportunity to work out the racial question without resort to force, but if that opportunity was missed the society was moving towards destructive racial war. In such a war, black people would undoubtedly suffer because of their minority position, but as an organised group they could wreak untold damage on the whites. The white racists and warmongers cannot drop their bombs on black people *within the U.S.A.,* and whatever damage is done to property means damage to white property. We have nothing to lose for they are the capitalists. Black people could not hope to, nor do they want to, dominate the whites, but large sections of the black youth realise that they cannot shrink from fighting to demonstrate the hard way that a 10 per cent minority of 22 million cannot be treated as though they did not exist. Already the limited violence of the past few years has caused more notice to be taken of the legitimate social, economic, political and cultural demands of black people than has been the case for the previous 100 years. The goal is still a long way off, for it is not only in a crisis that the blacks must be considered. When decisions are taken in the normal day-to-day life of the U.S.A., the interests of the blacks must be taken into account *out of respect for their power* – power that can be used destructively if it is not allowed to express itself constructively. This is what Black Power means in the particular conditions of the U.S.A.

Black Power – Its Relevance to the West Indies

About a fortnight ago I had the opportunity of speaking on Black Power to an audience on this campus[7]. At that time, the consciousness among students as far as the racial question is concerned had been heightened by several incidents on the world scene – notably, the hangings in Rhodesia and the murder of Dr. Martin Luther King. Indeed, it has been heightened to such an extent that some individuals have started to organize a Black Power movement. My presence here attests to my full sympathy with their objectives.

The topic on this occasion is no longer just 'Black Power' but 'Black Power and You'. Black Power can be seen as a movement and an ideology springing from the reality of oppression of black peoples by whites within the imperialist world as a whole. Now we need to be specific in defining the West Indian scene and our own particular roles in the society. You and I have to decide whether we want to think black or to *remain* as a dirty version of white. (I shall indicate the full significance of this later.)

Recently there was a public statement in *Scope* where Black Power was referred to as 'Black supremacy'. This may have been a genuine error or a deliberate falsification. Black Power is a call to black peoples to throw off white domination and resume the handling of their own destinies. It means that blacks would enjoy power commensurate with their numbers in the world and in particular localities.

Whenever an oppressed black man shouts for equality he is called a racist. This was said of Marcus Garvey in his day. Imagine that! We are so inferior that if we demand equality of opportunity and power that is outrageously racist! Black people who speak up for their rights must beware of this device of false accusations. Is it intended to place you on the defensive and if possible embarrass you into silence. How can we be both oppressed and embarrassed? Is it that our major concern is not to hurt the feelings of the oppressor? Black people must now take the offensive – if it is anyone who should suffer embarrassment it is the whites. Did black people roast six million Jews? Who exterminated millions of indigenous inhabitants in the Americas and Australia? Who enslaved countless millions of Africans? The white capitalist cannibal has always fed on the world's black peoples. White capitalist imperialist society is profoundly and unmistakably racist.

The West Indies have always been a part of white capitalist society. We have been the most oppressed section because we were a slave society and the legacy of slavery still rests heavily upon the West Indian black man. I will briefly point to five highlights of our social development: (1) the development of racialism under slavery; (2) emancipation; (3) Indian indentured labour; (4) the year 1865 in Jamaica; (5) the year 1938 in the West Indies.

Slavery. As C.L.R. James, Eric Williams and other W.I. scholars have pointed out, slavery in the West Indies started as an economic phenomenon rather than a racial one. But it rapidly became racist as all white labour was withdrawn from the fields, leaving black to be identified with slave labour and white to be linked with property and domination. Out of this situation where blacks had an inferior status in practice, there grew social and scientific theories relating to the supposed inherent inferiority of the black man, who was considered as having been created to bring water and hew wood for the white man. This theory then served to rationalise white exploitation of blacks all over Africa and Asia. The West Indies and the American South share the dubious distinction of being the breeding ground for world racialism. Even the blacks became convinced of their own inferiority, though fortunately we are capable of the most intense expressions when we recognise that we have been duped by the white men. Black Power recognises both the reality of the black oppression and self-negation as well as the potential for revolt.

Emancipation. By the end of the 18th century, Britain had got most of what it wanted from black labour in the West Indies. Slavery and the slave trade had made Britain strong and now stood in the way of new developments, so it was time to abandon those systems. The Slave Trade and Slavery were thus ended; but Britain had to consider how to squeeze what little remained in the territories and *how to maintain the local whites in power*. They therefore decided to give the planters £20 million compensation and to guarantee their black labour supplies for the next six years through a system called apprenticeship. In that period, white society consolidated its position to ensure that slave relations should persist in our society. The Rastafari Brethren have always insisted that the black people were promised £20 million at emancipation. In reality, by any normal standards of justice, we black people should have got the £20 million compensation money. We were the ones who had been abused and wronged, hunted in Africa and brutalised on the plantations. In Europe, when serfdom was abolished, the serfs usually inherited the land as compensation and by right. In the West Indies, the exploiters were compensated because they could no longer exploit us in the same way as before. White property was of greater value than black humanity. It still is – white property is of greater value than black humanity in the British West Indies today, especially here in Jamaica.

Indian Indentured Labour. Britain and the white West Indians had to maintain the plantation system in order to keep whites supreme. When Africans started leaving the plantations to set up as independent peasants they threatened the plantation structure and therefore Indians were imported under the indenture arrangements. That was possible because white power controlled most of the world and could move non-white peoples around as they wished. It was from British-controlled India that the indentured labour was obtained. It was the impact of British commercial, military and political policies that was destroying the life and culture of 19th century India and forcing people to flee to other parts of the world to earn bread. Look where Indians fled – to the West Indies! The West Indies is a place black people want to leave not to come to. One must therefore appreciate the pressure of white power on India which gave rise to migration to the West Indies. Indians were brought here solely in the interest of white society – at the expense of Africans already in the West Indies and often against their own best interests, for Indians perceived indentured labour to be a form of slavery and it was eventually terminated through the pressure of Indian opinion in the homeland. The West Indies has made a unique contribution to the history of suffering in the world, and Indians have provided part of that contribution since indentures were first introduced. This is another aspect of the historical situation which is still with us.

1865. In that year Britain found a way of perpetuating White Power in the West Indies after ruthlessly crushing the revolt of our black brothers led by Paul Bogle.[8] The British Government took away the Constitution of Jamaica and placed the island under the complete control of the Colonial Office, a manoeuvre that was racially motivated. The Jamaican legislature was then largely in the hands of the local whites with a mulatto minority, but if the gradual changes continued the mulattoes would have taken control – and the blacks were next in line. Consequently, the British Government put a stop to the process of the gradual takeover of political power by blacks. When we look at the British Empire in the 19th century, we see a clear difference between white colonies and black colonies. In the white colonies like Canada and Australia the British were giving white people their freedom and self-rule. In the black colonies of the West Indies, Africa and Asia, the British were busy taking away the political freedom of the inhabitants. Actually, on the constitutional level, Britain had already displayed its racialism in the West Indies in the early 19th century when it refused to give mulattoes the power of Government in Trinidad, although they were the majority of free citizens. In 1865 in Jamaica it was not the first nor the last time on which Britain made it clear that its white 'kith and kin'[9] would be supported to hold dominion over blacks.

1938. Slavery ended in various islands of the West Indies between 1834 and 1838. Exactly 100 years later (between 1934–38) the black people in the West Indies revolted against the hypocritical freedom of the society. The British were very surprised – they had long forgotten all about the blacks in the British West Indies and they sent a Royal Commission[10] to find out what it was all about. The report of the conditions was so shocking that the British government did not release it until after the war, because they wanted black colonials to fight the white man's battles. By the time the war ended it was clear in the West Indies and throughout Asia and Africa that some concessions would have to be made to black peoples. In general, the problem as seen by white imperialists was to give enough power to certain groups in colonial society to keep the whole society from exploding and to maintain the essentials of the imperialist structure. In the British West Indies, they had to take into account the question of military strategy because we lie under the belly of the world's imperialist giant, the U.S.A. Besides, there was the new and vital mineral bauxite, which had to be protected. The British solution was to pull out wherever possible and leave the imperial government in the hands of the U.S.A, while the local government was given to a white, brown and black petty-bourgeoisie who were culturally the creations of white capitalist society and who therefore support the white imperialist system because they gain personally and because they have been brainwashed into aiding the oppression of black people.

Black Power in the West Indies means three closely related things: (i) the break with imperialism which is historically white racist; (ii) the assumption of power by the black masses in the islands; (iii) the cultural reconstruction of the society in the image of the blacks.

I shall anticipate certain questions on who are the blacks in the West Indies since they are in fact questions which have been posed to me elsewhere. I maintain that it is the white world which has defined who are blacks – if you are not white than you are black. However, it is obvious that the West Indian situation is complicated by factors such as the variety of racial types and racial mixtures and by the process of class formation. We have, therefore, to note not simply what the white world says but also how individuals perceive each other. Nevertheless, we can talk of the mass of the West Indian population as being black – either African or

Indian. There seems to have been some doubts on the last point, and some fear that Black Power is aimed against the Indian. This would be a flagrant denial of both the historical experience of the West Indies and the reality of the contemporary scene.

When the Indian was brought to the West Indies, he met the same racial contempt which whites applied to Africans. The Indian, too, was reduced to a single stereotype – the coolie or labourer. He too was a hewer of wood and a bringer of water. I spoke earlier of the revolt of the blacks in the West Indies in 1938. That revolt involved Africans in Jamaica, Africans and Indians in Trinidad and Guyana. The uprisings in Guyana were actually led by Indian sugar workers. Today, some Indians (like some Africans) have joined the white power structure in terms of economic activity and culture; but the underlying reality is that poverty resides among Africans and Indians in the West Indies and that power is denied them. Black Power in the West Indies, therefore, refers primarily to people who are recognisably African or Indian.

The Chinese, on the other hand, are a former labouring group who have now become bastions of white West Indian social structure. The Chinese of the People's Republic of China have long broken with and are fighting against white imperialism, but *our* Chinese have nothing to do with that movement. They are to be identified with Chiang-Kai-Shek[11] and not Chairman Mao Tse-tung. They are to be put in the same bracket as the lackeys of capitalism and imperialism who are to be found in Hong Kong and Taiwan. Whatever the circumstances in which the Chinese came to the West Indies, they soon became (as a group) members of the exploiting class. They will have either to relinquish or be deprived of that function before they can be re-integrated into a West Indian society where the black man walks in dignity.

The same applies to the mulattoes, another group about whom I have been questioned. The West Indian brown man is characterised by ambiguity and ambivalence. He has in the past identified with the black masses when it suited his interests, and at the present time some browns are in the forefront of the movement towards black consciousness; but the vast majority have fallen to the bribes of white imperialism, often outdoing the whites in their hatred and oppression of blacks. Garvey wrote of the Jamaican mulattoes – 'I was openly hated and persecuted by some of these coloured men of the island who did not want to be classified as Negroes but as white'. Naturally, conscious West Indian blacks like Garvey have in turn expressed their dislike for the browns, but there is nothing in the West Indian experience which suggests that browns are unacceptable when they choose to identify with blacks. The post-1938 developments in fact showed exactly the opposite. It seems to me, therefore, that it is not for the Black Power movement to determine the position of the browns, reds and so-called West Indian whites – the movement can only keep the door open and leave it to those groups to make their choice.

Black Power is not racially intolerant. It is the hope of the black man that he should have power over his own destinies. This is not incompatible with a multi-racial society where each individual counts equally. Because the moment that power is equitably distributed among several ethnic groups then the very relevance of making the distinction between groups will be lost. What we must object to is the current image of a multi-racial society living in harmony – that is a myth designed to justify the exploitation suffered by the blackest of our population, at the hands of the lighter-skinned groups. Let us look at the figures for the racial composition of the Jamaican population. Of every 100 Jamaicans,

76.8% are visibly African

0.8% European

1.1% Indian

0.6% Chinese   91% have African blood

0.1% Syrian

14.6% Afro-European

5.4% other mixtures

This is a black society where Africans preponderate. Apart from the mulatto mixture all other groups are numerically insignificant and yet the society seeks to give them equal weight and indeed more weight than the Africans. If we went to Britain we could easily find non-white groups in the above proportions[12] – Africans and West Indians, Indians and Pakistanis, Turks, Arabs and other Easterners – but Britain is not called a multi-racial society. When we go to Britain we don't expect to take over all of the British real estate business, all their cinemas and most of their commerce as the European, Chinese and Syrian have done here. All we ask for there is some work and shelter, and we can't even get that. Black Power must proclaim that Jamaica is a black society – we should fly Garvey's Black Star banner and we will treat all other groups in the society on that understanding – they can have *the basic right of all individuals* but *no privileges to exploit Africans* as has been the pattern during slavery and ever since.

The present government knows that Jamaica is a black man's country. That is why Garvey has been made a national hero, for they are trying to deceive black people into thinking that the government is with them. The government of Jamaica recognises black power – it is afraid of the potential wrath of Jamaica's black and largely African population. It is that same fear which forced them to declare mourning when black men are murdered in Rhodesia, and when Martin Luther King was murdered in the U.S.A. But the black people don't need to be told that Garvey is a national hero – they know that. Nor do they need to be told to mourn when blacks are murdered by White Power, because they mourn every day right here in Jamaica where white power keeps them ignorant, unemployed, ill-clothed and ill-fed. They will stop mourning when things change – and that means a revolution, for the first essential is to break the chains which bind us to white imperialists, and that is a very revolutionary step. Cuba is the only country in the West Indies and in this hemisphere which has broken with white power. That is why Stokely Carmichael can visit Cuba but he can't visit Trinidad or Jamaica.[13] That is why Stokely can call Fidel 'one of the blackest men in the Americas' and that is why our leaders in contrast qualify as 'white'.

Here I'm not just playing with words – I'm extending the definition of Black Power by indicating the nature of its opposite, 'White Power', and I'm providing a practical illustration of what Black Power means in one particular West Indian community where it had already occurred. White Power is the power of whites over blacks without any participation of the blacks. White Power rules the imperialist world as a whole. In Cuba the blacks and mulattoes numbered 1,585,073 out of a population of 5,829,029 in 1953–i.e., about one quarter of the population. Like Jamaica's black people today, they were the poorest and most depressed people on the island. Lighter-skinned Cubans held local power, while real power was in the hands of the U.S. imperialists. Black Cubans fought alongside white Cuban workers and peasants because they were all oppressed. Major Juan Almeida,[14] one of the outstanding leaders of Cuba today, was one of the original guerrillas in the Sierra Maestra, and he is black. Black Cubans today enjoy political, economic and social rights and opportunities of exactly the same kind as white Cubans. They too bear arms in the Cuban Militia as an expression of their basic rights. In other words, White Power in Cuba is ended. The majority of the white population naturally predominates numerically in most spheres of activity but they do not hold dominion over blacks without regard to the latter's interests. The blacks have achieved power commensurate with their own numbers by their heroic self-efforts during the days of slavery, in fighting against the Spanish and in fighting against imperialism. Having achieved their rights they can in fact afford to forget the category 'black' and think simply as Cuban citizens, as Socialist equals and as men. In Jamaica, where blacks are far greater in numbers and have no whites alongside them as oppressed workers and peasants, it will be the black people who alone can bear the brunt of revolutionary fighting.

Trotsky once wrote that Revolution is the carnival of the masses. When we have that carnival in the West Indies, are people like us here at the university going to join the bacchanal?

Let us have a look at our present position. Most of us who have studied at the U.W.I. are discernibly black, and yet we are undeniably part of the white imperialist system. A few are actively pro-imperialist. They have no confidence in anything that is not white – they talk nonsense about black people being lazy – the same nonsense which was said about the Jamaican black man after emancipation, although he went to Panama and performed the giant task of building the Panama Canal – the same nonsense which is said about W.I. unemployed today, and yet they proceed to England to run the whole transport system. Most of us do not go to quite the same extremes in denigrating ourselves and our black brothers, but we say nothing against the system, and that means that we are acquiescing in the exploitation of our brethren. One of the ways that the situation has persisted especially in recent times is that it has given a few individuals like you and … [me] … a vision of personal progress measured in terms of front lawn and the latest model of a huge American car. This has recruited us into their ranks and deprived the black masses of articulate leadership. That is why at the outset I stressed that our choice was to *remain* as part of the white system or to break with it. There is no other alternative.

Black Power in the W.I. must aim at transforming the Black intelligensia into the servants of the black masses. Black Power, within the university and without must aim at overcoming white cultural imperialism. Whites have dominated us both physically and mentally. This fact is brought out in virtually any serious sociological study of the region – the brainwashing process has been so stupendous that it has convinced so many black men of their inferiority. I will simply draw a few illustrations to remind you of this fact which blacks like us at Mona prefer to forget.

The adult black in our West Indian society is fully conditioned to thinking white, because that is the training we are given from childhood. The little black girl plays with a white doll, identifying with it as she combs its flaxen hair. Asked to sketch the figure of a man or woman, the black schoolboy instinctively produces a white man or a white woman. This is not surprising, since until recently the illustrations in our textbooks were all figures of Europeans. The few changes which have taken place have barely scratched the surface of the problem. West Indians of every colour still aspire to European standards of dress and beauty. The language which is used by black people in describing ourselves shows how we despise our African appearance. 'Good hair' means European hair, 'good nose' means a straight nose, 'good complexion' means a light complexion. Everybody recognises how incongruous and ridiculous such terms are, but we continue to use them and to express our support of the assumption that white Europeans have the monopoly of beauty, and that black is the incarnation of ugliness. That is why Black Power advocates find it necessary to assert that BLACK IS BEAUTIFUL.

The most profound revelation of the sickness of our society on the question of race is our respect for all the white symbols of the Christian religion. God the Father is white, God the Son is white, and presumably God the Holy Ghost is white also. The disciples and saints are white, all the Cherubim, Seraphim and angels are white – except Lucifer, of course, who was black, being the embodiment of evil. When one calls upon black people to reject these things, this is not an attack on the teachings of Christ or the ideals of Christianity. What we have to ask is 'Why should Christianity come to us all wrapped up in white?' The white race constitute about

20 per cent of the world's population, and yet non-white peoples are supposed to accept that all who inhabit the heavens are white. There are 650 million Chinese, so why shouldn't God and most of the angels be Chinese? The truth is that there is absolutely no reason why different racial groups should not provide themselves with their own religious symbols. A picture of Christ could be red, white or black, depending upon the people who are involved. When Africans adopt the European concept that purity and goodness must be painted white and all that is evil and damned is to be painted black then we are flagrantly self-insulting.

Through the manipulation of this media of education and communication, white people have produced black people who administer the system and perpetuate the white values – 'white-hearted black men', as they are called by conscious elements. This is as true of the Indians as it is true of the Africans in our West Indian society. Indeed, the basic explanation of the tragedy of African/Indian confrontation in Guyana and Trinidad is the fact that both groups are held captive by the European way of seeing things. When an African abuses an Indian he repeats all that the white men said about Indian indentured 'coolies'; and in turn the Indian has borrowed from the whites the stereotype of the 'lazy nigger' to apply to the African beside him. It is as though no black man can see another black man except by looking through a white person. It is time we started seeing through our own eyes. The road to Black Power here in the West Indies and everywhere else must begin with a revaluation of ourselves as blacks and with a redefinition of the world from our own standpoint.

NOTES

1. Moise Tshombe (1919–69), supported by Belgian mining interests, became president of the state of Katanga which broke away from the Congo (1960–63), and then prime minister of the Democratic Republic of the Congo until he was exiled after a military coup in 1965.
2. Patrice Lumumba (1925–61) was the first prime minister of the Democratic Republic of the Congo after it achieved independence in 1960 but he was soon dismissed by President Joseph Kasavubu. He was arrested and imprisoned in Katanga and then assassinated, probably with the connivance of Belgian officials and the US Central Intelligence Agency.
3. The period known as Reconstruction is generally agreed to be 1865–77, after which a combination of fraud and violence was used to deny black citizens their right to vote.
4. Malcolm X, born Malcolm Little (1925–65), was a leader of the Nation of Islam in the United States in the 1950s. His father, who was a follower of Marcus Garvey, was murdered by the Ku Klux Klan. In 1964, Malcolm X broke with the Nation of Islam and formed the Organization of Afro-American Unity (OAAU). After a pilgrimage to Mecca, he adopted the name El-Hajj Malik El-Shabazz. While speaking to an OAAU

rally in New York City in 1965, he was assassinated, allegedly by members of the Nation of Islam.

5. The Student Nonviolent Coordinating Committee was formed by black college students in 1960 as a direct action wing of the civil rights movement, emerging in sit-ins and voter registration campaigns for black people in the US south. In 1966, Stokely Carmichael (who later adopted the name Kwame Toure, 1941-98) became the leader of SNCC and issued the call for Black Power, which was the name of a book he wrote with Charles V. Hamilton, *Black Power: The Politics of Liberation in America* (1967).

6. Martin Luther King (1929–68), one of the founders and leaders of the Southern Christian Leadership Conference in 1957 and the dominant personality of the US civil rights movement, was assassinated on April 4, 1968, shortly before Rodney gave this lecture in Jamaica. The shock and anger provoked by news of King's murder resulted in massive demonstrations and riots in more than a hundred US cities.

7. The University of the West Indies campus in Mona, Jamaica.

8. Paul Bogle, a small farmer and leader of a Native Baptist Church, was the leader of the rebellion at Morant Bay in 1865. Bogle, along with other rebels and many people who had not been involved, was executed but he was declared a National Hero of Jamaica in 1965.

9. Ian Smith unilaterally declared independence for the colony of Southern Rhodesia in 1965, with a white-minority government. He used the expression 'kith and kin' in order to emphasise the historical connections between the white settlers and Britain. However, Britain did not recognise Smith's regime and joined the United Nations in a trade embargo. The collapse of Portugal's African empire in the 1970s left Smith's government isolated, except for South Africa. An armed struggle forced Smith into negotiations and he conceded to black-majority rule. Elections followed in 1978, and Robert Mugabe led Zimbabwe to independence in 1980.

10. This was known as the Moyne Commission, after its chairman, Lord Moyne.

11. General Chiang-Kai-Shek (1887–1975) was the leader of the Nationalist Party (Kuomintang) that was defeated by the communists, led by Mao Tse-tung, in 1949. His army retreated to the island of Taiwan and created the Republic of China. With the support of the United States, Chiang ruled Taiwan until his death and Kuomintang was the only legal party until 1989.

12. In the proportions, that is, of the non-black minorities in Jamaica.

13. Stokely Carmichael, who was born in Trinidad, was banned from entering Trinidad or Jamaica, and all his writings, along with those of Malcolm X and others, were banned by the government of Jamaica in the 1960s.

14. Major Juan Almeida, who commanded the third front of the revolutionary forces around Santiago de Cuba in 1958, was a member of the original group that attacked the Moncada barracks on July 26, 1953. After the revolution, he became head of the Revolutionary Armed Forces and one of the eight members of the politburo.

Thirty-Four

Michael Manley

Michael Manley (1924–97) was born in Kingston, Jamaica, the younger of two sons of Edna Manley (1900–87) and Norman Washington Manley (1893–1969), a distinguished sculptor and politician, respectively. Michael Manley attended Jamaica College, a prestigious secondary school, and joined the Royal Canadian Air Force in 1943. After the war he studied at the London School of Economics where he formed lasting friendships with two other future West Indian leaders, Errol Barrow of Barbados and Forbes Burnham of Guyana. In 1950, he lectured students on the importance of a West Indian federation, to which his father was deeply committed. He began a career in journalism at the Observer in 1951 but at the end of that year he returned to Jamaica and worked for Public Opinion, a progressive Jamaican paper that supported his father's People's National party (PNP). In 1952, the party expelled its left wing, among whom were some of its best labour organisers, and formed a new trade union, the National Workers Union (NWU), for which Manley began to work.

Between 1952 and 1955, the NWU, affiliated with the party that was out of power, was competing with the Bustamante Industrial Trades Union (BITU) and the Jamaica Labour party (JLP). From 1955 to 1962, however, the NWU was affiliated with the party in power and the government was led by Manley's father. In 1961, Norman Manley staked his government's standing on a referendum about whether Jamaica should stay in the West Indies Federation and he lost. The pro-federation PNP narrowly lost the 1962 general election (50 per cent of the vote went to the JLP and 49 per cent to the PNP) and Alexander Bustamante led Jamaica into independence.

During the 1960s, Michael Manley continued his leadership role in the *NWU while becoming increasingly involved in party politics. His father appointed him a senator in 1962 and he was elected to the House of Representatives in 1967. He replaced his ailing father as the PNP leader in February 1969 and in September his father died. In October 1969, at the PNP's annual conference, Michael made economic nationalism the centre of his party's policy and his article in the prestigious journal* Foreign Affairs *(1970) focused on the importance of economics in international relations. He urged Jamaica to abandon the insularity that had led it to turn its back on the West Indies Federation and to participate in a coordinated Caribbean strategy of development.*

The PNP won the general election in 1972 with 56 per cent of the vote, winning 37 of the 53 seats in the House of Representatives, and Manley became the prime minister at the age of 47. Manley's government launched a series of domestic reforms and his economic and foreign policy, which followed from the arguments he had made in the Foreign Affairs *article in 1970, moved towards greater independence, Caribbean cooperation and participation in the Non-Aligned Movement. The United States, which was involved in the overthrow of the democratically-elected socialist government of Chile in 1973, reacted negatively. Manley's first book,* The Politics of Change: A Jamaican Testament *(1973), emphasised his commitment to the principles of equality, social justice, self-reliance and participatory democracy. In 1974, he declared that the PNP, which had been a nominally socialist party under his father's leadership since 1940, was committed to 'democratic socialism'. Manley's second book,* A Voice at the Workplace: Reflections on Colonialism and the Jamaican Worker *(1975), presented his views and experience of trade unionism and its relations with capitalism. He became an articulate advocate of the New International Economic Order, a proposal to reform the unfair trade relations between the rich and poor nations of the world. When Manley praised Cuba's efforts in helping to defeat a South African army that tried to overthrow the Marxist government of Angola in 1975, this was the last straw for the US secretary of state, Henry Kissinger, and Jamaica was subjected to immense economic and political pressure.*

The political polarisation of Jamaica in 1975 and 1976 was exacerbated by US involvement in attempts to destabilise the government and reflected in increasing violence. A respected Jamaican political scientist, Carl Stone, later described three stages to the political violence that continued through the 1970s: first, the JLP used 'armed thugs to destabilize the PNP's popularity prior to the 1976 election', then 'the PNP organized retaliation but mainly as defensive responses', and third, 'both were on the offensive and pushed the country on the verge of civil war' (Daily Gleaner, March 17, 1986). In the 1976 elections, the

PNP won 57 per cent of the vote and 47 of the 60 seats in the House of Representatives, a clear victory which even the conservative newspaper, the Daily Gleaner, *acknowledged was an endorsement of the PNP's programme of democratic socialism.*

Jamaica faced an economic crisis in 1976 and Manley turned to the International Monetary Fund (IMF) for credit. The IMF imposed harsh and unpopular conditions on Jamaica and this helped undermine the government without improving the economy. With growing unemployment and poverty, and a media campaign that made the most of human rights scandals and Manley's friendship with Fidel Castro, the economic and political crisis deepened. Opposition to the government intensified and there were 889 murders in 1980, many of them due to political violence. Despite widespread fear, 77 per cent of the eligible voters participated in the 1980 elections, giving the JLP 59 per cent of the vote and 51 of the 60 seats.

During his years as leader of the opposition (1980–89) Manley was an active lecturer on an international circuit, an influential vice-president of the Socialist International, and the author of many articles and three books, Jamaica: Struggle in the Periphery *(1982),* Up the Down Escalator: Development and the International Economy - A Jamaican Case Study *(1987) and* A History of West Indies Cricket *(1989). Meanwhile, Edward Seaga's JLP government became increasingly unpopular and in 1989 Manley and the PNP were returned to power, winning 57 per cent of the vote and 45 of the 60 seats in the general election. By then, Manley had changed his policies on many issues and he avoided the ideological confrontations of the 1970s. In 1992, ill health led him to leave politics and he died of cancer five years later.*

*O*vercoming Insularity in Jamaica

I

In the long run it may yet transpire that the differences between stages of economic development as between various nations and regions of the world are a more important determinant of history than differences in ideology or systems of government. Religious wars are contested with fervor at the time; so are wars to make the world safe for democracy. But sooner or later, the economic historian presents an alternative analysis which seems to put the hysteria of yesteryear in a more realistic frame.

And so today, press, pulpit and politician would have us believe that a new ideological focus is at the heart of the uncertainties, tensions and conflicts of the second half of the twentieth century. Once again, I suggest that tomorrow's historians will point out that behind the hysteria lay economics and that the real battleground was in that largely tropical territory which was first the object of colonial exploitation, second, the focus of non-Caucasian nationalism and more latterly known as the underdeveloped and the developing world as it sought euphemisms for its condition. It has now proclaimed itself the third world to mark its transition from an age of apology to one of assertiveness.

To the extent that all this is true, any development in any part of the third world has an importance that far outweighs the size, wealth or power of that particular part of that world. And so, recognizing that this explanation may be required, I do not apologize for writing about Jamaica with its 4,000 square miles and two million people and its relationship to the English-speaking Caribbean which covers many more square miles but still adds up to only a little more than five million people.

Because Jamaica and the Caribbean are a part of the third world, they are best understood if one first isolates certain basic features that are common to that world and its general condition at this moment of history.

I think that four factors can be distinguished. First of all, the third world has joined the other two worlds in one feature that is common to both: nationalism. Basic to attitudes in the third world is the fear of foreign domination. Inevitably, in the second half of the twentieth century, foreign domination is understood in economic terms just as clearly as it used to be understood in political terms. And no consideration of third-world politics can proceed unless this is borne clearly in mind.

The second factor, in the area of economics, is the adverse movement in the terms of trade between the third world and its highly industrialized and developed neighbors of the North, encompassing not only price trends as they relate to exports and imports between groups but also the terms on which capital is exported from one world to the other.

The third factor inheres in a paradox: the fact that the new taste of nationalism and political independence coexists with a need for external capital. Common to every former colonial territory is a shortage of internal capital resources, a release of popular expectation and an urge toward complete national independence. The paradox consists in the fact that popular expectation cannot be satisfied without capital, and capital cannot be generated from internal sources alone. Thus, the urge for independence and the need for capital come into conflict.

The fourth factor which I contend is common to the third world is that in its dealings with the industrialized nations, the third world desperately needs the strength that can come from regional economic groupings; and, more generally, the development of a common economic diplomacy. This obvious need, however, conflicts with the tendency of all 'new' nations to be separatist and insular.

It is against this background that Jamaica's recent history, present posture and future possibilities must be judged.

II

The recent past has been remarkable for three things. A Crown Colony within the British Empire up to 1944, Jamaica became a part of the colonial revolt in 1938. Riots precipitated a trade union movement on the one hand and the island's first mass political party on the other. Alexander Bustamante was the charismatic focus for a unique brand of mass trade unionism and Norman Manley was the equally charismatic force behind a movement dedicated to political independence and social and economic reconstruction. In time, the trade union group formed a political party and the political group began to organize in the field of trade unionism. Less surprisingly than might appear at first blush, the trade union group, which later formed a political party, became the conservative focus and the nationalists who later became union organizers became the radical focus. The net effect was a polarization of the island's politics and the most effective two-party system among the countries then fighting for national independence.

This two-party system, driven by the two astonishing personalities mentioned, embarked upon what is probably the most orderly transition from colonial status to political independence in modern history. In fact, the transition was so orderly, was handled with such sophistication and poise that many young Jamaicans today feel cheated by history. Deprived of the psychological rallying point of an heroic episode, they feel that they entered upon the estate of freedom so silently, with so little drama, that many question whether it has happened at all.

The formation of this deeply entrenched two-party system, along with the orderly transition from political colonialism to political freedom, are two of the three significant features. The third is Jamaica's part in the West Indies Federation which was launched with more doubt than fanfare in 1958 and collapsed by the end of 1961.

The English-speaking Caribbean is effectively bounded by the Bahamas to the north, British Honduras[1] (in Central America) to the west, Barbados to the east and Guyana (on the South American mainland) to the south. However, the area has hitherto been dominated by its largest island, Jamaica (population, two million), just south of Castro's Cuba, and its second largest island, Trinidad (population, one million), just north of Guyana. Jamaica consists of the city of Kingston with half a million people, an entrenched plantation system mainly centering on sugar, a booming bauxite and alumina industry and a burgeoning tourist trade, all of which coexist with the country's rural peasant majority whose small-scale hillside agriculture is falling further and further behind the progress achieved by the rest of the country. Kingston itself is a classic example of urban life in a developing country, with beautiful suburbs, a growing and expert middle class, a skillful but restless industrial proletariat and huge, smoldering slums all packed together around a port which boasts one of the greatest natural harbors in the world and rests on a plain surrounded by mountains of spectacular beauty.

Trinidad is like Jamaica except that it has no rural peasantry to speak of, and whereas Jamaica has a new bauxite industry, it has a much older oil industry. Like Jamaica, it has extensive sugar plantations, massive unemployment and a growing but more recent investment in tourism. Jamaica has, however, in a subtle but real way, a more practical population. Trinidad, with its carnival tradition and stronger Latin influence, tends to be more volatile.

These, along with the smaller islands of the Leeward and Windward chain, share a predominantly African ethnic origin and a common political and institutional history as ex-British colonies. However, the area consists of eight clearly defined sub-regions, at least one of which has a thousand islands and all of which have separate senses of identity. All this adds up to one of the most tantalizing political problems in the world today.

It is in this regional focus and within the broad perspective of third-world politics that one must now consider Jamaica's part in the abortive West Indies Federation. During the 1940s and 1950s the question of such a Federation was much talked about in Caribbean politics; but however central it was in the rest of the Caribbean, it was always an afterthought in the dialogue of Jamaican politics.

The truth is that Jamaica all along had been preoccupied with its internal problems which were, and are, legion. Once in the Federation, which was not independent in 1958 and whose central government was then largely impotent, the issue had to be faced: 'What sort of constitution shall we have when we become an independent nation shortly and how shall the powers of a central government ruling over many separate islands compare with the power remaining with the government of each island?' In the event, geography defeated political logic; Jamaican nationalism proved too strong for the federal principle. The two parties which dominate Jamaican political life failed to agree on federation and in a referendum insularity won. Jamaica voted herself out of federation, and without Jamaica the Federation collapsed.

But federation is a technique. It is a means rather than an end, a point of departure rather than of arrival. Behind this particular federal experiment, which collapsed in 1961 (the vote was approximately 230,000 against to 210,000 for the federation), lies the still larger question of regionalism. Do Jamaica and the Caribbean stand to lose or gain by regional cooperation?

III

Becoming an independent nation in 1962, Jamaica has nonetheless remained a classic example of what is sometimes described as a 'two tier' economy. Equally important, our economy has remained firmly cast in the colonial mold. The bauxite and alumina industry is entirely North American owned. More than half the tourist and sugar industries are under foreign ownership. Foreign trade continues to grow faster than internally consumed production and remains oriented toward traditional lines of exchange with North America and Great Britain. And those who manage the economy continue to look outward for ideas and expertise.

In spite of dramatic expansions in the bauxite and tourist industries, a balance-of-payments situation in surplus, the rapid development of a sophisticated network of financial institutions and a basically sound civil service, Jamaica remains a prey to many of the evils which beset it in colonial times.

Unemployment runs at a dangerous 20 percent, and is believed to be over 30 percent in the 16 to 25 age group. Agriculture lags badly and is virtually stagnant in an otherwise booming economy. Since approximately half the population depends upon agriculture, either as small farmers or as agricultural workers, this means that half of the population are condemned both to a total defeat of their expectations ever to become independent and to a growing awareness of the widening gap between their condition and that of the rest of the population.

Inevitably, this has led to growing tensions in the society. The older peasantry tends to be bitter, but resigned. The youth, on the other hand, are increasingly disillusioned but by no means resigned. Instead, the anger of the youth tends to focus increasingly on the presence of a dominant structure of foreign capital and contends that we have not altered the equation of our problems in spite of the considerable sacrifice of sovereignty involved in the acceptance of foreign capital. In short, they feel that we are sacrificing economic independence for the explicit purpose of solving our internal problems, but that in the event, since the problems are growing worse, the sacrifice is in vain.

Of course, both the perception of the problem and disappointment with the result involve dangerous oversimplifications in economic terms. Basically, the economy needs to be restructured. This should involve land reform, import substitution in relation to food consumption and the planned use of inter-industry linkages so as to ensure a growing measure of internal viability to the economy. A largely agricultural country, Jamaica is exporting J$62 million of sugar, bananas, citrus and coffee, while it imports J$60 million of food; and this in a context where some 20 percent of its arable land is either totally idle or seriously under-used. In addition, much of the industrial development of the last 20 years has been of the last stage assembly 'screw-driver' type, while virtually no attention has been paid to agro-industrial development, which is the most obvious area for establishing inter-industry linkages. The total result has been that agriculture, while supporting more than half of the population, contributed 13 percent to the gross national product in 1960 just before the attainment of independence but only nine percent in 1969.

Broadly speaking, Jamaica has fallen into the same trap as many other developing countries by thinking that the indiscriminate granting of tax incentives to foreign capital – regardless of the contribution which the particular capital can make to development, or of the posture of that capital in the society – will necessarily contribute to progress. Even in recent times, when experiments in forms of joint ownership ventures between foreign and local capital have become the vogue in response to nationalist pressures, there is still no evidence of realistic national planning as to the sort of ventures that are needed and, in particular, industries which seek to exploit local raw materials and by-products. If unemployment is to be significantly reduced and the dangerous gap between the agricultural population and the industrial élite is to be narrowed, radically different policies have to be pursued. These will have to involve new thinking about the use to which internal resources are to be put; a complete reexamination of the sort of foreign capital which should be invited to participate, and the relationship between foreign capital and the national interest as regards ownership and control.

The question arises as to the frame in which these objectives can best be secured. As a consequence of the federal experience, Jamaica is undergoing a period of ambivalence toward the rest of the Caribbean. In less fanciful terms, the party in power, the Jamaica Labour Party (JLP), is hostile to regionalism partly in response to the parochial instincts which lay behind its anti-federal fight and partly because it is a prisoner of its success in that fight. The opposition People's National Party (PNP) tends to be afraid of regionalism because its own loss of power was attributable to its support of federation in the 1961 referendum. And yet history has its own inexorable logic. In spite of all these factors which seem to conspire against regionalism, Jamaica has already joined the Caribbean Free Trade Area[2] and is a founding member of the Caribbean Development Bank.

Exploratory talks are already under way as the region makes the first tentative approaches toward a formula for a common external tariff and common policies toward foreign investments. Although many counsel caution – and indeed, this may be the price of ultimate success – one wishes that a greater sense of urgency attached to the whole exercise. Where gross disparities in wealth, massive unemployment, showpiece industries and conspicuous consumption coexist in one overpopulated island, violence and even revolution must lurk in the wings. Clearly, regional economic development provides a more ample prospect in a situation where peaceful progress cannot be more than a marginal possibility. Yet, although the aisle is clearly marked, we seem to come to the altar of history like a reluctant bride with faltering step and lowered gaze.

What is needed, I suggest, is a tough-minded recognition that national survival, like business survival, is a matter of margins and that regionalism can provide the framework in which internal markets are increased, external bargaining power enhanced and international recognition maximized. The fact that all these differences may be marginal, far from disproving the case, represents the limit of what is possible in any event and should be pursued relentlessly in a world which does not offer more than marginal opportunities at best. Perhaps, then, we might now consider what Jamaica stands to gain from regionalism.

IV

As indicated earlier, Jamaica cannot hope to provide the basis of a decent society unless it substantially restructures its economy. The plantation system condemns those who depend upon it to a life of insecurity and is a constant focus for hostility and tension for any society which it dominates. Hence it is almost a precondition of progress to reduce dependence on fly-by-night foreign capital which will come in briefly for a 'quick buck' while wages are low and the conditions for exploitation ideal. But the search for alternatives is no easy matter and a regional economic bloc unquestionably provides a larger frame within which to pursue the restructuring of the Jamaican economy along with those of its Caribbean neighbors. Apart from the obvious advantages of size that come with regional cooperation, there are four other major areas that must be considered.

The English-speaking Caribbean will not benefit from its size until its territories learn to act in unison in matters of common concern. Thus, it is urgent that its governments develop techniques for handling trade and other relations with the outside world on the basis of a common policy. Beginnings have been made in this direction with an annual Heads of Government conference and in certain areas of trade, such as sugar, which are handled collectively. These tentative beginnings have to be pursued with vigor so that the region speaks more and more to the outside world with one voice.

Secondly, the region would benefit enormously if it could learn to handle major foreign capital interests secondary to a common policy. A classic example is the bauxite and alumina industry. The Caribbean region, including the Dominican Republic, Haiti and Surinam (which is next door to Guyana), produces 52 percent of the bauxite consumed in the Western world and 43 percent of world consumption. As the raw material of the aluminum industry, bauxite has a critical part to play in the economic future of Jamaica and certainly of Guyana and Surinam. But it is a wasting asset, which has to make its contribution to general development as rapidly as possible. Interestingly enough, the workers of the region have been much quicker to recognize this than the politicians.

Perhaps because bargaining power is 'the name of the game' in trade unionism, the Bauxite Workers Union in Jamaica (a section of the National Workers Union and affiliated with the PNP) pursued a more than ordinarily aggressive wage policy against the giants of the industry – Alcoa, Kaiser and Reynolds of the United States and Alcan of Canada – from the very outset of bargaining in 1952. Later, when the companies began quoting wage rates in Guyana and Surinam against Jamaican union claims in the mid-1950s, the Jamaican Union responded by forming the Caribbean Bauxite Mining and Metal Workers' Federation. In the last ten years, this body has played a significant part in bringing regional strength to the collective bargaining process, and this in turn has led to spectacular gains in wages and fringe benefits for the region's 15,000 bauxite and alumina workers.

Clearly, this is a lead that the politicians and governments of the region would do well to follow. In terms of royalties, taxes and general contributions to infrastructure, the aluminum companies can do far more in the Caribbean region. The ability of the region to bargain, however, to increase the contribution of the industries to general welfare, has been considerably affected by the fact that no coherent policy within a united political front exists. And here, let me make it clear that I am not talking in the spirit of wreaking some sort of spiteful vengeance on the aluminum industry; rather, I am concerned to find by legitimate bargaining that point at which the conflicting interests of the industry and the region may be reasonably resolved.

So long as this and similar industries remain exclusively owned by foreign, multinational corporations, the search for this point of 'mutual justice' will be virtually impossible. The very presence of such economic power in foreign hands represents a threat to the sense of independence of a country and a serious obstacle to its freedom of action in economic planning. On the other hand, the corporations have made large investments and provide access to markets and technology. The key, therefore, must lie in joint ownership. It is only when control and ownership are shared reasonably between those who supply the initial capital and know-how on the one hand, and those who supply the raw material and the labor on the other, that mutuality of interest can exist. There is perhaps no greater challenge to man's capacity for wisdom than this. Indeed, the future of the world may be profoundly influenced by the ability of the third world to pursue this goal with calmness and with skill and equally by the ability of the metropolitan world to comprehend the aspirations that lead to the claim for joint ownership and to cooperate wholeheartedly with the process. Where the metropolitan world and its overseas corporations have not learned this lesson in the past, expropriation has often sooner or later been the result. If the world refuses to learn from the past, the old device of revolutionary expropriation may continue to be invoked, not as dogma, but out of practical necessity.

And so to the third proposition. As I said at the outset, it is my conviction that the fundamental problem of the world today is not so much a question of conflicting ideologies as of the economic relationship between the developed economies of the metropolitan world and the less developed economies of the third world. This is not the place to attempt to outline the argument. Suffice it to say that for a variety of well-understood reasons the terms on which trade and capital move between the two worlds do so constantly to the disadvantage of the developing nations and make the problem of real economic progress for small independent countries crushingly difficult.

Clearly, therefore, the ability of the Caribbean to achieve progress goes beyond regionalism to the necessity for the developing world as a whole to evolve a common strategy with regard to its economic dealings with the metropolitan nations. The fundamental rationale of third-world politics is economic. The imperative of the future must be the search for a common economic diplomacy in which, to put it at its simplest, the Caribbean must be as concerned about the fate of Ghana's cocoa as Ghana should be concerned about the fate of Caribbean sugar. And both should be concerned to see that they do not act in such a manner as to undermine each other's possibilities as they trade with the metropolitan world. When we consider the inherent economic power of the United States, Great Britain, the European Common Market and Russia, we see what India, Africa, Latin America and the Caribbean are up against. What is not recognized is that fundamentally they are all up against exactly the same thing. To the extent that the Caribbean region can proceed more coherently and more cogently in acting not only as a part of the third world, but as a sophisticated leader in the development of relevant third-world policies, to that extent can it help to underwrite its own survival.

Obviously, a Caribbean voice will carry more weight in the third world than the sum total of the area's separate voices. And so, therefore, regionalism is important to Jamaican development because it is the natural avenue through which it can enter and influence the stream of third-world politics. What is more, I suggest that third-world politics would benefit enormously from the tough-minded pragmatism which characterizes Jamaican political leadership.

I turn finally to an idea that is not often in general discussion at all. Because it has something to do with human psychology and a lot to do with attitudes and the scars left by past wounds, it is not an easy one to present with clarity. I begin with the premise that national power and success tend to breed a confident man and that lack of power and success tend to have the reverse effect. Obviously, this will not operate where two societies are unaware of each other. However, colonialism and technology have combined to make all the societies of the world acutely aware of each other. To be a member of a small struggling nation, isolated within the difficulties that beset small struggling nations, puts the ordinary citizen at a psychological disadvantage. And I mean by this something quite different from the straightforward problems that arise from poverty and lack of economic opportunity. There is a sense in which the reality of metropolitan power invades the feeling of security and dignity of members of a fragmented third world.

It is clear that the youth of the metropolitan world are increasingly concerned with the moral quality of life in wealthy countries in spite of the growing economic power of their system. On the other hand, the youth of the Caribbean are increasingly uncomfortable with a situation in which they feel trapped in a helpless isolation and yearn to be part of a system that has a chance because it can face the world from a position of strength. I suggest that not all of the brain drain is a response to higher salaries. Nor is all of it merely discontent with the lack of progress at home. If you talk to young migrants you sense behind and beyond these obvious problems a deeper feeling of futility, as if they are tired of belonging to something which does not amount to much in the world. I believe this tendency to despair will grow in the future unless we wake up to the harsh facts of life and grapple with them. Jamaicans must learn to see beyond the narrow focus of insularity and realize that self-interest must be organized in the wider world because it is there that the battle is going to be won or lost. Jamaica's problem is to organize the conditions for its own survival now and it must do so in a context where the revolution of rising expectations, a revolution that is necessarily intolerant of failure, is the dominant reality of politics. The choice, therefore, in the long run of history lies between a low road of self-imposed, insular impotence and a high road of adventure into Caribbean regionalism leading on to the wider possibilities of third-world strength.

NOTES

1. British Honduras was officially renamed as Belize in 1973 and became an independent nation in 1981.
2. The Caribbean Free Trade Area (CARIFTA) was started in 1968. In 1973, it became the Caribbean Community and Common Market (CARICOM), which consisted of 15 countries by the end of the twentieth century: Antigua, Bahamas, Barbados, Belize, Dominica, Grenada, Guyana, Haiti, Jamaica, Montserrat, St Kitts-Nevis, St Lucia, St Vincent, Suriname and Trinidad and Tobago. The goal of this organisation is to achieve regional economic cooperation and greater coordination of services, such as education and health, and of foreign policy.

Thirty-Five

Kamau Brathwaite

Edward Kamau Brathwaite, born in 1930 in Barbados, is one of the outstanding poets and historians of his generation. Educated at Harrison College, he won the Barbados Scholarship in 1949 and studied at Cambridge University. Subsequently he worked as an education officer in Ghana, an experience which inspired him to explore African cultural traditions. In the 1960s, several poets were writing poems based on their understanding of the oral tradition, including rhythmic inspiration from African and jazz musicians. Brathwaite's trilogy, The Arrivants *(Rights of* Passage, Masks *and* Islands *were published separately between 1967 and 1969 and together in one volume in 1973), is one of the richest examples of this vein. A five disc set of his reading of this trilogy was issued by Argo in the 1970s. His many other volumes of poetry include* Black and Blues, *which won the 1976 Casa de las Americas prize for poetry,* Mother Poem *(1977),* Sun Poem *(1982) and* Third World Poems *(1983), which includes his famous 'Poem for Walter Rodney', the Guyanese historian who was assassinated in 1980. Brathwaite was a co-founder of the Caribbean Artists' Movement (CAM) in London in 1966 and an editor of the journal* Savacou.

Brathwaite completed his doctoral dissertation in history at the University of Sussex in 1968. It was published with the same title, The Development of Creole Society in Jamaica, 1770–1820, *in 1971. His argument that the development of new creole cultures from European and African elements created a distinctive kind of society during the era of plantations and slavery has been highly influential. He was appointed a lecturer in history at the University of the West Indies in Jamaica where he later held a chair as*

Professor of Cultural History. Later he moved to New York University as a professor of poetry.

His essay 'Timehri,'published in Savacou, *the journal of CAM, in 1970, grew out of a talk he gave in connection with an exhibition by the distinguished Guyanese painter, Aubrey Williams, in Kingston, Jamaica. Building on some comments about creolisation and his own artistic and intellectual development, Brathwaite identifies some of the possible roots of an authentic Caribbean culture and identity.*

imehri

I

The most significant feature of West Indian life and imagination since Emancipation has been its sense of rootlessness, of not belonging to the landscape; dissociation, in fact, of art from act of living. This, at least, is the view of the West Indies and the Caribbean that has been accepted and articulated by the small but important 'intellectual' élite of the area; a group – call it the educated middle class – ex-planter and ex-slave – that has been involved in the post-plantation creolizing process that made our colonial polity possible. To understand the full meaning of this dissociation of the sensibility, and why it has primarily affected our middle classes and the so-called intellectual élite, it will be necessary, in the first place, to look briefly at our colonial heritage within the context of the process of creolization.

The concept and process of creolization has been treated in some detail by (among others) Richard N. Adams in a paper, 'The Relation Between Plantation and "Creole Cultures"' in *Plantation Systems of the New World.*[1] 'Creolization' is a socio-cultural description and explanation of the way the four main culture-carriers of the region: Amerindian, European, African, and East Indian: inter-acted with each other and with their environment to create the new societies of the New World. Two main kinds of creolization may be distinguished: a *mestizo-creolization*: the inter-culturation of Amerindian and European (mainly Iberian) and located primarily in Central and South America, and a *mulatto-creolization:* the inter-culturation of Negro-African and European (mainly Western European) and located primarily in the West Indies and the slave areas of the North American continent. The crucial difference between the two kinds of creolization is that whereas in mestizo-America only one element of the interaction (the European) was immigrant to the area, in mulatto-America both elements in the process were immigrants. In mestizo-America, there was a host environment with an established culture which had to be colonized mainly by force – an attempted eradication of Amerindian spiritual and material structures. In mulatto America, where the indigenous Indians were fewer and more easily destroyed, and blacks were brought from Africa as slaves, colonizing Europe was more easily able to make its imprint both on the environment (the plantation, the North American city), and the cultural orientation of the area. As the effects of force began to wear off in mestizo-America, the process of creolization began to reverse itself: Europeans became Indianized. In mulatto America, where force had always been a more secondary factor or had, in a sense, been exerted by remote control, the process of creolization began to alter itself with the waning of the colonial régime. It simply fragmented itself into four main socio-cultural orientations: European, African, indigeno-nationalist and folk.

The problem of and for West Indian artists and intellectuals is that having been born and educated within this fragmented culture, they start out in the world without a sense of 'wholeness'. Identification with any one of these orientations can only consolidate the concept of a plural society, a plural vision. Disillusion with the fragmentation leads to a sense of rootlessness. The ideal does not and cannot correspond to perceived and inherited reality. The result: dissociation of the sensibility. The main unconscious concern of many of the most articulate West Indian intellectuals and artists in the early post-colonial period was a description and analysis of this dissociation: C.L.R. James' *Minty Alley*, the work of George Lamming, V.S. Naipaul, Orlando Patterson and M.G. Smith's *The Plural Society in the British West Indies*. The achievement of these writers was to make the society *conscious* of the cultural problem.[2] The second phase of West Indian and Caribbean artistic and intellectual life, on which we are now entering, having become conscious of the problem, is seeking to transcend and heal it.

My own artistic and intellectual concern is, I think, not untypical of this new departure in West Indian and Caribbean cultural life. As such, I shall briefly describe it, since I believe that in doing so, I will be able to throw some direct and personal light upon our present stage and forum. I was born in Barbados, from an urban village background, of parents with a 'middle class' orientation. I went to a secondary school originally founded for children of the plantocracy and colonial civil servants and white professionals; but by the time I got there, the social revolution of the 30's was in full swing, and I was able to make friends with boys of stubbornly non-middle class origin. I was fortunate, also, with my teachers. These were (a) expatriate Englishmen; (b) local whites; (c) black disillusioned classical scholars. They were (with two or three exceptions) happily inefficient as teachers, and none of them seemed to have a stake or interest in our society. We were literally left alone. We picked up what we could or what we wanted from each other and from the few books prescribed like Holy Scripture. With the help of my parents, I applied to do Modern Studies (History and English) in the Sixth Form. Since Modern Studies had never been taught at this level before (1948), and there were no teachers to teach it, I (with about four others) was allowed to study the subject on my own with only token supervision and succeeded, to everyone's surprise, in winning one of the Island Scholarships that traditionally took the ex-planters' sons 'home' to Oxbridge or London.

The point I am making here is that my education and background, though nominally 'middle class', is, on examination, not of this nature at all. I had spent most of my boyhood on the beach and in the sea with 'beach-boys', or in the country, at my grandfather's with country boys and girls. I was therefore not in a position to make any serious intellectual investment in West Indian middle class values. But since I was not then consciously aware of any other West Indian alternative (though in fact I had been *living* that alternative), I found and felt myself 'rootless' on arrival in England and like so many other West Indians of the time, more than ready to accept and absorb the culture of the Mother Country. I was, in other words, a potential Afro-Saxon.

But this didn't work out. When I saw my first snow-fall,[3] I felt that I had come into my own; I had arrived; I was possessing the landscape. But I turned to find that my 'fellow Englishmen' were not particularly prepossessed with me. It was the experience later to be described by Mervyn Morris, Kenneth Ramchand and Elliot Bastien in *Disappointed Guests* (OUP, 1965). I reassured myself that it didn't matter. It made no difference if I was black or white, German, Japanese or Jew. All that mattered was the ego-trip, the self-involving vision. I read Keats, Conrad, Kafka. I was a man of Kulture. But the Cambridge magazines didn't take my poems. Or rather, they only took those which had a West Indian – to me, 'exotic' – flavour.[4] I felt neglected and misunderstood.

Then in 1953, George Lammings's *In the Castle of My Skin*[5] appeared and everything was transformed. Here breathing to me from every pore of line and page, was the Barbados I had lived. The words, the rhythms, the cadences, the scenes, the people, their predicament. They all came back. They all were possible. And all the more beautiful for having been published and praised by London, mother of metropolises.

But by now this was the age of the Emigrant. The West Indies could be written about and explored. But only from a point of vantage outside the West Indies. It was no point going back. No writer could live in that stifling atmosphere of middle class materialism and philistinism. It was Lamming again who gave voice to the ambience in *The Emigrants* (1954), and in *The Pleasures of Exile* (1960). His friend Sam Selvon made a ballad about it in *The Lonely Londoners* (1956), and Vidia Naipaul at the start of his brilliant career could write (in *The Middle Passage*):

> I had never wanted to stay in Trinidad. When I was in the fourth form I wrote
> a vow on the endpaper of my Kennedy's *Revised Latin Primer* to leave within five
> years. I left after six; and for many years afterwards in England, falling asleep in
> bedsitters with the electric fire on, I had been awakened by the nightmare that I
> was back in tropical Trinidad . . . .
>
> I knew [it] to be unimportant, uncreative, cynical . . . . (p.41).

For me, too, child and scion of this time, there was no going back. Accepting
my rootlessness, I applied for work in London, Cambridge, Ceylon, New Delhi,
Cairo, Kano, Khartoum, Sierra Leone, Carcassone, a monastery in Jerusalem. I was
a West Indian, rootless man of the world. I could go, belong, everywhere on the
world-wide globe. I ended up in a village in Ghana. It was my beginning.

Slowly, slowly, ever so slowly; obscurely, slowly but surely, during the eight
years that I lived there, I was coming to an awareness and understanding of
community, of cultural wholeness, of the place of the individual within the tribe, in
society. Slowly, slowly, ever so slowly, I came to a sense of identification of myself
with these people, my living diviners. I came to connect my history with theirs, the
bridge of my mind now linking Atlantic and ancestor, homeland and heartland.
When I turned to leave, I was no longer a lonely individual talent; there was
something wider, more subtle, more tentative: the self without ego, without I, without
arrogance. And I came home to find that I had not really left. That it was still Africa;
Africa in the Caribbean. The middle passage had now guessed its end. The
connection between my lived, but unheeded non-middle class boyhood, and its
Great Tradition on the eastern mainland had been made.

The problem now was how to relate this new awareness to the existing, inherited
non-African consciousness of educated West Indian society. How does the artist
work and function within a plurally fragmented world? How can a writer speak
about 'the people', when, as George Lamming dramatises in *In the Castle of My
Skin*, those to whom he refers have no such concept of themselves?

> 'I like it,' I said. 'That was really very beautiful.'
> 'You know the voice?' Trumper asked. He was very serious now.
> I tried to recall whether I might have heard it. I couldn't.
> 'Paul Robeson',[6] he said. 'One of the greatest o' my people.'
> 'What people?' I asked. I was a bit puzzled.
> 'My People', said Trumper. His tone was insistent. Then he softened into a smile.
> I didn't know whether he was smiling at my ignorance, or whether he was smiling
> his satisfaction with the box and the voice and above all Paul Robeson.
> 'Who are your people?' I asked. It seemed a kind of huge joke.
> 'The Negro race,' said Trumper. The smile had left his face, and his manner had

turned grave again . . . . He knew I was puzzled . . . . At first I thought he meant the
village. This allegiance was something bigger. I wanted to understand it . . . . (p.
331).

What kind of product will emerge from this gap and dichotomy; from conscious
vision and the unwillingly envisioned? It is a problem that Derek Walcott, never
leaving the Caribbean and aware of it from his very first lines in 1949,[7] was increasingly
to face. On the one hand, aware of the material and restricting influences around
him, he wanted, as 'Letter to Margaret' (*Bim* no. 12, 1955) suggests, to cut himself
off:

> Daily, my gift to a nervous crowd of roars
> Conceals raw anger under lip-thin laughter,
> As when the pavilion of pigments applauds after
> Some skin-surpassing stroke, I itch to scratch the sores
> Under the green epidermis of the lawn.
> But single, am helpless . . . .

On the other hand, in 'Hic Jacet' (*The Gulf and Other Poems*, 1969), he seems
certain in the knowledge that the source of his art was and is with the people, and
now 'Convinced of the power of provincialism', he says: 'Commoner than water I
sank to lose my name . . . .'

But Walcott is a brilliant exceptional, creatively expressing through his work
the pressures and dilemmas of his plural society. He is a humanist in the sense that
the scholars and artists of the Italian Renaissance were humanists. He is concerned
with converting his heritage into a classical tradition, into a classical statement. But
as the folk movement from below his outward looking position begins to make itself
felt, there is heard, in the title poem of *The Gulf*, a growing note of alienation and
despair:[8]

> Yet the South felt like home. Wrought balconies,
> the sluggish river with its tidal drawl,
> the tropic air charged with the extremities
>
> of patience, a heat heavy with oil,
> canebrakes, that legendary jazz. But fear
> thickened my voice, that strange, familiar soil
>
> prickled and barbed the texture of my hair,
> my status as a secondary soul.
> The Gulf, your gulf, is daily widening,

each blood-red rose warns of that coming night
where there's no rock cleft to go hidin' in
and all the rocks catch fire, when that black might,

their stalking, moonless panthers turn from Him
whose voice they can no more believe, when the black X's
mark their passover with slain seraphim.

So the question of communal, as opposed to individual wholeness still remains. And returning to London in 1965, I was more than ever aware of this. For there were the West Indian writers and artists, still rootless, still isolated, even if making a 'name'. It seemed that flung out centrifugally to the perimeter of their possibilities, our boys were failing to find a centre. Salkey's *Escape to an Autumn Pavement* (1960), and *The Adventures of Catullus Kelly* (1968), Naipaul's *The Mimic Men* (1967), and Orlando Patterson's *An Absence of Ruins* (1967), were moving witnesses to this realization.

II

Then in 1966/67, two events of central importance to the growth and direction of the West Indian imagination took place. Stokely Carmichael,[9] the Trinidadian-born American Black Power leader visited London and magnetized a whole set of splintered feelings that had for a long time been seeking a node. Carmichael enunciated a way of seeing the black West Indian that seemed to many to make sense of the entire history of slavery and colonial suppression, of the African diaspora into the New World. And he gave it a name. Links of sympathy, perhaps for the first time, were set up between labouring immigrant, artist/intellectual, and student. Sharing, as he saw it, a common history, Carmichael produced images of shared communal values. A black International was possible. West Indians, denied history, denied heroes by their imposed education, responded. From London, (and Black America) the flame spread to the university campuses of the archipelago. It found echoes among the urban restless of the growing island cities. Rastafari art, 'primitive' art, dialect and protest verse suddenly had a new urgency, took on significance. Walter Rodney published *Grounding with my Brothers* (1969); Marina Maxwell started the Yard Theatre; Olive Lewin's Jamaican Folk Singers began to make sense; Mark Matthews in Guyana in poems like 'Portia Faces Life' (to be published in *Savacou*, Vol. 1, Nos. 3-4), was doing with the dialect of the tribe what critics like Louis James[10] had declared to be impossible. The artist and his society, it seemed, were coming closer together.

The second event, of late 1966, was the founding, in London, of the Caribbean

Artists Movement. The object of CAM was first and foremost to bring West Indian artists 'exiled' in London into private and public contact with each other. It was a simple thing, but it had never happened before. The results were immediate, obvious and fruitful. Painters, sculptors, poets, novelists, literary and art critics, publishers, for the first time saw and could talk to each other. Wilson Harris and Aubrey Williams, both of Guyana, both miraculously working on the same kind of theme, had never met each other. Now they could engage in long dialogues. Harris and Michael Anthony, natural opposites, met and talked and talked. John Hearne and Orlando Patterson clashed. We all heard and came out of it the richer. Jerry Craig was invited to illustrate Andrew Salkey's '*Jonah Simpson*' (1969); Williams, for the first time in his life, was asked to provide a cover for a West Indian publication, *The Islands in Between*.[11] After this, he collaborated with Sam Selvon over the illustrations for *A Drink of Water* (Nelson, 1968), and with Longman's for a school edition of Jan Carew's *Black Midas* (1969). Conferences were held at the University of Kent in 1967 and 1968 and at the West Indian Students Centre in 1969. Academics interested in West Indian art and literature came into the picture. Some who knew nothing about us, became interested. Art exhibitions of West Indian work – never seen collectively before – were arranged in a variety of places: the WI Students Centre, the Theatre Royal, the Universities of Kent and Sussex, the House of Commons and in Birmingham. New artists like Clifton Campbell and Errol Lloyd made their appearance; grand old men like Ronald Moody, creator of the Savacou, a sculpture of the Carib bird placed outside the Epidemiological Research Unit at the Mona campus, made their reappearance. Poetry readings were held almost monthly. West Indian students and their friends became interested; joint sessions were held between CAM and the WI society at LSE.[12] The West Indian Students Centre became CAM headquarters; its presence rejuvenated the place. Soon CAM-like organizations were being formed at the Students Centre, in Nottingham, Edinburgh and later in some of the London ghettos. A relationship between artist and audience had become possible. And John La Rose's[13] bookshop, his book service, and finally his New Beacon Publications venture were all, too, to come out of this new mood and movement.

All this was possible because CAM came at a time when several artists and writers then in London had something new to say. I was about to start publishing my trilogy of long poems, influenced by those resurrectionary years in Ghana, and tightened by my contact with Jamaican society with its black consciousness and its controlled rage and implosive violence, the sound of ska, rock-steady, reggae, and Orlando Patterson's *The Children of Sisyphus* (1964). John La Rose was about to launch the New Beacon Press with his own collection of poems, *Foundations*. Patterson had completed his second novel *An Absence of Ruins* (1967), and was working on *The Sociology of Slavery* (1967). Andrew Salkey, already moving to new directions with *The Late Emancipation of Jerry Stover* (1968), was soon to visit Cuba and return with an urgent sense of the Third World Revolution, which he connected with Stokely Carmichael's ideas.[14] Marina Maxwell was working on 'Violence in the Toilets' (*Race Today*, Sept. 1969), *Play Mas* and 'Towards a Revolution in the Arts of the Caribbean' (in this issue of *Savacou*). All these artists were concerned primarily with the ex-African black experience, slavery, the plantation, and their consequences.

But there was also Harris and Aubrey Williams, both black, both from Guyana, who were contributing if not a different vision, then at least a different approach to that vision. Coming from mainland South America, they found themselves involved not with the problem of mulatto-creolization, but with mestizo-creolization. Their starting point, was not the Negro in the Caribbean, but the ancient Amerindian. Williams, speaking at a CAM Symposium in June 1967 had said:

> In art, I have always felt a wild hunger to express the rather unique, human state in the New World . . . . I find there an amalgam of a lot that has gone before in mankind, in the whole world. It seems to have met there, after Columbus, and we are just on the brink of its development. The forces meeting in the Caribbean .
> . . . will eventually, I feel, change this world... not in the sense of a big civilisation in one spot, but as the result of the total of man's experience and groping for the development of his consciousness.[15]

In articulating this faith in the Caribbean, and in emphasising roots rather than 'alien avenues', Williams was connecting with what many West Indian writers are now trying to do. And in emphasising the importance to himself of primordial man, *local* primordial man, he, like Harris, was extending the boundaries of our sensibility. Most of us, coming from islands, where there was no evident lost civilisation – where, in fact, there was an 'absence of ruins', faced a real artistic difficulty in our search for origins. The seed and root of our concern had little material soil to nourish it. Patterson's view was that we should accept this shallow soil, (we begin from an existential absurdity of nothing) and grow our ferns in a kind of moon-dust. Fertility would come later; if not, not. Naipaul refused to plant at all.[16] He watered the waste with irony. But Williams, coming from Guyana, where he had lived intimately for long periods with the Warraou Indians of the Northwest District, had a more immediate and tactile apprehension of artistic soil.

It was not only a matter of getting to know the people – although that was a crucial element in his growth. He didn't only come to an understanding of tribal custom and philosophy – although that too was essential to him as continuing creator. But he could actually *see* the ancient art of the Warraou Indians. Living with them placed him in a significant continuum with it; for high up on the rocks at

Tumatumari, at Imbaimadai, people, who were perhaps of Maya origin – the ancestors of the Warraou and others in the area – had made marks or *timehri*: rock signs, paintings, petroglyphs; glimpses of language, glitters of a vision of a world, scattered utterals of a remote *gestalt*; but still there, near, potentially communicative. Sometimes there were sleek brown bodies that could have been antelope or ocelot; there were horns and claws of crabs. There were triangular forms that might have been the mouths of *cenotes*. But hints only; gateways to intuitions; abstract signals of hieroglyphic art. To confirm that these marks were made by man, imprints of the etcher's palm were left beside the work; anonymous brand in living stone, imperishable witnesses from past to conscious present. It is from these marks that Aubrey Williams' art begins:

> I feel that these pre-Columbian influences are so strong, that we couldn't possibly shut them off. We might be attracted to alien avenues, but we're not really trying to shake off primordial life; and this primordial life is still manifest in Caribbean life today and I hope that it will inform and strengthen what we will become.[17]

This vision, coming from these sources, has made Williams a unique artist. In the first place, he is grounded, in the Rastafarian and African religious and cosmic electrical sense. He starts from the rock. His abstracts are not eclectic, are not the result of a loss or faltering or failure of vision or direction, a dissociation of sensibility. The marks he makes are deliberate but organically involuntary. They relate to a living source. What we are confronted with in Williams, is a modern artist working in an ancient form; or – and this is the only way we can understand the truth and paradox of the statement – an ancient artist working in a modern form. There is no difference. Form, content, technique, vision – all make a seamless garment for the mind and senses. Like a worshipper possessed at shango or vodun, as with a jazz musician, time past and future speak to the community in the trapped and hunting moment of awareness. We become the Maya who were already us. Williams is the medium. His paint brush is the door, the *porte cabesse* or central pole, down which the gods often descend into the *tonnelle* during *vodun* worship.[18] Like jazz musicians, still tunnelling the ancient African tone scales and rhythms on European instruments, Williams uses note, tone, rhythm, improvisation. Every one of his paintings is a variation on a central theme; his source's central vision.

For Williams, this central source is Amerindian. For others of us, the central force of our life of awareness is African. As black people in the Caribbean, that is how we feel it should be. But Williams' choice of the Amerindian motif does not exclude the African. For one thing, Williams claims ancestry from both peoples – he is spiritually a black Carib. Secondly (and this point has been made already) it was the specific Warraou experience, with the impinging *timehri*, that was most meaningfully available to him when he needed something most at that first crucial stage of his development. Africa in the Caribbean at that time, was still hidden and/ or ignored. But what Williams' work has revealed – and what in my analysis of it I have largely unconsciously stressed – is that the distinction between African and Amerindian in this context is for the most part irrelevant. What is important is the primordial nature of the two cultures and the potent spiritual and artistic connections between them and the present. In the Caribbean, whether it be African or Amerindian, the recognition of an ancestral relationship with the folk or aboriginal culture involves the artist and participant in a journey into the past and hinterland which is at the same time a movement of possession into present and future. Through this movement of possession we become ourselves, truly our own creators, discovering word for object, image for the Word.

NOTES

1. Richard N. Adams 'On the relations between plantation and "Creole cultures" ', in *Plantation Systems of the New World* edited by Vera Rubin (Washington, 1959).73–82.
2. Author's note: The achievement of Elsa Goveia, expressed in her *A Study of the Historiography of the British West Indies to the End of the Nineteenth Century* (Mexico: 1956) is that she described the state of Caribbean disnomia without herself being trapped in its effects.
3. Author's note: See 'The Day the First Snow Fell', *Caribbean Quarterly* 5:3 (1958), p.128.
4. Author's note: See 'A Caribbean Theme', in *Poetry from Cambridge* (Cambridge, 1950).
5. George Lamming, born in Barbados in 1927, wrote his first novel, *In the Castle of My Skin* (London, 1953), shortly after arriving in England in 1950. It won the Somerset Maugham award for literature in 1958. (See chapter 44 in this volume).
6. Paul Robeson (1898 – 1976) was an African-American actor and singer who appeared in many roles and concerts in Europe and the United States, and whose recordings, especially of spirituals, were famous. He was a supporter of the Soviet Union, which he believed was not racist like his own country, and he was persecuted in the United States for his social and political beliefs.
7. Author's note: See Derek Walcott, *25 Poems* (Bridgetown, 1949); *Epitaph for the Young* (Barbados, 1949).
8. Author's note: For this, from two different points of view, see Gordon Rohlehr's review of *The Gulf* in the *Trinidad Guardian*, December 10, 11, 13, 1969; and Lloyd King, 'Bard of the Rubbish Heap: The Problem of Walcott's Poetry,' in *Tapia*, No. 5 (Feb. 1, 1970), p.7-8.
9. Stokely Carmichael (1941 – 98) was born in Trinidad, where he lived his first 11 years. In 1952 he joined his parents in Harlem, New York. While a student at Howard University, from which he graduated in 1964, he participated in the civil rights movement. In 1966, he became chairman of the Student Nonviolent Coordinating

Committee (SNCC), which he had helped to create several years earlier, and he became a leading spokesman of Black Power. With Charles Hamilton he wrote a book, *Black Power* (1967), and in 1968 he became prime minister of the militant Black Panther party. He resigned this post in 1969, and moved to Conakry in the Republic of Guinea in West Africa. He changed his name to Kwame Toure, in honour of Kwame Nkrumah of Ghana and Sekou Toure of Guinea, and worked for 'One United Socialist Africa' until his death.

10. Author's note: *The Islands in Between* (London, 1968). For a refutation at some length of the Euro-centred academic view of West Indian literature and society in this book, see my 'Caribbean Critics', *New World Quarterly*, Vol. 5, Nos.1-2 (1969); *The Critical Quarterly*, Autumn 1969.

11. Aubrey Williams (1926-90) was an abstract painter from Guyana who used Amerindian and Mesoamerican (Olmec and Maya) symbols and motifs in much of his work. As a young agricultural extension officer he had lived with the Warau Indians in the interior of Guyana and this experience was a key influence on his work even after he moved to the UK in 1952. In addition to the cover of *The Islands in Between*, to which Brathwaite refers, one of Williams's paintings was used for many years on the covers of a series of books, Warwick University Caribbean Studies, that were edited at the Centre for Caribbean Studies of the University of Warwick.

12. London School of Economics and Political Science, the University of London.

13. John La Rose, a poet who was born in Trinidad in 1927, was the general secretary of the West Indian Independence party and an executive member of the Federated Workers Trade Union. He migrated to the UK in 1961, where he founded New Beacon Books and was a co-founder of the Caribbean Artists Movement in 1966. He was also a founder of the Caribbean Educational and Community Workers Association (1969) and the Black Parents Movement (1975) and the director of the International Book Fair of Radical and Third World Books, which was first held in London in 1982.

14. Andrew Salkey (1928 – 95) was a novelist, born of Jamaican parents in Colón, Panamá, who moved to London in 1952. He wrote *The Quality of Violence* (1959), *Escape to an Autumn Pavement* (1960) and *The Late Emancipation of Jerry Stover* (1968), and also poems and short stories. His visit to revolutionary Cuba, between December 1967 and January 1968, is recalled in his *Havana Journal* (1971).

15. Author's note: Aubrey Williams, *CAM Newsletter* No.3 (June 1967).

16. Author's note: I make, however, an exception of Naipaul's major work so far, *A House for Mr Biswas*. Here, despite the futility, it seems to me, there is clear evidence of planting.

17. Author's note: Williams, *CAM Newsletter* No.3 (June 1967).

18. The *porte cabesse*, or *poteau-mitan*, is the centre post holding up the roof of the building, usually an open annexe of the *humfo* or shrine, where the Vodou dances and ceremonies take place. The centre post is the *axis mundi* which both separates and connects 'heaven' and 'earth', and is a 'ladder' for the passage of those spirits who may descend when they are invoked to the *tonelle*, which is the covering of the ritual stage.

Thirty-Six

W. Arthur Lewis

W. Arthur Lewis (1915–91) was born in St Lucia and went to England at the age of 18. He earned his bachelor's degree in 1937 and doctorate in 1940 at the University of London, where he taught for ten years. From 1948 to 1958 he was a professor at the University of Manchester and, between 1959 and 1963, he was the vice chancellor of the University of the West Indies. He joined the faculty of Princeton University in 1963, where he was the James Madison Professor of Political Economy until he retired in 1983. In addition to these academic positions he held several advisory positions and directorships, including director of the Colonial Development Corporation of the UK (1950–52), economic advisor to the prime minister of Ghana (1957–58), deputy managing director of the United Nations Special Fund, now the UN Development Programme (1959–60), special advisor to the prime minister of the West Indies (1961–62), director of the Central Bank of Jamaica (1961–62) and, while on leave from Princeton University, the president of the Caribbean Development Bank (1970–73).

Lewis was noted for his contributions to the economics of development and the relations of economic growth to social and political change. His most famous book is The Theory of Economic Growth *(1955). He wrote eleven other books, including* The Evolution of Foreign Aid *(1972) and* The Evolution of the International Economic Order *(1978), and over eighty monographs, articles and chapters. Among many honours, he was knighted in 1963, awarded the Nobel Prize in Economics in 1979, and was a president of the American Economic Association (the first black person to head that organisation). Lewis, a committed West Indian regionalist, gave the 1970 graduation address, 'On Being Different', at the campus of the University of the West Indies, Cave Hill, Barbados.*

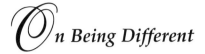n Being Different

A constant theme in today's West Indies is that we should stop imitating other peoples, and do our own thing. We should be different, and West Indian. It is an attractive theme; has indeed become almost a bandwagon theme; every other public speaker takes the chance of recording his adherence to it. I too want to get into this popular stream, but I am also a little more anxious to find out just what it is all about. Obviously West Indians cannot be different from other men in everything, since we all belong to *homo sapiens*, so one has to ask where we should draw the line; in what respects should we be the same as other peoples, and in what respects should we strive to be different?

My only qualification for talking about this subject is that I have probably thought about it more than most other West Indians. Since no job was available for me here when I graduated, I have had to spend most of my life out of the West Indies. And in striving to earn my living in the great wide world I have had to try to master the highly competitive skills of my profession. In the process I have become what is now called in the West Indies an Afro-Saxon. The term is meant to be abusive, but what in practice it seems to mean is a black man who can hold his own in competition with white people on their own ground. Facing this difficult challenge, I have had to ask myself over and over again over the past thirty years what sort of person I ought to be trying to be. West Indian, yes, but just what does this mean that is intended to distinguish us from other human beings?

Obviously one must not take to its extreme conclusion the proposition that West Indians must live differently from other men. If so, it would be wrong for Barbadians to play cricket, which is an Englishman's invention; or if Barbadians do play cricket, they should make their own special rules. Taken to the extreme, the proposition would prevent Trinidadians from playing in steel-bands, since the steel from which the instruments are made comes from iron ores which are not found in Trinidad. Trinidadians should make music instead exclusively from bamboos, which grow luxuriantly in that island, and which make splendid musical instruments.

I do not wish to make fun of the proposition that we should be different, which, as I have said I accept: I am merely emphasising the fact that the proposition is not as universal as some make it out to be. There are people who worry at the level of the commodities we use, and insist that it is wrong to use imported materials, or to eat imported food – which to me seems an economic question rather than one for nationalist emotions. Other people are het up about the clothes we wear, or about our hairstyles, which seem to me to be trivial and ever-changing phenomena which are hardly worth the glance of the philosopher or statesman, even though I recognise that difference in these respects gives emotional comfort to a great many people:

men have fought bitterly about the wearing of a turban. That we should be different seems to me a good proposition, and yet one which is easily nonsensical or trivial, unless one defines rather carefully what it is we are to differ in.

Before I tackle this question let me first note that the ground is not entirely occupied by Afro-Saxons and the advocates of an exclusively West Indian culture. We have in our midst a third group who advocate that we should model ourselves on the Africans, since Africa is where most of our fathers came from some two centuries ago. I will leave aside the complication that there are more Indians than Africans in Guyana and nearly as many Indians as Africans in Trinidad[1] – and follow the proponents of this idea in arguing as if West Indians were all descended from Africa.

Even with this fatal simplification, the proposition is hardly meaningful, and always bemuses Africans who make its acquaintance. In the first place, Africa is the most diversified of all the continents in terms of strictly indigenous institutions, languages, food patterns, clothes or any other index which you care to choose. There are hundreds of tribal and national groups, very different from each other, so there is no unique African model that West Indians could imitate. In the second place Africans themselves are trying hard to get into the modern world, and are in the process of shedding a great number of the characteristics which they developed in isolation. The idea that we should choose as models what they are discarding seems to them a little quaint. To use the popular jargon, the Africans are having as big a crisis of identity as we are. In stretching out to them we shall find sympathy and understanding, but hardly remedies for the condition in which we both find ourselves.

However, let me come back to my theme, the proposition that we strive to be ourselves, not Englishmen or Africans or Indians or Chinese, but West Indians.

Different in what ways? Since we are not racists, we are committed to the proposition that we are essentially the same as other men. Societies differ not in the underlying humanity, but in what they make of themselves and of their environment. What differs is the human achievement. So when we say that West Indians are to be different, we mean that they must make something different – our achievement must be unique.

In framing the problem in this way I am automatically ruling out what is in practice the most obvious difference between peoples, namely their manners and customs, especially their clothes, language, accent, mannerisms and food. Here for instance is a standard anthropological problem. When you meet your friend should you shake hands with him? The traditional answer is: If he is an American, Yes. If he is an Englishman, No. If he's a Frenchman, shake hands with him every five minutes. When we say that a man is typically German, or Chinese, or that we can always recognise a West Indian on the streets of Harlem, it is to these superficial characteristics that we refer.

Inevitably, manners have strong local roots and differ from place to place. Inevitably the local manners are menaced by foreign importations, and inevitably local conservatives and local revolutionaries get very excited with every new importation. Traditionally it used to be the most highly educated and well travelled who were least identifiable by these local mannerisms, since they tend to follow the precept that when in Rome one does as the Romans do; but today, thanks to records, television and films, it is the masses of the population who seem to be quickest in adopting the new international life styles of the world's young adults, and the whole world is now coming to look and sound alike.

No doubt West Indians will and should evolve their own ever-changing systems of manners, but this is not what we have to examine. The charge against the Afro-Saxon is not that he does not dress like a West Indian or speak with a West Indian accent, but that he does not *think* like a West Indian. Hence our question has to be: how should West Indian thinking differ from other thinking? And to answer it we have to look at the whole realm of human thought, and to ask what opportunities it offers for national characteristics. This is a very appropriate question for a university community, since thought is our stock in trade.

The human achievement is all the product of thought, applied to work. It is rather small. Man has existed for a million years, but it is only within the last 5,000 years that we have made significant progress. This is because nature is hard and cruel, and has had to be fought every step of the way. The fight has not been led by any one nation; nations have had very little to do with it, and nationalism has been more often destructive than helpful. Individuals of many nations have contributed, each building on the work of his predecessors from many different nations at many different times. What has resulted from this is a body of knowledge which is now the heritage of all mankind. This knowledge divides into three areas – first, knowledge of how phenomena work, which includes the natural and social sciences; secondly, moral knowledge, or if you like, opinion as to how human beings are to behave towards each other if human society is to be tolerable; and thirdly aesthetic knowledge, or how to be creative in the arts. Each of these three kinds of knowledge combines elements of universality with some opportunity for differences between national groups.

Let us take first science, natural and social. The evolution of natural science was delayed for a long time by prejudice, or as we would now say by lack of objectivity. Indeed the very notion that science should try to be objective was bitterly resisted, by those who thought that we should accept only results which seemed consistent with what was already revealed about God. Science was to serve religion, or as we might now say, to serve the purpose of history. The social sciences are fighting the same struggle today against those, including many social scientists, who not only deny that social scientists can be objective, but also argue that they should not try to be objective, since their science should serve the purposes of history. If they are right, social science would differ from society to society; but they are not right. Genuine social scientists, gathered together from all parts of the world, have no difficulty in understanding each others' concepts, and in my profession of economics we have found that any tool which is illuminating in one part of the world – like monetary theory or linear programming or the discounting of future returns – is equally illuminating everywhere, whether in the Soviet Union, or the U.S.A. or Tanzania.

I am of course talking about theory. The applied part of any science is naturally environment-related. Any scientific group is bound to contribute more to the study of its own environment, or its own history, than will be contributed by other groups elsewhere. Every colony has had to fight the battle to have its own curriculum in its schools and colleges. This is obviously right, but is also easily overdone. We make progress in science not only from studying the local environment, but also from elaborating our basic theory. This kind of theoretical elaboration frequently derives from wide comparison. Particularly, if you want to be a revolutionary in science, achieving some great new breakthrough, you have to understand the existing system which you wish to overthrow better than it is understood by its supporters, not less so. Keynes[2] was able to invent a new economics because he thoroughly understood the old. If any new physics or sociology is going to come out of the West Indies it will be from people who have mastered the old physics or sociology, and not just from people who have rejected the old without really coming to grips with it.

In sum, we will make our special contribution to applied science, but we must first master the basic universal theoretical principles of the disciplines we use. And our chance of contributing to those basic disciplines will depend very largely on the excellence of our secondary schools and the respect accorded to basic theoretical studies in our university colleges. In this respect West Indians will not differ from other men.

I have dwelt somewhat on this point because there is a strong current of thought that West Indians should study only things West Indian. This is an egregious error, and a danger to the young. The old are not so easily moved, since we have learned each to go his own way; but the young are very conformist, and are easily bulldozed into acting against their better judgment.

Let me turn now to the second area of human thought, that of morals, or of what behaviour towards each other should be. This itself divides into two parts, personality and social structure. Manners could also be included here, but I have already dealt with this topic.

There is a distinct West Indian personality, marked by its aggressive nature, which in turn derives from the insecure family life in which such a large proportion of our children are reared. Not all West Indians are aggressive, but it is the quality we most admire in our leaders. This aggressive personality has some advantages; it is the chief reason why West Indians figure disproportionately in the black leadership of the United States. But it also has its disadvantages. For example, as Sir John Mordecai's book[3] on the breakdown of our federation shows, the chief reason was the inability of our three leaders in the same federal political party to maintain normal personal relations, and compromise with each other. We also make rather poor business men, compared with say the Nigerian Ibos, because unlike the Ibos we are spendthrift, and not very reliable in keeping our commitments punctually.

On the whole I do not think that it is an advantage for West Indians to have a distinct personality of our own. Philosophers and religious thinkers have meditated for five thousand years on what ideal human beings should be like, and there is no reason to believe that these ideals should differ from one country to another. For my part I think our aggressive personality makes us inferior to our African brethren, who bring up their children in warm, stable and secure family situations, and who therefore produce a stable personality. If we must imitate the Africans, this is what I would urge our countrymen to imitate. Also, if we continue to be unbusinesslike and spendthrift, our society will have no long term future, since it will not survive in this Darwinian world.

In the moral area we have also the subject of social structure – family relations, the political system, class, economic relations and so on. There is an immense variety of social structures, as one moves from place to place. None embodies perfection, and all change nowadays with unprecedented rapidity. Men have imagined and written for five thousand years about every kind of social system, and it seems highly improbable that West Indians will come up with some new kind of social structure which has never been heard of before; this is why those of us who do not like our existing structures find ourselves having to import our ideas from abroad instead of trying to invent some unique West Indian social system. If perchance we did invent something new of our own (which is admittedly possible even though unlikely) and it proved to be good, it would soon be widely imitated elsewhere, since what was good for us would be equally good for many other social groups. For my part, I believe in the open, egalitarian, raceless society which we do not now have, but to which most of our leaders are committed. But when we get there we shall find ourselves in company with many other nations.

In sum, in the area of human relations, national difference is either trivial, in so far as it relates to manners, or undesirable in so far as it relates to personality or to social structure. This is because the underlying principles of ethics are of universal validity; what is good for one society is likely to be good for every other. It would be nice if West Indians could have a better community life than other nations, but there is no reason to expect our struggles to be easier than anybody else's.

Finally I come to aesthetics. Music, literature and art are as important a part of the heritage of mankind as are science and morals. They differ from science in that they do not represent what is, but are products of the creative imagination. They have therefore infinite scope for variation. And yet they tend to be distinctively national in character. This is because artists live in colonies, like ants or porpoises. Some great artistic figure attracts other artists to his school; they see or hear alike; they help and criticise each other. And their product is clearly distinct from that of other schools.

It is thus of the very nature of the game that as aesthetic activity burgeons in the West Indies, our art and music and literature will be clearly distinguishable from that of other peoples. We shall have our own schools of painting and music and poetry and drama and the rest. This is the essential and most valuable sense in which West Indians must be different from other peoples. This is the contribution which above all others we know we can make to the common human heritage.

I stress the word common to avoid misunderstanding. The human heritage includes Chinese art, European art, African art; Hindu music, which is quite different from Ashanti music, which in its turn differs from the diatonic structure of jazz and the European classics. This is our common heritage, because the civilized man learns to appreciate as many of these different styles as he can, just as he learns to like French cooking and Chinese cooking and Malay cooking, which are essentially different. For any person to wish to exclude himself from any part of the human artistic heritage, in favour of his local nationalism, is simply boorish. And what is one to say of the incident in South Africa last year where three African pianists were turned away from a Beethoven competition on the ground that Beethoven is not part of African culture? Beethoven belongs to all of us.

We must also note that it is true of the arts, as it is of science, that one learns most by comparison. Our writers must study other writers – not just in English but in other languages – when they are young, in order to have a basis for developing their own styles. Difference must be grounded in wide knowledge and not in ignorance of all except the local effort.

Fortunately we have already established the beginnings of an artistic heritage. In literature we have had the great explosion of novels since the 1950's. In art, starting also in the '50's, a steadier pace has been maintained, but we have already reached the position of having established artists who manage to make a living just by selling their works. In music we are still far behind, since despite our great contributions to popular music, we have a dearth of well trained musicians, and especially a dearth of the string players needed to maintain a symphony orchestra.

The principal handicap is of course that there are so few people who understand and enjoy the creative arts in our communities, that our artists, musicians, writers, actors and so on, have too small a market. So they have to go abroad and scatter instead of making their little colonies here, at home, which would be very much more productive. The smallness of the market is the fault of our secondary schools, which fail to develop this part of our children's personalities. A society without the creative arts is a cultural desert. I would commend to our statesmen that they put a lot more money into the creative arts departments of our secondary schools.

To conclude, as I look ahead at the evolution of the West Indies, I see many respects in which we should strive to be like other peoples – like having a well rounded personality, or scientists and scholars of world repute – and many respects in which we will be different – like having some distinctive manners and customs, our own curricula in schools, our own applied science, natural and social, and our own musical and other artistic achievements. The main point that I would leave with you is that our chance to make something good of our own depends on our studying carefully what other peoples have done, and learning from their mistakes and their successes. If we are going to close our minds in a box of pure West Indianness, we shall achieve nothing worthwhile.

NOTES

1. About 51 per cent of the population of Guyana and 40 per cent of the population of Trinidad and Tobago are of Indian descent, compared to 30.5 per cent and 40 per cent African, respectively. Most of the remainder in both cases are 'mixed'.
2. John Maynard Keynes (1883–1946) was a British economist who served in the treasury department from 1915 to 1919. When the UK was in economic difficulties in the 1920s and 1930s, Keynes wrote a series of books and essays which attacked the government's economic policies. These culminated in his *General Theory of Employment, Interest, and Money* (1936), which is one of the most important books on economic theory and policies in the twentieth century. Keynes argued that governments should intervene in economic affairs, especially to counter a depression, by lowering interest rates and increasing spending.
3. Sir John Mordecai, *The West Indies: The Federal Negotiations* (London, 1968).

Thirty-Seven

Merle Hodge

Merle Hodge was born in 1944 in Trinidad. She won the Trinidad and Tobago Girls' Island Scholarship in 1962 and studied French at University College, London, earning a BA in 1965 and MPhil in 1967. She has travelled widely in Europe, living for long periods in France and Denmark, and has lived in Senegal and Gambia. She has translated a collection of poems, Pigment, *by Léon Damas of French Guiana and has taught West Indian, French Caribbean and French African literature at schools in Trinidad and Grenada and also at the University of the West Indies in Jamaica and Trinidad.*

Hodge's first novel, Crick Crack, Monkey, *about a girl growing up in Trinidad, was published in 1970. It describes the alienation created by a colonial education by placing the young protagonist between the Creole folk culture in which she was nurtured and the middle-class culture of metropolitan manners and values towards which she is pushed. Hodge has also published essays, short stories, and the novel* For the Life of Laetitia *(1993).*

$\mathcal{T}$he Shadow of the Whip: A Comment on Male-Female Relations in the Caribbean

The man-woman relationship is nowhere a straightforward, uncomplicated one – it is always perhaps the most vulnerable, the most brittle of human relationships. And in the Caribbean this relationship has been adversely affected by certain factors of our historical development, notably, I think, by the legacy of violence and disruption with which our society has never adequately come to terms.

Caribbean society was born out of brutality, destructiveness, rape; the destruction of the Amerindian peoples, the assault on Africa, the forced uprooting and enslavement of the African; the gun, the whip, the authority of force. Yet the Caribbean area today is not particularly noted for any large-scale, organized violence. Caribbean governments sit securely and complacently, with or without popular support.

But the violence of our history has not evaporated. It is still there. It is there in the relations between adult and child, between black and white, between man and woman. It has been internalized, it has seeped down into our personal lives. Drastic brutality – physical and verbal – upon children is an accepted part of child rearing in the Caribbean. 'Gavin,' threatens Laura of *Miguel Street*[1] to one of her children, 'Gavin, if you don't come here this minute, I make you fart fire, you hear.' And C.L.R. James in his novel *Minty Alley*[2] describes a hair-raising scene of violence upon a child which contains not an inch of exaggeration.

Our capacity for verbal violence is limitless. Teasing and heckling are taken to lengths which would shock in another society. For example, we award nicknames on the basis of hopeless physical deformities – 'Hop-and-Drop', for example, for a polio victim who walks with a pathetic limp. Our expressions of abuse would fill catalogues. Quarreling is a national pastime – quarrels are spectacular: a great deal of energy and artistry are applied to body movements, the ingenuity of insults, the graphic recitation of the antagonist's crimes; a good quarrel will provide a morning's dramatic diversion for a whole neighborhood, for quarrels often emerge onto the street as if in search of an adequate stage.

And the fact that a physical fight between a man and a woman – or more accurately, a woman-beating – may erupt into the open air and rage for hours without any serious alarm on the part of onlookers for the safety of the woman, without attracting the intervention of the law, is a strong comment on our attitudes:

Never never put yu mouth
In husband-and-wife business.

runs the refrain of one calypso, a word of warning to the sentimental, to those who may be naïve enough to think that a woman minds being beaten by her man. It is the message of many a calypso. Another song recounts with mock disapproval a public 'licking'. The thinly veiled sexual imagery is a stock device of calypso, but here it illustrates effectively the idea of violence being part and parcel of the normal relations between man and woman: a policeman who would intervene is rebuffed by none other than the 'victim' of the licking:

> Constable have a care
> This is my man licking me here
> And if he feel to lick me
> He could lick me,
> Dammit, don't interfere.

Of course, calypsonians are mainly men, and men are largely responsible for perpetuating the myth of women thriving on violence from their men:

> Every now and then cuff them down,
> They'll love you long and they'll love you strong.
> Black-up their eye
> Bruise-up their knee
> And they will love you eternally.

The idea is not far removed from the maxim coined in the era of slavery: 'Battre un négre, c'est le nourrir'– a beating is food to a nigger.

But of course, violence in its narrowest definition, namely, physical violence, is only a visible manifestation of a wider disruption, a basic breakdown of respect. For violence to women includes the whole range of mental cruelty which is part and parcel of women's experience in the Caribbean.

Every now and then our attention is drawn to this existing situation when a woman, known to her neighbors as a devoted, hard-working, self-sacrificing mother, of no particular wickedness, appears trembling and speechless before a judge for having killed her man.

And the familiar, almost humdrum details roll out again – a history of intolerable ill-treatment by the man both upon her and upon her children: neglect, desertion, humiliation, tyranny, unreasonableness, lack of consideration . . . the last straw falls and the woman runs at him with a kitchen knife.

It would seem that the precedents of this case stretch far enough back into our history to have entered our folklore – there is the folk song about Betsy Thomas who killed her husband stone cold dead in the market and had no doubt that she would be absolved of crime:

I ain't kill nobody but me husband.

In fact, our society implicitly acknowledges the permanent situation out of which husband killings arise, in the leniency the court generally affords to a woman who has been driven to this act. Of course, killing your man is an extreme measure, but, again, it is a crisis which is but the visible tip of the iceberg or, to bring our imagery home, the eruption of a volcano that all along has been silently cooking.

The black man in the role of Dispenser of Violence is very likely a descendant of the white slave-overseer asserting an almost bottomless authority over the whipped. But there is one fundamental difference, for whereas the overseer beat and tortured his victim because he had power over him, the black man ill-treating his woman is expressing his desire for power, is betraying a dire insecurity vis-à-vis the female.

In the Caribbean the 'war of the sexes' takes on a very special character. It is not a straight fight between handicapped Woman on the one hand and omnipotent Man on the other. From the very beginning of West Indian history the black woman has had a *de facto* 'equality' thrust upon her – the equality of cattle in a herd. We became 'equal' from the moment African men and women were bundled together onto galleys, men and women clamped to the floor alongside each other for the horrifying middle passage. A slave was a slave – male or female – a head of livestock, a unit of the power that drove the plantation. The women worked equally hard out in the fields with the men, were equally subject to torture and brutality. The black woman in the Caribbean has never been a delicate flower locked away in a glass case and 'protected' from responsibility. Of course, the African woman in Africa is no delicate flower either, wielding a tremendous physical force in her daily chores of pounding, planting, etc., all the while carrying around her latest child upon her back.

From the very beginning of our history on this side of the Atlantic, woman has been mobilized in the society's work force. But there was, of course, some division of labor or functions, and this is where the male-female trouble began.

In the first place, the whole humiliation of slavery meant an utter devaluation of the manhood of the race; the male was powerless to carry out his traditional role of protector of the tribe, he was unable to defend either himself or his women and children from capture and transportation, from daily mishandling. His manhood was reduced to his brawn for the labor he could do for his master and to his reproductive function.

And the function of fatherhood was limited to fertilizing the female. Gone was the status of head of the family, for there was no family, no living in a unit with wife and children. A man might not even know who his children were, and at any rate they did not belong to him in any sense; he was unable to provide for them – their owner performed the function of provider. The black man had no authority over his children, but the woman did. The children's mothers, or female child-rearers, were responsible for the upbringing of the race. Women became mother and father to the race.

And it is this concentration of moral authority in the person of the woman that has influenced relations between men and women of African descent in the Caribbean. For today the average Afro-West Indian is still reared more or less singlehandedly by a mother, or aunt, or big sister, or god-mother – the men have still not returned to the functions of fatherhood. Fathers are either physically absent – the prevalent pattern of concubinage and male mobility results in a man not necessarily staying put in one household until the children he has deposited there have grown up – or, even when the father is present in the home, his part in the bringing up of the children is a limited one. His role is not clearly defined and not binding. One of the roles he may play is that of Punisher, administering beatings at the request of the mother; but the strongest influence in the home is usually female.

The society may be called a matriarchal one – many of our ancestors were in fact brought from West African societies which were matriarchal in structure, although there this by no means implied an abdication of responsibility on the part of the males. But this meant that our women had precedents of matriarchy upon which to draw in the new situation of male defection.

The Caribbean, and indeed black America on the whole, has produced the new black matriarch, the strong female figure who is responsible not only for the propagation of the race but by whose strength our humanity has been preserved.

Most Afro-West Indians have grown up 'fatherless' in one way or another, most have been reared under almost exclusive female influence. So in the society moral authority is female, an authority that may sometimes be harsh and driven to extremes by the situation of stress in which a Caribbean mother often finds herself – often ill-feeling against a deserting man is vented upon the children he has left in her lap.

Caribbean writing teems with the strong woman type. Many of Samuel Selvon's immigrants[3] are our feckless, happy-go-lucky men now and then marshaled into responsibility by brisk, matter-of-fact women. The female figures of James's *Minty Alley*, the dignified, almost statuesque Mrs. Rouse; Maisie the wraith, invincible in any situation. The women of *Miguel Street*, bawling out, battering (as well as being battered by) or working to support their unstable men. And I have discovered that my own book, *Crick Crack, Monkey*, is full of strong woman figures and that men are, like Auntie Beatrice's husband, 'either absent or unnoticeable'– even the heroine's succession of 'uncles' do not constitute any solid presence. And I had once intended to give the children a grandfather – Ma's husband – but I had conceived of him as an invalid in a rocking chair, ably looked after by Ma!

Caribbean woman has developed a strong moral fiber to compensate for the weakening of the male. Hence the desire of the man to do her down, to put her in her place, to safeguard his manhood threatened by the authority of the female upstart.

The black man in the Caribbean is capable of deep respect for his mother and for older women in general. The worst insult in our language is to curse a man's mother. An 'obscenity' flung in the heat of quarrel is, quite simply, 'Yu mother!' Authority is female, a man will have instinctive qualms about disrespecting his mother or, by extension, her contemporaries, but he will take his revenge on the black female by seeking to degrade women within reach of his disrespect.

Young men at a loose end (usually unemployed – the devaluation of black manhood is perpetuated in economic frustration) will position themselves on a culvert, at a street corner, on a pavement, and vie with each other in the ingenuity of their comments to embarrass women going by. The embarrassment of woman is part of the national ethos, stemming, I am convinced, from a deep-seated resentment against the strength of women.

In Trinidad the calypsonian, the folk poet, is assured of heartfelt, howling approval when he devotes his talent to the degradation of woman:

> Clarabelle,
> She could chase the Devil from Hell
> With the kind of way she does smell
> Anytime she pass yu could tell.

Our folk poet is rarely given to flattering and extolling the qualities of womanhood – woman and her sexual attributes are almost only a stock dirty joke in his repertoire. And the calypsonian mirrors collective attitudes – he is the product of his society and sings to please his audience.

There has, however, been one major development in our contemporary history which promises to have a salutary effect upon relations between black men and women in the Caribbean. This is the advent of black power ideology.

An important element of the history of male-female relations in the Caribbean has been the imposition of European standards of physical beauty – the tendency of the man to measure the desirability of women by these standards, and the corresponding struggle of black women to alter their appearance as far as possible in the direction of European requirements for beauty but of course still falling short of these requirements. A large part of male disrespect for the black woman was an expression of his dissatisfaction with her, 'inferior' as she was to the accepted white ideal of womanhood.

This bred a great deal of destructive dishonesty, a canker eating away at the roots of our self-respect. For these attitudes were especially destructive as they were to a large extent disavowed or even entirely subconscious. A man would vehemently deny that he could be the victim of this mesmerism. His cousin, yes, damn fool who went to England to study and could find nothing else to get married to but a white woman – but *he* would never be found putting milk in his coffee, unthinkable, *he* had a healthy attitude toward these white people.

It was indeed a difficult burden to bear – his very deep-seated resentment of whitedom and this hopeless involvement with them.

Today's ideology has begun to liberate us from this particular dishonesty. It has forced into the open, and at popular level (a success not achieved by the literary movements of the first half of the century), the discussion of our polarization toward whiteness, and it has effectively set about revising our concepts of physical beauty. The progressive abolition of hair-straightening in the Caribbean is a momentous revolution. It is part of the revaluation of the black woman.

And the revaluation of black womanhood inevitably also implies a restoration of black manhood, when the black man no longer forcibly evaluates his women by the standards of a man who once held the whip hand over him. It is one stage of his liberation from the whip hand.

And it is only when our lives cease to be governed by the shadow of the whip that we can begin to heal the grave disruption of relations between men and women that we have suffered in the Caribbean.

NOTES

1. V.S. Naipaul's *Miguel Street* (London: Andre Deutsch, 1959) won the Somerset Maugham Award.
2. C.L.R. James' *Minty Alley* (Trinidad: Heinemann, 1936), one of the first works to establish social realism in West Indian fiction, was republished in 1971 by New Beacon Books.
3. Sam Selvon's *The Lonely Londoners* (Harlow, Essex: Longman, 1956) and *Moses Ascending* (Trinidad: Heinemann,1975) are about West Indian immigrants in Britain.

Thirty-Eight

Maurice Bishop

Maurice Bishop (1944–83) was born in Aruba of middle-class Grenadian parents who returned to Grenada in 1951. After being head boy of the Catholic Presentation College in St George's, where he was already known as a magnetic speaker, he went to London to study law in 1963. He became chairman of the West Indian Students' Society and was an active member of the Campaign Against Racial Discrimination. After earning his law degree in 1966, he worked for the civil service and co-founded a legal aid clinic for West Indians in the Notting Hill district of London. In 1970 Bishop passed through Trinidad, on his way back to Grenada, during the mass demonstrations that became known as the Black Power Revolution.

Grenada, meanwhile, was moving towards independence under the leadership of Eric Gairy, who had created the Grenada Manual and Mental Workers' Union in 1950 and the Grenada United Labour Party (GULP), which won the first elections under universal adult suffrage in 1951. Gairy's support ebbed in the mid-1950s but the GULP swept back in 1967 and Gairy became increasingly exploitative and authoritarian. Bishop and another lawyer, Kenrick Radix, created the Movement for the Advancement of Community Effort (MACE) in 1972 while an economics teacher, Unison Whiteman, led the Joint Endeavour for Welfare, Education and Liberation (JEWEL). In 1973, these groups merged to form the New Jewel Movement (NJM) and it soon attracted activists among the youth and working class, including Hudson Austin, Jacqueline Creft, George Louison, and Selwyn Strachan. The NJM and other anti-Gairy organisations feared independence under Gairy but the British government decided in favour of accelerated decolonisation. NJM rallies were broken up and its leaders arrested and beaten. Early in 1974, Rupert Bishop, Maurice's father, was shot by Gairy's notorious police 'aides' who were really his private army.

Grenada became independent on February 7, 1974 and the NJM, suffering increasing repression, was reorganised as a Marxist vanguard party. In 1976, it was joined by Bernard Coard, who had been teaching at the University of the West Indies in Jamaica and Trinidad, and his wife Phyllis, both of whom were Marxist-Leninists. The NJM joined the Grenada National Party and the United People's Party in the People's Alliance to contest the 1976 elections. Despite massive and blatant electoral fraud, the Alliance won 48 per cent of the vote, but Gairy remained in power. Opposition to Gairy increased as his regime became more openly oppressive. After the NJM's newspaper was declared illegal it became clear that another electoral contest would be ineffectual because of fraud and intimidation.

In the early hours of March 13, 1979, while Gairy was in New York lobbying the United Nations to create an agency to investigate unidentified flying objects from outer space, a group of 40 to 45 NJM members attacked the Defense Force barracks. The NJM leaders had learned that they were to have been arrested while Gairy was away so they decided to strike first. Within twelve hours and with only three casualties, one of which was accidental, the NJM took over and created a Provisional, later the People's, Revolutionary Government (PRG). The people's response was overwhelmingly positive. Five days later, at a rally of 25,000 people (about a quarter of the island's population), the PRG was proclaimed, with Maurice Bishop as prime minister and Bernard Coard as minister of finance, and Gairy conceded defeat.

There was widespread relief among Commonwealth Caribbean countries that an embarrassing leader had been ousted, and Michael Manley and Forbes Burnham, on behalf of Jamaica and Guyana, respectively, welcomed the change and offered support. Fidel Castro also welcomed the PRG and when the Sandinista forces overthrew the Somoza dictatorship in Nicaragua in July 1979 these three countries established a close relationship. The response from the United States became increasingly negative and, after Ronald Reagan became president in 1981, openly hostile. The United States, which had played a leading role in destabilising elected governments in Chile and Jamaica in the 1970s, turned its focus on Grenada and Nicaragua in the early 1980s. Bishop's response to US pressure was proud and defiant: 'We are a small country, we are a poor country, with a population of largely African descent, we are a part of the exploited Third World ... Grenada is a sovereign and independent territory ... and we expect all countries to strictly respect our independence just as we will respect theirs. No country has the right to tell any other country what to do. We are not in anybody's backyard, and we are definitely not for sale ... Though small and poor, we are proud and determined' (speech on April 13, 1979, in Maurice Bishop Speaks, *1983, 30–31).*

Bishop remained a very popular leader in Grenada not only because he was a dynamic speaker and an attractive personality, but also because the PRG addressed many of Grenada's problems which Gairy had neglected. The World Bank praised the financial and economic achievements of the PRG in a report in 1982, and unemployment fell while real living standards rose. Education received the highest priority, as evidenced by the challenging National In-Service Teacher Education Programme (NISTEP), introduced in October 1980, and the Centre for Popular Education which improved adult literacy. Strong support was given to women, including the introduction of maternity leave, and to the expansion of public health with community-based health centres. The United States, however, defined the PRG as 'hostile to American interests' and planned its overthrow. A full-scale rehearsal of the Grenada invasion, called Ocean Venture '81, was carried out by the United States at Vieques, Puerto Rico, in August 1981.

Under the persistent pressure and threats from the United States one faction of the PRG, led by Bernard and Phyllis Coard, turned against Bishop and his supporters. Although Bishop had agreed to share leadership with Bernard Coard in September 1983, he was placed under house arrest on October 12. A week later, a huge crowd released Bishop and took him into St George's, where he intended to use the army transmitter at Fort Rupert to broadcast to the people. Three armoured cars were sent by Hudson Austin, the head of the army, from Fort Frederick, the other army base, where Bishop's opponents were located. They arrived at about 1pm and, by 1:15pm, Bishop and five other leaders of the PRG had been shot, murdered in cold blood. Austin announced the formation of a Revolutionary Military Council at 3pm and the PRG was dissolved. The United States took advantage of this situation and invaded the shocked nation with about 6,000 troops on October 25. After four days of resistance, the United States established a military occupation and began reversing the Grenadian revolution. Reactions within Grenada and among nations of the Caribbean to the US invasion differed sharply. Some countries, including Barbados, Dominica and Jamaica, supported the invasion, while others, including the Bahamas, Belize, Guyana, and Trinidad and Tobago, opposed it. One consequence of this event, therefore, was the weakening of regional unity, a goal which had been shared by leaders as politically diverse as Grantley Adams of Barbados, Norman and Michael Manley of Jamaica, C.L.R. James and Eric Williams of Trinidad and Tobago, and T. Albert Marryshow and Maurice Bishop of Grenada. The speech by Bishop that follows was given on November 7, 1982, to celebrate Marryshow and establish the first National Day of Culture.

⸙⸙⸙

$\mathscr{A}$ddress Celebrating the First National Day of Culture

The great Grenadian whom we are honouring today, in every sense of the word can be described as a genuine original. Our dear and veteran comrade, Cacademo Grant, who worked, organized and struggled side by side with this man, once had this to say about him: 'Marryshow was truly a great man, a man you would like to be near. Those of you who didn't live one day with Marryshow, then you didn't live a satisfactory life.' Comrades, T. Albert Marryshow[1] is physically with us no longer, but his inspiration and example is something we must invoke every day of our lives, his undying commitment and love for the people of *his* and *our* Caribbean must burn in us continually, his presence must always be inside us and alongside us. In this way, remembering our brother Cacademo's words, we can at least begin to lead satisfactory lives, – lives, like that of Marryshow, that give everything to our people.

Why is the memory and example of T.A. Marryshow so vital for us now in Grenada, and now throughout the Caribbean region? It is because Marryshow was the creator of a tradition, a set of principles and attitudes that since March 13th, 1979 we have struggled to implement, consolidate and extend. In a sense, of course, Marryshow, himself was also the inheritor of a great tradition. He grew from the earth of Fedon,[2] a great revolutionary who fused the humanism and hatred of tyranny sweeping from the French masses in 1789 by way of the great Haitian upsurge, with the fury of the rebel slave ground down in his own island by slavery and British colonialism. The huge courage of Fedon and his comrades in 1795 gave birth to Marryshow in 1887, and perhaps we should note that almost a century divided them, and that Marryshow's birth in 1887 was in fact almost the mid-point in time between Fedon's Revolution and our Revolution. So in every sense, comrades, he was also a continuer, a link, a great bridge between two massive blows at imperialism.

This great son of our soil was also a son of the working people, born just a stone's throw from here in Lucas Street in St. George's. There was nothing special about his birth, he inherited no money or property, his only inheritance was that great fighting tradition of Fedon that runs in the blood of every Grenadian. Alongside his great contemporary, Tubal Uriah Buzz Butler,[3] he lit the way for all of us present in this commemoration in his honour tonight. Apprenticed to a carpenter, he later shifted trades and became a compositor and then a trainee printer. But Marryshow soon found that his love for words and writing was uncontrollable, and as a teenager he turned to the tool and weapon that was going to serve the Caribbean people and cause them to marvel at him and admire him for the rest of his days – his pen.

The Man and His Pen

Here was a man of complete eloquence, whose power of speech was only matched by his power with the written word. As he levelled his pen at them, colonial administrators and governors who had sat behind the most expensive desks in England and idled their way through Oxford and Cambridge universities, through right of birth, quaked and trembled. And yet Marryshow had no university education, not even a secondary school education. He learned to read and write without the benefit of electricity, he had no money to buy books, he had no access to vast libraries, bookshops or museums. He learned his brilliance from the streets of St. George's and the great hills and forests of our beloved Grenada. He studied the hearts and hopes of his people.

His first great influence was the man whose newspaper he began to work for at the age of 17 years in 1904 – William Galway Donovan, the editor of the *Federalist and Grenada People*. And what a fantastic combination that was! Here was W.G. Donovan, half black Grenadian and inheritor of Fedon's mighty struggle, half Irishman, and inheritor of Wolfe Tone, of O'Connell, of the Fenians and the great Irish rebels and republicans, who like the Caribbean people had spent centuries trying to free themselves from the British colonial stranglehold and who are still fighting, up until now![4] And here was Donovan and his paper, which in its very title, was articulating the great dream of Marryshow – a united, federal Caribbean, *one* Caribbean, one indivisible people. Again comrades, the more we look at our history, the more we see the connections we have with the rest of the struggling people of the world, the more we realise our destiny remains integral with the fortunes of the oppressed of the world.

And Marryshow more than anyone before him realised this and expressed this. By 1909, at the age of 22, he was editor of the *St. George's Chronicle and Grenada Gazette*, and by 1915 he had helped found *The West Indian*, and stayed as editor of that pioneering journal for nearly twenty years, headlining on *every single* issue the slogan that was to be his watchwords for the rest of his fighting life! *THE WEST INDIES MUST BE WEST INDIAN!* And yet his unquestionable commitment to the Caribbean did not make him simply a regionalist. In 1917, he wrote a ferocious and historic attack on the racist state of South Africa, in his *Cycles of Civilisation*. And never forget that at this time there was no world-wide movement against Apartheid, no United Nations, no great cluster of independent African States to support him.

The man he was attacking, General Jan Smuts, one of the early architects of the emerging Apartheid state, was seen by the ruling class of the British Empire as an important ally, and bastion of the Empire, and Marryshow's great defence of the African people came in the middle of the 1914–1918 imperialist war, when millions upon millions of people from all over the world were uselessly dying.

Such words from an impertinent, unknown black man in an outpost of the empire would have been seen as treason. And yet none of this deterred Marryshow, man of Grenada, man of the Caribbean, man of the rising world, from his defence of justice and truth, and his undaunted assault on all things racist, oppressive and inhuman. In fact, in 1917, when the pillars of the ancient order were being torn down in Soviet Russia and when Lenin was directing the Russian masses to storm the palaces of the Tzar, T.A. Marryshow was sitting writing words in a small island in the Eastern Caribbean, a forgotten and remote part of the British Empire. And the words pouring out from the great Grenadian's pen read like an extraordinary prophecy of what has happened in Ghana, in Mozambique, in Angola, in Guinea Bissau, in Libya, Zimbabwe, in Cuba and Grenada – and what will storm through South Africa and Namibia in the months and years that are approaching.

Here are his words written in 1917 after he had heard and read about the great events taking place in Russia in 1917, a revolution which took place exactly 30 years after Marryshow's own birth:

> Africa! it is Africa's direct turn. Sons of New Ethiopia scattered all over the world, should determine that there should be new systems of the distributions of opportunities, privileges and rights, so that Africa shall rid herself of many of the murderous highwaymen of Europe who have plundered her, raped her and left her hungry and naked in the broad light of the boasted European civilisation. Africa would then be free again to rise her head among the races of the earth and enrich humanity as she has done before. . .

Comrades, thus spoke Grenada in 1917. Thus speaks Grenada in 1982.

Man of the Caribbean, Man of the World

T.A. Marryshow never forgot the rest of the world as he spent his life struggling for a united Caribbean. In his own words, he was an enemy of old style bramble politics, or as he called it 'parish pump politics', and his anti-parochialism was manifested in his ceaseless struggles to unite the Caribbean, culturally and politically. As founder and president of the *Grenada Working Men's Association* formed in 1931, he became a prominent figure in Caribbean Labour Organisations, and his energy and commitment was instrumental in setting up the *Caribbean Labour*

Congress. As president of this body in 1946 he persuaded it to take a supportive stand on the Federation. In every forum in which he participated he condemned the political tribalism that put territory against territory and one section of working people against another. It made no sense to him, he saw it as reactionary and foolish – his whole life was dedicated to unifying and bringing together all of his people, who had been scattered and separated by the interests of British imperialism.

In 1921 he travelled to London, using his own money and under his own initiative. He sought out the colonial office, marched in with all the dignity and independence that marked his entire character, and brought his eloquence to bear on the men behind the desks at the hub of Empire. At that time, the legislative councils of the Caribbean islands – with the exception of Barbados and Jamaica – had no *elected* members, and were all appointed by the British governor. Marryshow spoke not only for Grenada, *not only for his own island but for the entire unfranchised Caribbean*. As a result of his reasoning and argumentation, achieved without pleading or begging, the Wood Commission[5] came to the Caribbean, and as a direct consequence of Marryshow's mission, a measure of representative government was achieved not only for Grenada, but also for the other Windward islands, the Leewards *and* Trinidad.

And it is important to remember, as Book I of our locally written CPE Adult Education Reader reminds us, that this historic victory of representative government for our region came as a direct result of dozens of years of struggles by T.A. Marryshow dating back to his formation in 1917 of the Grenada Representative Government Association.[6]

The creation of a representative section of the legislative council meant that T.A. Marryshow became the elected member for St. George's and stayed in that seat for 33 tireless, brilliant and self-sacrificing years, until his death in 1958. He had struck a great blow for democracy throughout the Caribbean, and given the people a foot in the door of freedom, a door which was to be thrown open fully on March 13, 1979 by the struggles of our people. But of course, the emphasis of his public and political life was firmly upon creating a structure of regional unity, which found expression in his vision of *FEDERATION*. It was a noble, democratic vision which sought to re-integrate a divided people to bind our islands together in one fraternal, united mainland. From 1929 when he attended the first regional conference on regional integration in Barbados, through the years until the West Indies Conference of the Caribbean Commission in St. Kitts in 1946 and the Montego Bay Conference in 1947, Marryshow personified Caribbean oneness, he was in himself the symbol and dynamo of unity, the 'Father of Federation'. In 1953, he was the advisor to the Federal Conference in London, and played an integral role in the Planning Conference for Federation in Jamaica in 1957. In 1958, when what had been just a compelling idea in his brain became a political reality and he himself became one of his country's two federal senators to the Federal Parliament, he could only utter the unforgettable words – 'This is my dream come true. Today, I am a member of that august body that I dreamed into existence'.

The Marryshow Standard

Marryshow died in the same year, 1958, and over his bones grew division, faintheartedness and a withdrawl to insularity. Suddenly there was no Marryshow to heal these wounds and bind the parts of the whole together once more. And so, comrades, we have to continue his unfinished work, to bring together again everything that was lost. That is not a mere sentimental or nostalgic gesture for us in Grenada, it is a part of our blood, ours mixed with Fedon's, mixed with Butler's, mixed with Marryshow's. It is a part of the responsibility of the tradition handed down to us, part of the task passed to us from the giants of our history who have laid the foundations for us and our progress.

For when we consider Marryshow, we see an extraordinary man who grew from the ordinary earth that we all share. In a way, we can see him as the *most ordinary* of men who grew from the most ordinary of backgrounds. And yet this working class boy of St. George's became the greatest journalist and prose stylist of his age, became the founder of our country's first labour movement, became in himself the standard of honesty, integrity and truth. One of the greatest singers of his generation, the mighty Paul Robeson, told him his voice was one of the most magnificent he had ever heard that he should become a professional singer. His poetry was compared to that of the great black American, Paul Lawrence Dunbar. He was a sportsman, a humourist, a democrat and a struggler for human progress: and perhaps the nearest to a complete human being that our region has ever produced.

He was not only a firm anti-colonialist, he also firmly refused to compromise his principles regardless of the consequences, a quality which always got him into the bad books of the British colonialists. In fact, up to 1921, the British never called his name but only referred to him as 'this dangerous radical'. And what a nice compliment that was! This strong kind of principle continued right through his life.

During the late 1940's the colonial system was challenged by a worldwide struggle which campaigned for placing all colonies under the rule of the League of Nations, (later to become the United Nations). The British therefore elaborated a scheme to get the West Indian colonies to say to the U.N. that they wanted to remain with Britain instead of obtaining independence. In pursuance of this trickery and deception, the British requested Marryshow to go to The Hague in Holland to read such a statement for them. Of course, Marryshow with his customary courage and uncompromising attitude to colonialism, bluntly refused, and so it fell to Grantley Adams to go before the Security Council to try to make out the British case that West Indian countries wanted to stay as colonies.[7]

And so comrades, in honouring and remembering him yet again tonight and as we do on this date every year, what does his message from the past bring us at this present moment, how is he speaking to us now? He is demonstrating to us and telling us a standard, that we, as Grenadians and Caribbean people, must seek to emulate. If we pause and examine ourselves and our Revolution by the Marryshow standard, we can, of course, find many places where we have fallen short, but we can also find other places where we are proud to have touched him. We know he would have approved of our declaration in the early hours of March 13th, 1979 that our Revolution, 'is for work, for food, for decent housing and health services, and for a bright future for our children and grandchildren'. He devoted his own life to those things, and we were merely carrying on his concerns and those of Fedon and Butler. We felt his closeness on July 14 and 15th of 1979 when we hosted the Grenada Summit and conferred with the Prime Ministers of St. Lucia and Dominica.[8] His same spirit of Caribbean solidarity was present at that meeting, when all three Prime Ministers spoke of the creation of one, united Caribbean, and when it was decided that travel restrictions between our islands would be eased, and in the future between our shores, passports would be irrelevances. T.A. Marryshow was with us when we signed the Declaration of St. George's, telling the region that we would erase the traces of colonialism in our countries and move *forward together in a non-aligned policy* towards peace and progress. And his spirit travelled with us to Lusaka in Zambia a month later. Following his example of a rejection of parochialism and national selfishness, we spoke not only for ourselves, but also for Zimbabwe's independence and for all small island states, not only in the Caribbean, but throughout the Commonwealth, the islands of the Pacific, the Atlantic, the Indian Ocean and any other small national territory like ourselves which had been set apart by both geography and imperialism. We asked that there should be more assistance for states like ours from the bigger and richer Commonwealth countries to give us free access to their markets, that they offer us greater financial help with less debt traps, that they create a Basic Needs Fund for the small island states, that they help us to be more self-sufficient in our energy supplies, and less dependent upon their oil by giving us the technical assistance to help us discover our own energy sources.

Not Only For Ourselves

Comrades, we spoke not only of Grenada and for Grenada. We wanted nothing for ourselves that our neighbours and brothers and sisters in the neighbouring islands couldn't enjoy too. We have never said that only Grenada matters because for us that would be impossible as the heirs of Marryshow, Fedon and Butler. We have always believed and still believe that what is good for us is also good for the entire Caribbean, although we would never force our view on our sister islands. But, we know, we all suffer from the same underdevelopment, the same scars of colonialism, the same trade imbalance, the same exploitation by the trans-national corporations that try to suck us dry. And so, what we labour to find for ourselves, we shall labour to find for the rest of the Caribbean.

And the fact is that three years after the Lusaka Conference the mighty presence of Marryshow still accompanies us when we travel around the world to seek assistance, cooperation, and friends and allies, who will help us without trying to dictate to us. When Comrade Coard was in London last month at the Commonwealth Finance Ministers' Conference, we saw the same pattern, the same insistence that Grenada fights for the entire Caribbean, that we saw with Marryshow's lone journey to London in 1921. There we spoke out for all small island states in the manner of Marryshow. We proposed that the Commonwealth appoint a panel of experts to conduct a special survey of the problems of small island states, recognising that over half of the nations of the Commonwealth fall inside this category – including Grenada, St. Lucia, Barbados, the Seychelles, Tonga, Kiribati, Ascension Island, Bermuda, the Bahamas, Montserrat and St. Vincent. Comrade Coard, like Marryshow of old, was fighting for all these countries, battling to secure more favourable repayment periods from the International Monetary Fund in Toronto a few days later, fighting to improve the situation of our small farmers and their counterparts right through our Caribbean, Marryshow's Caribbean.

T.A. Marryshow was with us too comrades, when we were in Paris a few weeks ago, inspiring us in our conversations with President Mitterand of France. We could feel his joy when the generosity of the French government was expressed in substantial aid from their Fund For Aid and Co-operation, secured *not only for us*, but for six of our closest neighbours too. This was the *first time* ever this fund had reached out towards the Eastern Caribbean, being normally directed to former French colonies and the Portuguese-speaking nations of Africa. As this month's *Caribbean Contact*[9] declares and acknowledges:

> Several million dollars' worth of economic aid will start trickling into the Eastern Caribbean early next year as part of the effort by France's new Socialist government to step up its aid to the Third World. This bonanza will be largely thanks to Grenada!

And we could add not only thanks to the Grenada of today but thanks to the Marryshow tradition, for we are simply carrying on his work, his sustaining love for the Caribbean – and not by words alone, for indeed Marryshow was a man of magnificent words, but every word was matched with a deed, with a real, concrete action. He did not simply compose elegant sentences and write emotional poems to

Caribbean unity. He lived that unity, worked tirelessly for it, travelled oceans and continents to bring it nearer and finally, if only temporarily, he helped to bring it about. That is our way too comrades, our tradition, our commitment. And that is what we pledge to continue and consolidate on this day, the day when we remember Marryshow.

Unite Or Perish

Comrades, like Marryshow, we recognise the strength and necessity of workers' organisations and have promoted their regeneration and re-invigoration by scrapping all the dictator's anti-trade union laws and giving the choice to all workers to join which trade union they please.

And Marryshow was also a great housebuilder. Next time you walk along the Carenage look at those houses next to the Empire Cinema. And next time you walk along Tyrrel Street watch the houses opposite the University of the West Indies centre – they are the houses that Marryshow built, workers' houses, and for just three dollars a month for twelve years, the houses were theirs!

Think what Marryshow would have done with our Sandino Plant, with our pre-fabricated houses from the government of Venezuela, with the no-interest loans of our House Repair Programme! We build them in the spirit of Marryshow. He promoted sports for all, like the Revolution does and he built parks. He was cheering with us in Tanteen when our Netball sisters played like lionesses this August, and he will be singing with our National Performing Company as they tour the U.S.A. right now and during the next month and he will undoubtedly soon be laying the bricks of our House of Culture.

And because he loved beauty, culture and sport, Marryshow was a man of peace. He knew that *peace* is the ideal of every working person. He was with Comrade Louison[10] in La Paz, Bolivia, at the O.A.S. conference when we first put forward our determination that the Caribbean shall be, and must be, a *zone of peace*, when we articulated the principle of ideological pluralism and friendship and co-operation between all nations of the Caribbean and of the wider world. He would have understood our concept of the *wider Caribbean*, that languages and national boundaries and the different identities of the ex-colonial powers must never be factors that separate the *one people* of the Caribbean Basin, whether, they are from the Bahamas or Suriname or Jamaica, from Mexico, Panama, Nicaragua or El Salvador, from Curacao, Haiti or Cuba, from Guatemala or Grenada – one people, one history, one Caribbean nation!

Tonight we remember comrades, what Marryshow's mentor, W.G. Donovan inscribed upon his newspaper, something that reached right through Marryshow and came directly to our Revolution, the remarkable words – '*Better a naked freeman, than a gilded slave'*. Tonight as we remember these words, we also remember that just as we do not interfere in the internal affairs of other nations, so we will accept no bullying, no intimidation, no interference, no bribery, no blackmail or whitemail from any person or government. We are certain that if Marryshow and Donovan could look around this meeting tonight and through the villages of our own country, and certainly be confident that they see no gilded slaves in Free Grenada! Only free men, free women, free children in our small island, a world of freedom.

A Vital Upcoming Period

Comrades, the next three weeks will be vital for us. We have over one hundred activities leading up to Bloody Sunday,[11] two major regional conferences here in Grenada, and the meetings of the heads of the Organisation of Eastern Caribbean States and the heads of the CARICOM states. And as we know the existence of these regional structures in themselves owe a huge amount to the vision and lifetime's work of Marryshow, which makes them of particular significance to us, as there is undoubtedly a huge amount to be done to carry on Marryshow's work.

For us in the People's Revolutionary Government, the continuation of Marryshow's visionary work is the priority for these meetings – to boldly extend and sustain his efforts, to build on his foundations, to make these meetings genuinely *meaningful* to the lives of the poor and working people of our Caribbean. We are not going to cuss or fight any other nation; we are going with our heads and hearts open to build upon our history, like Marryshow went to Barbados in 1929, like he went to St. Kitts in 1946 and Montego Bay in 1947. We go to St. Lucia and Jamaica in 1982 to continue Marryshow's work, to find real answers to the massive problems facing our people.

What can we do *as a Caribbean people* to help our farmers sell their products? What can we do *as a Caribbean people* to develop much more just and equitable terms of trade with the European countries? What can we do *as a Caribbean people* to secure better prices for our cocoa, our bananas, our nutmegs – or our arrowroot, our sugar or our bauxite? How can we bring closer the New International Economic Order?[12] How can we begin to control the massive imperialist cultural onslaught on our people's minds and consciousness? We shall be recommending plans to develop a regional maritime transport system, recalling the days when we had the *Federal Maple* and the *Federal Palm* plying between our islands.

We Shall Defend U.W.I

We shall be resolutely defending our regional university, the University of the West Indies, arguing that it must stay intact for the benefit of all Caribbean people, as it is a part of our Marryshow inheritance that we cherish and hold dearly. We shall be putting forward proposals for much greater cultural and sporting interchanges. We shall be recommending ways of promoting much deeper friendship and understanding between our people, and putting forward a policy of bulk-buying of certain expensive imported goods for the region, so that we can collectively cut our import bills and ease strain on all our budgets.

In other words comrades, we are approaching these meetings in the Marryshow tradition, with positive, unifying proposals. We want nothing to do with sectarianism, conspiracies or cliques, we want an agenda which serves our people, the Caribbean people, and confronts and seeks to resolve their multiplicity of problems. We remember the words of the man whose life and work we are celebrating today:

> A West Indies in a world like this must unite or perish. This is not the time for parish pump politics. We must think nobly, nationally, with special regard for the first fundamentals of a West Indian unity, and a West Indian identity.

Comrades, we go to St. Lucia and Jamaica with these words ringing clearly in our minds.

The Intellectual Worker

As you know comrades, for you have been at many openings and public sessions – Free Grenada has been the venue of many Caribbean conferences. We have had conferences of Caribbean workers, Caribbean and American lawyers, Caribbean trade unionists, Caribbean journalists, just to name a few. Later this month we shall be hosting two more regional conferences. One will be the first ever international conference to be held in our sister island of Carriacou, on the subject of Education and Production, in which we aim to demonstrate the excellence of Camp Carriacou as a Conference Centre, while emphasising the meaning behind our slogan, that *Education is Production Too!* The other is a conference of Caribbean Intellectual Workers, some of the most remarkable and talented people of our region, who will come together here in Grenada to discuss and affirm the cultural sovereignty of the Caribbean.

Historically, intellectuals, or what we used to know as the 'intelligentsia' – authors, journalists, artists, poets, and scholars – have seen themselves as alienated, apart from the ordinary working people of the region. As such, they tended to distance themselves from the people's struggles, living abroad or in ivory towers of dreams and sheer individualism. This conference is designed to help to create intellectual workers out of intellectuals, to form a policy and a plan of action that will make cultural and intellectual work, in the words of one of the conference's organisers, the brilliant Barbadian novelist George Lamming, 'an essential part of the lives of all our people'. We shall be host to many outstanding minds and imaginations: from Michael Manley of Jamaica to the great Caribbean poet, Martin Carter of Guyana, from Paul Keens-Douglas to the Minister of Culture in Nicaragua, Ernesto Cardenal, from Trevor Farrell to George Beckford and Don Robotham,[13] from the 1982 Nobel prize winner for literature Gabriel Garcia Marquez of Colombia, to the legendary Harry Belafonte[14] who was last here in 1955. Scarcely have so many extraordinary Caribbean people come together for such an event, and comrades, they are coming together in Free and Revolutionary Grenada!

So earlier on this evening we formed a *Committee of Grenadian Intellectuals*, which will formulate its own programme and proposals for bringing the Arts, all aspects of National Culture, and scholarship, closer to our people, so that intellectual work stands beside manual and productive work and takes us towards the same ends and objectives: the full economic, social and political emancipation of our people, and a way of life which imitates none, which mimics none, which is slave to none, but which reflects the originality and genius of our struggling people and our developing nation. Thus our intellectuals, like our workers, farmers and fishermen, will be producers too, and catalysts in creating and reflecting a new life for our people, as well as guardians of our culture who ensure that the imperialist cancer cannot penetrate and destroy the new values and definitions we are building for ourselves through our own unique process.

A Very Special Day

Without doubt, today is a special day in many ways. It is the day of T.A. Marryshow, but it is also a day in which we also remember great events and other gigantic people. Today is the 65th Anniversary of the Great October Socialist Revolution, that epoch-making event in Russia in 1917, which has paved the way for so many enormous changes, not only for the Soviet people, but for the entire world. In 1917, as Marryshow wrote his *Cycles of Civilisation*, he knew of the massive blow struck against backwardness and tyranny in Russia. Listen to Marryshow as he expressed his joy in his unforgettable language and style as he beheld the triumph for the masses of St. Petersburg and Moscow an ocean and a continent away:

> A great spirit of Democracy and Socialism is coming to do God's work of levelling up and levelling down.

Today, we also commemorate Palestine Liberation Day, and we are happy to have a Palestinian comrade with us, who has given us the latest information of the heroic struggles of their people against the murderous Zionist aggression backed up to the cowardly hilt by U.S. imperialism. We can hardly find words to express our shock and shame at the barbarous forces that massacred your people in Beirut. We mourned with you for the loss of your innocent lives but we also clench firmly our Caribbean fists to fight on with you. We can only say that your agony was also our agony, but that your certain and inevitable victory and joy will also be ours.

Our Party, our People's Revolutionary Government, and our Free people are with you. Last month we marched through our streets in solidarity with you, and one day, just as you are visiting free and revolutionary Grenada, we shall be visiting you in free and revolutionary Palestine.

Our Culture Is Our Dignity

Comrades, in our presentation this evening we have truly traversed the world. In dealing with Marryshow, this is inevitable, because of his worldliness, his universal vision. But let me end by saying that this day, Marryshow Day, will from this year, also be known as *National Day of Culture* in our country. Marryshow, as we have noted, was a cultured man, and a true forerunner of the organized intellectual who strives to use his brain, his art, his scholarship to serve his people. He would have been the first to sponsor and take part in the intellectual conference on culture and sovereignty we are hosting later this month. For our culture is how we live, how we produce, what we grow, how we make our democracy and freedom, how we change and transform our earth, how we organise our hopes, dreams and aspirations, how we love one another. And how, as we change the world, we are changed ourselves, into new men, new women, new Caribbean people.

The great man once said and it was on March 13th that he said it, comrades, as if he already knew what that day would mean for us, March 13th, 1950, in the Market Square where we have had so many of our own meetings:

> From earliest times I had thought in terms of human dignity, that a man no matter how poor could lift himself and become somebody in the world. I read avidly in my youth, and the quotation: 'I never did believe, nor do I now believe that Providence ordained one set of men, spurred to ride and others saddled to be ridden', had a profound influence and inspired me!

Our culture is our dignity, the dignity the Revolution has brought us and the dignity it sustains in us. We are sovereigns of our dignity, of *our pride in being we,* and we are proud of our consistent victory over the forces that try to make us their imitators, their mimics and their puppets. Our Revolution has put on the agenda of the Caribbean people a new way, a new view of ourselves, a new determination in our destiny. For this we thank and honour T.A. Marryshow, the Prince of West Indian journalists, the father of the West Indian Federation, the oldest statesman of the West Indies, and all those Caribbean masses, our ancestors and their ancestors, that have brought us to the freedom of being what we are and being what we are, determined we shall be, and determined we shall walk in a conscious, organised, productive and united way along the glorious new path that will bring peace, happiness, justice and social progress to all of our free and patriotic people.

Long live the struggle for Caribbean Integration and unity!
Long live the spirit, memory and example of T.A. Marryshow!
Long live the Palestine Liberation Organization!
Long live the struggles of the Palestinian people!
Long live the Grenada Revolution!
FORWARD EVER, BACKWARD NEVER!
FORWARD EVER, BACKWARD NEVER!
FORWARD EVER, BACKWARD NEVER!

NOTES

1. T. Albert Marryshow (1887–1958), a Grenadian journalist, was one of the first West Indian federalists. He founded the Representative Government Association in Grenada in 1918 and the Grenada Workingmen's Association in 1931. As the president of the Grenada Labour Party he attended a regional labour conference in 1944 and the next year, at the founding conference of the Caribbean Labour Congress in Barbados, he was elected its first president.
2. Julien Fedon, a free coloured planter, led a revolution that controlled much of Grenada between March 1795 until its defeat in June 1796.
3. Tubal Uriah 'Buzz' Butler (1897–1977) was born in Grenada, but in 1921 he migrated to Trinidad where he worked as a pipe-fitter in the oilfields. He was a preacher and then, by 1937, the chief leader of the oilfield workers in the great labour rebellion. Interned during the Second World War, he created the British Empire Workers and Citizens Home Rule Party and was elected in 1950 to the legislature. Although his party won more seats than any other, the governor and other members of the Legislative Council excluded him and the other five members of his party who had been elected from the Executive Council.
4. Ireland was conquered by England in the sixteenth century and, after a series of revolts, was officially made part of the United Kingdom of Great Britain and Ireland in 1801. Daniel O'Connell (1775–1847) was elected to the British Parliament in 1828 but could not take his seat because he was Catholic. Pressure from his Catholic Association helped bring about the Catholic Emancipation Act in 1829. In 1843, O'Connell, known as the Liberator, was convicted of conspiracy for advocating a free Ireland. The Irish Free State, without the six counties of Ulster which had a Protestant majority, was created in 1921 and became an independent republic in 1949. Catholics in Northern Ireland continued to struggle for unification with the rest of Ireland.
5. The Wood Commission, named after its chair, Major E.F.L. Wood, made its report on constitutional reform in the British Caribbean colonies in 1922. It repeatedly referred to 'responsible opinion' and the 'substantial elements' in the colonies to justify its

recommendations of reforms which would be so limited as to leave real imperial power intact.

6. The Representative Government Association was, in fact, established at a meeting on November 10, 1918, with D.S. DeFreitas as president and Marryshow as treasurer.

7. Adams gave his speech as a member of the British delegation at the United Nations General Assembly meeting in Paris on October 13, 1948. In response to a Russian proposal calling upon the colonial powers to provide information concerning the political and constitutional status of non-self-governing territories, Adams declared, as the British government wanted him to, that Britain was making changes but these should not be the subject for debate at the UN. Adams' speech, which was an early manifestation of the global cold war, provoked a split within the Caribbean Labour Congress between himself, as the organisation's president, and Richard Hart, its secretary.

8. Dominica and St Lucia became independent in 1978 and 1979, respectively. The prime minister of Dominica at that time was Oliver Seraphin. Seraphin was replaced by Eugenia Charles, the Caribbean's first female prime minister, when her Dominican Freedom Party won the election on July 20, 1980. She played a leading role in October 1983 when, as Chair of the Organisation of Eastern Caribbean States, founded in 1981, she invited the United States to intervene in Grenada after Bishop's murder.

9. *Caribbean Contact* was the monthly newspaper of the Caribbean Conference of Churches, published in Barbados. Rickey Singh, who was its editor from 1974 to 1983, was expelled from Barbados by Tom Adams's government for criticising the invasion of Grenada.

10. George Louison, one of the early members of the NJM, was the PRG's minister of agriculture, rural development and cooperatives. He supported Bishop to the end and was imprisoned by the Revolutionary Military Council after Bishop's murder. After Gairy returned to Grenada in January 1984, Louison and Kenrick Radix formed the Maurice Bishop Patriotic Movement.

11. 'Bloody Sunday' was November 18, 1973, when several leaders of the NJM were arrested and badly beaten by Gairy's thugs. Bishop suffered persistent double vision as a result of head injuries he received that day.

12. The proposals for a New International Economic Order, which would restructure the world economic system in order to deliver a more equitable share of benefits to the lower income countries of the South, were promoted in the 1970s by Michael Manley of Jamaica, among others.

13. Trevor Farrell and George Beckford, economists, and Don Robothom, sociologist, taught at the University of the West Indies.

14. Harry Belafonte was born in New York City of West Indian parents in 1927 and lived in Jamaica from the age of 8 to 13. He became famous in the 1950s as a singer of folk music, especially West Indian songs, blues and spirituals, and he starred in several films.

Michelle Cliff

Michelle Cliff was born in Jamaica in 1946, grew up in Jamaica and the United States, and studied in New York and at the University of London. She is the author of three novels, Abeng *(1984),* No Telephone to Heaven *(1987) and* Free Enterprise *(1993), and three collections of short stories, poetry and prose. In the autobiographical essay, 'If I Could Write This in Fire, I Would Write This in Fire,' she explores some of the complexities of identity, association and culture, and the dividing lines of class, colour, gender and sexual orientation, as they are created in the connections between the personal, national and transnational levels.*

$\mathcal{I}$f I Could Write This in Fire, I Would Write This in Fire

I

We were standing under the waterfall at the top of Orange River. Our chests were just beginning to mound – slight hills on either side. In the center of each were our nipples, which were losing their sideways look and rounding into perceptible buttons of dark flesh. Too fast it seemed. We touched each other, then, quickly and almost simultaneously, raised our arms to examine the hairs growing underneath. Another sign. Mine was wispy and light brown. My friend Zoe[1] had dark hair curled up tight. In each little patch the riverwater caught the sun so we glistened.

The waterfall had come about when my uncles dammed up the river to bring power to the sugar mill. Usually, when I say 'sugar mill' to anyone not familiar with the Jamaican countryside or for that matter my family, I can tell their minds cast an image of tall smoke-stacks, enormous copper cauldrons, a man in a broad-brimmed hat with a whip, and several dozens of slaves – that is, if they have any idea of how large sugar mills once operated. It's a grandiose expression – like plantation, verandah, out-building. (Try substituting farm, porch, outside toilet.) To some people it even sounds romantic.

Our sugar mill was little more than a round-roofed shed, which contained a wheel and woodfire. We paid an old man to run it, tend the fire, and then either bartered or gave the sugar away, after my grandmother had taken what she needed. Our canefield was about two acres of flat land next to the river. My grandmother had six acres in all – one donkey, a mule, two cows, some chickens, a few pigs, and stray dogs and cats who had taken up residence in the yard.

Her house had four rooms, no electricity, no running water. The kitchen was a shed in the back with a small pot-bellied stove. Across from the stove was a mahogany counter, which had a white enamel basin set into it. The only light source was a window, a small space covered partly by a wooden shutter. We washed our faces and hands in enamel bowls with cold water carried in kerosene tins from the river and poured from enamel pitchers. Our chamber pots were enamel also, and in the morning we carefully placed them on the steps at the side of the house where my grandmother collected them and disposed of their contents. The outhouse was about thirty yards from the back door – a 'closet' as we called it –infested with lizards capable of changing color. When the door was shut it was totally dark, and the lizards made their presence known by the noise of their scurrying through the torn newspaper, or the soft shudder when they dropped from the walls. I remember most clearly the stench of the toilet, which seemed to hang in the air in that climate.

But because every little piece of reality exists in relation to another little piece, our situation was not that simple. It was to our yard that people came with news first. It was in my grandmother's parlor that the Disciples of Christ held their meetings.

Zoe lived with her mother and sister on borrowed ground in a place called Breezy Hill. She and I saw each other almost every day on our school vacations over a period of three years. Each morning early – as I sat on the cement porch with my coffee cut with condensed milk – she appeared: in her straw hat, school tunic faded from blue to gray, white blouse, sneakers hanging around her neck. We had coffee together, and a piece of hard-dough bread with butter and cheese, waited a bit and headed for the river. At first we were shy with each other. We did not start from the same place.

There was land. My grandparents' farm. And there was color.

(My family was called *red*. A term which signified a degree of whiteness. 'We's just a flock of red people,' a cousin of mine said once.) In the hierarchy of shades I was considered among the lightest. The countrywomen who visited my grandmother commented on my 'tall' hair – meaning long. Wavy, not curly.

I had spent the years from three to ten in New York and spoke – at first – like an American. I wore American clothes: shorts, slacks, bathing suit. Because of my American past I was looked upon as the creator of games. Cowboys and Indians. Cops and Robbers. Peter Pan.

(While the primary colonial identification for Jamaicans was English, American colonialism was a strong force in my childhood – and of course, continues today. We were sent American movies and American music. American aluminum companies had already discovered bauxite on the island and were shipping the ore to their mainland. United Fruit bought our bananas. White Americans came to Montego Bay, Ocho Rios, and Kingston for their vacations and their cruise ships docked in Port Antonio and other places. In some ways America was seen as a better place than England by many Jamaicans. The farm laborers sent to work in American agribusiness came home with dollars and gifts and new clothes; there were few who mentioned American racism. Many of the middle class who emigrated to Brooklyn or Staten Island or Manhattan were able to pass into the white American world – saving their blackness for other Jamaicans or for trips home; in some cases, forgetting it altogether. Those middle-class Jamaicans who could not pass for white managed differently – not unlike the Bajans in Paule Marshall's *Brown Girl, Brownstones*[2] – saving, working, investing, buying property. Completely separate in most cases from Black Americans.)

I was someone who had experience with the place that sent us triple features of B-grade westerns and gangster movies. And I had tall hair and light skin. And I was the granddaughter of my grandmother. So I had power. I was the cowboy, Zoe was my sidekick, the boys we knew were Indians. I was the detective, Zoe was my 'girl', and the boys were the lost boys.[3] And the terrain around the river – jungled and dark green – was Tombstone, or Chicago, or Never-Never Land.

This place and my friendship with Zoe never touched my life in Kingston. We did not correspond with each other when I left my grandmother's home.

I never visited Zoe's home the entire time I knew her. It was a given: never suggested, never raised.

Zoe went to a state school held in a country church in Red Hills. It had been my mother's school. I went to a private all-girls school where I was taught by white Englishwomen and pale Jamaicans. In her school the students were caned as punishment. In mine the harshest punishment I remember was being sent to sit under the *lignum vitae* to 'commune with nature'. Some of the girls were out-and-out white (English and American), the rest of us were colored – only a few were dark. Our uniforms were blood-red gabardine, heavy and hot. Classes were held in buildings meant to recreate England: damp with stone floors, facing onto a cloister, or quad as they called it. We began each day with the headmistress leading us in English hymns. The entire school stood for an hour in the zinc-roofed gymnasium.

Occasionally a girl fainted, or threw up. Once, a girl had a grand mal seizure. To any such disturbances the response was always 'keep singing'. While she flailed on the stone floor, I wondered what the mistresses would do. We sang 'Faith of our Fathers', and watched our classmate as her eyes rolled back in her head. I thought of people swallowing their tongues. This student was dark – here on a scholarship – and the only woman who came forward to help her was the gamesmistress, the only dark teacher. She kneeled beside the girl and slid the white web belt from her tennis shorts, clamping it between the girl's teeth. When the seizure was over, she carried the girl to a tumbling mat in the corner of the gym and covered her so she wouldn't get chilled.

Were the other women unable to touch this girl because of her darkness? I think that now. Her darkness and her scholarship. She lived on Windward Road with her grandmother; her mother was a maid. But darkness is usually enough for women like those to hold back. Then, we usually excused that kind of behavior by saying they were 'ladies'. (We were constantly being told that we should be ladies also. One teacher went so far as to tell us many people thought Jamaicans lived in trees and we had to show these people they were mistaken.) In short, we felt insufficient to judge the behavior of these women. The English ones (who had the corner on power in the school) had come all this way to teach us. Shouldn't we treat them as the missionaries they were certain they were? The creole Jamaicans had a different role: they were passing on to those of us who were light-skinned the creole heritage of collaboration, assimilation, loyalty to our betters. We were expected to be willing subjects in this outpost of civilisation.

The girl left school that day and never returned.

After prayers we filed into our classrooms. After classes we had games: tennis, field hockey, rounders (what the English call baseball), netball (what the English call basketball). For games we were divided into 'houses' – groups named for Joan of Arc, Edith Cavell, Florence Nightingale, Jane Austen.[4] Four white heroines. Two martyrs. One saint. Two nurses. (None of us knew then that there were Black women with Nightingale at Scutari.) One novelist. Three involved in whitemen's wars. Two dead in whitemen's wars. *Pride and Prejudice.*

Those of us in Cavell wore red badges and recited her last words before a firing squad in World War I: 'Patriotism in not enough. I must have no hatred or bitterness toward anyone.'

Sorry to say I grew up to have exactly that.

Looking back: To try and see when the background changed places with the foreground. To try and locate the vanishing point: where the lines of perspective converge and disappear. Lines of color and class. Line of history and social context. Lines of denial and rejection. When did *we* (the light-skinned middle-class Jamaicans) take over for *them* as oppressors? I need to see when and how this happened. When what should have been reality was overtaken by what was surely unreality. When the house nigger became master.

'What's the matter with you? You think you're white or something?'

'Child, what you want to know 'bout Garvey for? The man was nothing but a damn fool'.

'They not our kind of people'.

Why did we wear wide-brimmed hats and try to get into Oxford? Why did we not return?

Great Expectations:[5] a novel about origins and denial about the futility and tragedy of that denial. about attempting assimilation. We learned this novel from a light-skinned Jamaican woman – she concentrated on what she called the 'love affair' between Pip and Estella.

Looking back: Through the last page of *Sula.*[6] 'And the loss pressed down on her chest and came up into her throat. "We was girls together," she said as though explaining something.' It was Zoe, and Zoe alone I thought of. She snapped into my mind and I remembered no one else. Through the greens and blues of the riverbank. The flame of red hibiscus in front of my grandmother's house. The cracked grave of a former landowner. The fruit of the ackee which poisons those who don't know how to prepare it.

'What is to become of us?'

We borrowed a baby from a woman and used her as our dolly. Dressed and undressed her. Dipped her in the riverwater. Fed her with the milk her mother had left with us: and giggled because we knew where the milk had come from.

A letter: 'I am desperate. I need to get away. I beg you one fifty-dollar.'

I send the money because this is what she asks for. I visit her on a trip back home. Her front teeth are gone. Her husband beats her and she suffers blackouts. I sit on her chair. She is given birth control pills which aggravate her 'condition'. We boil up sorrel and ginger. She is being taught by Peace Corps volunteers to embroider linen mats with little lambs on them and gives me one as a keepsake. We cool off the sorrel with a block of ice brought from the shop nearby. The shopkeeper immediately recognizes me as my grandmother's granddaughter and refuses to sell me cigarettes. (I am twenty-seven.) We sit in the doorway of her house, pushing back the colored plastic strands which form a curtain, and talk about Babylon and Dred. About Manley and what he's doing for Jamaica. About how hard it is. We walk along the railway tracks – no longer used – to Crooked River and the post office. Her little daughter walks beside us and we recite a poem for her: 'Mornin' buddy/ Me no buddy fe wunna/ Who den, den I saw?' and on and on.

I can come and go. And I leave. To complete my education in London.

II

Their goddam kings and their goddam queens. Grandmotherly Victoria spreading herself thin across the globe. Elizabeth II on our tv screens. We stop what we are doing. We quiet down. We pay our respects.

1981: In Massachusetts I get up at 5 a.m. to watch the royal wedding.[7] I tell myself maybe the IRA[8] will intervene. It's got to be better than starving themselves to death. Better to be a kamikaze in St. Paul's Cathedral than a hostage in Ulster. And last week Black and white people smashed storefronts all over the United Kingdom. But I really don't believe we'll see royal blood on tv I watch because they once ruled us. In the back of the cathedral a Maori woman sings an aria from Handel,[9] and I notice that she is surrounded by the colored subjects.

To those of us in the commonwealth the royal family was the perfect symbol of hegemony. To those of us who were dark in the dark nations, the prime minister, the parliament barely existed. We believed in royalty – we were convinced in this belief. Maybe it played on some ancestral memories of West Africa – where other kings and queens had been. Altars and castles and magic.

The faces of our new rulers were everywhere in my childhood. Calendars, newsreels, magazines. Their presences were often among us. Attending test matches between the West Indians and South Africans. They were our landlords. Not always absentee. And no matter what Black leader we might elect – were we to choose independence – we would be losing something almost holy in our impudence.

WE ARE HERE BECAUSE YOU WERE THERE
BLACK PEOPLE AGAINST STATE BRUTALITY
BLACK WOMEN WILL NOT BE INTIMIDATED
WELCOME TO BRITAIN…WELCOME TO SECOND-CLASS CITIZENSHIP
(slogans of the Black movement in Britain)

Indian women cleaning the toilets in Heathrow airport. This is the first thing I notice. Dark women in saris trudging buckets back and forth as other dark women in saris – some covered by loosefitting winter coats – form a line to have their passports stamped.

The triangle trade: molasses/rum/slaves. Robinson Crusoe was on a slave-trading journey. Robert Browning[10] was a mulatto. Holding pens. Jamaica was a seasoning station. Split tongues. Sliced ears. Whipped bodies. The constant pretense of civility against rape. Still. Iron collars. Tinplate masks. The latter a precaution: to stop the slaves from eating the sugar cane.

A pregnant woman is to be whipped – they dig a hole in the ground to accommodate her belly and place her face down on the ground. Many of us became light-skinned pretty fast. Traced ourselves through bastard lines to reach the duke of Devonshire. The earl of Cornwall. The lord of this and the lord of that. Our mothers' rapes were the thing unspoken.

You say: But Britain freed her slaves in 1833.[11] Yes.

Tea plantations in India and Ceylon. Mines in Africa. The Cape-to-Cairo Railroad. Rhodes scholars.[12] Suez Crisis.[13] The whiteman's bloody burden. Boer War. Bantustans.[14] Sitting in a theater in London in the seventies. A play called *West of Suez*. A lousy play about British colonials. The finale comes when several well-known white actors are machine-gunned by several lesser-known Black actors. (As Nina Simone says: 'This is a show tune but the show hasn't been written for it yet.')

The red empire of geography classes. 'The sun never sets on the British empire and you can't trust it in the dark'. Or with the dark peoples. 'Because of the Industrial Revolution European countries went in search of markets and raw materials.' Another geography (or was it a history) lesson.

Their bloody kings and their bloody queens. Their bloody peers. Their bloody generals. Admirals. Explorers. Livingstone. Hillary. Kitchener.[15] All the bwanas. And all their beaters, porters, sherpas. Who found the source of the Nile. Victoria Falls. The tops of mountains. Their so-called discoveries reek of untruth. How many dark people died so they could misname the physical features in their blasted gazetteer. A statistic we shall never know. Dr. Livingstone, I presume you are here to rape our land and enslave our people.

There are statues of these dead white men all over London.

An interesting fact: The swearword 'bloody' is a contraction of 'by my lady' – a reference to the Virgin Mary. They do tend to use their ladies. Name ages for them. Places for them. Use them as screens, inspirations, symbols. And many of the ladies comply. While the national martyr Edith Cavell was being executed by the Germans in 1915 in Belgium (called 'poor little Belgium' by the Allies in the war), the Belgians were engaged in the exploitation of the land and peoples of the Congo.

And will we ever know how many dark peoples were 'imported' to fight in whitemen's wars? Probably not. Just as we will never know how many hearts were cut from African people so that the Christian doctor might be a success[16] – i.e., extend a whiteman's life. Our Sister Killjoy observes this from her black-eyed squint.

Dr. Schweitzer[17] – humanitarian, authority on Bach, winner of the Nobel Peace Prize – on the people of Africa: 'The Negro is a child, and with children nothing can be done without the use of authority. We must, therefore, so arrange the circumstances of our daily life that my authority can find expression. With regard to Negroes, then, I have coined the formula: "I am your brother, it is true, but your elder brother."' (*On the Edge of the Primeval Forest,* 1961)

They like to pretend we didn't fight back. We did: with obeah, poison, revolution. It simply was not enough.

'Colonies . . . these places where 'niggers' are cheap and the earth is rich.' (W.E.B. DuBois, 'The Souls of White Folk')[18]

A cousin is visiting me from Cal Tech[19] where he is getting a degree in engineering. I am learning about the Italian Renaissance. My cousin is recognizably Black and speaks with an accent. I am not and I do not – unless I am back home, where the 'twang' comes upon me. We sit for some time in a bar in his hotel and are not served. A light-skinned Jamaican comes over to our table. He is an older man – a professor at the University of London. 'Don't bother with it, you hear. They don't serve us in this bar.' A run-of-the-mill incident for all recognizably Black people in this city. But for me it is not.

Henry's eyes fill up, but he refuses to believe our informant. 'No, man, the girl is just busy'. (The girl is a fifty-year-old white woman, who may just be following orders. But I do not mention this. I have chosen sides.) All I can manage to say is, 'Jesus Christ, I hate the fucking English'. Henry looks at me. (In the family I am known as the 'lady cousin'. It has to do with how I look. And the fact that I am twenty-seven and unmarried – and for all they know, unattached. They do not know that I am really the lesbian cousin.) Our informant says – gently, but with a distinct tone of disappointment – 'My dear, is that what you're studying at the university?'

You see – the whole business is very complicated.

Henry and I leave without drinks and go to meet some of his white colleagues at a restaurant I know near Covent Garden Opera House. The restaurant caters to theatre types and so I hope there won't be a repeat of the bar scene – at least they know how to pretend. Besides, I tell myself, the owners are Italian *and* gay; they *must* be halfway decent. Henry and his colleagues work for an American company which is paying their way through Cal Tech. They mine bauxite from the hills in the middle of the island and send it to the United States. A turnaround occurs at dinner: Henry joins the whitemen in a sustained mockery of the waiters: their accents and the way they walk. He whispers to me: 'Why you want to bring us to a battyman's den, lady?' (*Battyman* = *faggot* in Jamaican.[20]) I keep quiet.

We put the whitemen in a taxi and Henry walks me to the underground station. He asks me to sleep with him. (It wouldn't be incest. His mother was a maid in the house of an uncle and Henry has not seen her since his birth. He was taken into the family. She was let go.) I say that I can't. I plead exams. I can't say that I don't want to. Because I remember what happened in the bar. But I can't say that I'm a lesbian either – even though I want to believe his alliance with the whitemen at dinner was forced: not really him. He doesn't buy my excuse. "Come on, lady, let's do it. What's the matter, you 'fraid?" I pretend I am back home and start patois to show him somehow I am not afraid, not English, not white. I tell him he's a married man and he tells me he's a ram goat. I take the train to where I am staying and try to forget the whole thing. But I don't. I remember our different skins and our different experiences within them. And I have a hard time realizing that I am angry with Henry. That to him – no use in pretending – a queer is a queer.

1981. I hear on the radio that Bob Marley is dead and I drive over the Mohawk Trail listening to a program of his music and I cry and cry and cry. Someone says: 'It wasn't the ganja that killed him, it was poverty and working in a steel foundry when he was young'.

I flash back to my childhood and a young man who worked for an aunt I lived with once. He taught me to smoke ganja behind the house. And to peel an orange with the tip of a machete without cutting through the skin – 'Love' it was called: a necklace of orange rind the result. I think about him because I heard he had become a Rastaman. And then I think about Rastas.

We are sitting on the porch of an uncle's house in Kingston – the family and I – and a Rastaman comes to the gate. We have guns but they are locked behind a false closet. We have dogs but they are tied up. We are Jamaicans and know that Rastas mean no harm. We let him in and he sits on the side of the porch and shows us his brooms and brushes. We buy some to take back to New York. 'Peace, missis.'

There were many Rastas in my childhood. Walking the roadside with their goods. Sitting outside their shacks in the mountains. The outside painted bright – sometimes with words. Gathering at Palisadoes Airport to greet the Conquering Lion of Judah.[21] They were considered figures of fun by most middle-class Jamaicans. Harmless – like Marcus Garvey.

Later: white American hippies trying to create the effect of dred in their straight white hair. The ganja joint held between their straight white teeth. 'Man, the grass is good.' Hanging out by the Sheraton pool. Light-skinned Jamaicans also dred-locked, also assuming the ganja. Both groups moving to the music but not the words. Harmless. 'Peace, brother.'

III

My grandmother: 'Let us thank God for a fruitful place.'

My grandmother: 'Let us rescue the perishing world.'

This evening on the road in western Massachusetts there are pockets of fog. Then clear spaces. Across from a pond a dog staggers in front of my headlights. I look closer and see that his mouth is foaming. He stumbles to the side of the road – I go to call the police.

I drive back to the house, radio playing "difficult" piano pieces. And I think about how I need to say all this. This is who I am. I am not what you allow me to be. Whatever you decide me to be. In a bookstore in London I show the woman at the counter my book and she stares at me for a minute, then says: 'You're a Jamaican.' 'Yes.' 'You're not at all like our Jamaicans.'

Encountering the void is nothing more or less than understanding invisibility. Of being fogbound.

Then: It was never a question of passing. It was a question of hiding. Behind Black and white perceptions of who we were – who they thought we were. Tropics. Plantations. Calypso. Cricket. We were the people with the musical voices and the coronation mugs on our parlor tables. I would be whatever figure these foreign imaginations cared for me to be. It would be so simple to let others fill in for me. So easy to startle them with a flash of anger when their visions got out of hand – but never to sustain the anger for myself.

It could become a life lived within myself. A life cut off. I know who I am but you will never know who I am. I may in fact lose touch with who I am.

I hid from my real sources. But my real sources were also hidden from me.

Now: It is not a question of relinquishing privilege. It is a question of grasping more of myself. I have found that in the real sources are concealed my survival. My speech. My voice. To be colonized is to be rendered insensitive. To have those parts necessary to sustain life numbed. And this is in some cases – in my case – perceived as privilege. The test of a colonized person is to walk through a shantytown in Kingston and not bat an eye. This I cannot do. Because part of me lives there – and as I grasp more of this part I realize what needs to be done with the rest of my life.

Sometimes I used to think we were like the Marranos – the Sephardic Jews forced to pretend they were Christians. The name was given to them by the

Christians, and meant 'pigs'. But once out of Spain and Portugal, they became Jews openly again. Some settled in Jamaica. They know who the enemy was and acted for their own survival. But they remained Jews always.

We also knew who the enemy was – I remember jokes about the English. Saying they stank. saying they were stingy, that they drank too much and couldn't hold their liquor, that they had bad teeth. were dirty and dishonest, were limey bastards, and horse-faced bitches. We said the men only wanted to sleep with Jamaican women. And that the women made pigs of themselves with Jamaican men.

But of course this was seen by us – the light-skinned middle class – with a double vision. We learned to cherish that part of us that was them – and to deny the part that was not. Believing in some cases that the latter part had ceased to exist.

None of this is as simple as it may sound. We were colorists and we aspired to oppressor status. (Of course, almost any aspiration instilled by Western civilization is to oppressor status: success, for example.) Color was the symbol of our potential: color taking in hair 'quality', skin tone, freckles, nose-width, eyes. We did not see that color symbolism was a method of keeping us apart: in the society, in the family, between friends. Those of us who were light-skinned, straight-haired, etc., were given to believe that we could actually attain whiteness – or at least those qualities of the colonizer which made him superior. We were convinced of white supremacy. If we failed, we were not really responsible for our failures: we had all the advantages – but it was that one persistent drop of blood, that single rogue gene that made us unable to conceptualize abstract ideas, made us love darkness rather than despise it, which was to be blamed for our failure. Our dark part had taken over: an inherited imbalance in which the doom of the creole was sealed.

I am trying to write this as clearly as possible, but as I write I realize that what I say may sound fabulous, or even mythic. It is. It is insane.

Under this system of colorism – the system which prevailed in my childhood in Jamaica, and which has carried over to the present – rarely will dark and light people co-mingle. Rarely will they achieve between themselves an intimacy informed with identity. (I should say here that I am using the categories light and dark both literally and symbolically. There are dark Jamaicans who have achieved lightness and the 'advantages' which go with it by their successful pursuit of oppressor status.)

Under this system light and dark people will meet in those ways in which the light-skinned person imitates the oppressor. But imitation goes only so far: the light-skinned person becomes an oppressor in fact. He/she will have a dark chauffeur, a dark nanny, a dark maid, and a dark gardener. These employees will be paid badly. Because of the slave past, because of their dark skin, the servants of the middle class have been used according to the traditions of the slavocracy. They are not seen as workers for their own sake, but for the sake of the family who has employed them. It was not until Michael Manley became prime minister that a minimum wage for houseworkers was enacted[22] – and the indignation of the middle class was profound.

During Manley's leadership the middle class began to abandon the island in droves. Toronto. Miami. New York. Leaving their houses and business behind and sewing cash into the tops of suitcases. Today – with a new regime[23] – they are returning: 'Come back to the way things used to be' ' the tourist advertisement on American t.v. says. 'Make it Jamaica again. Make it your own'.

But let me return to the situation of houseservants as I remember it: They will be paid badly, but they will be 'given' room and board. However, the key to the larder will be kept by the mistress in her dresser drawer. They will spend Christmas with the family of their employers and be given a length of English wool for trousers or a few yards of cotton for dresses. They will see their children on their days off: their extended family will care for the children the rest of the time. When the employers visit their relations in the country, the servants may be asked along – oftentimes the servants of the middle class come from the same part of the countryside their employers have come from. But they will be expected to work while they are there. Back in town, there are parts of the house they are allowed to move freely around; other parts they are not allowed to enter. When the family watches the t.v. the servant is allowed to watch also, but only while standing in a doorway. The servant may have a radio in his/her room, also a dresser and a cot. Perhaps a mirror. There will usually be one ceiling light. And one small square louvered window . . . .

The houseworker/mistress relationship in which one Black woman is the oppressor of another Black woman is a cornerstone of the experience of many Jamaican women . . . .

We are women who come from a place almost incredible in its beauty. It is a beauty which can mask a great deal and which has been used in that way. But that the beauty is there is a fact. I remember what I thought of the freedom of my childhood, in which the fruitful place was something I took for granted. Just as I took for granted Zoe's appearance every morning on my school vacations – in the sense that I knew she would be there. That she would always be the one to visit me. The perishing world of my grandfather's graces at the table, if I ever seriously thought about it, was somewhere else.

Our souls were affected by the beauty of Jamaica, as much as they were affected by our fears of darkness.

There is no ending to this piece of writing. There is no way to end it. As I read back over it, I see that we/they/I may become confused in the mind of the reader: but these pronouns have always co-existed in my mind. The Rastas talk of the 'I and I' – a pronoun in which they combine themselves with Jah. Jah is a contraction of Jahweh and Jehova, but to me always sounds like the beginning of *Jamaica*. I and Jamaica is who I am. No matter how far I travel – how deep the ambivalence I feel about ever returning. And Jamaica is a place in which we/they/ I connect and disconnect – change place.

NOTES

1. 'Zoe' appears also in Cliff's novel of childhood, *Abeng* (1984), in a similar relationship with the character Clare Savage.
2. Paule Marshall, whose parents migrated from Barbados to the United States, was born in 1929 and grew up in Brooklyn, New York. Her novel, *Brown Girl, Brownstones,* published in 1961, is about Barbadian immigrants in Brooklyn during the Great Depression and the Second World War. She has written three other novels, *The Chosen Place, The Timeless People* (1969), *Praisesong for the Widow* (1983) and *Daughters* (1991), and two collections of short stories.
3. Peter Pan, Wendy and the lost boys appear in Never-Never Land in the fairy-tale play, *Peter Pan* (1904), by J.M. Barrie (1860–1937). It is a play about childish innocence and never growing up.
4. Joan of Arc (1412–31) is a national heroine and patron saint of France, Edith Cavell (1865–1915) was an English nurse who was executed by German soldiers, Florence Nightingale (1820–1915) was an English nurse who organised and directed nursing services during the Crimean War in Turkey, and Jane Austen (1775–1817) was an English author who wrote *Pride and Prejudice* (1813) and other novels.
5. *Great Expectations* (1861) is a novel by Charles Dickens (1812–70) in which a poor boy, Pip, befriends the haughty Estella.
6. *Sula* (1973) is the second novel by Toni Morrison (born in 1931), an African-American writer whose other works include *The Bluest Eye* (1970), *Song of Solomon* (1977), *Tar Baby* (1981), *Beloved* (1987) and *Jazz* (1992). She won the Nobel Prize for literature in 1993.
7. The wedding between Charles, the Prince of Wales, and Lady Diana Spencer.
8. The Irish Republican Army was very active in the 1980s and it was feared it would disrupt the royal wedding.
9. Kiri te Kanawa, a soprano from New Zealand, sang 'Let the Bright Seraphin' from Handel's 'Samson' at the royal wedding in St Paul's cathedral.
10. Robert Browning (1812–89) was one of Victorian England's greatest poets, known especially for *The Ring and the Book* (1869).
11. The Emancipation Act was passed in July 1833 but did not take effect until August 1, 1834, and even then the former slaves remained tied to their masters in a system of coerced labour called apprenticeship which lasted until 1838.
12. Rhodes scholarships, named after the British imperialist Sir Cecil Rhodes, were established in 1902 to enable students from the empire, Germany and the United States to study at Oxford University.
13. The Suez War occurred in 1956 when Britain, France and Israel tried to overthrow the Arab nationalist leader of Egypt, Gamel Abdel Nasser (1918–70), in order to control the Suez Canal. Under pressure from the United States, the war was aborted.
14. The Boer War (1899–1902) was fought between the British and the Boers who were descended from Dutch settlers in southern Africa. When the Boers were defeated, their

republics became part of the British colony of South Africa. The Bantustans were 'black homelands' established as part of the apartheid system from the 1950s to 1994 to keep the 'races' separate in South Africa.

15. David Livingston (1813–73) was a Scottish doctor and missionary; Sir Edmund Hillary (born in 1919), a New Zealander, and a Sherpa guide, Tenzing Norgay, were the first people to climb to the summit of Mount Everest, in 1953; and Lord Kitchener (1850–1916) was a British military officer known for his brutal conquest of Sudan (1895–98) and his incompetent leadership as the secretary of state for war from 1914 to 1916.

16. Dr Christiaan Barnard (1922–2001) was a South African surgeon who performed the first human heart-transplant operation in 1967.

17. Albert Schweitzer (1875–1965) was a German philosopher, theologian, musician, doctor and missionary who established a hospital in Lambarene, French Equatorial Africa (now Gabon) in 1913.

18. W.E.B. DuBois (1868–1963), an African-American historian and sociologist, and a leading Pan-Africanist, wrote 'The Souls of White Folk' (1910) and some 20 books, including *The Souls of Black Folk* (1903), *Black Reconstruction* (1935) and an autobiography, *Dusk of Dawn* (1940).

19. Cal Tech is short for the California Institute of Technology, a university in Pasadena that was founded in 1891.

20. These are offensive terms for a gay or homosexual man.

21. When Haile Selassie, the Emperor of Ethiopia, one of whose titles is the Conquering Lion of Judah, visited Jamaica in 1966, he was greeted at the Palisadoes airport by thousands of enthusiastic Rastafarians.

22. The Minimum Wage Law (1975) provided for the regulation of hours and minimum wages, possibly tripling the lowest wages in private homes and sweatshops.

23. When Cliff wrote this, the Jamaica Labour Party was in power and Edward Seaga was the prime minister.

Forty

Clive Y. Thomas

Clive Y. Thomas, born in 1936 in Guyana, earned a BSc in Economics from the University of London and PhD from the London School of Economics in 1964. He has taught at the University of the West Indies in Jamaica, the University of Dar-es-Salaam in Tanzania, Colgate University in the United States and has directed the Institute of Development Studies at the University of Guyana. His many publications include Dynamics of West Indian Economic Integration *(with Havelock Brewster, 1967),* Dependence and Transformation *(1974),* Plantations, Peasants, and State *(1984),* The Rise of the Authoritarian State in Peripheral Societies *(1984) and* The Poor and the Powerless *(1988). He has been a consultant to the International Labour Office and a member of the Coordination Committee on the Caribbean Technology Policy Studies Project. He has been an advisor to trade unions, a member of the Ratoon group, and an executive member of the Working People's Alliance in Guyana. Thomas had personal experience of the 'democratic authoritarian state': he was expelled from Jamaica in 1969, about ten months after Walter Rodney was banned, and he survived an attempt to kidnap him when he was a member of the Movement Against Oppression in Guyana in the early 1970s.*

An Alternative Conception of Development

Development: Meaning and Purpose

I conclude this book by outlining an alternative conception of development in the region . . . . One of the points I hope that this book has made is that development is about people, about the concrete context of their existence, and that this is largely influenced by the social conditions they inherit and the movements and rhythms underlying them. Even though people make history with their daily lives, they do not and indeed cannot expect to start with a clean slate. But if development and change are about people, then it is they who should ultimately choose what path they wish to pursue. Individuals and groups can offer ideas, suggestions and leadership, but the ultimate test of their efficacy lies in the willingness of the people to adopt them as part of their daily existence. What I offer here, therefore, is no more than a tentative starting point for a pathway to be carved out by the willing actions of the people themselves, working as much in concert as is socially and politically possible at a given time.

It is important to remember that the pattern and rhythm of growth the region has inherited is also the point of departure for constructing a new economy and society and that if new economic and social foundations are to be built, the old ones must be pulled down. Consequently, any plans or programmes that act outside the historical possibilities of these inheritances and the radical (revolutionising) zeal of the people are bound to be frustrated. It is also important not to underestimate just how depressing daily life is for the broad mass of Caribbean people who are poor and powerless and how stark the contrast between their life styles and those of the small minority who make up the rich and powerful. The existence of this inequality is a clear reminder of how easy it has been for social forces of underdevelopment and dependency to reproduce themselves and how, under conditions of negative real growth and declining per capita real incomes, a minority can still prosper. The mushrooming of black-market goods and foreign currency in Jamaica and Guyana show that even in the context of widespread deprivation and shortages, a small minority has been able to 'capture' supplies for themselves and to monopolise the scarcity values these commodities generate in the market place.

The region's economic policies are still largely based on the assumption that development and a satisfactory growth rate of per capita product are one and the same thing, with the main constraint to its achievement (maintaining a balance-of-payments equilibrium) being externally induced and internal imbalances (such as unemployment and domestic inflation) holding far less significance. While a number of different options have been espoused on what constitutes a satisfactory rate of growth, it is only recently that popular forces have sought to challenge this line of argument with a double line of attack.

The first advances the view that, although perhaps willing to agree on what constitutes an acceptable rate of growth, it is important to know whether the chosen rate can be *sustained* before deciding whether or not development is taking place. Posing this issue in this way raises some ancillary questions. For example, is the rate of increase of per capita national product brought about by the existence in the country of some non-renewable resource for which there happens to be a world demand, such as oil in Trinidad-Tobago or bauxite in Jamaica and Guyana? If so, what are the reserves of these resources and their current and projected rates of exploitation? How far into the future can favourable demand conditions be projected? Does the satisfactory rate of increase depend on foreign borrowing? If so, what are the prospects of it continuing? Is per capita national product increasing because of reduced population pressure brought about by the mass emigration which has taken place since the Second World War? If so, what are the prospects of the political and social conditions that make this possible continuing?

The second line of attack argues that such a formulation of development ignores the region's internal problems, such as growing unemployment, the worsening distribution of income and wealth and the persistence of poverty. This criticism was particularly marked during the unprecedented rates of increase per capita nation product in the 1950s and 1960s in the region as a whole and in the 1970s and early 1980s in Trinidad-Tobago.[1]

Liberal tendencies among the ruling strata have responded to these challenges by introducing social and political considerations into the development analysis, but these usually remain somewhat incidental to the interpretation of development and the debate continues to be conducted at an institutional level, at best. The approach adopted in this book, however, differs from the liberal approach in that it expressly includes class and social relations as integral dimensions of development. The liberals never ask for whom the development is supposed to take place, but it is important to recognise early on that how development is interpreted, defined and measured goes a long way towards determining what development path is pursued. Asking who the development is for also helps determine the criteria for future development strategies and policies.

Our *first task*, therefore, is to identify the essential rhythms of underdevelopment in the region so that *strategic* choices can be made about how these rhythms should be altered. Thereafter, the development of lines of production, consumption and social organisation can be deduced.

As I have repeatedly argued throughout this book, development in the Caribbean cannot be studied in isolation. The question of alternative paths of development has to be raised within the historical context of the concrete manifestation *on a world scale* of a group of countries described as 'underdeveloped' (as distinct from undeveloped which might have been the condition of Europe before the development of capitalism). For our purpose, this underdevelopment (when used to describe the condition of the region) refers to the consequences of the long period (16th–18th century) during which capitalism became an international system of production and created a world market. During this process of internationalisation, two important divergences emerged in the way in which the material conditions of social life in the Caribbean were reproduced.

The first was that as market relations became more and more generalised and entrenched in the regional economy, a systemic divergence occurred between the pattern of resource use and the demand structure. This happened because European conquest and settlement destroyed the communal and other pre-capitalist production relations which prevailed at that time in the Caribbean. Thereafter, domestic resources were systematically garnered to service overseas markets in Europe and elsewhere. The development of tropical export cash crops (sugar, cotton, spices, cocoa and coffee), mineral production for export (oil and bauxite), services (offshore finance and tourism) and even the recent wave of export-processing firms operating from regional enclaves, are all reflections of this orientation.

The second was that the export sector became highly specialised in producing and selling what is still essentially a very narrow range of products to one or two major capitalist markets. Even now, when there is so much talk about revitalising the region's agriculture, the focus is either on non-traditional exports (such as exotic flowers) to special access markets (CBI),[2] or on reviving dying speciality crops (such as sea-island cotton and arrowroot). The internal regional market is thus neglected at a time when masses of small farmers are living in poverty and over US$1,000 million is spent on food imports from outside the region. This divergence developed as the market economy spread and the ability to purchase (to command money incomes) became the principal determinant of consumption. As a result, ever since colonisation, the needs of the broad mass of poor people have played virtually no part in directing the course of production, for, apart from a few residual subsistence sectors in some territories, commodities from both local production and imports are allocated on the basis of purchasing power. In the context of widespread poverty and unemployment, this has resulted in a systemic bias in favour of servicing the needs of the relatively better off. Even where commodities have become popular consumer items (for example, poultry and consumer durables such as radios, televisions and cookers), their import content remains high (over 80 per cent in several territories for the above items) with the result that domestic production of these products has become a thinly-disguised form of importation.

If this is the dynamic for reproducing the material needs of the society as a whole, then it follows that the complex set of political, social and legal relations (patterns of ownership of productive factors); institutions, organisations and other decision-making structures; and ideas and ideologies have grown out of and dialectically interact with this rhythm of production. It is therefore only through understanding this expression of the condition of underdevelopment that we can begin to understand what constitutes development.

The *second task*, therefore, is to indicate what development (as the negation of underdevelopment) means in the Caribbean context. Eight points seem critical. In the first instance, and in direct contrast to what prevails, development requires a system of ownership, control and production oriented towards satisfying the basic needs of the masses. By the masses is simply meant all those who are poor and who do not have any power in society derived from property, wealth, religion, caste, expertise or other sources not widely shared, including political party affiliation. This definition recognises that, in the past, property relations and production have benefited too few at the expense of too many. It explicitly states that redistribution, social equality and a participatory political process should be the cornerstone of another kind of development in which the concerns of the poor and powerless are central rather than incidental items on an agenda for some other disembodied abstraction, such as export competitiveness, building an industrial sector, or developing a new and appropriate technology. In other words, production aimed at providing for the basic needs of the masses, in the first instance, implies a systematic, conscious, deliberate and planned attack on poverty. Eliminating poverty should not be treated merely as a possible or desirable consequence of production, which is what happens when profit is the main determinant of output.

The basic needs of the masses are either personal (food, clothing, housing) or public/collective (health, sanitation, education, culture, recreation), or seen differently, both material (food, clothing, housing) and non-material (health, education). During the heyday of Bishop's rule in Grenada, Burnham's in Guyana and Manley's in Jamaica,[3] there was much talk of a 'basic needs' approach to development, but in practice such programmes failed to reorient the system of production, although they probably did in some instances heighten concern about social equality. In Guyana, the basic needs programme coincided with a period in which the real incomes of the masses actually fell. In fact Cuba is the only territory in the region where redistributive ideals and popular enhancement of the status of the masses is a motive force in economic production. The effects of this are particularly obvious in areas such as health care, recreation, sport and education. Apart from this, there are only a few isolated examples of communities where this conception of the purpose and meaning of social production is accepted . . .

Second, there can only be real development in the region if these basic needs are satisfied through planned and effective implementation of the right to work. This implies not only that all those who want jobs have them, but that they also have (i) the right to a job without coercion as to place and type of work (given their particular skills); (ii) a framework of industrial relations that permits free collective bargaining and effective (as distinct from nominal) representation within bargaining units; (iii) a work process that allows for effective worker involvement and control; (iv) health protection and guaranteed education and training for tasks they are engaged in; and (v) an end to discrimination based on sex, colour, ethnicity, age or physical disability.

The objective is to situate work within a process of self-realisation, so that for West Indians work is both an end in itself and a means of development. The persistence of high levels of unemployment (ranging from 18 to 40 per cent and more in some instances) is an unacceptable social scourge which will not simply 'disappear' as per capita incomes grow. It has to be tackled as a separate objective. The stress on making work more meaningful is to counteract the humiliating and degrading practice sometimes employed by governments in the region of paying a limited number of people to perform meaningless tasks for brief and uncertain periods of time to 'ease the unemployment problem'. Not surprisingly, this has often degenerated into a form of political patronage. It is also to restrain progressive forces from directing labour from above as a short-cut to development and full employment, a practice which, as experience in Guyana has shown, can degenerate into enforced labour, often requiring state employees to abandon their rights to choose a job without coercion or to select the place of their employment.

Third, to reverse the region's authoritarian tradition, the material conditions of life should be reproduced within a self-reliant and endogenous pattern of growth. This is in fact the only sustainable pattern of growth given the particular historical formation of underdevelopment (with its resultant pattern of producing what is not consumed locally and consuming what is not produced locally) and the widespread foreign ownership and domination of production in the region. It is premised on the need to reverse dependency relations and to situate development in the Caribbean in the context of the capacity of people of all regions to develop themselves. Various forms of cooperation and self-organisation, such as the community councils in Jamaica, the sou-sou land societies in Trinidad-Tobago,[4] the agricultural cooperative movement in Dominica and the activities of the Caribbean Conference of Churches should be encouraged and regarded as mainstays in the organisation of economic activity. Fortunately, a regional research project is being launched to study these phenomena in Guyana, Grenada, Jamaica, Belize, Cuba and Nicaragua.

Fourth, development also implies that work, politics and social organisations are based on democratising power in society and on the effective (as opposed to nominal) exercise of fundamental rights, such as those to free expression and organisation, respect of an individual's privacy and the abolition of repression and torture. The democratisation of power also implies the democratisation of all the decision-making structures in the society, from the level of the workplace and community right through to central government. An equitable distribution of wealth and income, equitable access to the use and management of society's resources and equitable access to information are, of course, necessary requirements for achieving this objective. Being in full possession of all the necessary information is absolutely vital if sound decisions are to be made, if control from below is to be assured and if popular participation in development is to be socially efficient.

This point explicitly seeks to negate certain aspects of social life in the Caribbean. One of these is the somewhat authoritarian view (held on the right and the left) that direct democracy can act as a substitute for the political democracy embodied in representative political institutions. In other words, direct democracy should complement rather than replace political democracy. Another is to conceive of political democracy as a colonial or local ruling-class 'trick'. Rights of representation and political forms of democracy do exist in the region (they were won through the heroic struggles of the masses), but are limited because they exist within a social context in which inequalities of income and wealth are systematically reproduced. Thus, as far as practical considerations go, they are severely constrained. The task in hand is to secure economic and social rights so as to negate these limiting considerations and not to reduce their significance by caricaturing them as a 'longing for British parliamentarianism', as certain left circles in the region are wont to do.

Fifth, development also implies preserving the stability of the environment and putting an end to the degradation it has suffered through the growth of national production in Caribbean societies. This is a simple and straightforward point which merely seeks to situate the region's development within the context of an unequivocal acceptance of our universal responsibility to protect the environment and sustain life.

Sixth, it is important to recognise that because of the polarity between the state and private sector, the state would have to play an important part in the development of the region, but only within the context of a participatory political process in which the ordinary West Indian's status as a citizen, producer and consumer of wealth was enhanced. To achieve this, the economic process would have to be based on workers having strong organisational and representational roles in their places of work. There is no doubt that, even when it has ostensibly been pursuing the public good, the West Indian state has revealed many weaknesses, which advocates of privatisation have successfully exploited (often through the use of Reaganite propaganda) in moulding the consciousness of the West Indian masses. So successful have they been that it is not generally recognised how frequently they turn to the state for help in promoting their own interests, in negotiating with foreign agencies and countries when they have difficulties gaining access for their products (often because of high local costs), or for providing domestic protection when competition from abroad adversely affects their operations.

The truth of the matter is that the private sector (the local capitalist class) in the region is incapable of directing a process of economic development that could ensure a sustained increase in the living standards of the broad mass of the population, reduce unemployment to the barest minimum and achieve an acceptable degree of social and political equality. The local capitalist class is limited in its vision (it does not even advocate the kinds of reforms many metropolitan capitalists uphold) and this is particularly evident in periods of crisis. Whereas Colonial Office officials looked inward for solutions during the Depression in the 1930s and the Second World War, all the solutions to the crisis of the 1980s are looked for outside the region, through measures such as more aid or better access for traditional crops. In Jamaica under Seaga,[5] for example, recourse to the CBI (Caribbean Basin Initiative) and the development of non-traditional exports are the two most frequently relied on strategies for trying to solve the country's economic impasse. Yet, despite the publicity, Jamaica's exports to the US have declined by 27 per cent since 1984. Bank credit to the much touted manufacturing sector declined by 64 per cent between 1983 and 1985 and imports of industrial raw materials fell by 19 per cent over the same period. The high rate of growth in non-traditional non-CARICOM exports has in reality meant an expansion from US$0.45 million in 1980 to US$0.88 million in 1986 – a pitiful amount in absolute values.

The new manufacturing bourgeoisie in the region operates much like the absentee planter class of old. Most of its members live in two societies, with assets in each, the local ones always hedged by foreign ones. Levels of inefficiency and corruption are high. On the Jamaican stock-market insider trading and conflicts of interest are rife . . . .

Whether or not the government intervenes *per se* is neither here nor there. What is significant, however, is the purpose of the government intervention and what class and social interests it serves or seeks to serve. It is pure fantasy to believe that political freedom in the region can be reduced to, or is in some way dependent on, the operation of unrestrained market forces. The interpretation of development advanced here is intended to subject the functioning of the state, as well as the development of the society as a whole, to what has been aptly termed the 'logic of the majority' . . . In other words, given the authoritarian traditions of colonial and plantation autocracies in the region, alienation is a characteristic feature of life for large sections of the population, particularly the poor and powerless. It is therefore important to avoid reinforcing this alienation by uncritically accepting the vague notions of development that seek to galvanise people into projects which then substantively marginalise them by turning them into the objects of the project.

Seventh, a realistic approach to development in the region must begin by recognising the stark reality of the hostile environment created by living in imperialism's backyard:

Whatever may be the economic logic of US policies towards Central America and the Caribbean, it is clear that geopolitical considerations predominate. Historically, the region has always been considered 'America's backyard'. So long as the area was thought to be secure, the US could afford to ignore it; but any threat to the status quo has always triggered an immediate response. US military intervention in the region has been more frequent than in any other part of the world . . . . the underlying assumption of US policy towards the region appears to be that its own geopolitical interests are incompatible with the emergence of genuinely independent states.[6]

Given this incompatibility, the future scope for development in the region is ultimately bound up with the survival and eventual success of the region's two major social experiments, Cuba and Nicaragua. It is important to recognise that this view does not imply that Cuba, Nicaragua, or even a combination of the two, have to be accepted as future models for the poor and powerless to adopt, but rather that the survival of the *very notion of experimenting to build new Caribbean societies is indissolubly linked to the survival of the only two surviving experiments*. It provides, as it were, a regional alternative and, as such, must remain a high priority in any development thrust. Given the historical circumstances, an effective regional alternative must at all times and in all situations seek to challenge the mechanisms that facilitate the absorption of the region into the US. And it must do so especially at this critical time when the US is pursuing the larger projects of engulfing Canada and Mexico and securing the submission of Central America through undeclared war against the region's popular forces.[7]

And eighth, the criticisms mounted against Lomé, CARIBCAN[8] and the CBI in the previous chapter should not be taken to mean that the external context is irrelevant to the region's successful development. On the contrary, the chosen path of development cannot realistically be separated from the outside world. The interface between internal class struggle and the international operation of capitalism is a crucially important consideration to take into account and it is for this reason that proposals designed to offer a 'global challenge' to existing structures are, I believe, of some importance[9] . . . The sad reality, however, is that multilateralism is in retreat and unilateralism is dominant; protectionism in the north is the order of the day, while monetarism and *laissez-faire* policies are prevalent in both the north and the south. In this context, therefore, it is all the more important to successful development that accumulation should take place within national boundaries, but given how small most of the region's economies are and the high social costs of small size, the only realistic solution is to develop a regional alternative as an essential part of the process of national transformation.

Accumulation: Basic Goods and Basic Needs

In outlining an alternative conception of development, the *third task* is to tackle three key problems identified above. These are (i) that the pattern of consumption in the region fails to satisfy the basic needs of the broad mass of the population (it instead reflects the unequal distribution of wealth and income, disparities in urban and rural development and the poverty and dispossession of large social groups, particularly the peasants and urban poor); (ii) that because imperatives for bringing resources into production in the past derived largely from the needs of international capitalist expansion, the pattern of resource use and resource endowment are improperly reconciled; and (iii) reflecting the situation in i and ii above, the pattern of property ownership and the social relations centring on this, show sharp and worsening inequalities both at the national/international level and within each national territory. Because of the systemic nature of these problems, it follows that the configurations of a transformed regional economy must be based on the *construction of a process of accumulation founded on the priorities required to ensure the eventual reversal of these divergences*. In other words, accumulation has to be founded on the logic of a dynamic convergence between social needs and the use of domestic resources.

In the past, even in revolutionary Cuba, this was taken to mean a simple sequence of import substitution. Beginning with the products in greatest demand, attempts were made through limiting imports to foster the development of local or joint-venture enterprises to produce these products. As my earlier critique of the industrialization process showed, this pattern of industrialization not only takes import demand (and hence the prevailing pattern of consumption) as desirable, but more often than not results in assembly and fabricating concerns with very little domestic value added and a very high import content. Its main weakness is its failure to grasp the source of the divergences. That source lies in the inability of the productive factors (as they currently exist) to produce the commodities used directly or indirectly in the production of all other commodities. The region's development strategies should at the very least aim to develop a domestic capability in this regard. Goods used directly and indirectly in the production of all other goods can be termed 'basic goods'.

It is often claimed that starting import-substitution industrialization with the final goods will, in the long run, create market incentives strong enough to produce backward linkages so that more and more inputs into the final process are attained. Nowhere, however, have market forces successfully induced this backward expansion . . .

A far more suitable alternative would be to create a basic goods sector. This approach is supported by a survey of world consumption patterns and their basic material input requirements, which shows that of the millions of products currently consumed around the world, only a dozen raw materials (iron and steel, cement, rubber, textiles, glass, leather, paper, plastics, industrial chemicals, aluminum, wood and fuels) account for more than 90 per cent of all the basic materials used in manufacturing. The list of basic foods is similarly short and the pattern is revealed in both capitalist and socialist economies.

The conclusion of all this is that for the region to embark on another development, three priorities have to be taken into account in the process of accumulation. These form the strategic choices or options to be pursued and it is from them that detailed programmes, sub-programmes and specific production activities should be based. They are (i) agricultural production oriented towards supplying the needs of the population in the *first instance* and with export specialization following on as an extension of this. (The population's needs include food as well as raw materials. This reorientation would require major social changes, including radical land reform, a generally enhanced social status for traditional small farmers and a scientific and technological capability in these domestically-consumed crops); (ii) developing a capacity to produce basic materials as a key element in the industrialisation strategy . . . and (iii) raising the level of economic and technical competence, although not necessarily increasing output, in the entrenched mineral and agro-exporting sector. (This is necessary to lower costs and enhance foreign-exchange inflows, to support the process of diversification, to extend the use of an internally developed scientific production capacity and to exploit the scope for innovation leading not only to lower costs but also to new products based on old lines of production.) Colonial policies and the downgrading of the region's technological capacity are not wholly responsible for the low level of technical competence in the traditional export sector. Petroleum was produced in Trinidad-Tobago for almost 80 years before a national research initiative was undertaken (nearly two decades after independence) in 1982, and here the focus of research has been on enhanced recovery methods.

It should be borne in mind that accumulation must be subordinated to socio-political priorities if it is to be interiorised in the society. Unless this happens, the material base of Caribbean social life will not complement the indispensable prerequisite of the move towards political and social change being generated from within the society. In the region, neither political nor economic decisions revolve around the issues of the society. This does not derive solely from its openness, as some presume, but essentially from the general marginalisation of the masses from social life. It is this marginalisation that allows the present ruling class to treat their hard-won independence (after centuries of slavery and exploitation) so carelessly.

Because the region is so open and vulnerable in the present world context, the approach outlined here encourages, but does not guarantee, its participation in the world system in such a manner that it does not automatically become a hapless victim of the system's systematic reproduction of inequalities. It is evident from the protectionism in the north, from the foreign-exchange and development pressures in the south (which are imposing more and more restrictions on imports), from the secular decline in primary commodity prices, from the former consumers of West Indian exports themselves becoming exporters of the same products (sugar from the EEC,[10] oil from Britain and rice from Indonesia) and from the technological changes which are undermining the region as an export-processing zone, that the traditional exports and the new exports from the EPZs cannot constitute an 'engine for the region's growth'. By creating both a *social base* (with the orientation towards needs) and a *material base* (with the emphasis on domestic resources) for the development of a scientific and technological capability in the region, this difficulty is overcome. One of the striking characteristics of the region is that even in its area of specialisation and comparative advantage in the world economy, it does not have highly-developed technical or scientific competences. An essential task of economic construction must be to create them, but this can only be done from a material base and within a logic of accumulation that explicitly promotes and accommodates it.

It is clear from the above that since size imposes an important constraint on the region's development, a reversal of its present balkanisation is essential to the task of successfully pursuing the path of another development. The resolute and relentless pursuit of the interests of the poor and powerless requires an equally resolute and relentless pursuit of regional unity. Indeed, in a real sense, neither is achievable by itself.

Given the nature of the Caribbean economies, transforming them will inevitably be an extended social project. Nevertheless, it is still necessary (as part of the mobilizing effort of the society) to incorporate, as early in the process as possible, a more or less definite *conception* of the main economic configurations of the economy the society is working to construct. Moreover, this conception should be elevated to the level of a *popular conception*, rather than simply remaining the possession of the economy's political leadership, technocrats and managers. Rooting the project in the popular culture is the only way of ensuring its success, of organising and promoting the development of a new social order.

Another reason for having a clear idea of the configurations of the economy under construction is that it provides a point of reference with which *to test and measure its performance and development. This is important since there are no purely technical tests of a process as profound as the transformation of an economy.* The crisis in the region accentuates the importance of this point, for there is an ever-present danger that, unless the popular consciousness embraces the vision of another development, the many 'quick-fix' solutions being offered and attempted will take on an impetus of their own and, in the process, become the end product of development itself.

The issue of property and social relations is central to the re-direction of the accumulation process. Contrary to popular left orthodoxy in the region, at this conjuncture the formulation presented here neither implies nor requires extensive state ownership, nor that the process be centrally planned and directed. On the contrary, it seeks to promote development from below, so that the vision of popular participation in a political democracy is translated into popular and participatory forms of ownership as well as economic policies and activities. In fact, at the present stage in the region's development, many factors work against extensive state enterprise and the possibility of being able to direct centrally planned economic change. These include a shortage of skills, lack of data and information, the instability of the region's price-formation process, the heterogeneity of production and the entrenchment of corruption and bureaucratisation in central government. The new development, however, envisages a different conjunction of state-society relations as the social complement to policies of economic transformation . . .

Views, popularly regarded as progressive in the past, which equate state ownership of the productive factors and state direction of the economy with the transition to a higher order of economic, social and political organisation are, in my view, dangerous and are consequently rejected in my formulation, as are those which equate the entrenchment of democratic social forms with the entrenchment of a state elite and/or vanguard group 'chosen' by the people to give leadership to the 'immense majority' – the poor and the powerless.

In conclusion, it should be stated that, at the philosophical level, this formulation, along with the critical analysis of economic policy which had preceded it, seeks to do two things. One is to challenge the traditional ways of perceiving the operation of economic processes in the region, and hopefully in other countries of the third world where the basic conditions are sufficiently similar. The other is to dramatise the 'poverty of the received doctrines' in which economic policy is more often than not framed. The 'poverty' is clearly revealed in the many 'irrationalities' and paradoxes which prevail within the economic order and which, as we have shown, public policy systematically reinforces. Thus we find that despite the widespread under- and unemployment of the labour force and the absence of any form of institutionalized unemployment relief, public policy continues to direct a high proportion of the region's resources into subsidising foreign capital, with little or no challenge. Similarly, one would imagine that a rational system would require a society to treat its people and its land as its premier resources. Yet with all the poverty and unemployment in the region, its small size, and the dearth of resources available to its poor and powerless, both land and labour continues to be systematically under- and unutilized.

This sort of paradox or irrationality is also observed in the present regional situation where the external debt continues to be posed as a critical element of the crisis, and to which governments have invariably responded by repressing the living standards of the poor. At the same time there is a substantial haemorrhage, as the reverse flow of foreign exchange has reached a stage where the region's economic and political elites probably possess more overseas assets than the value of the public external debt. In the face of this, the current real wage of the poorest sections of the population in many countries (which include all those on the minimum wage or less and the unemployed) cannot purchase at today's prices the rations of protein (salted fish and beef), carbohydrates (corn, flour and cassava), shelter, wood fuel, working implements etc, allocated to the typical slave more than a century ago.

The prevalence of the 'black market', 'informal', 'underground' sector in some of the region's economies has reached a stage where in at least two territories (Guyana and Jamaica) it accounts for a substantial share of employment, importation of basic goods, ownership of financial assets, 'illegal' exports and earnings of foreign exchange. It includes the well-known marijuana trade and the not so well-known illegal export of precious metals from Guyana . . .

Perhaps the ultimate symbolic manifestation of these paradoxes is revealed in the appeal of the Prime Minister of St Vincent in his opening address to the CARICOM Heads of Government Conference, held in July 1987:

> Let us invite Canada, the United States and those countries of Europe which have historical links to the Caribbean to put together a development plan for this region to be called the Columbus Plan, to be launched on the anniversary date of the first landing of Christopher Columbus in this hemisphere.

As that event sparked the wanton slaughter of the region's indigenous peoples and the later enslavement of millions of Africans and Asians, it stands in cruel paradox to all our aspirations to sovereignty, independence and self-worth. It is, in other words, the very negation of the idea of a free West Indian people.

NOTES

1. When the international price of oil suddenly went up in the early 1970s, creating a crisis in those Caribbean countries that had to import oil, Trinidad and Tobago received huge revenues from its oil exports. This boom was followed by a bust after 1982 when the oil economy began to stagnate. Despite the massive windfall gains and substantial investment in industries at Point Lisas, unemployment stood at 15 per cent in 1985.
2. The Caribbean Basin Initiative (CBI) was a package of aid, trade and investment incentives, initiated by the United States in 1983. It operated on a bilateral basis, thereby creating the opportunity for the United States to play one Caribbean country

against another and to reward those governments that cooperated with the United States.

3. Maurice Bishop was prime minister of Grenada from 1979 to 1983, Forbes Burnham became premier of Guyana in 1964 and president from 1980 until his death in 1985, and Michael Manley was prime minister of Jamaica from 1972 to 1980 (and again between 1989 and 1992, after Thomas wrote this).

4. The Sou-Sou Lands project was designed to allow poor people to buy land cheaply. Sou-sou, or susu, which originated among the Yoruba of Nigeria, is a system of savings in which a number of persons each deposit a certain sum every week, with one of them taking the entire collection each week until every member of the group has received his or her share, at which point the sequence begins again.

5. Edward Seaga was prime minister of Jamaica from 1980 to 1989.

6. G. Irwin and Xavier Gorostiaga, *Towards an Alternative for Central America and the Caribbean* (London, 1985), 28.

7. The United States was negotiating the North American Free Trade Agreement (NAFTA) with Canada and Mexico, which became effective on January 1, 1994, while supporting reactionary forces in El Salvador, Guatemala, Honduras and Nicaragua.

8. Lomé, the capital of Togo, was the site of a trade agreement, called the Lomé Convention, between African, Caribbean and Pacific countries and the European Economic Community in 1975. CARIBCAN is a trade agreement between Caribbean countries and Canada, made in 1986. Thomas' criticism stems from the fact that the goal of the CBI is to integrate Caribbean countries more closely into the US orbit of capitalism. Because it operates on a bilateral basis, it enables the US to play one Caribbean country off against another. CARIBCAN, though less threatening than the CBI, would not be able to significantly transform the Caribbean economy and Lomé cannot make the poor countries 'equal partners in trade' with Europe or affect their basic poverty and underdevelopment.

9. *Global Challenge* is the name of the report by an international committee chaired by Michael Manley on economic relations between North and South (London 1985).

10. The European Economic Community.

Forty-One

Stuart Hall

Stuart Hall was born in 1932 in a middle-class family in Jamaica. He described his father as belonging to the 'coloured lower-middle-class ... ethnically very mixed – African, East Indian, Portuguese, Jewish', and his mother's family as 'much fairer in colour' and 'English-oriented' (Hall 1996, 484). He went to the UK in 1951 where he studied at Oxford University, 'was saturated in West Indian expatriate politics' (Ibid., 492), met African students, and associated with what became known as the New Left - Alan Hall, Raymond Williams, Raphael Samuel, Peter Sedgewick and Perry Anderson. He became an editor of the Universities and Left Review *which became the* New Left Review. *He moved to London in 1957 where he taught in a secondary school and edited the review until 1961. He taught media, film and popular culture at Chelsea College, University of London. He moved to Birmingham University in 1964 where he worked with, and then succeeded, Richard Hoggart as the director of the new Centre for Cultural Studies. In 1979, he became a professor of sociology at the Open University, an institution that pioneered the use of television and distance learning in higher education.*

Hall's work has been important in the formation and development of cultural studies as an interdisciplinary and international field. He is well-known for his work on questions concerning the relations between race, ethnicity, culture and identity, particularly in connection with West Indians at home and abroad.

*M*yths of Caribbean Identity

I want to talk about questions of culture and identity, specifically questions of Caribbean culture and identity, and to suggest that such questions are not in any sense separate or removed from the questions of political mobilisation, of cultural development, of national identification and of economic development. The more we know and see of the struggles of the societies of the periphery to make something of the slender resources available to them, the more important we understand the questions and problems of cultural identity to be in that process. I want to examine some of the themes of this enormous topic, which has been richly explored especially by Caribbean writers and artists – the question of cultural identity as it has presented itself always as a problem to Caribbean people.

Why it should be a problem is not a mystery, but I want to probe this question of identity and why Caribbean writers, politicians, civic leaders, artists and others have been unable to leave worrying this problem. And in doing so, I want to analyze the way we think about identity, and to explore the term 'myth' itself. The English are not good at myth; they always oppose it on the one hand to reality, on the other hand to truth, as if you have to choose between them. I specifically do not want to choose between myth and reality, but to talk about the very real contemporary and historical effects of the myths of identity, and to do so with one other purpose which I hope will come through more clearly at the end. My own view is that the issue of cultural identity as a political quest now constitutes one of the more serious global problems as we go into the twenty-first century. The re-emergence of questions of cultural identity, of ethnicity, of nationalism – the obduracy, the dangers and the pleasures of the rediscovery of identity in the modern world, inside and outside of Europe – places the question of cultural identity at the very centre of the contemporary political agenda. What I want to suggest is that, despite the dilemmas and vicissitudes of identity through which Caribbean people have passed and continue to pass, we have a tiny but important message for the world about how to negotiate identity.

There is a very clear and powerful discourse about cultural identity, especially in the West . . . But the discourse of identity suggests that the culture of a people is at root (and the question of roots is very much at issue) a question of its essence, a question of the fundamentals of a culture. Histories come and go, peoples come and go, situations change, but somewhere down there is throbbing the culture to which we all belong. It provides a kind of ground for our identities, something stabilised, around which we can organise our identities and our sense of belonging. And there is a sense that modern nations and peoples cannot survive for long and succeed without the capacity to touch ground, as it were, in the name of their cultural identities.

The question of what a Caribbean cultural identity might be has been of extraordinary importance, both before but especially during the twentieth century, partly because of the dislocations of conquest, of colonisation and slavery, and partly because of the colonial relationship itself and the distortions of living in a world culturally dependent and dominated from some centre outside the place where the majority of people lived. But it has also been important for counter-identities, providing sources from which the important movements of decolonisation, of independence, of nationalist consciousness in the region have been founded. In a sense, until it is possible to state who the subjects of independence movements are likely to be, and in whose name cultural decolonisation is being conducted, it is not possible to complete the process. And that process involves the question of defining who the people are. In *Black Skin White Masks,* Fanon[1] speaks of what he calls 'a passionate research directed to the secret hope of discovering beyond self-contempt, resignation and abjuration, some beautiful and splendid area whose existence rehabilitates us both in regard to ourselves and others'. And as I have said, that passionate research by Caribbean writers, artists and political leaders, that quest for identity, has been the very form in which much of our artistic endeavours in all the Caribbean languages has been conducted in this century.

Why then is the identity of the Caribbean so problematic? It is a very large question, but let me suggest some of the reasons. First of all, if the search for identity always involves a search for origins, it is impossible to locate in the Caribbean an origin for its peoples. The indigenous peoples of the area very largely no longer exist, and they ceased to exist very soon after the European encounter. This is indeed the first trauma of identity in the Caribbean. How many of you know what the coat of arms of Jamaica is? It has two Arawak Indian figures supporting a shield in the middle, which is crossed by pineapples surmounted by an alligator. In 1983 the then Prime Minister of Jamaica, Edward Seaga, wanted to change the coat of arms on the ground that he could not find represented in it a single recognisable Jamaican identity. 'Can the crushed and extinct Arawaks,' he asked, 'represent the dauntless inhabitants of Jamaica? Does the low-slung near-extinct crocodile, a cold-blooded reptile, symbolise the soaring spirits of Jamaicans? Where does the pineapple, which was exported to Hawaii, appear prominently either in our history or in our folklore?' I read that quote simply to remind you that questions of identity are always questions about representation. They are always questions about the invention, not simply the discovery of tradition. They are always exercises in selective memory and they almost always involve the silencing of something in order to allow something else to speak . . .

Silencing as well as remembering, identity is always a question of producing in the future an account of the past, that is to say it is always about narrative, the stories which cultures tell themselves about who they are and where they came from. The one way in which it is impossible to resolve the problem of identity in the Caribbean is to try looking at it, as if a good look will tell you who the people are. During the period in which I was preparing my BBC series,[2] I had the occasion in a relatively short space of time to visit a large number of Caribbean islands, several of which I had not seen before. I was absolutely staggered by the ethnic and cultural diversity I encountered. Not a single Caribbean island looks like any other in terms of its ethnic composition, simply from the point of view of the different genetic and physical features and characteristics of the people. And that is before you start to touch the question of different languages and cultural traditions, which reflect diverse colonising structures.

It may be a surprise to some people that there are several Caribbean islands, large ones, in which blacks are nowhere near a majority of the population. There are now two important ex-British Caribbean nations where Asians are in a majority, and in Cuba, what strikes you first of all is the long persistence of white Hispanic settlement and then of the mulatto population, and only later of the black population. Haiti, which is in some ways the symbolic island of black culture, and where one feels closer to the African inheritance than anyone else, has a history in which mulattos have played an absolutely vital and key historical role. Martinique is a bewildering place, it is in my experience more French than Paris, just slightly darker. In the Dominican Republic it is possible to feel closer to Spain and to the Spanish tradition of Latin America than anywhere else I have been in the Caribbean. The melting-pot of the British islands produced everywhere you look a different combination of genetic features and factors, and in each island elements of other ethnic cultures – Chinese, Syrian, Lebanese, Portuguese, Jewish – are present. I know because I have a small proportion of practically all of them in my own inheritance. My inheritance is African, also I'm told Scottish – of pretty low descent, probably convict – East Indian, Portuguese, Jew. I cannot summon up any more but if I searched hard I expect I could find them.

What is more, in another sense, everybody there comes from somewhere else, and it is not clear what has drawn them to it, certainly not whether the motives were ever of the highest level of aspiration. That is to say, their true cultures, the places they really come from, the traditions that really formed them, are somewhere else. The Caribbean is the first, the original and the purest diaspora. These days blacks who have completed the triangular journey back to Britain sometimes speak of the emerging black British diaspora, but I have to tell them that they and I are twice diasporised. Furthermore, we are not just living in a diaspora where the centre is always somewhere else, but we are the break with those originating cultural sources as passed through the traumas of violent rupture. I don't want to speak about the trauma of transportation, of the breaking up of linguistic and tribal and familial groups; I don't want to talk about the brutal aftermath of Asian indenture. I simply want to say that in the histories of the migration, (forced or free, of peoples who now compose the populations of these societies, whose cultural traces are everywhere intermingled with one another), is the stamp of historical violence and rupture.

Of course, the peoples thus inserted into these old colonising plantation societies instantly polarised. And if anyone is still under the illusion that questions of culture can ever be discussed free and outside of questions of power, you have only to look at the Caribbean to understand how for centuries every cultural characteristic and trait had its class, colour and racial reference. You could read off from the populations to the cultures, and from the cultures to the populations, and each was ranked in an order of cultural power. It is impossible to approach Caribbean culture without understanding the way it was continually inscribed by questions of power. Of course that inscription of culture in power relations did not remain polarised in Caribbean society, but I now understand that one of the things I was myself running away from when I came to England to study in 1951 was a society that was profoundly culturally graded; that is what the old post-colonial society I grew up in was like. Of course those cultural relations did not remain fixed, and the relative cultures were quickly open to integration, assimilation and cross-influence. They were almost never self-contained. They became subject at once to complex processes of assimilation, adoption, adaptation, resistance, reselection and so on. That is to say, they became in a deep sense diasporic societies. For wherever one finds diasporas, one always finds precisely those complicated processes of negotiation and cross-influence which characterise Caribbean culture. I don't want to try and sketch the cultural relations of that period, but simply to identify three key processes which are at work creating the enormously refined and delicate tracery, the complexes of cultural identification, in Caribbean society in that time.

First, and especially with respect to the populations that had been enslaved, there has been the retention of old customs, the retention of cultural traits from Africa. Customs and traditions which were retained in and through slavery, in plantation, in religion, partly in language, in folk customs, in music, in dance, in all those forms of expressive culture which allowed men and women to survive the trauma of slavery. These were not intact, never pure, never untouched by the culture of Victorian and pre-Victorian English society, never outside Christianity or entirely outside the reach of the church, never without at least some small instruction in the Bible, always surrounded by the colonising culture, but importantly (and to some extent today imperatively) retaining something of the connection, often unrecognised, often only in practice, often unreflected, often not knowing that people were practising within a tradition. Nevertheless, in everyday life, insofar as it was possible, maintaining some kind of subterranean link with what was often called the other Caribbean, the Caribbean that was not recognised, that could not speak, that had no official records, no official account of its own transportation, no official historians, but nevertheless had an oral life which maintained an umbilical connection with the homeland and the home culture.

But let us not forget that retention characterised the colonising cultures as well as the colonised. For if you look at the Little Englands, the Little Spains and the Little Frances that were created by the colonisers, if you consider this kind of fossilised replica, with the usual colonial cultural lag – people are always more Victorian when they're taking tea in the Himalayas than when they're taking tea in Leamington – they are keeping alive the memory of their own homes and homelands and traditions and customs. This very important double aspect of retention has marked Caribbean culture.

Secondly, the profound process of assimilation, of dragging the whole society into some imitative relationship with this other culture which one could never quite reach. When one talks about assimilation in the Caribbean, one always feels Caribbean people constantly leaning forward, almost about to tip over, always just going somewhere else. My mother used to tell me that if she could only get hold of the right records, she would be able to stitch together a kind of genealogy for her household – not one that led to the West Coast of Africa, believe me, but a genealogy which would connect her, she wasn't quite sure, to the ruling house of the Austro-Hungarian empire or the lairds of Scotland, one way or the other. She probably thought that maybe in the quadrangle of Merton College, Oxford I might stumble across one of these secret stones that would somehow convert me into what clearly I was formed, brought up, reared, taught, educated, nursed and nurtured to be, a kind of black Englishman. When I first went home in the mid 1950s, my parents said to me, 'I hope they don't take you to be one of those immigrants over there.' And the funny thing is, I'd never called myself, or thought of myself as an immigrant before. But having once been hailed or interpellated, I owned up at once; that is what I am. In that moment I migrated. Again, the word black had never been uttered in my household or anywhere in Jamaica in my hearing, in my entire youth and adolescence – though there were all kinds of other ways of naming, and large numbers of people were very black indeed – so it was not until the mid 1960s, on another visit home, that my parents said to me, 'There's all this black consciousness, black movement in the United States, I hope it's not having an influence over there', and I realised I had just changed identity again. I owned up once more and said, 'Actually you know, I am exactly what in Britain we are starting to call black'. Which is a sort of footnote to say, identity is not only a story, a narrative which we tell ourselves about ourselves, it is stories which change with historical circumstances. And identity is far from the way in which we think and hear them and experience them. Far from only coming from the still small point of truth inside us, identities actually come from outside, they are the way in which we are recognised and then come to step into the place of the recognitions which others give us. Without the others there is no self, there is no self-recognition.

So given the skewed structures of growing up in such a society, of attempting whatever social rank or position in the racial colour structure you occupy, of trying to negotiate the complexities of who out of these complicated sets of stories you could possibly be, where you could find in the mirror of history a point of identification or recognition for yourself, it is not surprising that Caribbean people of all kinds, of all classes and positions, experience the question of positioning themselves in a cultural identity as an enigma, as a problem, as an open question. There are many writings about this question, but for me the overwhelmingly powerful statement is in Fanon's book *Black Skin White Masks,* for only in Fanon do you understand the internal traumas of identity which are the consequence of colonisation and enslavement. That is to say, not just the external processes and pressures of exploitation, but the way that internally one comes to collude with an objectification of oneself which is a profound misrecognition of one's own identity. Consequently, against that background, in the New World and in the Caribbean, the attempts in the twentieth century to reach for independence, to decolonise, the movements in the nineteenth century in the Hispanic Caribbean societies for independence from Spain, the attempts to regenerate and ground the political and social life of the society, not in an absent picture or image which could never be fulfilled, not in the nostalgia for something outside the society, but in the complicated realities and negotiations of that society itself, is a question which had to entail the redefinition of identity. Without it there could have been no independence of any kind. And one of the complexities or perplexities of the independence movement certainly in the British Caribbean islands is that in my view in the early phases of those movements so-called political independence from the colonial power occurred, but the cultural revolution of identity did not.

For the third process, which will form the rest of my talk, I want to start by looking at some of the other attempts to name the unnameable, to speak about the possibilities of cultural identification, of the different traditions of the peoples for whom on the whole there were no cultural models, the peoples at the bottom of the society. And as you can imagine, that always involved a renegotiation, a rediscovery of Africa. The political movements in the New World in the twentieth century have had to pass through the re-encounter with Africa. The African diasporas of the New World have been in one way or another incapable of finding a place in modern history without the symbolic return to Africa. It has taken many forms, it has been embodied in many movements both intellectual and popular. I want to say a word about two or three of them only. Perhaps best known in an intellectual sense is the movement around the notion of *négritude*, around the discovery of blackness, the affirmation of an African personality, very much associated with the name of Aimé

Césaire,[3] and of the group around Césaire in Paris and afterwards, coming out of Martinique, a tiny society which I described earlier on in a rather pejorative way, the most French place I have encountered in the Caribbean, certainly, but also the home-place of both Fanon and of Aimé Césaire. Césaire's work lay in plucking out of that Caribbean culture with which he was most familiar the strands that related most profoundly back to the valorisation of the African connection, the rediscovery of the African connection, of African consciousness, of African personality, of African cultural traditions.

I was fortunate enough in the programme on Martinique to be able to include an interview with Aimé Césaire, who must be nearly twice my age and looks about half of it, wonderfully fit and resilient at this moment. In that interview you can see the enormous pleasure with which he describes the story of having gone to Africa and rediscovered for the first time the source of the masks of the Martinique carnival which he had played in and helped to make when he was a boy – suddenly the flash of recognition, the continuity of the broken and ruptured tradition. The enormously important work that flowed from his involvement in the *négritude* movement, not only the poems and the poetry and the writing which has come out of that inspiration, of the renegotiation of a Caribbean consciousness with the African past, but also the work which he has inspired in Martinique amongst poets and painters and sculptors, is a profound revelation of how creative this symbolic reconnection has been. And yet of course the paradox is that when Aimé Césaire opens his mouth you hear the most exquisitely formed lycée French. I hardly know anyone who speaks a more perfect French, it is beautifully articulated. 'I am', he says, 'French, my mind is French'. Looking out for the right word, he says, 'like if you went to Oxford you would be English. I went to a French school, I was taught the French language, I wasn't allowed to use kréyole at home, I learned only French classical culture, there's a strong tradition of assimilation, I went of course to Paris where all bright young Martiniquans went'. And because of the tradition of political assimilation, he has in fact done what no black British Caribbean has ever done, which is to sit in the parliament of his own metropolitan society. Nevertheless when Aimé Césaire started to write poetry, he wanted, because of his interest, alerted and alive to the subterranean sources of identity and cultural creativity in his own being, to break with the models of French classical poetry. And if you know his notebook, the *Return to My Native Land,* you will know how much that is a language which in its open roaring brilliance, has broken free from those classical models. He becomes a Surrealist poet. Aimé Césaire has never, as you perhaps know, argued for the independence of Martinique. Martinique has a very particular position, it is an internal department of France, and those of you who want to be crude and materialist about it had better go and see the kinds of facilities which that gives Martiniquan people, and compare them with the facilities available to most of the other peoples of the Caribbean islands, before you begin to say what a terrible thing this is. Nevertheless, my own feeling, though I have no enormous evidence for this, is that the reluctance of Césaire to break the French connection is not only a material one but a spiritual one. He went to the Schoelcher lycée. Schoelcher[4] was an important early Martiniquan figure, and in celebrating an anniversary of Schoelcher, Césaire said, 'He associated in our minds the word France and the word liberty, and that bound us to France by every fibre of our hearts and every power of our minds'. He said, 'I know only one France, the France of the Revolution, the France of Toussaint L'Ouverture. So much for gothic cathedrals'.

Well, so much indeed for gothic cathedrals. The France with which Césaire identifies, and it has played of course a most profound role in Caribbean history, is one France and not another, the France of the Revolution, the France of *liberté, égalité, fraternité*, the France that Tousssaint L'Ouverture heard, the France that mobilised and touched the imagination of slaves and others in Haiti before the Revolution. And yet in the actual accounts of the revolution that we have, one of the most difficult, one of the trickiest historical passages to negotiate is precisely how much in the spark of the various things that went into the making of the Haitian Revolution can be attributed on the one hand to the ruptures sweeping out in the wake of the French Revolution, and on the other hand to the long experience of a severe and brutal regime on the plantations themselves, what you might call the revolutionary school of life itself. There were also, of course, the traditions of Africa and of African resistance, and of *marronage* in the plantation villages themselves. We don't know. It is an impossible enigma to sort out, in one of the momentous historical events of Caribbean history, to what can be attributed the different elements that come together in that revolutionary conjuncture.

Césaire was influenced in part by his contact at an early stage with an important movement in the United States which now goes under the title of the Harlem Renaissance.[5] I don't know how much you know about the writers of the Harlem Renaissance, of Langston Hughes and Countee Cullen and van Vechten, an important movement of writers, intellectuals and artists in New York in the early phases of the twentieth century, that had an important influence on a variety of Caribbean writers, poets and artists. One of the important things that the movement of the Harlem Renaissance did, was on the one hand to speak about the importance and the distinctiveness, the cultural and aesthetic distinctiveness of the black American contribution to American culture. The other important thing that movement did was to stake a claim for American blacks in the centre and at the heart of modernism itself. The writers of the Harlem Renaissance did not wish to be located and ghettoised as ethnic artists only able to speak on behalf of a marginal experience confined and immured in the past, locked out of the claim to modern life. What they said was, the experience of blacks in the New World, their historical trajectory into and through the complex histories of colonisation, conquest and enslavement, is distinct and unique and it empowers people to speak in a distinctive voice. But it is not a voice outside of and excluded from the production of modernity in the twentieth century. It is another kind of modernity. It is a vernacular modernity, it is the modernity of the blues, the modernity of gospel music, it is the modernity of hybrid black music in its enormous variety throughout the New World. The sound of marginal peoples staking a claim to the New World. I say that as a kind of metaphor, just in case you misunderstood the point I was trying to make about Aimé Césaire. I am anxious that you don't suppose I see him as an assimilationist Frenchman, deeply in bad faith because he is invoking Africa. I am trying to do something else. I am talking about the only way in which Africa can be relived and discovered by New World blacks who are diasporised irrevocably, who cannot go back through the eye of the needle.

Let me talk about finally going back through the eye of the needle. There was a very famous moment during the explosion of Rastafarianism in Jamaica in the sixties when a somewhat beleaguered Prime Minister said, 'Well perhaps you ought to go back to Africa. You've talked about it so much, you say you came from there, you say you're still in slavery here, you're not in a free land, the promised land is back there where somebody took you from, perhaps you ought to go back and see'. Well, of course some people did go back and see, as you perhaps know. Of course they did not go back to where they came from, that was not the Africa they were talking about. Between the Africa that they came from and the Africa that they wanted to go back to, two absolutely critical things had intervened. One is, that Africa had moved on. Africa – one has to say it now and again to somewhat nostalgic and sentimental nationalists in the Caribbean – Africa is not waiting there in the fifteenth or seventeenth century, waiting for you to roll back across the Atlantic and rediscover it in its tribal purity, waiting there in its prelogical mentality, waiting to be awoken from inside by the returning sons and daughters. It is grappling with the problem of AIDS and underdevelopment and mounting debt. It is trying to feed its people, it is trying to understand what democracy means against the background of a colonial regime which ruptured and broke and recut and reorganised peoples and tribes and societies in a horrendous shake-up of their entire cognitive and social world. That is what it's trying to do, twentieth-century Africa. There is no fifteenth-century mother waiting there to succour her children. So in that literal sense, they wanted to go somewhere else, they wanted to go to the other place that had intervened, that other Africa which was constructed in the language and the rituals of Rastafarianism.

Now as you know, the language and rituals of Rastafarianism speak indeed of Africa, of Ethiopia, of Babylon, of the Promised Land, and of those who are still in suffering. But like every chiliastic language which has been snatched by the black people of the New World diasporas out of the jaws of Christianity, and then turned on its head, or read against the grain, or crossed by something else – and the New World is absolutely replete with them – it is impossible in my experience to understand black culture and black civilisation in the New World without understanding the cultural role of religion, through the distorted languages of the one book that anybody would teach them to read. What they felt was, I have no voice, I have no history, I have come from a place to which I cannot go back and which I have never seen. I used to speak a language which I can no longer speak, I had ancestors whom I cannot find, they worshipped gods whose names I do not know. Against this sense of profound rupture, the metaphors of a new kind of imposed religion can be reworked, can become a language in which a certain kind of history is retold, in which aspirations of liberation and freedom can be for the first time expressed, in which what I would call the imagined community of Africans can be symbolically reconstructed.

I said to you that when I left Jamaica in the 1950s it was a society which did not and could not have acknowledged itself to be largely black. When I went back to Jamaica at the end of the sixties and in the early seventies, it was a society even poorer than when I had left it, in material terms, but it had passed through the most profound cultural revolution. It had grounded itself where it existed. It was not any longer trying to be something else, trying to match up to some other image, trying to become something which it could not. It had all the problems in the world sticking together, finding the wherewithal to get to the next week, but in terms of trying to understand ordinary people – I'm not now talking about intellectuals, I'm talking about ordinary people – the important thing was the new realisation that they could speak the language that they ordinarily spoke to one another anywhere. You know, the biggest shock for me was listening to Jamaican radio. I couldn't believe my ears that anybody would be quite so bold as to speak patois, to read the news in that accent. My entire education, my mother's whole career, had been specifically designed to prevent anybody at all, and me in particular, from reading anything of importance in that language. Of course, you would say all kinds of other things, in the small interchange of everyday life, but important things had to be said, goodness knows, in another tongue. To encounter people who can speak with one another in exactly that transformation of standard English which is patois, which is creole – the hundreds of different Creole and semi-creole languages which cover the face of the Caribbean in one place or another – that these have become as it were the languages in which important things can be said, in which important aspirations and hopes can be formulated, in which an important grasp of the histories that have made these places can be written down, in which artists are willing for the first time, the first generation, to practise and so on, that is what I call a cultural revolution.

And it was in my view made by the cultural revolution of Rastafarianism. What

I mean by that is certainly not that everybody became Rasta, although there was a moment in the sixties there when it was pretty hard not to be. I once interviewed a very old Rastafarian figure about the large numbers of Kingston intellectuals and students who were growing their locks down to their ankles. And I said to him, as part of a long interview about the nature of Rastafarianism, how he'd got into it, and so on, 'What do you think of these weekend Rastas, these middle-class Rastas, do you think they're up to anything, do you think they can reason?' and he said, 'You know, I don't say anything about them, I don't think anything about them, because in my church everybody reasons for themselves. So if they want to reason in that way, that's their business'. Well I thought that was a nice gentle remark, but I wanted to nail him, so I said, 'Listen to me now, isn't Haile Selasse dead, so the bottom has just fallen out of this whole Rastafarian business? He's dead, how can the Son of God be dead?' And he said to me, 'When last you hear the truth about the Son of God from the mass media?'

You see, it was not the literal place that people wanted to return to, it was the language, the symbolic language for describing what suffering was like, it was a metaphor for where they were, as the metaphors of Moses and the metaphors of the train to the North, and the metaphors of freedom, and the metaphors of passing across to the Promised Land, have always been metaphors, a language with a double register, a literal and symbolic register. And the point was not that some people, a few, could only live with themselves and discover their identities by literally going back to Africa – though some did, not often with great success – but that a whole people symbolically re-engaged with an experience which enabled them to find a language in which they could describe and appropriate their own histories.

I want to close. I have said something about the intellectual movement of *négritude*, I've referred to another important movement, not in the Caribbean but with influence on the Caribbean, the Harlem Renaissance of the twenties, and I've talked about the cultural revolution in the wake of Rastafarianism. One of the most important things that people on this side of the Atlantic know about Rastafarianism is that it produced the greatest reggae artist in the world, Bob Marley.[6] And I think many Europeans believe that reggae is a secret African music that we've had tucked in our slave knapsacks for three or four centuries, that we hid out in the bush, practised at night when nobody was looking, and gradually as things changed we brought it out and began to play it a little, feed it slowly across the airwaves. But as anybody from the Caribbean would know, reggae was born in the 1960s. Actually it was the answer to ska. When I returned to Jamaica I heard these two musical traditions. In *The Invention of Tradition,* the collection edited by Eric Hobsbawm and Terence Ranger,[7] it's explained that many British traditions which people believed have been around since Edward I were actually developed by Elgar or Disraeli,[8] the day before yesterday. Well, reggae is a product of the invention of tradition. It is a sixties music, its impact on the rest of the world comes not just through preservation – though it is rooted in the long retained traditions of African drumming – but by being the fusion, the crossing, of that retained tradition with a number of other musics, and the most powerful instruments or agencies of its world propagation were those deeply tribal instruments, the transistor set, the recording studio, the gigantic sound system. That is how this deeply profound spiritual music of Africa that we've been treasuring got here.

It's not part of my story to tell what it did here in Britain, but actually it not only provided a kind of black consciousness and identification for people in Jamaica, but it saved the second generation of young black people in this society. Is this an old identity or a new one? Is it an ancient culture preserved, treasured, to which it is possible to go back? Is it something produced out of nowhere? It is, of course, none of those things. No cultural identity is produced out of thin air. It is produced out of those historical experiences, those cultural traditions, those lost and marginal languages, those marginalised experiences, those peoples and histories which remain unwritten. Those are the specific roots of identity. On the other hand, identity itself is not the rediscovery of them, but what they as cultural resources allow a people to produce. Identity is not in the past to be found, but in the future to be constructed.

And I say that not because I think therefore that Caribbean people can ever give up the symbolic activity of trying to know more about the past from which they come, for only in that way can they discover and rediscover the resources through which identity can be constructed. But I remain profoundly convinced that their identities for the twenty-first century do not lie in taking old identities literally, but in using the enormously rich and complex cultural heritages to which history has made them heir, as the different musics out of which a Caribbean sound might one day be produced . . .

NOTES

1. See chapter 17 in this volume
2. Hall produced a seven-part television series about Caribbean culture called 'Redemption Song' for the British Broadcasting Corporation (1991).
3. See chapter 16 in this volume
4. Victor Schoelcher (1804–93), the son of a French porcelain manufacturer, encountered slavery first-hand when his father sent him to the Caribbean in 1829 in search of colonial outlets. He wrote accounts of what he saw to a Paris magazine, describing slave markets and punishments, and advocating the gradual abolition of slavery. He became the leading French abolitionist and, when he became a member of the revolutionary government of 1848, he organised emancipation. The freed slaves were declared citizens of France and adult males had voting rights in the Second Republic

(1848–51). Schoelcher fought against the coup of Louis Napoleon, which ended their rights along with the republic, and he was exiled from France in 1852.

5. The African-American cultural movement centred in New York City and known as the Harlem Renaissance was influenced by Marcus Garvey's ideas. One of its major figures was the Jamaican poet and novelist Claude McKay (1890–1948), author of *Banjo* (1929), *Banana Bottom* (1933) and many other works.

6. Bob Marley (1945–81), a Jamaican singer and songwriter, was the first reggae performer to achieve international stardom. He joined a group, the Rudeboys, in 1961, that later became the Wailers. By 1967, when Marley became a Rastafarian, reggae had emerged from a succession of musical styles, including ska, which incorporated elements of rhythm and blues from the southern United States and a kind of Jamaican folk song called mento. Many of Marley's songs convey messages of cultural revolution and spiritual redemption. His albums include 'Catch a Fire' (1972), 'Natty Dread' (1975), 'Rastaman Vibrations' (1976), 'Exodus' (1977), 'Kaya' (1978) and 'Uprising' (1979).

7. Eric Hobsbawm and Terence Ranger, editors, *The Invention of Tradition* (New York: 1983).

8. Sir Edward Elgar (1857–1934) was a distinguished English romantic composer whose popular 'Pomp and Circumstance' marches came to symbolise the British Empire. Benjamin Disraeli (1804–81), a British writer and prime minister, shaped the modern conservative party and supported traditional institutions such as the monarchy. He emphasised Britain's imperial policy by creating the title 'Empress of India' for Queen Victoria in 1876.

Forty-Two

Derek Walcott

Derek Walcott, born in St Lucia in 1930, was already a successful poet and playwright, and also a fine painter, at an early age. When he was 19, he wrote Henri Christophe, *a play about the 'slave-king' of Haiti, and published his first collection of poems. There followed a steady and prolific flow of poems and plays. Among the collections of poems are* In a Green Night *(1962),* The Castaway *(1965),* The Gulf *(1969),* Another Life *(1973),* Sea Grapes *(1976),* The Star-Apple Kingdom *(1979),* The Fortunate Traveller *(1981),* Midsummer *(1984),* The Arkansas Testament *(1987) and* The Bounty *(1997). He has also published the volume of* Collected Poems, 1948-1984 *(1986) and* Omeros *(1990), his ambitious epic poem, in seven books. His most famous plays include 'Dream on Monkey Mountain', 'Ti-Jean and His Brothers', 'Remembrance', 'Pantomime', 'The Last Carnival' and his stage version of Homer's poem* The Odyssey *(1993), which was commissioned by Britain's Royal Shakespeare Company. He also published a collection of essays,* What the Twilight Says *(1998).*

In 1959, Walcott founded the Trinidad Theatre Workshop, a touring company of which he was the director and chief playwright for nine years. His plays have been produced throughout the English-speaking world, in Canada, the UK, the United States and Nigeria as well as the West Indies. He has been honoured with many distinguished awards and prizes, including the Guinness Award for Poetry, the Royal Society of Literature Award, the Queen's Medal for Poetry in 1988, and in 1992 the Nobel Prize for Literature. His Nobel lecture was published as The Antilles: Fragments of Epic Memory *(1992).*

*Among the many subjects and themes he has addressed, a recurring one
concerns the relations between language, culture and identity. In one of his
early poems, 'A Far Cry From Africa', in which he reflects on a brutal colonial
policy and national liberation struggle in Kenya in the 1950s, where 'corpses
are scattered through a paradise', he refers to his own mixed origins and heritage:*

*Again brutish necessity wipes its hands
Upon the napkin of a dirty cause, again
A waste of our compassion as with Spain,
The gorilla wrestles with the superman.
I who am poisoned with the blood of both,
Where shall I turn, divided to the vein?
I who have cursed
The drunken officer of British rule, how choose
Between this Africa and the English tongue I love?
Betray them both, or give back what they give?
How can I face such slaughter and be cool?
How can I turn from Africa and live?*
(In a Green Night *1962, 18)*

*In 1962, Walcott wrote that 'the poet in the West Indies, exiled from a
mythically fertile past, must first explore his origins before he can purify the
dialect of the tribe' (*Trinidad Guardian *June 18, 1962). In his essay 'The Muse of
History', he expressed the ambivalent feelings he has when exploring his origins,
in a poetic eulogy to the fruit born of the pain of the Middle Passage:*

*I accept this archipelago of the Americas. I say to the ancestor who sold
me, and to the ancestor who bought me, I have no father, I want no such
father, although I can understand you, black ghost, white ghost, when
you both whisper 'history', for if I attempt to forgive you both I am
falling into your idea of history which justifies and explains and expiates,
and it is not mine to forgive, my memory cannot summon any filial love,
since your features are anonymous and erased and I have no wish and
no power to pardon. You were when you acted your roles, your given,
historical roles of slave seller and slave buyer, men acting as men, and
also you, father in the filth-ridden gut of the slave ship, to you they were
also men, acting as men, with the cruelty of men, your fellowman and
tribesman not moved or hovering with hesitation about your common
race any longer than my other bastard ancestor hovered with his whip,
but to you, inwardly forgiven grandfathers, I, like the more honest of my*

race, give a strange thanks. I give the strange and bitter and yet ennobling thanks for the monumental groaning and soldering of two great worlds, like the halves of a fruit seamed by its own bitter juice, that exiled from your own Edens you have placed me in the wonder of another, and that was my inheritance and your gift. (1974, 27)

Walcott's Nobel lecture, in contrast, is a song of praise to the multiple cultures that meet in the Caribbean. He acknowledges the sources of his art while concluding that he could have been a greater writer had he 'contained all the fragmented languages' of the region, and he celebrates the literature that, in several languages, is emerging 'in the early morning of a culture'.

⌒⟨✦⟩⌒

The Antilles: Fragments of Epic Memory

Felicity is a village in Trinidad on the edge of the Caroni plain,[1] the wide central plain that still grows sugar and to which indentured cane cutters were brought after emancipation, so the small population of Felicity is East Indian, and on the afternoon that I visited it with friends from America, all the faces along its road were Indian, which, as I hope to show, was a moving, beautiful thing, because this Saturday afternoon *Ramleela*, the epic dramatization of the Hindu epic the *Ramayana*,[2] was going to be performed, and the costumed actors from the village were assembling on a field strung with different-coloured flags, like a new gas station, and beautiful Indian boys in red and black were aiming arrows haphazardly into the afternoon light. Low blue mountains on the horizon, bright grass, clouds that would gather colour before the light went. Felicity! What a gentle Anglo-Saxon name for an epical memory.

Under an open shed on the edge of the field, there were two huge armatures of bamboo that looked like immense cages. They were parts of the body of a god, his calves or thighs, which, fitted and reared, would make a gigantic effigy. This effigy would be burnt as a conclusion to the epic. The cane structures flashed a predictable parallel: Shelley's[3] sonnet on the fallen statue of Ozymandias and his empire, that 'colossal wreck' in its empty desert.

Drummers had lit a fire in the shed and they eased the skins of their tablas nearer the flames to tighten them. The saffron flames, the bright grass, and the hand-woven armatures of the fragmented god who would be burnt were not in any desert where imperial power had finally toppled but were a part of a ritual, evergreen season that, like the cane-burning harvest, is annually repeated, the point of such sacrifice being its repetition, the point of the destruction being renewal through fire.

Deities were entering the field. What we generally call 'Indian music' was blaring from the open platformed shed from which the epic would be narrated. Costumed actors were arriving. Princes and gods, I supposed. What an unfortunate confession! 'Gods, I suppose' is the shrug that embodies our African and Asian diasporas. I had often thought of but never seen *Ramleela*, and had never seen this theatre, an open field, with village children as warriors, princes, and gods. I had no idea what the epic story was, who its hero was, what enemies he fought, yet I had recently adapted the *Odyssey* for a theatre in England, presuming that the audience knew the trials of Odysseus, hero of another Asia Minor epic, while nobody in Trinidad knew any more than I did about Rama, Kali, Shiva, Vishnu, apart from the Indians, a phrase I use pervertedly because that is the kind of remark you can still hear in Trinidad: 'apart from the Indians'.

It was as if, on the edge of the Central Plain, there was another plateau, a raft on which the *Ramayana* would be poorly performed in this ocean of cane, but that was my writer's view of things, and it is wrong. I was seeing the *Ramleela* at Felicity as theatre when it was faith.

Multiply that moment of self-conviction when an actor, made-up and costumed, nods to his mirror before stopping on stage in the belief that he is a reality entering an illusion and you would have what I presumed was happening to the actors of this epic. But they were not actors. They had been chosen; or they themselves had chosen their roles in this sacred story that would go on for nine afternoons over a two-hour period till the sun set. They were not amateurs but believers. There was no theatrical term to define them. They did not have to psych themselves up to play their roles. Their acting would probably be as buoyant and as natural as those bamboo arrows crisscrossing the afternoon pasture. They believed in what they were playing, in the sacredness of the text, the validity of India, while I, out of the writer's habit, searched for some sense of elegy, of loss, even of degenerative mimicry in the happy faces of the boy-warriors or the heraldic profiles of the village princes. I was polluting the afternoon with doubt and with the patronage of admiration. I misread the event through a visual echo of History – the cane fields, indenture, the evocation of vanished armies, temples, and trumpeting elephants – when all around me there was quite the opposite: elation, delight in the boys' screams, in the sweets-stalls, in more and more costumed characters appearing; a delight of conviction, not loss. The name Felicity made sense.

Consider the scale of Asia reduced to these fragments: the small white exclamations of minarets or the stone balls of temples in the cane fields, and one can understand the self-mockery and embarrassment of those who see these rites as parodic, even degenerate. These purists look on such ceremonies as grammarians look at a dialect, as cities look on provinces and empires on their colonies. Memory that yearns to join the center, a limb remembering the body from which it has been severed, like those bamboo thighs of the god. In other words, the way that the Caribbean is still looked at, illegitimate, rootless, mongrelized. 'No people there,' to quote Froude,[4] 'in the true sense of the word.' No people. Fragments and echoes of real people, unoriginal and broken.

The performance was like a dialect, a branch of its original language, an abridgement of it, but not a distortion or even a reduction of its epic scale. Here in Trinidad I had discovered that one of the greatest epics of the world was seasonally performed, not with that desperate resignation of preserving a culture, but with an openness of belief that was as steady as the wind bending the cane lances of the Caroni plain. We had to leave before the play began to go through the creeks of the Caroni Swamp, to catch the scarlet ibises coming home at dusk.[5] In a performance as natural as those of the actors of the *Ramleela*, we watched the flocks come in as bright as the scarlet of the boy archers, as the red flags, and cover an islet until it turned into a flowering tree, an anchored immortelle. The sigh of History meant nothing here. These two visions, the *Ramleela* and the arrowing flocks of scarlet ibises, blent into a single gasp of gratitude. Visual surprise is natural in the Caribbean; it comes with the landscape, and faced with its beauty, the sigh of History dissolves.

We make too much of that long groan which underlines the past. I felt privileged to discover the ibises as well as the scarlet archers of Felicity.

The sigh of History rises over ruins, not over landscapes, and in the Antilles there are few ruins to sigh over, apart from the ruins of sugar estates and abandoned forts. Looking around slowly, as a camera would, taking in the low blue hills over Port of Spain, the village road and houses, the warrior-archers, the god-actors and their handlers, and music already on the sound track, I wanted to make a film that would be a long-drawn sigh over Felicity. I was filtering the afternoon with evocations of a lost India, but why 'evocations'? Why not 'celebrations of a real presence'? Why should India be 'lost' when none of these villagers ever really knew it, and why not 'continuing', why not the perpetuation of joy in Felicity and in all the other nouns of the Central Plain: Couva, Chaguanas, Charley Village? Why was I not letting my pleasure open its windows wide? I was entitled like any Trinidadian to the ecstasies of their claim, because ecstasy was the pitch of the sinuous drumming in the loudspeakers. I was entitled to the feast of Husein, to the mirrors and crêpe-paper temples of the Muslim epic,[6] to the Chinese Dragon Dance, to the rites of that Sephardic Jewish synagogue that was once on Something Street. I am only one-eighth the writer I might have been had I contained all the fragmented languages of Trinidad.

Break a vase, and the love that reassembles the fragments is stronger than that love which took its symmetry for granted when it was whole. The glue that fits the pieces is the sealing of its original shape. It is such a love that reassembles our

African and Asiatic fragments, the cracked heirlooms whose restoration shows its white scars. This gathering of broken pieces is the care and pain of the Antilles, and if the pieces are disparate, ill-fitting, they contain more pain than their original sculpture, those icons and sacred vessels taken for granted in their ancestral places. Antillean art is this restoration of our shattered histories, our shards of vocabulary, our archipelago becoming a synonym for pieces broken off from the original continent.

And this is the exact process of the making of poetry, or what should be called not its 'making' but its remaking, the fragmented memory, the armature that frames the god, even the rite that surrenders it to a final pyre; the god assembled cane by cane, reed by weaving reed, line by plaited line, as the artisans of Felicity would erect his holy echo.

Poetry, which is perfection's sweat but which must seem as fresh as the raindrops on a statue's brow, combines the natural and the marmoreal; it conjugates both tenses simultaneously: the past and the present, if the past is the sculpture and the present the beads of dew or rain on the forehead of the past. There is the buried language and there is the individual vocabulary, and the process of poetry is one of excavation and of self-discovery. Tonally the individual voice is a dialect; it shapes its own accent, its own vocabulary and melody in defiance of an imperial concept of language, the language of Ozymandias, libraries and dictionaries, law courts and critics, and churches, universities, political dogma, the diction of institutions. Poetry is an island that breaks away from the main. The dialects of my archipelago seem as fresh to me as those raindrops on the statue's forehead, not the sweat made from the classic exertion of frowning marble, but the condensations of a refreshing element, rain and salt.

Deprived of their original language, the captured and indentured tribes create their own, accreting and secreting fragments of an old, an epic vocabulary, from Asia and from Africa, but to an ancestral, an ecstatic rhythm in the blood that cannot be subdued by slavery or indenture, while nouns are renamed and the given names of places accepted like Felicity village or Choiseul. The original language dissolves from the exhaustion of distance like fog trying to cross an ocean, but this process of renaming, of finding new metaphors, is the same process that the poet faces every morning of his workingday, making his own tools like Crusoe, assembling nouns from necessity, from Felicity, even renaming himself. The stripped man is driven back to that self-astonishing, elemental force, his mind. That is the basis of the Antillean experience, this shipwreck of fragments, these echoes, these shards of a huge tribal vocabulary, these partially remembered customs, and they are not decayed but strong. They survived the Middle Passage and the *Fatel Rozack*, the ship that carried the first indentured Indians from the port of Madras to the cane fields of Felicity, that carried the chained Cromwellian convict and the Sephardic

Jew, the Chinese grocer and the Lebanese merchant selling cloth samples on his bicycle.

And here they are, all in a single Caribbean city, Port of Spain, the sum of history, Trollope's 'non-people', A downtown babel of shop signs and streets, mongrelized, polyglot, a ferment without a history, like heaven. Because that is what such a city is, in the New World, a writer's heaven.

A culture, we all know, is made by its cities.

Another first morning home, impatient for the sunrise – a broken sleep. Darkness at five, and the drapes not worth opening; then, in the sudden light, a cream-walled, brown-roofed police station bordered with short royal palms, in the colonial style, back of it frothing trees and taller palms, a pigeon fluttering into the cover of an eave, a rain-stained block of once-modern apartments, the morning side road into the station without traffic. All part of a surprising peace. This quiet happens with every visit to a city that has deepened itself in me. The flowers and the hills are easy, affection for them predictable; it is the architecture that, for the first morning, disorients. A return from American seductions used to make the traveller feel that something was missing, something was trying to complete itself, like the stained concrete apartments. Pan left along the window and the excrescences rear – a city trying to soar, trying to be brutal, like an American city in silhouette, stamped from the same mould as Columbus or Des Moines. An assertion of power, its decor bland, its air conditioning pitched to the point where its secretarial and executive staff sport competing cardigans; the colder the offices the more important, an imitation of another climate. A longing, even an envy of feeling cold.

In serious cities, in grey, militant winter with its short afternoons, the days seem to pass by in buttoned overcoats, every building appears as a barracks with lights on in its windows, and when snow comes, one has the illusion of living in a Russian novel, in the nineteenth century, because of the literature of winter. So visitors to the Caribbean must feel that they are inhabiting a succession of postcards. Both climates are shaped by what we have read of them. For tourists, the sunshine cannot be serious. Winter adds depth and darkness to life as well as to literature, and in the unending summer of the tropics not even poverty or poetry (in the Antilles poverty is poetry with a V, *une vie*, a condition of life as well as of imagination) seems capable of being profound because the nature around it is so exultant, so resolutely ecstatic, like its music. A culture based on joy is bound to be shallow. Sadly, to sell itself, the Caribbean encourages the delights of mindlessness, of brilliant vacuity, as a place to flee not only winter but that seriousness that comes only out of culture with four seasons. So how can there be a people there, in the true sense of the word?

They know nothing about seasons in which leaves let go of the year, in which spires fade in blizzards and streets whiten, of the erasures of whole cities by fog, of reflection in fireplaces; instead, they inhabit a geography whose rhythm, like their music, is limited to two stresses: hot and wet, sun and rain, light and shadow, day and night, the limitations of an incomplete metre, and are therefore a people incapable of the subtleties of contradiction, of imaginative complexity. So be it. We cannot change contempt.

Ours are not cities in the accepted sense, but no one wants them to be. They dictate their own proportions, their own definitions in particular places and in a prose equal to that of their detractors, so that now it is not just St. James but the streets and yards that Naipaul commemorates, its lanes as short and brilliant as his sentences;[7] not just the noise and jostle of Tunapuna but the origins of C.L.R. James's *Beyond a Boundary*, not just Felicity village on the Caroni plain, but Selvon Country, and that is the way it goes up the islands now: the old Dominica of Jean Rhys still very much the way she wrote of it; and the Martinique of the early Césaire; Perse's Guadeloupe, even without the pith helmets and the mules; and what delight and privilege there was in watching a literature – one literature in several imperial languages, French, English, Spanish – bud and open island after island in the early morning of a culture, not timid, not derivative, any more than the hard white petals of the frangipani are derivative and timid. This is not a belligerent boast but a simple celebration of inevitability: and this flowering had to come.

On a heat-stoned afternoon in Port of Spain, some alley white with glare, with love vine spilling over a fence, palms and a hazed mountain appear around a corner to the evocation of Vaughn or Herbert's[8] 'that shady city of palm-trees', or to the memory of a Hammond organ from a wooden chapel in Castries,[9] where the congregation sang 'Jerusalem, the Golden'. It is hard for me to see such emptiness as desolation. It is that patience that is the width of Antillean life, and the secret is not to ask the wrong thing of it, not to demand of it an ambition it has no interest in. The traveller reads this as lethargy, as torpor.

Here there are not enough books, one says, no theatres, no museums, simply not enough to do. Yet, deprived of books, a man must fall back on thought, and out of thought, if he can learn to order it, will come the urge to record, and in extremity, if he has no means of recording, recitation, the ordering of memory which leads to metre, to commemoration. There can be virtues in deprivation, and certainly one virtue is salvation from a cascade of high mediocrity, since books are now not so much created as remade. Cities create a culture, and all we have are these magnified market towns, so what are the proportions of the ideal Caribbean city? A surrounding, accessible countryside with leafy suburbs, and if the city is lucky, behind it, spacious plains. Behind it, fine mountains; before it, an indigo sea. Spires would pin its centre and around them would be leafy, shadowy parks. Pigeons would cross its sky in alphabetic patterns, carrying with them memories of a belief in augury, and at the heart of the city there would be horses, yes, horses, those animals last seen at the end of the nineteenth century drawing broughams and carriages with top-hatted citizens, horses that live in the present tense without elegiac echoes from their hooves, emerging from paddocks at the Queen's Park Savannah[10] at sunrise, when mist is unthreading from cool mountains above the roofs, and at the centre of the city seasonally there would be races, so that citizens could roar at the speed and grace of these nineteenth-century animals. Its docks, not obscured by smoke or deafened by too much machinery, and above all, it would be so racially various that the cultures of the world – the Asiatic, the Mediterranean, the European, the African – would be represented in it, its humane variety more exciting than Joyce's Dublin.[11] Its citizens would intermarry as they chose, from instinct, not tradition, until their children find it increasingly futile to trace their genealogy. It would not have too many avenues difficult or dangerous for pedestrians, its mercantile area would be a cacophony of accents, fragments of the old language that would be silenced immediately at five o'clock, its docks resolutely vacant on Sundays.

This is Port of Spain to me, a city ideal in its commercial and human proportions, where a citizen is a walker and not a pedestrian, and this is how Athens may have been before it became a cultural echo.

The finest silhouettes of Port of Spain are idealizations of the craftsman's handiwork, not of concrete and glass, but of baroque woodwork, each fantasy looking more like an involved drawing of itself than the actual building. Behind the city is the Caroni plain, with its villages, Indian prayer flags, and fruit vendors' stalls along the highway over which ibises come like floating flags. Photogenic poverty! Postcard sadness! I am not recreating Eden; I mean, by 'the Antilles', the reality of light, of work, of survival. I mean a house on the side of a country road, I mean the Caribbean Sea, whose smell is the smell of refreshing possibility as well as survival. Survival is the triumph of stubbornness, and a spiritual stubbornness, a sublime stupidity, is what makes the occupation of poetry endure, when there are so many things that should make it futile. Those things added together can go under one collective noun: 'the world'.

This is the visible poetry of the Antilles, then. Survival.

If you wish to understand that consoling pity with which the islands were regarded, look at the tinted engravings of Antillean forests, with their proper palm trees, ferns, and waterfalls. They have a civilizing decency, like Botanical Gardens, as if the sky were a glass ceiling under which a colonized vegetation is arranged for quiet walks and carriage rides. Those views are incised with a pathos that guides the engraver's tool and the topographer's pencil, and it is this pathos which, tenderly ironic, gave villages names like Felicity. A century looked at a landscape furious with vegetation in the wrong light and with the wrong eye. It is such pictures that are saddening rather than the tropics itself. These delicate engravings of sugar mills and harbours, of native women in costume, are seen as a part of History, that

History which looked over the shoulder of the engraver and, later, the photographer. History can alter the eye and the moving hand to conform a view of itself; it can rename places for the nostalgia in an echo; it can temper the glare of tropical light to elegiac monotony in prose, the tone of judgment in Conrad, in the travel journals of Trollope.[12]

These travelers carried with them the infection of their own malaise, and their prose reduced even the landscape to melancholia and self-contempt. Every endeavor is belittled as imitation, from architecture to music. There was this conviction in Froude that since History is based on achievement, and since the history of the Antilles was so genetically corrupt, so depressing in its cycles of massacres, slavery, and indenture, a culture was inconceivable and nothing could ever be created in those ramshackle ports, those monotonously feudal sugar estates. Not only the light and salt of Antillean mountains defied this, but the demotic vigour and variety of their inhabitants. Stand close to a waterfall and you will stop hearing its roar. To be still in the nineteenth century, like horses, as Brodsky[13] has written, may not be such a bad deal, and much of our life in the Antilles still seems to be in the rhythm of the last century, like the West Indian novel.

By writers even as refreshing as Graham Greene,[14] the Caribbean is looked at with elegiac pathos, a prolonged sadness to which Levi-Strauss has supplied an epigraph: *Tristes Tropiques*.[15] Their *tristesse* derives from an attitude to the Caribbean dusk, to rain, to uncontrollable vegetation, to the provincial ambition of Caribbean cities where brutal replicas of modern architecture dwarf the small houses and streets. The mood is understandable, the melancholy as contagious as the fever of a sunset, like the gold fronds of diseased coconut palms, but there is something alien and ultimately wrong in the way such a sadness, even a morbidity, is described by English, French, or some of our exiled writers. It relates to a misunderstanding of the light and the people on whom the light falls.

These writers describe the ambitions of our unfinished cities, their unrealized, homiletic conclusion, but the Caribbean city may conclude just at that point where it is satisfied with its own scale, just as Caribbean culture is not evolving but already shaped. Its proportions are not to be measured by the traveller or the exile, but by its own citizenry and architecture. To be told you are not yet a city or a culture requires this response. I am not your city or your culture. There might be less of *Tristes Tropiques* after that.

Here, on the raft of this dais, there is the sound of the applauding surf: our landscape, our history recognized, 'at last'. *At Last* is one of the first Caribbean books. It was written by the Victorian traveller Charles Kingsley.[16] It is one of the early books to admit the Antillean landscape and its figures into English literature. I have never read it but gather that its tone is benign. The Antillean archipelago was there to be written about, not to write itself, by Trollope, by Patrick Leigh-Fermor,[17] in the very tone in which I almost wrote about the village spectacle at Felicity, as a compassionate and beguiled outsider, distancing myself from Felicity village even while I was enjoying it. What is hidden cannot be loved. The traveller cannot love, since love is stasis and travel is motion. If he returns to what he loved in a landscape and stays there, he is no longer a traveller but in stasis and concentration, the lover of that particular part of earth, a native. So many people say they 'love the Caribbean', meaning that someday they plan to return for a visit but could never live there, the usual benign insult of the traveller, the tourist. These travellers, at their kindest, were devoted to the same patronage, the islands passing in profile, their vegetal luxury, their backwardness and poverty. Victorian prose dignified them. They passed by in beautiful profiles and were forgotten, like a vacation.

Alexis Saint-Léger Léger, whose writer's name is St.- John Perse,[18] was the first Antillean to win this prize for poetry. He was born in Guadeloupe and wrote in French, but before him, there was nothing as fresh and clear in feeling as those poems of his childhood, that of a privileged white child on an Antillean plantation, *'Pour fêter une enfance', 'Eloges',* and later *'Images à Crusoe'.* At last, the first breeze on the page, salt-edged and self-renewing as the trade winds, the sound of pages and palm trees turning as 'the odour of coffee ascends the stairs'.

Caribbean genius is condemned to contradict itself. To celebrate Perse, we might be told, is to celebrate the old plantation system, to celebrate the *bequé*[19] or plantation rider, verandahs and mulatto servants, a white French language in a white pith helmet, to celebrate a rhetoric of patronage and hauteur; and even if Perse denied his origins, great writers often have this folly of trying to smother their source, we cannot deny him any more than we can the African Aimé Césaire. This is not accommodation, this is the ironic republic that is poetry, since, when I see cabbage palms moving their fronds at sunrise, I think they are reciting Perse.

The fragrant and privileged poetry that Perse composed to celebrate his white childhood and the recorded Indian music behind the brown young archers of Felicity, with the same cabbage palms against the same Antillean sky, pierce me equally. I feel the same poignancy of pride in the poems as in the faces. Why, given the history of the Antilles, should this be remarkable? The history of the world, by which of course we mean Europe, is a record of intertribal lacerations, of ethnic cleansings. At last, islands not written about but writing themselves! The palms and the Muslim minarets are Antillean exclamations. At last! the royal palms of Guadeloupe recite *'Eloges'* by heart.

Later, in *Anabase,* Perse assembled fragments of an imaginary epic, with the clicking teeth of frontier gates, barren wadis with the froth of poisonous lakes, horsemen burnoosed in sandstorms, the opposite of cool Caribbean mornings, yet not necessarily a contrast any more than some young brown archer at Felicity, hearing the sacred text blared across the flagged field, with its battles and elephants and monkey-gods, in a contrast to the white child in Guadeloupe assembling fragments of his own epic from the lances of the cane fields, the estate carts and oxens, and the calligraphy of bamboo leaves from the ancient languages, Hindi, Chinese, and Arabic, on the Antillean sky. From the *Ramayana* to Anabasis, from Guadeloupe to Trinidad, all that archaeology of fragments lying around, from the broken African kingdoms, from the crevasses of Canton, from Syria and Lebanon, vibrating not under the earth but on our raucous, demotic streets.

A boy with weak eyes skims a flat stone across the flat water of an Aegean inlet, and that ordinary action with the scything elbow contains the skipping lines of the *Iliad* and the *Odyssey,* and another child aims a bamboo arrow at a village festival, and another hears the rustling march of cabbage palms in a Caribbean sunrise, and from that sound, with its fragments of tribal myth, the compact expedition of Perse's epic is launched, centuries and archipelagos apart. For every poet it is always morning in the world. History a forgotten, insomniac night; History and elemental awe are always our early beginning, because the fate of poetry is to fall in love with the world, in spite of History.

There is a force of exultation, a celebration of luck, when a writer finds himself a witness to the early morning of a culture that is defining itself, branch by branch, leaf by leaf, in that self-defining dawn, which is why, especially at the edge of the sea, it is good to make a ritual of the sunrise. Then the noun, the "Antilles" ripples like brightening water, and the sounds of leaves, palm fronds, and birds are the sounds of fresh dialect, the native tongue. The personal vocabulary, the individual melody whose metre is one's biography, joins in that sound, with any luck, and the body moves like a walking, a waking island.

This is the benediction that is celebrated, a fresh language and a fresh people, and this is the frightening duty owed.

I stand here in their name, if not their image – but also in the name of the dialect they exchange like the leaves of the trees whose names are suppler, greener, more morning-stirred than English – *laurier canelles, bois-flot, bois-canot* – or the valleys the trees mention – *Fond St. Jacques, Mabonya, Forestièr, Roseau, Mahaut* – or the empty beaches – *L'Anse Ivrogne, Case en Bas, Paradis* – all songs and histories in themselves, pronounced not in French – but in patois.

One rose hearing two languages, one of the trees, one of schoolchildren reciting in English:

I am monarch of all I survey,
My right there is none to dispute;
From the centre all round to the sea
I am lord of the fowl and the brute.
Oh, solitude! where are the charms

That sages have seen in thy face?
Better dwell in the midst of alarms,
Than reign in this horrible place . . . .[20]
While in the country to the same metre, but to organic instruments, handmade
violin, chac-chac, and goatskin drum, a girl named Sensenne singing:

Si mwen di 'ous' ça fait mwen la peine
'Ous kai dire ca vrai.
(If I told you that caused me pain
You'll say, 'It's true'.)
Si mwen di 'ous ça pentetrait mwen
'Ous peut dire ça vrai.
(If I told you you pierced my heart
You'd say, 'It's true'.)
Ces mamailles actuellement
Pas ka faire l'amour z'autres pour un rien.
(Children nowadays
Don't make love for nothing.)

It is not that History is obliterated by this sunrise. It is there in Antillean
geography, in the vegetation itself. The sea sighs with the drowned from the Middle
Passage, the butchery of its aborigines, Carib and Aruac and Taino, bleeds in the
scarlet of the immortelle, and even the actions of surf on sand cannot erase the
African memory, or the lances of cane as a green prison where indentured Asians,
the ancestors of Felicity, are still serving time.

That is what I have read around me from boyhood, from the beginnings of
poetry, the grace of effort. In the hard mahogany of woodcutters: faces, resinous
men, charcoal burners; in a man with a cutlass cradled across his forearm, who
stands on the verge with the usual anonymous khaki dog; in the extra clothes he
put on this morning, when it was cold when he rose in the thinning dark to go and
make his garden in the heights – the heights, the garden, being miles away from his
house, but that is where he has his land – not to mention the fishermen, the footmen
on trucks, groaning up mornes, all fragments of Africa originally but shaped and
hardened and rooted now in the island's life, illiterate in the way leaves are illiterate;
they do not read, they are there to be read, and if they are properly read, they create
their own literature.

But in our tourist brochures the Caribbean is a blue pool into which the republic
dangles the extended foot of Florida as inflated rubber islands bob and drinks with
umbrellas float towards her on a raft. This is how the islands from the shame of
necessity sell themselves; this is the seasonal erosion of their identity, that high-

pitched repetition of the same images of service that cannot distinguish one island from the other, with a future of polluted marinas, land deals negotiated by ministers, and all of this conducted to the music of Happy Hour and the rictus of a smile. What is the earthly paradise for our visitors? Two weeks without rain and a mahogany tan, and, at sunset, local troubadours in straw hats and floral shirts beating 'Yellow Bird' and 'Banana Boat Song' to death. There is a territory wider than this –wider than the limits made by the map of an island – which is the illimitable sea and what it remembers.

All of the Antilles, every island, is an effort of memory; every mind, every racial biography culminating in amnesia and fog. Pieces of sunlight through the fog and sudden rainbows, *arcs-en-ciel*. That is the effort, the labour of the Antillean imagination, rebuilding its gods from bamboo frames, phrase by phrase.

Decimation from the Aruac downwards is the blasted root of Antillean history, and the benign blight that is tourism can infect all of those island nations, not gradually, but with imperceptible speed, until each rock is whitened by the guano of white-winged hotels, the arc and descent of progress.

Before it is all gone, before only a few valleys are left, pockets of an older life, before development turns every artist into an anthropologist or folklorist, there are still cherishable places, little valleys that do not echo with ideas, a simplicity of rebeginnings, not yet corrupted by the dangers of change. Not nostalgic sites but occluded sanctities as common and simple as their sunlight. Places as threatened by this prose as a headland is by the bulldozer or a sea almond grove by the surveyor's string, or from blight, the mountain laurel.

One last epiphany: A basic stone church in a thick valley outside Soufrière,[21] the hills almost shoving the houses around into a brown river, a sunlight that looks oily on the leaves, a backward place, unimportant, and one now being corrupted into significance by this prose. The idea is not to hallow or invest the place with anything, not even memory. African children in Sunday frocks come down the ordinary concrete steps into the church, banana leaves hang and glisten, a truck is parked in a yard, and old women totter towards the entrance. Here is where a real fresco should be painted, one without importance, but one with real faith, mapless, Historyless.

How quickly it could all disappear! And how it is beginning to drive us further into where we hope are impenetrable places, green secrets at the end of bad roads, headlands where the next view is not of a hotel but of some long beach without a figure and the hanging question of some fisherman's smoke at its far end. The Caribbean is not an idyll, not to its natives. They draw their working strength from it organically, like trees, like the sea almond or the spice laurel of the heights. Its peasantry and its fishermen are not there to be loved or even photographed; they are trees who sweat, and whose bark is filmed with salt, but every day on some island, rootless trees in suits are signing favourable tax breaks with entrepreneurs, poisoning the sea almond and the spice laurel of the mountains to their roots. A morning could come in which governments might ask what happened not merely to the forests and the bays but to a whole people.

They are here again, they recur, the faces, corruptible angels, smooth black skins and white eyes huge with an alarming joy, like those of the Asian children of Felicity at *Ramleela*; two different religions, two different continents, both filling the heart with the pain that is joy.

But what is joy without fear? The fear of selfishness that, here on this podium with the world paying attention not to them but to me, I should like to keep these simple joys inviolate, not because they are innocent, but because they are true. They are as true as when, in the grace of this gift, Perse heard the fragments of his own epic of Asia Minor in the rustling of cabbage palms, that inner Asia of the soul through which imagination wanders, if there is such a thing as imagination as opposed to the collective memory of our entire race, as true as the delight of that warrior-child who flew a bamboo arrow over the flags in the field at Felicity; and now as grateful a joy and a blessed fear as when a boy opened an exercise book and, within the discipline of its margins, framed stanzas that might contain the light of the hills on an island blest by obscurity, cherishing our insignificance.

NOTES

1. Seven major rivers flow south out of Trinidad's northern range into the Caroni River which flows west into the Gulf of Paria. The Caroni plain is just south of the most heavily urbanised area of Trinidad which lies between Port of Spain and Arima.
2. The *Ramayana* is one of the two great epic poems of India, the other being the *Mahabharata*. The hero of the *Ramayana* is Rama, the human form of the god Vishnu, who is the son and heir of an Indian king. The central episode describes the conflict between Rama and Ravana, the demon-king who has captured Sita, Rama's beautiful and devoted wife. Rama kills Ravana with an arrow, rescues Sita and returns home to become king.
3. Percy Bysshe Shelley (1792–1822) was one of the greatest English lyric poets of the romantic era. His poem 'Ozymandias' refers to an ancient, once-powerful king, whose broken statue lying in a desert is all that remains of his greatness.
4. James Anthony Froude (1818–94), the Regius Professor of Modern History at Oxford University, wrote *The English in the West Indies, or the Bow of Ulysses* (London, 1888), a prejudiced view of the people of the Caribbean.
5. There is a bird sanctuary in the Caroni Swamp where hundreds of scarlet ibis come to roost at twilight on an island in the middle of a lagoon.
6. The Muslim community commemorates the deaths of the grandsons of the prophet Mohammed, Hussein and Hassan, at the Hosay festival in which elaborately decorated *tadjahs*, representing their tombs, are paraded through the streets, accompanied by the vigorous rhythms of *tassa* drums.

7. St James, a western suburb of Port of Spain and the location of the main Hindu Mandir, or temple, is a centre of Trinidad's Indian community. The writers Walcott refers to are V.S. Naipaul, author of many novels about Indian Trinidadians (see chapter 28 in this volume), C.L.R. James, whose *Beyond a Boundary* (1963) is about cricket and culture in Trinidad (see chapter 29 in this volume), Sam Selvon, whose novels include *A Brighter Sun* (1952), *An Island is a World* (1955) and *The Plains of Caroni* (1970), Jean Rhys, who is best known for her novel *Wide Sargasso Sea* (1966), and the poets Aimé Césaire (see chapter 16 in this volume) and St John Perse, from the French islands of Martinique and Guadeloupe, respectively.

8. Henry Vaughn (1622–95) and George Herbert (1593–1633), who wrote largely on religious subjects, were among the chief of the English metaphysical poets in the seventeenth century.

9. Castries is the capital of St Lucia.

10. Queen's Park Savannah is 200 acres of open grassland in the middle of Port of Spain, surrounded by the Botanic Gardens and Emperor Valley Zoo, the President's House, Queen's Royal College and other landmarks. Once the site of horse races, it is now the centre of carnival competitions and parades.

11. The stories and novels of James Joyce (1882–1941), an Irish writer, celebrate the city of Dublin and make it a symbol of modern urban life. His novel *Ulysses* (1922), like Walcott's *Omeros*, establishes parallels with the wanderings of the hero of Homer's *Odyssey*.

12. Joseph Conrad (1857–1924), an English author of Polish birth, is famous for his stories about the sea and adventures in Asian, African and Latin American locations. His novel *Nostromo* (1904) relied on his memories when he was a sailor in the Caribbean. Anthony Trollope (1815–82) was an English author whose most popular novels were set in the imaginary county of Barsetshire. In 1859 he published a book about his travels, *The West Indies and the Spanish Main*.

13. Joseph Brodsky (1940–96), a Russian poet and a close friend of Walcott, won the Nobel Prize for literature in 1987.

14. Graham Greene (1904–91), a prolific English author, set his novels *Our Man in Havana* (1958) and *The Comedians* (1966) in Cuba and Haiti, respectively.

15. Claude Levi-Strauss (born in 1908), a French anthropologist who worked in Brazil, wrote an intellectual autobiography, *Tristes Tropiques* (1955), or the sad tropics.

16. Charles Kingsley (1819–75), an English clergyman and novelist, wrote *Westward Ho!* (1855), an adventure story on the high seas in the days of Sir Francis Drake, and *At Last: A Christmas in the West Indies* (1874).

17. Patrick Leigh Fermor wrote *The Traveller's Tree* (1950) about his travels in the Caribbean islands.

18. St-John Perse (1887-1975) won the Nobel Prize in 1960. He wrote symbolist verse, much of it dealing with his feelings of solitude and exile.

19. *Bequé*, or *béké*, refers to 'local whites' in the French Caribbean.

20. This is the first verse of 'The Solitude of Alexander Selkirk' by William Cowper (1731–1800), about the Scottish sailor who took part in privateering expeditions in the Caribbean and Pacific in the early eighteenth century. After a dispute with his captain he was put ashore on an island in 1704 and he lived alone until he was rescued in 1709. This episode suggested to the English novelist Daniel Defoe the plot of *Robinson Crusoe* (1719).

21. Soufrière is a small town in the southwest of St Lucia.

Forty-Three

Shridath Ramphal

Sir Shridath Ramphal, born in 1928 in Guyana, is one of the Caribbean's leading international statesmen. He studied law at King's College and Gray's Inn in London and Harvard University's Law School. He was Assistant Attorney General in the West Indies Federation and the first Attorney General and then Minister of Foreign Affairs and Justice in independent Guyana. As Secretary-General of the Commonwealth (1975– 1990) he was prominent in that organisation's efforts to help South Africa's struggle for freedom and to promote better policies towards developing countries. In the 1980s, Ramphal served on all of the five independent international commissions which reported on global issues: the Brandt Commission on International Development, the Palme Commission on Disarmament and Security Issues, the Brundtland Commission on Environment and Development, the Commission on Humanitarian Issues, and the South Commission, chaired by Julius Nyerere.

Ramphal was the chair of the West Indian Commission, created by the heads of government of CARICOM countries and composed of prominent regional figures, which travelled all over the region and to Canada, the UK and the United States, discussing the future of the Caribbean. Its report, Time for Action *(Kingston, 1993), recommended deepening and widening the regional integration movement, but it was rejected by the heads of government on the grounds that it would interfere with the national sovereignty of member states. However, Ramphal continued to advocate a 'Commonwealth of the Caribbean' that would draw all the nations of the region together. In 1994, a year after he gave the speech that follows to the Caribbean Hotel Industry Conference, a new organisation, the Association of Caribbean States (ACS) was created, consisting of 25 member states, including Cuba, the Dominican Republic, Haiti, the Central American states, Colombia, Mexico and Venezuela as well as the CARICOM members. Ramphal also co-chaired the Commission on Global Governance which resulted in the report* Our Global Neighbourhood *(Oxford, 1995) and he was appointed CARICOM's Chief Negotiator for international negotiations with Europe, the Americas and the World Trade Organization. Two collections of his speeches have been published:* Inseparable Humanity, *edited by R. Sanders (London, 1988) and* No Island is an Island, *edited by David Dabydeen and John Gilmore (London, 2000).*

A Commonwealth of the Caribbean for the Twenty-first Century

[T]he north coast of Jamaica holds for me special memories of occasions like this, that look ahead to our Caribbean future. I remember particularly an evening at the end of June 1975, which was to be my last home-based evening in the Caribbean, before leaving for the Commonwealth Secretariat,[1] when in some valedictory remarks I pleaded that we 'care for CARICOM'.[2] I seem to have been pleading ever since: most recently through the West Indian Commission's public consultations and our report *Time for Action*.

Today, however, I plead the cause of a wider vision, not just the vision of integration of the English-speaking countries of the Caribbean, but the vision of a Commonwealth of the entire Caribbean. I speak to the need for us to take steps now to make 'the Caribbean' more than a geographical description of a scattered archipelago – to make it a functional description of a community of Caribbean peoples harmonising identities and working together as an extended family. I plead for a process by which the Caribbean itself ceases to be the dividing sea it has been for centuries and becomes instead a uniting lake. It is of that Commonwealth of the Caribbean that I shall speak – a Commonwealth from the Bahamas in the north to Suriname in the south, from Central America in the west to Barbados in the east; a Caribbean Commonwealth encompassing the states, the governments, the people of the entire Caribbean: a Commonwealth of the islands of the Sea and the coastal states whose shores are washed by that Sea.

In that Caribbean Commonwealth, let me say immediately and without reservation, that I would see all the islands, including those not yet independent, playing a substantive part. Those islands which are not fully independent have to acknowledge, it is true, the paramountcy of their metropoles in crucial areas of national policy. But the fully independent ones have to acknowledge no less the *realpolitik* of shrinking sovereignty – that they have been made to bend to even more demanding paramountcies than one erstwhile colonial master. At least, in our Caribbean home, let us acknowledge there is no place for an upstairs-downstairs arrangement.

But I go further. May there not be value in a Caribbean system which draws in some of the strengths that the non-independent countries can bring through their continuing links with the metropoles – provided we have the clarity of purpose and steadfastness of resolution to stand against any semblance of neo-colonialism? We have to look to the future with new eyes and new understandings and abandon the habits of an era that has passed. When I speak, as I have done, with Caribbean brothers and sisters in Curaçao or in St. Thomas, in Puerto Rico or from Martinique, I am not speaking with unequals. Whatever our separate but different strengths, our weaknesses unite us. And there have been changes, as well, in the roles of the metropoles in relation to more autonomous Caribbean countries. The vision of a Community of Caribbean States cannot exclude, I believe, the American, British, Dutch and French islands – once they are allowed to participate in their own right and once, of course, they wish to do so. In a Commonwealth of the Caribbean there must be a place for all, and a welcome to all who wish to occupy it.

As a son of CARICOM – perhaps, more accurately, a father – I envisage the strengthening of CARICOM within that enlarging Commonwealth. It is to this strengthening that much of the West Indian Commission's report *Time for Action* speaks. Both for CARICOM's sake, as well as for the advancement of the vision of a wider Caribbean, such a strengthening is desirable, indeed, probably necessary. And it will come; if not through a dynamic of political vision then certainly through the compulsions of economic, social and cultural realities – a faith in the future which looks, you might think, to the old wisdom that politicians can be relied upon to act in courageous, enlightened and statesmanlike ways, having exhausted all other alternatives.

The motto of the West Indian Commission, established for us by CARICOM leaders in the Grand Anse Declaration, was: 'Let All Ideas Contend'. Although our formal work is over, ideas will continue to contend; and, ultimately, that process will lead CARICOM along the path of progress. My concern is about the pace of the journey. We may not have as much time as our languid style suggests. But that is CARICOM's domestic challenge. Let me turn to the challenge that looks beyond ourselves.

Looking to our relations with the wider Caribbean was a specific dimension of the West Indian Commission's mandate from Grand Anse. In requiring us to do so, CARICOM leaders were charting an enlightened course. In responding, the

Commission confirmed the central relevance of inter-Caribbean relations to the future of CARICOM. Last October we invited CARICOM leaders to agree that this 'widening' process must proceed on a dual track through the deepening of integration and the strengthening of CARICOM itself. The one, we said, cannot await the other – either way. They are complementary processes and both are now impatient of delay. Quite simply, CARICOM must take a position on our place in the Caribbean whose geographic description our 'Community' has arrogated. It is time, we said, to fill out that description with a clear sense of what the 'Caribbean' means to us and the role we must play in fulfilling our vision of it. Our CARICOM countries are accustomed to being characterised as drops in the ocean; in the Caribbean Basin we are still only a tea-cup. But, if you will forgive the xenophobic overtone, it is a tea-cup of Caribbean essence that gives flavour to the whole.

The West Indian Commission was not hesitant in asserting that beginning the process of integration of the entire Caribbean Basin is the most important Caribbean idea, and could be the most important Caribbean enterprise since Columbus committed us to a history of European dominion and a destiny bound up with European nationalism. The Commission's conversations beyond CARICOM – in Cuba, in Curaçao, in the Dominican Republic, in Martinique, in Puerto Rico, in Suriname, in Venezuela, in the US Virgin Islands – left us in no doubt of the need to provide space for the evolution of integrationist relationships with a wide range of countries for whom membership of CARICOM is not necessarily the relationship best suited to our own interests or theirs. In its section on 'Compulsions for widening integration', the report had this to say:

> As the world has grown smaller with the communications revolution and the compulsions of interdependence, those already small are in danger of being miniaturised. It is a danger that will continue. In the process, individually small West Indian countries become depreciated in the global balance sheet. Time was when Caribbean Islands held high value in metropolitan scales – higher than the 'icy wastes' of Canada or the small outpost of Manhattan.[3] That time is gone. Regionalism, however, can be our essential value added; but regionalism in CARICOM terms alone is no longer enough. Altogether, we are a market of 5.5 million, smaller than any but the very smallest economy of Latin America. The wider Caribbean –including Cuba in the north and Suriname in the south – is a market of 32 million: still not a giant in the world economy with which we must interact, but with a better chance of survival. The region of the Caribbean Basin, including Venezuela, Colombia and Central America, is a community of 112 million; with Mexico, almost 200 million.
>
> In this wider market we have important advantages, including among them larger opportunities for trade and investment that become open to our fast developing

indigenous business community. Already, the region as a whole has produced entrepreneurs who hold their own internationally. Some of them are beginning to move into the wider Caribbean area. On our visit to Cuba, we were proud to see the part Jamaican entrepreneurs are playing in the dynamic opening up of the tourist industry there. It should be a purpose of regional policy to give that process every encouragement.

The West Indian Commission's proposal for an Association of Caribbean States has been adopted by CARICOM heads of government. Initiating, evolving, negotiating and bringing to fulfilment that Association of Caribbean States will not be a simple matter. It will call for interaction with the wider Caribbean at a high level and at many levels – such as this one. Caribbean leaders individually will have to make major contributions; but there will be need for the continuous development of ideas and co-ordination of action and there will be roles for everyone. A part of the democratic reality of our Caribbean lives is not only that we choose our national leaders, but that we are empowered to encourage (indeed require) them to act as we wish them to do – and to act ourselves. Quite often, what is most needed is not the empowerment of people, but the exercise of the power that people already have. Too often, we seem to believe that we have spent our power after two minutes in the ballot box, and need five years to replenish our energies for any other meaningful political activity.

Caribbean countries – the islands, the mainland states, the independent and non-independent countries – will all have many windows on the wider world beyond our region: multiple entry points to Europe, to North America, to Asia and the Pacific, to Africa and to the rest of Latin America. The Commonwealth of the Caribbean States is not an alternative to them. It does not seek to diminish the opportunities they offer and to turn us inwards. I know, in particular, how strongly CARICOM countries value their cultural and political ties with Africa and Asia and how strong are the bonds of the Hispanic Caribbean with Spain. All such ties, for us and others, will continue to be strengthened over the entire field of relationships, including economic ones. But the world has already changed. We cannot live by ancient links alone.

The Europeans in particular are drawing together. They will argue fiercely in the process; but let us have no illusions; at the end of the day, they will find a way of uniting and being stronger as a result. Even when they fall apart, as in the Balkans or in Eastern Europe, they do so now within a wider process of coming together. They will be harder for us to deal with if they are one and strong, and we are many and weak. We are all experiencing such vulnerabilities already. ASEAN (the Association of South-East Asian Nations), not unlike the wider Caribbean in some respects, is consolidating its regional arrangements to face the new world of economic power blocs; and the entire Pacific Rim is developing its own configuration of collective strength. In our hemisphere, the reality of NAFTA[4] – whatever the arguments before it is fully consummated – is already a factor in our Caribbean destiny.

We tend to take comfort in other people's arguments, believing that they will frustrate the consolidation of their unity and release us from the need to respond to it, at least for the time being. But other people's arguments tend not to frustrate, but to refine the development of their unity – unlike ours, which have a potential for interminable postponement of action. These external developments will unfold: in Europe, in North America, in Asia. We cannot afford to simply wait and see how the rest of the world changes and settles down in the twenty-first century and then develop a response to that new world. A new world order is taking shape. I am personally co-chairing an international commission on aspects of that future shape – the Commission on Global Governance. Nineteen ninety-five will be the fiftieth anniversary of the signing of the Charter of the United Nations. We have, as a region, to be involved in these developments – in thinking about them, in trying to shape them so that they help and not hinder our prospects in the new era. Drawing together, as CARICOM heads have agreed, into an Association of Caribbean States – a Commonwealth of the Caribbean – is a very practical and fundamental step in this direction. The alternative is an ever enlarging danger of marginalisation.

The ACS will not answer to any single blueprint. There must be much discussion, and not only between governments. It must be pragmatic and evolutionary; it must not overreach itself in ambition; it must have the capacity to grow and to engender confidence in that capacity. But we must start. I see the Association of the Caribbean States permitting the creation, within the wider Caribbean, of special trade and functional co-operation arrangements in a whole variety of areas. Tourism will be prominent among them; but sea and air transportation, education, complementary health services, co-operation in environmental protection are all among them. Those arrangements should be integrative in character but pragmatic enough to acknowledge and accommodate the relative weakness of smaller economies in relation to larger partners.

I believe, of course, that it ought to be the vocation of CARICOM to take a lead in this matter, and now that CARICOM heads of government are committed to this cause, a special duty falls on us to give such leadership. CARICOM's track record in these respects is a good one. Despite our relative powerlessness, the four larger CARICOM countries played the principal role nearly twenty years ago in ending the hemispheric diplomatic embargo against Cuba.[5] More recently, the West Indian Commission played an effective good offices role in contributing to a resolution of outstanding problems between Grenada and Cuba, facilitating Cuba's membership of the Caribbean Tourism Organisation. CARICOM must remain in the vanguard of the Caribbean movement – not for reasons of vanity, but as a duty that history has bequeathed to us.

But the effort is not one for governments alone. The Caribbean's tourism community, in which the private sector rightly plays such a dominant role, has shown the way in which leadership can be given to the Caribbean movement. The Caribbean Tourism Organisation, your own Caribbean Hotel Association, your collective responses to governmental initiatives for developing co-operative approaches in tourism have helped to open the eyes of Caribbean people to the practical possibilities of working together to mutual benefit on a pan-Caribbean basis. Your efforts at marketing the Caribbean as a single vacation destination has been an enlightened act of emancipation. I am certain that it is one that will lead you to further areas of joint action and encourage governments and other non-governmental elements in our Caribbean community increasingly to act together.

The link with the environment is an absolutely inescapable one and I congratulate the CTO for its efforts in this area. I was particularly gratified – not just as President of the World Conservation Union, but more directly as a Caribbean person – by the conclusions of the Third Caribbean Conference on Eco-Tourism in the Cayman Islands just a month ago. It was encouraging that agreement was reached on the establishment of a CTO Eco-Tourism Society to monitor implementation of the decisions of the CTO's Eco-Tourism Conference; where the need for harmonisation of Caribbean-wide environmental controls was so heavily stressed and where governments were called upon to create incentives which promote environmentally sensitive behaviour. The communiqué stressed that 'while focusing on the Caribbean Sea, the Conference arrived at the concept of regional unity and collective responsibility'. That says it all. Our natural environment, quite apart from all the other compulsions, requires us to act together and with a sense of shared responsibility. There are many respects in which we shall have to exercise that responsibility with enlightenment and in doing so, take hard decisions.

The issue of disposal of solid waste from cruise ships is one of these, and it is a concern which troubles many Caribbean minds. A cruise ship industry which seeks to operate in the Caribbean must accommodate itself to Caribbean environmental regulation. But first must come the regulation – and it can only come by the joint action of all.

An even larger menace looms in the passage of hazardous cargoes through the Caribbean Sea, as nuclear waste, in particular, is transported through our waters from Japan to Europe. CARICOM heads of government have already spoken out against this; but if ever there was an issue that calls for sustained, concerted Caribbean-wide action, it is this. Our only chance of preventing the Caribbean from becoming a nuclear highway is if all who reside in and around it are resolved that it shall not become one.

As in so many other respects, we have to be clear about our priorities. If eco-tourism, for example, is to be a significant dimension of Caribbean tourism, we have to relate our other policies to that priority. When Caribbean delegations vote in international bodies on such issues as the resumption of commercial whaling, we have to recognise the implications of that support for what many nations and people in the world believe to be an unacceptable and retrograde policy towards nature and the marine environment. We have to think what it says about our posture as environmentally sensitive island communities inviting the world to share our ecological treasures. We must ask how we can expect to sell the Caribbean as a destination of eco-tourism when we accept with only the most muted demurral that the Caribbean Sea can be a safe haven for the transportation of nuclear wastes. There are pressures, of course, in all of these areas – on Governments, on enterprises, even on communities. My point is that so long as we remain separate and solitary in our responses to these pressures, we will remain weak and unable to withstand them.

That was the kind of consideration that led the West Indian Commission to propose that steps be taken at the level of the wider Caribbean community, the countries of the entire Basin, to declare the Caribbean a zone of environmental protection. We saw this as the first step towards ensuring that the precious national assets of the Caribbean are used sustainably by our generation. That should not be a matter of argument. We have a duty to pass on to the next generation a Caribbean that is pristine and not defiled, that has a capacity for continued economic growth, not one whose resources are overexploited and desecrated and diminished in its economic potential. To so devastate the Caribbean heritage would be a monumental crime for which future generations of Caribbean people will ever condemn us. But the essential point is that we have to preserve the Caribbean together, if we are to preserve it at all.

I mentioned cruise tourism in the context of the environment. But you know, even more accurately than I, that these are not the only aspects of this new dimension of Caribbean tourism with which we have to grapple. You have taken an enormously significant step in establishing the Caribbean Tourism Development Task Force and you have been fortunate, indeed, in having it chaired by former Prime Minister Michael Manley. That there is a negative impact of cruise tourism on the land-based tourism sector is not a conclusion but a starting point of any consideration of this matter. Cruise tourism must be a net gain to the Caribbean, not a net loss; and, to justify its claim on Caribbean support, that gain must be a substantial overall gain – not one that produces diminishing returns for the primary tourism sector. To ensure that it is, we will require sensitivity and understanding on the part of cruise ship operators at the level of boardrooms beyond the Caribbean. But, perhaps most of all, it will require unity of purpose and action on the part of Caribbean governmental and non-governmental authority.

This is a matter that goes beyond CARICOM and is a test case of our capacity not only to market the Caribbean as a single vacation destination, but also to act together to defend the concept itself – for example, against the erosion of shore-based vacation infrastructure. You will spend some time at this conference debating these matters. It has become essential that the issues be addressed on a basis that is factual not fanciful; in terms of social, economic and political realities not dogma; and, above all, with an acknowledgement that the primary interests to be served are those of the people of the Caribbean, who have a primordial claim on the resources of the Caribbean Sea.

Let me end with an observation of rather wider import, but one which is centrally relevant to how and why we should act as a community of Caribbean people. As the twentieth century draws to a close, our human society is being reminded that we retain our primitive capacities for perpetrating in the name of 'us' and 'them' the most fearful acts of inhumanity. At a time many will say is a high point of human civilisation, we act in brutal and gruesome ways against each other in the name of race, of tribe, of colour, of religion, of language – in short, of ethnicity broadly understood in terms of 'otherness'. The Caribbean has had its demographic character established by historical forces that were themselves examples of such base human instincts. But from this crucible has emerged a multi-cultural, multi-racial, multi-lingual society – one that allows the Caribbean to be a working model of ethnic co-existence and harmony. Perfecting that model is not a small contribution.

It would be far-fetched to say that we are a melting pot of all the diverse elements among us; but it would not be far-fetched to describe all our enriching varieties of race, of culture, of language, of religion and of social and political traditions as a Caribbean bouquet of flowers. It is a bouquet of many exotic blooms – flowers of which we can all be proud as examples of what the Caribbean can help the world to be.

The record is impressive and we owe it to ourselves to recognise it and be proud of it. Costa Rica, for instance, has given an example to the world in living without weapons and armies and a military culture. Cuba leads the Third World in the quality of health care and the infrastructure of education. Of the fifty-five countries worldwide, ranked 'high' by UNDP[6] in terms of human development – including, that is, all the countries of the industrial world – seven are from the Caribbean. Of the total number of developing countries that make that category, almost half are from the Caribbean – and Barbados first among them. In the attainment of excellence in many disciplines, including the advancement of peace, the Caribbean in our own time has produced some of the most renowned Nobel Prize winners – Oscar Arias, Arthur Lewis, Rigoberta Menchu, Gabriel García Márquez, Octavio Paz, Alfonso García-Robles, Derek Walcott: their achievements all came out of a

Caribbean experience and a Caribbean connection. As part of human society, we may be powerless at many levels; but we are strong in the quality of our human endowment. As we pool those resources in a Commonwealth of Caribbean States, we are bound to enlarge our other strengths and endow ourselves with a new capacity to overcome our vulnerabilities.

The West Indian Commission had developed a slogan for CARICOM that 'we do it better when we do it together'. It is a slogan I offer to our wider community as we pursue the vision of a Caribbean Commonwealth.

NOTES

1. The Commonwealth of Nations, whose activities are coordinated by the Commonwealth Secretariat based in London, is an association of over 40 independent countries, most of which are in Africa and the Caribbean, that used to be parts of the British Empire.
2. CARICOM, the Caribbean Community and Common Market, is a regional grouping consisting of 15 countries: Antigua, Bahamas, Barbados, Belize, Dominica, Grenada, Guyana, Haiti, Jamaica, Montserrat, St Kitts-Nevis, St Lucia, St Vincent, Suriname, and Trinidad and Tobago. It was established in 1973, replacing the Caribbean Free Trade Area (CARIFTA), which was formed in 1968, in order to achieve economic cooperation and greater coordination of services, such as education and health, and of foreign policy.
3. By the Treaty of Breda in 1667, the Dutch ceded New Amsterdam, which became New York, in exchange for Suriname. In the peace treaty signed at the end of the Seven Years War (1756–63), England returned Guadeloupe, Martinique and St Lucia to France in exchange for all those parts of north America east of the Mississippi that had been French territories.
4. The North American Free Trade Agreement, inaugurated on January 1, 1994, was passed by the Canadian, Mexican and United States governments in 1993. A triumph for US neo-liberal policies, it increases opportunities for US corporations which seek hemispheric free trade agreements.
5. In 1972, Barbados, Guyana, Jamaica, and Trinidad and Tobago signed a joint diplomatic agreement with Cuba.
6. United Nations Development Programme.

Forty-Four

George Lamming

George Lamming, born in Barbados in 1927, is one of the pioneers of literature in English in the Caribbean. His first novel, In the Castle of My Skin *(1953), is a classic of Caribbean civilization that is widely read around the world. After leaving Combermere School, Lamming taught English and French at a school in Trinidad and then went to England in 1950, where he worked in factories in the London area. He had work published in several English and West Indian magazines and he broadcast on the BBC's Caribbean Service. His other novels include* The Emigrants *(1954),* Of Age and Innocence *(1958),* Season of Adventure *(1960),* Water with Berries *(1971) and* Natives of My Person *(1972). He has also written many essays, a collection of which,* The Pleasures of Exile, *was published in 1960.*

Lamming has held visiting professorships at several US universities and has been writer-in-residence at the University of the West Indies. He has won many prestigious awards and fellowships, including a Guggenheim Fellowship, the Somerset Maugham Award, a Canada Council Fellowship, and an honorary doctorate from the University of the West Indies. He is well known internationally as an outspoken intellectual and spokesman for the cultural sovereignty of the region. 'Caribbean Labor, Culture, and Identity' was originally the keynote address at the first Humanities Festival at the Cave Hill, Barbados, campus of the University of the West Indies on March 6, 1994. It was edited by Glyne Griffith for publication.

*C*aribbean Labor, Culture and Identity

Introduction

Before addressing concerns relating to Caribbean identity, the question of a festival of the humanities also concerns me. I was asking my host whether this was the first humanities festival at the University of the West Indies, and I was both surpised to hear that it was the first such festival at the institution and puzzled that some institution called a university, existing for almost four or five decades, should have its first humanities festival in 1994. And then I am curious as to the extraordinary, euphoric response to the fascinating series of lectures on cricket, in the name of and on behalf of Sir Garfield Sobers.[1] I have listened very carefully to the series of broadcasts on the radio, and what I'm struck by is the thematic repetition of these lectures. They do not vary in any emphasis; there is no variation in theme, and you get the feeling that there is a theme to be presented to the society which could only be presented in the capsule of cricket if it were to be digestible to that society. An interesting paradox here is that what the lectures are critiquing is the very code within which they are constrained. The theme is the role of race as a material form of expression in the determining of social relations and individual attitudes. But that obviously could not be presented with approvable posture, if put in that way. Cricket is the capsule that makes it digestible.

In addition, the fascinating blend of alcohol and the cricket bat and ball, with cricket symbolized in the face of Sir Garfield Sobers appearing as an advertisement strategy on bottles of that most popular of Barbadian spirits, rum, is the sort of thing that would be very worthy of research . . . What I want to do now, therefore, is not so much to lecture, but to take you on a kind of journey which I comprehend as the ongoing theme of what I call the humanities.

If we have at one and the same time embarked on such a journey and indulged in regret about it, we understand that it is a journey which is both autobiographical and historical. In addition, I also want to say something else in relation to the cricket lecture series I mentioned above. It is an observation which is rather different from what I am going to focus on, but it is pertinent to this main focus, and it derives from an interesting comment cited by the historian Edward Hallet Carr in his collection of lectures entitled *What is History?*[2] In this text, Carr indicates that he was reminded by A.E. Housman,[3] himself a very extraordinary sort of poet and classicist, that for the historian, accuracy is a duty, but it is not a virtue. It is very important to get these priorities right, that is, to determine whether accuracy takes precedence over virtue in the practice of that profession, or whether virtue ought to resist any tendency to be swamped by accuracy.

On an occasion such as this (and I wish to say here that I was born in Barbados, which is not usually believed), I always imagine that I am talking to a composite Caribbean audience. Whether I see you or not, what is in front of me as I speak is Trinidad and Guyana and Jamaica, Cuba, the Dominican Republic, and so on. That is the audience I consider myself to be most obviously addressing. What I want to do or try to do in going through this narrative journey is to pinpoint areas of confrontation within the concept of humanities in order to lead to a possible ideology which a university might have about the concept of the humanities. I assume that since this is the first occasion of a humanities festival at this institution, there may be no clarity about the University of the West Indies relation to that area of commitment.

Indian Presence in the Caribbean

My childhood in Barbados did not have on its agenda any question which related to a concept of the Caribbean beyond the most elementary requirements of geography. Jamaica was remote and derived its reality almost entirely from the achievements of a cricketer named George Headley, whom none of us as young people in Barbados would have seen. Guyana, better known then as a place called Demerara, was a place where people in distress often went to consult with obeah men on questions about marriage and the inheritance of property. If you were in any doubt about 'catching' your man or woman, you went to Demerara to get advice on this. Trinidad was a more frequent experience due largely to annual visits of people who were then called tourists. The Trinidadians are no longer tourists, but this territory was at that time a place to be wary of, since the name 'Trinidad' was associated with trickery, sexual license, and a general resistance to all forms of order. That is why during those earlier times the policemen in Trinidad were often recruited from Barbados . . .

In the case of my boyhood/schoolhood recollections, what I am describing is an acute form of insularity which was cultivated in Barbados as a virtue: it was a virtue to be insular. We believed all these things to be true because we were taught that we occupied a place of special favor in the judgment of the ruling Empire. It was the careful work of systematic cultural indoctrination. But if this insularity assumed an extreme form in Barbados, the experience of travel would later warn me that it was, in varying degrees, a fairly general condition throughout the Caribbean region.

If the metropole once encouraged it as a strategy for divide and rule, we Caribbean peoples would later convert it into a convenient device for electoral advantage, until the supreme triumph of backwardness, self-imposed, was realized in the creation of a series of independent ministates, more dependent, more vulnerable, more mendicant than their authors could have imagined. Our particular multiparty system, with its seasonal 'cockfights' for political office, offered us an experiment in democratic participation, but became the most effective instrument of national and regional divisiveness.

My childhood in Barbados did not evoke in me any awareness of an Indian presence in the Caribbean or the concept of the Caribbean as a concrete human reality; yet today, I hold no stronger conviction than that the Caribbean is our own experiment in a unique equation of human civilization. My experiences in Trinidad (to which I owe deep-felt gratitude), not in Barbados, first awoke in me an awareness of this Caribbean world. It started in 1946 with my introduction to Trinidadian families, who were largely of African visibility. It was not always easy for the untutored eye to detect the other ingredients, and I could not always tell who were or were not Indian. They were faces totally black, with a slant of eyes and rigidity of cheekbone which belonged, it seemed, to another race. But it was not the evidence of miscegenation that fascinated so much as the discovery that many of the households I visited during that time were, in fact, a family of islands. The mother in the house would be Grenadian, the father Vincentian, the grandfather Barbadian; there would be an aunt seeking refuge from Antigua, and so on. Sometimes the only Trinidadians by birth were the children. Indeed, perhaps the only real Trinidadians with a length of continuity are Indians. Being the only ones who could trace two or three generations born in the country, and since this lineage, if we consider this aspect only, could trace its branches in a variety of territories, it dawned on me that this region, this Caribbean, was already a fact of continuity.

After what was for me the feudal authority of white Barbados, and it is difficult to communicate to those who did not live there how profoundly feudal that authority was, I had some difficulty recognizing which faces in Trinidad were white. There were certainly such faces, but it seemed as though they moved always through shadows of some other variety. But throughout those four or five years that I lived in Trinidad, I existed in an involuntary, almost unconscious, segregation from the world of Indians in Trinidad. I had not met any Indians, certainly not through casual encounter or as a result of common interests, but these individual relationships had a certain autonomy which did not make for access to that other world of India in Trinidad. And if I did not enter that world of Indians in Trinidad, it was also true to say that I never had any experience of rejection by it. Indeed, that world started to register its absence on me as I became more cognizant of the workplace in certain areas of Trinidadian public life. I rarely, if ever, met an Indian civil servant in the 1940s. I have no recollection of seeing an Indian policeman. But the reality of that world of India in Trinidad came home to me in the very early hours before dawn. I used to enjoy what West Indians call 'liming' (an Anglophone colloquialism meaning to 'hang out', to socialize) in a place called St. James. Since I lived in Belmont, I would be returning from St. James[4] somewhere between two and three in the morning.

The reality came to me in those early hours when the pavement outside what was then the George Street Market would be crowded with what could barely be perceived as human shapes, and boxes, and crocus bags with every variety of fruit and vegetable the earth could produce – and the shapes, these people in the shadows of early morning, were all Indian traders. I recall that I would, in my innocence, wonder how far they had traveled, when they had started on that journey with such a cargo, and whether the country in which I now lived realized that it was these invisible hands which fed it?

Indian Labor: A Creative Caribbean Reality

If labor is the foundation of all culture, then the Indian presence in Trinidad was the ground floor on which that house was built. Fundamental to all of my thinking, this concept of labor and the relations experienced in the process of labor is the foundation of all culture, and this is crucial to what I mean by the Indian presence as a creative Caribbean reality. For it is through work that men and women make nature a part of their own history. The way we see, the way we hear, our nurtured sense of touch and smell, the whole complex of feelings which we call sensibility, is influenced by the particular features of the landscape which has been humanized by our work; there can be no history of Trinidad or Guyana that is not also a history of the humanization of those landscapes by Indian and other human forces of labor.

I have from time to time taken a view that the most serious obstacle for the realization of the late Eric William's triumph as prime minister of Trinidad,[5] and perhaps the greatest explanation for what will have to be seen as his failure to transform the People's National Movement in Trinidad into a national movement, had something to do with the fact that although he recognized the importance of labor, he was not a labor-oriented man. There is no way, in the context of Trinidad, that you could work toward a national movement without coming to a clear understanding of the Indian presence as labor. This had nothing to do with Williams being anti-Indian; he was not pro-black labor either. He simply did not have a labor orientation. This situation was, upon reflection by historians and intellectuals, indeed very sad, because he was at the time and probably still is by today's standards, if you look at who came after, perhaps the most regional of all our leaders in the Caribbean, and the one with the most profound intellectual conviction of the absolute necessity for regionalism.

It was this critical role of labor in the transformation of society which came alive for me again during my first visit to Guyana in the 1950s. These were very, very dark days which revived for me that earlier scene of the 'invisible' hands in the George Street Market in Trinidad. It was the experience really of that visit to Guyana that made possible the novel *Of Age and Innocence* in which I was exploring a reflection, and then not very much later, looking at what were the inherent possibilities that existed there in what was then that movement in Guyana of the PPP.[6] But something quite extraordinary happened in Guyana in the early fifties. What was new and I think without precedent was the forging of two separate armies of labor, African and Indian, into a single political force, and the creation of a consciousness born of that collaboration which led these armies of labor to understand that they were the foundation on which the social order rested. It was, no doubt, this newly forged consciousness that combined with their numerical superiority and the morality of their purpose to equip them to challenge and ultimately dismantle the colonial, authoritarian structure of rule in what was then British Guyana. In the early fifties the People's Progressive Party in Guyana created an environment – expectations and a sense of possibilities – which affected in one way or another every section of the society. It set the agenda of intellectual discourse that influenced the mood and themes of creative expression. This was the soil from which the early and the strongest poems of Guyana's Martin Carter[7] would blossom.

The Creative Potential of Labor

There is for churches and universities an even more precise claim to be made on behalf of organized labor and the informing influence it had on those who have to establish the creative potential of this region in the field of cultural work. It is not often recognized that the major thrust of Caribbean literature in English rose from the soil of labor resistance in the 1930s. The expansion of social justice initiated by the labor struggle had a direct effect on liberating the imagination and restoring the confidence of men and women in the essential humanity of their simple lives. In the cultural history of the region, there is a direct connection between labor and literature, but this dream of Martin Carter suffered a traumatic collapse from which, in my view, the peoples of Guyana have never quite recovered. I am aware of the external forces which were hostile to this dream, the manipulative power of those forces able to intervene and erode what was in the making. However, I do not think we can settle for this as the sole explanation for the collapse of that radical movement against colonialism. A fundamental part of the weakness of that historical moment resulted from the party leadership assuming a human solidarity which had not yet been consolidated. This attribute of human solidarity is not a given; this attribute of human solidarity does not arise by chance or miracle. It has to be learned; it has to be nurtured; it has to be cultivated. This requires a kind of educational work, a kind of indoctrination, the reciprocal sharing of cultural histories which has never been at the center of our political agendas in the Caribbean.

Perhaps there was not time enough. Perhaps it was a misfortune that they came to power, such as it was in 1953. Perhaps the period of opposition, without consuming their energies in the emergencies of administration, might have allowed for that fundamental ground-work in political education and cultural dialogue. This recent consciousness of possibilities among the ranks of labor would have given a new dimension in the most substantial content. Tolerance was the adjustment they made in struggle, but tolerance is a fragile bond, and when the leadership broke, the armies turned with tribal and atavistic fury on each other. We ourselves had fertilized the ground for the enemy to plant further mischief. I think it is a profound illusion and a tragic error to transfer this act of self-mutilation to a foreign conscience we call imperialists. There are certain defeats for which we must be prepared to take full responsibility.

Race: A Force Used to Segregate Labor

The factor we call race has always been a component in our political history. It has been the device which the old plantocracy used to segregate the forces of labor which derived from a different cultural formation. The plantocracy successfully employed such strategies to maintain control over those divisions, and this historical circumstance has been the cultural appeal which certain nationalists, who had no other claims to speak, have made. The consequence of these antagonisms led inevitably to mutual charges of racism. Trinidad, for example, has become increasingly a battleground for this conflict of accusations, but to me it is interesting how Trinidad allows for a certain flexibility in the way these charges are formulated. I take two examples from two distinguished Trinidadians of Indian ancestry. In an interview in the twenty-fifth-independence edition of the *Express* newspaper, Mr. Panday,[8] now Prime Minister of Trinidad and Tobago, states:

> I still maintain that the late Dr. Eric Williams created one of the 'most racist' organizations. As I explained earlier, the politics of the society has been organized around the expediency of this political fact. The fact of the matter is that the two numerically dominant groups – the Africans and Indians – have both been disadvantaged as a result of the politics which the Williams design bred.

And in the same newspaper, Kenneth Ramchand,[9] a literary critic and professor of West Indian Literature at the University of the West Indies, indicates that:

> For all of its failings, many of them serious, the party of Dr. Eric Williams must be given credit of a sort. It has never gone so far as to undermine in a decisive way, either the possibility of the idea of racial harmony or the non-partisan status of the army or the police. We take these things for granted at our peril.

I take the word *racism* to have a specific and historical meaning. It defines those individuals and groups who have a profound conviction, accumulated over a long period of time, that they possess an inherent superiority over others, and furthermore they have the power to impose that conviction. It is therefore very different from racial consciousness, and it is not my experience that this kind of conviction informs and determines the relations between Afro- and Indo-Trinidadians. The factor of race as a component in our politics has always given national struggle – even the struggle for equality – a racial component. But the acute sectional rivalry for the distribution of spoils and power in Trinidad does not constitute, in my view, a racist confrontation.

Seeds of Caribbean Identity Formation

A concept of a people or a place does not arise out of the blue. How you come to think of where you are and how you come to think of your relation to where you are is dependent on what is the character and the nature of power where you are situated. You yourself do not, at a certain stage, decide who you are and what your relationship to where you are should be, and it is an illusion to think that you do. These relations are experienced within a specific context of power, and this experience always poses fundamental questions: to what extent have we been able to organize in the interest of our own welfare? to what extent can we control those who have acquired the power to organize our lives?

West Indian economists will frequently identify the problems of scarcity which justify their own professional experience. If you could find a society where there was no problem of scarcity, there could be no such thing as an economist. There would be no raison d'etre for the existence of any such expertise. It is the existence of the problem of scarcity that justifies that function, and economists are quick to identify the problems of scarcity. They are much more reluctant to explore and reveal the nature and the exercise of the power which determines that scarcity. And so, if you are trying to think of concepts of the Caribbean, these concepts you find will undergo a certain change. They will differ according to either the centers of power that are shaping them or to the centers of resistance against that power.

If you read the history naively and you hear about a sailor named Columbus whom you receive as hero and discoverer of worlds, your reading participates in a concept that has been shaped by some authority. It is very interesting to me, and I hope it will be for you, to draw attention here to two remarkable books carrying exactly the same title – *From Columbus to Castro* – both published in 1970 and written by two distinguished Caribbean scholars: Juan Bosch[10] of Santo Domingo and Eric Williams of Trinidad. Both books were published in the same year, yet neither author was aware that the other was doing the same thing.

The Williams version is a predominantly Anglophone experience. Bosch, however, presents a drama that takes place in what appears to be a Spanish sea. The index of names and places is a remarkable contrast in emphasis. As a result, Bosch offers more of a glimpse of the aboriginal peoples in their response to Spanish invaders than we find in Williams's work, whose book of some five-hundred-odd pages makes only four brief references to the Caribs, a people who had continued to offer the fiercest resistance to the Spanish invaders for more than two hundred years after the arrival of the admiral. Just four references to the Caribs in Williams's *From Columbus to Castro* – yet we have evidence that these people had been around the Americas from about 300 B.C.; and up until around A.D. 1000, the Caribs were still arriving in the Caribbean.

This cross-fertilization was the seed of our journey, and thus, people who are talking about roots, are not really talking about our formation. This cross-fertilization is the seed of all the journeys, not exclusively the encounter of Europe and Africa or Europe and Asia. And it is this encounter of Europe, Africa, and Asia in the Americas, with its resulting violence, which precipitated Maroon escape from bondage; and, in our time, it is the contemporary challenge of creolization that continues to haunt the energies of many Caribbean writers of African and Indian descent. Within thirty or forty years of the admiral's arrival, we have the almost total destruction of an indigenous population. In other words, what we know of the modern Caribbean, that is, the Caribbean over the last five hundred years, is an area of the world that begins with an almost unprecedented act of genocide. So now what you are talking about or looking at when you contemplate history and the movement of history and the concepts which are used to define historical events depends on the center of power that is your defining marker or the center of resistance that is your redefining marker.

The early arrivants may look heroic if you are looking at one part of what they did. Their achievement in navigation is remarkable; that cannot be devalued or undermined, but at the receiving end, there is a somewhat different story. There is a great deal of repetitive, elaborate complaint and lament about the cruelty of these men in the West Indies. But what I think we sometimes either fail to recognize, or recognize but perhaps do not want to put on the agenda, is their own formation. What sort of world did these men come out of?

If you take, for example, the Dutch historian, Johan Huizinga,[11] you are provided with insight into the cruel harshness of the world from which these men of Europe would come. Here is a passage from Huizinga's *The Waning of the Middle Ages*:

> Tortures and executions are enjoyed by the spectators like an entertainment at a fair ... The people of Bruges, in 1488, during the captivity of Maximilian, king of the Romans, cannot get their fill of seeing the tortures inflicted, on a high

platform in the middle of the market-place, on the magistrates suspected of treason. The unfortunates are refused the death-blow which they implore, that the people may feast again upon their torments.

This is the world, the environment, that shaped the sensibilities of the men who would arrive on the scene in the Americas. And so, what this devastation leaves us with is a territory settled and regimented by those who achieve, lose, and later recover possessions. What it leaves us with are territories that did not exist in and for themselves; what it leaves us with is the concept of the Caribbean as an imperial frontier.

The Caribbean: An Imperial Frontier

I think that the teachers in our schools, if they are aware of all this, may not always think it prudent to bring home to their students that this history, our history, has been one of almost unprecedented violence. This violence has marked this terrain as imperial frontier: territories of infinite beauty whose material life would be controlled in the interest of a center, we would learn, called the metropole. It is a concept that would be contested by insurrection, by rebellion, by riot, and by intellectual argument from native centers of resistance. The alternative center of resistance has been planted and has gradually expanded. In a way, I suspect there are elements within the university structure of all our territories which have been the agents of this expansion, creating and fertilizing this concept of the Caribbean as one's own historical experience, whose fundamental cultural links are within the region, waiting to be identified and explored. But this legacy of the imperial frontier remains formidable. Yesterday it was Empire; today it is market idolatry. Professor Gordon Rohlehr,[12] in an introduction to a remarkable anthology, *Voice Print*, states in a subdued tone of bitterness that:

> It is only since the 1970s that the term 'oral tradition' began to be consistently used in connection with certain developments in West Indian poetry. Before then the debate concerned the viability of 'dialect' as a medium for poetry, and was an extension of the troubled issue of the nexus between education, speech, class, status and power. Creole dialects were thought of as belonging to the semi-literate and poor. To argue, as some linguists did and still do, that Creole is simply another language, neither better nor worse than any other, was to ignore the social and political nature of language. To speak about the vitality and expressiveness of Creole was to sentimentalise warm folksiness without wanting to share in the anguish of its decrepitude, and to display the contempt of a complacent intelligentsia, who secretly wanted to reinforce their superior social status by keeping the mass of the people uneducated.

A very serious problem is articulated here in that there was a strong current within the population which was hostile to the notion of elevating something called dialect and Creole speech.

I will move now into what I consider to be the metaphor at work in this Caribbean imagination. There seems to me to exist a geography of imagination which imposes on the Caribbean artist a unique location in time and space. The island is a world whose immediate neighborhood is the sea. The landscape of the mainland, vast and cluttered by a great variety of topography, achieves its individuality by the erection of boundaries and the appropriation of frontiers. The island knows no boundary except the ocean, which is its gateway to eternity. If the frontier astonishes by its wealth of wonders and the infinite promise of marvels to be revealed, the island is a reservoir of secrets. The secret is simultaneously its shield and the pearl which it is often forced to barter. It is too visible for comfort and its size makes it vulnerable to the most casual of pirates in pursuit of fortune.

There is a peculiar sensibility that is nurtured by this paradoxical need to participate in novel encounters while it protects that area of privacy which gives it its special character. The island is a private place which attracts multiple forms of intrusion. So there is a Caribbean sensibility whose undiscovered history resides in its fiction, whose history achieves authenticity through the intricacies of metaphor. What the imagination implies achieves a greater force of persuasion for truth than the statistical evidence which measures this evasive and mesmerizing reality which history records. There is, therefore, this most paradoxical relation to place where each island signals the origin of a disaster and is also a seed which fertilizes an extraordinary faith in the possibility of recovering worlds of the spirit which yet remain obscured and entombed. A stranger sees from the cruiseline, now the more fashionable mode of loitering in the region, these isolated pebbles designed for the causal pleasure of men and women who seek a temporary distraction from the tedium of wealth, but in the imagination of poet Aimé Césaire,[13] for example, each island is an eye whose gaze the ocean has extended to embrace all continents as though geography had gone to war:

> Mine too the archipelago bent like the anxious desire for self-negation as if with material concern for the most frail slenderness separating the two Americas, and the womb which spills towards Europe and the good liquor of the Gulf Stream, and one of the two incandescent slopes through which the equator walks its tight rope to Africa. And my unfenced island, its bold flesh upright at the stern of the Polynesia, and right before it, Guadeloupe split in two by its dorsal ridge and as miserable as we ourselves; Haiti where Negritude stood up for the first time and swore by its humanity; and the droll little tail of Florida where a Negro is being lynched, and Africa caterpillaring gigantically up to the Spanish foot of Europe: its

nakedness where the scythe of Death swings wide. And I say to myself Bordeaux and Nantes and Liverpool and New York and San Francisco. Not a corner of this world but carries my fingerprint.

This theme of the inward journey is taken up by one of the most extraordinary intellectuals of this region, Fernando Ortiz, and there is a work of his which I believe should be at the center of reading for any scholar of the Caribbean, *Cuban Counterpoint*.[14] In this work, Ortiz looks at the evolution of a Caribbean society through the lens of two crops, sugar and tobacco. Through this lens, Ortiz arrives at a notion with which I want to conclude. It is an idea that separates us from the traditional concept of humanities, and brings us, not to the notion of acculturation, but to the idea of transculturation – the notion that if you consider what was already the mixed element in the people who came, and if you consider what was already the mixed elements in the very early stages of arrival, what you then observe is not only what impact x had on y, but also importantly what influence y had on x. This notion, which I think should be at the heart of the concept of the humanities – and which of course it would have been difficult for Europe to acquire – presents us with a particular and special kind of opportunity.

Caribbean Transculturation

This conjecture of worlds, Amerindian, European, African, and Asian, concentrated within this enclosure, reveals this persistent feature which is a continuing challenge to the native imagination, and I refer to the depth and durability of European hegemony. Thus Columbus was not only a courageous sailor, but a leader and the emissary of a new epoch. He was the carrier of a virus to which the people of the Caribbean would have no adequate immune response. The fundamental truth behind such conclusions is that this materialism, linked to human progress, allowed the Western world to accept that even the enslavement of a people was morally justifiable if it contributed to the march toward economic development, so that the universalizing power of capital reduced labor to a state of fugitive suspense.

Our concept of the humanities, shaped by the European Renaissance from the fifteenth century onwards, and the concept from which this institution, the University of the West Indies, would have been founded, was intended to provide some concrete insight into the nature of the human mode of being. What did it mean to be human? It is a concept which was intended to provide us some perspective from which we might be able to understand human life as a total meaning, expressed in the various manifestations which human existence might take, so that through the intellectual disciplines of art, music, history, religion, and philosophy we would acquire the necessary data which would illuminate all those issues relating to the fundamental question of being human. But for the greater part of the Western triumph that I have been discussing above, this data was circumscribed by those perceptions which had emerged almost exclusively from the Hebraic, Greek, and Christian forms of culture. Indeed, this data would acquire the authority to establish the normative meanings and definitions of all human worlds. It means, therefore, that an enormous body of scholarship and the intellectual staples through which almost everybody taught in these institutions would have been shaped fell within the context of this ideological construct. This concept of the humanities, therefore, has a history that is inseparable from the history of Western imperialism from the fifteenth century to the present. The world was divided between the West and those imperial 'others'.

There is a story of the Nigerian poet, dramatist, and essayist, Nobel laureate, Wole Soyinka,[15] which illustrates what I'm saying. Soyinka was invited to give a series of lectures at Cambridge University, and when he arrived, he discovered that the faculty members of the Department of English were surprised that he had chosen to lecture on African literature, though he was at the time a professor of literature in Nigeria. Cambridge did not yet consider or had not yet arrived at considering that there was such a category as African literature. When he decided not to go on with the lectures, they asked him to stay, but arrangements were made for the lectures to be given under the auspices of the Department of Anthropology.

Alternatively, our own experience of the Fernando Ortiz concept of transculturation in the Caribbean would help to put some distance between ourselves and that ideological construct which is so fundamental to experiences such as Soyinka's at Cambridge . . . These questions of the boundaries and the borders of the humanities are, I think, very urgent, since the university, and here I am speaking of the University of the West Indies, as an intellectual community, will find that it has to operate in the context of an increasingly aggressive market ideology.

In this connection, I would like to draw your attention to some of the conflicts and contradictions raised by the American economist Kenneth Galbraith[16] in an interesting work, *The New Industrial State*. These conflicts and contradictions have to do with what we imagine to be free choice and the organized management of consumer demand:

> But there remain more general sources of conflict between the educational and scientific estate . . . One is the management of individual behavior. In the absence of a clear view of the nature of this conflict, much of the dispute centers not on its ultimate causes but on the techniques of management. Management requires extensive access to means of communication – newspapers, billboards,

radio and especially television. To insure attention these media must be raucous and dissonant. It is also of the utmost importance that this effort convey an impression, however meretricious, of the importance of the goods being sold. The market for soap can only be managed if the attention of consumers is captured for what, otherwise, is a rather incidental artifact. Accordingly, the smell of soap, the texture of its suds, the whiteness of textiles treated thereby and the resulting esteem and prestige in the neighborhood are held to be of the highest moment. Housewives are imagined to discuss such matters with an intensity otherwise reserved for unwanted pregnancy and nuclear war. Similarly with cigarettes, laxatives, pain-killers, beer, automobiles, dentrifices, packaged foods and all other significant consumer products . . . The economy for its success requires organized public bamboozlement.

And finally, Galbraith speculates on a matter that I think would be very close to our own experience when he says that where the society approves and applauds money-making as the highest social purpose, public servants will often think it appropriate that they sell themselves or their decisions for what they are worth to the buyers.

Now here is a central paradox for the University of the West Indies as an intellectual community which is called upon to train people in the skills which support this system. Here is a critical challenge for this university as an intellectual community in its intercourse with the advertising complex which has, and will continue to have, a power to determine the scale, the content, and the direction of all cultural activity.

NOTES

1. Sobers, widely considered to be one of the greatest all-round cricketers ever, was captain of Barbados, Nottinghamshire, and the West Indies. During 1994, a series of radio talks on West Indies cricket was broadcast in Barbados in honour of Sobers.
2. E.H. Carr. *What is History?* (New York 1961).
3. A.E. Housman (1859–1936) was an English poet and classical scholar who taught at University College, London, and Cambridge University. He is best known for his collections of poems *A Shropshire Lad* (1896) and *Last Poems* (1922).
4. St James, to the west of downtown Port of Spain, is the urban centre of Indian life, and Belmont lies to the east of Queen's Park Savannah.
5. Eric Williams (1911–81), the founder and leader of the People's National Movement, was the prime minister of Trinidad and Tobago from 1956 until his death (see chapter 26 in this volume).
6. The People's Progressive Party, led by Cheddi Jagan and Forbes Burnham, formed the government after winning the first election under universal adult suffrage in April 1953, with 51 per cent of the votes, but the British government suspended the constitution in October. Burnham later split the PPP and, from 1956, race emerged as

the central issue in Guyana's politics, with the largely Indian PPP, led by Jagan, opposed by Burnham's largely African People's National Congress (see Chapter 31 in this volume).

7. Martin Carter (1927–97) was a Guyanese poet and nationalist who was jailed by the British. He became well-known for his *Poems of Resistance* (1954), including 'University of Hunger', some of which he wrote in prison. His *Selected Poems* was published in 1989.

8. Basdeo Panday, leader of the United National Congress, became Trinidad and Tobago's first prime minister of Indian origin in 1995 and remained in power until 2001. The quote is from *The Sunday Express Independence Magazine*, Aug. 30, 1987, pp.46–7.

9. Kenneth Ramchand, author of *The West Indian Novel and its Background* (1970), taught West Indian literature at the University of the West Indies in Trinidad and Colgate University in the United States. The quote is from *The Sunday Express Independence Magazine*, Aug. 30, 1987, pp.17-18.

10. Juan Bosch, born in the Dominican Republic in 1909, lived in exile from 1937 to 1961, a democratic opponent of the dictator Rafael Trujillo. He went home after Trujillo's death and was elected president in 1962. He was overthrown by the army after only seven months and again went into exile. When his supporters attempted to overthrow the military government and restore him to power in 1965 there was massive US intervention, ordered by President Lyndon Johnson. Busch criticised US foreign policy in a book, *Pentagonism: A Substitute for Imperialism* (1968).

11. Johan Huizinga (1872–1945) taught at universities in Amsterdam, Groningen and Leyden. His best-known book, *The Waning of the Middle Ages*, was first published in Dutch in 1919 and in English in 1924. The quote is from the Peregrine Books edition (1965), pages 22-3.

12. Gordon Rohlehr teaches West Indian literature at the University of the West Indies in Trinidad. An expert on calypso, he is the author of *Calypso and Society in Pre-Independence Trinidad* (1990) and co-editor with Stewart Brown and Mervyn Morris of *Voiceprint: An Anthology of Oral and Related Poetry from the Caribbean* (1989), from which comes the quote, p.1.

13. See chapter 16 in this volume. The quote is from *Aimé Césaire: The Collected Poetry*, translated by Clayton Eshleman and Annette Smith (Berkeley:1983), p.47.

14. See chapter 4 in this volume

15. Wole Soyinka, born in Nigeria in 1934, is a playwright, poet, novelist and essayist, who won the Nobel Prize for literature in 1986, the first African to do so. Among his best-known plays are *A Dance of the Forests* (1963), written to celebrate Nigeria's independence, *The Lion and the Jewel* (1963), *The Road* (1965), *Kongi's Harvest* (1967) and *Death and the King's Horsemen* (1975). His other works include the novels *The Interpreters* (1965) and *Season of Anomy* (1973), and several volumes of memoirs and collections of essays, including *Ibadan* (1994) and *Myth, Literature and the African World* (1976).

16. John Kenneth Galbraith, born in Canada in 1908, taught economics at Harvard and Princeton universities and was the US ambassador to India from 1961 to 1963. Among his best-known books are *American Capitalism* (1951), *The Affluent Society* (1958) and *The New Industrial State* (1967), from which this quote is taken, p. 293.

Forty-Five

Orlando Patterson

Orlando Patterson was born in Jamaica in 1940 and graduated from the University of the West Indies in 1962, the year his country became independent. He went on a scholarship to the London School of Economics where he completed his doctorate in sociology and became a member of the faculty in 1965. He also wrote two novels during that time, The Children of Sisyphus *(1964), which won the first prize for fiction at the Dakar Festival of Negro Arts in 1966, and* An Absence of Ruins *(1965). In 1967, he returned to the University of the West Indies in Jamaica to teach sociology and his book,* The Sociology of Slavery: An Analysis of the Origins, Development and Structure of Negro Slave Society in Jamaica *(London, 1967) was published. He left Jamaica to teach at Harvard University where he became a professor of sociology. Among his other books are* Slavery and Social Death *(Cambridge, Mass., 1982) and* Freedom Vol.1: Freedom in the Making of Western Culture *(New York, 1991).*

In his essay, 'Ecumenical America', Patterson explores the implications for ideas of culture, nation and identity of the mass migration of Caribbean people into the United States and Canada and the new forms of mass communication between these regions. Through the diffusion between these regions of popular culture, such as music, and the movement of people, both migrants and tourists, a new 'ecumenical America' is emerging in the West Atlantic system, which he calls a 'regional cosmos,' in which new cultural forms and flexible identities are created in a 'transnational space.' Among other issues, these changes include a challenge to the traditional binary conception of 'race' which predominates in the United States but not in the Caribbean.

$\mathscr{E}$cumenical America: Global Culture and the American Cosmos

The modern process of global cultural interaction has repeatedly been subjected to two criticisms. The first is that it threatens the diversity and particularism of the world's cultures, resulting in a deadening homogenization of the human cultural experience. The other is that this growing global uniformity results from the dominance of America's culture – that, in effect, global culture is nothing more than American cultural imperialism . . . Both objections are without foundation.

The argument that Americanization is resulting in the homogenization of the world ignores the increased vitality of local cultures and ethnicities in recent times and the complexity of global cultural diffusion, in particular the extent to which so-called peripheral regions are increasingly contributing to American popular culture and to the world music scene. Nor does it explain the emergence of a special kind of regional system, what I shall call the regional cosmos, or the great cultural divisions in America itself. The American cosmos, as we shall see, is not a single cultural space, but is divided among three Americas: a traditional America, multicultural America, and ecumenical America.

The Diffusion of Global Culture

Industrialization and modernization both entailed the spread of common sets of behaviors and attitudes within the context of economic change. However, the globalization of culture also takes place independent of whatever economic changes are occurring in a particular region or society. Traditionally, the transmission of culture across societies was facilitated by two main media: migration and literacy. People learned about other cultures either through traveling themselves or from travelers, or by reading about other cultures and adopting or adapting what they learned. These traditional media could, under certain circumstances, be effective means for the transmission of cultures across the globe.

The distinctive feature of literary transmissions, and all diffusions through individuals except during mass migrations, is that they tend to be largely confined to elites, or, where not, to enclaves of non-elite persons cut off from the mass of their societies. This was true of the diffusion of Hellenism[1] in the Mediterranean world and was largely true of the imperial influence on the societies of Asia and Africa. Until the end of the Second World War, Westernism was largely confined to a tiny minority of the populations of these continents, largely the educated native elites and urban workers. Since the fifties, however, this has changed radically. The globalization of culture, largely (although by no means solely, as the spread of

Islam indicates) through the impact of, and *reaction to*, the diffusion of Western popular and elite culture, has not only greatly increased in terms of its spread over the surface of the world, but in terms of the depth to which it has influenced the populations of other societies.

Four factors account for this sudden change of pace. The first is the spread of mass literacy throughout the world, which resulted from the new nations of the post-colonial era investing vast sums and human energy in their educational systems, the structure and content of which were largely influenced by Western models. The second is the rise of mass communication. The third is the growth of global organizations, both private and public, such as the multinational corporation, the United Nations, the World Bank, the IMF, and the large number of regional agencies, themselves often modeled on and directly influenced and promoted by the former. The fourth is the revolution in long-distance transportation, which has resulted in the emergence of an entirely new kind of global, or more properly, subglobal system, the regional cosmos. The most remarkable of these emerging regional cosmoses is the West Atlantic system,[2] encompassed by the eastern seaboard of North America and the circum-Caribbean societies of Central America and the islands.

The Global Popular Music Culture

The emergence of the regional cosmoses provides perhaps the best evidence of the complexity of global cultural diffusion. But before turning to the subject of their development, let us consider one example of global cultural diffusion – namely, how mass communication has facilitated the diffusion and creation of global popular musical culture. I choose to focus on popular music because it is in this area of the globalization process that the strongest claims of homogenization have been made. Its classic statement was given by the musicologist Alan Lomax who, in 1968, lamented the presumed passing of the great local cultures of the world under the impact of American popular culture, which, he feared, would lead to global rootlessness and alienation as the peoples of the earth all sank into the desolate gloom of the great, global 'cultural grey-out.'[3]

As someone who has studied this process in a Third World society that has perhaps been more exposed to the full glare of American culture than nearly any other – namely, Jamaica – I can say unequivocally that such charges are utter nonsense. It is simply not true that the diffusion of Western culture, especially at the popular level, leads to the homogenization of the culture of the world. Indeed, my research, and that of the best scholars working in this area, suggests that just the opposite is the case. Western-American cultural influence has generated enormous cultural production, in some cases amounting to near hypercreativity in the popular cultures of the world.

If what I say is correct, it must be wondered where the popular misconception of the homogenizing effect of the Western impact came from. One source is the propagandistic reaction of traditional cultural gatekeepers in Third World societies whose monopoly and influence has been threatened by the Western cultural impact. That impact, in generating new cultural forms, invariably stimulates the emergence of new and competing cultural agents and managers. To monopolize the cultural resources of a country is to exercise enormous power, not to mention to control economic resources. What usually upsets traditional cultural gatekeepers about the Western impact on their mass cultures is less the content of Western culture – because this is invariably transformed – and more the choice it immediately offers to the consumers of culture.

The second source of misconceptions about the impact of Westernism comes from important segments of the cultural gatekeepers in the West itself, on both the right and the left, who think and talk about this issue. The more abstract of these complaints about the influence of American global popular culture stem from elitist, postmodernist pessimism, of the sort that stimulates similar complaints about the stultifying effects of popular culture on the working class of the West. Cultural critic Paul Willis has recently taken issue with these pretentious criticisms. He notes that people never simply passively absorb cultural messages[4]. . .

There is a great deal of sloppy and ill-informed criticism of Americanization in what passes for serious, empirically based research. It is simply assumed that illiterate and semi-literate Third World peoples are powerless in their responses to Western popular culture. Experts on the subject have in mind a world of passive consumers, homogenized and manipulated into Marx's notorious sack of (Westernized) potatoes.[5] It is nothing of the sort. The semi- and non-literate masses of the Third World invariably react to Western cultural influence in a nonpassive manner, reinterpreting what they receive in the light of their own cultures and experience . . .

Either the Western cultural form is reinterpreted in light of traditional meanings, or Western meanings are adapted to traditional patterns. In any case, something new, although still local, emerges. As the musicologist Peter Manuel points out, not only do local cultures 'adapt foreign elements in distinctly idiosyncratic ways that substantially alter their function, context and meaning', but even what appears to Western ears and perception to be a major intrusion, may, in fact, be so shallow functionally to the native listener as to not even be perceived. This is true, for example, of the influence of American music on the thriving Indian pop culture.[6]

In their comparative analysis of eight cultures, musicologists Deanna Robinson, Elizabeth Buck, and others have demonstrated, in my opinion conclusively, that 'world musical homogenization is not occurring'. As they put it, 'even though information-age economic forces are building an international consumership for centrally produced and distributed popular music, other factors are pulling in the opposite direction. They are encouraging not only what we call "indigenization" of popular music forms and production but also new, eclectic combinations of world musical elements, combinations that contradict the continuing constraints of national boundaries and global capitalism'. [7]

Furthermore, the common notion that the globalization of culture, especially on the popular level, is a one-way process, from the Western metropolis to the passive and vulnerable periphery, is simply not the case, although it is certainly true that the major diffusionary source of this culture is a single Western country: the United States.

Not homogenization, then, but the revitalization and generation of new musical forms has been the effect of the global exchange process. Some of these forms remain local, providing greater choice and stimulus to the local culture. Examples of such revitalization include the modernization of the traditional Camerounian *makassi* style with the introduction of the acoustic rhythm guitar; the development of the *highlife* music of Ghana, which fused traditional forms with jazz, rock, and Trinidadian calypso rhythms; the vibrant local modernization of traditional Afro-Arab music in Kenya. Elsewhere, musical forms under Western impact have broken out of their provincial boundaries to become regional currency, as, for example, the Trinidadian and American pop influenced *kru-krio* music of Sierra Leone, which swept West Africa and beyond during the sixties and seventies; the Brazilian *sambo*, the pan-American *salsa*; *merengue* (the latter of Dominican Republic origin); the originally Cuban *nueva trova*, which became a radical pan-Latin form, stimulating the even more radical and pan-Latin *nueva cancion*; and the Colombian *cumbia*, which has become an important part of the music of the Tex-Mex regional cosmos . . .

Out of Jamaica

One of the most globally successful cultural creations of a Third World people is the musical form known as *reggae*. Indeed, the development of reggae perhaps more than any other musical form illustrates the complexity of global cultural interaction. The creation of the Jamaican working classes and lumpen proletariat, reggae emerged in the late fifties from a variety of influences, especially American. Jamaica had always had a rich musical tradition, originating mainly in the music of West Africa brought over by the slaves, but also influenced in its lyrical and melodic lines by British, especially Celtic, popular music of the late eighteenth and nineteenth centuries. At the turn of the century, a popular secular form, *mento*, ideal for dancing, emerged. Similar to the Trinidad calypso in its topical and satirical lyrics and in its reliance on the guitar for a Latinate ostinato, *mento* soon established itself as *the* traditional popular music of the island.

By the late fifties, however, young working-class Jamaicans had grown weary of *mento*. What they did like were the rhythm-and-blues records being brought back by farm laborers returning from cutting cane in Florida and the 'cowboy music' or bluegrass they picked up on short-wave early in the mornings. Aspiring young Jamaican singers – including the teenage Bob Marley, Peter Tosh, Bob Andy, and numerous others – began singing imitations of American soul songs at the many talent parades that preceded the weekend triple bills at the working-class cinemas. These imitations were, at first, ghastly renditions of the original. (I can still recall hearing a pimpled, short-haired Bob Marley singing an American soul song hopelessly out of tune.) At this point, Jamaica would seem to have had the worst of all possible worlds. A delightful native musical tradition had been abandoned, and in its place the island found its middle class swooning over syrupy white American ballads while its lower class sang imitations of African American music.

What happened next, however, demonstrates just how complex the dialectics between local and foreign influences that generate the global culture are. First of all, the imitations were so bad that they were unwittingly original. Furthermore, the Jamaicans instinctively brought their own local musical cadences and rhythms to bear on the tunes being imitated. This coincided with an infusion of the very African music of the Afro-Jamaican cults, which was lifted straight from the 'laboring' movements made by cult celebrants as they worked themselves up to the point of spirit possession. Both the movement and the accompanying rhythm were secularized (in a manner similar to the crossover from gospel to soul music among African Americans), and a wholly new musical form and accompanying dance, known as *ska*, was created.

At the time – the late fifties and early sixties – the vast majority of working-class Jamaicans were still too poor to buy record players or expensive imported records. This led to the formation of the *sound system*, a hi-fidelity system outfitted with enormous bass speakers, which the owners rented out, along with their record collections and themselves in the role of disc jockey. The disc jockeys, partly out of boredom, partly out of increasing dissatisfaction with the rhythmic patterns of the imported African American records, but above all, out of a desire to give a 'live' quality to the performance of their systems, started to deliberately play around with the records as they were being played. They voiced over the imported records with their own rhythmic commentary, improving their 'riddim' as they understood it, either through grunts and screams, or through an accompanying screed that sometimes made sense, sometimes was mere nonsense lyrics, which mattered little since the voice was actually being used as an additional bass instrument. This was rapidly to become a distinctive feature of reggae. The disc jockey would also 'play' the turntable, stopping and pushing the record as it turned on the platter in order to induce strange new sounds. This, too, was later to become an essential part of the music, except that the strange noises were to be made through the manipulation of sophisticated studio electronics.

What emerged from these activities was another distinctive musical form, *dub*. When the disc jockeys were unable to match the love lyrics of the imported black American rhythm-and-blues songs, they resorted to what they knew best, local politics. Thus was born reggae dub, with its strong emphasis on the political, a clear departure from popular American music, black or white.

At about the same time that these developments were taking place, the Ras Tafari cult, a millenarian back-to-Africa movement that was the religious component of the reaction to Western influence, was taking hold among the Jamaican proletariat of the Kingston shanties. The spiritualism and radical racial ideology of the cult – a religious form of negritude, exemplifying Sartre's 'anti-racist racism' – greatly appealed to the very people developing the music, and it was not long before the two merged, Rastafarian theology giving substance and ideological content to what were previously soppy imported lyrics or garbled political chatter.

The music swiftly went through several formal changes, first from ska to *rock-steady*, a more complex slow-tempo music, and finally, in response to the demands of the entrepreneurs who ran the weekend dance halls and who wanted music with a faster beat so their patrons would drink more of the Red Stripe beer on which they largely depended for their profits, to reggae.

Reggae swiftly caught on, not only among locals, but with the American tourists who were now visiting Jamaica in increasing numbers. Several major singers emerged in the late sixties and early seventies, the most successful of whom was Bob Marley, whose enormous showmanship and song-writing ability were important in internationalizing the music. However, one other factor was equally important in explaining the rapid spread of reggae and its eventual emergence as a global musical form. This was the mass movements of Jamaican working-class migrants. The first such movement was to Britain, where Jamaicans effectively transformed what was a previously all-white country into a multiracial society. By 1964, a thinly Anglicized version of ska known as *blue beat* was already in vogue.[8] Today, reggae has been completely embraced by white British youth, who now view it as an integral part of their culture.[9] From its British base, it was to spread rapidly throughout continental Europe and north and sub-Saharan Africa.

Similarly, reggae spread to the United States as a result of a second mass migration of the Jamaican working class, which began with the liberalization of American immigration laws in the early 1960s. A new kind of West Indian migrant now entered America, not the relatively well-educated, highly motivated petty-bourgeois migrants of previous generations, but the working-class and lumpen-proletarian people from the Kingston slums. Eventually, the reggae music these new migrants brought over with them, along with their disk jockeys and dance halls (as well as their gangs, the notorious posses), were to influence black American youth, but what is interesting is how long it took to do so. Black Americans, in fact, strongly resisted most versions of reggae. Reggae, however, rapidly caught on among the white college students of America, especially after the enormous success of the reggae movie, *The Harder They Come*, and soon broke out of the campus circuit with the success of Bob Marley and other international stars, such as Jimmy Cliff and Peter Tosh.[10]

Eventually, by the late 1970s and early 1980s, even the underclass African American young began to respond to reggae. They were simply unable to prevent themselves from listening to the version of reggae brought over to the ghettoes by the latest wave of underclass Kingston migrants: the dance-hall music. The fact that they also soon developed a healthy respect for the violent Jamaican posses also explains their changed attitude.

The music had gone full circle, from its beginnings in the crude imitations of 1950s' African American lower-class music, to the late 1970s' and early 1980s' imitations of dance-hall dub by the New York underclass. The American music that emerged from this extraordinary proletarian cross-fertilization was *rap*, the first popular American music to have an explicitly political lyrical content. The Jamaicans have repaid their debt.

The West Atlantic Regional Cosmos

The transmission of reggae to the American center from the Jamaican periphery not only illustrates the complexity of global cultural interaction, but was a forerunner of a much more complex process that has now integrated parts of the United States with other countries as deeply or more deeply than those parts are integrated with other regions of America. This aspect of the globalization of culture, which has resulted in the development of regional cosmoses, is entirely new. Indeed, it has emerged only over the past two decades or so, largely because it was dependent upon the revolution in cheap mass transportation.

The regional cosmos is best conceived of as a system of flows between a metropolitan center and a set of politically independent satellite countries within what the urban sociologist Saskia Sassen calls a 'transnational space.'[11] People, wealth, ideas, and cultural patterns move in both directions, influencing both the metropolitan center as well as the peripheral areas, although asymmetrically. Although they are similar in many respects to other migratory systems, such as those of the Mediterranean, there are several unique features of the regional cosmoses that are of special importance to the problem of the globalization of culture.

In the West Atlantic regional cosmos, made up of eastern America and the circum-Caribbean societies, the peripheral areas are either contiguous with or within easy reach of the dominant metropolitan society.[12] The separate units are legally autonomous, but sovereignty becomes merely a resource to be used in the interaction between the main collective actors. In spite of legal restrictions on the movement of peoples, there is a vast flow in both directions – legal and illegal migrants from the periphery, tourists and investors from the center. There is no simple flow of cheap labor to capital in this system, as in the classic colonial regimes. Skilled and cheap labor flow in both directions. Legal and illegal capital also moves in both directions.

The Third World countries of the periphery are only too eager to attract such capital, but with capitalization their economies become dualized, as is true of the center, between an urban-modern sector and a traditional-rural sector. This disrupts traditional labor patterns at a much faster rate than it provides new job opportunities. The result is massive unemployment, the rise of the urban slums – marking the first stage in the migration process – and from there the mass movement to the center. These migrants rarely compete directly with native workers in the center; instead, a wholly new sector – what sociologist Alejandro Portes calls the immigrant enclave – is created for them.[13] Thus, dualization at the center reinforces, and is reinforced by, dualization in the periphery.

An important aspect of the regional cosmos is the rise of the cosmopolis – a major urban center that shifts from being a major metropolis of the center to being the metropolis of the entire regional cosmos. This is precisely the role that Miami has come to play in the West Atlantic regional cosmos.[14] Miami is no longer an American city: it is a West Atlantic city, more vital to, and more dependent on, the needs of the circum-Caribbean societies and cultures than it is on the other sectors of the U.S. economy. It is the political, cultural, social, and economic hub and heart of the Caribbean.

Culturally, the periphery is greatly influenced by the society of the center, but the reverse is also the case, as the example of reggae demonstrates. Another example of periphery-to-center cultural flows is the transmission of Spanish and Haitian creole, which has resulted not simply in the creation of a multilingual center where English once prevailed but, more broadly, in the Latinization of English and the Anglicization of Spanish. This process of creolization, in turn, has resulted in the creation of wholly new cultural forms in the transnational space, such as 'New Yorican' and Miami Spanish. The same process of cosmopolitan creolization can be found in other areas of culture: in the rapid spread of Spanish-American food, Franco-Haitian-American dishes, and the recent diffusion of the Jamaican 'jerk' method of cooking in both Jamerican (Jamaican-American) and mainstream American cooking; in the Latin and West Indian carnivals that are now a standard part of the festivals of the cosmopolis; in the infusion and transformation of Afro-West Indian and Afro-Latin cults, whose animal sacrifices were recently offered constitutional protection by the Supreme Court after a major nativist challenge;[15] in the ironic revival of the game of cricket, once an elite sport among the dominant Anglo-Americans, under the impact of the Afro-West Indian working-class immigrants; in the spread of the dreadlocks style of hair grooming among African Americans and, increasingly, among white Americans from the Jamaican Rastafarian immigrants. These are only some of the more visible expressions of this extraordinary process of periphery-induced creolization in the cosmopolis.

Afro-Caribbean Intellectualism

One of the most fascinating, and neglected, areas of cultural exchange between the cosmopolis and the West Atlantic periphery is in intellectual and professional life. The British, Spanish, and French academic and professional cultures have traditionally dominated the countries of the periphery, the result of their respective colonial experiences. The ruthlessly selective nature of these European traditions created intellectual cultures that were at once highly sophisticated and elitist. What emerged in the black Caribbean – a vibrant engagement with European intellectualism in which the culture of Europe was critically embraced, dissected, and reintegrated through the filter of a creolized neo-African sensibility and aesthetic – had no parallel in the American mainland. It was possible only because of the overwhelming demographic presence of blacks in the West Indies, in contrast with the minority status of blacks in the mainland cosmopolis. In the periphery, the neo-European culture of the elite was mediated through agents of the hegemonic powers, who were themselves black or light-skinned. Hence race, per se, was muted as a factor in the cultural conflict that accompanied the decolonization process.

The ironic effect was that the European experience could be adjudicated, and dialectically explored, in purely cultural terms, devoid of the confounding effects of racial segregation and rejection. In contrast with the black American condition, where any engagement with the dominant culture always ran the risk of the loss of racial identity and the fear of racial betrayal, resulting in an understandable rejection of all intellectualism, the West Indian intellectual developed a love-hate relationship with the culture of the 'mother country' that was mediated through fellow blacks. The paradigmatic challenge in this situation became, not the rejection and suspicion of all intellectualism, but a desperate need to outdo the imperial culture at its own game. Intellectualism, however, went far beyond mere anti-imperial one-up-manship. For the ambitious black West Indian, it was, until recently, the only path to mobility, given the paucity of resources and the monopolization of the limited commercial positions by whites and Asians.

The net result has been a virtual hotbed of intellectualism among Afro-Caribbean peoples. These small, poor islands have, arguably, the highest per capita concentration of scholars, professionals, and real, as well as would-be, intellectuals as any place in the world. It is not Germany, Switzerland, or the United States that has produced the greatest proportion of Nobel laureates per thousand, but the tiny, dirt-poor island nation of St. Lucia. With an at-home population of under 100,000, it has produced two Nobel laureates, the economist Sir A.W. Lewis and the poet Derek Walcott. And they are merely the tip of the iceberg: Trinidad's V.S. Naipaul is generally considered one of the two or three best novelists writing in English; its late scholar-statesman, Eric Williams, was a major historian; its late radical intellectual C.L.R. James one of the foremost Marxist theoreticians. The poet-novelists Edward Brathwaite and George Lamming are only the most recent in a long line of internationally acclaimed writers from Barbados; indeed, Barbados was used by the colonial British as the seedbed for black professionals and missionaries in its cultural penetration of Africa and Asia and still lives to a considerable degree on the remittances of its large number of professional emigrants. What is true of the English-speaking Caribbean holds equally for the French-speaking islands where, to take the most noteworthy example, the poet-statesman Aimé Césaire has long been recognized by French critics as one of the best poets in their language.

This extraordinary intellectual and professional tradition is now being rapidly incorporated into the West Atlantic cosmopolis. American educational aid has been accompanied by American models of education, transforming the elitist nature of these systems. At the same time, there has been a massive redirection of the flow of talent from the region. All roads no longer lead to the old colonial metropoles of London and Paris but increasingly to the great East Coast cosmopolitan centers. Budding West Indian intellectuals now experience their required period of creative exile, not in Europe, but in America, where many take up permanent residence. What is more, a disproportionate number of American academic and other professionals are of West Indian ancestry. Paralleling the cross-fertilization of African American lower-class popular culture by West Indian immigrants is the interaction of Afro-Caribbean and African American traditions within the cosmopolitan academe, which has significant implications not only for the cultures of both traditions, but for the wider culture of the cosmopolis.

The special contribution of West Indian intellectualism in the cosmopolitan context will be a transference of its distinctive strategy of aggressive engagement with the dominant tradition of neo-European civilization – a strategy that, at its worst, generates enormous identity crises and self-destructive emotional and physical violence, but at the same time, and at its best, is the crucible for the explosively competitive syncretism that finds expression in Rastafarianism and *voudon*, reggae and merengue, and negritude, magical realism, *omeros*,[16] and the self-loathing genius of V.S. Naipaul. Such engagement African Americans have independently achieved so far only in the universalizing vitalism of rock music and the jazz aesthetic. My prediction is that the West Indian presence in the cosmopolis will act as a catalyst for the promotion of this transcendent Afro-European contribution to the emerging global culture.

In structural terms, the mass migration of peoples from the periphery in this new context of cheap transportation and communication has produced a wholly different kind of social system. The migrant communities in the center are not ethnic groups in the traditional American sense. In the interaction between center and periphery, the societies of the periphery are radically changed, but so is the traditional immigrant community of the center. What has emerged is, from the viewpoint of the peripheral states, distinctive transnational societies in which there is no longer any meaningful identification of political and social boundaries. Thus, more than a half of the adult working populations of many of the smaller eastern Caribbean states now live outside of these societies, mainly in the immigrant enclaves of the United States. About 40 per cent of all Jamaicans, and perhaps half of all Puerto Ricans, live outside of the political boundaries of these societies, mainly in America. The interesting thing about these communities is that their members feel as at home in the mainland segment as in the original politically bounded areas.

These communities are more like self-contained colonies . . . . within the body politic of the United States, and it is a serious error to confuse them with the traditional ethnic communities, including Native Americans. They are what the Jamaican folk poet, Louise Bennett, calls 'colonization in reverse'.[17] The former colonies now become the mother country; the imperial metropolis becomes the frontier of infinite resources, only now the resources consist not simply of unexploited land but of underutilized de-industrializing capital and the postindustrial service and professional sectors. There is no traumatic transfer of national loyalty from the home country to the host polity, since home is readily accessible and national loyalty is a waning sentiment in what is increasingly a post-national world. Jamaican, Puerto Rican, Dominican, and Barbadian societies are no longer principally defined by the political-geographical units of Jamaica, Puerto Rico, the Dominican Republic and Barbados but by *both* the populations and cultures of these units and their postnational colonies in the cosmopolis.

Other Regional Cosmoses

In addition to the West Atlantic system, there are at least three other emerging multi-national spaces within the body politic of contemporary America: the Tex-Mex cosmos of the Southwest, incorporating northern Mexican and Southwestern Euro-Indian cultures, peoples, and economies; the Southern California cosmos, with its volatile, unblended mosaic of Latin, Asian, and Afro-European cultures; and the newly emerged Pacific Rim cosmos of the Northwest, which integrates the economies and bourgeois cultures of industrial Asia and traditional Euro-America.

While the processes of incorporation and creolization are broadly similar in all four regional cosmoses, they differ sharply in their degrees of integration, in the volume and velocity of cultural, economic, and demographic flows, in the levels of asymmetry in the transfer of ideas, cultural products, and skills, in the patterns and stages of creolization, and in the nature and extent of the social and cultural conflicts that inevitably accompany the process of cosmopolitanization.

On all these indices, the West Atlantic cosmos is, in my view, the most advanced, especially in the degree of integration and the extent to which the nation-state has been transcended as a major basis of collective commitment and constraint on livelihood. The major outliers in this system are Haiti and Cuba, but in light of the already large contingent of Cubans and Haitians on the mainland, it is best to see their integration as a temporarily halted process, the one on ideological, the other on racist grounds. It is only a matter of time before both these restraints are eroded . . .

The American Cosmos

What are the implications of all this for our understanding of contemporary America? I believe it is best to conceive of not one, but three Americas, traditional America, multicultural America, and ecumenical America – a vast sociological cosmos bounded by a single, powerful polity. The three are obviously related, but it is important not to confuse them, especially in discussions of multiculturalism.

Multicultural America is made up of the mainland or metropolitan populations of the four 'transnational spaces' or regional cosmoses described above. It has been called immigrant America by Portes and others, and while this term obviously captures an important dimension of this sector, it is likely to be misleading to the degree that it invites too close a comparison with the immigrant America of earlier years. As I have pointed out, there is something fundamentally different in the relationship between these immigrant communities with both their home societies (to which they remain strongly linked socially and culturally) and the broader American society, with which they are permanently intertwined. Multicultural America is a great socio-cultural concourse, a space where all the cultures from the center's several regional cosmoses meet, resist, embrace, display their cultural wares at annual parades, gawk at, fight, riot, and learn to live with each other, sometimes even learn a little something from each other.

By traditional America, I mean the Euro-African world that emerged from the Puritan North, the industrial smokestacks, the prairie farms, and the slave South. It is the America of the Midwestern main street, of the old and new South, and of the ethnic working classes. It is the America of Richard Nixon, J. Edgar Hoover, and Louis Farrakhan. But it is also the America of Jimmy Carter and the Congressional Black Caucus, of the land grant colleges and the United Negro Colleges.[18] Socially, it is committed to enhanced opportunities and intergenerational mobility, but it is also historically racist, though changing in this regard, and profoundly separatist in its basic orientation. It embraces all races and classes, and today a great many African Americans are as committed to the separatist ideal as their Southern white counterparts. There has been some progress: instead of 'separate and unequal', the ethic of this America, as a result of African American pressure, is now 'separate but *truly* equal'.[19] There is profound disagreement about how such an America is to be achieved – witness the war over affirmative action – but all parties, except for the fringe extremists, are in agreement in their desire to live peacefully and separately.

Ironically, traditional America does have a common culture. At the elite level, it is largely the Anglo-American tradition modified by interactions with the older, more traditional ethnic groups, including mainstreaming African Americans, and by continental European influences. At the popular level, traditional America has been deeply influenced by the African American working class: in its language, music, art, and religion, and in many of its attitudes. For a long time, it simply refused to acknowledge this influence, but in recent decades it has come to do so. It does so even while remaining committed to a separatist society, though one less and less rationalized in racist terms. The persisting racial segregation among black and white traditional Americans is today as much a product of class as of race and is in many ways more voluntary than imposed.

Perhaps the strongest unifying cultural feature of traditional America is its Christian heritage. Originally and still largely Protestant, traditional America is rapidly losing its hostility toward Catholicism, as an overriding convergence of conservative religious values becomes more important: the belief in a Christian God and regular churchgoing; the commitment to patriarchy; the demonization of abortion rights; the preference for punitive law-and-order forms of childrearing and justice; the neo-Puritan fear of sex; uncritical patriotism; reverence for, and for many, dependence on, the military; and the parochial suspicion of the foreign. Even while firmly settled in their separate communities, the many different white ethnic groups and the large core of working- and middle-class blacks who make up traditional America are fully committed to this still thriving system of values.

The Meaning of Race

In one important area, traditional America is under strong pressure from the multicultural sector to change one of its central values, namely, the meaning and conception, though not the significance, of race. Traditionally, race has been defined among both black and white Americans in binary terms: the so-called one-drop rule sociologically excluded any intermediary racial groups on a continuum between blacks and whites. While the binary rule was originally constructed and rigidly imposed by whites out of their commitment to notions of racial purity and exclusion, it is one that traditional African Americans have come to embrace for political and cultural reasons. The rule operated with extraordinary tenacity not only because both the traditional 'races' came to accept it, but because later immigrant groups quickly conformed. Jews, dark-skinned southern Europeans, and Caucasoid Hispanics, once rejected as 'true whites', eagerly struggled for, and eventually won, acceptance within the Caucasian chalk circle[20] of white people – in contrast with the excluded blacks, whose presence is required for the extraordinary valorization of whiteness. (The point is best made by noting that for the average Irishman in non-black Ireland, whiteness has no social meaning; Ireland is, in fact, one of the least racist of European societies, as any well-traveled African American or West Indian tourist will attest; however, whiteness is instantly embraced as a valued social, cultural, and economic asset by the marginal, socially insecure Irish immigrant in America, as the well-documented historical negrophobia of working-class Irish Americans, their liberal politics notwithstanding, will also readily attest.)

The rise of the multicultural sector strongly undermines the binary rule in two important respects, one demographic, the other cultural. One reason why the binary rule worked so well was that African Americans were, by and large, the only significant 'other' in the American population for most of the nation's history. Until recently, Asians and dark-skinned Latin and South Asian immigrants were an insignificant demographic presence; and Native Americans – who up to the end of the eighteenth century constituted the second significant racial 'other' – were removed from consideration through decimation and confinement on reservations.

All this has changed dramatically with the rise of the regional cosmos and the multicultural sector. Visibly nonwhite Asians and Latin Americans, who by no stretch of the imagination can be socially redefined and incorporated within the social category of 'white people', now exist in significant numbers in society; indeed, they will outnumber blacks by the turn of the century. Since these groups are clearly neither whites nor blacks, a serious crisis of racial definition now confronts those clinging to the binary conception of race.

Quite apart from the purely demographic factor, however, is the cultural refusal of most of the new immigrants to play by the binary rule, as early streams of immigrants have done. On the one hand, most of the new Asian immigrants have a strong sense of their own racial identity, are proud of the way they look, and do not wish to be redefined racially as anything else. And this sense of racial pride is further reinforced by the multicultural celebration of ethno-racial differences. On the other hand, most immigrants from Latin America bring with them, in addition to their racial heterogeneity, their own highly developed nonbinary or 'interval-type' notions of race. That is, socially significant distinctions are made among persons on a continuum between obviously black and obviously white persons. A visibly nonwhite, but light- or brown-skinned Puerto Rican, Dominican, Jamaican, or Brazilian does not consider himself 'black'. One only has to observe the elaborate shade gradations and mating and marriage patterns of Cuban, Puerto Rican, and other Latin immigrants to recognize that a wholly different principle of racial classification is at play. A similar nonbinary pattern prevails among South Asians between black-skinned 'Dravidian' types and fair-skinned 'Aryan' types.[21] And the same holds for East Asians. Indeed, nonbinary racial classification is the norm among the vast majority of non-European peoples . . .

Ecumenical America

Ecumenical America is not merely cosmopolitan, for it goes beyond the simple embrace of many cultures maintaining their separate identities. It is, rather, the universal culture that emerged and continues to develop in the great cities and university towns of the nation. This culture is a genuinely ecumenical one: it draws from everywhere, not just from the local cultures of the traditional ethnic and immigrant sectors and the traditional Euro-American culture at its doorstep. The image of the melting pot fails to describe the process by which it emerges, for it does not indiscriminately absorb all and everything into some common stew. There is a complex process of selection and universalization of particular cultural forms and styles generating its great cultural innovations for itself and for the world: in science, technology, literature, dance, painting, music, and cuisine.

Like traditional America, it has both a formal or elite and a popular or vernacular level. English, both of the streets and the academy, is its common language. Its shared art thrives in the works of a Jasper Johns or an Andy Warhol[22] (with their ironic ecumenization of traditional America's most beloved icons) but, perhaps most quintessentially, in the musical form of jazz. On the popular level, the shared art of ecumenical America is also strongly influenced by African Americans. Increasingly, the products of the regional cosmoses are selected out for universalization, as in the ecumenization of Chinese and Mexican cuisine, the poetry of Derek Walcott, the fiction of Saul Bellow and Maxine Hong Kingston, and the drama of Eugene O'Neill.[23] Ecumenical America also draws directly from the wider world in meeting the needs of its art and its technology. The culture it produces, in turn, has become the koine, or common currency, of the world, the first genuinely global culture on the face of the earth.

Ecumenical America is based primarily in the postindustrial economy, with its advanced technological plants, complex services, and multinational corporations. It is no utopia, as the legion of previously secure unemployed workers and managers of the smokestack industrial regions and rapidly obsolescent high-tech sectors can attest. It is almost as class-ridden as traditional America. It is politically mainly liberal, but it includes the politically very conservative elites and middle managers of the multinational corporations and silicon suburbs. It also includes the elite managers, scientists, and intellectuals from all over the world – Indian engineers, Japanese and Hong Kong businessmen, Argentinean doctors, European managers and artists, and Caribbean intellectuals – who enter this sector at the top and are not to be confused with the working-class or sweatshop entrepreneurs of the immigrant enclave economy.

A New Cultural Policy

Let me conclude with a few reflections on the kind of cultural policy that this interpretation of the American cosmos implies. In the first place, it seems to me that any attempt at a single policy for all of America is a nonstarter. Any cultural policymaker must begin by recognizing the fundamentally tripartite nature of America. . . .

Second, it should now be clear that the multicultural social philosophy and approach to the arts and culture is wholly inadequate for the American cosmos. It very adequately addresses the needs of immigrant or multicultural America but is inappropriate as a strategy for the other two cultural systems that embrace the vast majority of Americans.

Indeed, it is questionable whether there can be a single policy even for the multicultural sector itself. In the first place, as we have seen, the American, cosmopolitan parts of the four regional cosmoses that together constitute the social bases of multicultural America are at different stages of development, especially in their degrees of integration. What holds true for the highly integrated West Atlantic cosmos, with its harmonizing processes of creolization, simply does not apply to the fissiparous Southern California cosmos.

But there is a more profound problem with regard to any attempt at a single multicultural policy. This is the inherent self-contradiction of all programs that adhere to the dogma of relativism. If all ideals, all values, and all art in all cultures and subcultures are of equal worth, there is no basis for the view that relativism – the basic value of the multicultural theorists and policy advocates – is of any greater worth than the basic values of any of the celebrated subcultures that deny the worth of others – including that of the relativists – in absolutist terms. Relativism requires the acceptance of its condemnation by the very antirelativists it embraces. . . .

In its extreme commitment to relativism, multiculturalism well serves the needs of immigrant peoples and cultures thrown upon each other and who must learn basic principles – often contrary to their own traditions – of tolerance for others. But discrimination is the essence of cultural creation, and this same relativism, when applied to the other two areas of the American cosmos, could be deadening in its impact.

The multicultural ideology, then, is certainly needed, but its limits must be understood. Making it the American creed would be a serious mistake. In general, art within the immigrant sector should be encouraged, preferably by private foundations rather than the government, but only where it looks toward, and strives to become, a part of the shared art of the ecumene. However, where the immigrant artist is atavistic, looking only back at his or her original culture, he or she should be tolerated, respected, and accepted in good faith, but not actively supported. It is not the business of the ecumenical to promote the atavistic.

Ecumenical America is no utopia. Nonetheless, it seems clear to me that this is the future of America, for better or for worse. There is no basis for the commonly heard criticism that associates the ecumenical with a grey, homogenized world. Nor is there any justification for the view that the ecumenical is dominated by a global financial elite having no responsibility to any local community. The ultimate thrust of the ecumenical is indeed transnational and, in many respects, postnational. But this is the way of the world in the twenty-first century, and such postnational orientation is by no means confined to the financial elite. Indeed, as I have shown, it is the migrant peasants, working classes, and intellectuals from the periphery of the world's transnational spaces who are most postnational in their attitudes and behavior. The typical Jamaican resident of Brooklyn or Mexican resident of Texas has already gone far beyond any transnational capitalist of New York in his or her attitudes, migratory movements, and life-style.

We have no choice but to accept the inevitable; but we do have choices in what we make of it. Ecumenical America and its advocates, among whom I count myself, should recognize its special place, not only as the most advanced part of the American cosmos, but as the vital source of the world's first truly global culture. It should support artists, scientists, and other cultural creators in and out of America whose work resonates and who are dialectically engaged with the emerging shared art and shared ways of the global ecumene, at both the advanced and vernacular levels of social and cultural life.

NOTES

1. Hellenism refers to an interest in and devotion to the culture of ancient Greece, especially that of Athens in the fifth and fourth centuries BC.
2. Patterson's idea of a transnational 'West Atlantic system' is comparable to the historian Philip D. Curtin's concept of the 'South Atlantic System', or what others have referred to as the 'Atlantic World', which draws attention to the important interrelationships that exist between societies and economies through trade, migration and the diffusion of culture.
3. Author's note: Alan Lomax, *Folk Song Style and Culture* (Washington, DC: American Association for the Advancement of Science, 1968).

4. Author's note: Paul E. Willis, *Common Culture* (Boulder: Westview, 1990).

5. Karl Marx referred to small peasants as people who live in similar conditions but without engaging in relations with each other, 'much as potatoes in a sack form a sackful of potatoes' (in 'The Eighteenth Brumaire of Louis Bonaparte', 1852).

6. Author's note: Peter Manuel, *Popular Musics of the Non-Western World* (New York: Oxford University Press, 1988), p. 20.

7. Author's note: Deanna Robinson, Elizabeth Buck et al., *Music at the Margins: Popular Music and Global Cultural Diversity* (Newbury Park, CA: Sage, 1991), p. 4.

8. Author's note: Orlando Patterson, 'The Dance Invasion of Britain: On the Cultural Diffusion of Jamaican Popular Arts', *New Society* 207 (Sept. 1966).

9. Author's note: See Simon Jones, *Black Culture, White Youth* (Basingstoke: Macmillan Education, 1988).

10. Author's note: See Stephen Davis and Peter Simon, *Reggae Bloodlines* (New York: Da Capo, 1979).

11. Author's note: See Saskia Sassen, *The Mobility of Labor and Capital* (New York: Cambridge University Press, 1988).

12. Author's note: For a detailed analysis of this cosmos, see Orlando Patterson, 'The Emerging West Atlantic System: Migration, Culture and Underdevelopment in the U.S. and Caribbean,' in *Population in an Interacting World*, edited by William Alonso (Cambridge, MA: Harvard University Press, 1987).

13. Author's note: Alejandro Portes and Ruben G. Rumbout, *Immigrant America* (Berkeley: University of California Press, 1990).

14. Author's note: For a spirited journalistic tour of this regional cosmos and Miami's central role in it, see Joel Garreau, *The Nine Nations of North America* (Boston: Houghton Mifflin, 1981), pp.167-206.

15. The city of Hialeah in Florida passed a series of ordinances in the early 1990s to make animal sacrifice illegal. Santería practitioners argued that these ordinances suppressed their religious practices. The Supreme Court overturned the city's ordinances in 1993, giving the practitioners the right to practice their religion under the protection of the First Amendment to the constitution.

16. Derek Walcott's *Omeros* (New York: Farrar, Straus and Giroux, 1990) is an epic poem in seven books. The figure of Omeros, which is the Greek for Homer, appears in various guises, as a Caribbean fisherman, an Indian shaman, and a vagrant in London, both in the present and the past.

17. Louise Bennett, 'Colonisation in Reverse', in *Jamaica Labrish* (Kingston: Sangster's Book Stores, 1966), p.179-80.

18. Richard M. Nixon (1913–94) and Jimmy Carter (born in 1924) were presidents of the United States, from 1969 to 1974, and 1977 to 1981, respectively. J. Edgar Hoover (1895–1972) was director of the Federal Bureau of Investigation for 48 years. Louis Farrakhan (born in 1933) is head of the Nation of Islam in the United States. The Congressional Black Caucus is a group of African-American members of the US Congress. The land grant colleges are those colleges and universities in the United States that were endowed under the Morrill, or Land Grant, Act of 1862, by which government land was sold and the proceeds invested to create and maintain the colleges. The United Negro Colleges are a group of predominantly African-American private colleges and universities in the United States that are supported by the United Negro College Fund which was established in 1944.

19. Racial segregation in the United States was supported by a series of decisions made by the Supreme Court, in particular in the case of Plessy v. Ferguson in 1896 when the court supported a Louisiana law requiring separate facilities for whites and blacks in railroad cars. These laws segregated the races in unequal schools, hotels, restaurants, recreational and transport facilities for over 50 years. Since the 1960s when various kinds of *de jure* segregation were abolished under pressure from the civil rights movement there has been widespread *de facto* segregation, for example, in residence and education, and millions of unskilled and low-income African-Americans have little chance of improving their situation.

20. This refers to Bertholt Brecht's play 'The Caucasian Chalk Circle', which was written in the mid-1940s and first published in 1949.

21. Dravidian refers to a linguistically related group of people in India, such as the Tamil. Aryan refers to Indo-European languages but is also used by white supremacists to refer to the 'white race'.

22. Jasper Johns (born in 1930) and Andy Warhol (1928–87) were leaders of the 'pop art' movement that took items of everyday life, such as the US flag and a Campbell's soup can, as the subjects of their paintings.

23. Saul Bellow (born in 1915), Maxine Hong Kingston (born in 1940) and Eugene O'Neill (1888–1953) are Jewish American, Chinese American and Irish American writers, respectively.

Bibliography

Aguilar, Luis E. *Cuba 1933: Prologue to Revolution.* New York: W.W. Norton, 1972.

Alleyne, Mervyn. 'A Linguistic Perspective on the Caribbean'. In *Caribbean Contours* ed. by Sidney W. Mintz and Sally Price 155-79. Baltimore: Johns Hopkins University Press, 1985.

Baxandall, Lee, ed. *Radical Perspectives in the Arts.* Harmondsworth: Penguin, 1972.

Benítez-Rojo, Antonio. *The Repeating Island: The Caribbean and the Postmodern Perspective.* 2nd edition, trans. by James Maraniss. Durham: Duke University Press, 1996.

Braithwaite, Lloyd. 'Social Stratification in Trinidad'. In *Social and Economic Studies* 2 (1953): 5-175.

Brathwaite, Edward Kamau. *The Development of Creole Society in Jamaica 1770-1820.* Oxford: Clarendon Press, 1971.

Brown, Stewart, Mervyn Morris and Gordon Rohlehr eds. *Voiceprint: An Anthology of Oral and Related Poetry from the Caribbean.* Harlow: Longman, 1989.

Carr, Raymond. *Puerto Rico: A Colonial Experiment.* New York: Vintage Books, 1984.

Césaire, Aimé. *The Collected Poetry* trans. by Clayton Eshleman and Annette Smith. Berkeley: University of California Press, 1983.

Dash, Michael. 'Introduction' to Edouard Glissant 1-17. In *The Ripening* trans. by Michael Dash, London: Heinemann, 1985.

_____. 'Introduction' to Edouard Glissant xi-xlv. *In Caribbean Discourse: Selected Essays* trans. by J. Michael Dash. Charlottesville: University Press of Virginia, 1989.

Dávila, Arlene M. *Sponsored Identities: Cultural Politics in Puerto Rico.* Philadelphia: Temple University Press, 1997.

Dietz, James L. *Economic History of Puerto Rico: Institutional Change and Capitalist Development.* Princeton: Princeton University Press, 1986.

Fanon, Frantz. *The Wretched of the Earth* trans. by Constance Farrington. New York: Grove Press, 1968.

Foner, Philip S. ed. *Our America by José Martí: Writings on Latin America and the Struggle for Cuban Independence.* New York: Monthly Review Press, 1977.

Garvey, Amy Jacques. *Garvey and Garveyism.* New York: Collier Books, 1970.

Glissant, Edouard. *Caribbean Discourse: Selected Essays* trans. by J. Michael Dash. Charlottesville: University Press of Virginia, 1989.

_____. *Poetics of Relation* trans. by Betsy Wing. Ann Arbor: University of Michigan Press, 1997.

Gordon, Shirley C. *Reports and Repercussions in West Indian Education, 1835-1933*. London: Ginn, 1968.

Griffith, Glyne, ed. *Caribbean Cultural Identities*. Lewisburg: Bucknell University Press, 2001.

Hall, Stuart. 'Cultural Identity and Diaspora' in *Colonial Discourse and Post-Colonial Theory* ed. by Patrick Williams and Laura Chrisman. New York: Columbia University Press, 1994.

_____. 'The Formation of a Diasporic Intellectual': An Interview with Stuart Hall by Kuan-Hsing Chen in *Stuart Hall: Critical Dialogues in Cultural Studies* edited by David Morley and Kuan-Hsing Chen, 484-503. London: Routledge, 1996.

Hennessy, Alistair ed. *Intellectuals in the Twentieth-Century Caribbean* vols. 1 and 2. London: Macmillan, 1992.

Henry, Paget. *Caliban's Reason: Introducing Afro-Caribbean Philosophy*. New York: Routledge, 2000.

Higman, B.W. *Writing West Indian Histories*. London: Macmillan, 1999.

Ho, Christine. 'Hold the Chow Mein, Gimme Soca: Creolization of the Chinese in Guyana, Trinidad and Jamaica'. *Amerasia* 15:2 (1989): 3-25.

Hobsbawm, Eric, and Terence Ranger eds. *The Invention of Tradition*. Cambridge: Cambridge University Press, 1983.

James, C.L.R. *At the Rendezvous of Victory: Selected Writings* 3-35. London: Allison and Busby, 1984.

_____. 'The Birth of a Nation'. In *Contemporary Caribbean: A Sociological Reader* ed. by Susan Craig. Maracas: Susan Craig, 1981.

James, Louis ed. *The Islands in Between: Essays on West Indian Literature*. London: Oxford University Press, 1968.

Kenner, Martin, and James Petras eds. *Fidel Castro Speaks*. New York: Grove Press, 1969.

King, Bruce. *V.S. Naipual*. Basingstoke: Macmillan, 1993.

Knight, Franklin W. *The Caribbean: The Genesis of a Fragmented Nationalism*. New York: Oxford University Press, 1978.

Lamming, George. *Season of Adventure*. London: Michael Joseph, 1960.

Lewis, Gordon K. *Main Currents of Caribbean Thought: The Historical Evolution of Caribbean Society in its Ideological Aspects, 1492-1900*. Baltimore: Johns Hopkins University Press, 1983.

Lewis, Rupert Charles. *Walter Rodney's Intellectual and Political Thought*. Kingston: University of the West Indies Press, 1998.

Marcus, Bruce and Michael Taber, eds. *Maurice Bishop Speaks: The Grenada Revolution 1979-83*. New York: Pathfinder Press, 1983.

Meeks, Brian and Folke Lindahl eds. *New Caribbean Thought: A Reader*. Kingston: University of the West Indies Press, 2001.

Mintz, Sidney W. 'The Caribbean as a Socio-cultural Area'. *Journal of World History* 9:4 (1966): 912-37.

_____. *Caribbean Transformations*. Chicago: Aldine Publishing, 1974.

Morales Carrión, Arturo. *Puerto Rico: A Political and Cultural History*. New York: W.W. Norton, 1983.

Pérez, Louis A. *Cuba: Between Reform and Revolution*. 2nd edition. New York: Oxford University Press, 1995.

Pfaff, Françoise. *Conversations with Maryse Condé*. Lincoln: University of Nebraska Press, 1996.

Reddock, Rhoda. *Elma Francois: The NWCSA and the Workers' Struggle for Change in the Caribbean in the 1930s*. London: New Beacon Books, 1988.

Renard, Rosamunde A. 'Immigration and Indentureship in the French West Indies, 1848-1870', in *Caribbean Freedom: Economy and Society from Emancipation to the Present* edited by Hilary Beckles and Verene Shepherd. Kingston: Ian Randle Publishers, 1993.

Shannon, Magdaline W. 'Introduction' to Jean Price-Mars *So Spoke the Uncle* trans. by Magdaline W. Shannon. Washington DC: Three Continents Press, 1983.

Smith, M.G. *The Plural Society of the British West Indies*. Berkeley: University of California Press, 1965.

Trouillot, Michel-Rolph. *Haiti, State Against Nation: The Origins and Legacy of Duvalierism*. New York: Monthly Review Press, 1990.

Turton, Peter. *José Martí: Architect of Cuba's Freedom*. London: Zed Books, 1986.

Wagenheim, Kal, with Olga Jimenez de Wagenheim, eds. *The Puerto Ricans: A Documentary History*. New York: Anchor/Doubleday, 1973.

Walcott, Derek. *In a Green Night*. London: Jonathan Cape, 1962.

_____. 'The Muse of History'. In *Is Massa Day Dead? Black Moods in the Caribbean* edited by Orde Coombs. New York: Anchor Books, 1974, 1-27.

_____. *Omeros*. New York: Farrar, Straus and Giroux, 1990.

_____. *What the Twilight Says: Essays*. New York: Farrar, Straus and Giroux, 1998.

Williams, Eric. *Capitalism and Slavery*. London: Andre Deutsch, 1964.

_____. *Inward Hunger: The Education of a Prime Minister*. London: André Deutsch, 1969.

Zanetti, Oscar, and Alejandro García. *Sugar and Railroads: A Cuban History, 1837-1959* trans. by Franklin W. Knight and Mary Todd. Chapel Hill: University of North Carolina Press, 1998.

Index

Aboriginal culture: destruction by European America, 130–131, 134n

Africa: alienation of, 238–239; Negritude and, 224–225; and the quest for a Caribbean identity, 583; in WI development, 400–406, 518

African diaspora: unity among the, 281

African heritage: and Caribbean culture, xxi

African immigration, xxi

African retentions: in the BLI slave society, 433–434; in Creole culture, 368–369; in Haiti, 208

African Society of Culture, 192

Africanness: and the Caribbean identity, 252

Afro-Caribbean intellectuals, 641–643

Afro-Cuban culture, 54, 56–57; 162–163, 164–165

Afro-Saxon: criticism of the, 519; definition of, 517

Agriculture: and land reform in Puerto Rico, 101–102

Albizu Campos, Pedro: and Puerto Rican culture, 71–73, 138, 140

Alliance for Progress, 351

American republics: Martí on governance of, 9–15

Americanization: process, 256; of Puerto Rico, 147–150, 159

Americanness: distinction between creoleness and, 255–257

Amerindian culture: and Caribbean identity, 512–514

Anglophone literature: defining West Indian, 282

Anacaona: legend, 288, 289, 290–291

Ancestral memory: in Caribbean literature, 274; and language, 601–605

Animism: in Voodoo, 197

Anthropology Society of Paris, 188n

Antillanité. See Caribeanness

'The Antilles: Fragments of Epic Memory', 593–605

Antoni, Robert: rhythm and performance in, 167–168, 169

Ariel: image in Latin American literature, 127–132

Aristede, Jean-Betrand, 290, 291n

Artist: Cuban revolution and the, 115–119

Assimilation: and Caribbean culture, 582–585

Association of Caribbean Historians (ACH), xii

Association of Caribbean States (ACS): proposal for the creation of a, 607–608, 611, 612; and regional unity, xx

Austin, Hudson: and the Grenada revolution, 533

Automatic Charter, 60

Bantu: in Haiti, 195–196

Barbados: similarity in economies of Cuba and, 30, 34

Barbarity: Albizu Campos on, 74; Césaire on colonization and, 213, 218

Basic needs approach: to economic development, 566–567, 571–575

Batista, Fulgencio, 38–39

Benítez-Rojo, Antonio, 160

Benítez, Jose Gautier, 78n

Bernabé, Jean, 250–251

Betances, Ramón, 100, 102, 104, 105n; and Puerto Rican culture, 138–139, 154n

Bishop, Maurice, 531–534

Black man: slavery and the devaluation of the, 527–528

Black Jacobins, 248n, 395

Black Power: definition of, 487, 488

Black Power Movement, 479–482, 510; in the West Indies, 476–490

Black Star Line, 323, 400

Blackness: awareness of, 229–231; definition of, 476; Fanon and myths of, 231–234; symbolism of, 231–232

Blacks: achievements of Jamaican (post-slavery), 317; in Jamaica, 466–469, 471–472; status of Jamaican, 319–323; Froude and the inferiority of, 296–311; and identity, 237; intellectual evolution of Haitian, 183–186; in Puerto Rican culture, 141–144, 150, in Trinidad and Tobago, 388–389, 390

Bloody Sunday: Grenada revolution and, 542, 547n

Bolívar, Simón, 16n, 185–186, 189n; and the

Mestizo concept, 125
Borinquen: definition of, 19–20n
Brathwaite, Kamau, 134n, 504–505, 506–507
Brau, Salvador, 138, 154n
Breton, André, 210
British Guiana; labour and race in, 455
British Guiana East Indian Association (BGEIA), 457, 458
British Guiana Labour Union, xix
British intervention: in British Guyana's politics, 455, 457–458
British Leeward Islands (BLI): slave society in the, 422–444
Broca, Paul, 188n
Burnham, Forbes, 447–448
Butler, Tubal Uriah Buzz, 332, 333, 534, 546n

Caliban: in Latin American literature, 126–134
Campeche José, 143, 154n
Capital: and labour in Caribbean history, 62
Capitalism and Slavery, 337, 338
Caribs: colonisers' vision of the, 126, 133n
Caribbean: defining the, xvii–xviii; definition of the English-speaking, 496; Williams on the future of the, 349–358
Caribbean Area Division of the Inter-American Regional Organisation of Workers (CADORIT), xix
Caribbean Artists Movement (CAM), 511–512
Caribbean cities: and the creative imagination, 598–601
Caribbean civilisation: birth of, xvi
Caribbean Commonwealth: Ramphal's vsion of a, 608–609
Caribbean Community and Common Market (CARICOM): and regional cooperation, xvii, xix-xx, 608–616
Caribbean Conference of Churches, xix
Caribbean creative imagination: geography and the, 597. *See also* Caribbean Culture and West Indian Culture
Caribbean culture: African heritage and, xxi; defining, xvii; development of indigenous, 342, 347–348; evolution of, 581–589; identifying 250–251; and self respect, 545–546. *See also* West Indian culture
Caribbean diaspora: and cultural identity, xvii, 580-581
Caribbean historiography: development of a, 421–422
Caribbean history: definition of, 250
Caribbean identity, 583–586, 588; Amerindian culture and, 511–514; and Caribbean literature, 414–417, 550–561; creolization and the evolution of the, 506; Cuban and Haitian revolutions and the quest for a, 397–406; history and the, 624-626; language and, 281–282, 294; myths of, 578–589; violence and the, 626–627
Caribbean Labour Congress (CLC), xix, 536
Caribbean literature: colour, class and identity in, 550–561; creoleness in, 259–260, 261; language and identity in, 596–598, 601–605; performance and rhythm in, 162–168; and the plantation system, 272–276; and the quest for identity, 414–417; theme of identity in, 237
Caribbean Sea: protection of the, 613–615
Caribbean Studies Association (CSA), xix
Caribbean Tourism Community (CTO): and environmental protection, 613
Caribbean writers: and pan-Caribbean scholarship, xxii-xxvi
Caribbeanness: concept of, 250, 252–254, 257; Glissant and the concept of, 268–269
Carmichael, Stokely, 491n, 510, 514n
Carpentier, Alejo, 163
Carter, Martin, 622
Casals Festival: Puerto Rican, 91–92
Casals, Pablo, 98n
Castellanos, Juan de, 15n
Castro, Fidel, 106–107, 112, 396, 399, 412: and the Mestizo concept, 129
Castro, Román Baldorioty de, 155n
Catholicism: and Voodoo, 206–207, 209n
Centrales system, 23–26, 46, 47, 48–49; sugar prices and the, 33
Césaire, Aimé, 210–211, 2449n; Condé on, 283–284; and Glissant, 267; and Negritude, 252; and the quest for a Caribbean identity, 584–586, 627
Chamoiseau, Patrick, 250–251; Condé on, 284–285, 285n
Chaos theory, 163, 169n
Chardin, Pierre Teilhard, 249n
Cheap labour: sugar and, 53–55
"Children of the Sea": rhythm and performance in, 166–167
Chinese: in Jamaica, 465, 466, 469
Christianisation: of Haitian peasants, 200; of Haitian slaves, 194; of slaves in BLI, 440–441
Christophe, Henri, 227n
Chritchlow, Hubert N., 457, 460

Ciboneys: in Cuba, 55

Cimarronage: and Caribbean cultural identity, 238, 248n

Cipriani, Captain Arthur.A., 331, 332, 406–407

Civilisation: Albizu Campos on, 74, 77; Césaire on European, 212–220; colonialism and, 297; defining Latin American, 123–133; Haiti and the search for a, 398, 399, 400; Muñoz Marin and good, 82, 89–90, 96–97

Class: and culture, 137, 140–141; and identity in Cliff, 551, 559; and race in the WI, 387

Class structure: in the BLI slave society, 423–424, 434–436, 439–440; and colour in British Guyana, 456–458

Cliff, Michele, 548

Coard, Bernard: and the Grenada revolution, 533

Code Noir, 200, 209n, 339, 358n

Coffee planter class: and Puerto Rican culture, 143–144

Columbus, Christopher: and the introduction of sugar cane into the WI, 52

Colonial writing, 273–274

Colonialism: Cesaire on civilization and, 213–220; and civilisation, 297; and identity in Cliff, 553–555, 557; and the loss of Black Power, 478; in post-WWII West Indies, 407–414; revolution against, 11–12; theme in Caribbean scholarship, xxiv

Colono system, 23–26, 29, 34n, 35n

Colour: and class in British Guyana, 456; and class in Jamaica, 463–471; and identity in Cliff, 550–561; and status in the BLI slave society, 424–426, 429, 439–440; and power, 477–479

Committee of Grenadian Intellectuals, 544

Commonwealth of the Caribbean. *See* Caribbean Commonwealth

Condé, Maryse, 279

Congo: effects of White Power on the, 478

Confiant, Raphaël, 250–251

Constitution: Puerto Rican, 89

Coolidge, President Calvin, 35n

Corretjer, Juan Antonio, 99, 154n

'Cosification': definition of, 238

Cox, S.A.G., 314

Creative marronage: in Caribbean literature, 274

Creole culture: definition of, 367–371

Creole language: and Caribbean cultural identity, 593–596; in Caribbean literature, 273; and Caribbeanness, 261–263; Condé and the use of, 281; and cultural identity, 626–627; Danticat and the, 290; Thomas and the, 294–295

Creole orality: concept of, 257–258

Creoleness: concept of, 251, 254–257, 263–265; and Creole literature, 263; and orality, 257–259; and politics, 264–265; role of, 285

Creolité. *See* Creoleness

Creolization: Benítez-Rojo on, 161–168; cosmopolitan, 640; definition of, 55–506; process, 256–257; theme in Caribbean scholarship, xvii; WI novelists and, 512–514

Crick Crack Monkey, 524

Crossing the Mangrove, 281

Crossing the River: performance and rhythm in, 164–165

Cuba: and Caribbean Development, 570, 571; CARICOM and, 612–613; coffee industry of, 22; independence, xvii, xviii 3; railroads and the sugar industry, 24; sugar industry of, 22-35; 46; transculturation in, 54–58; USA relations 17n

Cuban Institute for the Art and Industry of Cinema, 122n

Cuban nationalism, 36–37

Cuban revolution (1903s), 38–39, 106–107, 112, 113–119, 341, 353–354; and artistic freedom, 115–119; and cultural identity, 247–248; José Martí and the, 3–8, 18; and the quest for a Caribbean identity, 369, 399, 412; USA and the, 112, 113

Cuban Revolutionary Party, 18, 20

Cuban sugar industry: competition between the US and the, 30–33

Cuban War of Independence, 58n; language and the, 129

Cultural Development: in Puerto Rico, 91–92

Cultural diversity: Caribbean, 615

Cultural heritage: Puerto Rican, 99

Cultural identity: Caribbean, 579

Cultural pluralism, xvi, xxi; Caribbean, 363; Martí on American, 14–15

Cultural policy: USA and the need for a new, 648–649

Cultural resistance: by West Indian Blacks, 240

Cultural revolution: Cuban, 113–121

Culture: concept of, 364, 366; globalization of, 633–649

D'Aguiar, Fred: performance in the work of, 165–166, 169n

Dahomey: Voodoo in, 196–197, 205

Damas, Léon, 210, 249n

Danticat, Edwidge, 287

Democratic Party: and Puerto Rico, 63
Democracy: and development, 567–568; race relations and the growth of, 341
Depestre, René, 211, 236, 253, 265n; and Glissant, 267
Dessalines, Jean Jacques, 209n 227n
Development: basic need approach to economic, 571–575; in the Caribbean context, 565–570
Development Bank of Puerto Rico, 80
Dia de la Roza, 73, 78n
Diaspora literacy: concept of, 282
Diego, José de, 147, 156n
Disalienation: Fanon and the theory of, 230–234
Domination: Césaire on colonization and, 214, 216
Dominican Republic: Trujillo and the, 411
Donovan, William Galway, 535, 541–542
Duvalier, Francois, 249n, 291n
Duvalier, Jean Claude, 288, 289, 291n
Duvalier regime, 411
Divina Trace: language of the plantation in, 167–168

East Indians: celebration of Hosein by T&T, 302–303; cultural identity of T&T, 389–390, 593–595n; in Jamaica, 465, 466; Lamming and the creative role of T&T, 620–621
Eco-tourism: Caribbean, 613–615
Economic relations: USA/Philippines, 86–87
Economic status: Puerto Rico's, 90–91
Economics: Caribbean, 346–347, 348
'Ecumenical America', 633–649; Patterson's definition of, 647–648, 649
Education: development in Puerto Rico, 89, 91; and governance, 10–12; problems of Cuban, 109
Eisenhower, President Dwight: and the Cuban revolution, 112
Elite culture: Puerto Rican, 141, 144–146
Eloge de créolité, 283
Emancipation, 437–439, 442–443, 483; and free black and free coloured planters, 304
Employment: patterns in sugar industry, 30; in Puerto Rico, 98n
England: and self-government in the colonies, 63
Environmental protection: and development, 568; regional cooperation and, 613–615
Estado Libre Associado: Puerto Rico's status as an, 81–82, 151
Ethnic diversity: and Caribbean identity, 580,

522. *See also* Caribbean diversity
Europe: Césaire on colonization by, 213–218
European America: and exploitation of aboriginal cultures, 130–131
European culture: in the BLI slave society, 434
European power, 477–478
Europeanness: and Caribbean identity, 252
Europeans: in Cuba, 55–56
Existence: creoleness and the thematics of, 259–260

Fanon, Frantz, 228–229, 253; and Caribbean cultural identity, 579
'A Far Cry from Africa': language, culture and identity in, 592
Farming class: decline of the Cuban, 25–30, 49
Fatherhood: slavery and the devaluation of, 527–528
Faulkner, William: and the plantation experience, 271, 277n
Fedon, Julian, 534, 546n
Field slaves: in the BLI slave society,, 429–432
Fernández Retamar, Roberto, 123
Finlay, Carlos Juan, 35n
Firmin, Anténor, 173–174
Foraker Act (1900), 61, 63, 66n, 70n
Foreign investment: in Cuba, 25–26; in T&T, 355
Fournier, Charles, 16n
Franc-Jeu: Glissant and the, 267
Franchise. *See* Negro franchise
François, Elma; 331–334
Free coloureds: in the BLI slave society, 427–428, 437
Freedom: Cuban revolution and artistic, 115–119; Muños Marín on, 84–85
Freeling, Governor Sandford, 299–300, 302–303
French aid: and the Grenada revolution, 540
French language: and Caribbeanness, 262
Frenchness: concept of, 258
'From Toussaint L'Ouverture to Fidel Castro', 396–417
Front Antillo-Guanais, 268
Froude, James Anthony, 295–296, 349, 359n; Thomas' criticisms of, 298–311

Gaínza, Gabino, 16n
Gairy, Eric: and Grenada's independence movement, 531, 532
Galan, Natalio: and rhythm, 165
García, Caturla, Alejandro, 163

Garvey, Amy Jacques, 324

Garvey, Marcus, 222, 313–314, 318–319, 323–324, 400–401; and the Black Power Movement, 480, 487; Jamaicans and, 469–470; and WI racism, 486

Gender equality: in the Caribbean, 527–528

Geography: and the creative imagination, 597–601; and cultural identity, 627

Glissant, Edward, 267–268; and the concept of Caribbeanness, 250, 253, 265n

Global culture: diffusion of, 633–634

Gobineau, Comte Joseph Arthur de, 359n

Goncourt Prize, 284, 286n

González, José Luis, 135–136

Gonzalez, Manuel, 103

Gordon, Governor Arthur, 299, 311n

Goveia, Elsa, 421–422

Grenada: independence movement in, 531–532; USA relations, 532–533

Grenada Representative Government Association, 537, 547n

Grenada revolution, 532–534; and the Marryshow tradition, 539–541

Grenada United Labour Party (GULP), 531

Grenada Working Men's Association, 536

'Griffes', 188n

Griot: definition of, 169n

Guerra y Sánchez, 21–22

Guillén, Nicholás, 151, 156n, 163, 249n

Guyana: 1953 elections, 451–454; plantation system in colonial, 448–450; race and labour in, 622; USA relations, 447

Haiti: Blacks in, 183–186; Danticat on socio-economic conditions in, 288–290; economic isolation of, 190–191; Firmin on the responsibility of Blacks in, 175–176; and Francophone Caribbean, xvii; historical development of, 199–200; mulattoes in, 177–179; Negritude and, 223–225; and the quest for a civilization, 398, 399, 400; as a symbol of black independence, 412

Haitian culture: defining, 191–192

Haitian Historical and Geographic Society, 192

Haitian independence, 223

Haitian revolution: cultural resistance in the, 240–242; and the quest for a Caribbean identity, 398–399

Haley, Alex, 277n

Hall, Stewart, 577

Hamilton, Alexander, 15n

Harlem Renaissance, 221, 222, 225, 277n, 585, 588, 590n

Harris, Wilson, 416–417, 420n; and the Amerindian culture, 512–514; and the CAM, 511

Havelock, Governor Arthur, 300

Hawaii, 35n

Hearn, Laficadio, 277n

Health services: in Cuba, 110

Heroism: Martí on, 11

Herskovits, Melville J., 248n

Hidalgo y Costilla, 16n

Hill, Richard, 186

Hispanic Caribbean: definition of, xvii-xviii

Hispanophile culture: definition of, 135–136

Hispañiola, 58n

Historical commonalities: features of Caribbean, xiii–xiv

History: writing of WI, 384–385. See also Caribbean historiography

"History Will Absolve Me", 107–113

Hodge, Merle, 524

Hoover, Herbert C., 35n

Hosein celebration: repression of (1884), 302–303

Hostos, Eugenio María de, 78n; and Puerto Rican culture, 138, 145, 146, 154n

House for Mr. Biswas, 415–416

Housing: problems of Cuban, 109, 111

Hughes, Langston, 222, 226n

Human races: artificial ranking of the, 182–183, 187–188

Human species: evolution of the, 180–182

Ideas: significance of, 8

'If I Could Write This in Fire, I Would Write this in Fire', 549–560

Immigration: into Cuban, 27, 34n–35n, 49, 53, 54, 58n; of Puerto Ricans into the USA, 81

Independence: Martí and nationalism, xviii; struggle for Puerto Rican, 83, 84–87, 99, 138, 151, 152

Identity: the Black man's search for, 237; language and, 386–387; towards a Caribbean, 349–350, 353–358. *See also* Caribbean identity and West Indian identity

Indentured labour: and the West Indies, 484

Indian civilization: Albizu Campos on the, 74

Indians: massacre of North American, 9–10, 11, 15n

Indegenization: of popular music, 630

Indigenous Caribbean peoples, xvi

Industrialisation: Puerto Rican, 80–81, 90, 354–

355;

Inferiority: myth of Black, 229–234, 440: race relations and the theory of Black, 340

Institute of Ethnology, 192

Instituto de Cultura Puertorriqueña, 98n, 154n–155n

Intellectual tradition: Caribbean, xxii–xxvi

Intellectuals: and the Cuban revolution, 116–121

International enforcement: and Caribbean development, 570

Internationalism: features of, 565

Inter-racialism: growth of Caribbean, 345–346

Irigoyen, President Hipólito, 73, 78n

Irving, Governor Henry, 299, 300

Iturbide, Augustín de, 16n

Jagan, Cheddi, 446–448, 450–451

Jagan, Janet, 446, 448

Jamaica: and the Black Power Movement, 487–488; economy of, 497, 498; history of, 316–318; political development of, 496; reggae and, 636–639; race and identity in, 463–471; and regional cooperation, 499

Jamaican identity: quest for a, 462; reggae and the, 589

James, C.L.R., 394–396; on the Caribbean experience, xvi

Jewish communities, xviii

Jones Act, 62

Juárez, Benito Pablo, 17n

Jung, Carl, 235n

Junta Cubana de Renovación Nacional, 36

King, Martin Luther, 491n

Knowledge: growth of, 519–520

Krik? Krak!: rhythm and performance in, 167

La Cruz, Juana, 248n

La Revue indigene, 221–222

Labat, Jean-Baptiste: and slavery, 271

Labour: Cuba and the importation of cheap, 49; Lamming and the creative role of, 621–630; latifundium system and the demand for cheap, 30–33; and race in British Guiana, 455; in the sugar and tobacco industries, 40–43

Labour Relations Bill (British Guiana, 1953), 453, 454

Labour revolt (1938), 496

Laleau, Léon, 248n

Lam, Wilfred, 163; and Glissant, 267

Lamming, George, 414–415, 420n, 617; and

the theme of rootlessness, 509–510

Land reform: and agricultural development in Puerto Rico, 101–102

Language: and ancestral memory, 601–605; Césaire and, 220; and cultural sovereignty, 125–126, 128–130, 135, 153; Condé on identity and, 281; Danticat on identity and, 290; Depestre on identity and, 239; Fanon on cultural identity and, 230; and identity, 261–263, 294, 386–387, 584–587, 588, 598; and identity in Haiti, 192, 196; and nationalism, 79n, 81, 82, 98n; and sovereignty, 158

Lares, Gritode, 100

Las Casas, Bartolomé de, 58n, 161, 162, 340, 359n

Latifundium system: emergence of the, 25; expansion of the, 27–34, 34n, 48–50

Latin American culture: defining, 130–132

Lebrón, Lolita, 72

Leeward Islands. *See* British Leeward Islands

Lewis, W. Arthur, 411, 420n, 421, 516

Liberal Party (Puerto Rico), 135

Liga Teminira Puertorriqeña, 156n

Linguistic diversity, xvii–xviii, xxi

The Longest Memory: scholastic performance in, 165–166

Los Macheteros. 20

L'Ouverture, Toussaint, 184–185, 189n, 227n, 241, 248n, 359n, 396, 399, 412

Love, Dr. Robert, 313

Lumumba, Patrice, 249n, 490n

Maceo, General Antonio, 359n, 399

Machado, General Gerardo, 21, 37

Malcolm X, 490n

Male-female relationships: ambiguities in, 529–530; violence in, 525–527

Mallarmé, Stéphane, 226n

Malinowski, Bronislaw, 59n

Mambi: definition of, 129, 134n

Manley, Michael, 492–494

Manuel de Céspedes, Carlos: USA government and, 38

Maran, René, 226n

Marley, Bob, 590n

Marronage, 277n. *See also* Cultural marronage

Marryshow Day, 545–546

Marryshow, T. Albert, 534–538, 539, 546n

Martí, José, 123, 399; and Cuban revolution, 3–8, 18; death of, 58n; and the Mestizo concept, 125, 129–131; philosophy of, 5–8; two Americas, 135–136

Mass Communication: and the diffusion of global music culture, 634–636

Matriarch: the evolution of the Caribbean, 528–529

McIntosh, George, 331

McKay, Claude, 222, 226n

Memory. See Ancestral memory

Mestizo: concept of, 124–132, 133n; definition of the, 249n

Mestizo-creolization: definition of, 505–506; Wilson Harris and Aubrey Williams and, 512–514

Miami: cosmopolitan creolization of, 640–641

The Middle Passage: excerpts from, 375–392

Migration: and Caribbean cultural identity, xvii; trends in West Indian, 280–281, 285n

Mill, John Stuart, 359n

Missionaries: in the BLI slave society, 440–441

Monogenism: theory, 176–181

Morant Bay rebellion: White Power and the, 484

Morel Campus, Juan, 78n

Morrison, Toni, 277n

Moton, Robert: Garvey's letter to, 319–323

Motherland: Castro's concept of, 112–113

Mulatismo: in Caribbean literature, 241, 242

Mulatto-creolization: definition of, 505–506

Mulattoes: race and Haitian, 177–179

Multicultural America: Patterson's definition of, 644, 648

Muños Marín, Luis, 80–82, 359n

Muños Rivera, Luis, 60–62

Munroe Doctrine, 67

Music: and the plantation, 276

'The Music of History', cultural identity in, 592–593

Naipaul, V.S., 283, 285n, 360n, 373–374, 415–416, 420n

Nation: Garvey on the need for a Negro, 326

National Council of Culture: and the Cuban revolution, 118–120

National Institute of the Motion Pictures Industry, 120

National Library of Cuba, 120

National Publishing House: of Cuba, 120

National Unemployment Movement (NUM), 332

National Union of Writers and Artists, 122n

National Workers Union: Michael Manley and the, 492

Nationalism: features of Caribbean, xvi-xvii;

and culture, 364–365; and independence, xviii; language and, 79n; Puerto Rican, 71–73, 74–76, 77–78; 125, 138–140, 147; in Surinam, 391; Third World, 495–496

Natural heritage: preservation of Puerto Rico's, 92–93

Nazism: Césaire on colonization and, 213–214

Negrismo: and Caribbean literature, 241, 242; and (Cuba), 221

Negrista literature: in Southern USA, 242

Négritude, 210, 221; and the African vision, 252–253; and the quest for a Caribbean identity, 240–241, 242–246, 398–399, 400, 583–586, 588; rejection of, 253; role of, 282, 284

Negro franchise: Froude and the WI, 296–298, 305–311, 313

Negro Renaissance Movement (USA). *See* Harlem Renaissance

Negro Welfare Cultural and Social Association (NWCSA), 332–334; objectives of the, 334–335

Negroes: and labour on sugar plantations, 53

Nettleford, Rex M., 460

New International Economic order, 542, 547n

New Jewel Movement (NJM), 531–532

Nietsche, Freidrich, 226n

Nkrumah, Kwame, 402, 418n

Non-governmental organisations: Pan Caribbean, xix-xx

North American Free Trade Area (NAFTA), 612

Oilfeild Workers Strike (T&T), 333

'Omeros', 286n

Operation Bootstrap, 80–81: Puerto Rico's, 354

Oral tradition: in Caribbean history, 626; in Caribbean literature, 272–273, 276; and creoleness, 257–258; in Haiti, 192–193

O'Reilly, Alejandro: and land reform in Puerto Rico, 101–102

Ortiz, Fernando, 36–39, 163, 399; and the concept of transculturation, 628

Padmore, George, 394, 401–402, 418n

Pales Matos, Luis, 248n

Pan-Caribbean organisations, xix-xx

Panama Canal: West Indians and the, 280–281, 285n

Pareto, Vilfredo, 134n

Partido Liberal Fusionista, 60

Partido Nueva Progressita, 157

Partido Popular Democratico, 80, 83–85, 157

Patria: concept of, 82
Patronata, 58n
Patterson, Orlando, 632
People: Castro's definition of, 107–109
People's National Congress (PNC), 447–448
People's National Movement (PNM), 337; Jamaica and the, 395; and race relations, 343
People's National Party (PNP), 493–494; WI Federation and the, 492
People's Political Party, 323
People's Progressive Party (PPP), 447–448, 454, 459, 460
People's Revolutionary Government (PRG), 532
Performance and rhythm: Benítez-Rojo on creolization and, 161–164
Permanent Treaty (1903), 37
Perse, St John, 601–602
Pétion, Alexandre, 185
Phillipines, 35n
Phillips, Caryl: performance and rhythm in the novel of, 164–165, 169n
Physical abuse, of women, 525–527
Piñero, Jesús, 88, 97
Plantation system: Benítez-Rojo on the, 161–164; creolisation and the, 257; and Caribbean cultural identity, 397; in British Guiana, 448–450, demise of the, 340; Glissant's analysis of the, 269–277. See also Laitifundium system
Platt Amendment (1904), 26, 37, 383
Political development: Puerto Rican, 102
Political education: and governance, 10–12
Political power: colonial Blacks and, 305–307
Political status: of Puerto Rico, 81–82, 85–89, 93–95, 98n, 158–159
Politics: and creoleness, 264–265; features of Caribbean, 345–346
Polygenism theory, 176–182
Popular culture: Cuban, 162–163; Puerto Rican, 141–145, 150
Popular music culture: global, 634–636
Population statistics: the British Leeward Islands', 423
Poverty: and Blacks, 478; in Cuba, 109; in Jamaica, 322
Power: and colour, 477–479
Price-Mars, Jean, 190–192, 222; and Négritude, 399
Private sector: and development, 568–569
Production costs: effects of lowering of, 32
Progress: Garvey on humanity and, 325, 326, 327
Property: race an ownership of, 339–339

Prospero complex: definition of, 127
Public Law 600, 88, 98n
Puerto Rican government, 60, 62
Puerto Rican cultural identity, defining a, 136–154, 157, 158–159; Corretjer on, 100; Muñoz Marín on, 84–85
Puerto Rican nationalism, 125, 138–140, 147; Muñoz Marín and, 81–82; Pedro Albizu Campos and, 71–73, 75–76, 77–78
Puerto Rican revolution: against Spanish domination, 100–105
Puerto Rico: independence struggle, 18, 20, 62, 99; industrialisation in, 80–81; and national identity, xviii; and operation Bootstrap, 354–355; political status of, 81–82, 85–87, 88–89, 93–95, 98n; USA economic relations, 411; USA relations, xvii, 62–70
Puerto Rico Development Company, 80

Queen Isabella: Albizu Campos on, 75
Quintero Rivera, Angel: on American imperialism in Puerto Rico, 140, 154n

Race: Albizu Campos' discussion on, 73–77and Caribbean culture, 369–371; and class in Jamaica, 319–323; and class in the WI, 310–311; definition of, 17n; Firmin on, 173–174, 175–188; Garvey on the Negro, 325–328; and the Jamaican identity, 462–471; and labour in British Guiana, 455; and labour in T&T and Guyana, 621–624; and politics in Guyana, 452–454; traditional America and, 645–647. See also Human races
'Race Relations in Caribbean Society', 337, 338–344
Race-relations: changing, 338–344; in the WI, 385–392
Racial integration: Cuban revolution and, 247–248
Racism: Fernández Retamar on USA, 124–125; in Jamaica, 465, 466, 469; and slavery, 483; in the West Indies, 486
Railroads: impact on the Cuban sugar industry, 24, 25, 26, 34n, 46–48
Ramphal, Shridath, 607–608
Rastafarianism: cultural revolution of, 587–589; and identity in Cliff, 556; reggae and, 638
Reciprocal Treaty (1902), 26
Reggae: development of, 636–639; and the Jamaican cultural identity, 589
Regional blocks: emergence of international, 611–612
Regional cooperation: benefits of, 500–503;

Caribbean, 497, 499; Grenada revolution and, 541–542; Marryshow and the, 539, 540; Ramphal and, 607–616
Regional integration, 355–358
Regional organisations. *See* Pan-Caribbean organisations
Reid, Vic, 414, 420n
Religion: and Caribbean cultural identity, xviii
Renan, Ernest: on colonization, 214–215
Republican Party: and Puerto Rico, 63
Resistance to slavery: in the BLI slave society, 436–438
Riggs, Colonel E. Francis: assassination of, 72
Rimbaud, Arthur, 238, 248n
Ritual: and identity, 593–596
Rivadavia, Bernadino, 16n
Rivera, Alejandro Tapia y, 155n
Rodney, Walter, 474–476
Rodo, José Enrique, 127, 133n
Rodríguez de Tío, lola, 18–19; poetry, 19–20
Rohler, Gordon: and language and identity, 626–627
Rojas, Manuel, 103
Roldán, Armadeo, 163
Roosevelt, President Franklin D.: and Cuba, 38
Roumain, Henri, 227n
Roumain, Jacques, 249n

Salkey, Andrew, 515n
Samba: rhythm of the, 165
Sánchez Villela, Roberto, 82, 83
Sandys, Duncan, 459–460
Santería: definition of, 169n
Santiago, Esmerelda, 157
Santiago Diaz, Vidal, 158, 159
Schoelcher, Victor, 189n
Scholarship: Caribbean, xxii-xxvi
Seaga, Edward: and the Jamaican cultural identity, 579
Season of Adventure, 414–415
Self-government: Puerto Rican, 81, 83–86, 88–90
Self-respect: Garvey on, 325–326, 327
Sénghor, Leopold, 210, 211, 222; and Négritude, 245–246, 249n
Sexual orientation: and identity in Cliff, 550–551, 556
Sexual relationships: in the BLI slave society, 426–427
Sieyè, Emanuel Joseph, 15n
Slave culture: in the BLI slave society, 432–434, 432–434

Slave resistance. *See* Resistance to slavery
Slave society: in the British Leeward islands, 423
Slave Society in the British Leeward Islands (BLI) at the End of the Eighteenth Century (excerpts), 422–444
Slave system: decline of the, 442
Slavery, 131, 397; abolition in Puerto Rico, 101–102, 105n; African immigration and, xxi; and Caribbean cultural identity, 238; in Jamaica, 316; devaluation of manhood under, 527; the latifundium and Cuban, 49, 52, 56–57; and the plantation system, 270, 276, 277n; racism and, 483: violence under, 525;
Slaves: and the plantation experience, 272–274, 276
Smith, M.G. (Jamaica), 362–363
Social protest: against colonisation in T&T, 412–413; and negritude, 243–244, 247; and the NWCSA in T&T, 333–334, 335
Social structure. *See* Class structure
Sovereignty: and creoleness, 264–265
Spain: Albizu Campos on, 74–76, 77–78; Puerto Rico relations, 18, 60, 62, 64
Spaniards: in Cuba, 54
Spanish Cortes: structure of the, 60, 62
Spanish culture: in Puerto Rico, 141
Speech: and the plantation system, 275–276
State power: and race relations, 339
'Statement of a Return to the Country Where I was born', 402–405
Stipendiary magistrates: oppression by, 301–303
Student Non-violent Coordinating Committee, 491n
Sugar cane: contrast between tobacco and, 39–40, 45; cultivation and manufacture, 42–43, 45–49, 51
Sugar industry: competition between the USA and the Cuban, 30–33; Cuban, 22–35, 46–54; Puerto Rican, 92
Sugar mills: influence of Cuban, 26–27, 46–48
Sugar prices: Cuban, 32
Superiority: myth of White, 229–234
Surinam: nationalism in, 391
Surrealism: Césaire and, 284; Césaire on liberation and, 220–221, 226n; and the revaluation of Africa, 253

Tainos: colonisors' vision of the, 126, 133n; in Cuba, 55
Teachers: Puerto Rico and recognition of, 89–90, 91
Ten Years War, 58n

Texaco, 284, 286n
The Tempest: and colonisation, 127, 133n–134n
Third World: definition of the, 133n, 249n;
features of the, 495–496; and the impact of
western culture, 635
Thomas, Clive Y., 562
Thomas, J.J. (T&T), 294–296, 349
Time for Action, 607, 609
'Timehri', 505–513
Tobacco, 58n; contrast between sugar cane and,
39–40, 45; cultivation, 40–42, 43, 45–49,
51
Tobacco industry: of the Cuban sugar industry,
47–50
Todd, Robert H., 155n
Truman, Harry S., 226n
Trade union movement: development of the,
496
Traditional America: Patterson's definition of,
644–647
Transculturation: Caribbean, 628–630; in Cuba,
54–58; Ortiz and the concept of, 54, 628
Treaty of Paris (1898), 25, 61, 67, 69
Tree of Life, 280, 282
Trinidad and Tobago (T&T), 497; colonial
governance in 19th century, 299–303; foreign
investment in, 355; Lamming on East Indians
and labour in, 620–622; race and class in, 387–
390; USA relations, 412–414
Tshombe, Morrse, 490n
Tydings Bill (1936), 81, 83, 85, 86
Tydings, Senator Millard, 72, 97n
Tydings-McDuffie Act (1934), 97

Underdevelopment: Thomas' definition of, 565
Unemployment: in Cuba, 37, 110, 111; in Puerto
Rico, 158
Union Party (Puerto Rico), 135
Unitarian theory: distinction between
monogenism and the, 180–181
United States of America (USA): Albizu on the,
77–78; Black Power Movement and the, 480–
482; Césaire on colonization by the, 219–
220; cosmopolitan creolization of the, 640–
641; Cuba relations, 353–354; and the Cuban
revolution, 4, 6–7, 17n, 36; defining the
contemporary, 644-645; Fernández Retamar
on racism in the, 124–125; and the Grenada
revolution, 532–533; Guyana relations, 447;
intervention in Jamaica's politics, 493;
invasion of Puerto Rico, 18; investment in
Cuba, 26; and need for a new cultural policy,

648–649; occupation of Haiti, 191;
Philippines relations, 86; Puerto Rico
economic relations, 354–355, 411; T&T
relations, 412–414; and the West Indies, 485
Universal Negro Improvement Association
(UNIA), 313, 318, 323–324, 325, 326–328
University of the West Indies (UWI), 421–422;
and regional unity, xix
Urban slavery: in the BLI slave society, 428
USA/Cuba relations, 36
USA/Puerto Rico economic relations, 61, 63,
77–78, 98n
USA sugar industry: competition between the
Cuban and the, 30–33

Violence: against Blacks, 481–482; in Caribbean
history, 626; in Caribbean society, 525
Virginia: tobacco industry, 53
Voodoo, 399; ceremony, 200–205; development
of, 193–199, 206; repression of, 206–207;
symbolism of, 205

Walcott, Derek, 283, 284, 591–593; and theme
of rootlessness, 509–510
Wealth: and White Power, 478
Wealth creation: Cuban economy and decline
in, 28–30; in Puerto Rico, 89
Welles, Ambassador Sumner: and Cuba, 38
West Indian: defining, 367
West Indian Commission: and regional
cooperation, 607, 609–616
West Indian culture: and the quest for identity,
521–522
West Indian diaspora, 281
West Indian history: development of, 421–422
West Indian identity: defining the, 517, 520;
ethnicity and the, 518. *See also* Caribbean
identity
West Indian intellectuals: and theme of
rootlessness, 506, 507
West Indian life: Froude on 19th century, 296–
311
West Indian literature: common themes in, 283
West Indian novelists: and the quest for identity,
414–417; and the theme of rootlessness, 509–
510
West Indian personality. *See* West Indian identity
West Indies: Black Power and the, 482–483,
485–490,
West Indies Federation: failure of the, xvii, 352,
366, 367, 395, 492, 496, 497, 499; the
colonial system and, 410; Marryshow and the,

537

The West on Trial, 446; excerpt of, 448–461

Western influence: and Third World culture, 635–636

White power: features of, 477–478; and the West Indies, 483–485

Whiteness: definition of, 485

Whites: in BLI slave society, 424–427; and the plantation experience, 271–272

Whitman, Walt, 359n

Williams, Aubrey: and Amerindian culture, 512–514, 515n; and the CAM, 511

Williams, Eric, 336–338, 374, 395

Wilson, Woodrow, 226n

Winship, Governor Blanton, 72

Women: Albizu Campos on civilization and, 75; in the BLI slave society, 426–427; and development in Puerto Rico, 156n; in Haiti, 289; physical abuse of, 525–527

Wood, General Leonard: and Cuba's sugar industry, 26–27, 34n

Zeno, Manuel Gandía, 138, 154

'Zombification': defining, 238, 247, 248n

Zorilla, José, 16n